Organizational Behavior

KENT Series in Management

Barnett/Wilsted, *Cases for Strategic Management*

Barnett/Wilsted, *Strategic Management: Concepts and Cases*

Barnett/Wilsted, *Strategic Management: Text and Concepts*

Berkman/Neider, *The Human Relations of Organizations*

Carland/Carland, *Small Business Management: Tools for Success*

Crane, *Personnel: The Management of Human Resources*, Fourth Edition

Davis/Cosenza, *Business Research for Decision Making*, Second Edition

Finley, *Entrepreneurial Strategies: Text and Cases*

Kemper/Yehudai, *Experiencing Operations Management: A Walk-Through*

Kirkpatrick, *Supervision: A Situational Approach*

Mendenhall/Oddou, *Readings and Cases in International Human Resource Management*

Mitchell, *Human Resource Management: An Economic Approach*

Nkomo/Fottler/McAfee, *Applications in Personnel/Human Resource Management: Cases, Exercises, and Skill Builders*

Plunkett/Attner, *Introduction to Management*, Third Edition

Punnett, *Experiencing International Management*

Roberts/Hunt, *Organizational Behavior*

Scarpello/Ledvinka, *Personnel/Human Resource Management: Environments and Functions*

Singer, *Human Resource Management*

Starling, *The Changing Environment of Business*, Third Edition

Steers/Ungson/Mowday, *Managing Effective Organizations: An Introduction*

Tosi, *Organizational Behavior and Management: A Contingency Approach*

KENT International Dimensions of Business Series

Series Consulting Editor, David A. Ricks

Adler, *International Dimensions of Organizational Behavior*, Second Edition

AlHashim/Arpan, *International Dimensions of Accounting*, Second Edition

Dowling/Schuler, *International Dimensions of Human Resource Management*

Folks/Aggarwal, *International Dimensions of Financial Management*

Garland/Farmer/Taylor, *International Dimensions of Business Policy and Strategy*, Second Edition

Litka, *International Dimensions of the Legal Environment of Business*, Second Edition

Phatak, *International Dimensions of Management*, Second Edition

Terpstra, *International Dimensions of Marketing*, Second Edition

KENT Series in Human Resource Management

Series Consulting Editor, Richard W. Beatty

Bernardin/Beatty, *Performance Appraisal: Assessing Human Behavior at Work*

Cascio, *Costing Human Resources: The Financial Impact of Behavior in Organizations*, Third Edition

Kavanagh/Gueutal/Tannenbaum, *Human Resource Information Systems: Development and Application*

Ledvinka/Scarpello, *Federal Regulation of Personnel and Human Resource Management*, Second Edition

McCaffery, *Employee Benefit Programs: A Total Compensation Perspective*

Wallace/Fay, *Compensation Theory and Practice*, Second Edition

Organizational Behavior

Karlene H. Roberts
University of California, Berkeley

David Marshall Hunt
University of Southern Mississippi

PWS-KENT PUBLISHING COMPANY
Boston

PWS-KENT
Publishing Company

20 Park Plaza
Boston, Massachusetts 02116

PWS-KENT Publishing Company is a division of Wadsworth, Inc.
Printed in the United States of America
1 2 3 4 5 6 7 8 9—94 93 92 91

Library of Congress Cataloging-in-Publication Data
Roberts, Karlene H.
    Organizational behavior / Karlene H. Roberts, David M. Hunt.
      p.   cm.
    Includes bibliographical references and index.
    ISBN 0-534-92249-X
    1. Organizational behavior.   2. Organizational effectiveness.
    I. Hunt, David (David Marshall)   II. Title.
    HD58.7.R624   1991
    658.4′063—dc20   90-20855
                                                      CIP

International Student Edition ISBN 0-534-98469-X

Managing Editor: Rolf Janke
Editorial Assistant: Marnie Pommett
Production Editor: Pamela Rockwell
Manufacturing Coordinator: Margaret Sullivan Higgins
Interior Designer: Julia Gecha
Cover Designer: Nancy Lindgren Associates
Typesetter: G&S Typesetting, Inc.
Print and Bind: Arcata Graphics, Halliday
Cover Printer: New England Book Components, Inc.

To Brett and Corey
whose needs determined ours

Contents

About the Authors

Karlene H. Roberts (Ph.D., University of California, Berkeley) is Professor of Business Administration at the University of California, Berkeley. Her research and other writing projects are in the areas of organizational communication, international business, the design and management of potentially hazardous organizations, and research methodology. She has served on the editorial boards of *Journal of Vocational Behavior, Journal of Applied Psychology, Academy of Management Journal, Organizational Behavior and Human Decision Processes, California Management Review*, and *Academy of Management Executive.*

Dr. Roberts was chair of the Organizational Behavior Division of the Academy of Management and served on the Board of Directors of the Academy. She is a Fellow in the Academy of Management and of the American Psychology Association.

David Marshall Hunt (Ph.D., University of Houston) is Professor of Management at the University of Southern Mississippi. He has taught courses at both the graduate and undergraduate levels in international management, organizational behavior, organizational theory, and human resource management.

A member of the Academy of International Business, Academy of Management, American Psychological Association, and Organizational Behavior Teaching Society, Dr. Hunt has also published numerous articles in related professional journals. Dr. Hunt was recently a visiting Fullbright Professor at the University of Nairobi (Kenya) and was posted in Korea, Japan, Okinawa, and Pakistan during his years as an international bank officer. He is currently a visiting professor at the University of Witwatersrand in Johannesburg.

Preface

Most of you hope to pursue domestic or international management careers. You are or soon will be concerned with understanding how organizations operate effectively in a world of global changes and ever greater competitive challenges. Within this context you will be concerned with the characteristics of organizations and of managing people in them. There are numerous ways to learn about these concerns including studying the experiences of real firms and their managers, examining organizational theory and research, and reading popular books on management. Rather than focusing on any one of these approaches, we have combined all three—the better to equip you for careers in management.

This book addresses different aspects of behavior in organizations and of organizing and managing people. Taken together, the chapters provide a clear description of those aspects of organizing and managing that must be attended to by professional managers if their organizations are to operate effectively in the challenging environment of the 1990s and beyond.

Students of management and organizational behavior are faced with a dynamic and complicated arena. Particularly in the last few years, organizations have grown larger and more complex partly because of the rush towards mergers and acquisitions in the 1980s, which included the formation of transnational partnerships between former rivals in world markets (such as the General Motors–Toyota joint venture). Another reason for organizational growth and complexity is the development of sophisticated communications technologies that can tie together far-flung domestic and international operations. Technologies are becoming so advanced that we are able to build extremely complex organizations in which the actions of different units can be closely coordinated and in which decisions and strategies can be tailored to fit rapidly changing situations even in the increasingly multicultural environment that organizations must face. On the other hand, small, highly specialized organizations that fit particular market niches in very segmented environments continue to form. Thus, we are simultaneously becoming a world of ever larger and ever smaller organizations.

Although this book does not resolve any of these complexities, it does intend to shed light on the underlying concepts and processes managers must think about in dealing with their employees and organizations. In doing so, the book introduces a systematic language and set of categories to define and bring order to the chaotic organizational processes we are exposed to in everyday life.

The Philosophy of This Book

We conceived of this book as addressing two major issues we had not seen satisfactorily addressed before in organizational behavior textbooks. The first is concerned with the growing trend of merging macro and micro perspectives. Historically, researchers interested in larger environmental and organizational questions have been called "macro" analysts. Those who study individuals and groups are "micro" analysts.

Some writers with micro interests are beginning to include macro variables in their research. While still studying individuals and groups, they are more clearly addressing and dealing with the environmental factors that affect individuals' experiences. Some are interested in organizations as environments, some take even larger perspectives addressing various issues concerned with the impact of societies on people and of people on their larger environments.

Some writers with macro interests are becoming more concerned with the impact of human beings on organizations, remembering that individuals live and work in organizations. We felt it was time to bring some integration to these two broad perspectives and have done so by giving the book a macro to micro flow and by heavily cross-referencing from chapter to chapter.

Second, in our judgment most textbooks in the field are too elementary. We wanted a book to challenge the minds of both aspiring managers and experienced managers. We also wanted to offer something that would give future managers pragmatic help.

Before beginning the book we asked a set of M.B.A. students about to enter management careers and a set of managers who either were changing jobs or had recently changed jobs to tell us the kinds of questions and issues they would want information about as they entered their new organizations. Together, their answers divided themselves into three categories:

- First, they wanted to know "how we're organized around here." When entering new organizations, they wanted something of an overall view. They wanted to know what the organization's goals are and how it is structured to attain these goals.

- Second, they wanted to know how they could expect to get things done in a general way. That is, "how do we, as a group of people, get things done?" For example, how do we communicate and make decisions together?

- Third, they wanted to know how they, as managers, could expect to get things done through other people. That is, "how do *I* get things done around here?" How could they encourage themselves and others to do a good job, and how could they manage on a one-to-one basis.

These three categories and the general chapter topics they include are illustrated in the figure on the inside cover of this book.

In sum, our informants told us they needed the "big picture" first. They only needed more specific information later as they became more experienced with their organizations and jobs. The three-pronged approach suggested by their responses determined the primary structure of our book.

It is our intent to provide balanced coverage of the way the field of organizational behavior research looks today and to overlay that coverage with application. Two techniques have been used in every chapter for providing that added spice of application. Detailed theme cases, reproduced largely from popular management sources, are placed at the beginning of each chapter to introduce the reader to the challenges and contemporary managers' approaches to them. These theme cases, drawn from both the public and private sectors and domestic and foreign sources, are integrated into the chapters and provide a basis for discussion. Next, we have ended each chapter with a "Managerial Insight." This feature provides the perspective of an experienced manager on one of the chapter's main topics and is designed to leaven theory(ies), which may seem too abstract at times, with some practical considerations that will prove valuable.

The Plan of the Book

The first of the three parts of the book addresses the issue of how we're organized around here. We asked ourselves, What do managers need to know when they first enter an organization? An important issue in thinking about "how we're organized around here" has to do with the bottom line. For economists, the bottom line is usually profit; but for organizational researchers and for managers, it is the goals of the organization and its effectiveness in reaching those goals. What is the organization trying to do, how explicit is it about what it is trying to do, and how well does it accomplish its aims? Chapter 1 addresses these issues.

The next issue concerned with the "how" of organization has to do with the way the organization puts itself together to realize its goals. In other words, What constitutes the parts of organizations, and how are these parts put together? These questions have to do with organizational structure, the topic of Chapter 2. Structure reflects fundamental inputs to, as well as activities taking place within, organizations. How do organizations structure themselves? How do specific structural arrangements affect the way people behave in organizations? What happens when those arrangements change? How can one change them? How do structural characteristics influence the jobs people do in organizations and individuals' responses to those jobs? These issues seem to us to be among the first that managers new to an organization need to confront.

Chapter 3 views the organization as a society and tries to understand how each organization establishes its own culture—partly influenced by the culture(s) of the surrounding society but also by a special set of beliefs, norms, and values that expresses what is unique about the organization. With some notion about what the culture of an organization is, we should gain some insights into the kind of people who will perform best in it. If anything is to be accomplished, we must have people who can work together. But can we just bring people in off the street, offer them a reasonable wage, and expect them to be responsible and dedicated to achieving our organization's goals? Managers engage in various activities that bring people to organizations and that bind them and keep them there. Thus, Chapter 3 also takes up issues of organizational socialization.

Once people are in organizations, managers need to find ways to use their various talents most effectively. This brings us to Part 2 and the issue of how we get things done together. Because many tasks are accomplished by groups of people, managers must know something about group processes. How are groups structured? How do they influence people? How are norms of behavior established and what factors are involved in attracting individuals to each other and to groups? These are some of the issues addressed in Chapter 4.

Communication is essential to the process of working together. Chapter 5 examines communication in organizations, exploring the characteristics of the communicator and the receiver of information, the effectiveness of various communication channels, and what we need to know about the content of communications.

The next issue in Part 2 deals with the development and use of power in organizations. What constitutes power, and how can it be managed? Who are the actors in the power game? What are various theories about the development and use of power in and between organizations? These issues, among others, are covered in Chapter 6.

Decision making—especially as it pertains to goals, action planning, and implementation—is also an important element of getting things done together. How do individuals and groups make decisions? When is it better to use individuals or groups to make decisions? How do decision makers process information? These questions are addressed in Chapter 7.

In Part 3 we address the third question raised by our respondents—how do we manage people as individuals? Once employees are in the organization, we must think about managing or leading them. This is the subject of Chapter 8. What is leadership and how does it emerge in organizations? What are various approaches to leadership? What environmental and organizational factors influence leadership? And how can we train good leaders?

Getting things done on a one-to-one basis depends not only on leadership but also on motivation. How do managers increase motivation to work to achieve the organization's goals? What strategies can we use to motivate employees? This is the central question of Chapter 9.

In order to work effectively with other people, we must know something about them as individuals. Chapter 10 addresses organizational behavior at the level of the individual, considering such topics as personality, people's social perceptions, how people attribute causes to their own and other's behaviors, and the importance of personal values. The chapter also presents several other important considerations: training, motivating, and evaluating employees. Once individuals come to us with their unique personalities, attitudes, and values, how do we need to use training, evaluation, rewards, and discipline to meld diverse people into a cohesive and effective work force.

Finally, after focusing on how people are organized in organizations, how we get things done as groups, and how we work with people one-on-one, we turn to how organizations and people in them can manage and cope with change. Renewal is critical in organizations and is discussed in our final chapter. What are the processes of change? What relationships arise between strategies for change and people who work in organizations? What model might we use for managing change? How can we identify the need to change? These issues are discussed in Chapter 11.

In all, we have used several approaches to discussing the issues raised in this book. The theme case that begins each chapter is referred to within the chapter for illustrations of the concepts being discussed. In addition, features—short illustrations, examples, or extensions of various points—are interspersed throughout each chapter. And each chapter concludes with a managerial insight addressing an issue raised in the chapter. Throughout, we have drawn as much as possible from the international and cross-cultural literature to reflect the realities of our interdependent world.

Answering the questions developed in this preface should provide managers and would-be managers with firm grounding in both the organizational and people issues they must consider in their jobs. We hope you will find the journey through these issues exciting, challenging, and rewarding and that you will return to *Organizational Behavior* as a valuable resource as you encounter specific situations in your managerial career.

Acknowledgments

The skills and time of many people was generously given to this project. First, at PWS-KENT our appreciation goes to Rolf Janke for constant encouragement and support and to Pamela Rockwell for skillful management of the production process. Dante Sands and Douglas Creed worked their magic with words to make each chapter flow more clearly. Many reviewers offered comments that greatly improved this effort. Our special thanks to the following:

Gib Akin
University of Virginia

Dan Brass
Pennsylvania State University

James Cashman
University of Alabama

Robert DeFillippi
Suffolk University

Christopher Earley
University of Minnesota

William Glick
University of Texas-Austin

Edward Morrison
University of Colorado-Boulder

Sheila Puffer
Northeastern University

Hannah Rothstein
Bernard Baruch College-CUNY

Ellen Singer

William Stevenson
Boston College

Joseph Weiss
Bentley College

Finally, we thank Patricia Murphy, Josef Chytry, Nina Jannik, Brendon Winstead, and Martha Dale Lee for their superb word-processing skills and assistance in other activities germane to the final product.

Organizational Behavior

How Organizations Are Organized

C H A P T E R

1

Organizational Goals and Effectiveness: What We Do

CHAPTER OVERVIEW

This chapter discusses two closely linked organizational concepts: goals and effectiveness. After outlining the nature and function of goals, we explore a more recent, alternative view that calls into question the idea of goals as rational expressions of organizational intention. We then turn to consider various conceptual models of organizational effectiveness, with the aim of encouraging readers to select and use the elements of these models that are suitable to their specific organizations.

THEME CASE

"The Mission of Provigo, Inc., of Canada"—contains a clear mission statement that is followed by four general objectives and information on the operational performance of this North American consumer-goods firm.

CHAPTER OUTLINE

- Why Do Organizations Form?
- The Study of Goals
- An Alternative View of Organizations
- Organizational Effectiveness
- Summary
- Managerial Insight

KEY DEFINITIONS

Organizations   social inventions formed for the purpose of accomplishing tasks or goals.

Goals   desired states of affairs or wishes for the future held by people or organizations.

Operative goals   ends sought through the actual operations of the organization, regardless of the stated or official goals.

Efficiency   the technical ability of the organization to minimize the costs of transforming specified inputs into acceptable outputs.

Effectiveness   the organization's ability to maximize its returns by whatever means, including not only efficiency but also management of its input and output environments.

Additional Terms

Management
Mission statement
Operational goals
Formal goals
Real goals
Competition
Bargaining
Cooptation
Coalition
External constituencies
Goal succession
Goal displacement
Means-end inversion
Law of the instrument
Iron law of oligarchy
Systems view
Variable analysis
Revelatory analysis

THE MISSION OF PROVIGO, INC., OF CANADA

Provigo, Inc. is a leading North American distributor of consumer goods at the wholesale and retail levels. The Company also provides retail support services and programs to its network of affiliated and franchised stores.

Provigo is structured into operating companies that enjoy a large degree of operating autonomy. The Food Group includes Horne & Pitfield Foods (Alberta), Loeb (Ontario and northwestern Quebec), Provigo Distribution (Quebec) and a distribution company specializing in the food service industry. Activities related to the health and pharmaceuticals sector are consolidated in Medis, and C Corp. is the convenience store and petroleum products retailing company. The Specialty Retailing Group consists of Sports Experts and Consumers Distributing, an affiliated company. Provigo Corp. is responsible for Provigo's operations in the United States.

Provigo's Head Office is located in Montreal, Canada. Its capital stock is divided into 42 million shares traded on the Montreal and Toronto Exchanges.

This Annual Report is the result of the outstanding work of some 21,000 employees at Provigo and its affiliated companies in Canada and the United States.

Results for the year ended January 31, 1987, best demonstrate the strength and vitality of your Company. Last year, we announced four particularly demanding corporate objectives. We are pleased to report that we met all of them.

We achieved a 20.5% return on equity as well as an 18% growth in earnings per share, lowered our ratio of debt-to-equity to 40% and increased our dividend by 20% to $0.346 per share. This was accomplished despite an additional tax burden of $5.3 million, stemming from tax surcharges and the elimination of the 3% inventory tax allowance.

It is the competency and dedication of each of the individuals working in our different businesses that made last year's performance possible. All the women and men who form the Provigo team must be thanked sincerely for a splendid job. By their commitment, effort and continued support, they ensure that Provigo remains a superior Company.

We are now living and managing in markedly uncertain times. The tempo of change has quickened. Competition and technology are reshaping markets and industries. Achieving consistent superior performance in such an environment requires that organizations define clearly and pursue their strategic focus, their core mission. Ours is now well defined: a leading North American distributor of consumer goods at both the retail and wholesale levels. This mission has become the leitmotiv of our Company, the symbol of our being and our evolution, of our present and our future. It carries several important messages.

Common Thread and Core Skills

Most importantly, our mission statement captures the unique character of Provigo, the common threads which run through all of our businesses are involved in the distribution of consumer goods and owe their success to a common set of skills. Provigo is established in different geographical regions and product markets. Our Company is now organized for operations of this breadth and magnitude. During the course of last year, we restructured the Company into distinct but homogeneous business Groups: Food, Health and Pharmaceuticals, Convenience, Specialty Retailing and USA. The rationale and objectives of this reorganization are straightforward. Each Group, comprised of companies operating in the same industry, was given a well-defined mandate. This reorganization has improved decision making, encouraged innovation, facilitated coordination and reinforced the ability of our operating companies to adapt the changes in their particular environments. As shown in this report, these changes in our structure and management approach have had a positive impact.

Recognizing the specificity of the sectors in which we are present does not diminish the similarity of the core skills that are the key success factors in the distribution of consumer goods. Conditions and dynamics differ from market to market. Management teams must be sensitive and receptive to changes in their markets in order to become and remain the recognized leader in their sector. For this reason the management teams of our operating companies are given a high degree of operating autonomy. The fact remains, however, that there are strong similarities in the core skills required to attain excellence in each of the sectors where we are active.

For the distribution dimension of our activities, the common thrust across the Groups is the effective implementation of an integrated approach to the management of the supply chain. This comprehensive view of the supply chain is the basis for our vigorous strategic actions in each business sector. Effective and flexible logistical support is a key element of our strategy. By making extensive use of applied information technology, we are achieving levels of coordination and control in the supply chain that, in the past, were only possible through single ownership of all firms concerned. We are also providing more effective means of harmonizing manufacturers' and retailers' goals with our requirements as a distributor.

The use of EDI (Electronic Data Interchange) is an excellent illustration of how our operating companies are making use of common technologies and similar core skills. EDI links the computers in our distribution centres with those of our suppliers, thus eliminating paperwork and offering both parties tremendous opportunities for enhanced productivity. Provigo is recognized as the Canadian leader in this area. Our target is to process 60% of the business going through our food and pharmaceutical distribution centres on EDI by January 1988 and 95% by the end of the next fiscal year.

Similarly, common core skills lead to success on the retail side of our operations. In the food, pharmaceutical, convenience and sporting goods sectors, 2,127 of the 2,264 stores in our networks are operated by affiliates or franchisees. These are remarkable local entrepreneurs. Our operating companies serving them are entirely dedicated to their success.

Our ability to support our retailers' myriad of needs, well beyond the basic supply of products, gives them, and Provigo, a competitive edge. Nowadays, retailers are looking for and need much more than simply a supplier of goods at low cost. In-store technology is fast becoming a major competitive tool and Provigo is and will continue to be at the leading edge in its development and application. At the same time, we are providing our retailers with other services including assistance in site selection, store planning and development, merchandising, promotional and advertising programs, in-store training, insurance and risk management, accounting and financial services. Although the specifics may differ from business to business and indeed between markets, the core skills in our retailing operations are remarkably similar.

A Clear Direction

Our mission statement also defines our future activities. We intend to focus our resources and energies on those areas at which we excel and where our skill base provides our shareholders with added value. We shall concentrate on the distribution of consumer goods at the exclusion of other types of activities such as processing or manufacturing. Accordingly, we have discontinued our meat processing activities and sold our holdings in the Montreal City and District Savings Bank.

The path of our development is delineated by our mission. First, we must take advantage of the substantial expansion opportunities that exist in our core businesses. This will have first call on available resources. We have also identified sectors with interesting growth opportunities which constitute a "natural" evolution or addition to our core businesses. A good example is the food service sector. This industry is entering a phase of rapid consolidation brought about by the implementation of more efficient procurement and management methods as well as the adoption of sophisticated information technologies. Through the recent acquisitions of Wald-man Fisheries Limited, Le Groupe Landry Inc., Pecheries St-Laurent Inc. and Bronstein Bros. (Quebec) Limited, we have already established our-selves as the leading company in this sector in Quebec. Our current activities in the food sector will both complement and benefit from our presence in the food service industry.

A Winning Team

Leading distributors of consumer goods share a number of characteristics. They have mastered information technologies and applied them in a large number of areas. They are recognized for their superior execution, which stems largely from a commitment to training and people development. They place a high value on innovation and risk-taking.

These are qualities that Provigo possesses. We strongly believe that they must be continually nurtured and sharpened. Accordingly, every effort is made to ensure that human resources, technology and the development of shared values are treated as high priorities. On the human resources front, one of our many initiatives involves the establishment of a re-muneration policy consistent with our high performance objectives and the considerable degree of operating autonomy given to each of our management teams. Our key managers will be given the opportunity to take an equity interest and thus participate to the extent that the performance of their operating company contributes to shareholders' wealth. As a result, the interests of shareholders and management will be congruent. Our policy is designed to attract and retain high achievers competent in all phases of our operations and to build a winning team, the Provigo team.

North America in Scope

Our mission statement states unequivocally that North America is the relevant market for Provigo. We are witnessing significant changes in the strategic orientation of corporations, on both sides of the border, as businesses look beyond their domestic markets. Our outlook, like our positioning, must reflect this evolution, this North Americanization of retail and whole-sale markets. Provigo already has operations in the United States and has performed as well as other American companies in the same industry. This experience should serve us well as we prepare to expand our presence in that market.

In short, both the present and the future are captured in our mission statement. It defines our value-creating focus. We intend to keep this focus and to grow within it.

Looking Ahead

Our performance in the year just ended shows that we have achieved a healthy balance between tasks which are often considered to be mutually exclusive. On the one hand, our riveted attention on the present, on the quality and excellence of our execution, has produced superior results. On the other hand, we are decidedly turned towards the future, determined to identify and implement the programs and systems which will give Provigo sustainable competitive advantages. The introduction of a rigorous strategic planning discipline imposes hard work and a heavy commitment of time on our management teams. It is intellectually demanding since it forces management to define the direction of the companies, while continually testing their assumptions against facts and reality of the marketplace. In this regard, it is noteworthy that the business opportunities available to our operating companies should allow us to meet during the next three years our four corporate goals. Clearly, considerable potential exists in our core activities.

Yet, there is much more to it. The applicability of the methods that characterize our operating modes and the nature of the core skills of our teams allow us to consider with confidence additional growth opportunities such as penetrating sectors that are closely linked to our present businesses, expanding geographically or increasing our presence in the Specialty Retailing sector.

Decidedly, Provigo's growth potential is considerable—and within the path defined by our mission.

Our aim is to build a dynamic, innovative and technologically adept distributor of consumer goods. A company driven by clear understanding of its role and direction. We are convinced that this approach is the best guarantee that Provigo will continue to be a market leader and a high performer, whatever the competitive circumstances.

Why Do Organizations Form?

Organizations begin with goals—people form into groups or organizations for a purpose. This formation may take place because one individual, an entrepreneur, has a vision of a new product or service to bring to the market and she recruits others to help her accomplish that goal. Or the organization may be based on the congruence of desires or interests of a number of individuals who band together to achieve their goal. Whatever the stimulus, the core of the organization is its goal.

Organizations are simply social inventions for accomplishing tasks or goals. Everyone is familiar with organizations because we live in them from the day we are born. Common examples are families, schools, churches, and clubs.

People form organizations because they realize that they can magnify their own abilities by working with others toward common objectives. Once people come together in groups, tasks must be differentiated and labor divided. Specialization and division of labor has two benefits: it permits the optimal use of group members' abilities, thus playing to their strengths; and it avoids redundancy of labor by clearly delineating who does what. The resulting structure, however, requires coordination of effort. It also becomes clear that results are more likely to be achieved if someone is in charge of keeping the group moving toward its goal. Thus, the essence of **management** is born. Today's most complex organizations reflect these essential building blocks.

The primacy of goals to organizations is clear; we hear them espouse goals every day. Pro football teams strive to win the Super Bowl and baseball teams the World Series. A political party in power has the goal of remaining there, while the minority party has the goal of claiming power for itself. NASA accomplished its goal of putting an American astronaut on the moon, and Lee Iacocca reached his goal of turning Chrysler Corporation around.

Goals are a person's or an organization's desired state of affairs; they are wishes people and organizations have about where or what they want to be at some future time. Goals have traditionally been closely linked to organizational effectiveness; the degree to which an organization attains its goals is, in the judgment of many analysts, a measure of its effectiveness. Provigo's annual report reflects this view; the company argues for its success based on the achievement of four goals, including high return on equity, growth in earnings per share, decreased leverage, and higher dividends.

In this chapter we will familiarize readers with different theories or views on goals as well as discuss the issues of goal formulation, succession, and displacement. We will point out the many functions and dysfunctions of goals. Finally, we'll examine models and measures of organizational effectiveness.

While we will discuss the functions of goals in greater detail later in this chapter, we can consider four general functions that goals possess:

1. They provide direction to the activities of individuals and groups.

2. They shape how organizations plan and organize their activities.

3. They are used to motivate people to perform at high levels.

4. They form the basis for evaluating and controlling organizational activities.

We have seen these functions at work in the Provigo case. The company's goals are used as (1) the ends that worker and unit effort are meant to attain; (2) rationales to determine whether a unit is part of the company's core business; (3) motivators to obtain peak employee performance; and (4) yardsticks to measure the company's success.

It is precisely because of their multiple uses—and the different activities they lead to—that the subject of goals constitutes one of the most complex and controversial topics in management. Given the variety of uses of goals, consensus about an organization's goal is highly important to that organization. But such consensus rarely exists. As we shall see, this lack of agreement constitutes just one of the problems involved in grappling with organizational goals. Some of the shortcomings of the goals approach have lead researchers to devise alternative approaches to the study of organizations.

The Study of Goals

To understand how goals are used, we must first analyze kinds of goals, differences between formal and real goals, and how goals are formulated and changed. This analysis will provide the fundamentals for discussing the functions and dysfunctions of the goals perspective.

Typologies of Goals

Goals can be viewed in a number of ways. One can focus on the matter of level, defining some goals as primary and others as subsidiary. With this approach we identify the goal at the top of the organization's hierarchy of goals as the **mission statement,** which defines the fundamental and unique purposes that differentiate the organization from others. Provigo was careful to define its mission clearly: it sees itself as "a leading North American distributor of consumer goods at both the retail and wholesale level." The feature "Mission Statements" has more examples of these fundamental goals.

FEATURE: *Mission Statements: Functions and Examples*

Developing a mission statement is an important first step in the strategic planning process, according to both practitioners and research scholars. An effective mission statement defines the fundamental, unique purpose that sets a business apart from other firms of its type and identifies the scope of the business's operations in product and market terms. It is an enduring statement of purpose, comprehensive in its coverage of broad organizational concerns. The limited evidence available suggests eight key approaches to mission statements. Following is a list of these components with examples of mission statements that illustrate each:

1. *The specification of target customers and markets:* "to anticipate and meet market needs of farmers, ranchers and rural communities within North America" (CENEX).

2. *The identification of principal products or services:* "Standard Oil Company (Indiana) is in business to find and produce crude oil, natural gas and natural gas liquids; to manufacture high quality products useful to society from these raw materials; and to distribute and market those products and to provide dependable related services to the consuming public at reasonable prices."

3. *The specification of geographic domain:* "We are dedicated to the total success of Corning Glass Works as a worldwide competitor."

4. *The identification of core technologies:* "The common technology in these areas relates to discrete particle coatings" (NASHUA).

5. *The expression of commitment to survival, growth and profitability:* "To serve the worldwide need for knowledge at a fair profit by gathering, evaluating, producing, and distributing valuable information in a way that benefits our customers, employers, authors, investors and our society" (McGraw-Hill).

6. *The specification of key elements in the company philosophy:* "We believe human development to be the worthiest of goals of civilization and independence to be the superior condition for nurturing growth in the capabilities of people" (Sun Company).

7. *The identification of the company self-concept:* "Hoover Universal is a diversified, multi-industry corporation with strong manufacturing capabilities, entrepreneurial policies, and individual business unit autonomy."

8. *The identification of the firm's desired public image:* "to contribute to the economic strength of society and function as a good corporate citizen on a local, state, and national basis in all countries in which we do business" (Pfizer).

Source: John A. Pearce II and Fred David, "Corporate Mission Statements: The Bottom Line," *Academy of Management Executive* 1, no. 2 (1987): 109–116.

The mission statement establishes other, more subordinate goals that are formulated to implement that mission. These secondary goals are called **operational goals.** Provigo states such goals in their 1987 Annual Report, which appear on a number of different levels. First, we learn of a larger operational goal: "making use of technologies and core skills." Later, this is translated into a far more specific goal: "our target is to process 60% of the business going through our food and pharmaceutical distribution centers on EDI by January 1988 and 95% by the end of the next fiscal year." The feature on overarching goals details the value of the link between operational goals and the mission statement.

FEATURE: *The Importance of an Overarching Goal*

The concept of an overarching goal is directly analogous to the concept of a superordinate goal or mission for the total organization (Pascale and Athos, 1982). Peters and Waterman (1982) found in their study of excellent companies that each had a chief executive officer who had articulated a goal that used only a few words to summarize what was unique and special about the company, what employees could focus on and use as a guideline, and what the company stood for. IBM, for example, has as its superordinate goal "customer service." Hewlett-Packard's is "innovative people at all levels." Sears stands for "value at a decent price." AT&T has been guided by the idea of "universal service." Bechtel, a huge construction company, prides itself on "a fine feel for the doable." GE is known for its "progress is our most important product" theme. . . .

. . . But the organization's goal needs to be translated, or specifically formulated, for each department or unit. Exactly what is the goal that General Electric's CAT scanner service department should follow to be consistent with the idea of progress as a product? What is the goal of the finance department within IBM's office products division that supports "customer service"? How does the contract estimating department at Bechtel run itself to have a "fine feel for the doable"? Even when the organization as a whole has a clearly articulated and well-supported superordinate goal—an all-too-rare occurrence in American companies—each unit must also have an overarching goal that does specifically for the unit's members what the corporate goal does for the company at large. Even if the organization has nothing more explicit than its generalized purpose, a unit can be greatly aided by adopting a goal.

The unit's goal must be consistent with overall corporate goals, but it is more than a mere restatement of a company purpose. Instead, it must be distinctive and suited to the specific unit's purposes and competencies. . . .

An overarching goal has several important effects. It builds a common frame of reference that allows people with different backgrounds and varying orientations to pull collectively toward the same ends. It is an important force for change; it describes what could be, what the department should strive for. Finally, it is highly motivational. It places individual tasks within a larger framework, thereby giving work greater significance. . . .

In some ways the overarching goal is the departmental parallel to a corporate strategic posture, in which a firm examines the environment and its opportunities, assesses its own capabilities, and then determines a market niche that will allow it to be successful. Just as the chief executive officer must lead the effort to formulate a strategy that can be encapsulated in an exciting, challenging superordinate goal statement, the middle manager needs to work toward the formulation and dissemination of a departmental overarching goal.

An effective overarching goal has four essential characteristics:

1. The goal reflects the core purpose of the department.

2. The goal is feasible—consistent with the general purposes of the organization as a whole, compatible with what other departments can deliver, and feasible in terms of the departmental manager's personal capacities.

3. The goal is challenging—tasks that are stretching—difficult but achievable—will pull the best from most subordinates.

4. The goal has larger significance—people will extend themselves for work that they see is important. Though not all tasks can have earth-shattering significance, most work can be put in terms that highlight its meaning to others.

One example of a useful, although unusual, overarching goal occurred in the maintenance and engineering department of a medium-size company. The leader saw his department as "the glue that holds the organization together." Normally, this opinion might be a bit presumptuous, but it was somewhat valid in this situation since the company was faced with stringent economic belt-tightening in order to survive. There would be no money in the foreseeable future for new equipment or major renovations. Engineering had to help other departments make do with what plant and equipment they had, so the department's ability to respond quickly to requests for repairs and refurbishing did much to boost morale in the struggling organization. Members of the department increasingly saw themselves as vital to the organization's survival rather than as the ones who had to do the dirty work. The manager found he needed far less time seeing that people actually put in their hours and more time jointly solving problems raised by subordinates who were eager to perform. When combined with challenge, a goal that underlines the larger organizational significance of everyday tasks can be highly motivating.

Source: David L. Bradford and Allan R. Cohen, *Managing for Excellence* (New York: John Wiley & Sons, 1984), pp. 100–105. Copyright © 1984 by David L. Bradford and Allan R. Cohen. Reprinted by permission of John Wiley and Sons, Inc.

Another way of looking at goals is based on their functions, or on whom they serve. One example of this approach classifies organizational goals on the basis of whose point of view is recognized (Perrow, 1970, pp. 135–136). This typology includes five categories of goals:

1. *Societal goals* refer to society in general. Examples: produce goods and services, maintain order, generate and maintain cultural values. This category deals with large classes of organizations that fulfill societal needs.

2. *Output goals* refer to the public in contact with the organization. This category deals with types of outputs defined in terms of consumer functions. Examples: consumer goods, business services, health care, education.

3. *System goals* refer to the state or manner of functioning of the organization, independent of the goods and services it produces or its derived goals. Examples: emphasis on growth, stability, profits, or modes of functioning, such as being tightly or loosely controlled or structured.

4. *Product goals* refer to the characteristics of the goods or services provided. Examples: an emphasis on quality or quantity, variety, styling, availability, uniqueness, or innovativeness of the products.

5. *Derived goals* refer to the uses to which the organization puts the power it generates in pursuit of other goals. Examples: political aims, community services, employee development, investment and plant-location policies that affect the state of the economy and the future of specific communities.

An organization is likely to have goals in each area of this typology—perhaps even more than one. Provigo's annual report mentions output goals (focusing on foodstuff, health and pharmaceuticals, convenience stores, and specialty retailing); system goals (growth, profits, maintaining autonomy); product goals (providing a high level of service to retailers); and derived goals (employee development).

Formal Versus Real Goals

Such goals as the mission statement and operational goals, created by management and specifically stated, are the organization's **formal goals.** Formal goals can be created on a number of different dimensions. Provigo had some quantifiable performance goals involving return on equity, earnings per share, leverage, and dividend levels. It also has formulated some qualitative human resource goals, such as nurturing innovation and risk-taking.

Although these formal statements of goals are useful, putting too much credence in formal goals may be misleading. First, it is clear that organizational goals will sometimes conflict with one another. For example, universities espouse such goals as faculty teaching, research, and public service. Yet for any faculty member these goals conflict; to the extent that she engages in one of these activities, the other two are left wanting. Large bureaucratic organizations, struggling to remain competitive, simultaneously try to encourage innovation while clinging to standard practices and controls that stifle creativity.

The constant tension between formal goals and actual organizational behavior adds to the difficulty of accepting the formal goal model of organizations. For example, Anderson, Clayton and Company (involved in cotton, vegetable oils, and coffee) spent many years formally pursuing the acquisition of a major company in the food industry, including such well-known firms as Stokely-Van Camp and Gerbers. However, their actual behavior indicated that they really wanted to avoid the heavy debt of a big acquisition that might make them less attractive to prospective buyers of their own firm.

Because of the shortcomings of the formal goal model of organizations, models began to appear that discussed operative or real goals. **Operative goals** are those ends "sought through the actual operating policies of the organization; they tell us what the organization is actually trying to do, regardless of what the official goals say are the aims" (Perrow, 1961, p. 855). Another researcher uses the term **real goals** to refer to these perhaps unstated but significant pursuits: "those future states toward which a majority of the organization's means and the major organizational commitments of the participants are directed, and which, in cases of conflict with goals which are *stated* but command few resources, have clear priority" (Etzioni, 1964, p. 7).

Taking the view of goals as operative or real has the advantage of recognizing that goals are distilled from both formal and informal sources and that they are the consequences of interactions and bargaining among organizational members. These views also recognize the importance of power to the formation of goals. Finally, they suggest that a way to understand organizational goals is to examine actual organizational processes, including the allocation of resources to specific programs and activities. For instance, a study of juvenile correctional institutions found that more resources were allocated to custodial aspects of the organizations than to professional personnel, suggesting that the real goal was not the stated goal, rehabilitation, but custodial care.

Figure 1.1 shows the relationship among formal goals, operational goals, and operative goals. It illustrates that the main difference is in the direction in which the goals are expressed.

A problem in attempting to identify operative or real goals has to do with measurement. One measures what is visible to measure, but this may have little to do with what is really important to the organization. Investigators must open themselves to unusual approaches in the search for operative goals. In the study of juvenile corrections previously mentioned, the researcher looked at the allocation of resources to tease out the real goals. In the investigation of a company, it may be necessary to look beyond such traditional measures as profitability to employee turnover ratios, product quality, or overall stability.

Other considerations complicate formal goal models. There is the problem of whose goals one has to consider. At one extreme it can be argued that the goals of organization members perfectly reflect organizational goals. But such is not the case, forcing the researcher to identify the disparity between individual and organizational goals. In fact, it seems obvious that any organization would have large numbers of individual goals, some of which may conflict with each other, and some of which are inconsistent with the organization's goals. The managerial difficulties are clear. The question

FIGURE 1.1
Mission,
Operational, and
Operative Goals

Formal Goals: Goals formally stated internally or externally

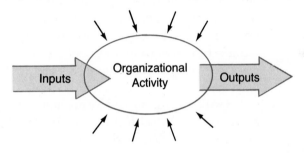

becomes, How does an organization accommodate these differences in formulating a clear set of goals? Some recent discussions of what organizations need to do to perform effectively focus on how top managers must reconcile competing values through using metaphors, images, and other integrative devices (Hampden-Turner, 1990; Pascale, 1990).

Goal Formulation and Changing Goals

The formulation of goals and their change over time involve complex issues. Since, in the goals approach, effectiveness is a function of the degree to which goals are met, the matter of how goals get established in the first place is important. Goal formulation is determined by factors that are both inside and outside the organization.

Internal Factors   As noted elsewhere (see Chapter 4), organizations are coalitions of groups and individuals who have diverse needs and desires. Within an organization, these coalitions bargain continuously, using side payments to induce others to join them in attaining their goals (Cyert and

March, 1963). These side payments can take many forms, such as money, status, power, or authority. In this view, conflicts among coalition members are settled through side payments as well; for a price, an individual or group adopts a goal. Thus, for money employees produce products, and for status they take on jobs that may not be entirely to their liking. The more power a coalition or an individual has, the larger the number of side payments available for use in cementing its position of dominance.

Goals are also influenced by prior commitments such as agreements that members of organizations make with one another or policies that are established and internalized. Such commitments include a wide range of past decisions or obligations and may embrace such issues as growth, minority hiring policies, research priorities, market selection, dividend policy, and other issues. These commitments directly affect future allocation decisions and may constrain future behavior, limiting major changes that an organization may make in its goals, because these commitments limit the organization's resources. As an example, if a company commits resources to a new product line, fewer resources are available for expanding markets in older lines.

Goals are also shaped by previous experience. For example, an organization may have had bad experiences in a market and be unwilling in the future to enter that market. Such was the case with Sears, Roebuck and Company, which failed in foreign markets in the past and has consequently decided not to enter such markets again.

External Factors   Factors outside an organization also have the potential to influence the organization's goals. One can view goal formulation primarily as a process in which managers attempt to maintain a favorable balance of power between the organization and its environment (Thompson and McEwen, 1958). The amount of power organizations have over their environments determines how they deal with those environments. Large multinationals typically have considerable power over their environments and can frequently dictate their own activities to those environments. Grassroots groups of any sort typically have little such power and must cooperate with their environments or use ingenious methods of exerting pressure on those environments.

Thompson and McEwen suggest a continuum of organizational power; where an organization sits on that continuum suggests the appropriate strategy for dealing with the environment. The optimum strategy is **competition** with elements in the environment. An organization in a position to employ this strategy has considerable power to determine its own goals and pursue them with little concern for other factors. Thompson and McEwen point out that hospitals, which compete with midwives, quacks, faith healers, and patent medicine manufacturers, are in a state of competition. As the health care industry has changed, with the addition of HMOs and emergency clinics, hospitals are meeting even more challenges in their environments.

As environmental forces come to have increasing power, one of three more cooperative strategies is called for. The first such cooperative mode is **bargaining,** in which organizations and environments engage in exchange relationships. Lobbying is an example of bargaining. Sometimes this approach can cross the line of ethical behavior, with disastrous results for both participants, as was seen in Japan's Recruit Company scandal.

As the proportion of organizational to environmental power decreases, **cooptation** is the appropriate strategy. In this approach, the organization absorbs environmental elements into itself in order to maintain stability. Firms in the military-industrial complex, for instance, often hire former officials of military agencies in an attempt to secure inroads into decision making.

The other strategy, employed when organizational power is at its weakest compared to the environment, is **coalition.** In this strategy, the organization is forced to join another organization for a common purpose. The auto industry is rife with joint ventures and combinations reflecting this strategy—combinations by General Motors and Toyota and by Chrysler and Mitsubishi are but two examples. The combination of Federal Express and Flying Tigers, creating the first air freight company with truly international reach, is another example.

It is essential that organizations read their environments and select the appropriate strategy. History is filled with examples of organizations unable to do so—in other words, of failed organizations. The Johnson administration was forced out of power by President Johnson's misreading of the country's position on the Vietnam war. The air traffic controllers were fired when they misread President Reagan's position and persisted in their strike. AT&T misread how the courts would interpret the pleas of its competitors and was ultimately broken up in the largest corporate breakup in modern times. The feature on SAS describes an organization that successfully interpreted and reacted to its environment.

FEATURE: *Clear Goal Unleashes Employee Energy for Scandinavian Airlines System*

The objective handed to us by the SAS board was to make the airline operation profitable even though the market couldn't be improved. We imposed one condition on ourselves: we wouldn't achieve short-term profitability by selling airplanes, which so many airlines do in hard times. We would become profitable by providing the best service in the market, thereby increasing our share of the stagnant overall market. . . .

First we needed a clear picture of the outside world and of SAS's position within it. This meant that we had to establish a goal and determine how to reach it. In other words, we had to create a new business strategy.

We wanted SAS to be profitable in its airline operations even in a zero-growth market such as we were then experiencing. To do this we chose to become known as "the best airline in the world for the frequent business traveler." We had pegged businessmen as the only stable part of the market. Unlike tourists, businessmen must travel in good times and bad. Perhaps most important, the business market has special requirements, and developing services to meet those requirements would enable us to attract their full-fare business.

This was not a particularly brilliant idea. All airlines know you cannot make a profit without attracting business travelers, because they are usually the only passengers who pay full fare. What was unique was the *way* we determined to achieve this goal. It was the opposite of the cheese-slicer approach.

We decided to stop regarding expenses as an evil that we should minimize and to begin looking at them as resources for improving our competitiveness. Expenses could, in fact, give us a competitive edge *if* they contributed to our goal of serving the business traveler.

So we scrutinized every resource, every expense, every procedure and asked ourselves, "Do we need this in order to serve the frequent business traveler?" If the answer was no, then we were prepared to phase out the expense or procedure, no matter what it was or how dear it was to those within the company. If the answer was yes, then we were prepared to spend *more* money to develop it further and make SAS more competitive. . . .

The result was a unique strategic plan for turning the company around. Far from cutting costs more, we proposed to the SAS board that we invest an *additional* $45 million and *increase* operating expenses $12 million a year for 147 different projects. . . .

Source: From *Moments of Truth*, pp. 23–27, by Jan Carlzon, copyright © 1987 by Ballinger Publishing Company. Used by permission of Harper Business, a division of HarperCollins Publishers.

The Formulation of Goals The two factors with the strongest influence on the formulation of goals are the nature of an organization's prior commitments and the power relationships within and outside the organization. Pennings and Goodman (1977) shed light on how these power relationships are involved in goal formulation in their insightful discussion of determinants of organizational effectiveness, which can be slightly modified to help us think about the determinants of organizational goals. Their discussion is developed from the strategic contingencies model of organizational structure and power (see Chapter 6).

Pennings and Goodman view organizations as conglomerates of subunits. This enlarges our view of goals "by not focusing exclusively on output parameters such as sales, patient mortality, or students' aptitude" (p. 149). Goals are defined and actualized depending on the power inherent in various subunits. The strategic contingency theory says that power is "some multiplicative function of each subunit's (1) coping with uncertainty, (2) substitutability, and (3) centrality." Powerful subunits obviously have more weight in determining the organization's goals than do weak subunits.

Dominant coalitions emerge from negotiation among groups. The importance of various goals is a function of the relative strengths that the various proponents of those goals have in the negotiated social order. Constituencies probably have competing and potentially incompatible goals, and these have to be worked through by negotiation or other means. Ultimately, the coalition that is formed adopts some set of these goals.

Organizational goals are also influenced from outside the organization. Other people and organizations in the environment of a focal organization influence its goals to the extent that they have some control over it. Organizations either adapt to existing environments or select other environments that are more congruent with their goals. **External constituencies** are those organizations, such as customers, suppliers, competitors, or regulatory agencies, that can influence the focal organization. These organizations set constraints and influence organizational goals.

Provigo very clearly recognizes that its retailers are a critical constituency when it states the following: "We are also providing more effective means of harmonizing manufacturers' and retailers' goals with our requirements as a distributor," and "our ability to support our retailers' myriad of needs, well beyond the basic supply of products, gives them, and Provigo, a competitive edge."

Figure 1.2 (page 22) illustrates this notion of interorganizational relationships. Organizations have dyadic relationships with other organizations in their environments. The figure presents a simplified representation of such a set of relationships. Rosabeth Moss Kanter (1989) calls for more pool-

FIGURE 1.2
*Schematic
Description of
Organizational
Environment*

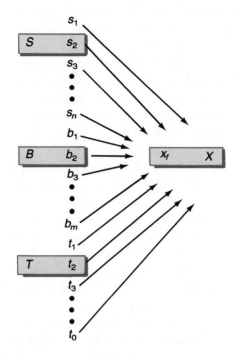

Meaning of symbols:
x_f = focal organization
x_i = member of X
$X = [x_1, x_2, x_3,..., x_p]$ competitors of focal organization
s_i = supplier
$S = [s_{21}, s_{22}, s_{23},..., s_{sq}]$ competitors of supplier 2 (secondary environment)
b_i = buyer
$B = [b_{21}, b_{22}, b_{23},..., b_{2r}]$ competitors of buyer 2 (secondary environment)
t_i = third party, for example, regulatory agency pressure group or
       government
$T = [t_{21}, t_{22},..., t_{25}]$ third parties associated with t_i but *not* interacting with
       x_f (secondary environment)

Source: From P. S. Goodman and J. M. Pennings, and Associates (eds.), *New Perspectives on Organizational Effectiveness* (San Francisco: Jossey-Bass, 1977), p. 158. Copyright © 1977 by Jossey-Bass, Inc. Reprinted by permission of Jossey-Bass.

ing, allying, and linking across companies to meet the competitiveness problem in a world in which the strategic challenge is to do more with less.

> The focal organization, *X*, has exchanges with suppliers, buyers, and third parties such as regulatory agencies and professional associations. Furthermore, the focal organization may be a monopolist, or an oligopolist, or it may face a large number of competitors. Thus, in Figure [1.2] *X* may be zero, a few, or many members. Organizations belonging to an industry or market may be represented in Figure [1.2] by the symbols *X*, *S*, *B*, or *T*. Figure [1.2] gives a representation of the environment from the perspective of the focal organization. (Pennings and Goodman, 1977, p. 157)

In this view, then, goals are a set of criteria, each reflecting evaluations made by various constituencies involved to a greater or lesser degree in the focal organization (Conolly, Conlon, and Deutsch, 1980) and its environment. The word *constituencies* is meant to reflect the fact that groups may or may not directly participate in organizational activities and that they have different amounts of power over the focal organization.

The issue of whether organizational goals are independent of individual goals is resolved by the idea of coalitions that define goals. A major shortcoming of this view, however, is that it is extremely difficult to study organizational processes, such as decision making, that underlie the allocation of key resources. Even if organizations let members or outsiders study these processes, interpretation of what is seen is frequently flawed. For example, in the late 1970s and early 1980s several large utilities in the West embraced energy conservation as a formal corporate goal because it helped them to defer the construction of expensive new power plants and at the same time helped customers manage their rising bills. Some outsiders, and even a few individuals within the utilities, were skeptical that management was sincere and doubted the utilities' commitment to making conservation effective. Only after several years of repeated pronouncements and the adoption of extensive programs that saved literally billions of dollars worth of energy were the skeptics finally convinced that the conservation goals were real.

Changing Goals   Another weakness in the goals approach is a possible mistaken impression that may derive from too much focus on goals. One might assume, incorrectly, that goals are static expressions of organizational intention when, in truth, goals change over time. Given turbulent environments and recurring conflicts among coalitions, it is easy to see why goals remain in a constant state of flux. Goals can change in one of two ways: intentionally or unintentionally.

Goal succession occurs when management consciously decides to change the course of the organization (Steers, 1977). The SAS case provided earlier is such a situation. Another clear example of goal succession is the experience of the National Foundation for Infantile Paralysis (Sills, 1957). The foundation was established in 1938 by Franklin D. Roosevelt to provide information about and find a cure for polio. Through its March of Dimes campaign the organization ultimately succeeded in providing sufficient resources to reach its goal. Having done that, it could have disbanded. To do so, however, not only would have put many people out of work but also would have meant the destruction of the organization's infrastructure, including communications networks and effective leadership. It was easier and more attractive to the organization to find a new mandate: fighting arthritis and birth defects.

The other kind of goal change is **goal displacement.** It occurs when energies are unintentionally diverted away from the original goals of the organization (Steers, 1977). Displacement can take a number of different forms, the simplest of which is the **means-end inversion,** which occurs when the means designed to facilitate goal achievement become the ends in and of themselves. Suppose that a city council decides to slow down automobile traffic by issuing more speeding tickets. Eventually, the goal becomes one of issuing a certain quota of tickets. A similar means-end inversion is the **law of the instrument,** once expressed succinctly as follows: "Give a small boy a hammer, and he will find that everything he encounters needs pounding" (Kaplan, 1964, p. 28). The use of workstations and personal computers in businesses today may suffer this kind of inversion; the goal may become having newer, faster equipment rather than focusing on how the equipment can facilitate work.

The **iron law of oligarchy** is another form of goal displacement (Michels, 1949). Here revolutionary political leaders may change because of their recognition that being in positions of leadership is associated with higher status, income, and power, which they did not enjoy in the past. The result is that the revolutionary goals are displaced in favor of maintaining the status quo. Successful entrepreneurs run the risk of this form of goal displacement; as a new, innovative business meets success, the temptation often arises to codify behavior rather than to rely on the less formal, more flexible approaches that brought success in the first place.

Steers (1977) elucidates a number of reasons for goal displacement:

1. The need to operationalize abstract goals

2. The interpretation of goals brought about through delegation

3. The uncertainty associated with new or tangible goals

4. The necessity for coordinated and controlled activities

5. The tendency to invent measures and evaluations, which can deemphasize qualitative goals

6. The existence of prior commitments and decisions

7. The absence of goal consensus

8. The existence of personal goals and aspirations

The Functions and Dysfunctions of Goals

Goals are both functional and dysfunctional; they can serve or detract from both individual and organizational performance. Steers (1977) has identified five functions that goals serve for organizations:

1. They focus attention or provide direction for managers in their attempts to acquire and use resources. The SAS case demonstrates the value of this function.

2. They serve as a rationale for organizing. We saw in the Provigo case how the overall goals helped define the way the company was organized.

3. They serve as standards of assessment for organizations, against which judgments can be made about organizational effectiveness and efficiency. Opening virtually any annual report reveals this function of goals.

4. They constitute a source of legitimacy for an organization that justifies its activities and existence to diverse groups (investors, members, customers, and so on). In the annual report from another year, Provigo (1988) carefully defined its efforts "to achieve higher standards of excellence . . . with all our partners," including customers, affiliated and franchised retailers, employees, shareholders, suppliers, and communities.

5. They assist the organization in acquiring human resources. Apple Computer's goal of creating a more formal corporate system led it to hire John Sculley, a manager successful in running consumer-goods companies.

Steers also defined five functions that goals can serve for individuals:

1. They provide direction for one's job.

2. They provide a rationale for working and sometimes a sense of meaning to an otherwise pointless job.

3. They may serve as a vehicle for personal attainment.

4. They provide a sense of psychological security.

5. They can provide a source of identification and status for employees.

Unfortunately, goals can be dysfunctional as well. One potential pitfall of organizational goals has been discussed already in the section on goal displacement: when the means becomes the end, the organization suffers. Further, the emphasis that goals place on the measurable can be harmful. Managers may ignore qualitative goals in favor of such measurable goals as profits and sales. A last dysfunction of organizational goals derives from their expression. Goals stated too ambiguously may fail to provide adequate direction, yet highly specific goals may constrain creativity.

These dysfunctions of organizational goals apply to individuals as well, but there are also other problems with goals that are unique to individual behavior. Where reward systems are not designed to reward goal-directed behavior directly, goal attainment will not be maximized. Instead, employees will pursue activities that they can expect will have greater personal payoffs. When reward systems attempt to reflect goal-directed activity, it is often difficult to identify performance criteria that can be used as evidence of goal attainment. For instance, if profit is a company's goal, how can one evaluate the company's public relations program that is designed to increase the public's perception of the company's involvement in the community? Clearly, it is important to define goals appropriately to the position of an individual to prevent this problem.

Another dysfunction occurs in establishing the level of a goal. While goals can be motivating factors, establishing an aim for individuals while making effective use of their motivating capability requires careful thought. The feature "Objectives That Emphasize the Achievable" discusses some of the fine points of the art of goal setting. A goal set too low provides inadequate challenge for motivation. A goal set too high, because it is perceived as impossible, is no motivator either.

FEATURE: *Objectives That Emphasize the Achievable*

Put a 5-foot-10-inch person into 6 feet 3 inches of water, and odds are he'll learn to swim. He may sputter and spit a bit, but he can always hop up off the bottom and get air. Put that same person in 7 feet 4 inches of water, and you may have a dead body on your hands.

In any managerial forum, the topic turns at some point to goal-setting. Most American managers seem all too ready to toss the people who report to them into the 7-foot-4-inch-deep tank. This is what I hear:

"You've got to push your people. Shoot for the moon. That's what motivates 'em. Give 'em half a chance and they'll sign up for a goal 10 percent less than last year's, even though the market is way up." And so on.

. . . I fervently believe in "stretch." I believe, however, in the 6-foot-3-inch variety for the 5-foot-10-inch participant. There is an attribute of goal-setting that stands out in creating a highly charged environment—teaching people that they are winners and that they can succeed, which in turn induces them to take on more, risk more. Thus, the prime objective of goal-setting should be to turn 90 percent of the people in your firm into confident winners who will take the new and always greater risks required by the chaotic times we live in.

That does leave room for "stretch"—it's a must. Without it, there is no sense of accomplishment. But the real art for the manager lies in creating challenging but achievable targets. . . .

The right attitude is one I call "degrees of winning," rather than "winners and losers." This is especially important today. We are required to teach so many fundamentally new things—how a manager can be a facilitator instead of a cop, how to stop emphasizing volume and enhance quality, how to manage a flexible organization instead of a stable one, how to make everyone rather than a handpicked few an agent for change and a risk taker responsible for constant improvement. Building new skills, when large numbers of people are involved, depends above all on generating momentum and commitment. Momentum and commitment come from learning that you can act as needed in—and succeed in—the brave new world. "Punishment," the behavioral scientists have long told us (with compelling documentation), is a futile strategy in general, but especially when new behaviors are required, as they are today. Punishment drives us to hide and be even more averse to risk.

A final word and pleasant surprise: If you work with your team to set achievable goals, you may find yourself managing goals downward—and "unstretching" them, if you will. Social psychology experiments reveal time and again that once people (singly or in groups) get on a roll, they set their objectives too high! They rapidly come to believe they can leap any building of any height in a single bound; by overreaching, they set themselves up for demotivating disappointments. The best route to long-term success, especially where new skills need to be learned, is therefore to meticulously set tailor-made targets that do indeed stretch, but which can be hurdled by almost everyone.

Source: from *Thriving on Chaos: Handbook for a Management Revolution* by Tom Peters. Copyright © 1987 by Excel, a California Limited Partnership. Reprinted by permission of Alfred A. Knopf, Inc.

A last dysfunction occurs when employees cannot identify with abstract goals. How can a student contribute to a university's goal of research excellence? A similar dysfunction occurs when company and individual goals are in conflict. The use of overarching goals for subunits of an organization is essential to prevent both types of dysfunction.

An Alternative View of Organizations

The goal-centered view of organizations assumes that organizations are in the hands of rational actors who have sets of goals that they are consciously pursuing. These goals are assumed to be few enough to manage, well enough identified to be understood, and common enough to be shared throughout the organization. Since goals can be identified, it should be possible to plan optimal management strategies for realizing them (Campbell, 1977). Indeed, Provigo's annual report details strategies for implementing its goals. But as we have seen throughout the prior section, an organization's goals are not always so clear.

Another view of organizations takes a different approach. Generally labeled the **systems view** (Ghorpade, 1971), this approach assumes that organizations of any size are so complex that it is not possible to define a finite number of goals meaningfully. Instead, organizations develop the overall goal of staying alive. Consistent with this approach is another view, which sees organizations as adaptable entities rather than goal-seeking entities (Weick, 1977).

The systems approach differs significantly from the goal-oriented view. The systems perspective pays primary attention to the "people" aspects of the organization, for instance, by encouraging participation in decision making at all levels or by assessing and changing an organization's work climate or workers' job satisfaction or employee health. Goal-achievement approaches emphasize such programs as management by objectives (Odiorne, 1969), cost-benefit analysis (Rivlin, 1971), military readiness (Hayward, 1968), and the direct realization of other goals. The systems approach, on the other hand, stresses survival and viability. These notions "are often extended to include a number of system properties that are seen as immediate causes of survival. Adaptability, maximization of returns, and even integration of subsystems are examples. These properties, like the notion of viability itself, have been difficult to work with" (Kahn, 1977, p. 236).

Viewing organizations as adaptable, viable systems requires the acceptance of some underlying assumptions not taken very seriously in the goals approach. Pondy (1977, p. 229) enumerates those assumptions:

1. Organizations are not material, substantive entities with objective properties: the organization is not an object. That idea is a trap in which our thing-oriented language has caught us. Organizations are sets of interlocked organizing processes that create order (remove equivocality).

2. The organization environment is, in part, enacted by the organization itself, not just given in a predetermined, independent variable sense. Some of those enactments are random, and some contradict the retained order.

3. Rational, goal-directed, instrumental behavior plays a relatively unimportant role in organizing. Instead, organizing is treated as an evolutionary process of variation (enactment plus ecological change) and selective retention. Rationales for behavior are developed retrospectively, after the behavior has been completed and is available for "bracketing" and sense-making.

4. Organizing is primarily an interpersonal process. Realities are *socially* constructed. Therefore, communication and the use of language are important processes. (Language also affects what is selected for our attention.)

5. . . . organizations are creative, problem-solving systems, not just performing systems. They have to figure things out, not just execute behaviors.

If we accept these assumptions, we would undoubtedly view organizations and organizational effectiveness in a different light than we do if we take the goal-oriented view. We might see organizations as behaving and making sense of their past behavior rather than anticipating their future behavior; organizations talk in order to discover what they are saying. Goals, then, are constructed not before but after the fact.

This approach leads to another recognition that has been mentioned earlier. When organizations adapt to specific situations, they lose resources for adapting to other situations down the road (Weick, 1977). The systems view sees a way out of this dilemma that provides for flexibility: organizations should maintain some deviance. Such variation on organizational norms may be healthy because it may promote survivability in a changed environment.

A goal-oriented perspective on organizations specifies integration of functions as a crucial organizational component. The systems approach, too, may see such coordination as essential. But as we will see in Chapter 2, researchers are developing new images of organizations, seeing them as loosely coupled systems that are fluid coalitions of competing interests

(Weick, 1976), or as sets of weak ties that emphasize the links between each coalition and groups external to the organization (Granovetter, 1973). To survive, organizations must have both independence and interconnectedness, gulfs and bridges. This emphasis on adaptability, which sees the benefit to the organization of keeping many options open, also accepts the value of nonintegrative systems.

Finally, one can argue that taking the view of organizations as goal directed is a confusion of means and ends and completely misses a crucial point about organizational behavior: the pleasure is in the process. "Organizations keep people busy, occasionally entertain them, give them a variety of experiences, keep them off the streets, and allow them to socialize. If they do that then they are effective. If the process absorbs time and energy and provides the pretexts for story telling, that is sufficient" (Weick, 1977, p. 216). From the systems perspective, then, organizational effectiveness is not so much a matter of a set of outcomes from goal-seeking behavior as it is the ability of the organization to remain viable in the face of multiple and conflicting goals. From the goals perspective, however, effectiveness is closely tied to the goals themselves.

Organizational Effectiveness

Managers need to judge the success of their organizations; higher-level management wants means to judge the success of its lower-level managers. The criterion often used takes the form of the construct effectiveness. Katz and Kahn (1978) proposed that a distinction be made between the terms *efficiency* and *effectiveness*. **Efficiency** refers to the technical ability of an organization to minimize the costs of transforming inputs into outputs. **Effectiveness,** on the other hand, refers to the organization's ability to maximize its returns by whatever means, including not only the technical efficiency of its throughput processes but also the management of its input and output environments (Scott, 1977, p. 179). Efficiency refers to costs incurred in striving to reach goals. Effectiveness is not conditional on resources the organization commits, but efficiency is. Our focus here is on effectiveness.

Effectiveness is a popular topic, significant not only for the amount of research attention it has received but also for its prevalence in popular media. During the 1980s a number of books about effectiveness reached the *New York Times* best-seller list, most being a good deal more concrete than their academic counterparts. Ouchi's *Theory Z*, Kanter's *The Changemasters*, and all the books authored or co-authored by Tom Peters have effectiveness as their themes. Peters and Waterman (1982) identified excellent organiza-

FIGURE 1.3
Eight Principles
for Excellence

One:	A bias for action: a preference for doing something—anything—rather than sending a question through cycles and cycles of analyses and committee reports.
Two:	Staying close to the customer—learning his preferences and catering to them.
Three:	Autonomy and entrepreneurship—breaking the corporation into small companies and encouraging them to think independently and competitively.
Four:	Productivity through people—creating in *all* employees an awareness that their best efforts are essential and that they will share in the rewards of the company's success.
Five:	Hands-on, value driven—insisting that executives keep in touch with the firm's essential business.
Six:	Stick to the knitting—remaining with the business the company knows best.
Seven:	Simple form, lean staff—few administrative layers, few people at upper levels.
Eight:	Simultaneous loose-tight properties—fostering a climate where there is dedication to the central values of the company combined with tolerance for all employees who accept those values.

Source: From T. R. Mitchell, "In Search of Excellence Versus the 100 Best Companies to Work for in America: A Question of Perspective and Values," *Academy of Management Review* 10(1985): 351. Reprinted by permission.

tions using a number of different criteria to establish eight principles of effectiveness (see Figure 1.3). Despite the prevalence of such examples, a number of writers have questioned these authors' strategies and findings (for example, Carroll, 1983; Hitt and Ireland, 1987). Critics point out that before the end of the 1980s many of these "excellent" companies were no longer excellent.

In addition to these best-sellers, a number of other books about effectiveness have been published, primarily aimed at managers. They take different views of the issue, ranging from economic results (Drucker, 1986), to employee satisfaction (Levering, Mokowitz, and Katz, 1984), to the issue of ethical behavior and profitability (Tuleja, 1985). The last of these views is discussed in the feature "Goals and Ethics."

FEATURE: *Goals and Ethics*

One aspect of goals that needs closer attention than it currently enjoys is the question of ethics. The issue comes under the general heading "corporate social responsibility," which embraces a number of different meanings. Here we suggest one typology.

A first distinction we might make is between actions judged permissible versus those judged impermissible from an ethical or moral point of view (Wokutch and Spencer, 1987). This judgment might be made by asking whether a corporation harms innocent people, keeps promises, shows gratitude, acts in just ways, and provides reparations to those harmed by its actions. Further, we might distinguish between two types of permissible action, that which is supererogatory, or virtuous, and that which is morally neutral.

Based on these notions, one author (Lehman, 1985) proposes a four-cell matrix that categorizes firms according to their involvement or non-involvement in virtuous and impermissible behavior. The four possibilities are:

1. Firms that engage in behavior that is both permissible and virtuous

2. Firms that engage in behavior that is both permissible and morally neutral

3. Firms that engage in behavior that is both impermissible and virtuous

4. Firms that engage in behavior that is both impermissible and morally neutral

One can argue about whether firms with good records of social responsibility perform better or worse than firms with poor records of social responsibility. Current evidence suggests no relationship between the two factors (Aupperle, Carroll, and Hatfield, 1985). Reidenbach and Robin (1989) agree that attempts to measure the success of ethical firms compared to that of other firms have produced questionable results. However, these authors do cite as potential evidence the performance of the so-called socially responsible mutual funds. These funds, which invest only in good corporate citizens, are typically not as successful as other funds in the short run.

Considerable interest has been focused on the relationship between organizational size and performance, about which there is a raging debate. This research is based on the interest economists have in organizational

economies of scale. They want to find the optimum size for a firm, the one that results in the lowest cost per unit of production. Some researchers find that small organizations produce the best economies of scale, others identify large organizations as the most effective, and still others point to medium-sized firms. Academic researchers, too, report contradictory findings on the size–performance relationship (Gooding and Wagner, 1985). Thus the battle continues; the feature "Think Big, Think Small" summarizes the two main lines of debate.

FEATURE: *Think Big, Think Small*

In the March–April 1988 issue of the *Harvard Business Review*, professor and editor Ted Levitt offered his view on the importance of size to organizational effectiveness. Management consultant and author Tom Peters answered Levitt with an article in the July 1988 issue of *Inc.* Here are highlights of the exchange.

> **Levitt:** . . . *It is easy to exaggerate what small new firms do. Their economic importance is obvious. Yet remarkably few are actually possessed of exceptional enterprise or new ideas.*

> **Peters:** . . . *But it is easier, and more conventional, to exaggerate what big companies do, and what they've done in the face of new competition and a technological revolution. And what* have *big companies done lately? Lost jobs. Innovated less. Moved operations mindlessly, and prematurely, offshore. Failed to protect their markets. Kept their leaders insulated from reality (although that may be changing, thanks largely to the effort of such financial entrepreneurs—pardon the expression—as T. Boone Pickens and the Hafts).*

> **Levitt:** *Mostly they are imitative, repeating what others have already done. Mostly they represent modest attempts to attain independence and self-employment by well-established routes.*

> **Peters:** *Now hold on, Ted. When it comes to imitativeness, lack of creativity, and aversion to risk, nobody can top your longtime friends at companies such as Procter & Gamble and NBC. I refer you to* The Bigness Complex *by Walter Adams and James W. Brock: "Nor do giant firms display any appetite for undertaking more fundamental and risky research projects. That is, contrary to the image that bigness is conducive to risk-taking, there is no statistically significant tendency for corporate behemoths to conduct a disproportionately large share of the relatively risky R&D or of the R&D aimed at entirely new products and processes. On the contrary, they generally seem to carry out a* disproportionately small *share of [that] R&D. . . ."*

Levitt: *Many are simply the illusionary creations of people seeking employment they cannot otherwise find, or escape from industrial disciplines they cannot abide.*

Peters: *Condescension is one thing, but this is perverse. Of course, many start-ups fail. So do most new products from large companies. And, yes, companies—as well as products—often start out as "illusionary creations." A dream is illusionary by definition. To become reality, it must be modified again and again. Even then, it may come to naught. But without such dreams, there is no progress—at IBM, at GE or at Microsoft.*

Levitt: *The world's work is done by all sizes of enterprise. None is constitutionally superior to any other. Enterprises of different sizes each do different needed and different newly imagined things.*

Peters: *. . . What that statement overlooks are the real problems large companies are having because they are large, and the challenges they are facing from smaller companies—which are producing better results with fewer resources. . . . These days, even executives of large companies are questioning the advantage of size. Consider Don Povejsil, retired vice-president at Westinghouse, who recently stated that "most of the classical justifications of large size have proved to be of minimal value, or counterproductive, or fallacious."*

Source: From "Thinking Big" by Tom Peters. *Inc. Magazine,* July, 1988, pp. 72–75. Copyright © 1988 by *Inc. Magazine.* Reprinted by permission. Excerpts from "On Agility and Stability" by Ted Levitt, *Harvard Business Review,* March–April, 1988, p. 7. Copyright © 1988 by the President and Fellows of Harvard College; all rights reserved. Reprinted by permission of *Harvard Business Review.*

Models of Organizational Effectiveness

Academic research has produced a number of approaches to organizational effectiveness. The first and most widely used defines effectiveness in terms of how well an organization accomplishes its goals. A second approach corresponds to the system perspective: it focuses on the internal processes and operations of the organization, or the integrity of the system; effective organizations are those whose internal functioning is smooth and without strain. Other approaches focus on other aspects of organizations. These many approaches to organizational effectiveness are summarized in Figure 1.4, which also indicates the circumstances under which each approach is most useful.

FIGURE 1.4
Common Models of Effectiveness

Model	Definition	When Useful
	An organization is effective to the extent that . . .	The model is most preferred when . . .
Goal Model	It accomplishes its stated goals.	Goals are clear, consensual, time-bound, and measurable.
System Resource Model	It acquires needed resources.	A clear connection exists between inputs and performance.
Internal Processes Model	It has an absence of internal strain with smooth internal functioning.	A clear connection exists between organizational processes and performance.
Strategic Constituencies Model	All strategic constituencies are at least minimally satisfied.	Constituencies have powerful influences on the organization, and it has to respond to demands.
Competing Values Model	The emphasis on criteria in the four different quadrants meets constituency preferences.	The organization is unclear about its own criteria, or changes in criteria over time are of interest.
Legitimacy Model	It survives as a result of engaging in legitimate activity.	The survival or decline and demise among organizations is of interest.
Fault-Driven Model	It has an absence of faults or traits of ineffectiveness.	Criteria of effectiveness are unclear, or strategies for improvement are needed.
High Performing Systems Model	It is judged excellent relative to other similar organizations.	Comparisons among similar organizations are desired.

Source: From K. Cameron, "Effectiveness as Paradox: Consensus and Conflict in Conceptions of Organizational Effectiveness," *Management Science* 27(1986): 542. Reprinted by permission of the Institute of Management Sciences and the author.

Most of these approaches are fairly abstract and can therefore embrace a wide range of possible evaluations. For instance, while both U.S. and Japanese companies emphasize profitability as a measure of effectiveness, U.S. firms have traditionally stressed short-term profitability and Japanese businesses long-term profits. This contrast suggests that the approach taken to measuring effectiveness must be defined clearly in order to achieve an accurate assessment.

Another way of dealing with the abstractness of these concepts is to reify organizations, or treat them as though they are concrete entities. We do this by focusing on activity that we call "organization behavior." Managers, in particular, need to keep in mind that *people* in organizations behave, not organizations themselves. Only when we focus on what people in organizations do can we gain any understanding of the effectiveness of the whole. People can behave in vastly different ways, although they may seemingly be pursuing the same goals. Consequently, it is necessary to look at what people do and say and combine their activities and interactions in some way that reflects organizational effectiveness. Managers should keep in mind that effectiveness studies rarely turn up clean relationships, as one would wish. That is, one hopes that employee commitment would be clearly related to effectiveness, but studies relating the two variables have revealed no such connection (see, for example, Angle and Perry, 1981; Jobson and Schneck, 1982).

The Study of Effectiveness

According to one author (Perrow, 1977), **variable analysis** is virtually the only kind of study of organizational effectiveness undertaken:

> In its simplest form, [variable analysis] designates Y as a legitimate goal or output of the organization and studies the effect upon Y of changes in X or a number of X's. Y may be the adaptability or flexibility of the organization, productivity, profitability, amount of job satisfaction, growth, or wealth, to cite the most common dependent variables. . . . X may be training, supervisory style, authority structure, integration, coordination, specialization, or any number of things. A typical study, then, might ask, What is the effect of centralization of decision making on job satisfaction? (p. 97)

Perrow goes on to identify two kinds of alternative studies that are never done. Most studies compare organizations within a narrow range of performance—thus, for example, fairly good hospitals or fairly good penal institutions are compared. No one ever studies the grossly malfunctioning organization.

There are three possible explanations for this phenomenon. First, social scientists do not consider themselves reformers and are consequently more interested in how organizations work than in how to fix the truly bad ones. Second, social scientists have contracts with organizations to investigate those aspects of the organizations in which the groups' leaders are interested. Most do not want to hear failure stories. Finally, grossly malfunctioning organizations are less interesting than adequately functioning ones because the reasons for failure can be easily determined. It is more revealing to identify the subtler dysfunctions in an otherwise well-run organization.

The second kind of study that is not done Perrow calls **revelatory analysis,** or "'who is getting what' from the organization, or 'effectiveness for whom?'" (Perrow, 1977, p. 101). This question presupposes a definition of organizations not as rational systems guided by official goals but as bargaining arenas, as systems of power, and as resources for other organizations (see Chapter 6). If you look at organizations as places where people and groups inside and out compete for outputs of interest to them under conditions of unequal power, the issue of effectiveness is posed differently. The obvious question to ask is, What does the organization produce?

> Take human services organizations, such as hospitals, prisons, social agencies, welfare departments, public schools, and so on. Some outputs that are probably far more critical for the organization than service to clients might be: providing employment opportunities in a society where business and industry cannot generate enough jobs, so tax money is used to employ people; segregating and controlling people who are defined as deviant while symbolically indicating something is being done for them; providing economic opportunities for legitimate business interests, political machines, and organized crime; providing employment opportunities for political parties or ethnic groups. (Perrow, 1977, p. 102)

Gaertner and Ramnarayan (1983) have expanded the notion of revelatory analysis and promoted its adoption by managers interested in assessing effectiveness.

Because the notion of effectiveness does not reflect the various interests of participants impartially, some effort has been made to incorporate into theories of effectiveness such notions as principles of justice or the minimization of harm (Keeley, 1984). Whether more work along these lines will better alert us to consider the different publics served by adopting various criteria of effectiveness is still unknown.

Measuring Effectiveness

To assess organizational effectiveness, one must first find outcome measures that truly reflect what an organization is doing and are as objective as possible. Although this may be self-evident, it is surprising how frequently organizations take stock of themselves by saying something like, "Well, it feels like we're doing okay."

The organization, then, must develop some model of what constitutes effectiveness for it (Campbell, 1977). From that model, it needs an explicit list of the actual decisions for which effectiveness data will be used. Campbell indicates six kinds of decisions for which organizational outcome data could be used. All except the last address practical problems that organizations face, yet, as Campbell notes, only the first and last have received any research attention.

1. Determination of whether some part of the organization is in a "good" or "bad" state. Among the possible outcome measures are profitability, turnover, and frequency of complaints.

2. Determination of why the system is in that particular state. In other words, what causes profitability, turnover, or complaints?

3. Decisions about plans that will change the system. What can be done to improve profitability, turnover rates, or the level of complaints?

4. Evaluation of an organizational change. Did the change provide the expected results?

5. Comparison of organizations for lawmaking or public-policy purposes. For example, the Bureau of Labor Statistics collects labor force data to help determine affirmative action and other laws.

6. Identification of the antecedents of effectiveness. This is the typical reason that scientists want effectiveness data; they wish to determine what factors can predict effectiveness.

Bear in mind that effectiveness data are often used to serve different and conflicting purposes, as when personal performance data are collected to inform the organization about training needs and performance appraisal. A single set of data cannot serve these two masters. Data used to determine training needs should point out deficiencies in performance; on the other hand, it is certainly in the performer's best interest to provide data supporting the view of superior performance when it comes to performance appraisal. The kinds of outcomes or criteria data collected, then, should be determined by the kinds of decisions that data will be used to help make and how they will be used. Data used to find out what went—or may have gone—wrong procedurally or operationally (as in identifying training needs) should be independent of data used to identify how well things are done (as needed for performance evaluations).

A number of investigations have used single measures of organizational outcomes such as overall effectiveness, readiness, productivity, stability, absenteeism, and so on. Three problems are inherent in this approach (Steers, 1977). First, it is virtually impossible to capture the essence of an organization's performance in a single measure. Second, these outcome measures may reflect researcher bias. If an organization sets high productivity as a goal, it is worth measuring. But for a researcher to state that high productivity is a goal and then measure it is to mislead. Third, though many measures are thought to contribute to effectiveness, no one knows exactly how. Single-measure studies are less complete in assessing this relatively amorphous construct than are multimeasure studies.

One might suspect that a number of variables are interrelated and have a complementary relationship to effectiveness. If so, one could design effectiveness studies that simultaneously assess these many variables. The specific variables chosen would depend on the specific goals of the organization under scrutiny and the researcher's hypotheses about the connections among the variables. Campbell and colleagues (1974) identified a number of different variables, which are listed in Figure 1.5 (pages 40–41). They are not all independent of one another, nor have all appeared to date in research. But taken together they provide an extensive list of criteria that might be selected.

As Campbell (1977) states, these indicators differ on a number of dimensions. There are a lot of them, and there have been few attempts to identify the overlap among them. The factors differ in the degree of specificity, and they vary in what might be called "closeness to final payoff" (p. 40). As yet it is impossible to specify a set of "core" outcomes that reflect effectiveness across the organizational board. Although we know that there appears to be no link between effectiveness and corporate social responsibility, various ways to measure the latter can be found elsewhere (Dierkes and Antal, 1986).

Managers might select from this list and add to it criteria that seem important in their organizations, or use it as a springboard for generating a completely different list. A manager with a systems orientation will emphasize different factors (participation, for example) than one with a goal perspective. The astute manager combines the two approaches in constructing an assessment program.

In using the list, one should be careful not to assume that criteria, like turnover, have only one meaning. In one setting turnover may reflect poor organizational performance, whereas in another it may be functional to the organization (Staw and Oldham, 1978). A second caution is to fight the tendency to search for "objective" measures of things. Economists engage in this search every day. Generally, this task is probably doomed to failure. Although conventional wisdom says that objectivity is good, what we think are objective criteria are simply subjective criteria once removed.

A Managerial Guide to Assessing Effectiveness

When devising a program to assess effectiveness, managers are immediately faced with a number of the issues that have been discussed in this section. Here we provide a set of steps managers can follow in constructing an effectiveness measure:

FIGURE 1.5

Criteria Used to Assess Effectiveness

Criterion	Explanation
Overall effectiveness	Takes into account as many factors as possible.
Productivity	Quantity of production or output for a given level of input. Because an individual's productivity may differ from a group's or an organization's, this measure must be used carefully.
Efficiency	The ratio of performance to cost.
Profit	Revenue from sales after the deduction of costs and obligations. Often measured by return on sales or return on investment.
Quality	Can take many forms, such as number of rejects or level of customer complaints; to be used carefully.
Accidents	Frequency of on-the-job accidents resulting in lost time.
Growth	Can take many forms: increase in staff, assets, market share, and so on.
Absenteeism	Can be used as a proxy measure of perceived quality of work life. Again, managers should be careful about what measures they select.
Turnover	Voluntary turnover and involuntary turnover (as when someone leaves because a spouse is transferred) can be caused by different factors.
Job satisfaction	The degree of a worker's satisfaction with the satisfaction amount and kinds of outcomes the job provides.
Motivation	The strength of effort one will apply to achieve group goals; very difficult to measure.
Morale	Difficult to define and separate from job satisfaction and motivation; often seen as a group phenomenon reflecting happiness with the job (whereas the other criteria are individual factors).
Control	Degree and distribution of control in influencing and directing behavior.
Conflict/cohesion	Existence of verbal or physical clashes versus degree of cooperation.
Flexibility/adaptability	Ability to change in response to environmental changes.
Planning and goal setting	Degree to which an organization plans its future.
Goal consensus	Degree to which members of the organization perceive the same goals.
Goal internalization	Degree to which members of the organization accept the same goals.
Role and norm congruence	Degree of agreement on performance expectations, role requirements, and so on.
Managerial interpersonal skill	Level of skills managers possess for dealing with others in terms of giving support, facilitating constructive interaction, and so on.
Managerial task skills	Level of skills with which leaders perform tasks.
Information management and communication	Completeness, efficiency, and accuracy of analysis of information and its distribution.
Readiness	Ability of the organization to perform well and in a timely way; a commonly used military measure.
Utilization of environment	Extent to which an organization interacts with its environment, acquiring and using resources.
Evaluation by external entities	Assessment of the organization by individuals and organizations in its environment.
Stability	Maintenance through time, particularly through periods of stress.
Value of human resources	Total worth of workers to the organization.

FIGURE 1.5
(*continued*)

Criterion	Explanation
Participation and shared influence	Degree to which individuals participate in making decisions that affect them.
Emphasis on training and development	Amount of resources devoted to these areas.
Emphasis on achievement	Degree to which the organization values achieving new goals.

Source: J. P. Campbell et al., "The Measurement of Organizational Effectiveness: A Review of Relevant Research and Opinion," Final Report, Naval Personnel Research and Development Center Contract N00022-73-C-0023 (Minneapolis, MN: Personnel Decisions, 1974). Reprinted by permission of Personnel Decisions.

1. Help the organization develop an explicit model or theory of effectiveness by helping it to describe explicitly the decisions or courses of action for which effectiveness data will be used. Two questions are important in this process: "Will the data base toward which we are moving really be useful for the purposes we have in mind? Are we inadvertently asking the same data to serve conflicting aims?" (Campbell, 1977, p. 47).

2. Specify the task objectives of the organization or of its subunits. (The list will probably be long.)

3. Decide which objectives are means and which are ends.

4. Specify the conditions under which the organization should be able to accomplish a particular objective.

5. Weight the importance of each objective and focus on the more important ones first.

6. Decide on the degree to which "ends" should be accomplished given prevailing conditions.

7. Decide on ways to measure objectives. Some will require simple counts, some more complex assessments.

Following these seven steps will provide managers with a clearer picture than most now have of how to uncover and assess effectiveness. Underlying those steps is the assumption that goals are not too difficult to know and deal with. Conflicts and tensions will come alive in this kind of analysis, and a systems perspective will be folded into the goals perspective. The result of such study is described in the feature "Measuring Productivity."

FEATURE: *Measuring Productivity: One Way to Assess Effectiveness*

Many sophisticated models developed by specialists to measure productivity are useless to managers because they ignore the real challenges managers face. They may measure what productivity is *not*, such as *wages*. In deciding how best to measure productivity, managers should focus not on dollars per hour but on labor dollars per product. That is, on labor content, not labor cost. Productivity measurement should focus on overall capabilities, not on one set of costs. How good is your company at taking a pile of raw materials, a bunch of machines, stacks of paperwork, and groups of employees, and turning out useful goods and services? That's what a productivity index should address.

The trouble with single-factor productivity measures (whether output per labor hour, output per machine, or output per ton of material) is that it is easy to increase the productivity of one factor by replacing it with another. Effective productivity measurement requires the development of an index that identifies the contribution of each factor of production and then tracks and combines them.

A multifactor index to track productivity gives managers a convenient scorecard to answer the question, "How are we doing?" But an index can play this role only if managers and workers understand it, which may require certain compromises in mathematical elegance and accuracy. When the chief goal is to study productivity behavior, as in statistical research, [logarithmic and multiplicative techniques] have theoretical advantages. But when the primary goal is to influence behavior, the simpler the better must be the rule. If the people who use an index can't understand it at a gut level, it probably will not affect their decisions and priorities.

Conventional systems to measure productivity often overlook two aspects of the production process that are becoming very important in determining international competitiveness: production time and the role of employees other than shop floor workers.

The first oversight, time, is not purchased, so it is usually ignored. But the production process certainly consumes time, and the fact that it is not purchased doesn't mean it's free. If two businesses use identical machines, the same number of people and equivalent materials to produce identical products, most productivity indexes would produce identical scores. But suppose one business ships orders within three days of receiving them and the other takes three weeks. Is their productivity the same? Obviously not.

The second crucial but often overlooked aspect of many productivity measurement systems regards whose performance is being measured. Engineers, supervisors, and other white-collar employees make significant contributions to manufacturing productivity, but few systems measure their roles. It isn't possible to measure white-collar outputs or inputs fully, but this fact doesn't mean that only blue-collar productivity should be measured. It does mean, however, that managers must be creative and open to new ways of thinking about an operation.

Things are often not as they first appear with productivity data. One big manufacturer, after introducing a multifactor productivity index, discovered that its plants had suffered a significant productivity decline in the early 1980s. Bad management, right? Wrong. Demand for its product had fallen sharply during the period and, given the fixed inputs, overall productivity had declined. One plant had an especially large drop. Bad management, right? Wrong again. The plant, located in a rural area lacking skilled labor, treated skilled and semiskilled employees as fixed costs. To lay off these workers would be to lose them permanently to other employers. The large decline in productivity in response to a six-month downturn was thus evidence of good management; the employees should have been kept on. Productivity measurement raises issues and highlights changes, but it does not tell the whole story.

Perhaps the most important use of productivity measurement is as an objective source of information about long-term operating trends. An index can draw attention to plants or departments experiencing unusual problems or uncommonly strong performance. Productivity comparisons can also inspire useful exchanges of ideas. Differences in the amount of vertical integration or subcontracting, accounting policies, and many other factors often obscure the relative productivity of companies. Nonetheless, if a business finds itself a lot less productive than a competitor, it probably has a real problem. Managers may insist that the productivity gap is overstated, and they may be right. They will be hard-pressed, however, to argue that it does not exist.

Source: Excerpt from W. Bruce Chew, "No-Nonsense Guide to Measuring Productivity," *Harvard Business Review*, January–February 1988, pp. 110–118. Copyright © 1988 by the President and Fellows of Harvard College; all rights reserved. Reprinted by permission of *Harvard Business Review*.

Peters, in *Thriving on Chaos* (1987), takes a different view of measurement. He argues that because modern systems are so complex, we need to simplify them by selecting just a few things to measure—but making sure that they are "the right stuff." Peters suggests that organizations may want to focus on quality, innovation, flexibility, and perhaps such unusual characteristics as "bureaucracy bashing" (p. 480).

Some argue that effectiveness is based on various external and internal environmental contingencies, a position based on structural contingency theory (explained in Chapter 2). Because the tenets of this theory are somewhat vague and measurement problems exist, studies both support and refute it (see, for example, Azma and Mansfield, 1981; Boseman and Jones, 1974; Negandhi and Reimann, 1972). As yet, it is unclear that this approach will offer managers practical guidance about what to change to improve effectiveness in their organizations.

SUMMARY

Organizations are formed to achieve goals, whether the providing of a good or service at a profit or the accomplishment of social change or simply the enjoyment of good company. Goals can be viewed in a number of different ways, either hierarchically or by analyzing to whom the goals are directed. Researchers find it useful to differentiate formal and real goals. The former are the official, stated goals of the organization; the latter are the goals that can actually be inferred from the actions of the organization. Managers should be sensitive to the real goals of their own and other organizations to ensure that they correspond to the desired formal goals. Looking at real goals provides advantages: if one sees goals as resulting from coalitions, the issue of individual versus organizational goals is resolved or can be approached in a constructive way. This perspective has a disadvantage, however. It can be difficult to devise methods to ascertain an organization's real goals.

To try to identify goals in this way, we explored the internal and external factors that contribute to goals. Prior commitments and power relationships have the greatest roles to play in the formulation of goals. Managers attempt to maintain a favorable balance of power with their external environments, engaging in strategies ranging from competition to cooptation to coalition forming. Goals change over time, either when managers intentionally alter course or when organizational energies are unintentionally diverted from the original goals. There are several forms of goal displacement, including means-end inversion, the iron law of oligarchy, and the law of the instrument.

Goals provide valuable functions for both organizations and individuals, among them being the establishment of a source of identity and a basis for motivation. They are dysfunctional as well, however. When goals are displaced, the organization may suffer. If too much reliance is placed on measurable goals, other, equally important, goals could be ignored.

With a thorough understanding of goals, we went on to examine alternative perspectives—the systems view. This approach recognizes the fact that in most large organizations goals are simply too numerous and possibly too conflicting to provide meaningful direction. This perspective focuses on adaptability and survival as criteria of effectiveness. Organizations are seen as sets of interlocked processes that are evolutionary and social, with participants working to make sense of those processes. Instead of searching for goals, we might be better off looking for such qualities as deviance, loose ties, and the pleasure of organizational processes.

In contrast, the goals approach sees effectiveness in connection with the goals themselves. Effectiveness studies tend to employ the method of variable analysis—researchers study how the manipulation of one variable changes the attainment of goals. Researchers have yet to employ two other possible approaches: the study of grossly malfunctioning organizations and the study of who gets what from the organization. To be useful, studies of effectiveness must carefully define what data are being used to study a variable; if the same data are used for more than one variable, the results could be misleading. We went on to describe a large number of criteria that could be used to assess effectiveness, noting that these measures differed from one another in a variety of ways. Managers might draw from this list, perhaps adding their own criteria, to devise a set of measures to use in their own organizations. We presented a managerial guide to effectiveness that focused on clearly identifying the goals, their relative weight, the data measures to be used, and the way data can be measured. Recently, there was a plea for the application of effectiveness research to help Third World organizations grow and develop (Khondwalla, 1989).

At the beginning of the chapter, we presented the case of Provigo, Inc., of Canada, a firm that combines goal attainment (growth as well as four clear financial objectives) with a system orientation that keeps an eye on the needs of external constituents and employee development. In essence, Provigo's management makes excellent use of multiple models to assess their organizational effectiveness and to provide guidance.

MANAGERIAL INSIGHT

To: *Student Manager*
From: *Veteran Manager*
Subject: *Goals*

The power of sharply defined goals to focus the effort of an organization cannot be overstated. The clearer the goals, the more concentrated the energies of the group can be, and the less wasted effort there will be.

That much is easy to say. What makes a manager's goal-setting responsibilities much tougher is that the challenge goes beyond being clear. You have to make sure that the goals of your department or unit are aligned with those of the whole organization or that key managers are harnessing tension. Neither alignment nor harnessing is always easy.

In the for-profit sector, more and more organizations are revising and restating their overall goals to meet the demands of an increasingly fast-moving, internationally competitive marketplace. In the not-for-profit sector, equally powerful social and governmental forces are requiring similar adaptiveness in every kind of organization, from hospitals to social agencies to trade associations.

Two concepts have been useful for me in trying to make sure that the goals of my department are aligned with the goals of the whole organization.

The first is to imagine that my department suddenly disappeared, but that management intended to replace whatever functions and positions were essential—one person and one function at a time. This exercise forces a manager to concentrate on the essential purpose of the whole organization and think of the contribution his or her department makes to that essential purpose. If it is difficult to find one or more factors that clearly contribute to the whole organization's success, some serious re-evaluation of the department is in order. Another benefit of the exercise is that it helps a manager to identify the functions that make low or marginal contributions. This helps the manager avoid setting departmental goals that emphasize the wrong things.

The second concept is for the manager to see his or her role as that of a translator or interpreter. The whole organization speaks in one language; the individual employee usually thinks and communicates in another language. The manager, or interpreter/translator, has to first understand what the larger organization is saying when it articulates its goals, then convert those goals into meaning for the employees in the department. Somebody has to understand and internalize the corporate goal and translate it into "Things for Our Department to Do Today." The CEO's vision may be grand and inspiring, but the man or woman doing the work has to be able to see how his or her individual part contributes.

A necessary prerequisite to either of these concepts working very well is that the corporate or organizational goal itself be clear and understandable. Unfortunately, this is not always the case in every organization. In any given organization, it is not always the case at all times. At times of dramatic change, such as those typifying most organizations in the 1980s and 1990s, the organizational goals may become fuzzy and indistinct. The manager trying to align department goals with those of the whole organization may feel that the task is impossible. In such a case, the department's goals may be all the employees have to direct their efforts.

When that happens, you will earn your salary and then some.

REVIEW QUESTIONS

1. How does Provigo, Inc., use its mission statement to structure its operations and generate other goals?

2. Distinguish among mission statement, operational goals, formal goals, and operative goals.

3. If operative goals are not explicitly stated, how can they be identified?

4. Give examples of each of Thompson and McEwen's four strategies for handling uncertainty in the environment.

5. The study of goal formulation through the influence of constituencies is also called the "stakeholder model." What does that term indicate about the reason that constituencies take part in goal setting?

6. How could the study of groups and power enhance your understanding of goals?

7. What are three types of goal displacement? Why is goal displacement a problem?

8. List five functions that goals serve for organizations.

9. What kinds of valuable behaviors can be overlooked if goals are expressed only in quantifiable terms?

10. What are the two alternate views of goals in organizations?

11. How can an organization be said to "enact" its environment?

12. Who do you think is right, Levitt or Peters?

13. How is Perrow's concept of revelatory analysis related to the idea of operative goals?

14. Distinguish between efficiency and effectiveness.

15. What are the three drawbacks of single-measure studies of effectiveness?

REFERENCES

Angle, H. L., and Perry, J. L. (1981). An empirical assessment of organizational commitment and organizational effectiveness. *Administrative Science Quarterly* 26:1–13.

Aupperle, K. E., Carroll, A. B., and Hatfield, J. D. (1985). An empirical examination of the relationship between corporate social responsibility and profitability. *Academy of Management Journal* 28:446–463.

Azma, M., and Mansfield, R. (1981). Market conditions, centralization, and organizational effectiveness: Contingency theory reconsidered. *Human Relations* 34:157–168.

Boseman, F. G., and Jones, R. E. (1974). Market conditions decentralization and organizational effectiveness. *Human Relations* 27:665–676.

Bruner, J. S., and Taguiri, R. (1954). The perception of people. In G. Lindzey (ed.), *Handbook of Social Psychology*, vol. 2. Reading, MA: Addison-Wesley, pp. 634–654.

Cameron, K. S. (1986). Effectiveness as paradox: Consensus and conflict in conceptions of organizational effectiveness. *Management Science* 27:539–553.

Campbell, J. P. (1977). On the nature of organizational effectiveness. In P. Goodman and J. Pennings (eds.), *New Perspectives on Organizational Effectiveness*. San Francisco: Jossey-Bass.

Campbell, J. P., et al. (1974). The measurement of organizational effectiveness: A review of relevant research and opinion. Final Report, Naval Personnel Research and Development Center Contract N00022-73-C-0023. Minneapolis, MN: Personnel Decisions.

Carroll, Daniel, T. (1983). A disappointing search for excellence. *Harvard Business Review*, November–December, pp. 78–79, 83–84, 88.

Collins, A. M., and Loftis, E. F. (1975). A spreading-activation theory of semantic processing. *Psychological Review* 82:407–428.

Conolly, T., Conlon, E. J., and Deutsch, S. J. (1980). Organizational effectiveness: A multiple constituency approach. *Academy of Management Review* 5:211–218.

Cyert, R. M., and March, J. G. (1963). *A Behavioral Theory of the Firm*. Englewood Cliffs, NJ: Prentice-Hall.

Dierkes, M., and Antal, A. B. (1986). Whither corporate social reporting: Is it time to legislate? *California Management Review* 28:106–121.

Drucker, P. F. (1986). *Managing for Results: Economic Tasks and Risk-taking Decisions*. New York: Harper & Row.

Etzioni, A. (1964). *A Modern Organization*. Englewood Cliffs, NJ: Prentice-Hall.

Gaertner, G. H., and Ramnarayan, S. (1983). Organizational effectiveness: An alternative perspective. *Academy of Management Review* 8:97–107.

Ghorpade, J. (ed.). (1971). *Assessment of Organizational Effectiveness*. Pacific Palisades, CA: Goodyear.

Gooding, R. Z., and Wagner, J. A. (1985). A meta-analytic review of the relationship between size and performance: The productivity and efficiency of organizations and their subunits. *Administrative Science Quarterly* 30:462–481.

Granovetter, M. S. (1973). The strength of weak ties. *American Journal of Sociology* 73: 1360–1380.

Hampden-Turner, C. (1990). *Charting the Corporate Mind.* New York: Free Press.

Hayward, P. (1968). The measurement of combat effectiveness. *Operations Research* 16:314–323.

Hitt, M. A., and Ireland, R. D. (1987). Peters and Waterman revisited: The unended quest for excellence. *Academy of Management Executive* 2:91–98.

Jobson, J. D., and Schneck, R. (1982). Constituent views of organizational effectiveness. *Academy of Management Journal* 25:25–46.

Kahn, R. L. (1977). Organizational effectiveness: An overview. In P. S. Goodman and J. M. Pennings (eds.), *New Perspective on Organizational Effectiveness.* San Francisco: Jossey-Bass, pp. 235–248.

Kanter, R. M. (1989). *When Giants Learn to Dance.* New York: Simon & Schuster.

Kanter, R. M. (1983). *The Changemasters.* New York: Simon & Schuster.

Kaplan, A. (1964). *The Conduct of Inquiry.* San Francisco: Jossey-Bass.

Katz, D., and Kahn, R. L. (1978). *The Social Psychology of Organizing,* 2nd ed. New York: Wiley.

Keeley, M. (1984). Impartiality and participant-interest theories of organizational effectiveness. *Administrative Science Quarterly* 29:1–25.

Khondwalla, P. N. (1989). OB for social development: A position paper. *International Studies of Management and Organization* 18:6–44.

Lehman, C. K. (1985). Some methodological problems in studies of corporate social responsibility and financial performance. Paper presented at Academy of Management National Meeting, San Diego, CA.

Levering, R., Mokowitz, M., and Katz, M. (1984). *The 100 Best Companies to Work For in America.* Reading, MA: Addison-Wesley.

Michels, R. (1949, 1911). *Political Parties: A Sociological Study of the Oligarchical Tendencies of Modern Democracy.* New York: The Free Press.

Mitchell, T. R. (1985). In search of excellence versus the 100 best companies to work for in America: A question of perspective and values. *Academy of Management Review* 10:350–355.

Negandhi, A. R., and Reimann, B. (1972). A contingency theory of organization reexamined in the context of a developing country. *Academy of Management Journal* 15:137–146.

Odiorne, G. S. (1969). *Management Decisions by Objective.* Englewood Cliffs, NJ: Prentice-Hall.

Ouchi, W. G. (1981). *Theory Z: How American Companies Can Meet the Japanese Challenge.* Reading, MA: Addison-Wesley.

Pascale, R. T. (1990). *Managing on the Edge.* New York: Simon & Schuster.

Pennings, J. M., and Goodman, P. S. (1977). Toward a workable framework. In P. S. Goodman and J. M. Pennings (eds.), *New Perspectives in Organizational Effectiveness*. San Francisco: Jossey-Bass, pp. 146–184.

Perrow, C. (1961). The analysis of goals in complex organizations. *American Sociological Review* 26:854–866.

Perrow, C. (1970). *Organizational Analysis: A Sociological View*. Belmont, CA: Wadsworth.

Perrow, C. (1977). Three types of effectiveness studies. In P. S. Goodman and J. M. Pennings (eds.), *New Perspectives in Organizational Effectiveness*. San Francisco: Jossey-Bass, pp. 96–105.

Peters, T. (1987). *Thriving on Chaos*. New York: Knopf.

Peters, T. J. and Waterman, R. H. Jr. (1982). *In Search of Excellence: Lessons from America's Best-Run Companies*. New York: Harper & Row.

Pondy, L. (1977). Effectiveness: A thick description. In P. S. Goodman and J. M. Pennings (eds.), *New Perspectives in Organizational Effectiveness*. San Francisco: Jossey-Bass, pp. 226–248.

Provigo, Inc. (1987). *Annual Report*.

Provigo, Inc. (1988). *Annual Report*.

Reidenbach, R. E., and Robin, D. P. (1989). *Ethics and Profits*. Englewood Cliffs, NJ: Prentice-Hall.

Rivlin, A. M. (1971). *Systematic Thinking for Social Action*. Washington, D.C.: Brookings Institution.

Scott, W. R. (1977). Effectiveness of organizational effectiveness studies. In P. S. Goodman and J. M. Pennings (eds.), *New Perspectives in Organizational Effectiveness*. San Francisco: Jossey-Bass, pp. 63–96.

Sills, D. (1957). *The Volunteers: Means and Ends in a National Organization*. New York: Free Press.

Staw, B. M., and Oldham, G. R. (1978). Reconsidering our dependent variables: A critique and empirical study. *Academy of Management Journal* 21:439–559.

Steers, R. M. (1977). *Organizational Effectiveness: A Behavioral View*. Santa Monica, CA: Goodyear.

Thompson, J. D., and McEwen, W. J. (1958). Organizational goals and environment. *American Sociological Review* 23:23–30.

Tuleja, T. (1985). *Beyond the Bottom Line: Leaders Are Turning Principles into Profits*. New York: Facts on File.

Weick, K. E. (1976). Educational organizations as loosely coupled systems. *Administrative Science Quarterly* 21 (no. 1):1–19.

Weick, K. E. (1977). Re-Punctuating the problem. In P. S. Goodman and J. Pennings (eds.), *New Perspectives on Organizational Effectiveness*. San Francisco: Jossey-Bass, pp. 193–226.

Wokutch, R. E., and Spencer, B. A. (1987). Corporate saints and sinners: The effects of philanthropic and illegal activity on organizational performance. *California Management Review* 29:62–77.

C H A P T E R

2

Organizational Structure: Who Works Under Whom

CHAPTER OVERVIEW

This chapter discusses how an organization structures itself to carry out its activities. Our purpose is to show how various factors shape an organization's structure and how structure in turn affects the organization's functioning and effectiveness.

THEME CASE

"Westinghouse Gets Respect at Last" relates how Westinghouse has taken over a decade to restructure and diversify at a time when the trend for U.S. corporations had been to return to core businesses. At the heart of this restructuring there has been a revolution in corporate values, culture, and management with dramatic increases in productivity and quality. What was once described as a stodgy and misshapen bureaucracy has now become a portfolio of streamlined and decentralized holdings designed to create quality and shareholder value. And these broadly diversified holdings are integrated by a Productivity and Quality Center that is at the core of a restructured Westinghouse.

CHAPTER OUTLINE

- What Is Organizational Structure?
- Static Structural Elements
- Dynamic Structural Elements
- Determinants of Structure
- Organizational Structures in the Future
- Summary
- Managerial Insight

KEY DEFINITIONS

Organizational structure   how an organization arranges its activities to accomplish its tasks and reach its goals.

Elements of structure   the static and dynamic building blocks used by organizations to create and express a structure—physical design, size, complexity, formalization, centralization, networks, clusters, and communication roles.

Determinants of structure   factors that shape how elements are used to structure an organization—goals, social customs, management beliefs and values, environmental constraints, and technology.

Complexity   the division of labor, the levels of hierarchy, and the physical location of an organization.

Formalization   the extent to which rules and procedures are followed in an organization; a way of increasing rationality.

Centralization   the degree to which decision-making and policy-making power is reserved to a small group of people at the highest organizational levels. In a *decentralized* organization, by contrast, decision making is pushed down to the lowest possible level and wide latitude is granted to managers below the top and away from the corporate center in interpreting policy.

Network   a set of linkages between organization members that do not follow strict hierarchical or departmental lines. There are many different kinds of networks in organizations, performing various functions. They frequently overlap.

"Loosely coupled" model   a view of organizational structure based on the assumptions that organizations are coalitions of various interests, that structure is an unplanned response to contests among coalitions, and that goals are numerous and conflicting.

Additional Terms

Physical design
Size
Horizontal differentiation
Vertical differentiation
Organizational chart
Flat and tall structures
Spatial dispersion
Professionalization

Matrix organization
Divisionalization
Grapevine
Coalitions
Cliques
Strength of weak ties
Boundary spanners
Gatekeepers
Stars

Isolates
Self-designing systems
Mechanistic and organic structure
Long-linked, mediating, and intensive
  technology
Strategic contingency theory
Population ecology
Resource dependency
Dynamic network

WESTINGHOUSE GETS RESPECT AT LAST

The plan was simple: Restructure to create value for shareholders, and make quality your company religion. But carrying it out took more than a decade.

Here's a test of your investment acumen. You have a choice of buying stock in one of two companies. Do you believe in return on shareholders' equity? For 1988, Company A had an ROE [Return on Equity] of 22%; Company B's was 18%. Do you like earnings per share? In the past five years Company A has increased them 123%, while Company B's have gone up 68%. You want dividends? In the same period, Company A's dividend has about doubled, while Company B's is up 55%. P/E ratios? Company A's stock has risen from 27 to 64 but still trades at a multiple of just 11 times earnings; Company B's stock has gone from 29 to 56 and trades at a P/E of 14. So which stock do you buy?

Easy, right? Then why did you buy Company B—General Electric—instead of Company A—Westinghouse?

Westinghouse? Talk to any top executive of Westinghouse Electric Corp., and before long you'll hear the same complaint: "We can't get no respect; we're the Rodney Dangerfield of industrial America." There's nothing funny about the numbers the Pittsburghers have put on the board—but maybe it's hard to get respect when you are unfashionably diversified. While today's trend is for American corporations to brag about returning to core businesses, Westinghouse executives refer proudly to their "portfolio" of enterprises—shades of yesteryear—that range from advanced radar technology and nuclear power to 7 Up bottling. The company is also still living down unhappy reminders of a messy past, such as a complex dispute with the Philippine government, now headed for arbitration, in which Westinghouse is battling charges of bribery and sloppiness in constructing a nuclear power plant.

But Westinghouse is not the misshapen conglomerate it was in the 1970s, when it ran a record club and built low-income housing. And it has been carrying on a revolution in management, dramatically raising quality and productivity in recent years. Chairman John C. Marous is convinced that by the end of 1990, when he hands the company over to his designated successor, Paul E. Lego, Westinghouse—stodgy old Westinghouse—will have become not just a good company but a great one.

In 1975 the company was barely profitable, with a 2.8% return on sales. (Westinghouse expects to hit 10% this year.) The new chairman, Robert E. Kirby, unclogged channels of communication—"To make sure that if there was bad news I heard it second"—then began pruning the corporation's more unprofitable blooms. When he retired in 1983, Douglas D. Danforth picked up the shears. Danforth moved factories offshore, bought back stock, took a couple of restructuring hits, and channeled capital away from sluggish businesses and into fast-moving ones. Light bulbs, cable television, and many others were cut away. Between 1985 and 1987 Westinghouse made 70 divestitures but held sales steady—and improved profits—through internal growth and 55 acquisitions.

One of Danforth's stars was Marous, who took over Westinghouse's biggest division, the troubled Industries segment, in 1983. There he joined forces with Lego. Both are engineers who had grown up in working-class neighborhoods (Marous in Pittsburgh, Lego in Johnstown), gone to the University of Pittsburgh, and spent their entire careers at Westinghouse. What the two did in Industries was surgery, though for a while it looked like butchery; between 1983 and 1985 they turned the segment from a $19 million loser into a $61 million winner. Lego's reward was a high-visibility staff job, where he learned to cultivate a bedside manner to go with his scalpel. Marous stayed with Industries and by the end of 1987 had quadrupled profits to $224 million. His wasn't the only success story at Westinghouse, but when it came time for Danforth to retire at the end of 1987 Marous got the chairmanship. Because of his age—he was 62—Westinghouse also named Lego, then 57, president and chief operating officer and announced that the big office would be his in 1990.

The housecleaning continued last year as Marous and Lego dumped businesses with $700 million a year in sales, including Westinghouse elevators. Now the company's still astonishing array of roughly 75 lines are arranged in seven groups:

- Industries (24% of company sales: circuit breakers, motors, transport refrigeration, hazardous waste management).

- Energy and utility systems (22%: fuel and service for nuclear power plants, waste-to-energy plants, turbines, defense materials production, and other products).

- Electronic systems (21%: defense and civilian radar, defense electronics, and more).

- Wesco (13%: commercial electrical supply stores).

- Commercial (9%: beverage bottling, office furniture, watches).

- Financial services (6%: corporate and real estate financing, land development).

- Broadcasting (5%: Group W radio and TV stations, programming, and satellite communications).

In structuring their portfolio Marous and Lego, like Danforth, have relentlessly aimed to create value for shareholders. "It's the whole basis of what we do," Lego says, boasting that Westinghouse has "the most sophisticated strategic planning process of any company in the United States." The process is called Vabastram (for VAlue-BAsed STRAtegic Management). Behind that Sanskrit-sounding acronym is an arsenal of techniques, mostly developed by Donald Povejsil, now retired as vice president for corporate planning. Vabastram, says Burton Staniar, chairman of Westinghouse Broadcasting, "forces internal units to make decisions that will increase shareholder value."

One technique involves calculating what Westinghouse calls a "warranted equity value" for each piece of the company—in essence, notional balance sheets the sum of whose assets equals the assets of the company as a whole. Westinghouse calculates these imaginary annual reports not only at the business unit level but *below* that level, in some cases down to individual product lines. This, Lego says, "allows us to portfolio-plan on a micro basis."

Acquisitions must pass a shareholder-value test and must complement existing lines of business. An example: hazardous-waste disposal, an outgrowth of the technical expertise and familiarity with complex regulatory environments that Westinghouse had developed from years of handling its own hazardous and nuclear waste. In the last two years the company has made a pair of acquisitions to get both on-site and off-site waste destruction capabilities. Now toxic and industrial waste disposal is a $200-million-a-year business (among the top five in the industry) and growing 30% a year. That snazzy growth is helped by snazzy new tools like the "pyro-plasma torch," installed in a truck trailer that can be driven to a waste site. Load the gunk into the truck, turn on the torch, and its 5,000°C. blast dissociates the molecules of nasty stuff like PCBs and renders them harmless. The torch, it turns out, was a happy accident: The Research and Development Center and the Power Circuit Breaker division invented it as a way to melt scrap metal.

Serendipitous discoveries seem to occur when a company sticks to what it knows. Another came when a decision to expand its boiler-service business led Westinghouse to buy Global Power in 1983. Global, in turn, owned 80% of O'Connor Combustor, which made a highly efficient rotary kiln. Says Theodore Stern, the executive vice president who runs Westinghouse's utility businesses: "Our original thought was to spin off O'Connor. We were expanding into service—O'Connor didn't really fit." But when Westinghouse engineers began playing with the big, spiraling O'Connor combustor, they realized that it could be used to convert municipal waste into energy. The result: a brand-new business for Westinghouse, which has grown to a $1 billion backlog in two years and is also targeted to grow 30% a year.

Thanks to the rigors of Vabastram, fast growth doesn't imply fast-and-loose management. Joseph Dorrycott, who runs the Resource Energy Systems division, bid on only half the contracts offered last year, and won half of those. Mindful of regulatory pitfalls, he'll bid only if he can show a profit at every phase from design to operation. As a result, Dorrycott's young division has made money from the start, while less disciplined competitors—some of which have offered to sell out to Westinghouse—are still smarting from losses they took in the early stages of construction.

Patience and discipline have been institutionalized. Three times in the past four years Westinghouse has tried to add a television station to the five owned by Group W, and three times it has backed away when the price got too high. Meantime Staniar, the group's boss, made a deal in April to buy ten radio stations from Metropolitan Broadcasting Corp. and Legacy Broadcasting Inc. (The deal, estimated at $375 million, hinges on whether the broadcasters can buy back some junk debt). Looking for TV and ending up with radio sounds like the plot of *Working Girl*, but it's smart business: Group W stands to pick up an estimated $35.6 million in cash flow and become the second-biggest radio network in the country (after ABC), with stations in nine out of the ten biggest markets and about $190 million in advertising billings.

Such dealmaking has won the respect of investment professionals. A year ago security analyst Linda Schuman at Prudential-Bache was expressing her "distrust in management's competence in the crucial areas of strategic planning, acquisition analysis, and financial controls." Today she says,

"They've gotten infinitely better than they were. Their acquisitions make sense. They're buying companies in areas where they're good—broadcasting, environmental services, defense." A favorite: The torpedo business of Gould Inc. was "a superb move—they paid $100 million for what's now $100 million in sales and going up."

Complementing Vabastram's discipline is a part of Westinghouse that pulls rabbits out of hats: It can make inventory disappear, levitate productivity, and turn red ink into black. Ten years ago Westinghouse set up a skunk-works it called the Productivity Center. Showing that it was serious, the center's leaders within months declared that productivity was a by-product of quality and changed its name to the Productivity and Quality Center. "When you accept the challenge of doing the same work in half the time, you *must* improve quality," says Carl Arendt, the center's marketing manager. "By definition bad quality is a waste of time." The message clearly got through: In company shorthand, the center is always referred to as the Quality Center. Installed in a former Chrysler warehouse outside Pittsburgh, the center is a SWAT team of some 130 computer gurus, consultants, and engineers whose job is to help business units "do the right things right the first time."

The center has a sweeping mandate. Says Lego: "When most people think of quality they think of the product; we try to think of the process." He means looking for ways to improve everything that goes into a product, from engineering to plant maintenance to billing. The goal is customer satisfaction—the result of emphasizing quality rather than productivity. Boasts John Yasinsky, executive vice president for World Resources and Technology: "In any major business that we're involved in, we're probably closer to our customers than any of our competitors."

A business unit can order a Total Quality Fitness Review for all or part of its operation whenever it wants to. The call goes out almost 100 times a year, bringing a team from the Quality Center to conduct interviews and analyses at all levels of the organization—and, notably, to survey customers. The team identifies weaknesses in training, processes, and products. The results are translated onto a Total Quality scorecard and presented to the manager. They are not passed up the chain of command; instead, the Quality Center helps managers to set up teams to discover and deploy improvements. Quality Center experts stand by to advise and measure results. The process can become an obsession. At one point the Thermo King factory in Galway, Ireland, which makes truck refrigeration units, had 300 employees and 48 quality teams; the Nuclear Fuel division, while waiting to hear if it would win the government's Malcom Baldridge Award for quality (it did), was busy with 19 new self-improvement projects.

The teams don't stop on the factory floor. Mainly because of the center's work, white-collar productivity is rising 6% a year at Westinghouse, twice the national average. In the company's service businesses, where the inventory rides up and down in the elevator, productivity is harder to quantify. The center is now working with the corporate finance staff to invent accounting techniques to capture the savings and identify ways to save still more. Even so, claims Arendt, Westinghouse can quantify enough to know that savings in services are "significantly larger than those in the factories."

The Productivity and Quality Center's work is winning fans outside Westinghouse. Says Tom Davenport, a senior research associate at the Harvard Business School: "The approach is unique. It has a heavy emphasis on process redesign and more of an information technology component than others." For example, the center helps its "clients" find new uses for the companywide electronic mail system. Westinghouse is also unusual, says Davenport, in applying the techniques to corporate staff. "They must be pretty good," he adds. "Consulting firms have tried to hire their people away." The Boston Consulting Group has already got one.

As Westinghouse gets its house in order, the Quality Center works more and more with customers. When Pacific Power, an Oregon utility, told Westinghouse rep Paul Shameklis that it wanted to set up a computer link with his company to get a 10% saving in ordering costs, Shameklis went one better: He put Pacific Power together with the center, which flow-charted and redesigned the utility's entire purchasing process. When the changes are all in place, the time it takes to send and process a purchase order will drop from 14 days to six hours, and the cost per order from $86 to $12. Shameklis proudly put in for one of the company quality awards. He came in fourth.

You can't spend time at Westinghouse without realizing that Total Quality is the house religion. The missionary zeal begins at the top. Marous set an example for the faithful by ordering a fitness review of his own office. "Total Quality is everything, it's everybody," he says. "It's a matter of survival. And it *is* almost like a religion. To have total quality you're going to have to change your culture. You can't change your culture without an emotional experience. The Japanese have given us that." He likes to tell about an employee in Columbia, South Carolina, who was asked by a visitor if he was a machine operator. "I used to be the machine operator," he replied. "I manage machines now."

Marous faces obstacles on the road to corporate greatness. Westinghouse's defense business cannot sustain the 13.5% growth rate of the Reagan years—the company is aiming for 8%—and the Utilities segment will grow more slowly, since hardly anybody is adding generating capacity.

Westinghouse keeps its nuclear engineers sharp by servicing and fueling existing power plants and managing government-owned reactors. This spring the company took over operation of the government's troubled Savannah River nuclear-weapons materials plant, the probable site of a new government production reactor.

Westinghouse has poured millions into developing a new-generation nuclear power plant, the AP600, and is confident that it represents the future of nuclear power in America—if there is a future for nuclear power in America. Even Robert Pollard, a nuclear engineer at the Union of Concerned Scientists and one of the industry's toughest critics, says that the AP600 is "a better deal" than conventional nuclear plants because, with 50% fewer moving parts and safety features that require little or no action by workers, "the probability of an accident occurring is lower." But for Westinghouse that better deal isn't a good deal until someone orders an AP600, and if Pollard and other critics have their way, that day will never dawn. Meanwhile the nation's 112 nuclear power plants get older and more worrisome. Such is the public's skittishness, Stern acknowledges, that few people distinguish between one kind of reactor and another. To the public an accident anywhere is proof of an accident-waiting-to-happen everywhere else.

The waste-to-energy business also has a superheated political and regulatory climate. Worried about air pollution and hazardous ash, several states are tightening standards for burning and disposal, and Massachusetts recently declared a moratorium on new waste-to-energy plants. Westinghouse builds "mass burn" plants, which consume most garbage straight from the truck. Competitors like Wheelabrator, Mitsubishi, and Waste Management are buying or licensing technologies that sort and mechanically process waste first; the resulting "resource-derived fuel" (RDF) produces more BTUs and recyclable byproducts along with less ash. Neil Seldman, who works for an advocacy group called the Institute for Local Self-Reliance, says the economic benefits of RDF are so clear "we no longer plan citizen protests; we just talk to the local Chamber of Commerce." Although so far no Westinghouse deal has been canceled, 35 to 40 cities have killed mass-burn plants. The Environmental Protection Agency is now being asked to declare that pretreatment of waste is a so-called best-available-control technology, which would make the process mandatory. If that happened, Westinghouse would have to add a costly processor to the O'Connor combustor, putting the gift horse in a whole new race.

Diversity should keep Westinghouse safe from the worst effects of an economic downturn—environmental and utility services, for example, are fairly recession-resistant. But the company is not immune to the business cycle. A recent dividend increase commits it to pay out 40% of profits, equal to about a 7.5% return on equity. Lego estimates that another 7.5% in ROE is needed to feed existing business. Whatever's left is free cash flow, available for stock buybacks, acquisitions, or still higher dividends. If it can keep ROE in its target range of 18% to 21%, Westinghouse will have plenty of money to play with or reinvest. This year, Marous says, the company will generate enough cash to make a billion-dollar acquisition. But that attractive financial picture could change if capital spending, defense, construction, and real estate—the markets that have given Westinghouse its fastest earnings growth over the past ten years—slow greatly.

If the machine starts to smoke and clank, Marous and Lego can open up a sophisticated tool chest. The Productivity and Quality Center guarantees a continuing stream of "work-smart" ideas. The R&D Center ranked second among American companies in new patents in 1987 and third in 1988, and almost a third of its budget goes to projects for which it does not yet have a "customer" in the company. Westinghouse can take a relatively long view—as a defense contractor and broadcaster, the company is shielded from a foreign takeover and sheer size makes it a difficult target for anyone else. Almost all senior managers are engineers or physicists comfortable with technology, so radar experts understand office furniture experts and vice versa. That helps support strong internal communications. Eight task forces, each sponsored by a top executive, have the job of cutting across the lines of command to insure that a "Eureka!" uttered anywhere in the company will be heard wherever it can be put to use.

So does an every-Monday-morning breakfast for the top 14 executives—from Pittsburgh, Baltimore, and New York City—who gather for a no-agenda hour and a half in which ideas are shared and problems talked out. If there's especially good news—a big contract won, an acquisition—Marous will uncork a bottle and pour everybody a little glass of champagne. The first time he did it, Marous says, it shook people up. But they're getting used to it.

Source: From "Westinghouse Gets Respect at Last" by Thomas A. Stewart, *Fortune*, July 3, 1989, pp. 92–98. Copyright © 1989 The Time Inc. Magazine Company. All rights reserved. Reprinted by permission.

What Is Organizational Structure?

Every organization must arrange its activities to reach its goals. **Organizational structure** is the blueprint for this arrangement. It is the way an organization is tied together. This chapter will show what organizational structure is, then examine both static and dynamic elements of structure and show how structure affects the performance of the organization. It will close by examining the determinants of structure and the structures that may develop in the future.

Managers need to know about structure for a variety of reasons. Knowledge about how organizations are put together helps managers understand "the big picture." Without some knowledge of structure, it is difficult to know how the human resources of an organization are deployed and where these resources are located, what information may be gained from them, and what contribution they might be expected to make to the organization. Structure gives clues to the location of power (see Chapter 6) and is an indicator of a company's management philosophy. Structure should reflect—and facilitate the achievement of—an organization's goals. In sum, a manager can better understand her own place in the fabric of the whole by knowing something about structure.

When people think of organizational structure, what immediately comes to mind is the hierarchy of authority and reporting relationships portrayed in an organizational chart, and sometimes who is accountable (Jacques, 1990). While this view of an organization is one part of structure, it is not the only aspect. Indeed, an organization is structured using many different **structural elements.** These elements are the basic building blocks of organizations; they are the ways of both creating and expressing structure. Management uses them to erect the structure; in turn, they can be analyzed to determine the true structure of an organization—as opposed to the structure professed by management.

Some elements of structure are static; that is, they reflect where, on a continuum of choices, an organization sits. These elements involve such characteristics as size, hierarchy, and centralization. Looking at these characteristics of an organization, however, only shows the organization at one point in time. To provide descriptions that more closely match the fluid, changing entities that organizations are, a number of researchers have focused on organizations as networks of relationships that develop over time. These studies reveal the dynamic elements of an organization's structure—structure as an expression of how people interact.

These two general views of organizational structure are derived from somewhat different premises, and they are not easily integrated with one another. One might think of them as roughly analogous to photographic slides and motion pictures: slides are useful for showing what a scene or person looks like at a single moment, and motion pictures show movement and change over time. That both views are useful is clear from the Westinghouse case that opened this chapter. Several static elements played key roles in the case, including size, hierarchy, and formalization of key policies. But studying such dynamic elements as communication channels, coalitions, and managerial values is also important to understanding a decade of change at Westinghouse.

A number of different factors are **determinants of structure;** they shape how these elements are used to structure the organization. These factors include goals, social customs and mores, beliefs and values of the founders or the current managers, environmental constraints, and available technology. Once we learn about the elements of structure, we will see how these various determinants affect how those elements are combined into actual structures.

Our notions of structure include the assumption that organizations have relatively impermeable and easy-to-find boundaries. That is, one can fairly easily differentiate the organization from its environment. This premise is true of most organizations today but may be less true tomorrow, when we may have to alter radically our notions about what constitutes structure (Blair, Roberts, and McKechnie, 1985; Guest, 1986). In industrialized nations we are quickly working ourselves into a world in which high technology office management systems are used to complete and integrate work. It may be difficult to define the boundaries of, say, a bank if many of its clerical personnel work at home on terminals and transmit their completed work into a central computer, if customers access the bank through automatic teller machines and personal computers at home, and if banking has become so deregulated that lines of demarcation between banks and other financial institutions have blurred or been erased. Because environmental and technological changes are likely to have a profound impact on organizational structure in the future, we will turn our attention to that topic after studying the elements and determinants of structure.

Static Structural Elements

Some elements used to structure organizations are static; they reflect where the organization sits on a continuum, but they acknowledge that the organization occupies only one point on that continuum at a given time (although, of course, the specific point occupied can change from one time to another). Company size, for instance, is usually fixed at any given time—for Westinghouse between 1985 and 1987 when they made 70 divestitures and 55 acquisitions size was clearly different from time to time. The static elements of structure are physical design, size, complexity, formalization, and centralization. Each has a number of different factors that managers must take into account.

Physical Design

The **physical design** of an organization has two dimensions, each influencing structure. These dimensions are the qualities of the organization's physical space—the atmosphere created by the space—and the arrangement of units within that space.

The Qualities of the Space   Most organizations are formed around an existing physical design, as when social clubs are designed to fit into the existing physical characteristics of a church or community center. A church with a large population of young families, for instance, will probably establish groups oriented toward children or toward giving support to parents. Similarly, a community center with such recreational facilities as a swimming pool and tennis courts will create groups that can use those facilities; another center, with gymnastics equipment, will form groups interested in that sport.

Occasionally, architects and decorators design a physical setting to express what they feel are the goals and needs of the organization. In this way, the qualities of the space can reflect—and influence—the desired organizational structure. The pyramidal TransAmerica Building in San Francisco certainly reflects and reinforces the hierarchical structure of the modern corporation. Similarly, the electronics firms in California's Silicon Valley have created campuslike architectural styles that fit the informal organizational structure they try to encourage.

Arrangement of Units Within the Space   The details of how units are distributed throughout a space are important as well. When laying out locations for an organization in a new or remodeled building, planners ask numerous questions about the interaction of various departments and subunits within departments. They know that proximity or distance can affect how well units communicate with one another. Locating units on the same floor or gathering in one building units that had been dispersed in separate buildings facilitates communication; the opposite practices erect barriers to communication. Managers about to design a new space—say, when a company is moving—are in an excellent position to manipulate such factors to achieve their goals for employee interactions.

Sometimes the proximity of a department to a chief executive's office reflects the importance of that department to the company's mission. Similarly, the distance between a desk chair and a visitor's chair reflects a manager's view of distance between himself and others (see Chapter 5).

Another factor in the arrangement of office space is the degree to which the space is flexible or fixed. Flexible partitioning in an open-space design speaks of an organization that encourages a flow of communication and perhaps a collegiality of decision making. The use of walls and private offices to define individual spaces may reflect an organization with a more rigid hierarchy and lines of communication.

Of course, these features of arrangement may be due to other, more mundane, factors as well. The number of people in various departments, the amount of equipment required by various units, or the relative cost of office space in different locations all influence how space is arranged. These factors may even shape a space in a way that is contrary to what would ordinarily be dictated by the organizational structure.

Size

The most frequently discussed static element of structure is **size,** which is also a determinant of structure (Scott, 1987). It is obvious that large organizations influence the people in them (and outside of them) differently than do small organizations. People in large organizations, however, protect themselves from influences of monumental size by subdividing. Size thus influences both horizontal and vertical differentiation, two facets of complexity, another structural characteristic. Successful organizations born in basements and garages find themselves not only expanding but subdividing into production, marketing, personnel, and other departments.

Size probably influences people most when they first join organizations. A familiar adjustment to size occurs when students enter large universities. Coming from high schools of several hundred to a few thousand students, many first-year college students are overwhelmed by the sheer size of a university campus that may have from 10,000 to 30,000 students. Soon, however, the newcomers categorize their environment, using cognitive, emotional, and intuitive processes. Investigations of how people categorize in organizations are not readily available, but the process may be similar to how people map cities such as New York and Paris. In a series of studies Milgram (1977) showed that such factors as architectural or social distinctiveness highlight an area enough to place it on a person's cognitive map of a city. Thus, in New York City, Columbus Circle and Rockefeller Center are remembered because of their architectural characteristics; Chinatown and Little Italy because of their cultural features.

Newcomers to an organization, then, will probably first become familiar with that which is distinguished from the rest of the organization, such as high-profile or distinctive individuals, units, or spaces. Thus an active manager stands a better chance of being noted than her office-bound, isolated colleague.

There are almost as many ways to categorize organizations by size as there are kinds of organizations. Financial institutions may measure size by assets, deposits, loans, number of employees, or number of branches. Airlines, such as American or Delta, use passenger miles, number of employees, or number of aircraft. Perhaps the major generalization one can make about size is that, in most cases, the larger the organization the more complex its structure.

Complexity

Like size, **complexity** is among the first characteristics of organizations to strike a newcomer. Complexity refers to the division of labor, or horizontal differentiation; the levels of hierarchy, or vertical differentiation; and the physical location of the organization, or spatial dispersion (Scott, 1987).

Horizontal Differentiation   The way tasks are assigned is by **horizontal differentiation**. Managers need to understand this notion whenever they restructure existing work or design new projects (see Chapter 11 for a discussion of job design). Basically, tasks can be structured in either of two ways. In one, a typical worker completes many aspects of a job, either sequentially (e.g., a worker in an ice-cream shop who takes the order, makes the ice-cream cone, serves the customer, and rings up the sale) or functionally (e.g., being responsible for planning, manufacturing, and marketing a product). In the other approach, the work is divided rather minutely among different workers who do each individual task (either sequentially or functionally), often very rapidly (Hage and Aiken, 1969). An example of the first approach is the manager's job, in which many different tasks are done daily; assembly line jobs illustrate the second approach. Because they handle a multiplicity of tasks, workers with jobs in the first group often need extensive training. This is less often the case with jobs in the second group, but may nevertheless be true. A word processor, for instance, while specializing in one narrow task, may nonetheless receive a significant amount of training to exploit fully the features of a word processing program.

Another aspect of horizontal differentiation is the breakdown of the organization into units and subunits (departments, divisions, sections, branches, groups, and so on). Complex organizations have more jobs and more subunits than other organizations (Blau and Schoenherr, 1971). Westinghouse is segmented horizontally, with departments for each of seven groups of product lines—industries, energy systems, electronic systems, Wesco, commercial, financial services, and broadcasting.

Vertical Differentiation   The number of levels in an organization, or its hierarchy, is referred to as **vertical differentiation** (Pugh, Hickson, Hinings, and Turner, 1968) and reflects the lines of authority and responsibility.

Authority is essentially a matter of power (about which more will be said in the discussion of centralization); the question is, Who has the right to make a given kind of decision? Responsibility goes hand in hand with authority; the worker or manager authorized to make a decision is also responsible for the consequences. Similarly, that worker's supervisor or that manager's manager has responsibility for the quality of the decision as well.

An organization's hierarchy is revealed in an **organizational chart,** which provides a picture of the formal relationships of authority and control. Boxes represent positions, and the lines that connect them demonstrate who directs—and who reports to—whom. The convention in preparing such charts is for the higher positions to appear at the top; as one moves down the chart, one is also moving down the organizational ladder. Positions that appear on the same level are assumed to be of equal stature, although this is not necessarily the case.

Charts can be prepared for any level of organization. To provide more manageable and intelligible charts, chart designers often divide the entire organization into a number of views, the first showing the organization's top management structure, and subsequent charts revealing the structure of individual units, be they departments, divisions, or product lines. Figure 2.1 (page 68) illustrates both types.

An organization can have either a **flat structure,** with little hierarchical differentiation among workers, or a **tall structure,** with many levels and increasing authority as the top is approached. A club with no officers, in which all decisions are made by majority vote, is a flat structure. The top view of the organizational chart shown in Figure 2.1 shows the very top layers of a tall structure.

Charts must be used with caution. While they are useful, it is important to remember that they are snapshots of an organization at one moment. As such, their accuracy is usually momentary; organizations constantly change, usually faster than chart makers can keep pace with. Furthermore, charts are limited by their two-dimensional nature and by the scope of relationships they can portray. Charts convey only lines of authority and reporting relationships, showing few, if any, of the diagonal and lateral ties and interworkings of organizations. As Meyer and Rowan (1977) point out, "A sharp distinction should be made between the formal structure of an organization and its day-to-day work activities."

Charts may also be deceptive if used as depictions of the locuses of power in organizations. Many organizations distribute power so that very little is held at the top. Consulting firms, brokerage houses, or research institutes, for instance, may place little power in the top position. In some organizations the real power to accomplish objectives (or to frustrate their accomplishment) lies not at the top but with middle managers, who decide

FIGURE 2.1
Examples of
Organizational
Charts

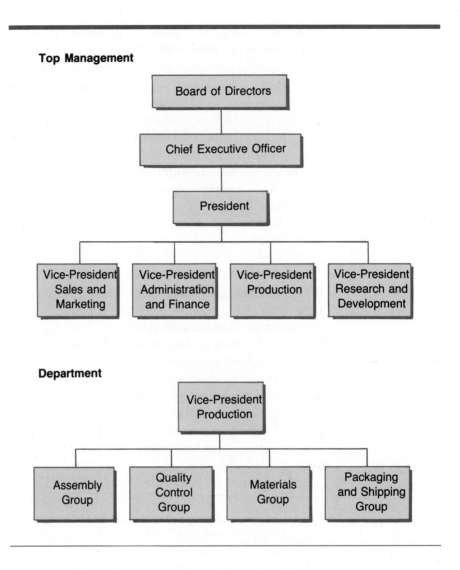

Top Management

Board of Directors

Chief Executive Officer

President

| Vice-President Sales and Marketing | Vice-President Administration and Finance | Vice-President Production | Vice-President Research and Development |

Department

Vice-President Production

| Assembly Group | Quality Control Group | Materials Group | Packaging and Shipping Group |

what work is done today and what gets put off until tomorrow. Senior management may find itself frustrated over having less power to control its middle management than it thinks it has. Recently, one author argued that, rather than flat organizations, managers need layers and layers of accountability and skill to unify systems (Jacques, 1990). Another author talked about how to practice democracy in a hierarchical organization.

Spatial Dispersion   The third dimension of complexity—**spatial dispersion**—may be either horizontal or vertical. The activities of an organization can be dispersed by separating power centers or by separating according to tasks. If an organization with a fully developed hierarchical form decides to clone itself in another location, its spatial dispersion is horizontal. On the other hand, if an organization has its company headquarters in Chicago, manufactures its products in Taiwan, and sells them in Western Europe, spatial dispersion is vertical. Assessing the nature of spatial dispersion may help a manager make decisions about the amount of autonomy given field personnel, the functions of central staff, entry into new markets, and other such strategic issues. Growing evidence shows that structural characteristics are related to organizational strategy.

Greater organizational complexity produces problems of communication, coordination, and control. Spatial dispersion of either sort (horizontal or vertical) increases the relative size of the administrative component of organizations (Anderson and Warkov, 1961). Spatial dispersion is negatively related to the standardization of work activities. Workers in dispersed organizations have more freedom in determining their work activities (Pugh, 1969).

Organizations tend to become more complex as their activities and their environments become more complex (Hall, 1977). This was true for Westinghouse, as they restructured their portfolio of holdings in the late 1980s in spite of trends by other U.S. firms to return to core business to meet greater competition from the Japanese.

Managers should be attuned to these results of complexity, particularly if their organizations are growing rapidly, because, as noted earlier, size affects complexity. In fact, expansion increases organizational complexity at geometric rates. A simple example illustrates this phenomenon. In an organization of three people, three interpersonal relationships are possible. If size doubles to six people, the number of interpersonal relationships goes up five times, to fifteen. Interactions create complexity.

Formalization

Formalization is the extent to which rules and procedures are followed in an organization. This element varies greatly across organizations. For example, in some organizations arrival and departure times to and from work are specified to the minute, with time clocks used to control deviant behavior. In other organizations it is understood that employees will spend sufficient time on the job to get the work done. In some organizations rules and procedures cover most activities, while in others people are allowed to exercise their own judgment.

In assessing the degree of formalization, one needs to use care. In some organizations many rules are codified in huge manuals, but no one pays attention to them. In others little is written down, but rules are informally understood and followed. Thus the most useful definition of formalization is that "it represents the use of rules in an organization" (Hage and Aiken, 1967, p. 79). The degree to which rules are followed—not the degree to which they are codified—is the key factor.

Organizations use formalization to increase their rationality. In one sense formalization is an attempt to make behavior more predictable by standardizing it. Standard procedures for production workers or quality control checklists that must be used and submitted before a product can be shipped are examples of this kind of formalization.

Formalization may also be an attempt to make explicit and visible the structure of relationships among organizational participants. It can establish status differences among organizational members in a way that is objective and external to the participants themselves. Formalization makes the process of succession routine and regular so that people can be replaced when necessary with minimal disturbance to an organization's functioning. The orderly selection of cardinals and popes in the Roman Catholic Church and the succession plan for the U.S. presidency are good examples of this function of formalization.

Alongside formal structures are "aspects of organizations that are not formally planned but that more or less spontaneously evolve from the needs of the people" (Litterer, 1963, p. 10). Thus, formal structures are the norms and behaviors that exist regardless of individuals; informal structures are interactions based on the personal characteristics or resources of the individuals involved (Scott, 1987). Informal structures are not without form; those forms are not determined simply by the organization but grow out of the relationships of the participants. Informal life is structured and orderly; it simply reflects the hearts and minds of an organization's members. We will study informal structures later in the chapter when we discuss networks.

Formalization in one area of an organization brings about pressures for less formalization in other areas. For example, one set of researchers studying employment security agencies found that strict conformity with civil service standards fostered decentralization, which permitted greater flexibility (Blau and Schoenherr, 1971). Perhaps there has to be some give and take if organizations are to function well.

Formalization is influenced by technology, size, and organizational traditions. One can categorize technologies as routine and nonroutine (Litwak, 1961; Perrow, 1967). Organizations or work units in which work is routine are more likely to be highly formalized than those in which technologies are less routine.

Obviously, size influences formalization. Large organizations have greater needs to formalize their activities than do small organizations. The mom and pop corner store that grows into a chain will experience a greater need for formalization, as rules will need to be created—and probably codified—to accommodate the increased relationships and interactions involved.

Tradition also influences formalization. If an early top executive believed that rules and procedures should be followed to the letter, this set of beliefs was codified into the organization's procedures manuals. The organization would then remain more formalized over time than existing conditions might have predicted.

What happens to members of rigidly formalized organizations or work groups? A classic study of two French organizations addressed this issue (Crozier, 1964). In these organizations strict rules limited the functioning of all individuals in the organization. Workers came to follow rules for the sake of the rules themselves since that determined how they were rewarded. More and more rules were created, with the result that the organizations became very unresponsive to customers and their environments. People failed to strive for autonomy and sought to decrease the amount of uncodified activity they performed. The consequences were declining competitiveness, lost worker productivity, higher operating costs, higher prices, and degradation of labor. These negative consequences of rigid formalization have long been recognized (Merton, 1957).

A number of studies show that professionalization is incompatible with formalization (e.g., Hall, 1968; Kornhauser, 1962). The greater the degree of formalization in organizations, the higher the alienation of members who are professionals. But formalization and professionalization are meant to do the same thing. Formalization is the internal process through which an organization sets rules, standards, and procedures to ensure that things get done correctly. **Professionalization** is an external means for accomplishing the same result: business schools teach future managers behaviors that will be expected of them in their work organizations. From an organization's viewpoint, both processes are effective. If it acquires a professional work force, the organization itself simply is not paying the costs of inculcating standardized practices. Nevertheless, there could be tension between the standards learned by the professionals and the demands of the organization.

Centralization

We have already touched briefly on the distribution of power; **centralization** is the structural element that actually describes that distribution. Power distributions are determined in advance of doing much else in organizations. For example, founders of organizations determine which decisions they will make and which will be made by those lower in the organizational echelon. Organizations in which all the important decisions are made by the headquarters or general office are centralized; those in which many important decisions are delegated to lower-level managers are decentralized. The feature on the *Challenger* shows how a lack of centralization can have disastrous results.

FEATURE: *Centralization as Insurance: The* Challenger *Disaster*

In January of 1986, the space shuttle *Challenger* exploded only seconds after launch, the single worst calamity to befall the American space program. The disaster set the shuttle program back for almost two years as engineers and managers tried to find out what went wrong and how it could be avoided in the future. The presidential commission that investigated the disaster found that management deficiencies at the National Aeronautics and Space Administration (NASA) were primarily responsible for the failure in the booster rocket that led to the explosion.

The commission learned that NASA allowed a great deal of autonomy for engineering and flight safety decisions to such subunits as the Marshall Space Flight Center, rather than retaining control at the Johnson Space Center in Houston. Thus, managers at Marshall had a wide latitude for decision making; indeed, they were not required to report information to higher levels at Johnson.

With so much leeway, Marshall managers declined on two issues to report potential problems to Houston. The explosion occurred precisely because of the problems about which Marshall did not issue warnings. Had a more rigidly centralized reporting system been established, the tragedy may have been averted.

Source: Adapted from "Rogers Commission Report Cites NASA Management Deficiencies" by Craig Covault, *Aviation Week and Space Technology* 124, no. 23 (June 9, 1986): pp. 16–18. Reprinted by permission.

The degree of centralization reflects what an organization thinks of its members. A high degree of centralization reflects an organization that feels its members need high degrees of control; decentralization implies that an organization feels its employees can govern themselves. Westinghouse was clearly restructured to reflect management's belief in decentralization—with a centralized Productivity and Quality Center, which consults but does not police.

Two aspects of centralization are most obvious in organizational life. The first is where decisions are made and what kind of decisions are allowed; the second is how those decisions are evaluated. Although evaluation is only one aspect of decision making, it is important enough in its own right to be singled out for attention. If all evaluation is done at the top, it does not matter whether decisions are made at lower levels. By definition, the organization is centralized.

Centralization and decentralization take a number of forms. One author (Melcher, 1975) discusses four:

1. *Autocracy.* Decision making is highly centralized, and few decisions are made by lower-level personnel.

2. *Collegial.* Decision making is highly decentralized. Many decisions are made at lower levels without policy restrictions.

3. *Centralized bureaucracy.* Decisions are made by operating personnel at lower levels but follow a framework of restrictive policies, procedures, and rules. When problems are not covered by existing policy, they are referred to higher levels for decisions or policy development.

4. *Decentralized bureaucracy.* Decisions are made at lower levels within the framework of policies, but lower-level personnel have discretion on problems not covered by policies.

Centralization is associated with size and technology as well as with environmental factors faced by organizations. One might think that increased size results in high degrees of centralization. The research, though, supports just the opposite notion (Blau, 1973; Blau and Schoenherr, 1971; Mansfield, 1973; Child, 1972); apparently increased size creates pressures to decentralize. Such pressure probably brings with it increased numbers of experts at lower levels who may demand more say in decision making and evaluation.

Technology is related to centralization in that when tasks have a high degree of clarity, predictability, and efficacy, they are assigned by directive and centralization is high. When tasks are low on these three factors, they are allocated by delegation and centralization is low (Dornbush and Scott, 1975).

The relationship of centralization to environmental conditions is not clear, possibly because environmental conditions are not specified in most existing research. A generalization we can make is that when environments change rapidly and it is critical to monitor them, decentralization is probably best; alternatively, when environments are stable, centralization is probably most effective. Centralization may also reflect the kind of society in which the organization exists. A society in which the majority of organizations are highly centralized is probably one in which its citizens have little say about their participation.

Manifestations of Static Structure

It is *task groupings* that illustrate how the static elements of structure are used in any organization. Positions can be grouped together based on quite different logics that often serve quite different purposes. Tasks can be grouped according to shared expertise or function, process, product, time horizon, or geographical location (Child, 1984).

When organizations are young and very small, they do not have very much structure. As they grow a little larger, structure is most frequently based on *functional* groups. Thus, production activities are grouped together, as are marketing activities and personnel activities. This organizational form is sufficient when all the organization's activities are focused on one product or service and if change is gradual.

When an organization diversifies its products or services, however, the functional form is inefficient. Various products are subject to different time constraints, diversification probably causes growth in size, and complexity is increased. Under these conditions, organizations often move to *product* organization. Figure 2.2 depicts such an organization, the Scandinavian-based conglomerate Euroc, an international industrial and trading group. The product form is appropriate when an organization produces two or more products or services that are different in their technical makeup, production requirements, and markets. Adaptation and change now focus on the product in each part of the organization. This organizational form may even cause competition among units in the same organization, as with the built-in competition among General Motors' Oldsmobile, Chevrolet, Buick, Pontiac, and Cadillac divisions.

The **matrix organization** is an alternative to the functional or product forms. In essence, when other structural forms do not work, a firm may try restructuring along matrix lines (Daft and Steers, 1986). Matrix management is an attempt to superimpose the logic of one approach to grouping onto the logic of another. A key point to remember is that no organization uses matrix management for the entire organization; rather, the form is an ancillary arrangement employed strictly for project- or product-specific work within the context of an organization that is structured in some other way.

Figure 2.3 illustrates matrix management. In this system, employees report not only to a functional manager but also to a project team leader or a product manager with regard to product issues. A key feature of the matrix

FIGURE 2.2
*Product Form of
Organization*

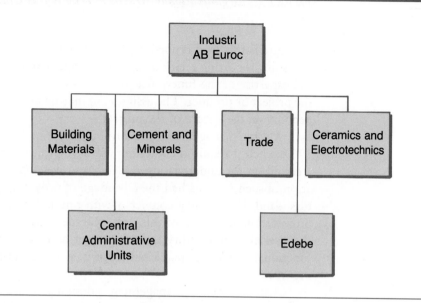

Source: From *Annual Report* (Malmo, Sweden: Industri AB Euroc 1989), p. 60. Reprinted by permission.

FIGURE 2.3
*Matrix
Management in
a Computer
Company*

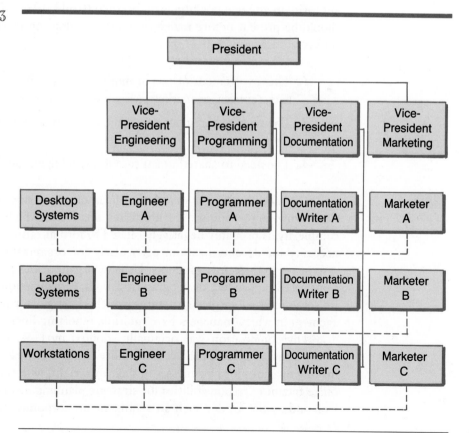

structure is this dual reporting, which violates a traditional principle of establishing reporting relationships. This radical step is taken because the special expertise of the functional worker is deemed essential to the success of the project or product. The assignment may be temporary or long term, depending on the nature of the project.

Matrix management was invented by the U.S. government in the 1960s when it required contractors to have project management systems as a condition for underwriting research and development projects. The creation of such systems had the advantage of providing government contractors—and their agency contacts—with one individual accountable for the project. The existence of this project leader or product manager, who has the overall responsibility for the project and the contributions of all the functional employees participating in it, is the other key feature of matrix management.

Although matrix management is designed to preserve flexibility, it creates a number of problems. First, people entering the system often need a long period of settling in, by which time the project may be complete. In addition, workers often feel confusion about reporting requirements, and authority in any one position is diminished (Child, 1984). Three conditions should be present before managers consider adopting matrix management (Davis and Lawrence, 1977, p. 21):

1. The involvement of two or more sectors (such as functions, products, services, or markets)

2. The need to carry out uncertain, complex, and interdependent tasks

3. The need to share human resources and maintain flexibility

Divisionalization is yet another form of structuring used as organizations grow larger. Figure 2.4 illustrates this form, which imposes further complexity, is probably negatively related to formalization, and imposes the necessity for decentralization, particularly for organizations that must be responsive to their environments. Usually, organizations partition into divisions based on product or geography or both. Organizations that divisionalize sometimes adopt grid structures, which are larger forms of matrix management in which managers have multiple reporting lines.

Divisionalization was originally adopted by U.S. business organizations. They assigned profit responsibility to division managers, essentially making divisions into businesses in their own right, with the main corporate office retaining responsibilities for strategic planning, overall financial control, and so on. Under such an arrangement, corporate managers become

FIGURE 2.4
*Division Form of
Organization*

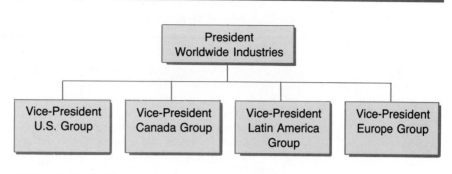

accountable for the performance of the company as a whole, rather than that of any individual division.

Divisionalization creates a number of problems (Child, 1984). First, there may not be an obviously superior way to divisionalize. Second, this kind of structuring is by definition divisive, creating all the problems that such strategies typically engender. Third, the greater the interdependence among divisions, the more difficult it will be to make the structure work. Fourth, the divisions themselves may grow large and diversified, losing the underlying logic of the original basis for divisionalizing.

Structure in Other Countries

There is considerable interest today in whether the structures of similar organizations in different cultures are similar—if, for example, a bank is a bank is a bank, regardless of the cultural values that spawned it. Alternatively, cultural norms and values may have considerable impact on organizational form. The evidence is mixed (e.g., Lincoln, Hanada, and McBride, 1986; Lincoln, 1989; Birnbaum and Wong, 1985), and there is considerable disagreement over whether U.S. theories and findings have applicability abroad.

Studies across the world find that organizational forms are becoming increasingly similar (Child, 1984). There are still national differences, however. Japanese organizations, for instance, seem to have a characteristic structure when one examines the abundance of qualitative data. In their review of the literature, Lincoln and McBride (1987) contrasted the characteristic Japanese organizational structure with those of American firms. The comparisons—made in terms of division of labor, hierarchy, span of control, and decision making—are listed in Figure 2.5 (page 78). Research also shows that in both the United States and Japan "tallness" (many levels) is

FIGURE 2.5

Japanese Versus American Organizational Structures

Factor	Structure
Division of labor	For U.S. firms, job titles proliferate and people pursue individual careers. Japanese firms promote generalist careers and job rotation. The work group is the key to cohesion, loyalty, and cooperation in Japanese companies. However, real responsibility is diffused among all members, according to one view. Others feel that Japanese firms are highly autocratic.
Hierarchy	In contrast with U.S. firms, heavy in middle management, Japanese organizations are viewed as leaner and flatter. Smaller size, greater specialization, and lower reliance on high-level finance and planning departments may explain this in part. Also, at the plant level, Japanese firms are often taller than their U.S. counterparts. Japanese firms also reflect a set of standard ranks, titles have much status, and all employees occupy these ranks and climb the same ladder, thus having a common reference point.
Spans of control	Whether structural spans do in fact differ between Japanese and U.S. firms, supervisor–subordinate relations show paternalism and strong bonds on and off the job between Japanese workers and supervisors.
Decision making	Japanese decision making is typically viewed by Americans as participative and consensual, with the lower levels showing initiative. There is some question, however, about how truly "bottom up" Japanese decision making really is.

Source: From "Organizational Structure in Japanese and U.S. Manufacturing" by J. R. Lincoln, M. Manada, and K. McBride. *Administrative Science Quarterly* 31 (1986): 338–364. Reprinted by permission.

associated with lower employee commitment and satisfaction than "flatness" (few levels) (Lincoln et al., 1986).

Other examples of national differences are apparent in the degree of centralization. European multinational firms favor local control, while American firms lean toward more centralized management. This contrast may reflect either differences in attitudes about obedience and authority, the histories of the countries, or other factors. With this orientation toward local control, European companies tend to use a national subsidiary structure rather than a system of international divisions, as favored by American companies. National subsidiaries report directly to the top without such intermediate or intervening levels as international or regional divisions. This structure, illustrated in Figure 2.6, helps grant autonomy to affiliates.

As companies increase product diversification and attempt to maximize gains from both domestic and international activity, worldwide structures

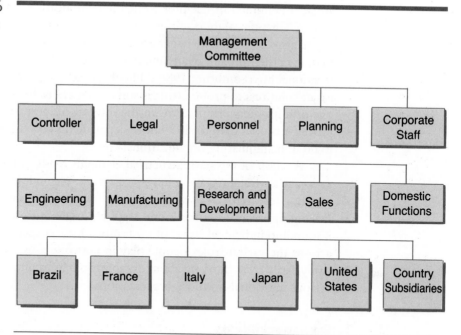

FIGURE 2.6
*Typical European
Multinational
Structure*

Source: From S. Ronen (1986), *Comparative and Multinational Management* (New York: Wiley),
p. 320. Copyright © 1986 by S. Ronen. Reprinted by permission of John Wiley and Sons, Inc.

replace divisional and subsidiary forms. A global orientation leads to the development of one of the following forms (Ronen, 1986, p. 322):

1. Global functional divisions such as manufacturing, marketing, and finance, responsible for worldwide operations in their own functional areas

2. Global geographic divisions, each responsible for all the products manufactured and marketed within a given geographical area

3. Global product divisions responsible for producing and marketing a product or group of products worldwide

4. Mixed structures with a combination of geographic operations, worldwide product divisions, and multiple functional links

Dynamic Structural Elements

As mentioned before, a number of management researchers have turned to examining organizations as networks of dynamic relationships. (Networks are also examined in Chapter 5 for their implications for communication, and in Chapter 6 for their implications for power.) This view offers a mechanism to enable managers to analyze the processes of interaction unfolding in their organizations and to think about the real complexity of organizational life (Fombrun, 1986). The dynamic perspective may also provide easier solutions to problems. It is sometimes easier for managers to change one or a few network patterns in the interest of increased efficiency or improved attitudes than to shift entire departments around, as one would have to do in manipulating organizational charts.

Analysis of the static structural elements tends to focus on the organization as a whole, to take a long-range view. A good deal more is added in network research. One can look more closely at individuals or subunits making up various networks and translate organizational issues of centralization into individual issues of centrality. One can specify in terms of interactions the various roles people play in networks. And one can move relatively easily from thinking about organizations as totalities to thinking about various individuals in those organizations.

Organizational Networks

A **network** is a set of linkages among a defined set of people in which the character of the linkages is specified. Thus, a network may be built around job requirements or how best to get things done. It may be structured by social interactions or how people interact informally.

Network observations began in laboratory research studies in the 1950s but were not done in real organizations. Groups of three, four, or five persons were studied to discover how variously imposed structures influenced problem solving and member attitudes (Shaw, 1964). Structure was varied by imposing rules about who could talk to whom. The kinds of structures imposed and the findings are given in Figure 2.7. The findings from these studies were consistent: for simple problems, centralized networks, in which information about the problem is sent to just one person, produced solutions faster with fewer errors than did decentralized networks, in which information was sent to everyone. However, when problems were complex, decentralized networks were superior. Unfortunately, findings from laboratory investigations such as these do not always generalize to people at work.

For many years the results of these small-group network studies were presented in management textbooks as the gospel about how to engage in efficient problem solving. The research exhausted itself, however, and a number of years passed before interest was renewed in organizations as networks of relationships. One reason for the stagnated research was that larger organizational networks could not be studied. Yet these networks (such as

FIGURE 2.7
Four Basic Types of Networks

Measure	CHAIN (Chain of command)	WHEEL OR STAR (Formal work group)	CIRCLE (Committee or task force; autonomous work group)	ALL CHANNEL (Grapevine; informal communication)
Centralization of power and authority	High	Moderately high	Low	Very low
Speed of communication	Moderate	Simple tasks; fast; complex tasks: slow	Members together: fast; members isolated: slow	Fast
Accuracy of communication	Written: High	Simple tasks: high; complex tasks: low	Members together: high; members isolated: low	Moderate
Level of group satisfaction	Low	Low	High	High
Speed of decisions	Fast	Moderate	Slow	—
Group commitment to decisions	Low	Moderate	High	—

Source: M. E. Shaw (1964), "Communication Networks." In L. L. Berkowitz (ed.), *Advances in Experimental Social Psychology* (New York: Academic Press). Copyright © 1964 by Academic Press. Reprinted by permission of Academic Press and the author.

the complex one shown in Figure 2.8, page 82) reflected the complex inter-relationships found in reality. Complex networks were ignored until the 1970s because reducing data from them to understandable forms required high-speed computers that were not readily accessible. Today a number of computer programs are available for describing networks (Tichy, 1981).

One kind of network of interest to managers is the **grapevine** (Davis, 1953; Sutton and Porter, 1968). Grapevines are naturally occurring networks that are familiar to all members of organizations. Efficient and fast, grapevines are an avenue for managers both to obtain information about what's going on in their organizations and to send out important information. Political leaders understand the value of pretesting their constituents'

FIGURE 2.8
*A Complex
Network*

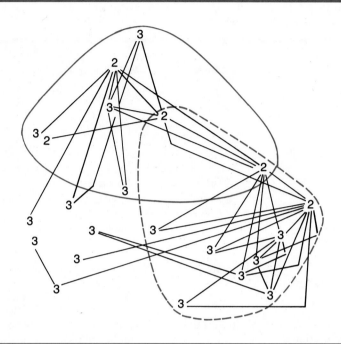

Source: N. Tichy and C. Fombrun, "Network Analysis in Organizational Settings," *Human Rela-tionships* 32 (11) (1979): 923–956. Reprinted by permission of Plenum Publishing Corporation.

acceptance of new programs and plans by leaking them to large-scale net-works. Grapevines offer informal ways for managers to move information for any of a variety of purposes.

Various networks coexist in organizations and are used for purposes other than moving information. The three types, aside from the grapevine, are task networks, authority networks, and social networks. All the types overlap and serve different organizational functions. One set of investiga-tions (Roberts and O'Reilly, 1978; O'Reilly and Roberts, 1977) of high-technology military organizations over a six-month period found that task networks developed more quickly and became stable sooner than other kinds of networks. These were closely followed by the development of social networks. Authority networks were much slower to develop and never reached the level of maturity of the other two kinds. These findings are somewhat surprising, particularly for military organizations. They suggest that managers should pay close attention, in particular, to the development of task networks, implementing change where these networks appear to be dysfunctional to the goals of the organization.

A number of network properties have been identified. Although it is not difficult to infer some of the consequences of these properties for organizations, little research relating them to organizational performance has been done. These network properties follow:

- *Connectedness*, or the extent to which people in networks are interconnected

- *Centrality*, or the degree to which network relations follow the formal organizational hierarchy

- *Reciprocity*, or the degree to which there is two-way communication

- *Vertical differentiation*, or the degree to which different organizational levels are represented in the network

- *Horizontal differentiation*, or the degree to which different job areas are represented in the network

Clusters Within Networks

Within a network are clusters that are more richly interconnected than the rest of the network. Coalitions and cliques are two types of clusters (see Chapter 4 for more on coalitions). **Coalitions** are temporary alliances among people for some distinct purpose, such as control over an activity. Coalitions often form in times of unusual or nonroutine demand, perhaps when firms develop new products or when the environment appears threatening. A joint venture is a coalition, as is the formation of a cartel such as OPEC. **Cliques** are permanent clusters, often involving friendships, in which all members are directly linked and may or may not exchange information about things other than friendship. Coalitions and cliques can both be used to maximize the power of some group in an organization (see Chapter 6). The feature on the clash between the Burger King and Pillsbury factions of Pillsbury Company demonstrates the difficulties that can arise from coalitions and cliques.

FEATURE: *The Dough Boy and the Burger King*

A cultural clash that could affect the fundamental structure of Pillsbury Co., a packaged-food and restaurant company, developed when the restaurant segment surpassed the packaged goods segment in contribution to profits. The company's packaged goods include Pillsbury flour and Green

Giant vegetables, and the restaurants include the Burger King and Steak and Ale chains. In 1986, for the first time, restaurant profits exceeded results from the 116-year-old grocery products business.

The packaged foods culture was that of a staid, midwestern (Minneapolis) grocery product company, steeped in tradition and given to dark suits and conservative colors in office decor. Burger King's culture was that of a brash, flamboyant Miami firm where colorful decor, flashy dress, and a hard-hitting marketing attack were the prevailing style.

For Pillsbury's packaged food executives, the stakes in the battle were high. "I suppose we wake up sometimes and don't want to work for a restaurant company," said one. "That wouldn't be right. I wouldn't want to be the foods president who let that happen at Pillsbury—the one who blows it."

Pillsbury's internal tension reflected an industry-wide war. Restaurant and packaged food marketers in the 1980s were battling hard for the stagnating consumer-food dollar. Packaged food businesses were on the defensive. Restaurants' share of the food market jumped from $2.50 of each $10 spent in 1955 to $4 in 1986. In 1986, 60% of Pillsbury's profit came from restaurants, up from 37% five years earlier.

The rivalry at Pillsbury seemed most intense when it came to discussing the corporate succession. One key was whether the head of Burger King could succeed to the chairmanship of the company. The incumbent chairman sought to minimize the friction by "blurring"—shifting executives from one part of the business to another.

Both support for and resistance to such cross-pollination developed. The senior vice president of growth and technology handed out business cards that listed his title as "Senior Vice President Blurring." A subsidiary senior vice president, however, said Pillsbury shouldn't try so hard to make all its pieces fit: "Companies who do that can get the round pieces where the squares belong."

Source: From "Cultural Clash: At Pillsbury Co., Restaurants Upstage Packaged-Food Group" by Robert Johnson. *Wall Street Journal*, October 23, 1986, pp. 1, 29. Copyright © 1986 by the Dow Jones Information Group. Reprinted by permission.

While managers should be sensitive to the development of coalitions and cliques in their organizations, helping them to develop or to deteriorate depending on the circumstances, they also need to be aware of how networks within organizations are tied to the outside. This issue has surfaced in the sociological literature under the rubric of the **strength of weak ties** (Granovetter, 1973).

The strength of a tie between two individuals within a network or in two different networks is defined by the amount of time, emotional intensity, intimacy, and reciprocal services that characterize the tie. The stronger the tie between any two individuals, the larger the proportion of people in a group to whom they will both be tied by either a strong or a weak tie. Strong ties produce dense networks, weak ties less dense networks. Strong ties are likely to create closed systems, impenetrable to outside information. Strongly tied groups cannot obtain or disseminate information, co-opt their environments, or develop coalitions with outsiders.

If organizations are to reach their goals, they must be permeable and sensitive to outside conditions, however. Thus, some persons in any given cluster need to have weak ties with persons in other clusters. These weak ties afford opportunities for the flow of information, ideas, innovations, and resources across groups, making them enormously important for diffusion in and across organizations (Rogers and Rogers, 1976). The importance of weak ties might suggest to a manager that he needs to develop them where they are nonexistent and that removing them by transferring or firing people or by changing their jobs may actually harm the organization. Alternatively, strong internal ties have been related to low internal conflict (Nelson, 1989).

Thus far, the strength of weak ties has been investigated only in friendship networks, but the results offer insight to managers. One example of the function of weak ties is demonstrated in finding a job (Granovetter, 1973). It has long been known that American blue-collar workers find new jobs more frequently through personal contact than through any other method. This appears to be true, too, for professional, technical, and managerial positions. One investigation asked a sample of such workers where they obtained information that helped them get new jobs. The researchers concluded that the vast majority of people who found new jobs through personal contacts used weak ties (they had been in touch with those contacts occasionally or rarely). Because those with whom we have weak ties move in different circles, they have different information than we do, making them valuable job contacts.

Communication Roles in Networks

Within networks, individuals can play a number of different communication roles. Individuals with weak ties are valuable because they are **boundary spanners.** Sales personnel in the field are boundary spanners for many firms; as customer relations specialists, they play a critical role in customer satisfaction and in identifying new product needs and competitive threats.

Other communication roles include gatekeepers, stars, and isolates, as explained below.

A secretary who decides what matters are to be brought to his boss's attention is the most common form of **gatekeeper.** Others include receptionists, nurses, and all other intermediaries between one individual and another. As we will discuss in greater detail later (see Chapter 6), having information provides power for the person holding the information; consequently, gatekeepers often are very powerful people. Some evidence suggests that new information often comes to organizations in a two-step flow, coming first to a gatekeeper who is tied both to the external environment and to the organization, and then going directly to others in the organization (Coleman, Katz, and Manzel, 1957). More recent research indicates a multistep flow in which information goes from the source to others, perhaps opinion leaders, and from them filters to yet others (Rogers and Shoemaker, 1971).

As environmental uncertainty increases, organizations create more gatekeepers. One public utility, facing a bewildering array of uncertainties ranging from regulatory policy to rapidly changing energy economics to local politics, created a network of employees who agreed to serve as "environmental scanners." Their job was to be on a more or less continual lookout for emerging issues that might affect the utility's operation. Systems were put in place for the scanners to regularly review certain publications or other information sources and report them to a central clearinghouse, which had the responsibility for either analyzing the issues or assigning them to other units for analysis. In this manner the utility hoped to heighten its sensitivity to its changing environment.

Stars are cluster members who are seen by others in the organization as having the most influence and who are the focus of most of the communication. In all likelihood stars become stars by reciprocating communication attempts: when someone communicates with them, they respond. Recall what we earlier said about information as a source of power. Stars have this source available to them.

Isolates are involved in almost no network communication. Isolates, with few contacts in their organizations, should concern managers. Although isolation is typical of certain jobs, such as computer programmer or night watchman, it can also indicate dissociation with the organization. Absence of communication can lead to alienation. In a study of isolation and participation in military organizations, researchers (Roberts and O'Reilly, 1979) found that isolates were younger, lower-ranking, less-educated personnel. They were also less satisfied and less committed to the military and performed their jobs more poorly than active participants. Often, managers can take steps to bring isolates back into the mainstream of organizational life and improve their functioning by doing so.

The Manifestation of Dynamic Elements

Two recent approaches to structuring organizations reflect the more fluid organizational processes—the dynamic elements—rather than the typical rational designs of organizations previously discussed. These approaches are possibly better observed through network strategies to uncover structure than by research methods used to obtain static pictures of organizational form.

"Loosely Coupled" Model   The first approach (Pfeffer and Salancik, 1977), which might be called the **"loosely coupled" model,** is posed as an alternative to a rational model of structure. The rational model is built on three assumptions: that organizations have one or a few goals, all consistent with one another; that information about various organizational contingencies can be obtained; and that environments are perfectly controlled. All these conditions, however, rarely exist.

An alternative model, say Pfeffer and Salancik, assumes that organizations are coalitions of various interests, that organizational designs are basically unplanned responses to contests among coalitions, and that organizational goals are numerous and conflicting. This view of organizations puts managers in the role of assimilators or processors of demands. The problem is that such managers are not in an action mode. To execute decisions requires more centralization, coordination, and order than would be possible in such a situation. Yet the attributes of structure that make action possible limit management's ability to visualize alternatives, inhibit the receipt of conflicting information, and minimize the possibility of other steps appropriate to a more fluid environment.

A frequent adaptation to this situation is to have line management worry about the day-to-day problems of running an organization and have staff engage in such support functions as gathering information and forecasting. All too often, however, this strategy fails because line and staff goals are not compatible with one another. Thus, information gathered never reaches decision makers, or does so but is not used in the decision process.

Fortunately, several strategies are open to managers. One is to bring together various sources of expertise, using a focused format to obtain heterogeneous information. Delphi or nominal group techniques might be applied (see Chapter 4 for descriptions of these techniques). Both techniques systematically query different experts about such factors as market characteristics, forecasts, potential actions, and environmental characteristics, with the goal of identifying a common body of information upon which to base action.

While this is an acceptable solution, a better one is to establish evaluation, reward, and incentive systems that define planning and environmental scanning as a part of a manager's job. One might also create internally differentiated, loosely coupled structures to confront various conflicting interests. When demands themselves are not tightly interconnected, it may be possible to satisfy conflicting claims by establishing subunits to do so. In this way, organizations typically establish consumer affairs or environmental impact departments to satisfy different demands (Pfeffer and Salancik, 1977).

Self-Designing Systems   Closely related to this view is the novel perspective of organizations as **self-designing systems** (Weick, 1977; Mohrman and Cummings, 1989). The notion underlying this view is that there are different ways to think about what is valuable and what is worthless in organizations.

As an illustrative problem of self-design, Weick cites *Skylab 3*, the first known example of a strike in space. In planning *Skylab* missions, Mission Control in Houston had reduced slack or discretionary time for the astronauts to the greatest degree possible. The astronauts were presented with a computer printout six feet long, with at least 42 separate sets of instructions for each day. They were programmed from the moment they awakened until the moment they went to sleep, with absolutely no room for the unexpected.

Unfortunately, by the time the *Skylab 3* astronauts arrived at the space station, they found that previous missions had failed to return tools and other materials to their proper bins. Thus, before the astronauts could even begin the required experiments, they had to search for the missing tools and materials. The grounds for conflict were clear: Mission Control knew exactly how long it was supposed to take an astronaut to perform each discrete task and had specifically planned every activity. They even wanted the astronauts to do additional tasks not included in the original plan. On the other hand, to the *Skylab* astronauts Mission Control seemed to view them as automatons with no needs of their own. Completely unplanned was the fact that astronauts were human beings complete with human needs and limitations. Thus, when illness overtook the astronauts early in the flight, they did not have the ability to meet the crisis. Finally, Mission Control failed entirely to be sensitive to the breakdown of relations between ground control and the *Skylab* inhabitants. In frustration, the astronauts refused to do further experiments until Mission Control retreated from its demanding schedule.

Skylab 3 became a sort of self-designing system when the astronauts aloft were given some authority to decide what was going to be done and in what sequence. Weick noted that the notion of self-design was so new that there were no business examples of it. He believed that organizations incapable of self-design are bound to suffer the same problems as *Skylab 3*. More recently, a study of five high-technology organizations provided an example of self-design (Schoonhoven and Jelinik, 1990). And Navistar International used self-design in its recent restructuring (Borucki and Barnett, 1990). The underlying assumption of self-design is that organizational participants are at once both teachers and learners. The essential problem is to design an ongoing process with six major characteristics:

1. Provides for arranging and re-arranging of elements to change consequences from those currently happening

2. Provides for the continuous evaluation of ongoing designs and supports that evaluation

3. Focuses on the process to determine how it reflects the need for people and creates possible alternative arrangements of people and activities

4. Recognizes that each adaptation restricts future adaptability

5. Creates designs without following specific performance criteria

6. Recognizes that design is inseparable from implementation

Weick (1977) summarizes both the obstacles to and benefits derived from self-design:

> Self-design involves some difficult managerial actions, including the management of anarchy, the encouragement of doubt, the fostering of inefficiency, and the cultivation of superstition. If an organization wants to take control of its own destiny and designs, the changes necessary to pull this off are substantial. But those changes are not impossible. The likelihood of pulling them off, however, depends heavily on the attitudes of the managers committed to self design. (p. 46)

The business community awaits examples of self-designing systems, but in an increasingly technological and sophisticated world they make sense. As the environment of organizations undergoes more and more change, self-design may provide the flexibility that organizations will require in order to survive (Courtright, Fairhurst, and Rogers, 1989).

Determinants of Structure

Six Determinants of Structure

A number of factors determine how organizations are structured. These include the organization's goals, social customs and mores, the beliefs and values of the founders or managers, environmental constraints, and available technology. As mentioned earlier, size, though an element of structure, is

FIGURE 2.9
*A Model of
Organizational
Structure*

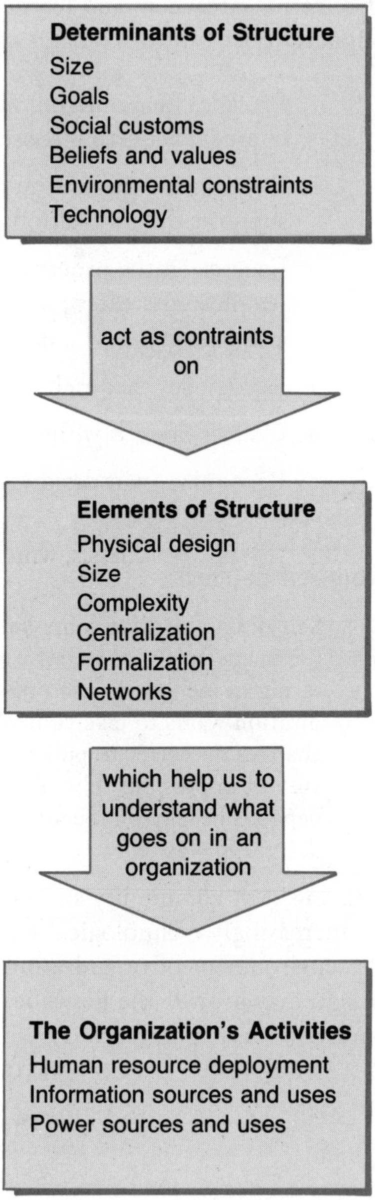

Determinants of Structure
Size
Goals
Social customs
Beliefs and values
Environmental constraints
Technology

act as contraints
on

Elements of Structure
Physical design
Size
Complexity
Centralization
Formalization
Networks

which help us to
understand what
goes on in an
organization

The Organization's Activities
Human resource deployment
Information sources and uses
Power sources and uses

also a determinant because it influences all the other elements. The relationship of these determinants and the structural elements is shown in Figure 2.9.

Organizational goals clearly influence the way an organization is designed. The high value placed on productivity and quality as well as shareholder value had a major influence on the redesign of Westinghouse as a more diversified and decentralized firm. Indeed, goals are the prime determinants of structure. If one is in the business of producing hamburgers, the goal of delivering a gourmet product at a moderate price leads to different structuring arrangements than does the goal of delivering a reliable product quickly at a low price. The feature on GE shows how goals can also be used to determine what activities the organization should pursue.

Social customs at the time of an organization's birth also determine how it is structured. This has been very important in the history of business. For example, the organizational forms adopted by the first companies in the automobile industry are not the same as the structures being adopted now. Historically production was structured around the assembly line. Some workers always built chassis, which were then sent down the assembly line to other workers, who did such jobs as putting axles and engines onto those chassis. Currently, many automakers are adopting the work-group or team concept (see Chapter 11 for more on these approaches to job design), in which a group of workers is responsible for more than just one portion of the car. At the time the auto industry began, no one thought about using a group approach to building cars, given that it was not consistent with the existing values about manufacturing.

FEATURE: *How Jack Welch Used Goals to Reshape General Electric*

When John F. (Jack) Welch became CEO of General Electric Co. in 1981, the company was ranked as the best-managed industrial company in the United States in a poll of Fortune 500 chief executives. But GE was also regarded as a company whose growth and prosperity could never do much better than the overall economy.

The strategy Welch adopted to make GE outperform the economy literally transformed the company. His goals were to emphasize technology and services and keep only those traditional GE businesses where the company could dominate the market. If a company could not be No. 1 or No. 2 in its market, it was put on notice that it would be sold or closed.

In his first five years at the helm of GE, Welch sold more than 190 subsidiaries worth nearly $6 billion, including Utah International and Family Financial Services, and spent $10 billion on 70 acquisitions, including Kidder Peabody, Employers Reinsurance and RCA.

When first articulated, Welch's goals were expressed by three circles covering services, high technology and core businesses. Businesses inside the circles were those that GE would nourish, while those outside were put on notice to become top players or cease to be a part of GE. The circles looked like this:

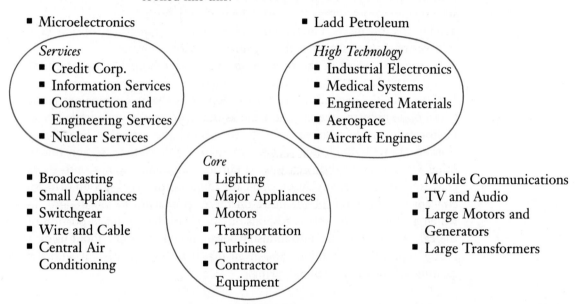

- Microelectronics

Services
- Credit Corp.
- Information Services
- Construction and Engineering Services
- Nuclear Services

- Broadcasting
- Small Appliances
- Switchgear
- Wire and Cable
- Central Air Conditioning

Core
- Lighting
- Major Appliances
- Motors
- Transportation
- Turbines
- Contractor Equipment

- Ladd Petroleum

High Technology
- Industrial Electronics
- Medical Systems
- Engineered Materials
- Aerospace
- Aircraft Engines

- Mobile Communications
- TV and Audio
- Large Motors and Generators
- Large Transformers

In Welch's shorthand, the traditional "core" businesses accounted for around 33% of profits, the high-technology businesses about 30% and rising, and the services about 29%. Around these three main groupings lay the remainder of the businesses. Some were profitable, some were losing money. Among them, they accounted for around 13% of total sales. These were the businesses that Welch told to fix themselves, become top players in their league, or they would be sold and closed. Some, like microelectronics and Ladd Petroleum, have links to all three main business circles. They were not on the threatened list. Many of the others were sold or are planned to be.

Source: Adapted from "What Welch Has Wrought at G.E." by Peter Petre. *Fortune*, July 7, 1986. Copyright © 1986 Time, Inc. All rights reserved. Reprinted by permission. Adapted from "General Electric Going with the Winners" by Howard Banks. *Forbes*, March 26, 1984. Reprinted by permission.

Once structures become common in an industry, they tend not to change. Certain social structures remain long after they are no longer suited to situations. For example, the railroad industry in the United States developed a structure that became dysfunctional as the engineering technology in the industry advanced. The tendency to stick with industry-specific structures may be changing with the proliferation of mergers and acquisitions and ever more rapid developments in engineering technologies. These developments may lead to the increased homogenization of structure as companies struggle to handle common problems of size. Alternatively, the need for structural change may become apparent more quickly due to technological advancement.

A third determinant of structure is comprised of the beliefs and values of the people forming the organization. Westinghouse chairman John C. Marous clearly believed in decentralizing, in giving employees decision-making freedom, and in a quality orientation as core managerial values to be built into the entire firm. Many firms in the computer industry, formed by young entrepreneurs who favor informal life-styles, have loose, informal, and collegial structures that reflect those values. Alfred P. Sloan put his personal stamp on the organization of General Motors in the 1920s, and it was not until the turbulent days of the 1970s that significant changes were made. Interestingly, these changes were brought about primarily as a response to the environment.

Environmental constraints include legislation, government regulation, court orders, market characteristics, social issues, and societal norms. For example, major incursions by Japanese auto manufacturers into the U.S. market have forced American firms to change their production methods as well as the underlying structures of their organizations. Laws concerning entry into or exclusion from certain businesses, the imposition or removal of regulations, and such court-ordered actions as the breakup of American Telephone and Telegraph Company affect the structure of organizations. The birth of People Express and other air carriers was the direct result of the Airline Deregulations Act of 1978, which enabled new carriers to enter the airline business for the first time in decades. How environmental changes affect structure is shown in the feature on the investment industry.

FEATURE: *How Explosive Growth Outran Systems and Structure in the Investment Industry*

The extended bull market in stocks and bonds in the mid-1980s showed many securities firms that they did not have the management systems and structures to control the rapid growth that occurred in the industry.

Wall Street historically had consisted largely of small partnerships selling stocks and bonds to institutions and individuals at fixed, noncompetitive prices. In the late 1960s, several securities firms collapsed because their managements had neglected to install the systems needed amid a bull-market surge in trading. Others did not survive the May 1975 move to competitive commission rates.

Though shaken, most surviving firms did not feel compelled to toughen their management practices. With this attitude toward management, Wall Street was largely unprepared for the vast changes that came in the 1980s. The bull market born in August 1982 saw the emergence of scores of new financial products, such as options, futures, and securities, backed by such assets as mortgages, car loans, and credit-card receivables. Deregulation of markets in London and Tokyo sent Wall Street firms scrambling to set up shop there. Many firms also sharply increased their capital by being acquired or making public offerings of securities. Anxious to generate high returns, the firms began taking larger and larger risks by betting more of their own money in the marketplace.

Fueled by entrepreneurs whose creative financial innovations drove the unprecedented expansion, Wall Street investment houses transformed themselves into powerful, worldwide corporations over a period of about five years. This go-for-broke strategy in many respects paid off. Salomon Brothers, for example, earned more than $1 billion in just two years.

But management skills did not keep pace with the growth, according to professionals in the industry. Many firms found they did not have the know-how or the systems to manage themselves adequately—especially to police large numbers of people, control costs, monitor and analyze risk, and plan for the future. A string of highly publicized management failings ensued.

Merrill Lynch lost $377 million after its mortgage department spun out of control. First Boston Corp. lost nearly $100 million in just two months, largely because a few loosely supervised, high-risk traders had put it in a vulnerable position in Treasury-bond options. Kidder, Peabody and Co. agreed to pay $25.3 million to settle government charges of insider trading and other securities law violations (Kidder neither admitted nor denied guilt). In firm after firm, the securities industry struggled with problems in controlling the activities of its brokers, traders, and investment bankers.

The fundamental problem, according to observers inside the industry, was that the huge profits made by all but the worst-managed firms during the market's rapid expansion allowed many to ignore the need for management systems to control the growth. There was no consensus, however, on just what management tools were needed. These firms had grown rapidly to become huge corporations, but were still dependent on the entrepreneurial flexibility most often found in small companies. Their dilemma was how to provide adequate supervision without creating stultifying layers of bureaucracy.

Salomon Brothers provided a good example of the difficulties in making the transition. Long known as a group of especially strong-willed traders with virtually no management hierarchy, the firm moved to change its structure by naming a president and two vice chairmen, creating an 18-member board of directors and forming two senior committees to monitor its balance sheet and investment risk. Later, it put in additional controls after its parent company, Salomon, Inc., reported an embarrassing 39 percent drop in quarterly earnings. It named its first chief financial officer and developed its first budget.

The changes have brought repercussions. Senior executives, who once spent much of their time on the trading desk, found themselves in what seemed to be endless meetings. One planning session lasted nearly 10 hours, such an unusual length that it sparked rumors that there had been a merger offer for the firm. One of the vice chairmen, an entrepreneurial former trader who often clashed with those trying to get control of the burgeoning enterprise, was asked to resign. A week later, his chief deputy was also ousted. The firm's highly respected economist resigned his top management position over a dilution of his authority and a management policy decision. "There's resistance here," said one young Salomon sales manager. "People don't want a lot of professional managers running around."

Many observers feel that Wall Street will not generally adapt to more disciplined management for some time, citing several reasons: (1) Installing such systems takes years; (2) strategic planning in the securities business is difficult because of the market's dependence on interest rates, stock market activity, and other unpredictable forces; (3) Wall Streeters are notorious prima donnas and difficult to lead; (4) most securities professionals disdain management jobs and scoff at anything smacking of traditional management techniques. Said one chief of investment banking at a major Wall Street firm: "I don't sit in my office and think up strategy and set up systems to control costs."

Source: From "Loose Bull: Wall Street's Growth Is Seriously Outpacing Management Systems" by Steve Swartz. *Wall Street Journal*, July 27, 1987, pp. 1, 7. Copyright © 1987 by the Dow Jones Information Group. Reprinted by permission.

Burns and Stalker (1961) studied structure in relation to the predictability of the environment. Analyzing firms in different industries, they concluded that the more stable the environment, the more rigidly structured the organization. They distinguished between organizations that are **mechanistic,** or rigidly structured, and those that are **organic,** or more fluid. Lawrence and Lorsch (1969) pursued similar lines of study, but focused on subunits within organizations. They found that a given organization may need differently structured subunits, each tailored to match, or fit, the degree of uncertainty in the environment. Close fit of the subunit's mission, technology, environment, and resources results in effectiveness. As the fit becomes less good, effectiveness suffers (David, Pearce, and Randolph, 1989). Burns and Stalker also pointed out that the more interdependence between subunits, the greater the need for integration of operations.

As alluded to previously, technology is another determining factor that will affect the new forms organizations will take. One example concerns organizations that were once a part of AT&T. Rapidly changing telecommunications technology and the removal of certain regulations are opening new market niches in which the regional telephone companies can compete. Another example is robotics and other modern production methods. As these technologies have developed, they have changed the American automobile industry as significantly as did foreign competition. Some research demonstrates that technological change offers occasions for restructuring (Barley, 1986).

Technology has received an extensive amount of study over the years. Woodward (1958) classified firms into one of three types of technology: small-batch or unit (such as the building of a ship or an airplane), mass production (an assembly line), and continuous process (oil refining). As a result of studies of scores of British manufacturing firms, Woodward (1965) concluded that increasingly complex technology required more levels of authority, a higher proportion of administrative workers, and more support personnel. She suggested that a fit between structure and technology contributes to organizational effectiveness.

While Woodward's work is useful, it is limited to firms engaged in production. Thompson (1967) provided another typology of organizations based on technology that embraces a wider range of activities. This approach identified three types of technology:

- **Long-linked technology,** in which many operations are interdependent, such as an assembly line

- **Mediating technology,** in which otherwise independent units are linked by following procedures, such as bank tellers who all serve customers in an isolated way but do so according to the bank's rules

- **Intensive technology,** in which the task sequence is unique and depends on feedback from the object being acted upon. Hospitals exhibit this technology in that patients are acted upon differentially and each action depends on their response (improvement or deterioration of their condition) to prior actions.

Clearly, as an organization moves from one type of technology to another, the demand for rigid rules or flexibility changes. While cooperation is significant in all three technologies—later stages of an assembly line cannot function smoothly if earlier stages falter, just as the surgical team requires intense cooperation to succeed—more flexibility and communication is needed in intensive technology than in the other two forms.

How the Determinants Are Used

A number of other views have recently emerged about why organizations are structured as they are. One view, the **strategic contingency theory,** assumes that organizations are open systems that respond to various opportunities and challenges from their environments. They develop various kinds of subunits to best respond to these opportunities and challenges. Organizational participants vary in their wishes, and the subunits to which they belong differ not only in their wishes but in their power. Power has many sources, one of which is environmental uncertainty. To the extent that a subunit can cope with uncertainty, thereby reducing it for everyone, it obtains power. Thus, "organizational structures are the outcomes of political contests within organizations" (Pfeffer, 1981, p. 266).

Four quite different explanations for organizational structuring come from an ecological perspective, two of which will be discussed here. The **population ecology,** or natural selection, model, which draws from biology, views organizations as populations rather than as individuals. In this view, environments differentially select organizations for survival based on the fit between organizational forms and environmental characteristics. Positively selected organizations survive and reproduce similar others, which then form the starting point for a new round of selection as mutants appear (Hannan and Freeman, 1977). As the environment changes, new structures are selected.

Where the population ecology approach stresses selection, both in terms of what kinds of organizations are created and which ones survive, the **resource dependency** model stresses adaptation. As does the population ecology view, this model argues that one cannot understand the structure or behavior of an organization without understanding the context within which it operates. Organizations are not self-sufficient. They must engage in exchanges with their environments as a condition of survival, and the need to acquire resources creates dependencies among organizations. Those organizations that survive are able to develop strategies to change and adapt to their environments, exploiting those dependencies. Organizations are active, not passive, in determining their own fates (Aldrich and Pfeffer, 1976). In this respect, the resource dependency model differs from the population ecology approach.

Organizational Structures in the Future

In industrialized nations we are increasingly working our way into a world that will require as yet unseen organizational structures. The most obvious development promoting change is the information revolution. It has already influenced the fabric and structure of every business organization. While the fact of such influence is undeniable, the dimensions are unclear, as are the dimensions of other technological change on organizational structure (Barley, 1990; Liu, Dennis, Kolodny, and Stymme, 1990). Since we have no way to know what future influences might be and no scientific data concerning the impact of widespread computing power on organizational structure, this section is speculative.

The structures of information and resource flows are surely being affected by integrated computer-driven robotic systems, automated office equipment, and computers. At the same time, computerization may be deskilling jobs (Zuboff, 1988). We predict that in the long run information will be decentralized and top-heavy static organizational forms will give way to less centralized, more fluid organizations. This will happen because important information will no longer be available to just a select few.

In a future in which organizations will probably be designed around their communication channels, the autonomy of peripheral units will increase, but so will the ability of organizational leaders to monitor subordinates. Simultaneously, some parts of the organization will become decoupled from one another while other parts will become more tightly linked. Formal and quasi-structural arrangements will increasingly occur simultaneously (Schoonhoven and Jelinick, 1990). A multinational corporation, for example, may choose to coordinate the activities of an affiliate while increasing its independence and teamwork because it can monitor the affiliate's progress and respond more quickly than before. People who were once isolates may find themselves in control of large amounts of information—and consequently power—and entire units that were once well integrated in organizations may lose their secure places.

Entire layers of organizations may disappear, shortening the distance from top to bottom and increasing the potential for less distortion of information between top and bottom. A supervisor's span of control (the number of people, computers, and robots he can supervise) will probably change. If an entire job can be done by a computer or robot, span of control is likely to decrease. If only part of a job is eliminated, a supervisor's span of control is likely to increase as the human–machine interface requires additional coordination. This change will require greater communication efforts than we see today.

Management information systems (MIS) or integrated computer-robotics systems have shown their potential to increase inter- and intradepartmental specialization and integration. Thus, coordination and control become more crucial. Information will move rapidly and have a more limited time value than it does today. Boundary spanners will be increasingly important.

On the other hand, many organizations are already resisting this kind of technological change. While such resistance will probably increase in coming years, it seems doomed. The hand-held calculator was seen as cumbersome and unusual when it entered the market in the early 1970s, but its frequency in the population is probably already similar to that of radios; indeed, probably as many people have calculators on their watches today as had any calculator at all 10 years ago. One technological liability of the resistance to change was described in *Business Week* as early as 1983. Line departments, tired of waiting for MIS departments to make computer purchase decisions, often purchased their favorite computers. Thus, while personal computers proliferated, so did problems of compatibility.

One set of authors addresses some of these problems and the changing nature of competition in the 1980s and 1990s. Miles and Snow (1986) point out that new organizational forms must arise to cope with new environmental conditions and that no new forms arrive full-blown. They usually result from a variety of experimental actions taken by innovative companies. Miles and Snow call this new organizational form the **dynamic network** to suggest that the components of the form can be assembled and reassembled to meet complex and changing competitive conditions.

The major characteristics of the dynamic network involve various kinds of businesses combining and recombining along the following lines:

1. *Vertical disaggregation.* Functions typically done in one organization are performed by independent organizations in the network. Thus, marketing, distribution, product development, manufacturing, and so on, may all be done by separate organizations.

2. *Brokers.* In situations in which all business functions are not necessarily carried out by a single group, brokers are needed to bring businesses together.

3. *Market mechanisms.* Market mechanisms rather than plans and controls are used to hold the major functions together.

4. *Full-disclosure information systems.* Because the need for short-term combinations does not lend itself to the long term needed to build trust, broad-access computer information systems will be used. Participants will agree on a general structure of payment for value added and hook themselves together in a continuously updated information system.

We cannot know for sure, of course, whether dynamic networks are indeed the organizational structure of the future—only time can tell. But if the pace of environmental change of the last decades continues—or accelerates, as it may do—the flexibility that is the hallmark of this structure seems mandatory.

SUMMARY

A brief profile of a decade long organizational restructuring at Westinghouse helped highlight the two main views of organizational structure: the static, rational approach and the dynamic network view. Managers need to be sensitive to structural issues if they are to know how to find their way around in organizations, where to go for information, and how to manipulate structure in the interests of optimizing performance and realizing their goals. The leaders of Westinghouse were clearly aware of the impact of size and growth on their portfolio and as the original design became more complex and as Japanese competition more severe, they restructured based on quality and shareholder value.

The basic static elements of organizational structure are physical design, size, complexity, formalization, and centralization. Physical design embraces the characteristics and arrangement of the physical space. Size is both an element of structure and a determinant, in that it influences other elements. Complexity includes the division of labor, or horizontal differentiation; the hierarchy, or vertical differentiation; and physical location, or spatial dispersion. Formalization describes not the extent to which rules are codified but the degree to which members of an organization follow rules, whether written or not. Organizations that focus the authority to make and evaluate decisions at higher levels are centralized; those organizations that disperse this authority throughout the entity are decentralized.

These concepts are manifested in the usual organizational designs seen today. Smaller organizations typically group by function; as they grow larger, they often find product grouping more appropriate. A number of mixed grouping strategies exist, among them the matrix organization, which typically groups simultaneously by function and product and provides for one individual as a focus of responsibility for a project or product. As organizations grow larger, they tend to form subunits or divisions, but one problem with divisionalization is that the underlying logic is frequently unclear. Also, that logic may change over time, rendering inappropriate a kind of divisionalization that was once functional.

A more recent view of organizational structure recognizes the often unplanned and very complex networks that are found within organizations. Components of networks include connectedness, centrality, reciprocity, vertical differentiation, and horizontal differentiation. Those networks in which the participants are densely linked—that is, coalitions and cliques— are often formed to maximize the power of some group. The openness of organizations to other organizations is probably more important than we think; organizations maintain their viability and flexibility by remaining permeable to environmental information and constraints.

Boundary spanners, gatekeepers, stars, and isolates are some of the roles manifested in networks. Boundary spanners link organizations to other organizations. Gatekeepers, by controlling access to leaders or to information, can play a vital part in promoting or shutting off communication. Centrality of an individual is often manifest in a person's role as a star. Some jobs lend themselves to isolation, but managers need to watch for isolation because it is frequently dysfunctional.

Two new approaches to organizational structure emphasize the fluidity of organizations. The first is based on a view of organizations as coalitions whose competing demands managers must work to accommodate; organizations are loosely coupled systems. This view embraces the notion that organizational goals are many and often conflicting and that organizational forms are frequently unplanned. It argues for a model of organizational design that is simultaneously capable of obtaining and acting upon environmental information and constraints. The second view sees organizations as self-designing systems, in which the teacher and the learner are one and the same. This view argues that organizations should structure themselves for constant change, so they can best respond to environmental conditions.

Certain factors—goals, social customs, beliefs or values of the founders or managers, environmental constraints, and technology—are determinants of organizational structure. They shape how those elements are used to build structure.

Current developments and trends in computers and robotics have profound implications for organizational structure in the future. These implications include simultaneous centralization and decentralization within organizations, the possible elimination of entire hierarchical levels, changes in span of control, and the potential for greater integration of organizational subunits. One organizational form—the dynamic network—has been proposed as being responsive to these developments and to the changing competitive environments of business.

Managerial attention to organizational structure will be more important in the future than in the past if for no other reason than larger, more technologically sophisticated organizations will have to design organizational forms undreamed of at this time. We will discuss managing change further in Chapter 11.

MANAGERIAL INSIGHT

To: *Student Managers*
From: *Veteran Manager*
Subject: *Organizational Structure*

There will be three times in your career when structure is very important to you:

1. When you are new to an organization and learning your way around

2. When you are managing a department or larger piece of the organization and need to make significant changes

3. When you want to use structure to help get something accomplished

The first occasion is the one most people associate with the concept of organizational structure: who reports to whom, which departments are grouped together, how close to the top certain functions are, which senior officers make up the top management team. Structure in this case is geographic; you study it as you would a map, with your reference points an arrow and a label that says, "You are here." The organizational chart is helpful, but it is equally important to get the interpretation of a veteran who can point out where the chart is out of date or where the appearance of structure and the reality are different.

The second use requires insight into how the structure is either helping or hindering you in achieving your goals. Cynics will say that the reason so many managers reorganize shortly after taking over is that they don't know what else to do. But a new manager may face real structural problems that require immediate attention—and sometimes the inability of the previous manager to deal with them is one reason the new manager has the job. The existing structure may prevent work units from communicating fully with each other. It may shelter key functions from direct managerial control. Or it may paralyze the manager with too many direct reports. Usually, some parts of the structure are working right. Wholesale changes, which impose a heavy burden on the organization in addition to its daily work, are rarely called for. In my experience, these observations apply whether the organization in question is a small company, a single department in a larger company, or an entire large firm.

The third use of structure could also be called a mixture of politics, motivation, and leadership. Structures are not airtight. Concepts discussed throughout this book—informal networks, sharing information, interdepartmental cooperation, deference to authority (either hierarchical or functional)—are all behaviors that give structure breathing room. My experience is that rarely in any organization can a manager accomplish anything of significance wholly within his or her own work unit without involving or affecting others. Sometimes you can't conveniently get to that other unit by going up your chain of command and down the chain of the other manager. You have to cross structural lines and territorial boundaries. Going across structural lines deliberately—for example, to invite another department in on a project early or to request the assistance of functional experts before the normal course of events brings them in—empowers others and usually positively motivates them to work cooperatively with you. Going around the structure may require sharing power or indicating vulnerability; it could entail some risk if your superiors are sticklers for bureaucratic protocol. While these behaviors may be uncommon in your organization, you may find that they are in fact a powerful means of accomplishing your objectives, especially if ultimate success is going to depend on the cooperation of many work units.

Structure exists to help the organization accomplish its goals. Use it to help you accomplish yours.

REVIEW QUESTIONS

1. What was the role of structure in the Westinghouse case?

2. Distinguish between the elements and the determinants of structure.

3. How is physical design an element of structure?

4. What are the three dimensions of complexity?

5. Why does professionalization clash with formalization?

6. What is the key negative feature of matrix management?

7. How can divisionalization promote entrepreneurism?

8. Contrast U.S. and Japanese firms on the basis of division of labor, hierarchy, span of control, and decision making.

9. Why would detailed information about an organization be required to establish a true picture of an organizational network?

10. What are the five properties of networks?

11. What is the difference between a coalition and a clique?

12. Identify the communication role played by each of the following hypothetical workers:
   a. President's chief of staff
   b. A very private worker who never communicates with others
   c. Top engineer who is respected by the sales department
   d. Union worker serving on company's board of directors
   e. Manager of MIS system

13. What three assumptions underlie the loosely coupled systems model of organizations?

14. What is the main characteristic of the self-designing system?

15. What are the six determinants of structure?

16. How is the environment a significant factor in both the population ecology and resource dependency views of organizational structure?

REFERENCES

Aldrich, H. E., and Pfeffer, J. (1976). Environments of organizations. In A. Inkeles, J. Coleman, and N. Smelsen (eds.), *Annual Review of Sociology* 2:79–105.

Anderson, T. R., and Warkov, S. (1961). Organizational size and functional complexity: A study of differentiation in hospitals. *American Sociological Review* 26:23–28.

Bamford, J. (1982). *The Puzzle Palace.* Boston: Houghton Mifflin.

Barley, S. (1990). The alignment of technology and structure through roles and networks. *Administrative Science Quarterly* 35:61–103.

Barley, S. R. (1986). Technology as an occasion for restructuring: Evidence from observations of CT scanners and the social order of radiology departments. *Administrative Science Quarterly* 31:78–108.

Birnbaum, P. H., and Wong, G. Y. Y. (1985). Organizational structure of multinational banks in Hong Kong from a culture-free perspective. *Administrative Science Quarterly* 30:262–277.

Blair, R., Roberts, K. H., and McKechnie, P. (1985). Vertical and network communication in organizations: The present and the future. In R. McPhee and P. Tomkins (eds.), *Organizational Communication: Traditional Themes and New Directions*. Beverly Hills, CA: Sage, pp. 55–78.

Blau, P. M. (1973). *The Organization of Academic Work*. New York: Wiley.

Blau, P. M., and Schoenherr, R. (1971). *The Structure of Organizations*. New York: Basic Books.

Borucki, C., and Barnett, C. K. (1990). Restructuring for self-renewal: Navistar International Corporation. *Academy of Management Executive* 4:36–.

Burns, T., and Stalker, G. M. (1961). *The Management of Innovation*. London: Tavistock.

Child, J. (1972). Organizational structure, environment and performance: The role of strategic choice. *Sociology* 6:1–22.

Child, J. (1984). *Organization: A Guide to Problems and Practice*, 2nd ed. London: Harper & Row.

Coleman, J. S., Katz, E., and Manzel, H. (1957). The diffusion of an innovation among physicians. *Sociometry* 20:253–270.

Courtright, J. A., Fairhurst, G. T., and Rogers, L. E. (1989). Interaction patterns in organic and mechanistic systems. *Academy of Management Journal* 32:773–802.

Crozier, M. (1964). *The Bureaucratic Phenomenon*. Chicago: University of Chicago Press.

Daft, R., and Steers, R. (1986). *Organizations: A Micro/Macro Approach*. Glenview, IL: Scott, Foresman & Co.

David, F. R., Pearce, J. A., and Randolph, W. A. (1989). Linking technology and structure to enhance group performance. *Journal of Applied Psychology* 74:233–241.

Davis, K. (1953). Management communication and the grapevine. *Harvard Business Review* 31:43–49.

Davis, S. M., and Lawrence, P. R. (1977). *Matrix*. Reading, MA: Addison-Wesley.

Dornbush, S., and Scott, W. R. (1975). *Evaluation and the Exercise of Authority: A Theory of Control Applied to Diverse Organizations*. San Francisco: Jossey-Bass.

Fombrun, C. (1986). Structural dynamics within and between organizations. *Administrative Science Quarterly* 31:403–421.

Granovetter, M. S. (1973). The strength of weak ties. *American Journal of Sociology* 78:1360–1380.

Guest, R. H. (1986). Management imperatives for the year 2000. *California Management Review* 28:62–70.

Hage, J., and Aiken, M. (1967). Relationship of centralization to other structural properties. *Academy of Management Journal* 30:7–32.

Hage, J., and Aiken, M. (1969). Routine technology, social structure and organizational goals. *Administrative Science Quarterly* 14:366–376.

Hall, R. H. (1968). Professionalization and bureaucratization. *American Sociological Review* 33:92–104.

Hall, R. H. (1977). *Organizations: Structures and Process*, 2nd ed. Englewood Cliffs, NJ: Prentice-Hall.

Hannan, M. T., and Freeman, J. H. (1977). The population ecology of organizations. *American Journal of Sociology* March: 929–964.

Jacques, E. (1990). In praise of hierarchy. *Harvard Business Review* 68:127–133.

Kornhauser, W. (1962). *Scientists in Industry: Conflict and Accommodation.* Berkeley: University of California Press.

Lawrence, P. R., and Lorsch, J. W. (1969). *Organization and Environment.* Cambridge, MA: Harvard University, Division of Research, Graduate School of Business Administration.

Lincoln, J. R. (1989). Employee work attitudes and management practice in the U.S. and Japan: Evidence from a large comparative study. *California Management Review* 32:89–106.

Lincoln, J. R., and McBride, K. (1987). Japanese industrial organization in comparative perspective. *Annual Review of Sociology* 13:289–312.

Lincoln, J. R., Hanada, M., and McBride, K. (1986). Organizational structures in Japanese and U.S. manufacturing. *Administrative Science Quarterly* 31:338–364.

Litterer, J. (1963). *Organizations: Structure and Behavior.* New York: Wiley.

Litwak, E. (1961). Models of bureaucracy which permit conflict. *American Journal of Sociology* 73:468–481.

Liu, M., Denis, H., Kolodny, H., and Stymne, B. (1990). Organizational design for technological change. *Human Relations* 43:7–22.

Mansfield, R. (1973). Bureaucracy and centralization: An examination of organizational structure. *Administrative Science Quarterly* 18:77–88.

March, J. G., and Simon, H. A. (1958). *Organizations.* New York: Wiley.

Merton, R. K. (1957). *Social Theory and Social Structure,* 2nd ed. Glencoe, IL: Free Press.

Miles, R. E., and Snow, C. C. (1986). Network organizations: New concepts for new forms. *California Management Review* 28:62–73.

Milgram, S. (1977). *The Individual in a Social World.* Reading, MA: Addison-Wesley.

Mohrman, S. A., and Cummings, T. G. (1989). *Self-designing Organizations.* Reading, MA: Addison-Wesley.

Nelson, R. (1989). The strength of strong ties: Social networks and intergroup conflict in organizations. *Academy of Management Journal* 32:377–401.

O'Reilly, C. A., and Roberts, K. H. (1977). Task group structure, communication, and effectiveness in three organizations. *Journal of Applied Psychology* 62:674–681.

Parsons, T. (1960). *Structure and Process in Modern Societies.* Glencoe, IL: Free Press.

Perrow, C. (1967). A framework for the comparative analysis of organizations. *American Sociological Review* 32:194–208.

Pfeffer, J. (1981). *Power in Organizations.* Marshfield, MA: Pitman, p. 266.

Pfeffer, J., and Salancik, G. R. (1977). Administrative effectiveness: The effects of advocacy and information on resource allocations. *Human Relations* 30:641–656.

Pugh, D. (1969). The context of organization structures. *Administrative Science Quarterly* 14:91–114.

Pugh, D. S., Hickson, D., Hinings, C. R., and Turner, C. (1968). Dimensions of organizational structure. *Administrative Science Quarterly* 13:65–105.

Roberts, K. H., and O'Reilly, C. A. (1978). Organizations as communication structures: An empirical approach. *Human Communication Research* 4:283–293.

Roberts, K. H., and O'Reilly, C. A. (1979). Some correlates of communication roles. *Academy of Management Journal* 22:42–57.

Rogers, E. M., and Rogers, R. A. (1976). *Communications in Organizations.* New York: Free Press.

Rogers, E. M., and Shoemaker, F. F. (1971). *Communication of Innovations: A Cross-Cultural Approach.* New York: Free Press.

Ronen, S. (1986). *Comparative and Multinational Management.* New York: Wiley.

Schoonhoven, C. B., and Jelenik, M. (1990). Dynamic tension in innovative high technology firms: Managing rapid technological change through organizational structure. In M. A. Von Glinow and S. Mohrman (eds.), *Managing Complexity in High Technology Organizations.* New York: Oxford, pp. 90–118.

Scott, W. R. (1987). *Organizations: Rational, Natural and Open Systems.* Englewood Cliffs, NJ: Prentice-Hall.

Shaw, M. E. (1964). Communication networks. In L. L. Berkowitz (ed.), *Advances in Experimental Social Psychology.* New York: Academic Press, pp. 111–147.

Sutton, H., and Porter, L. W. (1968). A study of the grapevine in a governmental organization. *Personnel Psychology* 21:223–230.

Thompson, J. D. (1967). *Organizations in Action.* New York: McGraw-Hill.

Tichy, N. M. (1981). Networks in organizations. In P. C. Nystrom & W. H. Starbuck (eds.), *Handbook of Organizational Design.* London: Oxford University Press.

Weick, K. E. (1977). Organizations as self-designing systems. *Organization Dynamics* 6:30–67.

Woodward, J. (1958). *Management and Technology.* London: Her Majesty's Stationery Office.

Woodward, J. (1965). *Industrial Organization: Theory and Practice.* Oxford: Oxford University Press.

Zuboff, S. (1988). *In the Age of the Smart Machines.* New York: Basic Books.

Organizational Culture and Socialization: Why Workers Stay

CHAPTER OVERVIEW

This chapter has three objectives: first, to examine theoretical and other issues associated with the concept of organizational culture; second, to describe the processes by which organizations socialize their workers to accept and internalize the organizational culture; and third, to explore the connection between socialization, commitment, and employee turnover.

THEME CASE

"The McDonald's Mystique" describes the philosophy and values behind McDonald's meteoric expansion worldwide. "Krocisms," stories, and award ceremonies are some of the ways in which this firm socializes its employees and strengthens its shared cultural values.

CHAPTER OUTLINE

- What Is Organizational Culture?
- The Cultural Context of Organizations
- Four Approaches to Organizational Culture
- Assessing Organizational Culture
- Organizational Socialization
- Organizational Commitment and Turnover
- Summary
- Managerial Insight

KEY DEFINITIONS

Cultural environment the economic, social, and political context established by the larger culture in which the organization resides.

Organizational culture no agreed-upon meaning, but two main views: culture is comprised of the behaviors and structures of a group (a component of the social system), or it is a mental construct (which influences how people think and view the world or find expression in symbols and shared meanings).

Socialization the process by which organizational culture is transmitted; how newcomers are taught and learn the ropes of the organization.

Commitment the capacity and willingness to act in ways that meet the organization's goals and interests.

Additional Terms
Culture
Tough guy, macho culture

Work-hard, play-hard culture
Bet-your-company culture
Process culture
Occupational communities
Rites of passage, degradation, enhancement, renewal, conflict reduction, and integration
Requisite variety
Thickness of culture
Extent of shared values
Clarity of order of values
Cultural scenes
Counterculture/subculture
Self-insurance
Culture insurance
Inclusion
Anticipatory socialization
Encounter
Change and acquisition
Moral, calculative, and alienative involvement
Continuance, cohesion, and control commitment
Attitudinal and behavioral commitment
Whistle-blowing

THE McDONALD'S MYSTIQUE

I was 8 years old, sitting in our brand-new cherry-red '57 Chrysler clutching a 15-cent hamburger and 10-cent fries. The crowded parking lot flickered under the most amazing neon sign Aurora, Illinois, has ever seen—twin golden arches with a little neon-legged man running in between them. The sign said these speedy McDonald's people had sold over 10 million hamburgers. As I sat there slurping on a milkshake so thick it made the straw collapse, I was in heaven.

I didn't know that this pioneering red-and-white tile building, sitting oddly on the prairie, would be an early link in a restaurant chain that has woven itself through our culture. It would go quickly from a curiosity to a tradition here, then spill across great oceans. Today golden arches beam out in Andorra, Kuala Lumpur, and Belgrade.

When entrepreneur Ray Kroc opened his first restaurant in Des Plaines, Illinois, on Friday, April 15, 1955, his cash register rang up $366.12. He noted in his ledger, now part of the McDonald's museum complex at the site, "It rained." But the rain stopped, and in two weeks sales had doubled. Last year the chain's restaurants, mostly franchises, grossed more than $14.3 billion, and the corporation took in $4.9 billion; it has to date logged 92 quarters of record earnings. It is the biggest owner of commercial real estate in America. It is the biggest food service corporation in the world. Over nine months recently, Wendy's and Pillsbury's Burger King closed 149 unprofitable restaurants. McDonald's during the same period opened a new restaurant every 17 hours.

What on earth is its secret? As the world of fast food turns, McDonald's should have run out its string a long time ago. It should have had its moment in the sun and then, in this crowded industry with notoriously fickle customers, should have been shoved aside.

Yes, Harvard MBAs will tell you that McDonald's better mousetrap was a unique partnership that strongly supported rather than bled franchises. They'll explain that McDonald's handles real estate cleverly, that it maintains strong central control over its restaurants and deals with suppliers in a straightforward manner that relies more on gentlemen's agreements than on signed contracts. It has gone after the kids' market. Right. Every competitor has known these things for decades.

So what is the real, deepdown reason McDonald's has prevailed? I think the question can be answered in part by me: The quintessential middle-class baby-boomer fast-food lover who grew up to be a quintessential almost middle-age, sometimes yuppie who can be felled on any given afternoon by a Big Mac Attack. McDonald's is a powerful sociological phenomenon that is not simple to grasp. Understanding it surely begins with the sociology of the company.

McDonald's folks attribute their success to devotion to their corporate creed of "quality, service, cleanliness, and value." They exude competence. Walking around the 80-acre Oak Brook, Illinois, headquarters complex brought out the heartland elitist in me. I can't help believing American efficiency reaches its apex right about where Illinois, Wisconsin, and Iowa come together and, with pockets of exception, declines in concentric rings moving toward both coasts. When asked if he could sum up the secret of McDonald's success in one sentence, chief financial officer Jack Greenberg—who can assemble a Big Mac as fast as lightning—says, somewhat shyly, "Well, for one thing, we're Midwestern."

Unlike many other franchise companies, McDonald's never bought anybody, and nobody bought it. Hamburgers were its business and its only business. Says Arthur Thompson, a senior vice president of National Westminster Bank and a man who finances a lot of McDonald's franchises: "The story of McDonald's success? They stuck to their knitting."

The chief knitter at McDonald's was—and is—Ray Kroc, an amazing man who, four years after his death at age 81, remains one of America's most powerful CEOs. He is quoted incessantly around headquarters. Jack Greenberg explains that the knitting "is not rocket science. It's rather plain-vanilla kinds of things, like don't take your eye off the basic business." He goes on to talk about Ray Kroc's ideals.

Chief executive officer Mike Quinlan talks about Ray too. "If there's one reason for our success, it's that Ray Kroc instilled in the company basic principles. Standards of excellence. Don't compromise. Use the best ingredients. The best equipment. Not galvanized metal, but stainless steel."

Ray is not only quoted, he is, uh, sort of there in Oak Brook today. In a headquarters exhibit called "Talk to Ray," a visitor can phone up Ray, as it were, on a videoscreen, and with a keyboard ask him questions. Over several years he recorded his thoughts for the company archives, and his appearances on talk shows were taped as well, so those left to carry on can find out nearly everything they might need to know.

I asked Ray about luck. Ray told me, "Luck is a dividend of sweat. The more you sweat, the luckier you get." Ray talks about the time he "washed the windows every day inside and out." Then there's a snip of him with Phil Donahue. "Did you really clean the johns?" Phil asks. "You're damn right I did," Ray shoots back, "and I'd clean one today if it needed it."

What Ray says still goes at McDonald's. Greenberg only sort of jokes that the bathroom standards may keep the corporate giant from diversifying. "We say around here we're not going to diversify until all of our

20,000 restrooms are in perfect order," Greenberg says. His wife reports to him upon exiting any McDonald's ladies' room. "Sometimes she'll come out and just shake her head and say, 'Jack, you can't diversify yet.'"

Bean counters with sharp pencils might snicker at Kroc's obsession with shiny windows and bathrooms. But we customers don't. Although I hadn't thought about it until I talked to Ray, I do appreciate clean johns. Then just the other day, a friend of mine seeing a McDonald's mused, "You know, when my kids were young, and we were heading somewhere on the road, nothing made me happier than finding a McDonald's. Fast food. Clean johns."

Ray Kroc was long on Krocisms, such as this one about competitors: "If they were drowning to death, I would put a hose in their mouth." Kroc also knew when not to compete. He took a look at other franchising systems and decided one major flaw was they competed with themselves. Some required franchises to buy equipment or supplies from them, then delivered overpriced or poor-quality merchandise. Sometimes the mother company sold large territorial franchises. The franchises then subdivided their districts. Soon there were layers of bureaucracy and—royalties skimmed off—between the top bananas and the lowly store. Left with little profit and direction, franchises rebelled, and soon droves of malcontents took down the glib franchise signs to become some variation of "Mom and Pop's Burger and Cones."

Kroc did it differently. He sold only single-unit franchises. They originally cost $950 and a 1.9% cut of revenues. In *McDonald's: Behind the Arches*, a lively corporate history, writer John Love explains, "The essence of Kroc's unique but amazingly simple franchising philosophy was that a franchising company should not live off the sweat of its franchises, but should succeed by helping its franchises succeed."

All of which helps explain why you would expect McDonald's to be a winner, but doesn't quite decipher the company's astonishing grip on the American—and increasingly the world—consumer. Something more must be going on. Let's see if we can figure it out.

After that first meal in 1957, McDonald's never left my life. Although my family moved about northern Illinois, we were never far from Mac's. I remember the whole family, with Grandma or an uncle in tow, remarking when the sign under Speedee's running legs changed . . . 100 million sold . . . 200 . . . 300 . . . 500. (The company went public; if I had bought 100 shares, for $2,250, I would today have 9,295 shares worth about $400,000.)

By the time I headed off to college in 1967, the sign had changed to three billion, and the chain comprised nearly 1,000 stores. By now all of America was heading for the golden arches. We boomers were hooked on the taste. Some of us were having kids of our own.

Several factors had been at work over those years to make McDonald's part of our culture. After the war, as everybody knows, America went car crazy, the suburbs sprawled, times were good, and in general we began to hurry. Carhop hamburger joints had reputations as teen hangouts with inconsistent food and slow service. At McDonald's, we little boomers could get out of the folk's car, walk up to the window, and order—a very grown-up thing to do. It was also more fun than having to sit in a restaurant, where there was nothing to do but shake salt on your sister.

We learned to hate to wait. Mark Friedman, director of the Nutrition Program at Philadelphia's Monell Chemical Senses Center, says that for people like me, "the golden arches may trigger a Pavlovian response to food. It's learned behavior: A Big Mac is a quick calorie payoff."

Rather than being bored with McDonald's sameness, we learned to appreciate it. In a world where one of my ancestral homes became an onramp for the Illinois tollway and another was claimed for an atomic accelerator site, McDonald's became a symbol of stability. A McDonald's meal tastes pretty much the same everywhere. It can cure homesickness and make strange places less strange. I brightened up considerably when after a long day on Guam earlier this year, the golden arches greeted me around a bend.

Another thing: The McDonald's folks have gained an edge by making you want to hug them. At my inner city yuppie McDonald's a few nights back, a young lawyer ahead of me pointed out to the cashier that she had undercharged him by $1.87. "Your mom would be proud of you," I joked with him. "Aw, I couldn't cheat McDonald's," he replied. "It'd be like stealing from Mickey Mouse."

McDonald's does good works. It backs community events. Ronald McDonald's Houses help the families of seriously ill children. Does any of this sell more burger? Probably not directly. But a new survey shows that, among 672 brands, consumers esteem McDonald's 68th most highly. Its closest fast-food competitor, Kentucky Fried Chicken, came in at no. 136. Whatever accounts for McDonald's rating, do-gooding can't hurt.

The McDonald's appeal is global and getting more so. The company's Hamburger University training center in Oak Brook, like a little United Nations, provides simultaneous translations of its two-week course in 17 languages. Last year at the 409th graduation ceremony, 230 students from all over America and the world sat in rapt attention as the achievement awards were handed out. When it came time for the award for technical merit in equipment handling, the room grew quiet as students waited to learn who among them had most quickly assembled the 57 parts of a milkshake machine—blindfolded. The crowd applauded third-place Johnnie Tsang, who had nailed it—or rather bolted it—in seven minutes 53 seconds to take a prize home to his hometown Hong Kong McDonald's.

They giggled a little when another Hong Konger, Winly Uip, came in second at 7:42. But they all just threw up their arms and laughed when first prize went to David Fung, whose 7:34 time sent him home victorious not to the Hong Kong McDonald's, but the new Kowloon McDonald's right across the harbor.

In March the first McDonald's in Belgrade, Yugoslavia, set an all-time opening day record by running 6,000 persons under the arches. About 40% of McDonald's franchises opening this year stand on foreign soil. The biggest franchise worldwide is in Rome (sales target for this year: $11 million).

How does McDonald's do it? They've got all the me's in the world, and they're keeping us. And getting us to come back again and again. On the same day. For dumb things like Monopoly game pieces.

Or are they dumb? After all, wasn't Monopoly the game we played when we weren't riding in our cherry-red Chryslers back in 1957? Aren't all of us boomers just a little nostalgic about Monopoly? And then don't we usually win fries or a drink, which gets us back for lunch again? I can almost feel Ray Kroc patting me on the head.

What Is Organizational Culture?

During the past 30 years McDonald's has risen from modest beginnings to occupy a global position in the fast-food business. Not the least of the reasons for this dramatic growth—and the accompanying profitability—has been the development and nurturance of a clear corporate creed, embodied in such diverse ways as tales of company humor and successes that nearly every McDonald's employee is told about, Krocisms that teach the company's philosophy, a company museum, and of course, Hamburger University, where new employees learn—and are awarded for learning—the core values and beliefs of the company. In sum, McDonald's has developed a strong corporate culture and a program for socializing employees to embrace that culture. The objective of all this effort is to ensure employee commitment and effective performance.

Organizational culture was one of the hot research topics in organizational science in the 1980s. It was a popular topic for business writers, who landed four books about it on the *New York Times* best-seller list (Ouchi,

1981; Pascale and Athos, 1981; Peters and Waterman, 1982; Peters, 1987). The subject also captured scholarly interest. In 1983 two scholarly journals (*Organizational Dynamics* and *Administrative Science Quarterly*) each devoted an entire issue to organizational culture. This interest derived in part from the changing competitive scene and the growth in market share enjoyed by foreign businesses, especially Japanese firms. How, observers wondered, might the company loyalty shown by Japanese workers contribute to their firms' success? What had the firm done to promote that commitment? In fact, one study showed that Japanese workers had stronger social bonds, which are related to commitment and the acceptance of similar norms (Lincoln, 1989).

As we will see, despite this intense interest, organizational culture is not yet a clearly defined area of study. Rather, it is an omnibus concept with numerous definitions reflecting many schools of thought (Malinowski, 1944). This variety of approaches has not helped either researchers or managers to understand exactly what constitutes culture in organizations. Culture is variously seen as a component of, equal to, or a determinant of organizational climate, a popular area of study until culture took its place in the late 1970s (Bates, 1984). Another difficulty is that culture and socialization are often discussed interchangeably. Another point of confusion involves the need to distinguish between organizational culture and national culture.

Although culture is just one of the many constructs managers must manage in organizations (along with structure, power, leadership, and so on), it has not been well differentiated from these other aspects of management. Neither culture nor socialization has been clearly linked through research to such outcome variables as turnover and commitment. Because these outcomes are important to managers and researchers alike, culture and socialization may wane as subjects of study unless such relationships can be shown (Staw, 1984).

In this chapter, we examine the complexity of organizational culture first, by exploring the various influences of the cultural environment on organizations. Then, after tackling the problem of defining culture, we study such issues as how to identify the elements of culture in an organization. With an understanding of corporate culture, we go on to discuss processes of socialization and to examine commitment and turnover.

The Cultural Context of Organizations

An organization does not exist in a vacuum. Any group of people—a business, hospital, charitable group, or government agency—is in part shaped by the society in which it was created. The values, ways of thinking, and customs of a culture, among other factors, are reflected in the structure and behavior of organizations within that culture. For example, compare the feistiness of the U.S. Congress to the rubber-stamp behavior of the Soviet legislature before Gorbachev's reforms. The **cultural environment** of an organization is the economic, social, and political context established by the larger culture in which the organization resides.

All three of these facets of culture are important to an organization's shape and functioning. The economic aspect of the cultural environment embraces such issues as how work is done, to whom the fruits of labor belong, and the relationship of the government to economic entities. In addition to demands for radical political changes, the upheaval that began in late 1989 in Eastern Europe included a kernel of economic revolution as well, as citizens of these formerly rigid communist countries campaigned, not just for democratic rights, but also for a market economy. Although the situation is much too volatile to permit predictions of what will occur, it is likely that organizations in Eastern Europe—or Western organizations attempting to enter these new markets—will have to adapt to new environmental conditions.

The social facet of culture embraces a range of fundamental influences on organizational life. Norms for human interaction, control (O'Reilly, 1989), the value placed on material versus spiritual life, the way language is used to express ideas and relationships, and the symbols that resonate in the minds of people in the culture, all are manifested in various ways—obvious or hidden—in the organizations formed within that culture. Thus the value placed in Japan on community and teamwork has found expression in such features of Japanese business as lifetime employment and work teams. And the opening of the first McDonald's in Moscow in 1990 revealed a fascinating glimpse of differences in social culture. Managers found that they had to teach the Russian patrons to form multiple lines for service; standing in just one line was habitual for Muscovites accustomed to stores barren of goods.

The political facet of culture is the relationship of individuals to the state and includes legal and political arrangements for maintaining social order. Political institutions take a variety of forms, as do the assumptions underlying them. Management's role in an organization is shaped by the form government takes. Government places constraints on certain industries in the United States—utilities, for instance, are heavily regulated by government agencies. The political form determines such things as the rights of individuals and organizations to hold property or engage in contracts and the availability of appeal mechanisms to redress grievances as well.

To understand the differences between domestic and international management, it is necessary to understand the major ways that cultures vary. Anthropologists see **culture** as patterns, explicit and implicit, of and for behavior acquired and transmitted by symbols, constituting the distinct achievement of human groups, including their embodiment in artifacts; the essential core of culture consists of traditional (i.e., historically derived and selected) ideas and especially their attached values; culture systems may, on the one hand, be considered as products of action, on the other as conditioning elements of future action. (Kroeber and Kluckhohn, 1952, p. 181)

Culture is shared by most if not all members of a group, it is passed from older to younger members, and it shapes behavior and structures one's perception of the world. Adler (1986) points out that six basic dimensions, each answering a fundamental question, describe the cultural orientation of a society:

1. *Who am I?* Or how do I see myself? This is the good–evil dimension.

2. *How do I see the world?* Am I dominant over my environment, in harmony with it, or subjugated by it?

3. *How do I relate to other people?* Am I an individualist? Do I come from a group-oriented society in which the welfare of the group predominates? Am I from a hierarchical group society, in which members of the group come from across generations?

4. *What do I do?* Do I value action? Do I value being in situations in which people, ideas, and events flow spontaneously? Or am I from a controlled society in which desires are restrained by detachment from objects in order to let each person develop as an integrated whole?

5. *How do I use time?* Is my culture oriented to the past, the present, or the future?

6. *How do I use physical space?* Is a conference room, an office, or a building viewed as private or public space?

The answers to these questions determine appropriate behaviors across cultures. For example, Americans hold important meetings behind closed doors and give important people private offices. In Japan, by contrast, bosses often sit amidst their employees, and no partitions divide working areas.

Cultural differences shape the behaviors of the people in those cultures. Management literature is informed primarily by studies done in the United States (or in North America) using primarily American workers, but a growing body of research either studies people and their organizations in other cultures (Japan being a recent favorite example) or compares the behaviors of people and organizations across cultures. Most organizational researchers who study groups across nationalities ignore definitional issues and equate the national culture with the existence of a nation-state. This approach misses important issues, however. The most common definition of culture that does not simply rely on identifying a nation-state concentrates on cultural content or shared values and the symbolic representation of shared meanings (Geertz, 1973).

Using this definition, one can distinguish two main types of national cultures: the homogeneous and the heterogeneous. "A homogeneous societal culture is one in which the shared meanings are similar and little variation in beliefs exists; that is, the culture has one dominant way of thinking and acting" (Enz, 1986, p. 177). In homogeneous societies the degree of consensus is strong. Examples are China, Japan, and Saudi Arabia. "A heterogeneous societal culture is one in which numerous population groups have specific and distinct values and understandings. In a heterogeneous society many sets of shared meanings make up the society" (Enz, 1986, p. 177). In a heterogeneous society, multiple cultures exist along with a dominant culture, the dominant set of values is not regarded as the only acceptable set of norms. Examples of heterogeneous nations are the United States, Canada, and Switzerland. (Bear in mind that even homogeneous societies include some subcultures that embrace values or norms deviant from the dominant culture; no society is so monolithic as to include one culture only.)

In homogeneous societies, organizations are likely to represent the societal culture; in heterogeneous cultures the diverse subcultures found in the work force will each shape the organizational culture, creating the possibility of a lack of congruence between the organizational culture and the dominant societal culture. In this case, a number of distinct corporate cultures will exist. Figure 3.1 illustrates the relationship between national and organizational culture under these two conditions. As the figure shows, beliefs and values in the societal culture find expression (or not, in the case of heterogeneous cultures) in beliefs and values of the organization. These, in turn, influence organizational functioning. In the homogeneous society, organizational functioning will fit with the societal culture as well as with the organizational culture. In the heterogeneous society, organizational functioning will reflect fit with the organizational culture, but there may be a gap between that culture and the dominant culture in the society.

Structural features of organizations may be similar across cultures, yet national differences among people are not diminished when they work in the same organization. One study (discussed in Chapter 9) found striking cultural differences among people working in a single multinational corporation (Hofstede, 1984). Another author (Laurent, 1983) found more pronounced cultural differences among employees of different nationalities working in the same multinational organization than among employees working for different organizations in their native lands. Managers working

FIGURE 3.1
*Cultural Fit and
Organizational
Functioning*

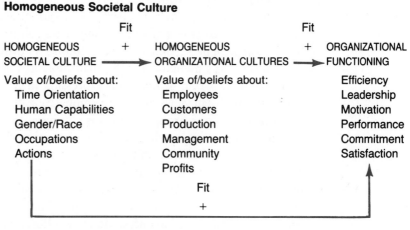

Homogeneous Societal Culture

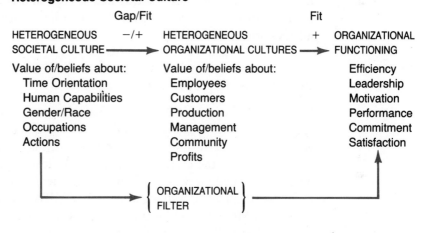

Heterogeneous Societal Culture

Source: Cathy A. Enz, "New Directions for Cross-Cultural Studies: Linking Organizational and Societal Cultures," *Advances in International Comparative Management*, vol. 2 (Greenwich, CT: JAI Press, 1986), p. 181. Copyright © 1986 by JAI Press. Reprinted by permission.

in other countries, then, must be aware of the cultural traits of their workers and perhaps try to adapt the corporate culture to the workers' characteristics.

Four Approaches to Organizational Culture

The notion of culture has a long history in anthropology (Malinowski, 1944; Radcliffe-Brown, 1952), and some of the constructs developed in that field are borrowed in the organizational literature. Among these constructs are two views of **organizational culture:** as sociocultural systems or as systems of ideas (Allaire and Firsirotu, 1984). The former approach emphasizes the behaviors and structures of a group and views culture as a component of the social system. The second view sees culture as distinct from social structures, instead as a mental construct that influences how people perceive and think about the world or that finds expression in symbols and shared meanings. Essentially, all views of culture emphasize a key point: culture is shared by all members of a group. From this common ground, we can investigate the different approaches that organizational researchers have pursued.

The research on organizational culture can be grouped into four approaches. Some scholars look for shared norms, beliefs, and values in organizations and work groups. A second group is interested in myths, stories, and language as manifestations of culture. The third perspective examines rites and ceremonies as manifestations of culture. The fourth group studies the interaction of members and symbols. We will examine each of these approaches to see what one might look for in his or her own organization as manifestations of culture.

Culture as Shared Norms, Beliefs, and Values

Peters and Waterman (1982) popularized the investigation of shared norms, beliefs, and values by showing similarities among management ideologies in very successful companies. They pointed out that in successful companies the product and the customer are of the utmost importance to managers. They also argued for the efficacy of management strategies that put into action "management by walking around," or MBWA. Peters (1987) extols the benefits of MBWA by citing a letter he received from a general parts manager for Caterpillar Tractor. The manager spent a week working in the warehouse of a customer and then spent two weeks working on the day and night shifts of his own company's warehouse. The experience, he said, opened his eyes both to the needs of his customers and the heroism of his company's warehouse workers, making him realize that he had to "think as my customers think" and "let the people I work with work, think, innovate, and do their best."

In her study of a successful electronics firm (called "Chipco"), Kanter (1983) notes that the existence of a culture of pride enhances the potential for innovation:

> To manage such change [innovation] as a normal way of life requires that people find their stability and security not in specific organizational arrangements but in the culture and direction of the

organization. It requires that they feel integrated with the whole rather than identifying with the particular territory of the moment, since that is changeable.

Thus, Chipco appeared conscious of itself as a culture, not just a technical system, and took steps to transmit its culture to newcomers in the managerial and professional ranks, through legends, stories, and special orientations at offsite meetings that were like boot camps. Just learning the job was not enough for success at Chipco; one had to learn the culture of the organization as well, and this could often be disorienting for the stream of new arrivals. (pp. 133–134)

Deal and Kennedy (1982), surveying a variety of companies, found that one third (25) had identifiable beliefs. (The feature on Procter & Gamble discusses the benefits of having such clear beliefs.) Of these 25 companies, two thirds had qualitative beliefs, such as "IBM means service," and one third had clear financial beliefs. These beliefs, which often express the company's mission statement (see Chapter 1), help give all employees a sense of direction.

FEATURE: *Forging a Value System at Procter & Gamble*

Many successful companies have a very rich tradition of values, beliefs, and themes that have developed over the years. Mostly these values come from experience, from testing what does and doesn't work in the economic environment. But individual people also have strong influence in shaping the standards and beliefs of the organization.

By almost any measure, Procter & Gamble is one of the best models of persistent long-term attention to building a strong culture, particularly in its emphasis on values. The first and most basic of these is "do what is right." As William Cooper Procter [once] said . . . , "Always try to do what is right. If you do that, nobody can really find fault." That rule has lived to this day, being passed on to every head of P&G since Cooper, and every new employee as well.

Other values embraced by the company include:

- *"The Consumer Is Important."* From its early discovery of the importance of brand identification and recognition, P&G has paid more attention to customers because over the years they learned that the more they did so, the greater the payback to the company. It was from customers that P&G learned that Ivory soap floated—the result of a production mistake that was incorporated into the manufacturing process after the company discovered that customers liked the feature. Since then they have always listened to customers, calling their obsession "consumerism: a response, after comprehensive market research, to what consumers need and want." P&G is a culture that glories in listening and listening well to consumers. They have developed more ways to listen to consumers than anyone else.

- *"Things Don't Just Happen, You Have to Make Them Happen."* P&G is the largest consistent advertiser among the giant consumer product companies. The company first learned the value of advertising with Ivory soap and has been hooked on it ever since. But it keeps testing, trying new ideas, evolving the basic idea year by year. In 1923, P&G was the first to capitalize on the use of what was then a brand new advertising medium—radio. Starting with informational radio spots, P&G went on to invent the daytime soap opera. Thirty years later, P&G did the same for television.

- *"We Want to Make Employee Interests Our Own."* P&G's dedication to improving labor relations began in the 1880s when William Cooper Procter, who was later to head the company, persuaded his father and uncle to give workers Saturday afternoons off without loss of pay, a radical idea at the time. Two years later the company instituted profit-sharing, and shortly thereafter a company-matching stock purchase plan. To promote two-way communication, P&G instituted an Employee Conference Plan and created one seat for a worker representative from each domestic plant on P&G's board of directors. Still later P&G offered its employees guaranteed employment, and, even during the Depression, was able to keep its workers on the payrolls.

Procter & Gamble has a long history of working hard on the "right" things. These values were formed and refined by years of experience in the marketplace. They didn't just appear overnight. The company's continuing experiences in the marketplace have evolved into a rich and varied culture that has sustained it through difficult times.

Source: Terence Deal and Allen Kennedy, *Corporate Culture* (Reading, MA: Addison-Wesley, 1982), pp. 25–30. Copyright © 1982 by Terence Deal and Allen Kennedy. Reprinted by permission of Addison-Wesley Publishing Co., Inc.

Based on their research, Deal and Kennedy provide a typology of organizational cultures. There is the **tough guy, macho culture,** or organizations in which people like to take high risks and get quick feedback on whether their actions are right or wrong. Examples include police departments or hospitals, where the stakes are life and death, or professional sports, where the financial stakes are high. There are **work-hard, play-hard cultures,** in which fun and action are the rule and employees take few risks. Sales organizations, including door-to-door sales businesses, and the sales departments in most organizations exemplify this culture. **Bet-your-company cultures** are those in which big-stakes decisions are made but years pass before employees know whether those decisions were right or wrong. These are high-risk, slow-feedback environments. Oil companies, dependent on large and long-term investment for exploration, are such cultures. Finally, there are **process cultures,** in which there is little or no feedback and employees find it difficult to measure what they do, concentrating instead on how it's done. Banks, insurance companies, and pharmaceutical firms are examples. Recently, an argument has been put forth that there is good reason for some ambiguity in meaning and for using images with multiple meanings because this allows employees to interpret meaning in the light of their own motives (Pascale, 1990).

An interesting application of the notion of shared norms and values involves **occupational communities** (Van Maanen and Barley, 1984). We usually describe occupations with terms such as engineer, mechanic, librarian, and so on, but these static descriptions fail to orient us to the dynamic meaning of work to people in particular jobs. In some jobs people leave social interactions and their own values outside when they walk into their organizations. But other jobs lay on their practitioners a whole set of cognitive, social, and moral meanings. For these jobs the idea of an occupational community is relevant.

> [An occupational community is] a group of people who consider themselves to be engaged in the same sort of work; whose identity is drawn from the work; who share with one another a set of values, norms and perspectives that apply to but extend beyond work related matters; and whose social relationships meld work and leisure. . . . Occupational communities are seen to create and sustain relatively unique work cultures consisting of, among other things, task rituals, standards for proper and improper behavior, work codes surrounding relatively routine practices and, for the membership at least, compelling accounts attesting to the logic and value of these rituals, standards and codes. (Van Maanen and Barley, 1984, p. 287)

The existence of occupational communities is significant because belonging to one may create a conflict of identification for the worker—what

pull demands his allegiance, that of the corporate culture or that of the occupational community? Academics provide an example. Although they identify with their universities, they tend to identify more strongly with their
field. An economist, for example, is more likely to view himself against other
economists rather than faculty on his own campus.

Geographic proximity is not necessary to the formation of an occupational community, even though it may help homogenize shared values and
beliefs. But a number of other factors can contribute to this kind of identification, each of which can be seen at work with Navy fighter pilots.

- *The use of distinctive accoutrements, costumes, and jargon.* The long
  white scarf of the pilot has long since been replaced by the standard
  flight suit, but even that government issue item is modified according to a certain style with badges, velcro, and other trappings. Pilots speak of *bolters*, *bingo fields*, *bears*, and *bogeys*, using their own
  special language to differentiate themselves from outsiders.

- *High involvement in work.* One has only to listen to fighter pilots
  complain of fatigue and long hours to sense their involvement in
  their work.

- *The possession of esoteric, scarce, socially valued, and unique abilities.* The
  esteem in which society holds pilots—embodied in the play of children and the fantasies of adults—reinforces their sense of identity.

- *Claimed responsibility for others.* Fighter pilots are not only responsible for their fellow airmen but feel responsible for the welfare of
  ships and forces they protect.

- *Confrontation with danger.* Pilots, catapulted off aircraft carriers only
  to land later on the rolling, pitching flight decks, clearly share the
  bond of a dangerous occupation.

The same principles can be seen at work with other occupational communities, such as police officers, doctors, and air traffic controllers. Investment
bankers, insurance agents, and managers, though they may not have the
bonds of shared danger, do include the other hallmarks of occupational
communities.

Culture as Myths, Stories, and Other Manifestations of Language

Organizational cultures and the stories that define them are said to be unique
to their locations. An argument for uniqueness is that each organization differs from the rest, a fact manifested in the stories created in organizations.
One set of research studies (Martin, Feldman, Hatch, and Sitkin, 1983),

however, shows that such stories may not be unique. Certain themes appear repeatedly in different organizations, and they seem to have a universal meaning.

According to Martin et al., seven kinds of stories exist across a variety of kinds of organizations:

1. *Stories that describe how organizations treat status considerations when rules are broken.* Such stories tell about how a high-status person breaks a rule and is confronted by a lower-status person who attempts to enforce the rule. The high-status person may become angry, conform to the rule, disregard the low-status person, or take some other action.

2. *Stories about whether the boss is human.* Such stories include three events. The status credentials of the central character are established, the character is presented with an opportunity to perform a status-equalization act, and the character does or does not abrogate status temporarily, exhibiting (or not exhibiting) "human" qualities (e.g., Ray Kroc cleaning a bathroom).

3. *Stories about whether a little person can rise to the top.* These stories describe the match between abilities and position. The most famous of these is the Horatio Alger hero, who, through hard work, rose from rags to riches.

4. *Stories about getting fired.* These stories include employees who fear losing their jobs and employees who must make the decision to lay off or fire people. A reason for the layoff or firing is given, and the company's decision is announced along with justification for the decision.

5. *Stories about whether the company will help an employee who has to move.* Such stories are implicit or explicit about the hardship the move will cause and indicate whether the company helps or does nothing for the employee.

6. *Stories about how the boss reacts to mistakes.* These stories include an employee who makes a mistake and one or more higher-level persons who learn of it. The stories conclude with foregiveness or punishment.

7. *Stories about how the organization deals with obstacles.* These are the most commonly found kinds of organizational stories involving employees at any status level. Attempts are usually made to deal with obstacles, and the stories end when the obstacles are either overcome or it is clear they are insurmountable.

We have seen some of these story motifs in the McDonald's case. Ray Kroc is humanized by the "talk to Ray" program still available after his death, and stories about the rags-to-riches growth of the firm are imbedded in the story about the rain stopping and sales doubling.

What themes do these stories convey? First, they appear to express the tensions that arise from conflicts between organizational requirements and the values held by employees. Second, they are related to concerns about status inequality. We live in a society that values equality, but the hierarchical nature of organizations often conflicts with this value; these stories embody, and show resolution of, that conflict. Third, such stories deal with security versus insecurity: people want to ensure themselves of security, and yet organizations must retain the right to deprive them of that security. Finally, these stories deal with the clash between our desire for control and events that indicate our inability to exert such control.

In addition to conveying themes that reflect important individual and organizational concerns, organizational stories offer self-enhancing explanations for organizational events. Here again we see how organizations use retrospective explanations of events, a view we encountered in Chapter 1's discussion of goals and effectiveness. Because reputations and self-esteem are on the line, organizational stories pound home the righteousness of organizations and their key players and reflect the myths organizations have (Mahle, 1988).

Culture as Rites and Ceremonials

Two authors (Trice and Beyer, 1984) note that in their rediscovery of culture, organizational researchers have provided a very narrow focus by concentrating their attention on such single, discrete elements as symbols, myths, or stories. To provide a broader view of cultural phenomena, these authors advocate studying rites and ceremonials that consolidate multiple cultural forms:

> The consolidation and interdependence of cultural forms is particularly evident in rites and ceremonials which combine various forms of cultural expression within coherent cultural events with well-demarcated beginnings and ends. In performing the activities of a rite or ceremonial, people make use of other cultural forms—certain customary language, gestures, ritualized behaviors, artifacts, other symbols, and settings—to heighten the expression of shared meanings appropriate to the occasion . . . a rite amalgamates a number of discrete cultural forms into an integrated, unified public performance; a ceremonial connects several rites into a single occasion or event. (Trice and Beyer, 1984, p. 654)

Rites and ceremonials have a number of consequences for organizations. Both do and say things about organizations, helping to establish a company identity, and both serve to ease people and their social groups through changes in roles and status. Hamburger University serves McDonald's ceremonially, providing awards, unifying employees, and helping socialize new employees by easing them through what Sathe (1983) calls the "culture shock" of entering a new company.

Trice and Beyer identify six kinds of rites in organizations:

1. **Rites of passage** show the altering of one's status. A good example of an organizational rite of passage is the events and behaviors involved in induction into the U.S. Army.

2. **Rites of degradation** sometimes accompany the removal of high-status people (Garfinkle, 1967). Generally, attention is directed to the person to be removed from office, and his behavior is publicly associated with the problems and failures of the organization. Subsequently, he is removed from office. The impeachment of Richard Nixon was a truncated rite of degradation, cut short by his resignation.

3. **Rites of enhancement** enhance the status and social identities of people. Public acknowledgment of a promotion would be such a rite.

4. **Rites of renewal** strengthen existing social structures and thus improve their functioning. Examples of such rites are most organizational development programs, such as management by objectives (MBO) and employee performance evaluations.

5. **Rites of conflict reduction** resolve the conflicts that inevitably arise among people or groups. Collective bargaining and arbitration are examples.

6. **Rites of integration** increase the interaction of potentially divergent subsystems with one another during participation in the rite and thus create or revive shared feelings of union and commitment to a larger system. Company Christmas parties and annual picnics are examples of such rites. Graduation ceremonies at Hamburger University serve not only as rites of passage but also as rites of integration.

Sensitivity to rites and ceremonials may help managers be more effective in their organizations. Managers can identify the purposes and encourage the expression of rites that benefit the organization. Paying attention to rites may be one of the first steps in developing the skills needed to be a good manager.

Culture as Symbolic Interaction

An amalgam of culture as shared norms and values, myths and stories, and rites and ceremonials is achieved by looking at organizations in terms of symbolic interaction (Pfeffer, 1981). From this perspective, managers provide explanations, rationalizations, and legitimation for the activities of the organization. Indeed, one writer sees management essentially as such an activity: "Managerial work can be viewed as managing myth, symbols, and labels. . . . Because managers traffic so often in images, the appropriate role for the manager may be evangelist rather than accountant" (Weick, 1979, p. 42). For managers to evangelize, there must be shared norms and values, which are manifested in the myths and stories, rites and ceremonials.

The task of management, then, is to help organizational participants arrive at shared norms and values or the shared paradigm of what the organization is all about. Its task is also to manage the social definition of the organization. Finally, its task is to break paradigms when they become dysfunctional. Figure 3.2 provides some examples of symbolic actions that managers may take and explains why those actions work to reinforce the organization's culture.

The reason for the effectiveness of the first action in Figure 3.2 is clear: managers invest an activity with significance by spending their own time on it or by changing the work environment to better accommodate it. The fourth action reveals an interesting power that managers may possess. By interpreting history, they can help shape workers' perceptions of an event or problem, using what then becomes a common view of the situation as a vehicle for consensus on the next steps to be taken. The other actions bear more discussion.

The second action demonstrates the well-known "Hawthorne effect," which refers to the finding that people who are subjected to observation, change, and special treatment may respond with better performance regardless of the content of the observation, change, or treatment. Observation and change signal that people are to be treated differently. This expectation results in increased motivation. (See Chapter 5 for a fuller discussion of the Hawthorne effect.)

The third example, symbolic actions, may be used to mollify dissatisfied groups in organizations. As Pfeffer (1981) notes, universities establish ombudsmen to handle student complaints about issues ranging from grades to sexual harassment, and privilege and tenure committees to protect professors from administrative capriciousness. IBM, among many other corpo-

FIGURE 3.2
Symbolic Actions and the Explanation for Their Effectiveness

Action	Explanation for Effectiveness
Spend time on activity that is to be emphasized or defined as important	Time spent is one measure of the importance of a goal, and goals and objectives become the reality defining managerial action; also, time spent conveys to others the importance of its focus.
Change or enhance the setting	A new setting conveys that something new is going on; an enhanced setting will convey the meaning that the activity now occurring is more consequential and important.
Exchange status for substance	Symbolic outcomes may be sufficient to ensure support of a relatively uninvolved group for the proposed action, if the conditions facilitating symbolic action are present.
Interpret history	Events have meaning only through interpretations; interpreting events as consistent with the definition of the problem or the solution can help develop a social consensus around the chosen course of action.
Provide a dominant value expressed in a simple phrase	Language can evoke support or opposition, can serve to organize social consensus, and can provide an explanation and rationalization for activity.

Source: J. Pfeffer, "Management as Symbolic Action: The Creation and Maintenance of Organizational Paradigms," in L. L. Cummings and B. M. Staw (eds.), *Research in Organizational Behavior* 3, 1–52 (1981): 37. Copyright © 1981 by JAI Press. Reprinted by permission.

rations, has open-door and speak-up programs to do the same thing. The aggrieved groups are mollified by the appearance of an administrative structure to deal with the problem, regardless of whether anything is done.

In manipulating symbols, managers can effect change simply by creating patterns of activity and staging the occasions for interaction (Peters, 1978). This activity may be a far more effective and common way to obtain change than any other we usually think about. On the other hand, managers must be cautious not to manipulate symbols without providing any content. Promising an open-door policy without delivering openness or access, or pledging to involve employees in decision making without doing so, can backfire by alienating workers.

Pfeffer's fifth example, expressing a dominant value in a simple phrase, underscores the importance of language. One way a manager can better understand the culture of his own organization is to examine the language and symbols within it. The language used in annual reports, for instance, reveals some facets of an organization's culture (Staw, McKechnie, and Puffer, 1983). At McDonald's, for instance, the corporate creed is "quality, service, cleanliness, and value." (See the discussion of mission statements in Chapter 1.)

The symbolic approach to culture is particularly visible in organizations in which reliability rather than productivity is the bottom line because the costs of error can be catastrophic. Examples are nuclear power plants, air traffic control systems, and complex weapons systems. A major aspect of these organizations is **requisite variety,** in which the complexities of the system and its operators must match the complexity required by the technology (Weick, 1987). High accountability and simultaneous centralization and flexibility are also part of the culture of these organizations (Roberts, Rousseau, and La Porte, in press).

Assessing Organizational Culture

With this understanding of the four broad theoretical approaches to organizational culture, we can now analyze how culture is actually exhibited in organizations. The issues we will address are the strength or weakness of the organization's culture and the identification of an organization's culture.

Strength of Culture

Sathe (1985) identified three features that determine a culture's strength. The first is **thickness of culture,** measured by the number of important shared assumptions. Thick cultures have many such assumptions, thin cultures few. The second dimension is **extent of sharing.** In strong cultures, layers and layers of beliefs are shared. **Clarity of ordering** is the third determinant of cultural strength. At McDonald's, product quality and customer service are clearly the highest priorities, but the two goals appear to be equally important. In some cultures, shared beliefs and values are clearly ordered, and their importance in relation to one another is known. Strength of culture is significant because strong cultures—that is, thick cultures in which the sharing of clearly ordered beliefs and values is pervasive—are more resistant to change than are weak cultures.

Two factors affect the strength of an organizational culture: the number of employees and geographic dispersion. Small work forces and more localized operations contribute to the development of strong cultures because beliefs and values easily develop and become shared. These characteristics are not essential for a strong culture, however. With 10,000 restaurants spread around the world, from Illinois to Yugoslavia to Russia, McDonald's clearly employs a large number of people and is very dispersed.

Nevertheless, it enjoys a strong organizational culture. Similarly, Nordstrom's, a department store chain from the Northwest that is expanding nationally, has cultivated a strong culture based on customer service. According to one story about the chain, "Salespeople have paid parking tickets for customers unable to find legal spots, delivered purchases to customers' homes on Christmas Eve and lent a few dollars to customers who have found themselves short at the cash register" (Stevenson, 1989, p. 38). The result was a tenfold growth in sales in the 1980s and a jump in size from 15 stores to 42.

Strong cultures are not always desirable. There appear to be organizational conditions that do not necessarily warrant them (Wilkins and Ouchi, 1983). If one looks at organizations as mechanisms for governing transaction costs (the organization requires something of the employee, who in turn benefits from the organization), there are three ways to manage those transaction costs. Whichever method is used to mediate costs, it must be viewed as equitable to everyone.

The first two mechanisms, the marketplace and bureaucracy, are used under conditions of fairly low uncertainty and complexity. The market form, appropriate in competitive situations, manages transaction costs with a price mechanism. Contracts are made and kept between parties at a "fair" price so that competitors won't take over the business. Bureaucracy creates the appearance of equity by creating an employment contract, whereby employees contract to receive wages and in turn submit to supervision, which is designed to reduce uncertainty and monitor employee performance. A hallmark of bureaucracy is the simplification of complex tasks into discrete, easily monitored activities. The bureaucracy uses the mechanism of rules or standards of behavior; as long as uncertainty is low, the rules in place can guide behavior.

When uncertainty or complexity increases, these mechanisms do not work. A third mechanism, a clan or culture, then becomes viable. The clan is a culturally homogeneous organization in which members share a common set of values, objectives, and beliefs; this common core empowers them to act with greater flexibility in a fluid situation. This approach addresses the social exchange problem quite differently than either the marketplace or bureaucracy method: it socializes parties to the exchange in such a way that all participants see their objectives in the exchange as congruent. Clans require a tremendous amount of group process activity (see Chapter 5).

Identifying Organizational Culture

Learning to identify an organization's culture can be a valuable tool to understanding what the organization is all about. Choosing an organization in which to work and being happy about that choice after the fact requires insight into organizational culture. A quick assessment of the culture might be obtained by examining the arrangement and feel of the organization's physical design (see Chapter 2 for a discussion of physical design) or examining its reward systems (Kerr and Slocum, 1987). Sathe (1985) has identified a set of questions that one could ask about an organization, as presented in the feature "Questions to Identify Organizational Culture." The answers should help provide insight into an organization's culture.

FEATURE: *Questions to Identify Organizational Culture*

1. What is the background of the founders and others who have followed them? Knowing something about the founders and the ideas they laid down in their organizations helps clarify our understanding about those organizations.

2. How does the organization respond to crises and other events and what has been learned from these experiences? Focusing on stressful events helps us understand how particular assumptions came to be formed and something about the ordering of cultural assumptions.

3. Who are considered deviant in the culture and how does the organization respond to them? Deviants define the boundaries of cultures and understanding them helps us decipher cultures.

4. What are the people in the organization like to work with? Such a question seeks a general understanding of the organization's members.

5. What is done to help a person along once he starts working in the organization? This question addresses the mechanisms of socialization, training, etc.

6. What does it take to do well in the organization? This question reveals performance necessary to get along well in the organization.

7. What are the mechanisms for finding out how one is performing in the organization? This question reveals something about performance and other feedback mechanisms.

8. How does one find out what is really going on in this organization? Answers to this question will reveal communication strategies and the existence of trust.

9. How does the organization make use of employee experience? Answers reveal something about how individual creativity is used, and the degree to which individuals participate in important organizational activities.

10. If the organization stopped doing some of the things it now does, what wouldn't change? Answers reveal critical organizational activities and functions.

11. What outside groups does the organization pay attention to? Answers reveal the extent and nature of the organization's dependencies.

12. What must the organization do particularly well? Critical organizational workings are uncovered by responses to this question.

13. How does one sell a new idea in this organization and who needs to be sold? Key decision makers are identified as is responsiveness to new ideas by answers to this question.

14. What are important strategies and tactics for getting things done in this organization? Political machinations and informal workings of an organization are addressed in answer to this question.

Source: V. Sathe, *Culture and Related Corporate Realities* (Homewood, IL: Irwin, 1985), *passim* (see especially pp. 19–20). Copyright © 1985 by Vijay Sathe. Reprinted by permission of the author.

Several of these assessment criteria are present in the McDonald's case. Ray Kroc, the founder of McDonald's, is memorialized and humanized for all to see (question 1). Hamburger University is clearly a powerful training and socialization tool (question 5). The Ronald McDonald Center clearly illustrates the importance of community to McDonald's (question 11). The emphasis on "quality, service, cleanliness and value" informs employees of what the company does well and what all workers should focus on (question 12).

Other approaches to assessing culture result in pictures different from this one (e.g., Wilkins, 1983). A manager might find it useful to catalog the myths and stories that circulate in his own organization and ask whether they share some common meaning purposeful to the organization. This method would be one way to get an idea about the culture of one's own organization. Schein (1985) states that there are no reliably quick ways to identify the cultural assumptions of people in organizations. He recommends observing, talking to people, collecting archival data, listening to stories, and so on, until a pattern finally emerges. Duncan (1989) argues for the same thing.

Other authors (Morey and Luthans, 1985) point out that organizations are embedded in larger cultures from which they draw values and assumptions and that we can learn much from going into organizations and examining **cultural scenes** (see the feature "Analyzing Culture with Scenes and Themes"). These examinations begin with a description of an interaction that took place and end with a meaningful explanation of that interaction, which may elucidate various themes. Sometimes the themes appear to contradict one another, but often contradictions can be resolved.

FEATURE: *Analyzing Culture with Scenes and Themes*

The use of "cultural scenes" and the analysis of themes demonstrate two techniques of analyzing an organization as if it were a culture.

Organizations are full of social situations or "scenes" that can be observed easily by both researchers (outsiders) and participants (insiders). Some such scenes are richer in their capacity to explain the culture of an organization than others. The process of selecting and analyzing them can be viewed as a two-step process requiring the point of view of, first, insiders and, second, outsiders.

Discovery of these scenes in the first place requires an insider orientation—someone who knows how the organization works, where and when the crucial events take place, and who participates. Once they are identified, the scenes are studied by the researchers, who seek to elicit from the participants, in a carefully structured but nondirective manner, the meaning of the scene.

This is the important first step in discovery of insider meanings for outsider-observed social situations. These insider descriptions can then be used and analyzed in "outsider" terms to produce culturally meaningful comparisons of organizational phenomena.

Theme analysis is another method for studying organizations. Themes are recurrent, and important principles occur in different cultural domains. They deal with core beliefs, values, and rules of behavior that cross boundaries and context.

Preliminary research indicates that themes probably reflect such ideas as beliefs about the realities of particular kinds of interpersonal relations within the organization. For most employees, the realities of organizational life revolve around interpersonal relations, not around the broad range of content issues found in cultural systems. Themes may include social conflict, cultural contradictions, informal techniques of social control, managing interpersonal relationships, acquiring and maintaining status, and solving problems.

Themes can be used within cultural analysis of organizations to identify and interpret common concerns of organization members and perhaps to diagnose areas of potential problems. They can be used to compare different groups within given organizations. Across organizations, themes may be found to have certain patterns of occurrence by organization or industry, geographic setting, and age of the organization.

Source: Adapted from Nancy C. Morey and Fred Luthans, "Refining the Displacement of Culture and the Use of Scenes and Themes in Organizational Studies," *Academy of Management Review* 10, no. 2 (1985): 219–229. Reprinted by permission.

Distinguishing Countercultures and Subcultures

Within any culture—including any organizational culture—a group of people may form a subculture different from the main culture. Certain values, rites, or symbols may be shared between the main culture and this subculture, but the subculture will, by and large, stress different beliefs and patterns of action. When the subculture contradicts the main culture, it is called a **counterculture.** A counterculture may develop for a variety of reasons (Sathe, 1985). First, a manager may simply be unaware of the prevailing culture and go against it unwittingly. More frequently, however, she goes against the grain of the culture because it is the right thing to do or for such personal reasons as rebelliousness. Let us take it for granted that managers are sufficiently astute and mature that if they attempt to create countercultures, they do so for good reasons. Then one might ask, How can one constructively deviate from the prevailing culture?

In general, going against the culture requires marshaling personal and organizational resources. We might view counterculture activities as falling into three camps. Those who use **self-insurance** in going against the culture do so on the basis of their credibility and acceptance by the dominant culture. As we discuss more fully in Chapter 5, one builds metaphoric credits over time by being compliant with the group's wishes; these credits can be cashed in at a later time through deviant behavior. The more deviance involved in the activity, the more one pays in credibility credits to carry out the attack successfully—and the larger the stock of credits one must have in the first place.

Yet another strategy, called the **culture insurance** strategy, requires support from others in high places. This strategy spreads the risk of nonconformity among the "old faithful."

In the third approach, managers can deviate from culture with the support of lower-status people, provided they are of sufficient number. The leader creates a subculture whose followers provide the clout needed to deviate from the company culture. The feature on counterculture at General Motors tells how John DeLorean established a subculture there.

FEATURE: *Counterculture at General Motors*

At General Motors, three related core values were repeatedly stressed as part of the dominant culture: respecting authority, fitting in, and being loyal. John DeLorean was a high-ranking executive who, before he left GM, took conscious steps to create an alternative culture with different values: productivity instead of deference, objective measures of performance instead of subjective indicators of conformity, and independence over blind loyalty. . . .

DeLorean wanted to replace deference to authority with task-oriented efficiency. As a step in this direction, he decided to discourage the practice of meeting superiors at airports. Instead of issuing an edict changing the policy, he role-modeled the new behavior when he was to speak to a luncheon of McGraw-Hill editors and executives in mid-Manhattan. He found his own ride from the airport to the McGraw-Hill offices, much to the surprise of his hosts, who were used to GM executives being regularly accompanied by large retinues. He later noted with some pride that the story of the "McGraw-Hill incident" had been retold many times, both in GM and in McGraw-Hill.

DeLorean was opposed to the domination of team play and fitting in. Instead, he valued dissent and independence. He changed the performance appraisal system in his division, replacing subjective criteria with measurements that were as objective as possible. To back up his beliefs, he promoted a man who was disagreeable but who had an outstanding performance record—not once but four times. When he was promoted to head the Chevrolet division, he used decor to symbolize his declaration of independence, installing bright carpets, restaining the paneling and bringing in modern furniture. In his own dress he wore suits with a continental cut, off-white shirts with wide collars and wider ties than the GM norm. His deviance appeared carefully calibrated to remain within, but test the limits of, the dominant culture's latitude of acceptance.

To express his distaste for unquestioning loyalty, DeLorean took no direct action but did retell the story of the company's Corvair misfortunes with pointed emphasis on the dangers of "groupthink" and an overemphasis on loyalty. This reinterpretation of history into a "boomerang" story—a tale of carrying cultural values to ridiculous or dangerous extremes to the detriment of the organization—is another way DeLorean established a counterculture.

Source: Joanne Martin and Caren Siehl, "Organizational Culture and Counterculture: An Uneasy Symbiosis," *Organizational Dynamics* Autumn (1983): 52–64. Copyright © 1983 by the American Management Association, New York. All rights reserved. Reprinted by permission.

Countercultures can serve some useful functions for the dominant culture, such as bringing into question old values and providing a safe haven for the development of innovative ideas. Some of the core values of the counterculture should present a direct challenge to those of the dominant culture; the two should exist in an uneasy symbiosis, taking opposite and critically important positions (Martin and Siehl, 1983). Recall from Chapter 1 the argument that organizations must include deviance in order to ensure survival. By embracing some deviance, organizations can adapt to environmental changes. In this view, countercultures could be valuable to an organization, rather than threatening.

As in any act of deviance (see Chapter 5), the prevailing culture may act to stop counterculture activity, initially devoting a great deal of attention to the deviant in an attempt to get him back into the fold. If this does not work, it frequently attempts to wall the deviant off, building a protective wall around the original culture, essentially isolating the deviant by other means.

If countercultures survive, the initial opposition to them may be replaced by a closing of the links between the counterculture and the top of the organization. In this way, the dominant culture attempts to minimize the counterculture's impact on the organization. The counterculture may then respond by attempting to develop other linkages, only to be met with several more rounds of obstruction. Gradually, a successful counterculture may even be granted more resources, autonomy, and legitimacy.

Organizational Socialization

Deciding which elements will characterize an organization's culture is not enough; management must pass on that culture to employees for it to matter. **Socialization** is the process by which culture is transmitted. To the extent that an employee is successfully socialized in the organization, she will be committed to and stay with that organization. Thus, socialization has implications for commitment and turnover.

Socialization is the process through which one is taught and learns the ropes of the organization. The process takes many forms; it may be long or slow, self-guided or elaborately staged. If we take seriously the notion that learning is continuous, whole careers may be characterized by socialization.

One author (Schein, 1971) provides a description of organizations along three dimensions. The first is a functional dimension and describes the things an organization must do (e.g., production, marketing, and so on). The second dimension is hierarchical and refers to the distribution of rank in the organization. Schein's third dimension, **inclusion,** illustrates the degree to which people are at the edge of an organization or near the "center of action." This is the dimension with which socialization is concerned.

Newcomers to most hierarchical levels and functional areas in virtually all organizations inevitably remain on the edge of organizational affairs for some time. The reasons are numerous (Van Maanen and Schein, 1979). New entrants may not be deemed trustworthy, they may not have had time to develop the kind of front expected by others, or they may need to be tested in some way as to their abilities, motivations, or loyalty. Newcomers must be judged acceptable to learn the organization's secrets and be able to separate the "presentational rhetoric" (used to relay to outsiders what's going on inside) from the "operational rhetoric" (used to communicate internally). Socialization is at once the mechanism by which newcomers are judged acceptable and the process by which they are taught. At Hamburger University, new employees are trained and socialized to carry the corporate philosophy back to their local franchises and to pass it on to their fellow employees. Each McDonald's employee is therefore privy to the secrets, stories, and Krocisms that are a part of the culture of the firm.

Because socialization is an ongoing process, it has a feedback loop. As newcomers are socialized, the socializer monitors the degree to which they fit the organization. Where fit is good, they are given more socialization. Where fit is too minimal—where the newcomer shows potential signs of deviance or at least nonacceptance of the corporate culture—the newcomer is either eliminated or given less of the secret information. Businesses want "team players."

Van Maanen and Schein suggest that socialization takes place on two dimensions. All roles are bundles of tasks that include both content characteristics (what people should do) and process characteristics (how they should do it). They write:

The content of a particular role can be depicted both in terms of a general, almost ideological mandate that goes with it and in terms of a general set of mandate-fulfilling actions that are supposed to be performed by the role occupant. Thus, doctors are thought to "heal the sick" by prescribing available "cures" to be found somewhere within the vast catalogue of "medical" knowledge. Similarly, the process associated with the performance of a role also has associated with it general strategies and specific practices. The doctor "does diagnosis" by taking a patient's blood pressure, eliciting a history, reading an X-ray, and so forth. Finally, linked to all these concerns are social norms and rules which suggest, for example, the appropriate mannerisms, attitudes, and social rituals to be displayed when performing various parts of the "bundle of tasks" called a role. Doctors, to continue our illustration, have "bedside manners," often assume a pose of distance or remoteness toward certain emotionally trying events in the lives of their patients, and take a characteristically "all knowing" stance toward most of the nursing personnel with whom they come into contact. (1979, pp. 226–227)

How People Are Socialized

Most of the available writing about organizational socialization assumes that a newcomer's adjustment to an organization is directly affected by early learning experiences in it and the organization's attempts at socialization. It seems fairly clear, however, that the individual differences people bring to organizations and the attributions they make about those organizations (see Chapter 10) also influence newcomer adjustment (Jones, 1983).

As in all aspects of life, the new situations that newcomers encounter provide uncertainty. The strategies they adopt to deal with this uncertainty and the way they make sense of the situations depend on how they have learned to deal with new situations. Newcomers who perceive themselves as personally competent and have the need to grow will interpret such situations differently than do people who see themselves as less able and who want to settle into a comfortable niche. Then, too, the attributions newcomers make of their new situations probably differ from those old-timers make of these same situations. These attributions are also dependent on the history of the newcomer. When newcomers and old-timers perceive the same situation differently, socialization becomes more difficult. Specific interactions among newcomers and insiders may be an important but overlooked influence on the socialization process (Reichers, 1987). Two major aspects of socialization are learning and modeling leaders (Schein, 1990).

FIGURE 3.3
The Multiple Socialization of Organization Members

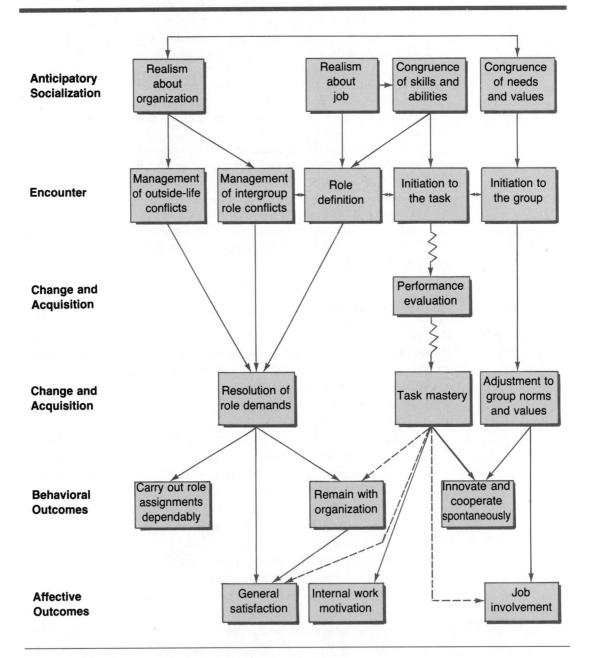

Source: D. C. Feldman, "The Multiple Socialization of Organization Members," *Academy of Management Review* 6 (1981): 311. Reprinted by permission.

Socialization includes several phases, according to Feldman (1981), as shown in Figure 3.3. The first, **anticipatory socialization,** encompasses the learning that occurs before a new member joins an organization and involves a recruiting process that attempts to select individuals who exhibit some fit with the organizational culture. In Chapter 4 we will see how the selection process was used to help cement a group identity.

The second phase of socialization is **encounter,** in which the new member sees what the organization is really like and changes some of his values and attitudes. This phase includes exposure of the new recruit to both task-related and group-related concerns. The socialization that takes place at Hamburger University is part of this phase.

The third phase of socialization is **change and acquisition,** a relatively long-lasting phase in which new recruits truly master the skills and roles required for their new jobs. A McDonald's franchise owner who begins to apply the principles learned at Hamburger University is in the midst of this part of the process. The success of socialization is exhibited in such behavioral and affective results as shown in Figure 3.3.

Pascale (1985) modeled a seven-step process to depict what goes on in organizations with strong cultures:

1. *Selection.* Trained recruiters carefully select entry-level candidates.

2. *Abandonment of past.* Experiences that give the new recruit humility break down the hold of past assumptions and traits, making the recruit ready to accept the organization's norms.

3. *Training.* On-the-job training helps the recruit master tasks, with mastery rewarded by promotion.

4. *Monitoring and reward.* Performance is monitored closely, and the reward system is geared toward reinforcing the values of the culture.

5. *Identification.* Employees begin to identify with the organization's values, thus making them able to justify any personal sacrifices required.

6. *Reinforcement.* Organizational legends reinforce the culture and goals.

7. *Role models.* Successful members of the organization provide role models for others.

Strategies for Socialization

One author (Van Maanen, 1978) delineated seven dimensions with which to view strategies that organizations often use to socialize new employees.

FIGURE 3.4
Kinds of Socialization

Dimension	Examples
Formal/Informal	Formal: Police academies; Marines in basic training; IBM executives
	Informal: On-the-job socialization, including that conducted by workers with other workers
Individual/Collective	Individual: Grooming of successor to CEO; religious training of minister or priest
	Collective: Hamburger University; group exercise programs of Japanese companies
Sequential/Nonsequential	Sequential: Banks rotating a potential manager through a variety of jobs prior to promotion
	Nonsequential: Line worker with no managerial training becoming a supervisor
Fixed/Variable	Fixed: Established durations for each grade in educational systems; set levels of experience associated with civil service grades
	Variable: Careers of business executives, which typically vary and are characterized by rumors about advancement
Tournaments	Fast-track executives who get preferential training; college-track high school students who get exclusive opportunity for certain courses
Serial/Disjunctive	Serial: Stability of police or military behavior patterns
	Disjunctive: Entrepreneurs; workers filling newly created jobs
Investiture/Divestiture	Investiture: Executive recruits chosen for their existing skills
	Divestiture: Professional football players; career military personnel; nurses

These dimensions are not independent of one another and are sometimes combined in inventive ways. Figure 3.4 exemplifies those seven dimensions:

1. *Formal (or informal)*. This dimension measures the degree to which the setting where socialization takes place is segregated from ongoing work. The more formal the process, the more the recruit is segregated and differentiated. Informal socialization takes place in the course of the job.

2. *Individual (or collective)*. The degree to which people are socialized individually or collectively is probably the most critical socialization variable. A group that is socialized together develops an "in the same boat" mentality.

3. *Sequential (or nonsequential).* Sequential strategies are based on a set of discrete steps through which a person must pass in order to obtain his role. Nonsequential strategies do not involve discrete steps; they could include one-time sessions or a more ad hoc approach to socialization.

4. *Fixed (or variable).* Fixed processes provide the recruit with precise knowledge about the time it will take him to complete a given step; variable processes do not. Since rate of progress is important in most organizations, people on variable schedules will try to figure out schedules using the flimsiest information.

5. *Tournament (or contest).* This is the practice of separating recruits into tracks on the basis of ability, ambition, and so on. Such tracking often occurs early in one's career, and shifts across tracks mainly occur downward—once off track, it is hard to get back on.

6. *Serial (or disjunctive).* The serial process is one in which old members of an organization groom new members to take over. It is a process guaranteed to result in little organizational change. Disjunctive processes give room for innovation and creativity.

7. *Investiture (or divestiture).* Investiture ratifies and establishes the validity of the characteristics a person already possesses. Divestiture denies and strips away characteristics of the entering recruit.

An organization wanting to promote relatively high similarity in thought and action among recruits would combine formal, serial, and divestiture strategies. An organization desiring dissimilarity should use informal, disjunctive, and investiture strategies. Relatively passive, hardworking, and undifferentiated workers are produced through the combination of formal, collective, sequential, tournament, and divestiture strategies. At McDonald's, socialization clearly is formal and collective (Hamburger University), sequential (the university's curriculum), serial (advice by Ray Kroc and other early leaders is handed down), and fixed (the university's set time period).

Pascale and Athos (1981) explored the Japanese method of socialization, which puts heavy emphasis on a kind of master–apprentice relationship, in which a junior worker (*kohai*) is linked with a senior worker (*sempai*). Unlike the traditional Western apprenticeship, though, this system emphasizes not the long-term mastery of tasks so much as the relationship itself whereby the mentor helps the protégé learn the organizational ropes. The relationship between the two becomes a firm bond that is not violated by interpersonal competition, as may occur in the West. Rather, the fates of the two are inextricably linked, and thus the junior rises along with the successful senior and, similarly, fades when the mentor falls into disrepute.

Organizational Commitment and Turnover

Definition of the Problem

If socialization ties individuals to their organizations, thereby resulting in committed employees, what constitutes commitment? In one view, **commitment** is the total capacity to act in ways that meet the organization's goals and interests (Wiener, 1982). Although a simple enough definition, it is inadequate. The problem is that commitment has now been defined in a number of widely varying ways. One set of writers (Mowday, Porter, and Steers, 1982) has reviewed three approaches to commitment in order to highlight its nature. Here we summarize those three approaches for better understanding of the term.

Etzioni (1961) argues that commitment—and the authority that organizations have over members—is rooted in the nature of employee involvement in the organization. Involvement takes one of three forms, ranging from total commitment to no commitment at all. **Moral involvement,** based on positive and intense orientation to the organization, results from internalization of the organization's values, goals, and norms. **Calculative involvement** is less intense and rests on an exchange relationship between the individual and the organization. People become committed to an organization to the extent that they perceive some beneficial or equitable exchange relationship. **Alienative involvement** is a lack of commitment, occurring when members feel constrained by circumstances to belong to the organization but do not identify with it.

Kanter (1968) takes a different view of commitment, arguing that different types of commitment result from different behavioral requirements placed on members by the organization. Again, involvement takes three forms, but here the forms may be interrelated. **Continuance commitment** has to do with a member's dedication to the survival of the organization and results from having people make sacrifices for and investments in the organization. **Cohesion commitment** is attachment to social relations in an organization; it can be enhanced by having employees publicly renounce previous social ties or engage in ceremonies that enhance group cohesion. **Control commitment** is a member's attachment to the norms of an organization that shape behavior in desired ways. It exists when employees believe that the organization's norms and values are important guides to their behavior.

Staw (1977) and Salancik (1977) discussed the fact that organizational researchers and social psychologists view commitment quite differently. Organizational researchers study **attitudinal commitment,** focusing on how employees identify with the goals and values of the organization. This is commitment viewed primarily from the standpoint of the organization. Social psychologists study **behavioral commitment,** focusing on how a person's behavior serves to bind him to the organization. Once behavior shows commitment, people must adjust their attitudes accordingly, which then influence their subsequent behavior. Thus a cycle begins: behavior shapes attitudes and the shaped attitudes in turn shape behavior.

Thus we have at least three different ways to view organizational commitment. If we accept all three notions, we will look in different places for evidence of commitment. We will look at exchange relationships as behaviors evidencing commitment, and acceptance of organizational norms and values as attitudes showing commitment. A broad view of commitment should lead managers to many different sources and manifestations of it. Most views of commitment treat it as a global concept: one is or is not committed to the organization as an entity. A more differentiated view, in which employees are thought to be more or less committed to various facets of the workplace, might be more helpful (Reichers, 1985; Meyer, Paunonen, Gellotly, Giffin, and Jackson, 1989).

The earlier discussion of occupational communities suggests that managers must consider employees' other commitments as well. Employees are not only committed to the organization to a greater or lesser degree, but as individuals with multiple roles also have other commitments. These include such obvious connections as those of family or community, but they also embrace membership in occupational communities or in other associations. Figure 3.5 (page 146) illustrates various constituencies to which a given employee may be committed. Managers need to be sensitive to these other motivations that may influence an employee's behavior or attitudes.

Another interesting manifestation of commitment is the phenomenon known as **whistle-blowing,** or publicizing unethical, illegal, or immoral behavior. The topic has gained prominence recently from the revelation of various government procurement and regulation scandals, including defense department contracting, the awarding of HUD contracts, and regulation of generic drugs by the FDA.

For the individual, whistle-blowing may be the last resort, the only step left open; for the organization it is extremely threatening when negative information reaches the press. Whistle-blowing may occur because the whistle-blower feels tremendously committed to the organization; it is, after all, borne of an impulse to reform an evil, and few people are willing to risk punishment to reform what they do not value. In this view the whistle-

FIGURE 3.5
*Various Commit-
ments of an
Organizational
Member*

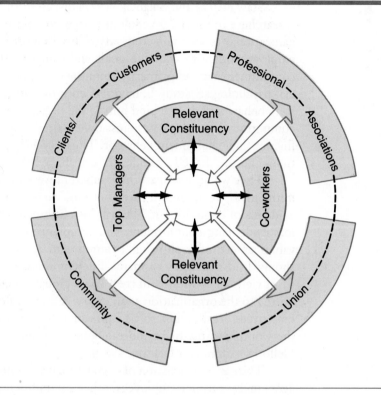

Source: A. E. Reichers, "A Review and Reconceptualization of Organizational Commitment,"
Academy of Management Review 10 (1985): 472. Reprinted by permission.

blower is the defender of the organization's true values and the management
that punishes the behavior is the deviant. Whistle-blowing may have the
beneficial effect for the organization, then, of spawning change, especially
when it can be made to overseeing bodies, as with all the government examples of whistle-blowing.

Most of the work on whistle-blowing is descriptive and philosophical.
Organizations are probably more apt to retaliate against whistle-blowers
they value, perhaps because of their potential threat. They may also retaliate
against those who are vulnerable because they lack public support. People
often fail to blow the whistle when organizational conditions suggest they
should. This hesitance undoubtedly results from fear of reprisal and skep-
ticism that their organizations will take ameliorative steps.

Antecedents to Organizational Commitment

Managers, once sensitive to the existence or nonexistence of commitment in
the organization, might want to know what causes it. We may be able to

FIGURE 3.6
*Antecedents to
and Outcomes of
Commitment*

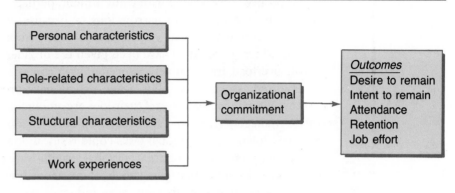

Source: R. T. Mowday, L. W. Porter, and R. M. Steers, *Employee-Organization Linkages: The Psychology of Commitment, Absenteeism, and Turnover* (New York: Academic Press, 1982). Reprinted by permission of Academic Press and the authors.

alter commitment by understanding its antecedents, of which there are four: personal characteristics, job- or role-related characteristics, structural characteristics, and work experiences (Mowday, Porter, and Steers, 1982). Figure 3.6 diagrams antecedents to and outcomes of commitment.

Research shows age and tenure to be personal characteristics positively correlated with commitment. As people get older and remain in their organizations, their commitment goes up, probably because alternative employment opportunities diminish for older people or because commitment may be a successful strategy in getting along. Or it may be, quite simply, that more committed employees stay with the organization longer. Higher education is associated with lower commitment, perhaps because educated people have expectations the organization cannot meet or are more committed to professions (their occupational community) than to organizations. It may also be that alternative work opportunities are greater. Women are usually more committed than men to their organizations, possibly because they have to overcome more barriers to getting into those organizations or because fewer alternatives are available to them. One multinational study of Asian, Western, and Arab workers in Saudi Arabia showed that Asians were more committed to work than the other two groups (al-Meer, 1989). This was probably because job opportunities were fewer in the six poor Asian countries from which these workers came.

A variety of personal attitudes are related to commitment, among them work-oriented life interests, achievement motivation, and a sense of competence. These kinds of relationships support the notion of exchange between the employee and his organization.

Several job role characteristics are correlated with commitment. Job scope is positively associated with commitment, perhaps because broad jobs challenge people more than narrow jobs or because people with broader jobs—managers and the like—often have already demonstrated their commitment, which is why they have been given the broader jobs. Role conflict and role overload are negatively associated with commitment; role ambiguity has mixed associations. Thus, when people have broad and clear jobs, commitment may increase, but if their jobs are ambiguous, commitment decreases. Managers need to watch their top performers; the temptation to load them down with additional tasks could result in lowered commitment.

Some characteristics of organizational structure are related to commitment, suggesting that managers should think about how the structural arrangements of their organizations may influence workers. Formalization, functional dependence, and decentralization are all related to commitment. Work experiences related to commitment include social involvement, organizational dependability, personal importance to the organization, pay equity, and group norms regarding hard work.

In summary, while we do not have very clear ideas about the process of commitment itself, we can identify a number of important antecedents to organizational commitment. They can alert managers to personal, work, and organizational characteristics they may wish to modify in the interest of improving commitment.

Consequences of Organizational Commitment

The consequences of organizational commitment group themselves into two main categories: job performance and turnover. One disappointing finding is that there is only a weak relationship between commitment and job performance. Satisfaction and commitment seem to be related, but whether one causes the other is still unknown (Curry, Wakefield, Price, and Muellen, 1986). Positive and negative consequences of various levels of commitment are summarized in Figure 3.7. Level of commitment may be related to the strength of an organization's culture and is almost certainly dependent on its socialization processes.

A great deal of attention has been devoted to the relationship between commitment and turnover. Taken together, the studies provide strong support that such a relationship exists and that it is negative. Thus, when managers spot declining commitment, they should also expect subsequent voluntary turnover. Low commitment, then, is a danger sign for turnover. It might be thought that employee commitment is higher in countries such as Japan, where turnover is lower than in the United States (Cole, 1979). Yet, one comparison of Japanese, Korean, and American workers (Luthans, McCaul, and Dodd, 1985) found that Japanese and Korean employee commit-

FIGURE 3.7
Consequences of Various Levels of Commitment

Level of Commitment	INDIVIDUAL		ORGANIZATIONAL	
	Positive	Negative	Positive	Negative
Low	*Individual* creativity, innovation, and originality *More* effective human resource utilization	*Slower* career advancement and promotion *Personal* costs as a result of whistle-blowing *Possible* expulsion, exit, or effort to defeat organizational goals	*Turnover* of disruptive/poor performing employees limiting damage, increasing morale, bringing in replacements *Whistle*-blowing with beneficial consequences for the organization	*Greater* turnover, tardiness, absenteeism, lack of intention to stay, low quantity of work, disloyalty to the firm, illegal activity against the firm, limited extrarole behavior, damaging role modeling, whistle-blowing with damaging consequences, limited organizational control over employees
Moderate	*Enhanced* feelings of belongingness, security, efficacy, loyalty, and duty *Creative* individualism *Maintenance* of identity distinct from the organization	*Career* advancement and promotion opportunities may be limited *Uneasy* compromise between segmental commitments	*Increased* employee tenure, limited intention to quit, limited turnover, and greater job satisfaction	*Employees* may limit extrarole behavior and citizenship behaviors *Employees* may balance organization demands with nonwork demands *Possible* decrease in organizational effectiveness
High	*Individual* career advancement and compensation enhanced *Behavior* rewarded by the organization *Individual* provided with a passionate pursuit	*Individual* growth, creativity, innovation, and opportunities for mobility stifled *Bureaupathic* resistance to change *Stress* and tension in social and family relationships *Lack* of peer solidarity *Limited* time and energy for nonwork organizations	*Secure* and stable work force *Employees* accept organization's demands for greater production *High* levels of task competition and performance *Organizational* goals can be met	*Ineffective* utilization of human resources *Lack* of organizational flexibility, innovation, and adaptability *Inviolate* trust in past policies and procedures *Irritation* and antagonism from overzealous workers *Illegal*/unethical acts committed on behalf of the organization

Source: D. W. Randall, "Commitment and the Organization: The Organization Man Revisited," *Academy of Management Review* 12 (1987): 462. Reprinted by permission.

ment to organizations is lower than that of their American counterparts, bringing into question the commitment–turnover relationship at least in these countries.

Turnover Reconsidered

Managers often become interested in commitment because they want to reduce voluntary turnover. In an organization like a McDonald's franchise, turnover is not expensive—and may even be desired—but in other organizations, training costs, the need for scarce skills, and so on, may be so high that turnover is not desirable.

Turnover is certainly one possible end response to low commitment, but it may also be a response to a number of other factors in the work situation. In its own right, turnover has enjoyed considerable research attention because it is assumed to engender large costs to organizations and to society as a whole. Researchers have, by and large, assumed that reducing turnover reduces these costs. However, some writers (Staw and Oldham, 1978; Staw, 1984) discuss turnover as a healthy factor in organizations. A moderate amount may positively influence organizational heterogeneity and flexibility by bringing in new ideas and circulating them throughout the organization.

Turnover rates and their correlates intrigue economists, whereas psychologists seem enamored by correlates of individual turnover. That is, economists want to know the causes and consequences of turnover in various sectors of the labor force; psychologists, on the other hand, are more interested in what causes workers to quit their jobs. Some attention has been given to merging these two approaches to turnover by examining the kinds of antecedents generally of interest to psychologists (such as organizational climate, age, tenure, education, and so on), not in relation to individual turnover, but in relation to turnover rates (Terborg and Lee, 1984). The results of this investigation showed that turnover rates can be reliably predicted using these variables for some occupations—for example, sales personnel and managers—but not for others. More of this research will bring economic and psychological traditions together and provide a more complete view of the antecedents of turnover.

One of the earliest studies of turnover in the organizational literature (March and Simon, 1958) found that people are more likely to stay in the organization when they perceive a balance between their efforts and their rewards (see Chapter 9). This balance is influenced by three factors: one's desire to leave the organization, the perceived ease of movement from the organization, and one's job satisfaction.

An interesting approach to turnover focuses on three possible responses to job dissatisfaction (Hirschman, 1970). Hirschman argues that people's activities during times of dissatisfaction can be the route by which management finds out about its failures. The first response to dissatisfaction is exit—members leave the organization or request transfers. The painful decision to withdraw or switch requires considerable effort and usually means the employee does not believe his situation will improve. The exit option is regarded as powerful. The second option, called the voice option, represents an attempt to change things rather than to escape. Appeals are usually made to higher authority as employees attempt to repair deteriorating conditions. The third response is loyalty, in which the employee confronted with deteriorating conditions does nothing, but rather suffers in silence, hoping things will get better.

A fourth response to deteriorating conditions has recently been identified: lax or neglectful behavior (Farrell, 1983). Temporary abandonment, just as full-fledged turnover, can be read by managers as a signal to look hard at the work situation.

The most frequently investigated model of turnover is the Mobley (1977) model (see Figure 3.8, page 152). It develops the following causal links: job dissatisfaction leads to thoughts about leaving, thoughts about leaving lead to intention to search for a new job, the probability of finding an acceptable job alternative leads to intention to quit, and intention to quit leads to turnover. A number of empirical tests support various linkages in the model. The model posits intention to quit as the strongest predictor of turnover. Thus, if a manager trusts the truthfulness of his employees' responses, the best indicator of turnover is to ask employees whether they intend to quit.

Extending upon Mobley's model and subsequent empirical work that tested it, and upon attribution theory (see Chapter 10), Steers and Mowday (1981) proposed a model of turnover that relies on attribution processes. This model (see Figure 3.9, page 153) proposes a complex interplay of factors involved in turnover decisions that the authors present in three general clusters. The first group of factors has to do with the employee's job expectations and values. Influences here are the characteristics of the employee, the amount of information available about the job and the organization, and the prevalence of alternative jobs.

The second set of factors influencing the turnover decision are the employee's responses to the job, which include job expectations, the characteristics of the organization and the employee's work experience, and the employee's level of job performance. The authors point out here that an individual who is dissatisfied with the organization may attempt to improve the situation not just by leaving but by trying instead to change the organization or by working to remove another employee or a supervisor perceived as an obstacle. Job expectations, Steers and Mowday point out, are influenced by practical considerations such as a spouse's career or family obliga-

FIGURE 3.8
The Employee Turnover Decision Process

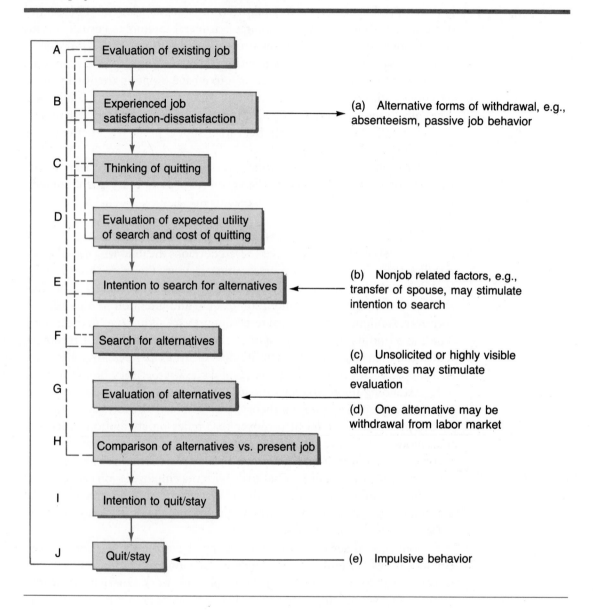

FIGURE 3.9
A Model of Voluntary Employee Turnover

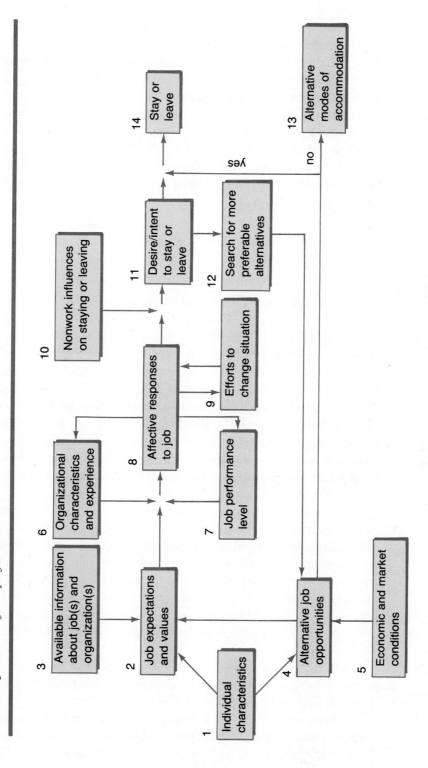

Source: R. M. Steers and R. T. Mowday, "Employee Turnover and Post-Decision Accommodation Processes," in L. L. Cummings and B. M. Staw (eds.), *Research in Organizational Behavior* (Greenwich, CT: JAI Press, 1981), p. 240. Copyright © 1981 by JAI Press. Reprinted by permission.

tions. It is important to remember that employees do not make decisions strictly on the basis of the job situation itself.

The third cluster of factors revolves around intent to leave, available alternatives, and the decision whether to leave. The authors suggest that the decision to leave is strongly influenced by the availability of alternatives, but they point out that intent to leave can make the employee more sensitive to alternatives and thus identify more opportunities. Nevertheless, the model proposes that the employee with few alternatives, however dissatisfied, will make some accommodation to stay. In this regard the model provides a useful balancing view of the turnover question—every worker who is dissatisfied does not leave.

SUMMARY

McDonald's efforts at socialization begin when new employees are hired; the efforts continue at Hamburger University, where employees learn about founder Ray Kroc's philosophy and the company creed of "quality, service, cleanliness, and value." Thus individual values and beliefs are meshed with the culture of McDonald's, whether the particular franchise is located in Des Plaines, Illinois, or Kuala Lumpur, Malaysia. With the death of McDonald's founder, Ray Kroc, one might well wonder whether this culture would continue unchanged or even if it should. The answer for McDonald's has been to keep Kroc's philosophy alive by establishing a corporate museum complete with recordings of "Krocisms." One might still be puzzled about how these committed employees will adjust to external pressures for change should they occur in the future.

Each organizational culture must be viewed within the context of its cultural environment; that larger culture will help shape the organizational culture. Economic, social, and political aspects of the cultural environment contribute to the structure of the organizational culture. That cultural differences among nations are real has significant implications for organizations. Researchers have found that multinationals can encounter significant differences among employees from different nations; thus managers must consider whether a given corporate culture can survive in a nation with conflicting values.

Organizational culture has been approached in four ways: as shared norms, beliefs, and values; as myths, stories, and other manifestations of language; as rites and ceremonials; and as symbolic interaction.

The strength of culture is reflected by its thickness, the extent to which values are shared, and the clarity with which the values are ordered. Sometimes strong cultures are undesirable, as when change is needed. Culture is a mechanism governing transaction costs between employees and their organizations. Of the three ways to manage transaction costs—the market, the bureaucracy, and the clan—the latter is the most flexible and the best suited to changing environments.

Organizational culture can be identified in a number of ways. One approach is to view an organization in light of a detailed set of questions aimed at revealing its values, norms, and behaviors. Other approaches consider whole scenes of interactions as rich sources of information about organizational beliefs.

Subcultures always and countercultures sometimes develop in organizations. They can be useful in bringing into question old values and providing a safe haven for the development of innovative ideas. Not surprisingly, dominant cultures tend to oppose the advent of countercultures.

Organizational socialization is the process through which organizational culture is inculcated in new employees; commitment and turnover are related to how well the job of socialization is done. In one view, socialization processes convey culture to the employee through three phases: anticipatory socialization, encounter, and change and acquisition. In another model, socialization covers seven steps, building from selection through removal of past attitudes, implanting new attitudes, monitoring and reward, and reinforcement of the culture using stories and role models. There are seven strategies for socializing people into organizations: formal/informal, collective/individual, sequential/nonsequential, fixed/variable, tournament, serial/disjunctive, and investiture/divestiture.

Commitment is the result of socialization. Various definitions of commitment have been offered, but essentially they provide two ways to view commitment, as behavior or as attitude. Antecedents to commitment are personal characteristics, job roles, and structural characteristics. Consequences of commitment are job performance, tenure with the organization, absenteeism, tardiness, and turnover.

Turnover is focused on because it is one possible outcome of low commitment and poor socialization attempts. It is also a mechanism employees use to dissociate themselves from organizational cultures with which they do not agree. A number of approaches to turnover exist. One focuses on the three options resulting from dissatisfaction with an organization: leaving (called exit), complaining (called voice), and staying but saying nothing (loyalty). Another view looks at temporary abandonment as opposed to full-fledged turnover. Thoughts of leaving precede actual turnover and underlie an interesting model that views withdrawal as an abrupt behavior. A final model of turnover focuses on causes, which are seen as characteristics of employees, characteristics of environment, and circumstances under which the behavior takes place.

MANAGERIAL INSIGHT

To: *Student Manager*
From: *Veteran Manager*
Subject: *Culture*

The chapter discusses culture primarily from the point of view of the whole organization. Those of you who achieve senior positions will have the opportunity to observe the phenomenon of culture from this very broad perspective. On the other hand, all of you who become managers should be able to experience culture in the small organization—the department, division, branch, or local office. This culture is one you as manager will be able to affect. You and your co-workers probably won't call it culture but "how we do things around here." On a unit level, it's the particular combination of overall culture, local customs, and individual stamp that you and others put on it.

Most of the principles discussed in the chapter apply to these subcultures. In some ways, the concepts are easier to see at the department level because the organizational unit itself is easier to see and comprehend. Depending upon the larger culture in which you find yourself, you may have a great deal of freedom to regulate the norms; establish the values, rites, and ceremonies; and create the myths, stories, and language in your unit.

You will probably find as manager that you affect these aspects of your department whether you consciously try to do so or not. You will be a leader and your followers will take many of their cues from you. At times you may feel they are doing just the opposite, but unless you manage a particularly recalcitrant group of rebels, you are certain to affect the mood and atmosphere of your department.

It will help you over your entire career to determine early on what values you will stand for. No attempt will be made here to prescribe a list, but there are many role models to choose from. In addition to the values you consciously choose, you will also put your own personality into the culture you create. The result will be a unique mix.

Study the principles in this chapter as they might apply to a department rather than to a whole organization. Think of them in terms of the organization's you've already been associated with. Think of the managers you've worked for—not the CEOs, but the first-line, department-level managers. What kind of culture did they create? Do you want your group to have the same "feel"?

The people you manage during your career will be like organizational culture laboratories. Keeping the larger goals of your organization in mind as well as the needs and aspirations of your people, don't be afraid to experiment. By trial and error—and success—you will gain a rich understanding of and appreciation for the many influences of culture on organizational behavior.

REVIEW QUESTIONS

1. What are the three facets of an organization's cultural environment?

2. In which kind of national culture, homogeneous or heterogeneous, are you likely to encounter a variety of organizational cultures? Why?

3. Apply each of the four approaches to culture to the theme case. What does each approach tell us about McDonald's?

4. Give three examples of a group that might constitute an occupational community.

5. What do organizational myths tell you about an organization's culture?

6. What are the six kinds of rites that may be used in an organization?

7. What is the potential danger of manipulating symbols?

8. Why might a strong culture be unhelpful in a time of environmental turbulence? Which of the three mechanisms for managing transaction costs discussed by Wilkins and Ouchi is appropriate in such times?

9. How might countercultures promote adaptability? What approach to deviance does this suggest for the organization?

10. What are Feldman's three phases of socialization?

11. Use Van Maanen's list to evaluate the socialization strategies of the military's basic training.

12. Contrast Etzioni's, Kanter's, and Staw and Salancik's views of commitment. What does each focus on?

13. What are the relationships found in research between job satisfaction and commitment and between job performance and commitment?

14. According to the research, does the relationship between commitment and turnover and between job satisfaction and turnover that is found in the United States hold true for other countries?

15. What four responses have been posited in the face of job dissatisfaction?

16. Why does the probability of finding an acceptable job figure in Mobley's turnover model?

REFERENCES

Administrative Science Quarterly. (1983). Vol. 28, no. 3.

Adler, Nancy J. (1986). *International Dimensions of Organizational Behavior.* Boston: PWS-KENT.

Allaire, Y., and Firsirotu, M. E. (1984). Theories of organizational culture. *Organizational Studies* 5:193–226.

Barley, S. R. (1983). Semiotics and the study of occupational and organizational cultures. *Administrative Science Quarterly* 28:393–413.

Bates, P. (1984). The impact of organizational culture on approaches to organizational problem-solving. *Organizational Studies* 5:43–66.

Cole, R. E. (1979). *Work, Mobility, and Participation.* Berkeley: University of California Press.

Curry, J. P., Wakefield, D. S., Price, J. L., and Mueller, C. W. (1986). On causal ordering of job satisfaction and organizational commitment. *Academy of Management Journal* 29:847–858.

Deal, T. E., and Kennedy, A. A. (1982). *Corporate Cultures: The Rights and Rituals of Corporate Life.* Reading, MA: Addison-Wesley.

Duncan, W. J. (1989). Organizational culture: Getting a fix on an elusive concept. *Academy of Management Executive.* In C. Hampden-Turner (1990), *Charting the Corporate Mind.* New York: Free Press.

Enz, C. A. (1986). New directions for cross-cultural studies: Linking organizational and societal cultures. In R. N. Farmer (ed.), *Advances in International Comparative Management,* vol. 2. Greenwich, CT: JAI Press, pp. 173–189.

Etzioni, A. (1961). *A Comparative Analysis of Complex Organizations.* New York: Free Press.

Farrell, D. (1983). Exit, voice, loyalty, and neglect as responses to job dissatisfaction: A multidimensional scaling study. *Academy of Management Journal* 26:596–607.

Feldman, D. C. (1981). The multiple socialization of organization members. *Academy of Management Review* 6:309–318.

Garfinkle, H. (1967). *Studies in Ethnomethodology.* Englewood Cliffs, NJ: Prentice-Hall.

Geertz, C. (1973). *The Interpretation of Culture.* New York: Basic Books.

Hirschman, A. O. (1970). *Exit, Voice and Loyalty: Responses to Decline in Firms, Organizations, and States.* Cambridge, MA: Harvard University Press.

Hofstede, G. (1984). *Culture's Consequences.* Beverly Hills, CA: Sage Publications.

Jones, G. R. (1983). Psychological orientation and the process of organizational socialization: An interactionist perspective. *Academy of Management Review* 8:464–474.

Kanter, R. M. (1968). Commitment and social organization: A study of commitment mechanisms in utopian communities. *American Sociological Review* 33:499–517.

Kanter, R. (1983). *The Changemasters.* New York: Simon & Schuster.

Kerr, J., and Slocum, J. W. (1987). Managing corporate culture through reward systems. *Academy of Management Executive* 1:99–107.

Kroeber, A. L., and Kluckhohn, C. (1952). *Culture: A Critical Review of Concepts and Definitions.* Cambridge, MA: Harvard University Press.

Laurent, A. (1983). The cultural diversity of Western conceptions of management. *International Studies of Management and Organization* 13:75–96.

Levi-Strauss, C. (1958). *Anthropologie Structurel.* Paris: Librairie Plon.

Lincoln, J. R. (1989). Employee work attitudes and management practices in the U.S. and Japan: Evidence from a large comparative survey. *California Management Review* 32:89–106.

Lincoln, J., Olson, J., and Hanada, M. (1978). Cultural effects on organizational structure: The case of Japanese firms in the United States. *American Sociological Review* 43:829–847.

Litwin, G. H., and Stringer, R. A. (1968). *Motivation and Organization Climate.* Boston: Harvard Business School of Divinity Research.

Luthans, J., McCaul, H. S., and Dodd, N. C. (1985). Organizational commitment: A comparison of American, Japanese, and Korean employees. *Academy of Management Journal* 28, no. 1: 213–219, 292.

Mahle, J. (1988). The quest for organizational meaning: Identifying and interpreting the symbolism in organizational stories. *Administration and Society* 20:344–368.

Malinowski, B. (1944). *A Scientific Theory of Culture and Other Essays.* New York: Galaxy Books.

March, J., and Simon, H. (1958). *Organizations.* New York: John Wiley.

Martin, J., Feldman, M. S., Hatch, M. J., and Sitkin, S. B. (1983). The uniqueness paradox in organizational stories. *Administrative Science Quarterly* 28:438–453.

Martin, J., and Siehl, C. (1983). Organizational culture and counterculture: An uneasy symbiosis. *Organizational Dynamics* Autumn:52–64.

al-Meer, A. R. A. (1989). Organizational commitment: A comparison of Westerners, Asians, and Saudis. *International Studies of Management and Organization* 19:74–84.

Meyer, J. P., Paunonen, S. V., Gellotly, I. R., Giffin, R. D., and Jackson, D. N. (1989). Organizational commitment and job performance: It's the nature of the commitment that counts. *Journal of Applied Psychology* 74:152–156.

Meyer, J. W., and Rowan, B. (1977). Institutionalized organizations: Formal structure as myth and ceremony. *American Journal of Sociology* 83:340–363.

Mobley, W. H. (1977). Intermediate linkages in the relationship between job satisfaction and employee turnover. *Journal of Applied Psychology* 62:237–240.

Morey, N. C., and Luthans, F. (1985). Refining the displacement of culture and the use of scenes and themes in organizational studies. *Academy of Management Review* 10:219–229.

Mowday, R. T., Porter, L. W., and Steers, R. M. (1982). *Employee-Organization Linkages.* New York: Academic Press.

O'Reilly, C. A. (1989). Corporations, culture, and commitment. *California Management Review* 31:9–25.

Organizational Dynamics (1983). Vol. 12, no. 2.

Ouchi, W. G. (1981). *Theory Z: How American Companies Can Meet the Japanese Challenge.* Reading, MA: Addison-Wesley.

Pascale, R. T. (1985). The paradox of 'corporate culture': Reconciling ourselves to socialization. *California Management Review* Winter: 29–33.

Pascale, R. T. (1990). *Managing on the Edge.* New York: Simon & Schuster.

Pascale, R. T., and Athos, A. G. (1981). *The Art of Japanese Management.* New York: Simon & Schuster.

Peters, T. J. (1978). Symbols, patterns and settings: An optimistic case for getting things done. *Organizational Dynamics* 7:3–23.

Peters, T. (1987). *Thriving on Chaos.* New York: Knopf.

Peters, T. J., and Waterman, R. H. (1982). *In Search of Excellence.* New York: Harper & Row.

Pfeffer, J. (1981). Management as symbolic interaction: The creation and maintenance of organizational paradigms. In L. L. Cummings and B. M. Staw (eds.), *Research in Organizational Behavior.* Greenwich, CT: JAI Press.

Radcliffe-Brown, A. R. (1952). *Structure and Function in Primitive Society.* London: Oxford University Press.

Reichers, A. E. (1985). A review and reconceptualization of organizational commitment. *Academy of Management Review* 10:465–476.

Reichers, A. E. (1987). An interactionist perspective on newcomer socialization rates. *Academy of Management Review* 12:278–287.

Roberts, K. H., Rousseau, D. M., and La Porte, T. R. (In press). The culture of high reliability: Quantitative and qualitative assessment aboard nuclear powered aircraft carriers. *Journal of High Technology and Management Research.*

Salancik, G. R. (1977). Commitment and the control of organizational behavior and relief. In B. M. Staw and G. R. Salancik (eds.), *New Directions in Organizational Behavior.* Chicago: St. Clair Press.

Sathe, V. (1983). Implications of corporate culture: A manager's guide to action. *Organizational Dynamics,* Autumn, 523.

Sathe, V. (1985). *Culture and Related Corporate Realities.* Homewood, IL: Irwin.

Schein, E. H. (1971). The individual, the organization, and the career: A conceptual scheme. *Journal of Applied Behavioral Science* 7:401–426.

Schein, E. (1985). *Organizational Culture and Leadership.* San Francisco: Jossey-Bass.

Schein, E. H. (1990). Organizational culture. *American Psychologist* 45:109–119.

Staw, B. M. (1977). Two sides of commitment. Paper presented at the National Meeting of the Academy of Management, Orlando, Florida.

Staw, B. M. (1984). Organizational behavior: A review and reformulation of the field's outcome variables. In M. R. Rosenzweig and L. W. Porter (eds.), *Annual Review of Psychology,* vol. 35. Palo Alto, CA: Annual Reviews, Inc., pp. 627–666.

Staw, B. M., McKechnie, P. I., and Puffer, S. M. (1983). The justification of organizational performance. *Administrative Science Quarterly* 28:582–600.

Staw, B. M., and Oldham, G. R. (1978). Reconsidering our dependent variables: A critique and empirical study. *Academy of Management Journal* 21:439–559.

Steers, R. M., and Mowday, R. T. (1981). Employee turnover and post decision accommodation processes. In L. L. Cummings and B. M. Staw (eds.), *Research in Organizational Behavior*. Greenwich, CT: JAI Press.

Stevenson, Richard W. (1989). "Watch out Macy's, here comes Nordstrom's." *The New York Times Magazine*, August 27, 1989, pp. 34–35, 38–40.

Terborg, J. R., and Lee, T. W. (1984). A predictive study of turnover rates. *Academy of Management Journal* 27:793–810.

Trice, H. M., and Beyer, J. M. (1984). Studying organizational cultures through rites and ceremonials. *Academy of Management Review* 9:653–669.

Van Maanen, J. (1978). People processing: Strategies of organizational socialization. *Organizational Dynamics* 7:18–36.

Van Maanen, J., and Barley, S. R. (1984). Occupational communities: Culture and control in organizations. In B. M. Staw and L. L. Cummings (eds.), *Research in Organizational Behavior*, vol. 6. Greenwich, CT: JAI Press.

Van Maanen, J., and Schein, E. H. (1979). Toward a theory of organizational socialization. In B. M. Staw (ed.), *Research in Organizational Behavior*, vol. 1. Greenwich, CT: JAI Press, pp. 209–265.

Weick, K. E. (1979). Cognitive processes in organizations. In B. M. Staw (ed.), *Research in Organizations*, vol. 1. Greenwich, CT: JAI Press, pp. 41–73.

Weick, K. E. (1987). Organizational culture and high reliability. *California Management Review* 29:112–127.

Wiener, Y. (1982). Commitment in organizations: A normative view. *Academy of Management Review* 7:418–428.

Wilkins, A. (1983). The culture audit: A tool for understanding organizations. *Organizational Dynamics* 12:24–38.

Wilkins, A. L., and Ouchi, W. G. (1983). Efficient cultures: Exploring the relationship between culture and organizational performance. *Administrative Science Quarterly* 28:468–481.

Zald, M. N. (1963). Comparing analysis and measurement of organizational goals: The case of correctional institutions for delinquents. *The Sociological Quarterly* 4:206–230.

How We Get Tasks Done

Groups and Group Conflict: How Workers Work Together

CHAPTER OVERVIEW

The objective of this chapter is to examine issues connected with how we get things done in organizations. The chapter examines concepts and evidence regarding the importance to organizations of groups and team efforts.

THEME CASE

"The Hardy Boys and the Microkids Create a New Machine" relates how a team of 30 young computer specialists were selected, hired, and challenged with the highly complex task of building a supercomputer in six months.

CHAPTER OUTLINE

- What Is a Group?
- Group Characteristics
- Group Effectiveness
- Intergroup Relations
- Intergroup Conflict
- Summary
- Managerial Insight

KEY DEFINITIONS

Group   any two or more people who interact with one another such that each person
influences and is influenced by the other.

Group norms   informal rules that groups
adopt to regulate group member behavior.

Conformity   yielding to group pressures
when no direct request to comply with the
group is made.

Cohesiveness   the spirit of closeness, or
lack of it, in a group.

Deviance   when individuals fail to respond
to pressures toward uniformity placed on
them by groups.

Conflict   disagreement, tension, or other
difficulties among two or more parties.

Additional Terms
Group structure
Position
Status
Ascribed vs. achieved status

Role
Idiosyncrasy credits
Expected, perceived, and enacted roles
Comparison levels
Groupthink
Return-potential model
Free-rider effect
Social loafing
Polarization
Social comparison
Persuasive argument
Group effectiveness
Social facilitation
Social inhibition
Ethnocentric relations
Dynamic conservatism
Goal, cognitive, affective, and behavioral
    conflict
Avoidance
Accommodation
Competition
Compromise
Collaboration
Mediation
Arbitration

THE HARDY BOYS AND THE MICROKIDS CREATE A NEW MACHINE

The basement of Westborough, subterranean at the front of Building 14A/B and at ground level in back, was one of the places in Data General's widening empire where machines were conceived, designed, labored over in prototypes, and sometimes brought to life. . . .

[Tom] West came to Data General in 1974, joining Carl Alsing and the other engineers who were attempting to bring the first Eclipse to life. To Alsing, West appeared to be just a good, competent circuit designer, but strikingly adept at finding and fixing the flaws in a computer. "A great debugger," Alsing considered him. "He was so fast in the lab I felt I was barely adequate to hold the probes of the oscilloscope for him." Alsing took a shine to his new colleague almost at once. . . .

When the first Eclipse went to market and the group's original leader began to take leave . . . , West asked that he be given command of the team. West seemed to Alsing the logical choice for the job: "He was the smartest guy around." . . .

West had a way of making ordinary things seem special; in one case a 32-bit Eclipse was being transformed into the occasion for an adventure. West's ardor for it seemed to spread the way his neologisms did. Others beside Alsing were affected.

For Rosemarie Seale, the main excitement began after EGO was canceled and everyone but West seemed ready to pack it in. "Tom's obviously made some decision which I know nothing about," she said. "He's decided he isn't gonna take his bat and ball and go home." Later, she would say, "I wanted to work for him. I could have gotten more pay elsewhere. I didn't understand it all, but I knew I wanted to work for him. I wanted to be part of that effort." . . .

Between the summer of 1978 and the fall of that year, West's team roughly doubled in size. To the dozen or so old hands—old in a relative sense—were added a dozen neophytes, fresh from graduate schools of electrical engineering and computer science. The newcomers were known as "the kids." West was the boss, and he had a sort of adjutant—an architect of the electronic school—and two main lieutenants, each of whom had a sublieutenant or two. One lieutenant managed the crew that worked on

From Tracy Kidder, *The Soul of a New Machine*, pp. 49–66, 111–122, 286–288. Copyright © 1981 by John Tracy Kidder. Reprinted by permission of Little, Brown and Co.

physical machine with the programs that would tell it what to do. To join this part of the group, which Alsing ran, was to become one of "the Microkids." There were also a draftsman and some technicians. The group's numbers changed from time to time. But usually they totaled about thirty.

There was, it appeared, a mysterious rite of initiation through which, in one way or another, almost every member of the team passed. The term that the old hands used for this rite—West invented the term, not the practice—was "signing up." By signing up for the project you agreed to do whatever was necessary for success. You agreed to forsake, if necessary, family, hobbies, and friends—if you had any of these left (and you might not if you had signed up too many times before). From a manager's point of view, the practical virtues of the ritual were manifold. Labor was no longer coerced. Labor volunteered. When you signed up you in effect declared, "I want to do this job and I'll give it my heart and soul." The vice president of engineering, Carl Carman, who knew the term, said much later on: "Sometimes I worried that I pushed too hard. I tried not to push any harder than I would on myself. That's why, by the way, you have to go through the signing-up. To be sure you're not conning anybody."

The rite was not accomplished with formal declarations, as a rule. Among the old hands, a statement such as, "Yeah, I'll do that," could constitute the act of signing up, and often it was done tacitly—as when, without being ordered to do so, Alsing took the role of chief recruiter. . . .

The Eclipse Group solicited applications. One candidate listed "family life" as his main avocation. Alsing and another of West's lieutenants felt wary when they saw this. Not that they wanted to exclude family men, being such themselves. But Alsing wondered: "He seems to be saying he doesn't want to sign up." The other lieutenant pondered the application. "I don't think he'd be happy here," he said to himself. The applicant's grades were nothing special, and they turned him away.

Grades mattered in this first winnowing of applications—not only as an indication of ability but also as a basis for guessing about a recruit's capacity for long, hard work—and with a few exceptions they turned down those whose grades were merely good.

Alsing hoped to recruit some female engineers, but in 1978 they were still quite scarce. Only a few young women applied, and Alsing hired one, who had fine credentials.

When they liked the looks of an application, they invited the young man—it was usually a young man—to Westborough, and the elders would interview him, one by one. If he was a potential Microkid, the recruit's interview with Alsing was often the crucial one. And a successful interview with Alsing constituted a signing up.

Alsing would ask the young engineer, "What do you want to do?"

Exactly what the candidate said—whether he was interested in one aspect of computers or another—didn't matter. Indeed, Alsing didn't care if a recruit showed no special fondness for computers; and the fact an engineer had one of his own and liked to play with it did not argue for him.

If the recruit seemed to say in reply, "Well, I'm just out of grad school and I'm looking at a lot of possibilities and I'm not sure what field I want to get into yet," then Alsing would usually find a polite way to abbreviate the interview. But if the recruit said, for instance, "I'm really interested in computer design," then Alsing would prod. . . .

"There's a thing you learn at Data General, if you work here for any period of time," said West's lieutenant of hardware, Ed Rasala. "That nothing ever happens unless you push it." To at least some people upstairs, this condition took the name "competition for resources." As a strategy of management, it has a long lineage. "Throw down a challenge," writes Dale Carnegie in that venerable bible of stratagems dressed up as homilies, *How to Win Friends and Influence People.*

In a sense, the competition between Eagle and North Carolina was institutionalized; each project lay in the domain of a different vice president. But that may have been accidental. West's boss, who was the vice president of engineering, Carl Carman, remarked that he had worked at IBM and that compared to competition among divisions there, rivalry among engineering teams at Data General resembled "Sunday school." Moreover, Carman said in a company with a "mature product line" like Data General's, situations naturally occur in which not enough large new computers are needed for every team of computer builders to put one of its own out the door. "And yeah," Carman continued, "the competition is fostered." He said that [Edson] de Castro [one of the three founders of Data General] liked to see a little competition stirred up among teams. Let them compete with their ideas for new products, and bad ideas, as well as the negative points of good ones, are likely to get identified inside the company and not out in the marketplace. That was the general strategy, Carman said. What it now meant downstairs, to the Eclipse Group, was that they not only had to invent their new computer but also had to struggle for the resources to build it. Resources meant, among other things, the active cooperation of such so-called support groups as Software. You had to persuade such groups that your idea had merit and would get out the door, or else you wouldn't get much help—and then your machine almost certainly wouldn't get out the door.

Here's how it looked to West: The company could not afford to field two new big computers; Data General had made a large investment in North Carolina as a place where major computers would be built; and although the Eclipse Group's engineers had good technical reputations, North Carolina's had better ones. The game was fixed for North Carolina and all the support groups knew it.

So West started out by calling Eagle "insurance"—it would be there in case something went wrong down South. Thus he avoided an open fight and thus he could argue that the support groups should hedge their bets and put at least a little effort into this project, too. As for North Carolina's superior reputation, West never stopped suggesting to people around Westborough that their talent had been slighted. His message was: "Let's show them what we can do."

"West takes lemons and makes lemonade," observed Alsing. From the first rule—that you must compete for resources—it followed that if your group was vying with another for the right to get a new machine out the door, then you had to promise to finish yours sooner, or at least just as soon as the other team promised. West had said that the Eclipse Group would do EGO in a year. North Carolina had said, okay, they'd finish their machine in a year. In turn, West had said that Eagle would come to life in a year. West said he felt he had to pursue "what's-the-earliest-date-by-which-you-can't-prove-you-won't-be-finished" scheduling in this case. "We have to do it in a year to have any chance." But you felt obliged to set such a schedule anyway, in order to demonstrate to the ultimate bosses strong determination.

Promising to achieve a nearly impossible schedule was a way of signing up—the subject of the third rule, as I saw it. Signing up required, of course, that you fervently desire the right to build your machine and that you do whatever was necessary for success, including putting in lots of overtime, for no extra pay.

The fourth rule seemed to say that if the team succeeded, those who had signed up would get a reward. No one in the group felt certain that stock options were promised in the case of success. "But it sure as hell was suggested!" said one of the Microkids. All members of the team insisted that with or without the lure of gold, they would have worked hard. But for a while, at least, the implied promise did boost spirits, which were generally high anyway.

I think that those were the rules they were playing by, and when I recited them to some of the team's managers, they seemed to think so, too. But Alsing said there was probably another rule that stated, "One never plays explicitly by these rules."

The attempt to turn those ideas into silicon and wire and microcode had begun. Now they had to create a complete design and do it in a hurry. Carman made it policy that members of the team could come and go more or less as they pleased. These were confident, aggressive young engineers—"racehorses," West liked to say—and they were about to be put under extreme pressure. Carman hoped that by allowing them to stomp out of the basement at any time without fear of reprisal, they would be providing an adequate "escape valve."

At last, by fall of 1978, the preliminaries were complete. The kids had been hired, the general sign-up had been performed, the promises suggested, and the escape valve established. Then West turned up the steam.

You're a Microkid, like Jon Blau. You arrived that summer and now you've learned how to handle Trixie [a computer used to write the code needed to build Eagle]. Your immediate boss, Chuck Holland, has given you a good overall picture of the microcode to be written, and he's broken down the total job into several smaller ones and has offered you your choice. You've decided that you want to write the code for many of the arithmetic operations in Eagle's instruction set. You always liked math and felt that this will help you understand it in new, insightful ways. You've started working on your piece of the puzzle. You can see that it's a big job, but you know you can do it. Right now you're doing a lot of reading, to prepare yourself. Then one day you're sitting at your desk studying Booth's algorithm, a really nifty procedure for doing multiplication, when Alsing comes by and tells you, "There's a meeting."

You troop into a conference room with most of the other new hires, joking, feeling a little nervous, and there waiting for you are the brass: the vice president of engineering, another lower-level but important executive, and West, sitting in a corner chewing on a toothpick. The speeches are brief. Listening intently, you hear all about the history of 32-bit superminis. These have been around for awhile, but sales are really picking up. DEC's starting to turn out VAXes like jelly beans, and the word is DEC'll probably introduce a new model of VAX in about nine months. No one's saying it's your fault, but Eagle's late, very late. It really must be designed and brought to life and be ready to go by April. Really. In just six months. That won't be easy, but the brass think you can do it. That's why you were hired—you're the cream of a very fine crop. Everything depends on you now, they say.

You feel good about yourself and what you're doing when you leave the meeting. You go right back to your desk, of course, and pick up Booth's algorithm. In a little while, though, you feel you need a break. You look around for another Microkid to share coffee with you. But everyone is working, assiduously, peering into manuals and cathode-ray tubes. You go back to your reading. Then suddenly, you feel it, like a trickle of sweat down your back. "I've gotta hurry," you say to yourself. "I've gotta get this reading down and write my code. This is just one little detail. There's a hundred of these. I better get this little piece of code done today."

Practically the next time you look up, it's midnight, but you've done what you set out to do. You leave the basement thinking: "This is life. Accomplishment. Challenges. I'm in control of a crucial part of this big machine." You look back from your car at the blank, brick, monolithic back of Building 14A/B and say to yourself, "What a great place to work."

What a way to design a computer! "There's no grand design," thinks [Hardy Boy] Josh Rosen. "People are just reaching out in the dark, touching hands." Rosen is having some problems with his own piece of the design. He knows he can solve them, if he's just given the time. But the managers keep saying, "There's no time." Okay. Sure. It's a rush job. But this is ridiculous. No one seems to be in control; nothing's ever explained. Foul up, however, and the managers come at you from all sides.

"The whole management structure," said Rosen. "Anyone in Harvard Business School would have barfed." . . .

In fact, the team designed the computer in something like six months, and may have set a record for speed. The task was quite complex.

From one angle, the task was to make an engine that could obey—without fail and at great speed—each of roughly four hundred chores named in Eagle's instruction set.

In the fall of 1980 the Eclipse Group was disbanded and its members dispersed into several new and smaller groups. Some of the old crew mourned the team's passing. Many others, however, shrugged. They felt that the group's demise had been inevitable.

West added: "It was a summer romance. But that's all right. Summer romances are some of the best things that ever happen."

Long before it disbanded formally, the Eclipse Group, in order to assist the company in applying for patents on the new machine, had gathered and had tried to figure which engineers had contributed to Eagle's patentable features. Some who attended found those meetings painful. There was bickering. Harsh words were occasionally exchanged. Alsing, who during the project had set aside the shield of technical command, came in for some abuse—Why should his name go on any patents, what had he done? Someone even asked that question regarding West. Ironically, perhaps, those meetings illustrated that the building of Eagle really did constitute a collective effort, for now that they had finished, they themselves were having a hard time agreeing on what each individual had contributed. But clearly, the team was losing its glue. "It has no function anymore. It's like an afterbirth," said one old hand after the last of the patent meetings.

Shortly after those meetings, Wallach, Alsing, Rasala, and West re-

clearly, the team was losing its glue. "It has no function anymore. It's like an afterbirth," said one old hand after the last of the patent meetings.

Shortly after those meetings, Wallach, Alsing, Rasala, and West received telegrams of congratulations from North Carolina's leader. That was a classy gesture, all agreed. The next day Eagle went out the company's door.

What Is a Group?

The task was to build a supercomputer in six months. To accomplish this complex task, a team of 30 engineers and computer specialists was assembled by Data General Corporation under the leadership of Tom West. Motivated by the excitement and challenge of the task, the Eclipse Group developed into a cohesive unit with its own culture and rites of initiation. The story of the Eclipse Group clearly illustrates many of the pitfalls, challenges, and successes of groups. We can observe group activities from task inception to group formation and development to cohesion, intergroup competition, and group dissolution. We can see group effectiveness measured as well.

To this point we have addressed issues concerned with how organizations are organized. We have seen organizations state goals, use those goals—along with other influences—to shape their structure, and define their own culture. We saw that organizations socialize their members, manipulating their acceptance of the organization's culture. Now we turn to some of the results of those early processes, the questions involved with how we get work done—how people work together. Among the topics to be explored are the dynamics of groups, communication among members of organizations, power, and decision making. We begin this examination by looking at groups and teams. The subjects to be covered include the group characteristics and formation; group conformity, cohesiveness, and deviance; group performance; intergroup relations; and group conflict.

Why is it important that we examine such issues? After all, we live in an individualistic society that highly values individual ability and effort and places less value on collective activity (Hofstede, 1980). We need to study groups because little work in the typical modern organization is done by individuals working alone. As we saw in the Data General case, a manager accountable for the accomplishment of certain tasks will find that he must deal at every turn with groups of anywhere from two to hundreds of people. Numerous studies show that managers spend most of their time dealing with other people, and a lot of that time in some sort of group function (see, for example, Mintzberg, 1973; Davis and Luthans, 1980; McCall et al., 1980).

Indeed, the importance of working together is likely to increase because organizations are becoming increasingly complex. They are often characterized by complicated procedures and interdependencies and the need for cooperative effort by people possessing many functional specialties. In such organizations, no one person or department can work on important matters in isolation. These functions require the interlinking of numerous groups, each possessing specialized skills that no one person can possess (Roberts and Gargano, 1989). Recently, some writers have focused on electronic groups at work or on groups formed through use of electronic mail systems (Finholt and Sproull, 1990). Some of the groups seem to behave like social groups.

Despite the obvious importance of groups, some writers believe that management literature has virtually ignored the subject of groups except in studies of organizational development and change (Schneider, 1985). One author (Leavitt, 1975) states that it is possible to ignore groups because American industry and American psychologists make individuals the focus of interest. Leavitt argues that if we took groups seriously, they, not individuals, would be the building blocks of organizations. We would select, train, pay, promote, design jobs for, and fire groups rather than individuals. Groups will not be an important focus of study in organizations until organizations are designed around the group.

What is a group, as far as organizations are concerned? The basic elements of the notion of a group have to do with interdependency or interaction. For a group to exist, its members must be aware that it exists and be motivated to join it (they expect that it will satisfy some of their needs). Over time, groups include role differentiation. Basically, though, a **group** can be defined as any two or more people who interact with one another such that each person influences and is influenced by the other (Shaw, 1981). Much of what follows will address the subject of groups from the assumption that they are formal structures created by management to accomplish a task. We should bear in mind that informal groupings, which evolve from interpersonal interactions not controlled by management, also appear in all organizations.

Group Characteristics

Groups have four basic sets of characteristics. They have to do with the structure of the group, the formation and development of the group, the norms of the group, and the degree to which members are bonded together. This latter characteristic encompasses three areas of study: conformity, cohesiveness, and deviance. It is with the structure, norms, and bonds of groups that we begin our study of groups.

Group Structure

When people begin to interact, individual differences appear. Some people talk more than others, some seem better able to lead, others seem to have more knowledge than the average group member. These differences, which produce inequalities among people along a variety of dimensions, are the basis for the formation of group structure. As differences become apparent, relationships are established among the various parts of the group; those relationships that become stable are referred to as **group structure.** The formation of group structure is one of the basic aspects of group development.

Three major factors influence group structure: (1) the requirements for efficient group performance, or for attaining the goals of the group; (2) the abilities and motivations of group members; and (3) the physical and social environments of groups (Cartwright and Zander, 1968). Groups form for any number of purposes, some to solve problems, as did the Eclipse Group, others for social reasons. Regardless of why they form, their members usually take their goals seriously, and the structures they invent are predicated by those goals. Structure is also influenced by the characteristics of the groups' members; for instance, individuals who like to dominate others may try to establish a centralized power structure with themselves at the center. People who appear knowledgeable may emerge as task leaders. Physical, cultural, and organizational climates directly affect group structuring and provide the opportunity for numerous other variables to influence it, too.

Any number of dimensions can be used to establish group structure. We have discussed many of these dimensions in Chapter 2. One could easily develop a list of characteristics that might be used to identify group structures from that chapter. Here we focus on only two sets of group structural variables: position (or status) and roles.

Position and Status   A person's **position** in a group is his place in the social system. It identifies his relative standing with regard to such dimensions as leadership, power, and knowledge. **Status** is the evaluation of that position by others. It is the rank or prestige accorded the position. **Ascribed status** is attributed to people through no action of their own, because of such factors as birth, sex, or age. **Achieved status** is based on individual accomplishment and includes such factors as education, work experience, and abilities.

Status contributes to a number of group processes and behaviors. For instance, high-status people both receive and initiate more communication than do low-status people and send more positive and more task-relevant messages. The high-status person is in a culturally valued position in the group. Once a person gains status in the group, she builds up **idiosyncracy credits,** or a bank account of credits that allows her to deviate without reprisal later on. These credits can be used to lead the group in a new direction (see Chapter 8). Status often, but not always, protects a person from severe sanctions for unacceptable behavior. For example, a study of destructive obedience in the military (in which an officer carries out orders from a superior with disastrous consequences) found that the superior officer who gave the orders was held more responsible for the outcome than his subordinate (Hamilton, 1978).

Role Each position in a group structure has associated with it a **role,** which is the set of behaviors expected of the occupant of the position. The boss is expected to do certain things that are not expected of the custodian. The reverse is also true. Roles have three aspects (Shaw, 1981). The **expected** role is what is expected of a person in a particular position. The **perceived** role is the set of behaviors the occupant of the position believes he should engage in. The **enacted** role is the set of behaviors the occupant actually carries out.

The role a person chooses to enact is, at least in part, a function of the impression he wants to make on other people. Roles exert important influences on the perceptions and evaluations of individuals made by other group members. Because role expectations specify the kinds of behaviors the occupant is expected to display, roles often bias perceptions about the role occupant. For example, students generally expect their professors to be smart and may assume that an English professor who makes a statement about the United States economy is right, even though economics is not his field of expertise.

Individuals occupy different roles in different groups. In most instances, the behaviors specified by these roles are not incompatible as long as different roles are not salient at the same time. Thus, for example, military officers are often seen in church even though they belong to an organization that specifically teaches people to kill. Under some circumstances, however, an individual with different roles in different groups is called on to enact incompatible roles simultaneously. This frequently happens to working mothers, who are expected to be at work while they need to care for a sick child. When this happens, the person will resolve the conflict by enacting the role required by the group that is most important to her (Killian, 1952).

Group structure has important implications for managers, who, like Tom West, are often in a position to structure new groups to do various things. West essentially structured the Eclipse Group based on the skills needed to accomplish each of its two primary tasks. A manager would do well to think about what he wants his group to accomplish and then analyze what structure will facilitate achieving those goals. Perhaps he wants to reduce (or increase) the possibility that structuring will take place on the basis of power. Perhaps he wishes to maximize differences on a particular dimension, such as knowledge. Managers must be sensitive to the effect status has on group members and to how information about status helps us understand what is expected of us in any situation and what is expected of other people. People play many different roles—usually more than one role in their work organizations. Managers should attempt to make these roles compatible and, where that is impossible, allow sufficient flexibility that employees do not get into terrible conflict situations. The feature "Temporary Groups" illustrates how managers might develop temporary groups with different structures to accomplish various goals.

FEATURE: *Temporary Groups*

A characteristic of many modern organizations is that they utilize a variety of working groups whose existence is a temporary situation, rather than a permanent part of the formal structure. These temporary groups are organized to achieve a specific purpose and usually go out of existence when they have completed their work. Members are brought together on either a full-time or part-time basis to comprise a specific blend of expertise, experience viewpoint, or implementation capability. They are expected to pool their knowledge and skill and attain objectives that no formal unit in the organization could achieve. Such systems are characteristic of the more flexible, innovative style of management being practiced by many organizations. They rely heavily on members' ability to function effectively in group settings.

One variety of temporary system is the task force, usually formed for the purpose of attacking a problem. They most frequently require a part-time commitment by members drawn together because of their ability to contribute to solving a problem. One authority points out that the distinguishing characteristics of task forces in contrast to ordinary committees are that they are formed to accomplish a task; they are temporary; they have operational responsibility to accomplish something, not just make suggestions; and they build collaboration by cutting across departmental boundaries and professional disciplines.

Kunde provides a case study that demonstrates use of task forces in local government [in Dayton, Ohio]. During the late 1960s and early 1970s urban areas began to experience many problems that traditional city governments were not organized to handle. . . . The existing structure and procedures appeared to be making little headway in resolving these problems. . . . A "Task Force on Task Forces" was created, and . . . it created the following task forces: Youth, Racism, Crime, Housing, Economic Development, Downtown Dayton, Future, and Organizational Improvement. . . .

The task force effort in Dayton lasted for two years. Many positive outcomes were reported as were some problems. New programs were developed, often in cooperation with community groups, and policy changes were made in the way the city operated. According to Kunde, the involvement of employees at all levels in the most significant issues of the organization also had a positive impact on the internal operations because it opened communication across units, levels, and subgroups.

Another variety of temporary system is the project team. Although similar to, or indistinguishable from, task forces in some situations, the project team is usually assembled to take responsibility for the management of a project from inception to conclusion. Rather than solving a specific problem or coming to grips with an issue, its role is to handle a project—the design and manufacture of a machine, the development of a new system, the creation of an organizational unit. . . .

Project teams often occur within the framework of "matrix structure," organizational designs in which specialists are affiliated with traditional functional units . . . but are also assigned to interdisciplinary teams to pool talents on their projects.

Source: From W. B. Eddy, *The Manager and the Working Group* (New York: Praeger, 1985), pp. 164–166. Copyright © 1985 by W. B. Eddy. Reprinted by permission of the author.

Group Formation

Groups form and develop over time, and people join groups because groups meet fundamental needs. At Data General, individuals joined the Eclipse Group for different reasons, though most joined because of the challenge of building a supercomputer in such a short time frame. Two researchers (Thibaut and Kelley, 1959) explained why people join groups, by proposing that interactions are evaluated by comparison to certain standards and that the most desirable possibility is the one chosen.

According to this view, each individual has internal standards called **comparison levels** (CLs) and a comparison level for an alternative (CL/alt).

The CL is a subjective standard against which an individual evaluates the attractiveness of an interpersonal relationship. The CL is a consequence of the individual's past interpersonal relationships and will be somewhere near the middle of the range of those relationships, ordered according to how satisfactory those relationships were. Once the CL is established, a person rates as positive any relationship that falls above it in terms of outcomes and as negative any relationship that falls below it. One can assume that each new experience modifies the CL in some way, though the movement of the threshold up or down that results from any one interaction may be negligible.

A person uses the CL/alt to decide whether to stay in a relationship or leave it. Conceivably, a person could choose to enter into or maintain an unattractive relationship if it is the most attractive one available at the time, that is, above his CL/alt. For example, a person may elect to remain the subordinate of a disliked boss if he works in an industry or region undergoing hard times.

Three facets of interpersonal attraction have been studied in relation to group formation: proximity, similarity, and perceived ability of others. Proximity and similarity will be discussed later in the chapter when we cover intergroup contact. Here we will look into perceived ability, which appears to be a determinant of the desire to affiliate.

People want to associate with others who are successful or others they judge to be similar in ability to themselves. Members of the Microkids and the Hardy Boys clearly identified with the enthusiasm, skills, and abilities of Tom West, as well as with each other's skills.

Until recently the standard model of group development (Heinen and Jacobson, 1976) focused on developmental stages and the interventions that might be appropriate to each stage. Stage one is the formation stage, when relationships among individuals and goals are formed (e.g., Jacobson, 1956) and methods of establishing boundaries for behavior are established (e.g., Tuckman, 1965). The second stage is a highly involved storming period, when disharmony develops from conflict over leadership and goals. If managed properly—not suppressed—this disharmony gives way in the third stage, characterized by a standardizing process, which brings about harmony and unity. The fourth and final stage is achievement of an effective, well-integrated group (McGrath, 1984).

This predictable schedule of group development has recently been challenged (Gersick, 1988). It was shown that group development proceeds in interaction cycles, not in some linear order (Bell, 1982; Poole, 1983), and that there are many possible sequences in which decisions can develop in groups. The initial meetings of groups seem important determinants of the way they will formulate and deal with problems. Groups make quick decisions about their strategies, suggesting that managers should plan initial group meetings carefully because norms will quickly develop. The feature "The Effective Use of Meetings" illustrates how meetings can be structured to maximize the benefits to be obtained from them.

FEATURE: *The Effective Use of Meetings*

Managers spend a great deal of time in meetings and are often frustrated with the time expended and lack of results. Studies on time management consistently indicate that meetings rank near the top (along with telephone calls) as a major time waster. Too frequently, goals and ground rules are not clear, there is chitchat that is unrelated to the topic, some members talk much more than necessary while others say nothing, and time runs out before the issue is solved. . . . [A]chieving effective meetings is a building and learning process that takes time.

Here is my laundry list of keys to having successful meetings. . . .

1. Remember that meetings are group phenomena, and that people come with more than just information about the topic. They bring their values, fears, habits, needs, and all the rest of their humanness.

2. Whenever possible, carefully select those who will be present. Many meetings suffer because too many people are present, the wrong people are present, or those present do not bring with them the necessary expertise. Most authorities place the optimal number for a problem-solving meeting at less than eight.

3. Be clear about the purpose of the meeting. Before the meeting, at the beginning, and throughout, if necessary, help the group be clear about why they are meeting, what the problem is, what is expected, what outcome is sought. . . .

4. Be specific about the kind(s) of meeting being held . . . : Informational . . . ; Consultation . . . ; Problem solving . . . ; Legislative . . . ; Social-emotional . . . Several of these may occur in the same meeting, and the leader may segment the agenda so that one portion is informational, another is problem solving, and so on. . . .

5. Build an agenda. An agenda sent out before the meeting is helpful.

6. Clarify the ground rules.

7. Keep in mind the stages in group development.

8. Help the group transition from divergence to convergence.

9. Deal with problem members.

10. Coping with conflict. [After problem members], the second most worrisome problem for many leaders is conflict. In meetings, conflict takes the form of disagreements, impasses, arguments, and hurt feelings. Social scientists have a fairly clear message: Don't try to avoid conflict, it will only smolder and crop up again. Face it, work on it, and try to resolve it. . . .

11. The leader's role. Those who would lead meetings must make a fundamental decision about the role they wish to play. . . .

Source: From W. B. Eddy, *The Manager and the Working Group* (New York: Praeger, 1985), pp. 158–162. Copyright © 1985 by W. B. Eddy. Reprinted by permission of the author.

Managers also need to monitor the group while the task is in progress. In the middle of the time period allotted to the task, groups reverse their frameworks. During the first half of a group's life it shows little progress, possibly because members do not know what the information they gather can be used for. At calendar midpoint groups experience transitions in their "ways of doing business," enabling them to capitalize on the gradual learning they did in the first half of their life (Gersick, 1988).

Group Norms

Group norms are the informal rules that groups adopt to regulate members' behavior. At Westborough, the Eclipse Group had not only West's "rules" to follow but also their own rites of initiation and behavioral norms. In Chapter 3 we examined these rites and cultural dimensions from the point of view of the entire organization. Norms are characterized by their evaluative nature; that is, they refer to what should be done. Norms represent value judgments about appropriate behavior in social situations. Although they are infrequently written down or even discussed, norms have powerful influence on group behavior. If each individual in a group decided how to behave in each interaction, no one would be able to predict the behavior of any group member; chaos would reign. Norms guide behavior and reduce ambiguity in groups. The feature on Dana Corporation illustrates the kind of norms an organization may have; these are unusual in that they are clearly identified.

FEATURE: *Dana Corporation: Making Norms Explicit*

Dana Corporation, under the leadership in the 1970s of Ren McPherson and [later] Gerry Mitchell, added an important chapter to the book on American management. . . . One of McPherson's first acts as chairman was to reduce the company's existing policy manuals to a one-page operational philosophy. In the mid-1970s that single page was culled to become "The Dana Corporation's 40 Thoughts"—not by the chairman but by a group of Dana employees acting entirely on their own initiative. They wanted to make it even easier for everyone at Dana to read and remember what made the company tick. The "40 Thoughts" are still vital to Dana's remarkable productivity:

> Remember our purpose—to earn money for our shareholders and increase the value of their investment - Recognize people as our most important asset - Help people grow - Promote from within - Remember—people respond to recognition - Share the rewards - Provide stability of income and employment - Decentralize - Provide autonomy - Encourage entrepreneurship - Use corporate committees, task forces - Push responsibility down - Involve everyone - Make every employee a manager - Control only what's important - Promote identity with Dana - Make all Dana people shareholders - Simplify - Use little paper - Keep no files - Communicate fully - Let Dana people know first - Let people set goals and judge their performance - Let the people decide where possible - Discourage conformity - Be professional - Break organizational barriers - Develop pride - Insist on high ethical standards - Focus on markets - Utilize assets fully - Contain investment - Buy, don't make - Balance plants, products, markets - Keep facilities under 500 people - Stabilize production - Develop proprietary products - Anticipate markets needs - Control cash - Deliver reliably - Do what's best for all of Dana.

Source: From T. Peters and N. Austin, *A Passion for Excellence* (New York: Random House, 1985), pp. 340–341. Copyright © 1985 by Tom Peters and Nancy Austin. Reprinted by permission of Random House, Inc.

Groups do not establish norms about every conceivable situation but only with respect to things that are significant to the group. Norms might apply to every member of the group or to only some members. Norms that apply to particular group members usually specify the role of those individuals. Norms vary in the degree to which they are accepted by all members of the group: some are accepted by almost everyone, others by some members and not others. For example, university faculty and students accept the faculty norm of teaching, but students infrequently accept the norm of faculty research. Finally, norms vary in terms of the range of permissible deviation; sanctions, either mild or extreme, are usually applied to people for breaking norms. Norms also differ with respect to the amount of deviation that is tolerable. Some norms require strict adherence, but others do not (Shaw, 1981).

Understanding how group norms develop and why they are enforced is important to managers. Group norms are important determinants of whether a group will be productive, as we saw at Data General. A work group with the norm that its proper role is to help management will be far more productive than one whose norm is to be antagonistic to management. Managers can play a part in setting and changing norms by helping to set norms that facilitate tasks, assessing whether a group's norms are functional, and addressing counterproductive norms with subordinates (Feldman, 1984).

Norms usually develop slowly as groups learn those behaviors that will facilitate their activities. However, this slow development can be short-circuited by critical events or by a group's decision to change norms (Hackman, 1976). According to one writer (Feldman, 1984), most norms develop in one or more of four ways: (1) explicit statements by supervisors or coworkers; (2) critical events in the group's history; (3) primacy, or by virtue of their introduction early in the group's history; and (4) carryover behaviors from past situations. Each of these methods was at work in the Data General case.

Why are group norms enforced? The most important reason is to ensure group survival (Feldman, 1984). They are also enforced to simplify or make predictable the expected behavior of group members. That is, they are enforced to help groups avoid embarrassing interpersonal problems, to express the central values of the group, and to clarify what is distinctive about it.

Conformity, Cohesiveness, and Deviance

Conformity, cohesiveness, and deviance are three key features of groups related to norms. In addition to studying these features, we will examine the free-rider effect and polarization, two group characteristics that reflect conformity and cohesiveness.

Conformity   **Conformity** refers to yielding to group pressures when no direct request to comply with the group is made. A classic study illustrates nicely what conformity is (Asch, 1956). Male college students were asked to participate in visual perception experiments, during which confederates of the experimenter gave incorrect judgments. What did the real subjects do? Thirty-two percent of all responses to this situation conformed to the incorrect answer. However, the distribution of responses is important because they showed a wide range. In one study 13 of the 50 subjects never yielded to the majority on any of the critical trials, whereas 4 subjects yielded on 10 or more trials. So, some subjects conformed, but others did not.

While Asch's work is instructive, it may be misleading. In that study the correct answer was obvious. In most group judgment situations, however, the right answer is not obvious, and groups struggle to reach some consensus. Conformity is more apt to occur in these relatively ambiguous situations than in unambiguous ones.

Four general classes of variables influence conformity to group norms: (1) personality characteristics of group members, (2) stimuli that evoke conformity, (3) situational factors, and (4) intragroup relations (Reitan and Shaw, 1964). Personality characteristics that influence conformity are intelligence, age, self-blame, and authoritarianism. People of low intelligence and those high on self-blame or authoritarianism are more likely to conform than are people with the opposite characteristics.

Stimulus characteristics include all aspects of the situation that are related to the norm to which the individual is conforming. As indicated previously, the more ambiguous these characteristics, the greater the conforming behavior. Situational factors include all aspects of the situation except the stimuli. Group size, unanimity of the majority, and group structure are situational characteristics. Conformity increases with group size up to some point; the point probably depends on the nature of the problem and of the setting. Unanimity of the majority increases conformity, as does decentralized group structure. Intragroup relationships include the kind of pressure exerted, the composition of the group, how successful the group has been in the past, and the degree to which the person identifies with the group. All of these variables influence conformity.

The **return-potential model** (Jackson, 1965) explains conformity to behavioral expectations. It suggests that for each relevant behavior, a curve can be drawn that specifies the amount of potential approval or disapproval (return) an individual will receive from the group. The model is illustrated in Figure 4.1 (page 184) with respect to a group's changing norm about talkativeness at meetings. At the beginning of a group's existence a moderately talkative person receives approval, and a person who shows extreme behavior—either too little or too much talkativeness—receives disapproval. As time passes, the return potential changes. At first, the point of ideal behavior

FIGURE 4.1
*The Return-
Potential Model*

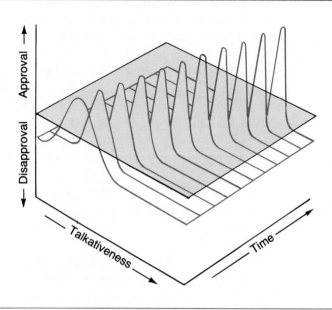

Source: From R. L. Moreland and J. M. Levine (1982), "Socialization in Small Groups," in L. Berkowitz (ed.), *Advances in Experimental Social Psychology* (New York: Academic Press), p. 142. Copyright © 1982 by Academic Press. Reprinted by permission of Academic Press and the authors.

increases; that is, to contribute to the group, people must become more talkative. Then the range of tolerable behavior decreases—the group grants approval for a narrower set of behaviors. Finally, the intensity of the group's feeling increases, and the person receives more positive evaluations for meeting the group's expectations or more negative evaluations for not doing so.

    The group may have the same expectations for all its members, or expectations may vary depending on the individual. Generally, however, those people occupying the same role in a group will be subject to the same expectations. A group's expectations for an individual are based on (1) the group's own characteristics, for example, the need for a particular set of skills; (2) the environment in which it operates, for example, resource availability; and (3) the characteristics of the person being evaluated, for example, her status or abilities (Moreland and Levine, 1982).

Cohesiveness   Another important group characteristic is **cohesiveness,** the spirit of closeness—or lack of it—in a group. Group cohesiveness is "the resultant of all the forces acting on members to remain in the group" (Festinger, 1950, p. 274). Studies of group cohesiveness emphasize the number, strength, and pattern of attractions of group members.

Groups with similar attitudes are more cohesive than groups with dissimilar attitudes, successful groups are more cohesive than unsuccessful groups, and groups with clear paths to goals are more cohesive than groups lacking clear paths. These are commonsense relationships. What is not common sense is that conflict within the group sometimes increases cohesiveness (Wheaton, 1974). It is the nature of this conflict that determines whether it helps or harms cohesiveness. Conflict over principles has negative effects; conflict over matters that assume adherence to principles enhances cohesiveness.

The most important consequences of cohesiveness are probably group viability and productivity. According to many theories of group functioning (e.g., Bennis and Shepard, 1955), a group's first order of business is resolving internal problems. Unless it solves these problems, the group will die. Thus, some minimal cohesiveness must exist if it is to continue to function as a group. One study suggests that homogeneity in group tenure provides a degree of cohesiveness (O'Reilly, Caldwell, and Barnett, 1989). Those who are attracted to a group presumably want it to succeed and thus work hard at helping it obtain its goals. Indeed, highly cohesive groups are more effective at achieving their goals than are uncohesive groups (Hackman and Suttle, 1977; Hare, 1976). Among management's most important tasks, then, are to ensure group cohesiveness and to keep group goals consistent with those of the organization. These tasks are among the functions of socialization (see Chapter 3).

Deviance   In our discussion of decision making (see Chapter 7), we note that groups exert tremendous pressure for uniformity among members, which often results in **deviance**. Although the pressure to conform is great, members of groups do deviate. A classic study of group problem solving illustrates what groups do to deviates (Schachter, 1951). The researcher arranged for one member of a group to maintain a position on a discussion topic quite at odds with the positions of the other group members. Initially, the deviate received a great deal of attention from the group, with members directing more communication to him than to each other. After it became clear that the deviate was not going to change, group members directed their communication to each other, even rejecting the deviate.

Pressures toward uniformity can be intense, particularly if the issues are important to the group. Nonetheless, deviates are important to organizations because they bring fresh ideas and provoke at least a sensitivity to differences. Thus managers should take care not to allow the stamping out of all deviance. Frequently, a group member will take a deliberately deviant or "devil's advocate" position to challenge or test a group's decision. Managers often play this role to test the quality of their subordinates' recommendations. Deviates sometimes find themselves playing the role of whistle-blower (see Chapter 3).

Related to deviance is multiculturalism. Adler (1991) notes that cultural diversity has both positive and negative effects on group functioning. Diversity hinders group functioning because it is more difficult for members to perceive situations and act on them in similar ways. Thus cohesiveness is difficult to obtain, and opportunities exist for higher levels of mistrust and communication problems than in single-culture groups. On the other hand, culturally diverse groups also have the potential to work more productively than homogeneous groups because their wide range of human resources allows them to function more creatively. To function effectively, groups need to perceive, evaluate, and interpret situations in a variety of ways and to evaluate many alternatives. Thus their diversity enables multicultural groups to invent more solutions than can monocultural or unicultural groups.

The Free-Rider Effect   "The term 'free rider' refers to a member of a group who obtains benefits from group membership but does not bear a proportional share of the costs of providing the benefits. 'Cheap rider' (Stigler, 1974) is a more accurate term for such a group member because receiving benefits from group membership typically involves some cost. . . . Free rider, however, is the more generally used term" (Albanese and Van Fleet, 1985, p. 244). The free rider is seen as someone who promotes self-interest—the desire for benefits—over public interest—the need to contribute to the activity that produces those benefits.

The assumption of classic economic theory that rational actors will try to minimize their costs relative to the benefits they receive is at the base of free-rider theory. The larger the group, the greater the **free-rider effect.**

What can managers do to counter free riding? Albanese and Van Fleet suggested that coercion and special incentives to promote desirable behavior will help. They also offered the following suggestions: "Through effective use of power, design of organizations (including the size of organizational units), and control of access to rewards and punishment, management influences the incentive system of group members. At a routine level, this influence may be achieved by offering financial incentives or special forms of recognition to particular group members. . . ." (1985, p. 253). Ultimately, say these authors, managers should attack the free-rider problem by attempting to broaden the individual's concept of self-interest. This can possibly be done through creating, communicating, and maintaining a strong organizational culture (see Chapter 3).

A concept related to free riding is **social loafing** (Latane, Williams, and Harkins, 1979), which is exemplified in two experiments. Subjects were asked to clap and cheer as loudly as they could, first alone and then in groups of two, four, and six people. As group size increased, individual effort dropped, presumably because individuals believed their own performance could not be identified. A cross-national study of social loafing showed that it was more prevalent in American managers, who generally have individualistic beliefs, than in Chinese managers, who hold collectivist beliefs (Early, 1989). Managers can counter social loafing by making the overall task more challenging, by assigning each person a somewhat different task, and by holding individuals accountable for specific aspects of performance.

Polarization   When groups really become cohesive over an issue, **polarization** occurs. A number of years ago Whyte (1956) contended that Americans are overly inclined to do things in groups, which creates undue conservatism because people in groups are often afraid to take risks. Research, however, showed a startling phenomenon (Stoner, 1961). Individuals in groups frequently made riskier decisions than if they had made the decisions alone. This shift toward group risk came to be known as the "risky shift."

Later research showed a shift not just toward risk but toward whatever was the dominant position of the group, thus producing group enhancement of a prevailing individual tendency. Apparently, the subjects of the original experiment were predisposed toward risk, but other groups are predisposed toward other things, including conservatism (Lamm and Myers, 1978). The phenomenon came to be known as group polarization.

There are two commonly accepted explanations of polarization (McGrath, 1984). The **social comparison** position argues that pressures toward accepting one position or the other result from learning about the position of others in the group. In the **persuasive argument** view, groups coalesce around a more forcefully argued alternative when initial discussions reveal no clearly favored argument. Managers should be aware that group polarization does take place and that it often leads to groupthink (see Chapter 7), which is best avoided.

Group Effectiveness

As is true of organizational effectiveness (see Chapter 1), there are no general theories of small-group effectiveness. We know very little about why some groups are more effective than others. **Group effectiveness** may be defined as the degree to which the group's output meets quantity and quality standards, the degree to which group processes enhance the capabilities of group members to work together in the future, and the degree to which the group experience contributes to the growth and personal well-being of team members (Walton, 1986).

Individuals and Groups

We frequently hear people say that individuals can complete tasks faster and more efficiently than groups. This "wisdom" is common, yet it is highly unlikely that even the most talented individual could have accomplished in six months what the Eclipse Group did at Data General. We will examine this issue by discussing two aspects of individual versus group behavior. The first issue is the influence the presence of others has on individual performance; the second has to do with individual versus group performance in making judgments and in problem solving.

The study of the effect of others on performance is one of the earliest areas of investigation in social psychology. In the 1890s, Triplett, a bicycle enthusiast as well as a psychologist, began reviewing the official records of bicycle races promoted by a bicycling organization. The group conducted three types of races: unpaced, in which a lone rider attempted to beat an established time; paced, in which a lone rider attempted to beat an established time with a swift motorcycle setting the pace; and competition, in which many riders competed. The records showed that times were fastest for competition, next fastest for paced events, and slowest for unpaced events.

At first the presence of other people was thought to enhance performance, and the term **social facilitation** was used to describe this phenomenon (Allport, 1920). Then researchers noticed that the presence of others sometimes interfered with individual performance. This effect was called **social inhibition** (Zajonc, 1965). The presence of others facilitates well-practiced, well-learned responses but inhibits those that are less well learned (Deaux and Wrightsman, 1984). Thus, when group work is required, managers should structure the tasks with an awareness of the potential of facilitation or inhibition.

A second strand of group research has asked to what extent the quality of group judgment exceeds or falls short of the judgment of individuals. This question has two subparts: (1) Does the quality of group judgment exceed that of the average individual performance of group members? and (2) Does the quality of group performance exceed that of the best member of the group? Researchers have found that group judgment is often superior to individual judgment and seldom less accurate. This may, of course, depend on the nature of the task. It is also evident that a single capable individual may do better than a group. In other words, the answer to the first subquestion is yes, and the answer to the second one is no. The feature "Crisis Management by Committee" illustrates the wisdom of the group—and also the benefits of group commitment.

FEATURE: *Crisis Management by Committee*

In August 1986, *INC.* published a story on Springfield Remanufacturing Corp., highlighting our success at reviving a dying division of International Harvester. "So much has happened so fast," the article noted, "that even Stack sometimes worries about the dream turning a little sour." Well, this past year we came about as close to a nightmare as I'd want to get.

In 1985 we signed a 10-year, $75-million agreement with General Motors to remanufacture automobile diesel engines. That first year was tough because of all the cash and energy we put into getting a new plant up and running. In '86, the production schedules went up every month, and we never had time to breathe. By '87, we were pretty burned out. So I promised everybody it would be The Year of Enhancement. . . . We'd spend 1987, our fifth year, fine-tuning the business. . . .

So we drew up a financial plan for '87, and it looked great. Very minimal growth, sizable cash-flow improvements, bonus programs for everybody. . . . I pictured a French village in the midst of springtime, with all the villagers out in the square celebrating the coming of spring.

And then, sometime that December, GM's Material Scheduling Division called to say "some decisions had been reached" that would affect its future cash flow. Effective immediately, 5,000 engines were being cut from our schedule.

Now to a seasoned pro, this might have seemed like a bump in the road. To me, however, it sounded like an earthquake. What are you *talking* about? I shot back. I told him we had material on order, that from our cash-flow standpoint this would paralyze us, absolutely cripple us. We did some quick financial projections and found out that the loss represented 100 people. With no time to reschedule, we'd have to lay them off indefinitely. GM was adamant at first, but we finally did get 90 days.

We spent the next two months shuffling paperwork, but we were in shock more than anything. In my entire career I'd worked very hard at this goal of job security. To us, it's as basic as the income statement and the balance sheet. We took great pride in the fact that when we brought somebody in here, we were putting food on somebody's table. One of the things I always wanted for this facility was to show people they were wanted, they were important. You can have all these glorious things, even be on the cover of *INC.*, but when a guy walks out the door, you're just a piece of shit to him. You can have the greatest severance package in the world, but you're still here and he's out there.

We went through a lot of agonizing. Could we cut down our non-people-oriented costs? Every time we'd flow it through our income statements, it all came down to having 100 people too many to absorb the overhead. The cold statistics said, all the rules said, lay them off. . . .

After about three months, I came up against decision time. Then it dawned on me: why am I sitting here trying to make this decision for all these people? Why shouldn't they be able to make the decision for themselves? So I called old-fashioned town meetings at all company sites, and asked my 350 employees what they wanted to do. I painted the bleakest picture possible. If we kept everyone around, I explained, we would have to go out and generate approximately 50,000 man-hours' worth of new business. But if that turned out to be the wrong direction, there was no contingency. Instead of having to lay off 100, we might have to lay off 200. Almost unanimously they said: go for it. Let's bring in new products, let's shoot craps. Let's keep the people.

It was incredibly hard. We took any job we could get. We sold in any kind of market we could sell into. We got into product lines we had no previous experience with. We worked an incredible number of hours to make sure that by the time that product went out the back door it would run right. Through it all, that entire year, they took it on. It was brutal. I remember in July, one guy called me on the phone and absolutely broke down, he was that burned out. It was that tense. But we ended up the year doing $40.8 million, $2 million more than '86—even with the $8 million GM drop. And we *increased* the work force by 100.

If we had done that layoff, I don't think we ever would have recovered. We'd have lost momentum. As tired as everybody is, they really feel great that they did it. We learned a lot about ourselves as people. That you can't really determine how far you can go. You always have a little bit left. You can always dig deeper. If there's a purpose, a deeper meaning to something you're doing, you can draw something out of yourself that you didn't think you had.

The neat thing about it was to realize that I couldn't make the decision myself. It was not a manager's decision, but a people's decision. It was their future and their company. The year before, they had gotten 7% to 9% of their salary in a bonus. Because we took this course of action, they only got 3.6%. That difference is a lot of money. But it was dedicated to the people who didn't hit the streets.

Source: J. Stack, "Crisis Management by Committee." Reprinted with permission, *Inc.* magazine, May 1988, p. 26. Copyright © 1988 by Goldhirsh Group, Inc., 38 Commercial Wharf, Boston, MA 02110.

Another factor in the individual-versus-group debate is efficiency. While groups produce more and better solutions than individuals, the time required to reach the solution is not consistently better for either groups or individuals (Shaw, 1981). When the amount of effort invested in solving the problem (measured by person-hours) is calculated, however, individuals are superior.

Implicit in studies of group judgment and problem solving is the notion that groups learn while performing tasks and, consequently, improve their performance. Groups do learn faster than individuals, both in natural situations and in contrived laboratory studies.

Nevertheless, a significant amount of research shows that groups are less effective than individuals at performing some tasks. In fact, many social psychologists talk about "process losses" and claim that group processes, for the most part, impair performance (e.g., Steiner, 1972). Others (e.g., Taylor and Faust, 1952) suggest that interaction helps groups to catch their errors, thus producing higher-quality solutions to problems than those produced by individuals. Of course, groupthink (see Chapter 7) can impair the ability of group interaction to find and correct errors. One view of groups (Collins and Guetzkow, 1964) proposes that in some circumstances interaction can result in "assembly effect bonuses." In other words, individual inputs may combine to yield an outcome better than what could be provided simply by summing the individual inputs. Hackman (1989) provides detailed descriptions of group characteristics of 27 diverse work groups, ranging from top management groups to production and customer and service groups. He provided insight into what leaders and group members can do to improve work group effectiveness.

Organizational psychologists involved with experiential training groups or team building tend to be optimistic about the possibility of enhancing group performance through changing group processes (Varney, 1989). (See the feature "Team Building," page 192, for one description of this process.) The available research does not support this optimism, however. One study of seven combat companies in the Israeli Defense Forces did find that team development workshops improved teamwork, conflict handling, and information about plans (Eden, 1985). But another study found team building to have negative effects on organizational functioning (Eden, 1986). Likewise, research on quality circles has produced both positive and negative relationships between these grouping strategies and performance (for more on these issues, see Chapter 11). The context in which teams or quality circles perform probably significantly influences them, but such factors as context, group boundaries, and group development have received little research attention (Sundstrom, De Meuse, and Futrell, 1990). One recent exception to this identifies national characteristics in Sweden, Japan, and the United States that impede and enhance group activities (Cole, 1989).

FEATURE: *Team Building*

Team building is a term used for training sessions to build collaboration skills in groups of people who work together. Few would dream of recruiting two dozen professional football players on Saturday morning and sending them onto the field that afternoon. Even if they were highly skilled in their individual specializations, their lack of training in working together as a team would be a serious detriment. Work teams, however, are frequently assembled from individuals with varying backgrounds and assigned complex tasks that require collaboration without any preparation in teamwork. Team building is a technique that combines training with practice on real problems to help members function together more effectively. A couple of examples will help to explain the concept.

The Up-In-The-Air Corporation has just received a government contract to build a component for a rocket. To get the project started a new project team will be assembled, pulling together experts from various branches and divisions. The head of the team realizes that none of his group has experience working with each other and that serious errors could occur because of garbled communication, confused roles, and professional jealousies. He decides to initiate team-building training at the beginning of the project. The group meets in a week-long retreat setting with a consultant. They get better acquainted and develop a clearer understanding of each other's backgrounds and competencies. They discuss and clarify the role each member will play. They decide how they will deal with potential group problems, such as conflicts. The leader clarifies with the group the assignment, including the corporation's expectations. He also discusses his leadership style and the ground rules about group decision making. At the end of the week the team members have improved their ability to collaborate on the project. . . .

[This example] demonstrate[s] the essence of team building. Through a combination of teaching the elements of group effectiveness, exercises in teamwork, and practice in real organizational issues, members learn to work together as a group. Team building is a component of a body of techniques commonly labeled organization development (OD). They seek to improve organizational functioning by focusing on the human interactional processes involved in getting work done.

Source: From W. B. Eddy, *The Manager and the Working Group* (New York: Praeger, 1985), pp. 163–164. Copyright © 1985 by W. B. Eddy. Reprinted by permission of the author.

The Human Resources View of Group Effectiveness

In the early 1930s a group of anthropologists at Harvard conducted research in the Hawthorne, Illinois, plant of Western Electric Company that is one of the classic studies in this area. These researchers attempted to establish that workers would work more efficiently with good lighting than with bad lighting. To their surprise, however, the researchers found that no matter how they varied lighting—by raising or lowering it—the workers produced more!

This outcome triggered five years of field research in which all kinds of variables were manipulated. In each case, the result was higher productivity. The researchers came to believe that productivity increased out of a sense of social support and the development of feelings of group identity and cohesion. They urged management to focus on the social and interpersonal aspects of work groups to improve performance.

With time, this "human relations" model came to be replaced by what was called the "human resources" model, in which workers are viewed as potential resources who perform best when effectively tapped. Two seminal theories from this school describe principles that managers can follow to enhance group performance. In *The Human Side of Enterprise* (1960), McGregor argued that effective managerial teams are characterized by "unity of purpose," which can be obtained only by closely knit groups. He argued that most management teams are not closely knit but rather are people vying with one another for power, prestige, recognition, and autonomy. McGregor's characteristics of an effective work team are listed in Figure 4.2 (page 194).

The second key work of this school came from Rensis Likert (1961), who developed a notion of organizations as a series of interlocking groups with managers as their "linking pins." Likert believed that managers should learn to cope with individuals as whole human beings and as members of

FIGURE 4.2
McGregor's Characteristics of an Effective Work Team

1. The "atmosphere" tends to be informal, comfortable, relaxed. . . . It is a working atmosphere in which people are involved and interested. . . .
2. There is a lot of discussion in which virtually everyone participates, but it remains pertinent to the task of the group. . . .
3. The task or the objective of the group is well understood and accepted by its members. There will have been free discussion of the objective at some point, until it was formulated in such a way that the members of the group could commit themselves to it.
4. The members listen to each other! . . . Every idea is given a hearing. . . .
5. There is disagreement. The group is comfortable with this and shows no signs of having to avoid conflict or to keep everything on the plane of sweetness and light. . . .
6. Most decisions are reached by a kind of consensus in which it is clear that everybody is in general agreement and willing to go along. However, there is little tendency for individuals who oppose action to keep their opposition private and thus let an apparent consensus mask real disagreement. . . .
7. Criticism is frequent, frank, and relatively comfortable. . . .
8. People are free in expressing their feelings as well as their ideas both on the problem and on the group's operation. . . .
9. When action is taken, clear assignments are made and accepted.
10. The chairman of the group does not dominate it, nor on the contrary, does the group defer unduly to him or her. . . . [T]he leadership shifts from time to time, depending on the circumstances. . . . The issue is not who controls, but how to get the job done.
11. The group is self-conscious about its own operations. Frequently, it will stop to examine how well it is doing or what may be interfering with its operation. . . .

Source: From Douglas McGregor, *The Human Side of Enterprise* (New York: McGraw-Hill, 1960), pp. 232–235. Copyright © 1960 by Douglas McGregor. Reprinted by permission of McGraw-Hill Publishing Co.

entire groups under them and not just manage individuals on a one-to-one basis. Likert's ideal management form is called "participative group management," identified by 24 properties and performance characteristics (see Figure 4.3).

Hackman and Morris's Theory

Hackman and Morris (1975) suggested how various classes of variables might combine to influence group task performance (see Figure 4.4, page 196). In offering their model, the writers stated the need for further research into the input-process-output sequence for different types of tasks in order to derive a better understanding of group processes that influence effectiveness. Hackman and Morris proposed that a major portion of the variation in measured group performance is controlled by three "summary" variables: (1) group members' knowledge and skills, (2) the group's strategies for performing tasks, and (3) the amount of group members' effort and coordination.

FIGURE 4.3
Likert's Characteristics of an Effective Work Group

1. Members are skilled in both leadership and membership roles and functions.
2. The group has been in existence long enough that members have well-established working relationships.
3. Members are attracted and loyal to the group and its leader.
4. Members and leaders have confidence and trust in each other.
5. Group values and goals integrate and reflect members' values and needs; members helped shape group values and goals.
6. Individuals who link different groups try to have, in harmony, the values and goals of both groups.
7. The more important a value to the group, the greater the likelihood that a member will accept it.
8. Members are highly motivated to achieve the group's goals and will do all in their power to do so.
9. All interaction, decision making, and problem solving occurs in a supportive atmosphere; criticisms are constructive, and they are listened to.
10. The group leader establishes the proper tone and atmosphere through his or her leadership practices.
11. The group helps each member develop his or her full potential.
12. Members accept the goals and expectations, which are set high enough to challenge members without generating anxiety.
13. The leader and members believe that the group can accomplish the impossible.
14. Members help each other out when necessary.
15. The supportive atmosphere stimulates creativity.
16. The group expects conformity on administrative matters to expedite them and preserve time for more salient group functions.
17. Members communicate fully and frankly with each other.
18. Communication is used to serve the interest of the group.
19. Members expect and are ready to receive and use communications.
20. Members try to influence each other and are open to influence from other members.
21. Members exert influence on the leader.
22. The group is flexible and adaptable.
23. Members feel secure in making decisions appropriate to them; initiative is encouraged.
24. The leader is selected carefully, perhaps using peer nominations and related methods to identify those with high leadership competence.

Source: Adapted from R. Likert, *New Patterns of Management* (New York: McGraw-Hill, 1961), pp. 166–169. Copyright © 1961 by R. Likert. Reprinted by permission of McGraw-Hill Publishing Co.

Group interaction can substantially influence each set of variables. Members' knowledge and skills are influenced in two ways. First, group interaction results in the assessment of individual contributions. Second, members learn from each other while working together, thus increasing the overall level of knowledge and skill in the group. Interaction also influences task performance strategies by aiding the implementation of preexisting strategies and reformulating existing strategies. Additionally, interaction influences individual effort through its coordination of member activities and its effect on effort individuals exert (which can be either positive or negative).

FIGURE 4.4
Hackman and Morris's Model of Group Effectiveness

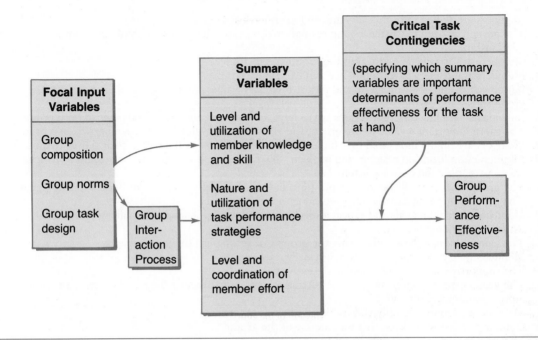

Source: J. R. Hackman and C. G. Morris, "Group Tasks, Group Interaction Process, and Group Performance Effectiveness," in L. Berkowitz (ed.), *Advances in Experimental Social Psychology* (New York: Academic Press, 1975), p. 88. Copyright © 1975 by Academic Press. Reprinted by permission of Academic Press and the authors.

Group interaction, and consequently the group summary variables, are influenced by three specific input factors: (1) the composition of the group, (2) group norms, and (3) the task design. Hackman and Morris proposed that each summary variable is especially responsive to changes in one of the input factors. For example, task performance strategies are usually codified in the task design. The effort that group members expend on tasks is powerfully governed by group norms. Finally, the single most powerful leverage on member knowledge and skill is group composition. A group made up of people competent to do the task at hand will perform better than a group composed of less competent people.

The effectiveness of the Eclipse Group in developing the Eagle demonstrates these principles. The task was achieved by following the original design, which differentiated the work into smaller units responsible for particular subtasks. The norms established by West clearly helped push group members to major effort. The initial selection process not only identified individuals who were willing to buy in but also picked highly skilled workers—the kind needed to get the job done.

FIGURE 4.5
A Conceptual Model of Team Performance

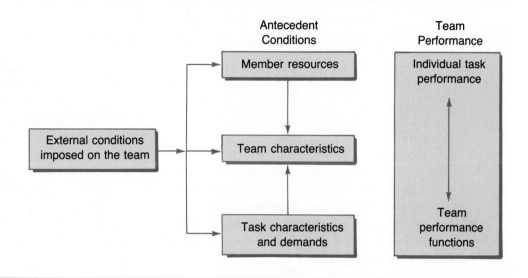

Source: V. F. Nieva, E. A. Fleishman, and A. Rieck, "Team Dimensions: Their Identity, Their Measurement, and Their Relationships," Final Technical Report for Contract No. DAHC19-78-C-0001 (Washington, D.C.: Advanced Research Resources Organization, 1978), p. 3. Reprinted by permission of the authors.

Other Models of Group Effectiveness

There are other models of group effectiveness (Goodman, Ravlin, and Argote, 1986). We briefly mention three of them as examples. Nieva, Fleishman, and Rieck (1978) suggest that team performance is a function of four variables:

1. External conditions, or the larger systems in which groups operate

2. Member resources, or the abilities, motivations, and personality characteristics of the members

3. Team characteristics, or the structural aspects of groups (such as gender, communication patterns, team climate, etc.)

4. Task characteristics and demands, or the specific kinds of activities that are permitted

The interactions among these variables are depicted in Figure 4.5.

Another model focuses on the effectiveness of task groups (Gladstein, 1984). This model begins with a series of inputs:

1. Group composition, measured by variables such as skills and tenure

2. Group structure, including group roles, size, leadership characteristics, and so on

3. Resources available, including the training and technical support that can be obtained and the markets served

4. Organizational structure, which addresses rewards and control

Note that the first pair of variables involve characteristics of the group itself, and the second pair involve characteristics of the organization. These variables influence group processes and effectiveness, as shown in Figure 4.6. Gladstein identifies three task-related variables as related to group effectiveness as well: task complexity, environmental uncertainty, and interdependence.

Gladstein, along with many other writers, sees group effectiveness in terms of performance and satisfaction. Shea and Guzzo (1987) focus strictly on task performance, arguing that while other approaches have studied group interaction, they have yet to establish any connection between interactions and task accomplishment. These writers see group effectiveness as arising from three factors:

1. *Potency.* Effectiveness increases as the group believes that it has or can acquire the resources needed to succeed. This belief affects the level of effort that members expend.

2. *Outcome interdependence.* Effectiveness increases as such outcomes as rewards and punishments are more directly related to the group's accomplishments of its task.

3. *Task interdependence.* Essentially a matter of the degree to which group members must work together to accomplish the common task, this factor influences effectiveness by influencing the other two factors.

The writers conclude that managers forming groups must pay careful attention to these variables. By ensuring that the group perceives itself as empowered to accomplish the task, by explicitly linking outcomes to accomplishing the task, and by structuring the work in such a way as to encourage interdependence, management can create effective groups.

Another model of group effectiveness, older than any of the others discussed here, is the sociotechnical model, discussed in Chapter 11. This model focuses on the optimal fit between technological and social characteristics.

Intergroup Relationships

Group interaction in organizations has largely been ignored as a field of study. Here we will draw on what is known about intergroup interaction and

FIGURE 4.6
*Gladstein's Model
of Group
Behavior*

INPUTS   PROCESS   OUTPUTS

Group Level

Group composition

- Adequate skills
- Heterogeneity
- Organizational tenure
- Job tenure

Group task

- Task complexity
- Environmental uncertainty
- Interdependence

Group structure

- Role and goal clarity
- Specific work norms
- Task control
- Size
- Formal leadership

Group process

- Open communication
- Supportiveness
- Conflict
- Discussion of strategy
- Weighting individual inputs
- Boundary management

Group effectiveness

- Performance
- Satisfaction

Organizational Level

Resources available

- Training and technical consultation
- Markets served

Organizational structure

- Rewards for group performance
- Supervisory control

Ⓧ indicates a moderated relationship

Source: D. Gladstein, "Groups in Context: A Model of Organizational Effectiveness," *Administrative Science Quarterly* 29 (1984): 499–517. Reprinted by permission.

ask ourselves how various facets of intergroup relations should play themselves out in organizations. In this section, we will explore how intergroup perceptions form, the effects of intergroup contact, and the characteristics of group exchanges. Most of this material will draw on research in social psychology and then attempt to relate these findings to organizational situations.

How do we differentiate intergroup interaction from other group phenomena? "Whenever individuals belonging to one group interact, collectively or individually with another group or its members *in terms of their group identification*, we have an instance of intergroup behavior" (Sherif, 1966, p. 12). That intergroup relations within the same organization can have an impact on organizational effectiveness is clear from what happened at Xerox, as described in the feature.

FEATURE: *How Intergroup Relations at Xerox Contributed to Corporate Stagnation*

The company [Xerox] was organized so that the functions of product planning, engineering, and manufacturing didn't come together until you got to Stamford [Connecticut; corporate headquarters] at the president's level. A lot of time was wasted in meetings and presentations. Many problems that should have been resolved in Rochester wound up going to Stamford for solution. "There was a lot of conflict," [Eric] Steenburgh [a Xerox personnel executive] says. "There were too many functional nits that became showstoppers. We had vice presidents yelling at vice presidents over nits."

Inside of its engineering organization, for instance, Xerox has a drafting function and a service engineering function. After a design engineer designed a part for a subsystem, he would pass it to the drafting department. The drafting department would do a drawing. The draftsman would then pass it to a detailer who would put the critical dimensions on it. Then the drawing would go to service engineering. They would determine if it was practical for maintenance out in the field. Could the tech reps around the world make that product work? If the answer was yes, then the drawing would go to the manufacturing engineering organization. They would determine if they could manufacture the part. If anybody along the line sent it back to the engineers who designed it, the design engineer would have to either redesign the part or try to convince the service or manufacturing engineers to see things his way. Each function had its own hierarchy. There was a vice president of service engineering and a vice president of advanced manufacturing engineering. The process chewed up a lot of time.

Unfortunately for Xerox, the groups were most interested in their own functional responsibility rather than meeting cost targets or getting the machines out the door on time.

Xerox marketing organizations around the world were the same. Rank Xerox had its own group of product planners as did the United States, Canada and Latin America. The idea was to be as close to customers in the various markets as possible and then bring all that information together in one place, a reprographics strategy office in Rochester reporting to Stamford. "All of that sounded beautiful, but what happened was you couldn't get that group to agree on what time of day it was if they were all looking at the same clock," Wayland Hicks says. "I can remember one argument over what the color of the paper tray should be."

One group would want reduction on a machine. Another would want eleven-by-seventeen [inch] capability. While the strategy office had responsibility for pulling everything together, it didn't have the same clout as the other groups, so it tried to compromise.

To make sure that things didn't get hopelessly bogged down, Xerox put a program manager on each product. He was accountable for delivering the product and pulling all the functions together—such as getting the sales and service forces trained and preparing the literature for sales promotions. He had these functional people reporting to him, but he didn't have any leverage if they were dropping the ball. . . .

Communications broke down as well. The Office Products Division (OPD) in Dallas didn't talk to the systems guys in El Segundo because they had competing technologies. People at Xerox's Palo Alto Research Center saw products coming out of OPD that they had never seen before. In many ways, the people of Xerox were working in two different worlds—a copier world and a computer world—separated by thousands of miles and layers of bureaucracy. "People in headquarters are like willows, moving every way the wind is blowing," James Campbell [founder of Xerox Computer Systems] said. "And the wind in El Segundo is a long damn way from Stamford."

Source: Reprinted with permission of Macmillan Publishing Company and Sterling Lord Literistic, Inc. from *Xerox: American Samurai* by Gary Jacobson and John Hillkirk (New York: Macmillan, 1986), pp. 76–78. Copyright © 1986 by Gary Jacobson and John Hillkirk.

How Intergroup Perceptions Form

Two factors seem important in the formation of intergroup perceptions: the knowledge structures people bring to the situation and the attributions they make about the situation. To illustrate, if an employee had never experienced a group in his company that made well-thought-out decisions, when confronted with a new group he would not be very optimistic about the quality of its decisions. Moreover, he would likely attribute poor decision quality to characteristics of group members rather than to situational constraints.

We categorize groups along social dimensions and assume they will behave in accord with some stereotype we have about the group. Gender, for example, is highly associated with status in our society. This stereotype leads to expectations that women will be more compliant and easily influenced than men, particularly when people's actual job status is unknown (Eagly and Wood, 1982). These expectations can foster interactions that promote behaviors conforming the stereotype, which contributes to a self-perpetuating cycle (Eagly, 1983).

This cycle is evident in the reciprocal relationship between the formation of categories and the consequences of being placed in categories. Belonging to a category tends to generate a feeling of sharing a common set of characteristics; at the same time, exposure to a common set of characteristics generates feelings of shared category membership. For example, a worker who is part of a very capable work group will perceive himself as very capable, and a worker who is newly assigned to that work group will begin to see herself as capable as well.

The relationship between intergroup differentiation and distinctiveness seems to be similarly reciprocal. Differentiation of a group into separate social categories reduces differences among individuals within the same category and enhances perceived differences between members of different categories. On the other hand, distinctiveness tends to induce categorization (Brewer and Kramer, 1985). In other words, birds of a feather flock together—and those who flock together are perceived as birds of a feather. The result is the establishment of an *in-group*—to which one belongs—and an *out-group*—to which "others" belong. People enhance the distinctiveness between social categories in ways that favor their group and further accentuate differences. Thus discrimination develops in favor of the in-group (Brewer and Kramer, 1985).

Cognitive processes alone do not account for intergroup stereotyping. "Social categorization entails much more than the cognitive classification of events, objects, or people. It is a process impregnated by values, culture, and social representations" (Tajfel and Forgas, 1981, p. 114). Cultural values and norms underlie stereotypes, which are triggered by cognitive processes.

Managers should try to understand the social categories that exist in their organizations and the relative status of each category. By being alert to the knowledge bases that employees are likely to bring to the organization and the attributions they are likely to make as a result, managers can develop an eye to understanding the kinds of prejudices that may develop. Grouping heterogeneous peoples together increases the likelihood of enhanced perception of cross-category differences, e.g., between departments, and of muted perceived differences, e.g., of cultural or social differences, within a category or group.

Contact Effects

Two schools of thought exist on the effect of contact on intergroup relations among ethnic groups. In one perspective, interdependent relations among groups assures intergroup conflict and within-group cohesiveness (Levine and Campbell, 1972). This point of view rests on the assumption that cohesiveness can exist only if group members have no negative interactions. An external enemy is then functional for any group by providing a target toward which internally generated negative feelings can be directed. Of course, it is possible that groups that can permit and deal with internal conflict have less need for enemies on whom to project negative feelings. These groups are less likely to form **ethnocentric relations** with other groups.

The second view is that contact between ethnic groups may facilitate better understanding and liking between the two. This hypothesis rests on the assumption that a shift from the abstract unfamiliar to the specific and more familiar will engender more positive intergroup attitudes. Research on the contact hypothesis is dominated by studies of desegregation, with mixed results.

Some evidence suggests that resegregation naturally occurs when intergroup contact takes place, leading researchers to ask what structural features of the situation influence segregated behavior and how these can be changed. The three features explored are the relative size of groups, group structure, and status differences among the groups.

There is little systematic information about the effects of proportional representation of different social categories in desegregated settings. The presence of distinct minorities appears to make membership in the minority more salient to nonminority persons and enhances in-group favoritism (Mullen, 1983; Sachdev and Bourhis, 1984).

Studies that vary structure in an effort to improve intergroup relations focus on altering learning techniques in school classrooms. In these studies, cooperative learning techniques seem to work better than traditional techniques at enhancing intergroup interaction, suggesting that comparable techniques for learning tasks in organizations may be effective in breaking down intergroup barriers.

Status difference studies have also been done using desegregated school populations. Most of this research has attempted to promote equal status conditions within the classroom, but to no avail. It is now recognized that structural equality does not equal psychological equality. People know that historically certain inequalities have existed; these status differentials carry over to new situations. Thus, it is difficult to manipulate equal status conditions in contact settings.

Intergroup Exchanges

Very little work on actual intergroup interaction exists. As mentioned previously, social psychology research typically deals with individual behavior in groups or in implied groups. Rarely does it deal with real group interaction and even less frequently does it concern itself with intergroup interaction. One author (Smith, 1983) offers an interesting account of intergroup exchanges among groups who are powerful (uppers), powerless (lowers), and caught-in-the-middle (middles):

> In exchanges of *upper* groups with middles and lowers, the key pattern was that uppers became protected from the consequences of their behavior. This was played through with uppers tending to split decision making from implementation; they tended to delegate responsibility without adequate authority for implementation; and they made decisions using trivial data. The major pattern involving the exchanges of *lower* groups with middles and uppers was the tendency of the powerless to develop strong norms of cohesiveness and unity to counter their experiences of helplessness. This dominant pattern was accompanied by strict rules about secrecy, the generation of deindividuating forces upon lower group members, and a paralyzing incapacity to deal constructively with dissension within their own ranks. For the exchanges of *middle* groups with uppers and lowers, the main pattern was the emergence of an imperative to develop and preserve functional relations with groups above and below them. This pattern had the middles struggling with the problem of keeping themselves together as a group, forever seeking to facilitate communication, and struggling to create a collective reality so that uppers and lowers could learn to understand and act towards each other in less polarizing ways. (Smith, 1983, pp. 200–201. Copyright © 1972 by JAI Press. Reprinted by permission.)

According to Smith, two general concepts guide intergroup interaction: social comparison processes and dynamic conservatism. One way a group develops an identity is to use another group (or itself) with which it interacts as a mirror. Thus, each group takes on both actor and performer roles. A problem evolves when groups use other groups to establish mirrors of themselves. Groups posture in such a way that the distances between them set the stage for what they can find out about themselves. If a group wants to feel good about something it feels bad about, it might position itself in such a way as to learn only those things that will make it feel good. And when a group learns something about itself it does not like, it may well find another group that can act as a more favorable mirror against which to compare itself.

Because each group in an interaction takes on actor and performer roles, the posturing of social distance between groups becomes critical. Each group wants to get close enough to the other to see what the other is doing, while remaining sufficiently distant to protect itself. In this interaction there is a shift from mutually proactive to mutually reactive postures. Smith calls this shift **dynamic conservatism** and identifies three main components.

The first is that the original goal of each group—to strike a posture offering the most advantageous position—becomes displaced by the defensive goal of not letting things get worse. The second component of dynamic conservatism is manifest in the structure of communication. When one does not have a way to say that some behavior will not occur, one must show the behavior and then stop it. For example, an animal cannot tell an adversary it is not fighting, so what it must do is show the adversary fighting behavior and then disengage from it. The third component of dynamic conservatism is illustrated when groups get closed in; although they seek alternative courses of action, they reject them precipitously. The fear of the unknown is more awesome than the restrictiveness of what is known. This behavior, called "value rigidity," triggers imprisoning frames of reference that are difficult, if not impossible, to change.

Theoretically, intergroup relations are power–dependency relationships (see Chapter 6) in which each group is dependent on the other for resources ranging from reflected self-knowledge to tangible resources. Groups with different amounts of power engage in social comparisons in different ways. In a situation involving just three groups, uppers try to keep their power, lowers try to destroy it, and middles attempt to alter the configuration of tensions between the other two groups. Most situations are extremely more complex than this, simply because they entail more than three groups. In addition, in a real world situation a group may simultaneously occupy an upper, middle, or lower position with respect to any number of issues. About all we can do in organizations is recognize that uppers, middles, and lowers exist and try to understand the dynamics of their relationships.

Intergroup Conflict

When two groups linked in a power-dependency relationship disagree about one or more aspects of their relationship, conflict results. Groups are differentiated along orientation lines involving task, technology, goal, and time. The elements that support differentiation among groups inhibit the integration of those groups. To illustrate, in a classroom group project some people are to obtain reading materials from the library, others to interview people knowledgeable about the project subject, others to write the report, and still others to edit and finalize the report for the instructor. During the beginning of the task, the research and interviewing groups want to work slowly, not only because it seems like a long time until the due date but because the technologies of their tasks require thought. The writing and editing groups want them to work fast, not only because they see the task from their perspective—in which the technology allows for quicker completion—but because they want time to complete their jobs before the end of the term. These groups are in conflict.

Conflict is disagreement, tension, or other difficulties among two or more parties. Some view conflict as preventable, but as the following brief example shows, a more realistic view seems to be that it is inevitable. Some writers even argue that conflict is healthy for organizations. Good managers can size up the potential for conflict and implement strategies for reducing it. By framing conflict in the context of tribal work force, one author (Neuhauser, 1988) provides a managerial guide to its reduction.

The intensity of conflict is, in part, a function of scarce resources. If one group can develop excess resources, it can buffer itself against other groups and reduce conflict. Thus the writing and editing groups plead for extra time after they receive the materials from the other groups; if they succeed, conflict is reduced. When extra resources are unavailable, conflict is likely to result, and the groups must use various methods to reduce it. Thus the causes of conflict are structural, but the solutions must take place between individuals representing groups.

Conflict is a dynamic process with a number of stages. The first stage involves the antecedent conditions, or the aspects of the situation that can trigger conflict. The second stage is a response to the first, in which at least one participant in the situation perceives that conflict exists and begins to express manifestations of conflict, such as taking defensive action. The third stage is conflict resolution or suppression. Finally come the aftermaths of conflict, or the effects and side effects of having been in conflict. These stages can be observed in the feature on the struggle for power over Getty Oil.

FEATURE: *Boardroom to Courtroom: Battling for Getty*

"Keep killing my son," John Paul Getty instructed his ferocious lawyer, Moses Lasky. The son was Gordon Getty, who'd had the tenacity to sue the old man to gain control of the stock dividends from the Sarah C. Getty Trust. . . .

Gordon survived his father's handling . . . and he even managed a reconciliation, so that before John Paul died, he appointed Gordon co-trustee of the family estate. Gordon launched a campaign to gain control of the corporation that had been his father's, to oust the sitting chief, Sidney Petersen, and he even utilized the razor talents of his father's old crony, Mr. Lasky. That's the sort of irony that Gordon, ever detached, must relish. Gordon's campaign, which eventually involved Texaco Inc., Pennzoil Co., a Texas jury, and an $11 billion award, is the starting point for "Oil & Honor: The Texaco-Pennzoil Wars" . . . by Thomas Petzinger, Jr. . . .

[Petzinger] contrasts the oil-patch ethic of Pennzoil with the maneuverings of the New York financial precincts in which Texaco did its business. In New York, Mr. Petzinger notes, a deal is done on paper, once the lawyers have filled in the last whereases and wherefores. In Texas, the creed runs differently: "If I give my word, no one can break it, but if I sign this contract, my lawyers can break it." Pennzoil and Texaco both thought they had bought Getty Oil Co., Mr. Petzinger concludes, one with a verbal agreement and the other with a paper deal. But the jury, Texans, decided it was Pennzoil's "gentleman's agreement" that deserved honoring. . . .

Mr. Petzinger has extended his reportage, and crafted a coherent and flowing narrative, but his book is more than a rehash. It goes deeper. One of its subplots is the drama of how Getty management "mismanaged" eccentric Gordon and converted his gentle yearnings into destructive passions.

Gordon would sit at the directors' table, his head thrown back and his lips silently moving. He would ask questions about items that had been on the agenda hours before. He once mistook a break in a meeting for an adjournment and left before business had been concluded. If the board was unanimously in favor of a proposition, he might vote against it on the grounds there should be some dissent.

And yet this hapless fellow had the guts to sue his father, and the ambition to grab for control of the corporation that bears his name. He is most elusive. In 1982, he toured New York's takeover houses, blithely chatting about Getty's problems. Was he naively seeking advice, or was he subtly showing that he was willing to go outside the firm for allies to oust the current management?

Unable to fit into an organization, unrealistic if innovative in his schemes, he felt compelled to persevere. He was perceived as an irritant when he was a junior executive, an annoyance when he was a spacey director, and then a major menace when he seemed on the verge of controlling the corporation.

Yet one perceives a hidden consistency in his behavior, as if he adheres to some non-Euclidean logic in a company of people restricted to narrow Euclidean rules. The Getty management continually misinterpreted and mishandled Gordon, and brought on its own demise.

The most pathetic image in the book is the sight of Sidney Petersen, then Getty Oil chief, as he tries to understand what Gordon is about. Mr. Petersen is a savvy executive, which means he seems to understand people like himself, but he comes off as unlettered, and therefore, solipsistic. He and his aides tried to explain Gordon in conventional business terms; Gordon's wife wears the pants in the family and is forcing him to grab for control; Gordon wants to live up to his daddy's image; he has an insatiable lust for power. But none of these explanations capture Gordon, because his motivations are alien to the management mindset and the Adam Smith world.

As the struggle between Gordon and Mr. Petersen escalated, management's antipathy took the form of xenophobia. T. Boone Pickens met with Mr. Petersen and his men and noticed their resentment toward their heir. "They won't be around very long," Mr. Pickens sagely noted, "This company is long gone."

Add one nonbusinessman to a corporate culture that understands only other businessmen, and all hell breaks loose.

Source: David Brooks, "From Boardroom to Courtroom: Battling for Getty," *Wall Street Journal,* June 19, 1987, p. 19. Reprinted by permission of the *Wall Street Journal.* Copyright © 1987 by Dow Jones & Company, Inc. All Rights Reserved Worldwide.

Types of Conflict

The circumstances of the fight between Gordon Getty and the company's managers reveal all four main types of conflict:

- **Goal conflict,** in which people disagree on the goals to pursue. Gordon's desire to gain control of Getty Oil clearly ran counter to Petersen's desires.

- **Cognitive conflict,** in which opponents perceive that their thoughts or ideas are incompatible. Writer David Brooks identifies a major difference in cognitive style between Gordon and Petersen as the underlying cause of the conflict.

- **Affective conflict,** in which people quite simply do not like each other. Pickens's meeting with the Getty managers revealed deep personal dislike for Gordon.

- **Behavioral conflict,** in which actions are incompatible. Gordon's conduct at board meetings was seen as inappropriate by the more traditional businessmen observing him.

The feature also reveals some of the levels of conflict: interpersonal, intergroup, and interorganizational. The competition between rival firms jockeying for larger market share or racing to develop new products is a kind of conflict. Given the value placed on competition in our culture, it may also serve as a reminder that conflict is not solely a negative phenomenon. Of course, such conflict can become negative if pursued single-mindedly. An interesting example of intergroup conflict is the complex story of the RVR Nabisco takeover in the late 1980s (Helyar and Burrough, 1990).

Conflict can also take place within the individual, group, or organization. A manager, for instance, can feel conflicting role demands, or a work group may experience the tension caused by a member not contributing adequately. Such conflicts are potentially more damaging because they can subvert the cohesion, coordination, and unity that an organization requires to a degree to function smoothly. Conflict within organizations stems from a number of causes, including different goals, competition for scarce resources, problems in communication, differences in status, the interdependency of individuals or groups, and differences in performance expectations.

Managing Conflict

People react to conflict in a number of ways, and several theories discuss reaction styles (Blake and Mouton, 1969; Filley, 1975; Hall, 1969; Thomas, 1979). The research has identified five methods for handling conflict and suggested when each is most appropriate in intergroup or interorganizational conflict:

1. **Avoidance.** Some people avoid conflict. Conflict avoidance is useful when the issues are insignificant or the costs of challenging someone outweigh the benefits.

2. **Accommodation.** Some people accommodate or give in to other's wishes. Accommodation is a good strategy when you decide you are wrong, because it permits the correct position to win.

3. **Competition.** Some people pursue their wishes at the expense of others or in competition with others. This style is useful in times of crisis, when there is no time for disagreement or discussion and a forceful style is needed.

4. **Compromise.** Compromise is the search for a middle ground, useful when two parties have mutually exclusive goals and relatively equal power.

5. **Collaboration.** Some people collaborate or accept the other party's needs while asserting their own needs. This style is useful when each party is strongly committed to different goals and when compromise is costly.

Outside parties may be employed to resolve conflict. Two common techniques employ third parties to help resolve conflict: **mediation** and **arbitration.** Mediators may make suggestions and monitor interaction among parties, or they may keep the parties apart. One objective of mediation is to reduce tension. Mediators do not impose solutions, but attempt to convince participants to compromise or collaborate. Unlike mediation, arbitrators make decisions that are binding on both parties.

A number of bargaining or negotiating strategies can be used to resolve conflict. Generally, bargaining varies in the degree to which it is distributive or integrative. Distributive bargaining occurs when one party's gain is another's loss. Integrative bargaining occurs when the parties work together to the benefit of both. Bargainers use many different strategies. Not uncommon is the strategy of beginning by demanding more than you expect to get.

Similarly, the integrated decision method (IDM) is a collaborative style that assumes that a solution exists that is acceptable to all parties (Filley, 1975). IDM draws on problem-solving principles (see Chapter 7). The first step in this method is to create an environment in which problems can be solved, for example, having the parties meet in a quiet unthreatening place. Then the parties are led to agree that a mutually agreeable solution is possible. They then discuss their attitudes and feelings about the problem, define the problem, search for alternative solutions, evaluate the solutions on the basis of quality and acceptability, and choose a solution. A variant of IDM is principled negotiation (Fisher and Ury, 1981).

Organizations can also take steps to reduce conflict. They can design specialized dispute systems (Brett, Goldberg, and Ury, 1990). Or they may adopt special roles or alter structure to resolve disputes; for example, special positions might be developed to manage conflict across departments. Liaisons or integrators one level above the conflict may take on the special job of managing conflict. Or an organization can relocate or recombine units to reduce conflict. Organizations can also reduce conflict by improving their management practices. They can help departments develop superordinate goals that draw the departments into collaborative efforts. They can help reduce ambiguities through techniques such as goal setting (see Chapter 1). They can make policies and rules clearer. They can reallocate or add resources or modify communication. Finally, they can rotate personnel and alter reward systems.

SUMMARY

The characteristics of groups were the first point of focus. The ways groups structure themselves depend on their need for effective performance. Two dimensions of structure discussed were status and roles. We introduced the notion of comparison levels for alternatives in our discussion of group formation. Individuals choose whether to enter a group—or whether to stay in a group—on the basis of which action provides them with the most desirable outcome or, when the two outcomes are both seen as undesirable, which is the less undesirable. Group formation is also affected by variables that influence the attraction of one person for another.

Group norms, the informal rules that regulate people's behavior, develop slowly through explicit statements by supervisors and co-workers, critical events in a group's history, primacy, and carryover behaviors from past situations.

Conformity, cohesiveness, and deviance are significant aspects of all groups. The return-potential model helps explain conformity to behavioral expectations. Factors that foster cohesiveness, or the spirit of closeness, were delineated, and cohesiveness was discussed as an important antecedent to viability and productivity. Deviance and group pressures that are brought to bear on deviance were mentioned.

We opened our discussion of group effectiveness with a review of investigations into the differences between individual and group effectiveness. The research indicates that, by and large, groups provide significant advantages over individual action, a significant finding given that the increasing complexity of work tasks probably will require group effort. Two extensive lists advocating certain behaviors as characteristics of effective groups were presented; then we examined a framework that proposed three classes of variables that influence group performance: (1) knowledge and skills of group members, (2) task performance strategies, and (3) effort expended by group members. Three additional models of effectiveness were given brief attention.

Intergroup perceptions are formed on the basis of the prior knowledge people bring to situations and on the attributions they make about those situations. We categorize groups along such social dimensions as gender or race and assume they will behave in accord with our stereotypes about how such groups behave. These categories help promote the establishment of in-groups and out-groups. Research into the effects of contact between different groups has proved to be inconclusive on whether contact resolves group conflict or engenders it.

One model of intergroup exchanges studies the interactions of powerful, powerless, and caught-in-the-middle groups. In these exchanges, social comparison processes develop in which each group comes to the situation with very different perceptions to guide behavior. The groups engage in what one author calls dynamically conservative behavior in which, while they intend to achieve different ends, they manage to perpetuate the status quo.

Because groups have differential power relationships, they can fall into conflict. This conflict can be related to differences in goals, cognitive factors, affective factors, or behaviors. Groups have five strategies for dealing with conflict, including avoidance, accommodation, competition, compromise, and collaboration. Two common conflict resolution techniques are mediation and arbitration.

MANAGERIAL INSIGHT

To: *Student Managers*
From: *Veteran Manager*
Subject: *Groups*

As a manager, one of your jobs will be to coordinate the efforts of groups of people. When you have several of them reporting to you, your whole area of responsibility can become dysfunctional if relations between your groups break down.

Consider this example from my experience. I had recently been named manager of a department that had three sections. Under the structure that existed, one section was responsible for planning customer programs, another section was responsible for marketing or implementing these programs, and the third section handled the paperwork that was generated by customer participation.

I quickly discovered that a serious communications problem existed between planning and marketing. The people in planning perceived the marketing section as "mere implementers," and considered the planning function the more important of the two. The marketing section felt that the planners were arrogant and didn't consider the real world when making or planning their programs.

Relations between the two sections had reached a point where they were hardly speaking to each other, even though their offices were just a few steps away. Instead, everything was put in writing.

When the planning supervisor advised me that he had unilaterally changed the name of his section to "Program Plans, Policy and Analysis," I realized that the planners had gotten too deeply into their role. Their group identity had overtaken them. Something had to be done.

The solution was made easy for me when the supervisor of the section was offered and accepted another position in the company. I brought in to succeed him a supervisor whose most important qualification was that he was admittedly not a planner. He was a pragmatic manager who was well grounded in the real world and who realized the necessity for groups in the same department to function smoothly together. The new name was quickly discarded in favor of the more mundane "Planning."

The communications barriers between the two groups came down within a few weeks of his appointment, and the output of both units improved substantially.

The lesson from this for me was that while group identity is important and can foster cohesiveness and teamwork, too much of it can be counterproductive. Members of groups in an organization must see themselves as units within a bigger entity with a higher purpose than that of their particular group. This principle holds true whether the group in question is a handful of people or a large division with hundreds of people.

Your task as manager becomes not only to foster positive "groupness" but to control it so that it stays in perspective. You can do this by the way you structure your groups, the norms you allow or promote, and the goals toward which you direct them. In this process, reflect on the discussions in this chapter about how groups are like and unlike individuals. A group is made up of individuals, but it has an existence and a personality of its own beyond the individuals in it. If the job of a manager is to get things done through other people, the job of a top manager is to get things done through *groups* of other people. Learn the techniques of doing both, and you will be well on your way toward one of those top jobs.

REVIEW QUESTIONS

1. How is signing up, as described in the theme case, related to socialization, discussed in the previous chapter?

2. What three factors influence group structure?

3. Distinguish between position and status and explain how each affects the effectiveness of group members.

4. Describe Heinen and Jacobson's stages of group formation. What criticism has been made of this model?

5. Carman allowed the members of the Eclipse Group to violate company norms for working hours. How might the creation of a new norm have added to the creation of group identity in the Eclipse Group? Would the creation of unique norms have presented any potential dangers to this group?

6. What four mechanisms did Feldman identify for the creation of group norms?

7. What personality or individual characteristics are associated with conformity?

8. What three techniques did Albanese and Van Fleet suggest to combat free riding?

9. What two explanations are offered for the development of risky shift?

10. Are groups more effective than individuals in making decisions? Are they more efficient?

11. What three variables did Hackman and Morris identify as influencing group performance? What three factors affect those three variables?

12. What is the effect of putting people in categories with others, and how can managers use that in building groups?

13. What does psychological research into desegregation say about the effects of intergroup contact? Which variable has research shown to be most effectively manipulated to promote desegregation?

14. Describe the two concepts that Smith argued guide intergroup interactions.

15. What four dimensions of group differentiation were identified by Brett and Rognes?

16. What are the four types of conflict? On what three levels may they take place?

17. Name five strategies for dealing with conflict.

REFERENCES

Adler, N. (1991). *International Dimensions of Organizational Behavior,* 2nd ed. Boston: PWS-KENT.

Albanese, R., and Van Fleet, D. D. (1985). Rational behavior in groups: The free riding tendency. *Academy of Management Review* 10:244–255.

Allport, F. H. (1920). The influence of the group upon association and thought. *Journal of Experimental Psychology* 3:159–182.

Asch, S. E. (1956). Studies of independence and conformity: Minority of one against a unanimous majority. *Psychological Monographs* 70 (9, Whole No. 416).

Bell, M. A. (1982). Phases in group problem solving. *Small Group Behavior* 13:475–495.

Bennis, W. G., and Shepard, H. A. (1955). A theory of group development. *Human Relations* 9:415–437.

Blake, R. R., and Mouton, J. S. (1969). *Building a Dynamic Corporation Through Grid Organization Development.* Reading, MA: Addison-Wesley.

Brett, J. M., Goldberg, S. B., and Ury, W. L. (1990). Designing systems for resolving disputes in organizations. *American Psychologist* 45:162–170.

Brewer, M. B., and Kramer, R. M. (1985). The psychology of intergroup attitudes and behavior. In M. R. Rosenzweig and L. W. Porter (eds.), *Annual Review of Psychology* 36:219–243. Palo Alto, CA: Annual Review, Inc.

Cartwright, C., and Zander, A. (1968). *Group Dynamics: Research and Theory.* New York: Harper & Row.

Cole, R. E. (1989). *Strategies for Learning: Small Group Activities in American, Japanese, and Swedish Industry.* Berkeley, CA: University of California Press.

Collins, B. E., and Guetzkow, H. A. (1964). *A Social Psychology of Group Processes for Decision Making.* New York: Wiley.

Davis, T. R. V., and Luthans, F. (1980). Managers in action: A new look at their behavior and operating modes. *Organization Dynamics* 9:64–80.

Deaux, K., and Wrightsman, L. S. (1984). *Social Psychology in the 80s*, 4th ed. Monterey, CA: Brooks/Cole.

Dyer, W. G. (1977). *Team Building: Issues and Alternatives*. Reading, MA: Addison-Wesley.

Eagly, A. H. (1983). Gender and social influence: A social psychological analysis. *American Psychologist* 38:971–981.

Eagly, A. H., and Wood, W. (1982). Inferred sex differences in status as a determinant of gender stereotypes about social influence. *Journal of Personality and Social Psychology* 43:915–928.

Early, C. (1989). Social loafing and collectivism: A comparison of the United States and the People's Republic of China. *Administrative Science Quarterly* 34:565–581.

Eden, D. (1985). Team development: A true field experiment employing three levels of rigor. *Journal of Applied Psychology* 70:94–100.

Eden, D. (1986). Team development: Quasi experimental confirmation among combat companies. *Group and Organizational Studies* 11:133–146.

Feldman, J. (1984). The development and enforcement of group norms. *Academy of Management Review* 9:47–53.

Festinger, L. (1950). Informal social communication. *Psychological Review* 57:271–282.

Filley, A. C. (1975). *Interpersonal Conflict Resolution*. Glenview, IL: Scott, Foresman.

Finholt, T., and Sproull, L. S. (1990). Electronic groups at work. *Organization Science* 1:41–64.

Fisher, R., and Ury, W. (1981). *Getting to Yes: Negotiating Agreement Without Giving In*. Boston: Houghton Mifflin.

Gersick, C. J. G. (1988). Time and transition in work teams: Toward a new model of group development. *Academy of Management Journal* 31:9–41.

Gladstein, D. (1984). Groups in context: A model of organizational effectiveness. *Administrative Science Quarterly* 29:499–517.

Goodman, P. S., Ravlin, E. C., and Argote, L. (1986). Current thinking about groups. In P. S. Goodwin and Associates. *Designing Effective Work Groups*. San Francisco: Jossey-Bass.

Hackman, J. R. (1976). Group influence on individuals. In M. D. Dunnette (ed.), *Handbook of Industrial and Organizational Psychology*. Chicago: Rand McNally, pp. 1455–1525.

Hackman, J. R. (ed.). (1989). *Groups That Work (And Those That Don't)*. San Francisco: Jossey-Bass.

Hackman, J. R., and Morris, C. G. (1975). Group tasks, group interaction process, and group performance effectiveness. In L. Berkowitz (ed.), *Advances in Experimental Social Psychology* 8:47–100.

Hackman, J. R., and Suttle, J. L. (1977). *Improving Life at Work*. Santa Monica, CA: Goodyear.

Hall, J. (1969). *Conflict Management Survey*. Houston: Teleometrics.

Hamilton, V. L. (1978). Obediance and responsibility: A jury simulation. *Journal of Personality and Social Psychology* 36:126–146.

Hare, P. (1976). *Handbook of Small Group Research*. New York: Free Press, p. 781ff.

Helyar, J., and Burrough, B. (1990). *Barbarians at the Gates*. New York: Harper & Row.

Heinen, J. S., and Jacobson, E. (1976). A model of task group development in complex organizations and a strategy of implementation. *Academy of Management Review* 1:98–111.

Hofstede, G. (1980). *Culture's Consequences: International Differences in Work-Related Values*. Beverly Hills, CA: Sage.

Jackson, J. (1965). Structural characteristics of norms. In I. D. Steiner and M. Fishbein (eds.), *Current Studies in Social Psychology*. New York: Holt, pp. 301–309.

Jacobson, E. (1956). The growth of groups in voluntary organization. *Journal of Social Science Issues* 12:18–23.

Killian, L. M. (1952). The significance of multiple-group membership in disaster. *American Journal of Sociology* 57:309–314.

Lamm, H., and Myers, D. G. (1978). Group-induced polarization of attitudes and behavior. In L. Berkowitz (ed.), *Advances in Experimental Social Psychology*, vol. 11. New York: Academic Press, pp. 145–195.

Latane, B., Williams, K., and Harkins, S. (1979). Many hands make light the work: The causes and consequences of social loafing. *Journal of Personality and Social Psychology* 37:822–832.

Leavitt, H. J. (1975). Suppose we took groups seriously. In E. L. Cass and F. G. Zimmer (eds.), *Man and Work in Society*. New York: Van Nostrand.

Levine, R. A., and Campbell, D. T. (1972). *Ethnocentrism*. New York: Wiley.

Likert, R. (1961). *New Patterns of Management*. New York: McGraw-Hill.

McCall, M. W., et al. (1980). *Studies in Managerial Work: Results and Methods*. Greensborough, SC: Center for Creative Leadership.

McGrath, J. E. (1984). *Groups: Interaction and Performance*. San Francisco: Jossey-Bass.

McGregor, D. (1960). *The Human Side of Enterprise*. New York: McGraw-Hill.

Mintzberg, H. (1973). *The Nature of Managerial Work*. New York: Harper & Row.

Moreland, R. L., and Levine, J. M. (1982). Socialization in small groups: Temporal changes in individual-group relations. In L. Berkowitz (ed.), *Advances in Experimental Social Psychology*, vol. 15. New York: Academic Press, pp. 137–184.

Mullin, B. (1983). Operationalizing the effect of the group on the individual: A self attention perspective. *Journal of Experimental Social Psychology* 19:295–322.

Neuhauser, P. (1988). *Tribal Warfare in Organizations*. New York: Harper.

Nieva, V. F., Fleishman, E. A., and Rieck, A. (1978). Team dimensions: Their identity, their measurement, and their relationships. Final Technical Report for Contract No. DAHC19-78-C-000. Washington, D.C.: Adraneed Research Resources Organization.

O'Reilly, C. A., Caldwell, D. F., and Barnett, W. P. (1989). Work group demography, social integration, and turnover. *Administrative Science Quarterly* 34:21–37.

Poole, M. S. (1983). Decision development in small groups. III: A multiple sequence model of group decision development. *Communication Monographs* 50:321–341.

Reitan, H. T., and Shaw, M. E. (1964). Group membership, sex-composition of the group, and conformity behavior. *Journal of Social Psychology* 64:45–51.

Roberts, K. H., and Gargano, G. (1989). Managing interdependencies in high reliability organizations. In M. A. Van Glimont and S. Morman (eds.), *Managing Complexity in High Technology Organizations*. New York: Oxford University Press, pp. 146–159.

Sachdev, I., and Bourhis, R. Y. (1984). Minimal majorities and minorities. *European Journal of Social Psychology* 14:35–52.

Schachter, S. (1951). Deviation, rejection, and communication. *Journal of Abnormal and Social Psychology* 46:190–207.

Schneider, B. C. (1985). Organizational behavior. In M. R. Rosenzweig and L. W. Porter (eds.), *Annual Review of Psychology*, pp. 573–612. Palo Alto, CA: Annual Review, Inc.

Shaw, M. E. (1981). *Group Dynamics: The Psychology of Small Group Behavior*. New York: McGraw-Hill.

Shea, G. P., and Guzzo, R. A. (1987). Groups as human resources. In K. M. Rowland and C. R. Ferris (eds.), *Research in Personnel and Human Resources Management*. Greenwich, CT: JAI Press, pp. 323–356.

Sherif, M. (1966). *In Common Predicament: Social Psychology of Intergroup Conflict and Cooperation*. New York: Houghton Mifflin.

Smith, K. K. (1983). Social comparisons in intergroup relations. In L. L. Cummings and B. M. Staw (eds.), *Research in Organizational Behavior*, vol. 5. Greenwich, CT: JAI Press.

Steiner, I. D. (1972). *Group Process and Productivity*. New York: Academic Press.

Stigler, G. J. (1974). Free riders and collective action: An appendix to theories of economic regulation. *Bell Journal of Economics and Management Science* 5:359–365.

Stoner, J. A. F. (1961). A comparison of individual and group decisions involving risk. Unpublished Master's Thesis, School of Industrial Management, M.I.T.

Sundstrom, E., De Meuse, K. P., and Futrell, D. (1990). Work teams. *American Psychologist* 45:120–133.

Tajfel, H., and Forgas, J. P. (1981). Social categorization: Cognitions, values, and groups. In J. P. Forgas (ed.), *Social Cognition: Perspectives on Everyday Understanding*. New York: Academic Press, pp. 113–140.

Taylor, D. W., and Faust, W. L. (1952). Twenty questions: Efficiency in problem solving as a function of size of group. *Journal of Experimental Psychology* 44:360–368.

Thibaut, J. W., and Kelley, H. H. (1959). *The Social Psychology of Groups*. New York: Wiley.

Thomas, K. W. (1979). Conflict. In S. Kerr (ed.), *Organizational Behavior*. Columbus, OH: Comd., p. 151–181.

Tuckman, B. (1965). Developmental sequences in small groups. *Psychological Bulletin* 63:384–399.

Varney, G. H. (1989). *Building Productive Teams*. San Francisco: Jossey-Bass.

Walton, R. E. (1986). A vision-led approach to management restructuring. *Organization Dynamics* 14:4–16.

Wheaton, B. (1974). Interpersonal conflict and cohesiveness in dyadic relationships. *Sociometry* 37:328–348.

Whyte, W. F. (1956). *The Organization Man*. New York: Simon & Schuster.

Zajonc, R. B. (1965). Social facilitation. *Science* 149:269–374.

C H A P T E R 5

Communication:
How Workers Talk Together

CHAPTER OVERVIEW

This chapter has two primary purposes: to delineate communication issues in organizations and to present steps for changing communication activities in organizations.

THEME CASE

"Bishop Rock Dead Ahead: The Grounding of the *U.S.S. Enterprise*" describes how a series of distractions, misperceptions, and a lack of communication among team members resulted in a failure of the organization to work in the designated manner.

CHAPTER OUTLINE

- **What Is Communication?**
- **The Sender**
- **Transmitting Information: Channels**
- **The Medium and Situation**
- **Message Content**
- **The Receiver**
- **Summary**
- **Managerial Insight**

KEY DEFINITIONS

Communication   getting, transmitting, and attaching meaning to information.

Channels   ways to transmit information.

Paralanguage   modifications in speech, including pitch, rhythm, intensity, pauses, and so on.

Additional Terms

Encoding
Decoding
Noise
Physical features
Stereotypes
Fundamental attribution error
Recency effect

Primacy effect
Socratic effect
Halo effect
Priming effect
Syntax
Technical language
Kinesics
Leakage
Interpersonal distance
Medium
Context
Attribution theory
Self-fulfilling prophecy
Feedback
Realistic job previews

BISHOP ROCK DEAD AHEAD:
THE GROUNDING OF THE *U.S.S. ENTERPRISE*

> When anyone asks me how I can best describe my experience in
> nearly 40 years at sea, I merely say, uneventful. Of course there
> have been winter gales, storms, fog and the like, but in all my expe-
> rience, I have never been in any accident of any sort worth speak-
> ing about. I have seen but one vessel in distress in all my years at
> sea. I never saw a wreck and have never been wrecked, nor was I
> ever in any predicament that threatened to end in disaster of any
> sort. (Captain E. J. Smith, *RMS Titanic*)

On November 2, 1985, the U.S.S. *Enterprise* was conducting an evaluated
exercise (ORE) in waters off Southern California. At 1745 hours, while
recovering aircraft, she sustained hull damage while steaming through shallow water near Bishop Rock.

To better display the context and processes that contributed to the
incident, the events that took place on the bridge are described from the
perspective of some of the key participants of the bridge team: the ship's
commanding officer (CO); the navigator; the assistant navigator (ANAV);
the officer of the deck (OOD); the junior officer of the deck (JOOD); and
the junior officer of the watch (JOOW).

CO. At the time of the grounding, *Enterprise* was recovering a small
flight of three aircraft. The captain, on the bridge, had spent most of the
day worrying about the need to sail his ship to a designated destination
called a choke point to the south, a journey that had to be completed if the
ship was to continue the ORE successfully. His efforts to move to the
choke point in a timely way had been thwarted repeatedly during the day
by morning and early afternoon fog patches, by the evaluations being conducted, and by surface winds that required changes of course for the sake
of air operations. The recovery currently under way was the last deviation
to the north the ship would have to make before a high speed dash to the
southwest to set up for the choke point transit.

This evaluation was the first one in the CO's memory to be con-

Adapted from K. H. Roberts, "Bishop Rock Dead Ahead: The Grounding of the *U.S.S. Enterprise*," Naval Institute *Proceedings*, in press. Reprinted by permission.

ducted at the beginning of a ship's final at-sea work-up period before the ship was deemed ready to be deployed overseas. Ordinarily, the ORE was a "graduation exercise." The timing of the evaluation was a major concern to the CO. He felt that neither the air wing nor the flight deck crews were ready for the evaluation's fast-paced, high-intensity air operations or for the "blue water" operations (which take place so far out to sea that no land-based air fields are available in emergencies). The ORE observers acknowledged this concern but declined to indicate whether their expectations would be adjusted accordingly. All the traditional first-day evaluations were scheduled, and when a persistent morning fog finally cleared, the senior ORE observer asked the CO to conduct a time-consuming drill for the recovery of a man overboard.

Just after 1600 hours the CO left the bridge for about 20 minutes for a meeting. When he returned to the bridge, he found the officer of the deck preparing for a downwind recovery of the three aircraft, contrary to what had been planned. Earlier in the afternoon the CO had returned to the bridge from another brief absence to find that a different OOD had unilaterally chosen a different course from planned.

He knew he was the only one on the bridge who could solve the wind vector problems mentally, but he had left instructions and the watch appeared to be disregarding them. This should have alerted the CO that the bridge crew was not operating normally, but he became involved in tactical conversations about the battle plan and did not follow up.

The CO asked the navigator for a course recommendation and was told 180°. Carriers cannot land their aircraft unless the wind over the deck is sufficiently strong; and the CO knew that course 180 would not provide enough wind. He remarked, "That's dumb," estimating that a course much farther to the east would be required. The CO instructed the conning officer to turn starboard. The proper course for recovery winds was ultimately found at 322°.

At that point the CO noted white flood lights, which he recognized as fishing boat lights, dead ahead. There was also a dim red flashing light among them, which the CO concluded was a net buoy marker from one of the boats. This conclusion was based on two previous encounters with fishing nets in this area. The CO discussed with the conning officer whether, once the last aircraft was landed, they should turn to port, inside the red flashing "net buoy marker," or turn starboard.

The navigator, who plotted the course himself, remarked that he would like to give Bishop Rock a wider berth than 1,000 yards. Since Bishop Rock had not been mentioned in earlier discussions, the CO was astonished to hear it mentioned now, but a look at the chart confirmed that the ship was steaming into shallow water at a speed of 20 knots.

As the CO returned to the port side of the bridge, he ordered a moderate shift to the right in the ship's course consistent with the ship's speed. He then told the conning officer to increase this shift to 20 degrees. In the darkness he still thought the Bishop Rock marker was a mile or more ahead, but as the ship turned starboard it was clear that the light was closer.

Navigator. The navigator notes that in setting up for the launch of aircraft at 1700 hours, the ship had turned from a northerly course to a southwesterly course of 220°. This looked good to him for two reasons: it would set the ship up nicely for a downwind leg for the aircraft recovery at 1730 hours, and it would open the distance to the Bishop Rock area. He was concerned about Bishop Rock because it had a lot of fishing boats around it, making it difficult to pick out the rock in the radar picture. He told the CO he wanted to come to port to open the distance to Bishop Rock and begin heading south to the choke point, but the CO, distracted by other events, did not hear any mention of Bishop Rock. According to the navigator, at 1710 both he and the junior officer of the deck had a good idea of the location of Bishop Rock.

The navigator recommended to the OOD to turn to port after the completion of the launch and set up for downwind recovery on course 140°. He told the OOD and the conning officer to consider the contact situation and evaluate a turn to course 180. He saw a fishing vessel on the port bow and thought they would pass it; he moved to the port side of the bridge. In reply to the CO's question about what he wanted, the navigator said "140." The CO stated something the navigator could not hear; the navigator was then surprised to see the conning officer turn starboard. Initially the navigator was concerned that the conning officer had confused port and starboard, but the OOD reported that the conning officer was following the CO's orders. No one attempted to reconcile these apparent contradictions with the CO.

The navigator then went to the chart to check the immediate area around the rock. The assistant navigator and OOD both spotted Bishop Rock bearing 319, at a range of 5,900 yards away. Neither informed the CO. The CO came to the chart and asked if this was a good course. The navigator pointed at Bishop Rock and stated that he wanted to open it up more to the right. The CO then went to the conning officer and said what the navigator thought was "right 10 degrees rudder," followed immediately by "make that 20 right." This appeared to the navigator to be a safe figure. Thinking the ship was still turning, the navigator checked the range again.

ANAV. The ANAV stood the 1600 watch as conning officer until relieved by another qualified officer at 1725. He reviewed the navigational plot chart before assuming the watch in order to get a picture in his mind of the general direction *Enterprise* needed to go.

The ANAV expected to come further right to the northwest to obtain the desired winds for the recovery of aircraft. Shortly after this his relief arrived for turnover. The ANAV briefed him on the situation, and during the brief heard something about a turn to 140–180 to launch and recover. He wanted to recommend a turn to the northwest, based on his experience earlier in the watch. He was becoming confused, but turned the watch over to his relief anyway.

The ANAV again checked the position of the rock and discussed this with the navigator. The navigator went to talk with the CO, and the ANAV assumed the navigator was telling the CO about the location of Bishop Rock. He did not confirm his assumption. He left the bridge at 1738 to get something to eat.

OOD. The OOD reports that at 1700, some 45 minutes before the grounding, he and the navigator were trying to estimate the bearing and the range to Bishop Rock from the dead reckoned position shown on the chart. A course of 180° would carry *Enterprise* away from Bishop Rock and aid in arrival at the simulated choke point, but the 140° course, while closing on the choke point, would take the ship too far east. The OOD assumed that the CO knew the flashing red light was Bishop Rock, but did not check his assumption with the CO. After the 1725 launch, the OOD ordered the conning officer to commence a slow turn to port to avoid a fishing boat on the port bow and try a new downwind track of 180°. (This is when the CO ordered the conning officer to turn to starboard, knowing that the 180° course would not provide the "hoped for" acceptable winds for aircraft recovery.)

The OOD then asked the JOOD if he had Bishop Rock on the radar. The JOOD replied that the Surface Plot in the Combat Information Center (CIC) had Bishop Rock, but he was personally unsure of its relative location. (Note that this is inconsistent with what the navigator thought the JOOD knew.)

At approximately 1735 the OOD (a lieutenant junior grade) was distracted from the situation when he accepted a telephone call from the Flag's Watch Officer (a lieutenant commander), who called to inform him that someone had spotted a man in a flight suit walking aft near the Admiral's quarters with a hand gun that looked like a 9 mm Uzi. The OOD spoke with the man making this report and told him to call the Master at Arms with the information. The Flag Watch officer spoke with the OOD again, keeping him on the phone until approximately 1747.

JOOD. The JOOD noticed that one of the surface contacts identified by radar had been redesignated from unidentified to "ISHROCK." Not knowing what that was, he asked the Surface Watch Officer, who informed him that it was Bishop Rock. He informed the OOD but could not tell him where the rock was on the radar because there was no contact where the status board said it was. There was confusion about which of the un-identified radar contacts really was Bishop Rock, and so the JOOD had "ISHROCK" redesignated as unidentified until he could gather more in-formation. A few minutes later the OOD saw the dim pulsating light of Bishop Rock. The navigator saw it, and the JOOD asked him for a bearing. The JOOD "then said out loud to no one in particular that 'CX' was Bishop Rock and changed it to that on the radar." At this time the turn to starboard for aircraft recovery commenced on the orders of the CO. The JOOD was briefing the oncoming JOOD when a mild shudder was felt as the ship sustained damage passing over shoal water of Bishop Rock.

JOOW. The conn had been in the hands of the junior officer of the watch since 1725. The CO ordered him to turn starboard to 300°. Later the CO told him to come 20° further right to 320°. To sweeten the winds across the deck for aircraft recovery, they ultimately decided on a course of 335°. The CO and JOOW noticed two fishing boats off the starboard bow, and the CO ordered the JOOW to turn starboard once again and lower the ship's speed. The JOOW was told by the CO to stay steady on a course of 020°. Moments later he felt a shudder. The JOOW remembers that the CO was unaware of Bishop Rock being in the area. Eventually, the navi-gator told the CO it was there, and the CO was "irritated" that he had not been informed earlier. The JOOW indicated that he was taking orders from the CO and not the OOD and that he was in the dark regarding the ship's intentions.

What Is Communication?

Three major factors contributed to the grounding of *Enterprise:* a series of distractions, misperceptions that led to confusion and misinterpretation of the situation, and lack of communication among the bridge team. These fac-tors resulted in the failure of the bridge team to work as the U.S. Navy has designed it to work.

The bridge team might have worked properly if the officers had had a better grasp of the probability of and potential for distraction, mispercep-tions, and lack of communication. If they understood these processes, they might have taken steps to prevent them from occurring. Many of these steps are already part of the navy rules and procedures and need only be reinforced.

For example, if a member of the bridge team does not completely understand the situation, as the junior officer of the watch did not, navy procedures require that he seek immediate clarification. An uncounted number of organizational difficulties are blamed on "communication problems." Yet those who use the label so easily rarely know how to dissect, analyze, and remedy failures in communication. "Communication" is simply the garbage can into which many tough—and some fairly simple—problems are thrown.

This chapter has two purposes. First, we will distinguish among and describe a number of communication issues that arise in organizations. Second, we will suggest steps that might be taken to change communication in organizations for the better. Clarifying these issues should help managers better understand various aspects of communication and should suggest ideas about how to increase organizational effectiveness. To accomplish these goals, we will examine in detail the various aspects of communication: the sender of information, the way information is sent, the content of the message, and the receiver of the message. This structure parallels the model of the communication process.

Communication is getting, transmitting, and attaching meaning to information. A simple model of the communication process is depicted in Figure 5.1: an individual encodes information and sends it to a receiver, who decodes it. **Encoding** is the process by which the communicator packages or translates ideas into a set of symbols. **Decoding** is the process by which the receiver interprets the information. Both encoding and decoding are influ-

FIGURE 5.1
A Basic Model of the Communication Process

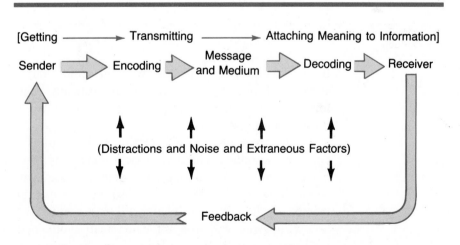

Source: Adapted with permission from C. Shannon and W. Weaver, *The Mathematical Theory of Communication* (Urbana: University of Illinois, 1949), p. 7. Copyright © 1949 by the University of Illinois Press.

enced by many factors, including personal characteristics and previous experiences of the people involved, aspects of the situation they are in, and predictions they can make about the future. Communication is further influenced by **noise**, or extraneous characteristics of the environment, and the entire process is characterized by feedback to the original communicator. In the Bishop Rock case, the lack of feedback prevented accurate message encoding and decoding. The CO, for instance, seems to have misunderstood the navigator's course recommendation.

Figure 5.1, which turns out to be more complex than it first appears, may describe a two-person interaction to some degree, but it is not sufficient to describe communication in organizations. In any organization many such interactions occur simultaneously, usually involving more than two individuals. Organizations are complex patterns of interwoven networks of exchange, as we saw in Chapter 2. The exchange in these networks is influenced by other factors, such as differences in authority of the communicators, the purpose of the communication, and such aspects of the external environment as markets and legal systems. Organizational communication, then, is more than encoding, transmitting, and decoding information. It is the social glue that helps the parts of the organization stay together. It is the vehicle by which goals, task assignments, and evaluations are transmitted. Without it, nothing else can happen in an organization. Given this complexity, it is understandable that we rarely try to untangle its elements. It is much easier to blame our ills on some vague "communications problem." In fact, it is probably a wonder that much communication in complex organizations is reasonably accurate.

The Sender

Because the message originates with the sender, our discussion will do so as well. Before that sender can communicate anything, he has to obtain information about it and interpret that information. This section focuses on those two processes.

The two sources of information available to us are our environments and our own minds. The environment includes information we obtain from books, newspapers, and magazines; television and radio; other people; our social and work environments; and so on. Our own minds provide us with memories, thoughts, and feelings. These mental creations really involve how we interpret and process the information obtained from the people and world around us. Before exploring how that information is stored and retrieved, let us examine the issues related to thinking, or how information is processed.

Forming Impressions

Although most of us believe that we are primarily rational actors, receiving and evaluating information from the environment, the truth is that much of the information that we receive is processed in less rigorous ways. People form extensive impressions, for instance, based on limited information. The exercise in the feature "Information Cues" demonstrates how this process takes place.

FEATURE: *Information Cues*

Select a person who is not well known to you or your friends. Ask that person to give you and your friends a short description covering *only* the nature of his or her home (where it is, the number of rooms, anything else that comes to mind), and his or her educational background (5 minutes). Then answer the following questions about this person and note the information you are basing your answers on in the "Cues" column (10 minutes).

	Cues	Weight Given Cues
How old is this person?		
_____	_____	_____
	_____	_____
What part of the country or what foreign country is this person from?	_____	_____
	_____	_____
_____	_____	_____
	_____	_____
Does this person work?	_____	_____
__yes __no	_____	_____
If yes, __full-time __part-time	_____	_____
What is this person's job?	_____	_____
	_____	_____
_____	_____	_____
	_____	_____
	_____	_____

What are this person's
hobbies?

_____   _____
_____   _____
_____   _____

_____   _____   _____
_____   _____   _____
_____   _____   _____
                             _____   _____
                             _____   _____
Is this person married?   _____   _____
                             _____   _____
—yes —no   _____   _____
                             _____   _____
                             _____   _____
                             _____   _____
Does this person have   _____   _____
children?   _____   _____
                             _____   _____
—yes —no   _____   _____
                             _____   _____
If yes, how many?   _____   _____
_____   _____   _____
What kind of car does   _____   _____
this person drive?   _____   _____
                             _____   _____
                             _____   _____

Now go back to each of the cues and weight the importance you attached to it (1 = very important, 3 = neither important nor unimportant, 7 = very unimportant) (5 minutes). Now discuss with the group the answers, the cues leading to those answers, and the weight given various cues. Have someone note on a blackboard or other available visible place the answers, cues, and weights (20 minutes).

Finally, have the target person answer the questions (5 minutes).

Afterward in a group discussion answer the following questions (15 minutes).

1. What kinds of information are given the most weight in forming first impressions (expressions, attire or other nonverbal cues, verbal cues, aspects of the environment, etc.)?

2. What did you already know that provided cues?

3. Why did you weight the factors the way you did?

4. What kinds of assumptions did you make in answering the questions?

5. What were the bases for those assumptions (e.g., people who live in four-bedroom houses usually have children)?

6. What expectations did you have that influenced which specific information you paid attention to?

7. What did you add to the information that "rounded it out"?

8. How did you summarize the information you had?

Source: Reprinted by permission of Macmillan Publishing Company from K. H. Roberts, "Communicating in Organizations," in F. Kast and J. Rosenzweig (eds.), *Modules in Management* (Chicago: SRA Associates, 1984). Copyright © 1984 by SRA Associates.

Physical features are among the first things we notice about other people; keep in mind, however, that the inferences drawn from physical characteristics are culture bound. The Japanese culture, for example, emphasizes a respect for elders, whereas American culture is more youth oriented. Thus an older, white-haired employee might be viewed by a Japanese manager as having valuable experience and by an American manager as being over the hill. The captain of the *Enterprise* was a tall, imposing person, which influenced how others communicated with him.

Long ago a psychologist devised a scheme for categorizing body type (Sheldon, 1940) that yielded three types: endomorphs, or heavy, fleshy people; ectomorphs, or skinny people; and mesomorphs, or muscular people. Inferences are commonly made about the personalities of these three types of people. Our society perceives mesomorphs to be energetic, well adjusted, and self-reliant, endomorphs to be lazy and unpopular, and ectomorphs to be ambitious, tense, and suspicious.

A large number of other physical characteristics are typically associated with certain personality traits. Bearded men are thought to be psychologically strong (Roll and Verinis, 1971). One study found that blondes are thought to have more fun, to be beautiful, and to be social and brunettes to be intelligent and dependable (Lawson, 1971). Blonde males are perceived as kind, but dark-haired men as strong and intelligent. Skin color is an important physical characteristic. In the United States people assign more negative traits to black- and brown-skinned people, and to a lesser extent to yellow-skinned people, than to white-skinned people (Brigham, 1976). One might hope that a future replication of this research would produce no such findings. *Black Like Me* (Griffin, 1961), the story of a white man who stained his skin dark and then toured the United States as a black man, poignantly tells what it is like to be treated differently solely on the basis of skin color.

It is no surprise that in our society different traits are ascribed to males and females and that males are assumed to have the traits required for effective management. Both men and women perceive men as calm, informal, logical, and ambitious. Women are seen as tactful, shy, and frivolous. Men are also seen as more normal and psychologically healthier than women. Women perceive female managers as more competent communicators than do males (Wheeless and Berryman-Fink, 1985).

Another important physical characteristic that triggers predispositions is physical handicap. An early study (Mussen and Barker, 1944) showed that handicapped people were thought to be more conscientious, persistent, religious, and unhappy than able-bodied people. They were also seen as more likely to feel inferior. In one study (Richardson, Hastorf, Goodmen, and Dornbush, 1961) people of different socioeconomic classes and geographic areas rank-ordered six pictures of a young child. The order consistently preferred was an able-bodied child, a child with a leg brace, a child in a wheelchair, a child with the left hand missing, a child with a facial disfigurement, and an obese child.

These **stereotypes**, based on body size, race, gender, or handicaps, are firmly rooted in U.S. society and color the way most individuals perceive and react to others. As powerful agents shaping our view of the world—and the people in it—stereotypes cannot be ignored. Since hundreds of possibilities arise every day for forming impressions based on limited information, these stereotypes are often called into play. The stereotype can then creep into the message we send to others about these encounters. Suppose we receive a directive from a higher-level manager to do something uncommon for the organization. If the manager is a man, we may pass it on as a sound new strategic thrust. But if the manager is a female, we may transmit it as an ill-advised move or, worse, as a foolish whim.

The literature on the impact of culture on stereotypes is vast, but few studies address intercultural communication and stereotypes in organizations. One example of such research is a study of the stereotypes of Japanese managers in Singapore (Everett, Stenning, and Longton, 1981). The researchers found that although no differences existed in the stereotypic view of these managers held by Americans, British, and Singaporeans who had little contact with them, those Singaporeans who had high contact with the Japanese managers held very different stereotypes. (See also the discussion of ethnocentrism in Chapter 4.) The increasing amount of global communications makes understanding intercultural communications all the more important.

When we form impressions about objects, we frequently form complex impressions that accept contradictions. In fact, faced with a complex subject like an organization, we usually form mixed impressions. An organization may be seen as large but informal, as having a poor management team while having a high-performance product, as conducting business ethically while having a negative impact on the environment nonetheless, and so on. When we form impressions about people, on the other hand, we tend to be consistent. We see others as good or bad, warm or cold, honest or dishonest—not both. Even when presented with inconsistent information, we tend to rearrange it, distort it, or eliminate some in an effort to be consistent.

Sources of Bias

Four sources of bias are also important determinants of how we process information (Ross, 1977):

1. We underestimate the impact of the situation on individual's behavior.

2. We perceive consensus where it does not exist.

3. We do not make allowances in our perceptions for the roles or positions people occupy.

4. We overlook the informational value of nonoccurrences or behavioral omissions.

The tendency to underestimate the impact of the situation and overestimate the impact of the individual on one's behavior is called the **fundamental attribution error**. As an example, you might observe that your secretary has of late been taking longer to produce reports or letters. You attribute this to laziness or lack of skill, when in fact the cause is a malfunction in the word processing software.

In the second source of bias, we see our own choices and judgments as relatively commonly held and appropriate to existing circumstances and we view other kinds of responses as uncommon, deviant, and inappropriate. For example, if you attend church regularly, are having an affair with a co-worker, and regularly cut people off in freeway traffic, you view these behaviors as more common than you would if you did not engage in them. A corollary of this bias, and of the fundamental attribution error, is that we judge people's actions that are unlike our own to be more distinctively revealing of their personalities than we do those actions that are like our own (Nisbett and Ross, 1980).

The third kind of bias is our failure to make adequate allowances for the influence of role advantages and disadvantages. Subordinates and supervisors interpret their interactions differently simply because of the role each occupies. In a sense this is a refinement of the fundamental attribution error. An experiment demonstrating this bias is featured in "The General Knowledge Quiz Game."

FEATURE: *The General Knowledge Quiz Game*

Ross, Greene, and House (1977) designed a general knowledge quiz game. The roles played in the game were questioner and contestant, with subjects randomly assigned to each role. The questioner's role was to make up questions based on his own knowledge, pose those questions to contestants, and provide accurate feedback when answers were wrong. Contestants, questioners, and observers were then required to rate each other's general knowledge. Everyone rated questioners as more knowledgeable— despite the fact that it was obvious to everyone that the contest was rigged to be unequal for the participants. Given the biases revealed by this experiment, imagine the errors in attribution likely to be made in superior– subordinate interactions or in the classroom.

Source: L. Ross, D. Greene, and P. House, "The 'False Consensus Effect': An Egocentric Bias in Social Perception and Attribution Processes, *Journal of Experimental and Social Psychology* 13(1977): 279–301.

Ample evidence suggests that the bias toward self-serving perceptions falls into this general category of biases (Larwood and Whittaker, 1977). Adam Smith noted that people overstate their chances of gain owing to "an absurd prescription of their own good fortune," which arises from "the overwhelming conceit which the greater part of men have of their own abilities" (Speigel, 1983, p. 243). People also tend to ascribe their own success to their superior abilities or intelligence but to attribute the success of others to good fortune or the use of influence. (The reverse is true for failure.)

The fourth kind of bias is overlooking the informational value of nonoccurrences. To illustrate, you meet a person of the opposite sex, chat with him or her, and come away with the vague feeling that he or she does not like you. But you search your memory for a reason and cannot find one. You fail to think about what the other person did not do—he or she did not prolong the interaction, did not meet your gaze, and did not show responses that normally signal liking.

When Do People Think?

The process of thinking includes asking how something happened, why something is the way it is, how things fit together, and so on. We know that people do not engage in thinking about all things. In fact, people are relatively miserly with their thinking resources. For example, you do not wake up in the morning and ask why you are in your pajamas, why you are brushing your teeth, or why you are listening to the radio while you dress.

One notion, in fact, is that the vast majority of our chatter is relatively unthinking and formed by a single salient event. In this view, our everyday attributions, opinions, and impressions are "top of the head" phenomena with little thought behind them. A good deal of evidence supports this position (see, for example, Taylor and Fiske, 1978). This view suggests that we often use irrelevant and trivial cues to draw sophisticated inferences and that we are unaware of doing this. In truth, however, such a strategy is useful to us: it helps us not to overthink about most matters and so prevents the waste of time by deferring action.

Alternatively, we all know of situations that demand all our thought processes (those in which we get tired of thinking). Under what conditions do people think? People ask why when something unexpected happens or when confronted by a problem. Both dependency and the unexpected motivate a search for answers. A subordinate is probably more concerned with what his supervisor is like than vice versa. After all, the subordinate is dependent on him for some, most, or even all the rewards of the job.

Some thinking takes place after the fact, as we attempt to understand what took place. Bad, painful, and unpleasant events cause us to search our thoughts: we ask why an accident occurred. The navy, trying to identify the events that led to the grounding of the *Enterprise*, asked the participants to review their thoughts. On such occasions, we must turn to our memories.

Some psychologists (Collins and Loftus, 1975) describe long-term memory as a network of concepts connected by paths. A concept is activated when excitation is transmitted to it from other concepts along these paths. After a concept is activated, it retains some residual excitation, and consequently, it requires less excitation to reactivate it again. Over time, when a concept is not used, the amount of excitation in it diminishes. Thus the likelihood of any concept being activated in the future depends on whether, and when, it was activated in the past.

Other psychologists (Wyer and Scrull, 1980) say that long-term memory is analogous to a set of mental storage bins, each bin containing information about a person, object, or event. The information is stored in the order in which it is deposited and subsequently is drawn out of the bins in a top-down manner. Hypothetically, a manager may have lots of information about "women employees" in some bin. The last piece of information stored is that they are "resourceful." When the concept "women employees" is activated, "resourceful" comes to the manager's mind. He uses that description and replaces it in the bin, ready to be activated again. If the manager sticks around the concept "women employees" long enough, other elements in the bin also reappear.

These two notions of long-term memory give us some idea about how we may retrieve information from our own heads. It appears that information stored last is frequently retrieved first (last in, first out, or LIFO). This theory is called the **recency effect**. Generally, we feel that a person's belief in a proposition is influenced more strongly by recently processed information than by "older" information. Thus politicians try to blitz voters just before the election. Likewise, we want the "last word" in an argument; the last position in a debate is seen as the stronger position. However, it is not always true that the last information in is the first out. Sometimes the first in is the first out (Luchins, 1957). General awareness of this **primacy effect** is evident in the common wisdom of mothers and job counselors everywhere— "first impressions are lasting." What that has to say about the content of our communications we will address later. Of course, another influence on memory is the intensity of the experience being remembered: the more intense the experience, the more easily remembered.

When searching for information to make a judgment, we sometimes retrieve a previous judgment relevant to the one under consideration (Higgins, Rholes, and Jones, 1977; Rosenberg and Sedlack, 1972). Since judgments come after evaluation of information (they are on top, in the memory, as it were), the old judgment, not the information on which it was based, may be what is used to make the new judgment. We saw this repeatedly in the Bishop Rock case, in which the major players used past judgments to make new ones, failing to go back to the original information. On the other hand, older information may also serve as an anchor against which new information is judged (Sherif, Sherif, and Nebergall, 1960).

Alternatively, it is possible that our own judgments and responses are more memorable than the external stimuli on which those judgments are based. That may be why we can often recall our subjective feeling about a person or event more easily than the things that produced those responses: "I like Jill, but I can't quite say why."

There is, too, the tendency for related thoughts to become more consistent over time. This factor is called the **Socratic effect**. For example, when we first walk into a large bank, we note its characteristics. Over time those characteristics become more homogeneous in our minds. We may also reorganize our thoughts to eliminate inconsistencies among them because inconsistencies are uncomfortable. If we judge Bill as perserverant, likable, and intelligent, we are likely to judge him high on almost all qualities, including neatness, though his office appears to have recently been hit by a tornado. This is known as the **halo effect**.

Concepts that have recently been used are more readily accessible than unused concepts, and those recently used concepts can affect other judgments. For example, suppose you are asked to judge how likable a potential co-worker might be. You know that he is able to do things well. The implication of this information for judging the man's likability depends on whether the information is interpreted as conveying that he is self-confident (a desirable trait) or conceited (an undesirable trait). One's interpretation depends on how recently he had thoughts regarding self-confidence or conceit. This is called **priming effect** because one concept primes another.

Besides being dependent on how information is presented, recall depends on a number of other factors. Among the most important is the amount of thinking devoted to the information in the past. The extent to which a proposition is processed depends on at least four factors: (1) the plausibility of the proposition; (2) the strength of its implications for other propositions; (3) the inconsistency between beliefs in one proposition and other beliefs; and (4) situational factors that lead one to think carefully about the objects of the belief.

First, a mental search for alternatives is less extensive when the proposition is highly plausible, because the information implying validity is already stored in one's memory and is quickly and easily accessible. "George Bush likes Ronald Reagan" is a plausible proposition, but "Edward Kennedy likes George Bush" is not. More thinking is required to evaluate implausible propositions than plausible ones. Highly improbable propositions that are discarded immediately may not follow this rule.

Second, if a person is required to recall proposition A in order to evaluate proposition B, the amount of recall work required influences later recall of proposition A. Both propositions are recalled best when the plausibility of the recalled proposition A is low and its implications for the validity of the second proposition B are weak. When the recalled proposition's plausibility is high, it and the second proposition are less likely to be recalled (Wyer and Henninger, 1978). Imagine the difficulties one has assessing information when the human mind favors recall of implausible information!

Third, as mentioned before, when people become aware of inconsistencies among their thoughts, they eliminate them. Inconsistent information is often better remembered than consistent information, but only if a person has a goal of forming a single impression about the content of the information (Higgins and Bargh, 1987).

Fourth, as a person thinks more about something, he brings to bear more previously acquired beliefs and concepts. If the implications of these beliefs are similar to those of the information under consideration, the person becomes more confident of his existing judgments. If the implications of the existing beliefs differ from those of the information under consideration, the disparity may weaken the existing opinion. Judgments are less extreme.

How does one integrate new information with existing beliefs? The manner in which this process occurs is not very clear (Wyer and Hartwick, 1980). We do know that it is almost impossible not to do, which probably comes as a relief to most of us. Beliefs evolve with the acquisition of new information.

The Implications for Messages

We need to know a number of things about information processing behavior and how we attach meaning to events before we can think about the transmission of information. Sensitivity to the issues discussed here can help us understand how we and our co-workers develop some of the useful—and some of the crazy—perceptions and evaluations of others we have. Understanding how impressions are formed can also help us mediate against flawed impressions. The biases and stereotypes discussed here are essentially the "noise" that interferes with the sender's transmission of a clear message.

Here are examples of how we might use this information to reduce communication distortion:

- Keep in mind that most of our day-to-day thoughts are superficial. We should guard against forming impressions based on a single piece of attention-getting information. Maybe the person we just labeled as kooky because of his long multibraided hair possesses valuable and useful qualities. Recognizing our own cognitive laziness could be helpful.

- Remember that our initial memories are limited. We would then take longer to examine a problem. At least we can think about information already in our heads that is likely to act as a magnet for new information.

- Know the kinds of biases we use in judgments. We then can take corrective action. Maybe we should not let our tendency toward consistency influence us as much as it does, and certainly we can correct for our proclivity to underestimate the impact of the situation and overestimate the impact of the person on our perceptions of another's behavior. In fact, it would be valuable to develop interviewer training programs or general management training programs that do more than simply sensitize managers to these biases.

Transmitting Information: Channels

Once we have a package of information we want to send someone, we can transmit it in a variety of ways. Most frequently, we use several *channels* together, as when we interact personally with someone by using both language and our body as mechanisms of transmission. The Chinese students who demonstrated in Tianamen Square in 1989 used both channels effectively to make their points, even if their efforts to achieve reform failed. It takes little effort to think of situations in which more complex channel use occurs. Take, for example, a presidential press conference in which a prepared statement might be handed to reporters and read aloud, followed by a question-and-answer period in which the President, dressed in stylish, conservative clothing, raises and lowers his voice, leans forward and back, makes various facial expressions, and uses other verbal and nonverbal means to convey his messages.

Verbal Communication

Speech is the most obvious form of communication, yet in organizations, memos and reports often run a close second. Whether oral or written, verbal communication includes both language and **paralanguage**, which is concerned not with what is said but with how it is said. Among the factors that affect verbal communication are social order, language factors, and paralanguage.

Social Order   Linguistic symbols act as indices of the social order among individuals. By observing verbal interactions among people we quickly identify who is the leader and who the led, when a person is angry with another and when he is pleased, and, in general, where people stand in relation to one another on a social scale.

Speech is in some ways like clothing. It situates us in a social field and helps establish a mode of relating. It also serves as a badge or index of social position. A self-demonstration of these uses of linguistic signs can easily be done while sitting in a busy area such as an airport or hotel lobby. Note the use of language to establish and maintain social and task interaction.

Big talkers get results in American society (Riecken, 1958). It has been shown that people who speak a great deal are better than taciturn people at imposing their opinions on problem-solving groups. Individuals who speak or communicate most also have a greater likelihood of being selected leaders than those who do not (Shaw and Gilchrest, 1956). It is even possible to place these people in visible positions or in positions to convey information in organizations, and thereby create the impression that those people are real leaders.

Changing the structure of an organization can have numerous consequences for the communications of people in that structure, as was demonstrated in an interesting experiment. Researchers assigned the task of writing a pamphlet to groups of three students. To some groups they emphasized teamwork, shared rewards, and interchangeable tasks. To other groups, the experimenters emphasized work efficiency, the individual nature of rewards, and assignment to different functions supposedly in accord with abilities. In other words, the former groups were teams and the latter groups followed a more traditional organizational structure with specialization. In the pamphlets prepared by groups to whom the more traditional relationships were emphasized, sentence variability was lower and the percentage of nouns and adjectives higher than in the pamphlets written by the less formal groups. Altering the structure of work groups, then, is reflected in the structure of the messages they produce.

Differences in status can have dangerous effects on communications, however. A problem that plagues all organizations is the need to communicate accurate—even if unpleasant—news from the lower levels to the higher. Peters (1986) analyzed the problem in two instances: the disastrous launch of the shuttle *Challenger* and the early years of the Peace Corps. He identified two causes for reluctance to send bad news up the ranks: fear of rejection by the superior and recognition that the task of solving problems is the subordinate's responsibility. Peters pointed out, too, that many leaders do not wish to hear bad news. Yet if they do not receive such information from within the organization, they run the risk of reading about it the next day in the paper. And bad news never gets better with time. Peters pointed to NASA's failure to act on safety warnings in the *Challenger* case as an example of succumbing to pressure to ignore unwanted messages. He used the Peace Corps as an example of effective communication management; Director Sargent Shriver created a team of inspectors to check on training programs and report—fully and frankly—to him.

Language Factors   A number of language factors help show how we phrase a message. One is redundancy. The frequency with which words occur—their rarity, abundance, or availability—directly influences learning and observation.

A second language variable to consider is **syntax**, or the grouping of words according to grammatical rules and to their roles as parts of speech. Structure helps convey meaning; in English sentences, subjects generally precede verbs and objects follow verbs. Sequence reveals the fundamentals of an event: actor, action, object. A passive sentence, which puts the object first and obscures the identity of the subject, can avoid a statement of responsibility. Managers should watch for such messages from their subordinates—good news is often in the active voice ("I closed the $1 million account"), whereas bad news is cloaked in the passive ("The project was not completed on time").

The kind of language we use depends on what we are trying to accomplish. If we are trying to change someone's attitude, communication is repetitive in content but varied in form. For instance, much of what is said at an antiwar rally or demonstration is redundant; the basic issues are the same, but the form varies in order to appeal to different listeners. If instead we are trying to get someone to do something, the content of our communication is varied but repetitive in form. For example, we offer several reasons for taking the same action. Perhaps this style is best exemplified by a campaign speech that uses a similar structure when making different promises to different groups.

Yet another aspect of speech that gives us clues about the thoughts of the speaker is immediacy (Mehrabian, 1972). An expression that is immediate establishes a close relationship between the sender and the receiver; one that is not makes that relationship more distant. "I like the flower on top of my wife's hat"—because it distances the speaker and his wife—is less immediate than "I like my wife." The use of nonimmediate or indirect expressions may well indicate the speaker's desire to create distance between himself and the subject. Nonimmediacy is also a common mode of negative expression. It has also been shown, however, that deceptive statements are usually less immediate than truthful ones, regardless of whether the deceivers attempt to convey positive or negative images.

When people speak similar sublanguages or argots (such as in engineering, business, law, or the navy) they can send fewer messages and still get their meaning across.

> The possession of a communication code, allowing an anticipation of answers and creating an awareness of the consequences of one's own verbal formulations, facilitates the whole process of encoding and decoding. The communication code and accompanying cognitive similarity simplifies the organization of messages, and the efficiency of communication as a whole is increased. (Moscovici, 1967, p. 242)

Technical language is thus a key vehicle for accurate communication within the group. It is a kind of code, a shortcut to communication. Understanding that code is a sign of membership in the relevant group. The CO of the *Enterprise* conveys a clear message as concisely as possible if he instructs the conn to "take right rudder angle." The Bishop Rock case contains much technical language to illustrate just how pervasive it is in organizations. An airplane crash in early 1990 showed the importance of using technical language precisely. An Avianca jet crashed on Long Island when it ran out of fuel, a disaster caused by a number of communications failures, according to the subsequent investigation. Among the causes was the pilot's failure to state clearly how dangerously low in fuel the plane was: he said that the fuel was low, but he did not use the prescribed phrases "minimal fuel" or "fuel emergency." Air traffic controllers, not hearing these alarm words, did not treat the plane's situation as one requiring immediate attention.

Technical language also has the tendency to block others from the group. Codes, after all, are also meant not to be understood. The language code used aboard ships functions, in part, to keep outsiders out. Conflicting technical language can lead to miscommunication in organizations—imagine the vice president of manufacturing, the plant site expert, and the vice president of marketing trying to tell the architect exactly what she should consider in designing a new plant. That most organizations of any size employ personnel from various subgroups heightens communication problems, especially in multinational organizations. People in different societies also differ in the extent to which they emphasize people, ideas, or actions in communications (Glenn, 1981). To an Arab, what you say is not nearly as important as whether you are a friend; the idea does not matter as much as the relationship.

Men and women also use language differently. For example,

> college men are more apt to use sentence cases that are neutral, objective, and describe the initiation of an action, whereas college women more frequently use cases referring to the experience and style of an actor. For instance, men might be more likely to talk about actions such as "he hit the ball" or "she kicked the vending machine." Women, in contrast, are more likely to describe feelings, such as "he hates the professor" or "she feels sad" (Deaux and Wrightsman, 1984, p. 111).

Given this difference, it is surprising that organizations are not Towers of Babel.

Paralanguage   Modification in speech, including pitch, rhythm, intensity, pauses, laughing, crying, and groaning, is known as *paralanguage*. Remember, paralanguage is concerned not with *what* is said but with *how* it is said. Each of these modifications contributes to the meaning of a message. When people speed up their speech, it may mean they are excited or anxious; when someone who is talking repeatedly looks away or glances at his watch, the message is that the listener is not important. Low pitch conveys pleasantness, boredom, or sadness; high pitch conveys anger, fear, surprise, or general activity. Extreme variations in pitch communicate pleasantness, happiness, or surprise, and moderate variations convey anger, boredom, or disgust. And silences can have a wide variety of meanings, from use as a weapon or tactic to close a deal or seek agreement, at one extreme, to serving simply as a pause so that others have time to carefully consider their thoughts or feelings (Duncan and Fiske, 1977; Knapp, 1978). Silence tends to produce discomfort, which may lead one participant in a conversation to remove the discomfort by talking. Questioners—for example, managers, interviewers, or lawyers—can use this tendency to advantage by not immediately following an answer with a new question. Upset by the lack of response, the responder may proceed to give more information.

It is often said that the acceptable voice of business in the United States is the paralanguage of the northeastern or farwestern businessman. To the extent this is true, women face one more difficult barrier to entering high levels in the work force. But consider for a moment the southern male businessman who needs to do business in other parts of the country. To what extent do listeners of our southern gentleman make the attribution, "slow speech, slow mind"? In this same way, we make attributions of people who speak English as a second language.

Communication is managed through paralanguage. As an example, vocal cues provide rules for taking turns. We rarely say to others, "Be quiet, I want to talk now." If we are talking and want to continue, we simply increase the volume or rate of speech and decrease the frequency and duration of pauses (Knapp, 1978; Rochester, 1973). At the same time, however, the listener may become a bit more aggressive and attempt to take over, using the buffers "ah" or "er" or increasing the rapidity of his or her responses as if to say, "Hurry, so I can talk."

Nonverbal Communication

Methods of nonverbal communication include body movements and gestures, touch, facial characteristics and expressions, and eye contact. Another nonverbal element that can be manipulated in communication is interpersonal distance. Nonverbal signals can be observed to try to identify deception.

Body Movements and Gestures   The study of body movement, called **kinesics**, parallels the study of verbal communication, or linguistics (Birdwhistell, 1970). Some body language is associated with spoken language. These movements are called *illustrators*. For example, if an employee asks where the water cooler is located, you might respond both verbally and by pointing. Movements can also substitute for a spoken phrase. These gestures, called *emblems,* are nonverbal acts typically understood by a majority of members of a culture or subculture. Obviously, emblems can differ dramatically across cultures (Ekman, Friesen, and Ellsworth, 1972) and thus cause confusion. The nuances of one culture's gestures may not be clear to someone from another culture. For example, Westerners are aware that Orientals bow but fail to recognize that variations in the depth of bows differentiate status. Roger Axtell (1985) described several gestures in his "International Gesture Dictionary." For example, an eyebrow raised in Tonga means "yes" or "agree"; in Peru this gesture means "money" or "pay me."

It is common for gestures to indicate the nature of relationships of people in a conversation. Status differences are often communicated by body position. In the United States the higher-status person typically is more relaxed, leans backward, and places arms and legs in a synchronized position. Attraction, too, is communicated by body movement. If I like you, I may lean forward, directly orient my body to yours, and am relaxed (Mehrabian, 1972).

A word of caution here. In the 1970s we saw an explosion of books and articles on "body language," telling us we can interpret easily what someone is thinking or wishes to say by observing movements. These writings were not based on scientific research and should be questioned. There is no reliable dictionary of gestures. Their meaning depends on the context, the actor, the culture, and other factors. The effective manipulation of context is shown in the feature on the Texaco-Pennzoil Trial.

FEATURE: *Nonverbal Communication in the Texaco-Pennzoil Trial*

In the celebrated case of *Pennzoil* v. *Texaco,* a jury ordered Texaco, Inc. to pay $10.53 billion to Pennzoil Company, a sum greater than the annual gross national product of 116 of the world's countries. In a stunning display of courtroom ingenuity that escaped virtually all public notice while it was happening, Pennzoil convinced the jury that Texaco had fraudulently induced Getty Oil Company to break a binding merger contract with Pennzoil, stealing a deal that would have given Pennzoil a billion barrels of choice oil reserves.

From mid-July to late August [1985], [Pennzoil lawyers Irv] Terrell and [John] Jeffers arduously added brick upon brick to Pennzoil's claim that it had a contract. Through the worst of Houston's sweltering summer months, the lawyers read aloud from one interminable document after another, trying to establish not only that the Getty people intended to be bound but that the Texaco people had *actual knowledge* of Pennzoil's deal. The evidence, however, added tedium to tedium, all the more so because much of it could be introduced only through a witness, and Pennzoil, of course, had no witnesses from Getty Oil or Texaco. As a result, Pennzoil spent days putting on evidence through a television screen.

Of the sixty-three depositions spanning fifteen thousand pages of transcript taken during the "discovery" phase of the case, fifteen had been videotaped by Jeffers and Terrell to assure that the jury got a firsthand look at "the flavor of these people." Besides permitting Pennzoil to introduce exhibits, the video depositions also enabled it to retell the story of the Getty Oil war—a story intended to depict [Sid] Petersen [Getty Oil chairman] and his people as double dealers.

Gordon Boisi, the investment banker who solicited Texaco's bid to defeat Gordon [Getty]'s deal with Pennzoil, fluttered his eyelids, sniffed and chuckled at the lawyers' questions and held forth in the gobbledygook of the takeover game. When asked in the videotape whether he would be testifying as a live witness at the trial, Boisi replied, "If my schedule allowed"—not the kind of answer that impresses jurors who by that time had given up nearly a month of their lives to the case. And when he was asked in the video whether he had come and gone during Gordon's absence from the "back door" board meeting, he swallowed before answering, "I guess that occurred."

Bart Winokur, the outside counsel for Getty Oil who had entered the Getty Oil board meeting in Houston in Gordon's absence, gave intelligent and straightforward responses but appeared a little shifty. He fidgeted in his seat. His eyes darted around the room. His voice at times adopted a somewhat sassy tone. He filled the sound track with the ring of tinkling ice cubes when raising a glass of fruit juice to his lips. There was something just a little unconvincing about Winokur; while he testified that it was not his practice to take notes during meetings, he was holding a pen in one hand.

Sid Petersen, an executive whose career had been scuttled just as it was reaching its peak, came off as smug and defensive, tossing his head, folding his arms across his chest, heaving sighs. When he was asked a question about [Pennzoil chairman Hugh] Liedtke's agreement to honor his golden parachute, Petersen snapped, "I don't give a damn what Mr. Liedtke approved. He had nothing to say about it. *I* had a contract."

Touch   Touch is surely one of the most basic forms of communication. After all, people learn to communicate through touching long before they learn to speak. It is an important form of communication for managers to learn about for two reasons. First, touch may be perceived differently than intended. It is easy for the communicator to encode one meaning to a touch and the receiver to decode another. Second, men and women perceive touch differently—an important factor in a work force in which the percentage of women is growing. A third reason is the variable interpretation that touch receives in different cultures.

Touch can be used to define status. Higher-status people are more likely to initiate touching and lower-status people to be touched. Perhaps in response to this tendency, people observing touching attribute status accordingly (Major and Heslin, 1978).

Women distinguish between touching that signifies warmth and friendship and touching that indicates sexual desire. Men may not be as likely to perceive the difference or to make the same distinctions. Even when the touch is brief, men and women respond to it differently. In one study, library clerks systematically briefly touched the hands of male and female students. The women who had been touched liked the clerk and the library more than did the women who had not. The men who had been touched did not increase their liking of either clerk or institution (Fisher, Ryttim, and Heslin, 1976). In another study male and female hospital patients were briefly and professionally touched by a nurse before an operation. After the operation, the women who had been touched reported less fear and anxiety and had lower blood pressures than the women who had not. In contrast, touched men had negative feelings after the operation and higher blood pressure than nontouched men.

Touch also means different things across cultural and subcultural groups. Russian men commonly hug; American men do not do so as commonly. In most Latin lands from Venezuela to Sicily, *abrazo* (hug) is as commonplace as a handshake. In Kenya a handshake is a social must between men even if they just saw each other moments before. The Japanese, though, have an aversion to body contact and prefer to bow. Touch is a form of communication riddled with possibilities for misunderstanding.

Facial Expressions   Facial expressions have been studied since the time of Charles Darwin, who stated in *The Expressions of Emotion in Man and Animals* (1872) that, due to evolutionary connections, some facial expressions may communicate the same message across species. One extensive research program (Ekman, Friesen, and Ellsworth, 1972) provided exact descriptions of the facial expressions associated with surprise, fear, anger, disgust, happiness, and sadness. This research further identified these expressions as existing across cultures.

Interestingly, both sides of the face may not show the same degree of emotional expression. Except for happiness, the left side of the face is more intense in emotional expression than the right side. One possible explanation is that the right hemisphere of the brain, which controls the left side of the body, may play a greater role in emotional expression than the left.

The wide agreement on the meanings of facial expressions of emotions does not mean the same emotion will be displayed in similar circumstances across cultures. We follow certain rules concerning the display of appropriate emotions. Called by Ekman and colleagues (1972) *display rules*, these norms vary across cultures and can result from personal habit, situational pressures, or cultural norms. We also need to distinguish between expressions as automatic, uncontrolled signals of emotion and as the deliberate communication of emotion. Work on smiling suggests that the major function of a smile is to communicate happiness to other people (Kraut and Johnson, 1979). That is, a smile reflects a conscious choice to communicate rather than an automatic response. Thus such facial expressions as a smile that are not altogether automatic can also be used to mask other emotions. Who has not been made uncomfortable by another person when some cues from that person said one thing about her emotions while other cues said other things?

Eye Contact   Eye contact is an important form of nonverbal communication. It is thought that we depend more on the eye behavior of other people in interpreting their communications than on any other form of behavior. As we discuss eye contact, however, we should keep in mind that it is difficult to differentiate between direct eye-to-eye contact and looking in the general direction of someone else's face. Thus some of the research findings on eye contact should be accepted with caution.

The average length of an individual gaze is three seconds, and the average duration of a mutual gaze is about one second (Argyle and Ingham, 1972). Ethnic differences affect patterns of gaze. The average white speaker gazes at another person more often when listening and less often when speaking; for blacks, this pattern is reversed. These differences can create substantial communication problems. One set of investigators (La France and Mayo, 1976) observed that when blacks and whites conversed, they often misinterpreted the signals for taking turns.

Eye contact serves four major functions in communication. It regulates the flow of communication, monitors feedback, expresses emotion, and indicates the nature of the interpersonal relationship (Argyle, Ingham, Aikens, and McCallin, 1973; Kendon, 1967; Knapp, 1978).

Gaze helps begin, maintain, and end conversations. Speakers often look away as they begin to talk, possibly to discourage the listener from responding or interrupting. They look up when they finish talking, perhaps to signal the end of a thought or to indicate it is all right if the other person now talks (Kendon, 1967).

Gazing also provides feedback to the speaker, who can interpret the action as a sign of attention, interest, or attraction. University professors are forever trying in the classroom to attract gaze to them and away from the newspaper. People with strong needs for approval gaze more than others, a behavior frequently perceived as an ingratiation strategy (Lefebvre, 1975). Surprisingly, some data indicate that even when we *think* a person has gazed at us, we feel liking for him. Males and females, however, may regard gazing differently. When women think some man has gazed too long at them, their liking for that person does not go up. For men the effect is the opposite; the longer they think a woman has gazed at them, the more attracted to her they are.

Lack of gazing is usually interpreted as lack of interest, but in reality this is not always the case. It may signal that a person is shy or frightened. People often avoid gazing when conveying bad news or saying something unpleasant. Lack of gazing provides a way of respecting another's privacy when discussing something intimate (Ellsworth, Carlsmith, and Henson, 1972).

The eyes are one of the three major areas of the face that convey emotions (the other two are the brow and forehead and the lower face and mouth). Because eyes are so important in this function, it is disturbing when we converse with someone and do not have their eyes as indicators of emotion. Think about the Darth Vader effect of mirrored sunglasses.

Like touch and body gestures, gaze serves to indicate the nature of the relationship between gazers. Gaze can be used to establish liking and disliking (we avert our eyes from those we dislike) and to indicate the intensity of a relationship. The more intense the relationship, the longer the mutual gaze (Efran and Broughton, 1966; Exline and Winters, 1965).

Status differences are indicated by gaze as well. High-status people spend less time looking at low-status people than vice versa, and they have a greater tendency to look at the other person when speaking than when listening. This pattern is called visual dominance behavior (Exline, 1971). Gender differences in gazing may be related to status differences. Women engage in more eye contact than men, consistent with their usually lower status in male–female interactions; also, women, unlike men, are more likely to avert the gaze of another.

Finally, eye contact can be used to threaten another person. A number of experiments have been done in which people were stared at more or less by another person (Ellsworth, Carlsmith, and Henson, 1972; Ellsworth and Carlsmith, 1968). People subjected to high, prolonged stares left the situation as soon as possible or behaved less aggressively than they otherwise might have. Here are two absolutely contradictory meanings of eye contact: attraction and threat. Their commonality is that they both signal great involvement and high emotional content. This is yet another example that nonverbal communication has no fixed meaning and is dependent on the situation.

Deception   Deception is conveyed through all manner of body and facial characteristics. For managers, understanding deception can often be important in implementing personnel policies. Generally, people are able to tell when others are lying at a better than chance level. Sometimes voice pitch gives the liar away; at other times it is gesture or facial expressions.

It has been suggested that certain nonverbal channels are less controllable than others (Ekman and Friesen, 1969, 1974). This lack of control is called **leakage**. The face is a fairly well-controlled channel compared with the body, making it less likely than the body to reveal deception. One reason is that we pay more attention to the messages we send with our faces than with our bodies. The voice is a leaky channel. People apparently do not really listen or attend to their own voices, as suggested by the fact that we do not react negatively to our own voices in everyday conversation, but when forced to hear tape recordings of our voices we often react negatively. Research indicates that tone of voice, not the content of the speech, leaks information (Zuckerman, De Paulo, and Rosenthal, 1981).

Some research on detecting deception in unemotional situations shows that people fare well in these situations, too, at telling whether another person is lying (Krause, Geller, and Olson, 1976). In one study, subjects pretended they were interviewing for a job (Kraut, 1978). Observers were moderately accurate in telling when someone was lying. Truthful answers tended to be longer, had fewer "ums" and "uhs," and began sooner after the end of a question than did false answers. People also have some knowledge about how they detect deception. In one research program, the following behaviors were mentioned more often as indicators of deception than of truthfulness: gaze aversion, smiling, nervous hand gestures, shifts in posture, longer response times, and hesitance of speech. Some respondents also mentioned length of responses as an indicator of deception. The next time you encounter someone you think is lying, ask yourself if he provided any nonverbal or paralanguage cues that made you suspicious.

Interpersonal Distance   A very important element of nonverbal communication in organizations is **interpersonal distance**. Probably the person most responsible for our attending to this issue is anthropologist Edward Hall. His books, *The Silent Language* (1959) and *The Hidden Dimension* (1966), are important readings, particularly for managers who are concerned about subcultural or cross-cultural management.

Hall proposed a set of distance zones to describe various patterns of interaction. There are cultural differences in the size of the zones. Germans typically put more distance between themselves in casual social interactions than do Italians. For Americans the four major zones and the distance they span are

1. *Intimate.* physical contact to 18 inches (.5 meter)

2. *Personal.* 1.5 to 4 feet (.5 to 1.25 meters)

3. *Social.* 4 to 12 feet (1.25 to 3.5 meters)

4. *Public.* 12 to 25 feet (3.5 to 7.5 meters)

The intimate zone is one in which the presence of another is unmistakable and bodies become highly involved with one another. The personal zone is the acceptable zone for friendly interaction or interaction with acquaintances. The greater distances of the social zone are used for business and casual social interaction, and the public zone is the distance acceptable for more formal interaction.

People strive in most situations to find and adhere to the appropriate level of intimacy. You can demonstrate this to yourself by engaging in what is known as the cocktail party game. Go to a party and select a stranger of the opposite sex with whom to talk. Establish between yourself and that person a distance that appears comfortable for you both, then move closer to the other person. You should observe him moving away. Alternatively, move away and he should move closer to reestablish the appropriate distance.

When people change the level of intimacy from the tacitly determined equilibrium to any other level, then, their partners compensate. One theory (Patterson, 1976) holds that when one person increases the intimacy of any channel, the other person experiences arousal. The latter person then looks at other aspects of the social situation. If he interprets his arousal as negative or threatening, he compensates. If he interprets it as positive, he reciprocates by increasing his own intimacy. For example, Jack sits down three feet from Jill. Jill interprets her arousal as nervousness, looks away, turns away, or runs away.

The Medium and the Situation

We have explored in depth various aspects of the individual's transmission of a message, including the verbal and nonverbal cues. What these discussions have not addressed are two key issues in communication: the **medium**, or the vehicle by which a message is delivered, and the **context** within which the communication takes place.

The Medium and the Message

There is some truth to Marshall McLuhan's (1967) comment that the medium is the message. Another writer noted:

> [Communication channels] are defined primarily by the technical characteristics of their functioning and the physical characteristics of the symbols they convey. . . . The social and psychological constraints of these characteristics are no less important than their physical and ecological dimensions. Writing is endowed with a certain aura of solemnity in our society, whereas gesticular expressions accompany more informal meetings. Reading books and even newspapers is generally an individual activity; going to the movies or watching television often are activities of a more collective nature. Thus, channels of communication are above all complex, psychological areas that call forth a set of stimuli and appropriate responses. (Moscovici, 1967, p. 238)

Television is a more effective transmitter of certain kinds of information (a rocket launch or a football game, for example) than magazines or newspapers. The fax companies tell us that fax is a better attention-getter than a first-class letter. The feature "Facsimile Machines" explores this relatively new medium.

FEATURE: *Facsimile Machines*

A boom in facsimile machines is sweeping the business world and beginning to alter the way people conduct their affairs.

Faster transmission speeds enable a document to be sent cross-country or around the world in about 20 seconds, using ordinary phone lines, while sharply lower prices have made the machines affordable to many small businesses and those who work at home.

Law firms are placing them in partners' homes so that important documents can be sent from the office on nights and weekends. Artists can send sketches to clients, who can make comments and send the sketches back for revisions. Commodities traders reduce international phone costs by sending a letter to a customer instead of conveying the information in a much longer phone conversation.

The facsimile machines are also appearing in hotel lobbies to enable business guests to communicate with the office and with clients.

Spreading along with the machines is the expression to fax, as in "I faxed the letter this morning."

In addition to replacing telephone calls, the machines are being used instead of computers for the transmission of data.

Because a document can be sent so rapidly, the machines seem certain to replace a sizeable portion of the overnight document delivery business carved out by companies like Federal Express and United Parcel Service.

To avoid lost or delayed mail, many businesses now send their bills by fax machine.

An indication of the facsimile machine's importance as a business tool is the growing number of businesses that include a fax number on their stationery and business cards.

The rapid growth in sales has been fueled by faster transmission speeds and lower long-distance rates. Most of the market growth has come from the low-priced machines aimed at small businesses and individuals who work at home—lawyers, freelance writers, artists, and advertising and public relations representatives. Analysts predict that as individuals purchase fax machines for home businesses they will also use the machines for personal tasks, such as banking or ordering merchandise by mail.

The more sophisticated machines have memory and can receive several documents, retain them and print them out later. Some can transmit photographs and half-tone reproductions used in the graphic arts industry. Some machines allow the user to send a document to numerous other facsimile machines. Corporations with their own data networks can use a master facsimile machine to distribute documents simultaneously to dozens or even hundreds of branch offices around the country.

Source: From "Coast to Coast in 20 Seconds: Fax Machines Alter Business" by Calvin Sims. *New York Times*, May 6, 1988. Copyright © 1988 by The New York Times Company. Reprinted by permission.

Personally available and easily transportable media can be used to circumvent mass media that are controlled by the powerful. In the late 1970s the Ayatollah Khomeini, in exile from Iran, taped inspirational speeches that were smuggled into the country on audiocassettes and helped foment the revolution that toppled the shah. Chinese protesters in 1987—both in China and the United States—helped spread the word of the democracy demonstrations by using fax transmissions.

The question of what media to use arises most often in the choice among speaking in person, writing, or phoning. All three methods use verbal communication but employ nonverbal methods to varying degrees. In organizations it is typically difficult to make a choice, so it is often ignored by saying that it all depends on the situation and the resources available to the sender of the message. You are more likely to drop a memo on somebody's desk if he is not around when you call on him.

Generally, when one's goal is to persuade someone to change an attitude, the most effective method is to appear in person. Phone communication is considered second best and written messages third (Cantril and Allport, 1935). Research shows that written messages are more likely to be understood than other kinds of messages; therefore, if you want to present a rather complicated message, put it in writing. Figure 5.2 (page 252) highlights some reasons for communicating in writing, by telephone, and in person.

Given the range of possibilities available, how does the manager choose the most effective media? Lengel and Daft (1988) proposed a framework for media selection based on a fit between the richness of the medium and the routine or nonroutine nature of the problem that the communication means to address. Richness is a matter of the medium's ability to handle simultaneously many information cues, to provide rapid feedback, and to create a personal focus. Media fall on a continuum from those low in richness, such as flyers and bulletins, to the method highest in richness, face-to-face contact. A match between media and message promotes good communication, but as the model in Figure 5.3 (page 253) shows, two of the four possibilities result in miscommunication.

One study showed cross-national differences in media use. It found English managers and workers to use more written communications than their French counterparts (Graves, 1972). It is not clear whether other cultural differences exist, but such is likely to be the case.

The development of new methods of message transmission is clearly affecting communication. The feature on car phones details how some of these new media are being used. "The development of new communication media, such as voice messaging, electronic mail, and teleconferencing, has been stimulated by technological advances in digital information technologies. . . . Digital representation of the units of communication considerably enhances their storage, processing, and transmission in time and space" (Culnan and Markus, 1987, p. 420). These new technologies extend the capabilities of verbal communication. The research on new technologies shows that they filter out communication cues found in face-to-face interaction and that substituting technology-mediated interaction for face-to-face interaction has predictable influences on a number of other aspects of organizational functioning. Generally, these interactions are less personal but allow more people at greater distances to be pulled into interactions. However, recent research finds that some electronic mail groups behave like real social groups (Finholt and Sproull, 1990). All in all, though, new communication

FIGURE   5.2
Reasons for
Choosing
Different
Methods of
Communication

Some Reasons for Communicating in Writing

When communicating with large numbers of people on the same subject.

When documenting a recommendation, analysis, or other set of facts.

When it is simply more convenient:

a. When dictating letters, memos and notes.

b. When it is difficult to see the other person (because of schedules, distance, available time, etc.).

When more formality is desired (because of etiquette, culture, emotional content, legal considerations, etc.).

When immediate face-to-face interaction or feedback is not necessary for ensuring understanding of the message.

Some Reasons for Communicating by Telephone

When it is more convenient.

When speed of communications is essential.

When it is not necessary to show or communicate messages that are highly visual (e.g., an advertising manager could communicate a radio commercial concept to a product manager by telephone, but would probably not attempt the same thing with a television commercial).

When you need a two-way exchange of information but visual exchange is not necessary.

For privacy.

Some Reasons for Communicating in Person

When the message is complex or sensitive and requires feedback and interaction.

When you wish to attach significance or importance to the message.

When the message may not be important, but paying attention to the message recipient is.

When you are uncertain about a message and need to "feel your way."

When you wish to invite the recipient into some situation and give or share "ownership" of an idea or project.

Source: Reprinted by permission of Macmillan Publishing Company from Karlene H. Roberts, "Communicating in Organizations," in F. Kast and J. Rosenzweig (eds.), *Modules in Management* (Chicago: SRA Associates, Inc., 1984), p. 14. Copyright © 1984 by SRA Associates, Inc.

FIGURE 5.3
*A Media
Selection
Framework*

Media Richness	Management Problem	
	Routine	Nonroutine
Rich	*Communication failure.* Data glut. Rich media used for routine messages. Excess cues cause confusion and surplus meaning.	*Effective communication.* Communications success because rich media match nonroutine messages.
Lean	*Effective communication.* Communication success because media low in richness match routine messages.	*Communication failure.* Data starvation. Lean media used for nonroutine messages. Too few cues to capture message complexity.

Source: R. H. Lengel and R. L. Daft, "The Selection of Communication Media as an Executive Skill," *Academy of Management Executive* 2, 3(1988):227. Reprinted by permission.

technologies are promulgating an explosion of off-site workers in the United States and overseas. This revolution has created a whole new set of communication problems (Metzger and Von Glinow, 1988).

FEATURE: *Car Phones Change the Way We Do Business*

(In preparation for a speech to a B. F. Goodrich business meeting, writer Jack Falvey spent a day with Goodrich sales rep Mike Rowland.)

As we drove away from our hotel rendezvous [Mike] pressed a pre-programmed button on his cellular phone that automatically dialed an 800 number in Cleveland. His territory customer service rep answered and told Mike that there were no messages. Sort of an expensive gimmick, I thought. But then the action began.

Mike asked for the shipping status of an order for his first call and also asked the customer service rep to call ahead for him and confirm our 9 A.M. appointment. Next, he asked if an appointment could be made for the following Thursday in a distant city and if so, could he get a hotel reservation there as well. He said he would check back in 15 minutes. The cheerful voice in Cleveland said, "Talk to you later," and a field day like no other I had ever experienced began.

A second preprogrammed button was pushed and a lab technician at another plant location answered. "Was the sample of the material that an account wanted to return for credit defective?" Not according to the tests, but it might be a good idea to take it back anyway because the application was not the best possible. "Okay, let's see how it goes."

About then it was time to check back with the customer service rep. The first account was expecting us, the last order had been delivered late the previous afternoon and the following week's appointment hadn't been set up yet. We pulled into the first stop of the day. We were ushered into a conference room where coffee and three engineers all arrived as we walked through the door. While Mike knew that company's last order had arrived late the previous afternoon, the customers hadn't realized it was in yet. They were impressed that we were right on top of things. A conventional sales call took place and soon we were back on the road and on the air again.

Mike called in a new order. The account would send confirming paperwork. A request to mail some specifications was fielded by the customer service rep at the same time and a message was passed back to Mike to call the vice president of sales on an expense account item. He decided not to return that call at once—well, not everything had changed since the old days. The whole process of the call-ahead confirmation for the next account was then repeated.

We stopped at the side of the road for about two minutes to make luncheon reservations for our noon clients. Mike explained that he didn't have the number preprogrammed, and that it was safer to stop the car to look up the number in his book and then dial it. By the middle of the afternoon he had trained me to make these kinds of calls. Twice during the day his all-present, all-knowing, hard-working support person in Cleveland was busy when he called. He left a message on the voice hold-and-forward system.

By this time I was checking my calendar to see what century we were in. How could so much change with just the addition of a car phone? It seemed as revolutionary as when the Model T Ford put salesmen on the road, allowing them to go to their customers rather than lugging their sample trunks from a train station to the local hotel so a potential buyer could visit them.

Why should a field sales rep have to write a call report if someone sitting in the home office in front of a computer terminal could enter the data firsthand? Why should a highly paid field sales representative enter orders or follow up on delivery when someone paid one-third as much, and supporting three or four sales people, can do it faster and far more effectively? The combination of cellular phone technology, a customer support person with a main-frame terminal and a field sales rep makes this technology cost effective for the first time.

Source: From "Car Phones Become the Sales Force's Fifth Wheel" by J. Falvey. Reprinted by permission of the *Wall Street Journal*, July 27, 1989. Copyright © 1989 by Dow Jones & Company, Inc. All rights reserved worldwide.

Whether this change in interactions adversely affects communication is not known because of the wide range of other influences on the communication process. In terms of getting messages to hard-to-reach people, these media may even improve communication. Further, the distancing effects vary from one new technology to another. Teleconferencing, for instance, gives a fuller communication than an old-fashioned phone call.

A number of predictions have surfaced about the use of these technologies. One is that the use of electronic media will increase the organization's ability to process information (Galbraith, 1973). Another is that these media will promote information overload and stifle the organization. Nearly every study shows that the new electronic media increase linkages among people in organizations, extending existing networks and forming new ones. Users of a Swedish electronic messaging and conferencing system reported that 50 percent of the messages they wrote and 75 percent of those they received would not have occurred before the system was in place (Palme, 1981). Finally, studies also show the ability of electronic media to affect the direction of communication. One study (Lippitt, Miller, and Halamaj, 1980) found an increase in upward and downward hierarchical communication with electronic messaging. Multinationals surely realize greater speed of interaction among their far-flung branches using computers and fax machines.

Context

All nonverbal and verbal communication must be thought about in terms of the context in which it takes place. Contexts are physical, social, and cultural determinants of behavior—they facilitate certain behaviors and constrain others.

People appear to understand that certain behaviors are appropriate to certain physical situations. Thus we act differently on board a ship at sea or in an office building than we do in a church or home, and we act differently in someone else's home than we do in our own. We usually do not try to carry on quiet, thoughtful conversations at football games, nor do we typically express our approval by cheering in churches.

When people perceive behavior as inappropriate to a situation, they are pushed to try to explain it. The kinds of explanations they come up with and the inferences they make are discussed by psychologists interested in **attribution theory**. (See the section on forming impressions and Chapter 10.) While we see people classify situations every day, as yet we have little knowledge about the classification schemes they use (Magnusson, 1976; Schneider, Hastorf, and Ellsworth, 1979).

Office environments communicate important facts about the people who work in them. The arrangement of objects in office spaces provides clues about how occupants see themselves and how they expect visitors to act. Desks, for example, provide barriers between occupants and their guests, and the positioning of chairs gives clues as to the roles of office occupants and their guests. The use of such personal items as family pictures also conveys information. All of these factors are devices through which office occupants manage their images.

An important aspect of the environment is the people in it. They comprise the social context of interaction. We often think about other people in our environments and forget that we, too, influence those environments. The CO of the *Enterprise* truly did not understand his impact on the bridge team. Our perceptions tend to influence others' behavior. For example, it is possible that if I perceive someone in my environment is hostile, she will engage in hostile behavior (Kelly, 1955). This is called a **self-fulfilling prophecy**. In an early experiment, Rosenthal and Jacobson (1968) went into classrooms and randomly identified some students as very bright and then informed their teachers of their intelligence. At the end of the class term, these students showed higher achievement than their peers (see the feature on the Pygmalion effect in Chapter 10). This particular research has been criticized, but similar demonstrations of the Pygmalion effect are numerous, particularly in educational and military organizations. Recent research shows that the effect may not be as pervasive in business organizations (Sutton and Woodman, 1989). However, we should monitor our communication in any situation in the workplace and be mindful of the biases we might introduce.

We infer characteristics of others by the contexts in which we find them. For example, we infer that people in student unions are either students or faculty, that people who go to certain resorts have money, that people who work for certain companies are high-technology oriented. Thus we use contexts to make snap judgments and to label behavior.

Context is a factor in a temporal sense as well—communications are judged in the light of past and other contemporary messages. In the feature on Chrysler, the company's embarrassment over some ill-timed announcements clearly shows the importance of context to effective communications.

FEATURE: *Chrysler's Ill-Timed Announcements*

Chrysler was scheduled to renegotiate its contract with the United Auto Workers during the summer of 1988 prior to the expiration of the existing agreement that September. The climate for those negotiations was strained considerably by the messages communicated to the union through several events and company announcements beginning in the summer of 1987:

- In July 1987, Chrysler agreed to pay a $1.6 million fine to the federal Occupational Safety and Health Administration for factory hazards, then the largest fine in the agency's history.

- In January 1988, the company announced that it would close the Kenosha, Wisconsin, plant, triggering cries of betrayal and lawsuits from workers and the Wisconsin state government.

- In February 1988, the company confirmed it was trying to sell its Acustar parts subsidiary, where one-sixth of Chrysler's UAW membership is employed. That unleashed protests, strike threats, and a halt to joint union-management programs.

- Chrysler tried to control the damage from these events in part through a series of concessions. It agreed to set up a special fund for laid-off Kenosha workers; it agreed not to sell Acustar; and it asked the UAW to open national contract talks early to diffuse tensions. But the day the talks started, Chrysler released its annual proxy statement, which contained information on top executive pay. The union learned, on the same day Chrysler said it wanted concessions from workers to help it remain competitive, that chairman Lee Iacocca had been paid $17.9 million the previous year in salary, bonus and stock options.

- A few days later, a story appeared in the *Detroit News* which said Chrysler planned to move production of its K-cars to Mexico from its Detroit plant, which was scheduled to start making other models (shifted from the soon-to-be-closed Kenosha plant). The story hit Detroit like a bombshell. The union for years has complained about outsourcing work to nonunion plants and operations abroad. The company's head of labor relations confirmed the newspaper story to reporters but argued that the shift to Mexico didn't involve many jobs.

- Finally, chairman Iacocca, trying to straighten out the confusion, said at a press conference that under the company's new plans, the

Kenosha plant would remain open until the end of the year and K-car production might only "possibly" be moved to Mexico.

Despite the communications snafus, the labor negotiations reached a satisfactory conclusion several weeks later when the company and union agreed on a settlement that matched those reached earlier at Ford and General Motors.

Source: From "Chrysler's First Quarter Net Dropped 32%: Two Production Changes are Postponed" by Gregory Witcher and "Chrysler's Public Relations Blunders on K-Car Moves Upset Talks with UAW" by Jacob M. Schlesinger and John Bussey. Reprinted by permission of the *Wall Street Journal*, April 28, 1988. And from "UAW's Tentative Accord with Chrysler Matches Contracts Made with Ford, GM" by Jacob M. Schlesinger. Reprinted by permission of the *Wall Street Journal*, May 5, 1988. Copyright © 1988 by Dow Jones & Company, Inc. All rights reserved worldwide.

The emotional context of communication is significant as well. Routine messages in routine situations are delivered in friendly, often elaborate terms. In stressful situations, however, messages may become clipped and the paralanguage of tone and gesture may convey urgency. Stress may also influence the receiver; someone under pressure may be too distracted to receive the message fully.

Message Content

The content of any message is always inextricable from the fabric of its context. People interested in changing attitudes or in marketing products probably know more than the rest of us how various kinds of content influence people. However, if we are to be effective managers, it is essential that we think about how to phrase the messages we send.

Good and Bad Feelings

One important aspect of any communication is the degree to which it elicits good feelings. Most of us assume that sending favorable information leads to better outcomes than does sending unfavorable information. This consensus is confirmed by a phenomenon social psychologists call the "mum effect"; people are unwilling to transmit to others bad news that will affect them (Tesser and Rosen, 1975). The classic example is the story of the Persian king's messenger who rode into camp from battle to inform the king his side was losing, and was slain. How many of the rest of us are victims of this effect every day?

Concepts that make us feel good need merely be associated with other entities and we become accepting of those other entities. Advertisers have learned this lesson well, and frequently associate a product with pictures of people having a good time regardless of whether the picture is relevant to the product. In an interesting experiment (Janis, Kaye, and Kirschner, 1965), researchers asked subjects to read messages designed to persuade the subjects of something. Some subjects just read the messages, but others were given snacks while they read. More of the snackers changed their minds in the direction of the message than did those not given the snacks. This finding might suggest something about the value of breakfast, lunch, and dinner meetings.

As mentioned before, it has been recognized for a number of years that we give more weight to unfavorable than to favorable information. In performance evaluations, then, we would expect employees to respond more to the negative than the positive (see Chapter 10).

Some information is designed to make us feel bad. The most frequently studied information in this category is that designed to arouse fear. Examples are "smoking causes cancer" and "cholesterol causes heart attacks."

A direct relationship between fear and behavior has been demonstrated in studies advocating safe driving practices (Leventhal, 1970), upgrading dental hygiene (Evans, Rozelle, Lasater, Dembroski, and Allen, 1970), and so on. Driving schools, required for traffic offenders, often show very frightening movies of accidents. Is there some point at which increasing fear further immobilizes action? No one yet knows the answer. We do know that arousing fear can be effective in changing behavior; its use, however, involves a number of trade-offs. If, for example, misuse of a piece of equipment is likely to lead to a serious accident, fear may be called for and should be communicated. Because deck operations aboard aircraft carriers, such as the *Enterprise*, are inherently dangerous, fear is conveyed to every man working the decks to increase his vigilance. There is scant evidence, however, that the warnings contained in product warning labels, disclaimers, and disclosures change behavior much or reduce liability risks or insurance premiums for businesses.

Feedback

Another frequently discussed aspect of content is **feedback**, which is studied in terms of source, timing, and content (Cusella, 1987; Erez, 1977). Because our focus here is on content, we will simply recognize the importance of source. For instance, hearing for the third consecutive time from your mother that you never write home has a different impact from hearing the same complaint from your boss in corporate headquarters. A number of studies have examined the influences of different sources of feedback (for example, Herold and Greller, 1977; Greller, 1980).

Some organizations provide employees with what are called **realistic job previews** (RJPs). The hope is that by stressing clearly to prospective employees what they can expect in their jobs, organizations can prevent job dissatisfaction, poor performance, and inappropriate hires prior to incurring training and development costs (Wanous, 1980). One study actually examined the message content of RJPs (Dean and Wanous, 1984). Researchers found that very specific job previews lower initial job expectations more than do more general previews, but that job survival rates do not appear to be influenced more by one content than by the other. Despite the lack of conclusive support for a connection to turnover, realistic job previews are probably a good idea for two reasons. They convey an interest by the company in the employee and they convey information that may otherwise be unobtainable to new employees.

Knowledge of performance is also important to helping employees set realistic goals once they are on the job (Cusella, 1987). If I know the quality of the widgets I produce is high and I am bored with my job, I might raise my production level. Alternatively, if I know quality is low, I may work on the quality, ignoring the production issue. Feedback is at the heart of most job redesign efforts tried in the United States today (see, for example, Hackman and Oldham, 1980, and Chapter 11). Certainly, the importance of feedback is the basic assumption underlying performance appraisals (see Chapter 10). It is unreasonable to expect people to perform well on complex jobs unless they have some mechanism for learning how well they are doing those jobs.

At one time or another most of us have felt that our responses to our jobs result from the way those around us see those jobs. My job as a neurosurgeon might not be so bad if it weren't that all the neurosurgeons I know were grousing about *their* jobs. My job as a garbage collector might be a lot worse if the other garbage collectors were not talking about how great their jobs are. Some evidence suggests that we can influence responses to jobs by manipulating information cues about those jobs.

Trust and Credibility

A number of studies have shown that the lack of interpersonal trust can negatively affect communication and other behaviors of people at work (Gibb, 1964; Loomis, 1959; Friedlander, 1970). When trust is nonexistent, people withhold or distort information, or both. This behavior leads to other serious problems. Trust—or the lack of it—is an important factor in cross-national transactions. Trust is low because the communicators do not perceive themselves as similar.

Most analyses of trust look at credibility as one of its components. Is credibility important? Subordinates receiving feedback from superiors with high credibility judge that feedback as more accurate and the source as more perceptive, they tend to express greater satisfaction with the feedback, and they are more likely to use performance suggestions offered in the feedback (Bannister, 1986; Earley, 1986).

One set of studies indicated that credibility is based on the dimensions of safety, expertise, and dynamism (O'Reilly and Roberts, 1974a,b). Workers in general-care medical practices were asked to assess the credibility of the information milieus of their practices. Safety, expertise, and dynamism were positively related to the openness and accuracy of messages, as perceived by respondents, and to the number of interactions among respondents in any one medical practice. The moral of the study is to try to design information milieus (content and context) in which the actors are seen as safe (just, kind, friendly, honest, agreeable), expert (trained, experienced, skilled, informed, authoritative, qualified), and dynamic (aggressive, energetic, active, bold, emphatic, forceful). That is a tall order!

Making Messages Understandable

Four issues should be addressed when trying to make messages understandable: (1) clarity versus ambiguity; (2) the number of sides of an argument; (3) whether to draw conclusions for a message recipient or let her draw them for herself; and (4) the style and organization of messages.

Are clear messages more influential than ambiguous messages? One would think so, but the research is not conclusive. On the whole, though, it appears that the clearer the message, the more arguments a recipient retains, and the less annoyed he becomes. One should strive to build messages with maximum clarity.

A considerable amount of attention has been devoted to whether to present one or two sides of an argument. A useful rule of thumb is to present two sides if you think the recipient will not hear the other side somewhere else (Worchel and Cooper, 1983). If you are successful in changing someone's attitude about something, a two-sided message has an additional advantage (Lumsdaine and Janis, 1953). People subsequently exposed to counterarguments later are more apt to retain the new attitude if they have heard both sides of an argument than if they have only heard one side. Two-sided arguments, then, "inoculate" the hearer against accepting the unwanted side later.

If more than one side is presented, presenting your side first is most effective (Lund, 1925). Also, consider the length of time between presentations of each side. Short-term memory is just that—short. If conditions allow your message to be forgotten while some other message is remembered, then the other message will prevail. Thus you are best off if you present both sides of an argument contiguously and your side first.

Does drawing conclusions for your audience insult its intelligence? President Richard Nixon's hallmark was to say, "I want to make one thing perfectly clear," at which he would draw conclusions for his audience. His strategy was sound. Messages are often more effective when conclusions are specifically drawn.

Communication style is undoubtedly important, but research is sketchy about the impact of style on understandability or on the effectiveness of various styles. Certainly, many of the nonverbal cues discussed previously are elements of style and are used in interpersonal interactions. Remember our southern businessman and the attribution, "talk slow, think slow"? What might be the results of speeding up his speech? It turns out that a fast rate of speech does make the communicator seem more expert and credible. If this is true, perhaps dynamic speeches are more effective than subdued speeches. We do not know the answer because of the difficulty of identifying exactly what might be perceived as dynamic versus subdued. Also, it is clear that some styles are inappropriate to some contexts.

The Receiver

Many of the characteristics of recipients of information are the same as those of senders. They obtain and integrate information the same way and engage in all the biases we discussed in connection with communicators. Keep in mind, that if any communication is really going on, an interaction is implied, and receivers quickly become senders. The discussion of impressions and biases is thus just as relevant to receivers as to senders. Receivers, too, give off nonverbal clues as they receive and send messages.

Personality and Message Acceptance

It is reasonable to think that different personalities will respond to the same messages differently. Personality traits are dispositions in people that are consistent across time and situations (see Chapter 10). Some researchers have sought a personality trait that could be called "persuasibility" and have looked for sets of people who are more persuasible than others regardless of the topic of the message. This trait has been found in some people, but it does not account for very much of their behavior (Hovland and Janis, 1959). Such factors as message content and characteristics of message sources influence responses to messages more than persuasibility. Although it may seem self-evident that higher intelligence will increase resistance to persuasion, research provides no such clear-cut evidence. Thus, in dealing with bosses, subordinates, and peers, we should not predict their acceptance or rejection of messages on the basis of our assumptions about or knowledge of their intelligence.

People with low self-esteem are more persuasible and are influenced more by negative information about themselves than are people with high self-esteem (Cohen, 1959; Silverman, 1964). People with low self-esteem are very sensitive to such information, but people high in self-esteem deny such information. One might do well to keep this in mind when conducting performance appraisals.

One reason personality characteristics alone do not account for very much of people's acceptance and rejection of messages is that they act in concert with situational characteristics. Thus, in communicating with some-one, I really have to think not only about what I think I am saying (sender characteristics), how I make the transmission (channel use), and how I say it (message content), but also what the recipient is like and what type of situa-tion we are in. In such loaded communication situations as job interviews and performance appraisals, all these dimensions are more important than they are in everyday casual transactions.

Methods of Presentation and the Recipient

In talking about one- versus two-sided communication we briefly men-tioned that presenting both sides of an argument can inoculate against later acceptance of the unwanted side. Consider the medical model of inocula-tion: by presenting a slight dose of the undesirable information to a person, you may inoculate her against heavier doses later. The mind is so immu-nized. On the other hand, we could really bolster an argument and hope it is sufficient to ensure that its counterpart will not be accepted later. It turns out that both strategies work, but inoculation works best. Forewarning someone that he will be exposed to a communication with which he will not agree is an inadvisable strategy; it allows him time to build defenses against it. He may develop counterarguments for what he expects to hear and fight off communication, as the body fights off disease. No doubt, military train-ers include this technique in training troops to withstand captivity by an enemy.

Common wisdom says that people should pay strict attention to what is being said to gain the maximum amount from it. It is good news for teach-ers and managers alike that such is not the case. People most often change their attitudes when messages are accompanied by mild distraction. The same may not be true for complex messages, however. Not to worry, then, about the effect of the large sign on your noisy, confusing plant floor that says, "Do Not Go Beyond This Point." It probably works as well or better than it would in a less distracting environment.

Ambiguity, too, often has a positive effect on message acceptance (Eisenberg, 1984). Clearly, this positive effect has its limits, however. Less, rather than more, ambiguous message transmission was called for aboard the *Enterprise* the night she hit Bishop Rock.

Obtaining Commitment

The simplest and most obvious way to get someone to accept a position contrary to one he now espouses is to ask him to make a public statement in favor of the contrary position. Totalitarian governments and other more benign organizations know this all too well. When Republican President Ronald Reagan was a young man he was a registered Democrat. Then General Electric paid Mr. Reagan to make conservative speeches to its constituents, and see what happened! A good deal of the research on role playing shows that when we play a role that is different from what we believe, in front of an audience, we change our views to match those of the role we play. The Patricia Hearst experience is a case in point. Hearst was abducted by the Symbionese Liberation Army and forced to comply with the group's demands. Over the course of her captivity, she came to behave as her captors did. Alternatively, we have examples of prisoners of war forced to give testimony contrary to their beliefs who never did come to believe the testimony.

Another way one might commit someone to something is through the "foot in the door" strategy (Worchel and Cooper, 1983). If I want you to do something that I know you are not going to like, I commit you first to a less onerous, related task and only later to the very objectionable task. Thus I want you, a pacifist, to write a position paper favoring the MX missile. It seems unlikely that I will be able to get you to do this task, but I might be successful if I begin by asking you to provide a short statement about the value of national defense.

Alternatively, if I have a rather moderate task in mind that I know you will not agree to, I could initially ask you to do an even larger task. The second task would seem less onerous than the first, and the probability is higher that you will do it than if I had not first asked for the more onerous task. This is called the "door in the face" technique (Worchel and Cooper, 1983). It has also been shown that for moderate tasks both the foot-in-the-door and the door-in-the-face techniques work. But if there is a delay between the first and second request, the second technique loses its value.

In preparing persuasive communication, we sometimes face the question of whether we should take positions either a little different or very different from those of the audience. Think of people's attitudes as consisting of a spider web or network of beliefs and values all somehow tied together.

Recall that we try to make our thinking as internally consistent as possible. We assimilate opinions we find tolerable, which fall into a range or latitude of acceptance, and we reject the rest (they are in the rejection range). For best success, we construct our messages from items within our audience's latitude of acceptance. Thus, if I wish you, an atheist, to represent our company at a special church function, perhaps I had best couch my request in statements about the good of the company or the best interests of all our employees. That way, I have woven my almost intolerable request into a network of ideas you already accept.

If a communication is far from the acceptable norms of a person or group, attitude change may still be obtained. In fact, such communications work well, but only when associated with highly credible sources. When President John Kennedy told us that Americans had to get to the moon, we believed him. But we may not have believed the same message delivered by Howard Fortsdeep. We experience distress when dealing with discrepancies; we can deal with such distress by saying the communicator is an idiot or by accepting him as an expert.

Listening

Listening is the one subject not taught in our schools, according to Mortimer J. Adler (1983). As another writer put it, "Listening is a rare skill, the most often used yet least understood and researched of the communicating processes" (DiGaetani, 1980). Listening is more difficult than speaking, reading, or writing because the speed of the activity is set by the speaker and the listener has to follow along without breaks in a direct flow, whereas we write, speak, or read at our own speed. Yet listening is an important skill. Adler estimates that business executives spend a third to half their time with one another and that half of *that* time is wasted due to ineffective speaking and listening. Keefe (1970), reviewing several studies, concluded that executives spend 45 to 63 percent of their day listening.

Adler further noted several things to avoid in effective listening:

- Avoid paying more attention to the speaker's mannerism than to the substance of what's being said.

- Avoid distractions.

- Avoid overreaction or a predisposition to be negative.

- Avoid initial lack of interest and daydreaming.

He further recommended that listeners take notes actively and ask speakers to explain jargon and hidden assumptions. In short, listen actively, but do not interrupt. One reason people do not listen effectively is because they think listening is passive. Being intellectually active and taking notes makes one an active listener.

One of the most difficult problems for many listeners is to formulate clear, well-structured questions. Pay attention to questions and be sure they are understood by the speaker, repeating and rephrasing them if needed. A number of books on communication directed to managers emphasize listening. One example is Donald Walton's *Are You Communicating?* (1990).

SUMMARY

The events leading to the grounding of the U.S.S. *Enterprise* on Bishop Rock illustrate how a series of distractions, confusion, and misperceptions combined with a general lack of communication to produce an accident. The case also illustrates the use of technical language in organizations. Communication is a key to an organization's effectiveness; because an organization by definition includes a multitude of individuals, the creation, transmission, and interpretation of messages is vital to those various participants working in concert. Communication may be summed up in a simple model: a sender encodes information and transmits it to a receiver, who decodes, or translates, it. This process takes place in a context of other events, called noise, and with feedback providing the communicator with cues as to the success or failure of the transmission. Although such a model overlooks much of the complexity of communication in organizations, it does provide a useful overview of what takes place.

The communicator constructs the message from a combination of information gleaned from the environment and memories in his own head. Environmental signals are interpreted through a filter of biases that, among other effects, categorize events and participants in existing schema. Similarly, various biases affect how individuals judge the people around them. When these judgments need to be recalled later, the recency or relatedness of memories promotes or hinders their accessibility.

Verbal and nonverbal communication are the major vehicles for delivering messages. Speech establishes social order among interacting people and situates them in a social field. Paralanguage—the way things are said—helps manage communication by providing cues for taking turns. Men and women, as well as people from different cultures, use paralanguage differently.

Nonverbal communication channels include the body, the face, the eyes, and interpersonal distance. Gestures and touch convey meaning, but they are also the aspects of nonverbal communication most subject to misinterpretation. No good dictionary of these meanings exists. We rely on faces, and especially eyes, to give us information about those with whom we are communicating. Eye contact regulates the flow of communication, monitors feedback, expresses emotion, and indicates the nature of the interpersonal relationship. Nonverbal cues are useful because they can reveal deception. The face is more easily controlled than the body and thus less likely to reveal deception. Relative distance and the organization of space convey messages as well.

The various media used to transmit messages affect the message because they include more or less of the verbal and nonverbal components of the message. Speaking in person is the method with the most impact, followed by phoning. Writing, however, is the best vehicle for complex messages. New technology is affecting message transmission in profound ways. Some media—teleconferencing, for instance—provide the benefits of in-person presentation; others, such as electronic mail, are similar to writing in that they strip away nonverbal cues, but they offer significant advantages in speed.

The content of any message is inextricable from the fabric of its context. Effective management requires that we think about how to phrase messages. Although we prefer to send favorable messages over unfavorable ones, fear campaigns often work. Feedback, especially about job performance, is an important aspect of message content. Trust and credibility seem to be related more to the sender than to the content of the message. When an attempt is made to persuade another, the message works best that includes other sides of the argument but presents the favored side first.

Many characteristics of receivers are the same as those of senders; both, after all, are people. Another reason is that receivers quickly become senders, and vice versa. Psychologists have long sought personality correlates of message acceptance, but found nothing. Obtaining commitment from receivers is important in the communication process. It can be done by asking people to make public statements about the desired position or by having them move toward it incrementally. A key aspect of receiving communications is listening, which is more of an active art than many people realize. Taking notes and asking questions are useful techniques to improving listening.

MANAGERIAL INSIGHT

To: *Student Managers*
From: *Veteran Manager*
Subject: *Communications*

Of all the skills you need as a manager, none is more certain to be used every day, no matter what your job, than communication. Unless you decide to sit in a closet and meditate your way to wealth, you will have to communicate.

And as a manager, you will have some very special communication demands placed on you.

This is especially true in times of dramatic and wrenching change, such as most organizations have experienced over the last decade. As change increases, communications becomes exponentially more critical to the success of the manager, the people working for the manager, and the organization employing the manager.

Why? Because change is disorienting, painful, and confusing. Disoriented, confused workers are ineffective at best and destructive at worst. Good communication can't stop change, but it can alleviate some of its negative side effects.

You will need to make extra efforts to explain the changes your organization is going through and what it is doing to cope with them. You'll also have an intensified need to listen closely to what your people are saying and help carry their feelings and reactions upward to senior management. In such times one of the most vital contributions you can make will be to help your people understand the "whys" and "whats" of the change you are going through, and help them figure out what they must do to cope with and master the change.

The manager-as-communicator has to be a *translator*. To understand this role, picture yourself as an interpreter at the United Nations: you must hear one language in your earphones—what senior management is saying—and simultaneously speak another language into a microphone—the language of your employees.

Senior management does not always speak the same language as the employees on the frontline of a company. But the frontline employees usually are precisely the people who must get the message, the people on whom the organization depends to carry out what senior management wants. Someone has to translate the message for them. That person is you, their manager.

You must take the corporate vision and organizational objectives and make them real in your department. You have to help your people figure out how their jobs and the work of your department fit into the organization's overall scheme and direction. You have to help your people find, in the wonderful phrase of a colleague of mine, a "clear line of sight to the company goals."

You do this through communication. You talk to them, preferably face to face and often. You help them see that their contribution fits in "right there" or "like this." You explain, listen, answer, explain, listen, answer—over and over and over again.

Management will be talking strategic direction and five-year plans and global competition and fundamental changes in the marketplace. Your employees will be talking actual customers and moving production lines and this problem right here, today, right now. You have to connect these two worlds.

You have to bridge the gap for your employees. Whether they are back-hoe operators or customer service representatives or salesmen or assembly line workers, they've got to understand, and ultimately support and agree with, senior management's directives. Without your intervention, there is little chance that they'll be able to do it.

As if this weren't enough, you also have to be a communicator in the other direction—simultaneously. You have to take in what your people are saying and translate it for your senior management, who may not believe what you tell them about your employees and their feelings. You will be counted on by your people to let senior management know what their views are and what the world looks like through their eyes.

Communicating in this direction may be even tougher than passing the word downward. Going up, you may well be the bearer of unwelcome tidings—gripes or confusion or "why don't we do it this way" kinds of questions. Your senior management won't always want to hear what you are saying when you are speaking for your people. All of which just makes your job as communicator that much more challenging.

Most freshly graduated MBAs plunge into their managerial duties without any formal training in how to communicate. You don't usually see it listed in the business school catalogs along with finance and marketing and accounting. Conventional wisdom is that because we've all been communicating since about age 1 or 2, we're pretty good at it and don't need to be trained to do it any better. Conventional wisdom is dead wrong. If you're not a good communicator—and there are evaluation instruments and other ways of finding out—you must try to learn to do better.

If there is one message in all these managers' memos that is paramount above all the others, it is this one: learn to communicate well. Believe me when I tell you this.

REVIEW QUESTIONS

1. What is the role of perception in communication, as evidenced in the theme case?

2. Briefly describe the simple model of communication in this chapter. What limitations does it present as far as describing communication in organizations?

3. How do stereotypes affect us? Are stereotypes of individuals more significant than impressions of objects? Why?

4. What is the fundamental attribution error? How does it affect our perceptions of others?

5. Name three other biases that make attributions inaccurate.

6. What three factors can influence the retention of an experience in long-term memory?

7. What three factors affect verbal communication?

8. Suppose you wanted to report a recent success to your supervisor. Which sentence does it more effectively: "I met the sales quota for the quarter" or "The sales quota for the quarter has been met"? Why?

9. How can technical language both enhance and impede communication?

10. What methods of nonverbal communication can be observed? What do these techniques say about the relative effectiveness of in-person communication rather than communication over the phone or by letter?

11. Which is more likely to "leak" information that a speaker is not telling the truth: the face, the voice, or the body?

12. What factors do Lengel and Daft suggest using to select an appropriate medium for a message? Explain what the two variables mean.

13. What is the goal of using realistic job previews?

14. Give two reasons why presenting two sides of an argument helps you persuade another person to accept your side.

15. What is a greater influence on the persuasibility of a message recipient, his or her personality characteristics or other factors?

16. Describe three techniques that can be used to obtain commitment from the recipient of a message.

17. What four pieces of advice does Adler offer about listening?

REFERENCES

Adler, M. (1983). *How to Speak, How to Listen.* New York: Macmillan.

Argyle, M., and Ingham, R. (1972). Gaze, mutual gaze, and proximity. *Semiotica* 6:32–49.

Argyle, M., Ingham, R., Aikens, F., and McCallin, M. (1973). The different functions of gaze. *Semiotica* 1:19–32.

Axtell, Roger. (1985). *Do's and Taboos Around the World.* New York: Wiley.

Bannister, B. D. (1986). Performance outcome feedback and attributional feedback: Interactive effects on receipt responses. *Journal of Applied Psychology* 71:203–210.

Birdwhistell, R. L. (1970). *Kinesics and Context.* Philadelphia: University of Pennsylvania Press.

Brigham, J. C. (1976). Ethnic stereotypes. *Psychological Bulletin* 76:15–38.

Cantril, H., and Allport, G. W. (1935). *The Psychology of the Radio.* New York: Harper.

Cohen, A. R. (1959). Some implications of self-esteem for social influence. In C. I. Hovland and I. L. Janis (eds.), *Personality and Persuasibility.* New Haven, CT: Yale University Press.

Collins, A. M., and Loftus, E. F. (1975). A spreading-activation theory of semantic processing. *Psychological Review* 82:407–428.

Culnan, M. J., and Markus, M. L. (1987). Information technologies. In F. Joblin, L. Putnam, K. H. Roberts, and L. W. Porter (eds.), *Handbook of Organizational Communication.* Beverly Hills, CA: Sage, pp. 420–444.

Cusella, L. P. (1987). Feedback, motivation, and performance. In F. Joblin, L. Putnam, K. H. Roberts, and L. W. Porter (eds.), *Handbook of Organizational Communication.* Beverly Hills, CA: Sage, pp. 624–678.

Darwin, C. (1872). *The Expression of Emotion in Man and Animals.* New York: D. Appleton and Company.

Dean, R. A., and Wanous, J. P. (1984). Effects of realistic job previews on hiring bank tellers. *Journal of Applied Psychology* 21:413–420.

Deaux, K., and Wrightsman, L. S. (1984). *Social Psychology in the 80s,* 4th ed. Belmont, CA: Brooks/Cole.

DiGaetani, J. L. (1980). The business of listening. *Business Horizons,* October, pp. 40–46.

Duncan, D., and Fiske, D. W. (1977). *Face-to-Face Interaction.* Hillsdale, N.J.: Erlbaum.

Earley, P. C. (1986). Supervisors and shop stewards as sources of contextual information in goal setting: A comparison of the United States with England. *Journal of Applied Psychology,* January 1986, pp. 111–117.

Efran, J., and Broughton, A. (1966). Effect of expectancies for social approval on visual behavior. *Journal of Personality and Social Psychology* 4:103–107.

Eisenberg, E. M. (1984). Ambiguity as strategy in organizational communication. *Communication Monographs* 51:227–242.

Ekman, P., and Friesen W. V. (1969). The repertoire of nonverbal behavior: Categories, origins, usage and coding. *Semiotica* 1:49–98.

Ekman, P., and Friesen, W. V. (1974). Detecting deception from the body or face. *Journal of Personality and Social Psychology* 29:288–298.

Ekman, P., Friesen, W. V., and Ellsworth, P. (1972). *Emotion in the Human Face.* New York: Pergamon Press.

Ellsworth, P. C., Carlsmith, J. M., and Henson, A. (1972). The stare as a stimulus to flight in human subjects: A series of field experiments. *Journal of Personality and Social Psychology* 10:15–20.

Ellsworth, P. C., Carlsmith, J. M., and Henson, A. (1972). The stare as a stimulus to flight in human subjects: A series of field experiments. *Journal of Personality and Social Psychology* 21:302–311.

Erez, M. (1977). Feedback: A necessary condition for the goal setting performance relationship. *Journal of Applied Psychology* 62:624–627.

Evans, R. I., Rozelle, R. M., Lasater, T. M., Dembroski, T. M., and Allen, B. P. (1970). Fear arousal persuasion to actual vs. implied behavioral change: New perspective utilizing a real-life dental hygiene program. *Journal of Personality and Social Psychology* 16:220–227.

Everett, J. E., Stenning, B. W., and Longton, P. A. (1981). Stereotypes of the Japanese manager in Singapore. *International Journal of Intercultural Relations* 5:277–289.

Exline, R. V. (1971). Visual interaction: The glances of power and preference. In J. K. Cole (ed.), *Nebraska Symposium on Motivation*, vol. 19. Lincoln: University of Nebraska Press.

Exline, R., and Winters, L. (1965). Affective relations and mutual glances in dyads. In S. Tomkins and C. Izarel (eds.), *Affect, Cognition, and Personality*. New York: Springer.

Finholt, T., and Sproull, L. S. (1990). Electronic groups at work. *Organization Science* 1:41–64.

Fisher, J. D., Ryttim, M., and Heslin, R. (1976). Hands touching hands: Affective and evaluative effects of an interpersonal touch. *Sociometry* 39:416–421.

Friedlander, F. (1970). The primacy of trust as a facilitator of further group accomplishment. *Journal of Applied Behavioral Science* 6:387–400.

Galbraith, J. (1973). *Designing Complex Organizations*. Reading, MA: Addison-Wesley.

Gibb, J. (1964). Climate for trust formation. In L. Bradford, J. Gibb, and K. Benne (eds.), *T-Group Theory and Laboratory Method: Innovation in Re-education*. New York: Wiley, pp. 279–309.

Glenn, E. (1981). *Man and Mankind*. Norwood, NJ: Ablex.

Graves, D. (1972). Cultural determination and management behavior. *Organizational Dynamics* 2:46–59.

Greller, M. M. (1980). Evaluation of feedback sources as a function of role and organizational level. *Journal of Applied Psychology* 65:24–27.

Griffin, V. H. (1961). *Black Like Me*. Boston: Houghton Mifflin.

Hackman, J. R., and Oldham, G. R. (1980). *Work Redesign*. Reading, MA: Addison-Wesley.

Hall, E. T. (1959). *The Silent Language*. New York: Doubleday.

Hall, E. T. (1966). *The Hidden Dimension*. New York: Doubleday.

Herold, D. M., and Greller, M. M. (1977). Feedback: The definition of a construct. *Academy of Management Journal* 20:142–147.

Higgins, E. T., and Bargh, J. A. (1987). Social cognition and social perception. *Annual Review of Psychology* 38:369–425.

Higgins, E. T., Rholes, C. R., and Jones, C. R. (1977). Category accessibility and impression formation. *Journal of Experimental Social Psychology* 13:141–154.

Hovland, C. I., and Janis, I. L. (1959). *Personality and Persuasibility*. New Haven, CT: Yale University Press.

Janis, I. L., Kaye, D., and Kirschner, P. (1965). Facilitating effects of "eating while reading" on responsiveness to persuasive communications. *Journal of Personality and Social Psychology* 1:181–186.

Keefe, W. F. (1970). *Listen, Management!* New York: McGraw-Hill.

Kelly, G. A. (1955). *A Theory of Personality: The Psychology of Personal Constructs.* New York: Norton.

Kendon, A. (1967). Some functions of gaze-direction in social interaction. *Acta Psychologica* 26:22–63.

Knapp, M. L. (1978). *Nonverbal Communication in Human Interaction,* 2nd ed. New York: Holt, Rhinehart and Winston.

Krause, R. M., Geller, V., and Olson, C. (1976). Modalities and cues in the detection of deception. Paper presented at the meeting of the American Psychological Association, Washington, D.C., September.

Kraut, R. G. (1978). Verbal and nonverbal cues in the perception of lying. *Journal of Personality and Social Psychology* 36:380–391.

Kraut, R. E., and Johnston, R. (1979). Social and emotional messages of smiling: An ethological approach. *Journal of Personality and Social Psychology* 37:1539–1553.

La France, M., and Mayo, C. (1976). *Moving Bodies: Nonverbal Communication in Social Relationships.* Monterey, CA: Brooks-Cole.

Larwood, L., and Whittaker, N. (1977). Managerial myopia: Self-serving biases in organizational planning. *Journal of Applied Psychology* 62:194–198.

Lawson, E. (1971). Hair color, personality, and the observer. *Psychological Reports* 28:311–322.

Lefebvre, L. (1975). Encoding and decoding of ingratiation in modes of smiling and gaze. *British Journal of Social and Clinical Psychology* 14:33–42.

Lengel, R. H., and Daft, R. L. (1988). The selection of communication medias as an executive skill. *The Academy of Management Executive* 2:3, 225–232.

Leventhal, H. (1970). Findings and theory in the study of fear communication. In L. Berkowitz (ed.), *Advances in Experimental Social Psychology,* vol. 5. New York: Academic Press, pp. 120–186.

Lippitt, M. E., Miller, J. P., and Halamaj, J. (1980). Patterns of use and correlates of adoption of an electronic mail system. Prepared for Proceedings of the American Institute of Decision Sciences, Las Vegas, Nevada.

Loomis, J. (1959). Communication, the development of trust and cooperative behavior. *Human Relations* 12:305–315.

Luchins, A. S. (1957). Primacy-recency in impression formation. In C. I. Hovland (ed.), *The Order of Presentation in Persuasion.* New Haven: Yale University Press.

Lumsdaine, A., and Janis, I. L. (1953). Resistance to counter propaganda produced by a one-sided versus two-sided presentation. *Public Opinion Quarterly* 17:311–318.

Lund, F. H. (1925). The psychology of belief: IV. The law of primacy in persuasion. *Journal of Abnormal and Social Psychology* 20:183–191.

McLuhan, M. (1967). *The Medium Is the Message.* New York: Random House.

Magnusson, D. (1976). The person and the situation in an interactional model of behavior. *Scandinavian Journal of Psychology* 17:253–271.

Major, B., and Heslin, R. (1978). Perceptions of same-sex and cross-sex touching: It's better to give than to receive. Paper presented at meeting of Midwestern Psychological Association. Chicago, May.

Mehrabian, A. (1972). *Nonverbal Communication.* Chicago: Aldine Atherton.

Metzger, R. O., and Von Glinow, M. A. (1988). Off-site workers: At home and abroad. *California Management Review* 30:101–111.

Moscovici, S. (1967). Communication processes and the properties of language. In L. Berkowitz (ed.), *Advances in Experimental Social Psychology*, vol. 3. New York: Academic Press, pp. 225–270.

Mussen, P. H., and Barker, R. G. (1944). Attitudes toward cripples. *Journal of Abnormal and Social Psychology* 39:351–355.

Nisbett, R., and Ross, L. (1980). *Human Inference: Strategies and Shortcomings of Social Judgment.* Englewood Cliffs, NJ: Prentice-Hall.

O'Reilly, C. A., and Roberts, K. H. (1974a). Information filtration in organizations: Three experiments. *Organizational Behavior and Human Performance* 11:253–265.

O'Reilly, C. A., and Roberts, K. H. (1974b). Failures in upward communication in organizations: Three possible culprits. *Academy of Management Journal* 17:205–215.

Palme, J. (1981). Experience with the Use of the Con Computerized Conferencing System. Stockholm, Sweden: Forsvarets Forskningsanstalt.

Patterson, M. L. (1976). An arousal model of interpersonal intimacy. *Psychological Review* 83:235–245.

Peters, C. (1986). From Ouagadougou to Cape Canaveral: Why the bad news doesn't travel up. *Washington Monthly*, April, pp. 27–31.

Richardson, S. A., Hastorf, A. H., Goodmen, N., and Dornbush, S. M. (1961). Cultural uniformity in reaction to physical disabilities. *American Sociological Review* 26:24–47.

Riecken, H. W. (1958). The effect of talkativeness on ability to influence group solutions to problems. *Sociometry* 21:309–321.

Rochester, S. R. (1973). The significance of pauses in spontaneous speech. *Journal of Psycholinguistic Research* 2:51–81.

Roll, S., and Verinis, J. S. (1971). Stereotypes of scalp and facial hair as measured by the semantic differential. *Psychological Reports* 28:975–980.

Rosenberg, S., and Sedlack, A. (1972). Structural representations of implicit personality theory. In L. Berkowitz (ed.), *Advances in Experimental Social Psychology*, vol. 6. New York: Academic Press.

Rosenthal, R., and Jacobson, L. (1968). *Pygmalion in the Classroom.* New York: Holt, Rinehart and Winston.

Ross, L. (1977). The intuitive psychologist and his shortcomings: Distortions in the attribution process. In L. Berkowitz (ed.), *Advances in Experimental Social Psychology*, vol. 10. New York: Academic Press, pp. 173–220.

Ross, L., Greene, D., and House, P. (1977). The "false consensus effect": An egocentric bias in social perception and attribution processes. *Journal of Experimental and Social Psychology* 13:279–301.

Schneider, D. J., Hastorf, A. H., and Ellsworth, P. (1979). *Person Perception*, 2nd ed. Reading, MA: Addison-Wesley.

Shaw, M. E., and Gilchrest, J. E. (1956). Intra-groups communication and leader choice. *Journal of Social Psychology* 43:133–138.

Sheldon, W. H. (1940). *The Varieties of Human Physique: An Introduction to Constitutional Psychology*. New York: Harper & Row.

Sherif, C. W., Sherif, M., and Nebergall, R. E. (1960). *Attitude and Attitude Change: The Social Judgment Approach*. Philadelphia: Saunders.

Silverman, J. (1964). Self-esteem and differential responsiveness to success and failure. *Journal of Applied Psychology* 69:115–119.

Spiegel, H. N. (1983 revised). *The Growth of Economic Thought*. Durham, NC: Duke University Press, p. 243.

Sutton, C. D., and Woodman, R. W. (1989). Pygmalion goes to work: The effects of supervisor expectations in a retail setting. *Journal of Applied Psychology* 74:943–950.

Taylor, S. E., and Fiske, S. T. (1978). Salience, attention, and attribution: Top of the head phenomena. In L. Berkowitz (ed.), *Advances in Experimental Social Psychology*, vol. 11. New York: Academic Press, pp. 249–288.

Tesser, A., and Rosen, S. (1975). The reluctance to transmit bad news. In L. Berkowitz (ed.), *Advances in Experimental Social Psychology*, vol. 8. New York: Academic Press, pp. 193–232.

Walton, D. (1990). *Are You Communicating?* New York: McGraw-Hill.

Wanous, J. P. (1980). *Organizational Entry: Recruitment, Selection, and Socialization of Newcomers*. Reading, MA: Addison-Wesley.

Wheeless, V. E., and Berryman-Fink, C. (1985). Perceptions of women managers and their communication competencies. *Communication Quarterly* 33:137–148.

Worchel, S., and Cooper, J. (1983). *Understanding Social Psychology*. Homewood, IL: Dorsey.

Wyer, R. S., and Hartwick, J. (1980). The role of information retrieval and conditional inference processes in belief formation and change. In L. Berkowitz (ed.), *Advances in Experimental Social Psychology*, vol. 13. New York: Academic Press, pp. 241–284.

Wyer, R. S., and Henninger, M. (1978). The effects of reporting beliefs on the recall of belief-related propositions. Unpublished manuscript, University of Illinois at Urbana-Champaign.

Wyer, R. S., and Scrull, T. K. (1980). Category accessibility: Some theoretical and empirical issues concerning the processing of social stimulus information. In E. T. Higgins, C. P. Herman, and M. P. Zanna (eds.), *Social Cognition: The Ontario Symposium on Personality and Social Psychology*. Hillsdale, NJ: Erlbaum.

Zuckerman, M., De Paulo, B. M., and Rosenthal, R. (1981). Verbal and nonverbal communication of deception. In L. Berkowitz (ed.), *Advances in Experimental Social Psychology*, vol. 14. New York: Academic Press, pp. 2–59.

6

Power and Politics in Organizations: Who Influences Whom

CHAPTER OVERVIEW

This chapter defines organizational power and shows how it differs from politics. The bases and types of power are discussed and then power relationships are explored within and between organizations. The tactics of power, or the way it is exercised, are also examined, followed by study of how managers view organizational politics.

THEME CASE

"Power Shift at Bank of America" relates how A. W. (Tom) Clausen regained and consolidated the reins of power after returning to the bank to replace Sam Armacost, the man he had picked to succeed himself just a few years before.

CHAPTER OUTLINE

- What Are Power and Politics?
- Sources of Power
- Intraorganizational Power
- Interorganizational Power
- The Use of Power: Power Tactics
- What Managers Think of Organizational Politics
- Summary
- Managerial Insight

KEY DEFINITIONS

Power   a relationship among people in which one person is able to get another to do something he would not otherwise do.

Politics   the study of who gets what, when, and how.

Authority   the right to command and decide.

External coalitions   groups outside an organization that exert power over the organization, e.g., owners, associates, unions, professional associations, publics.

Internal coalitions   power inside the organization. Alliances among CEO, middle line managers, operators, analysts, and support staffs.

Strategic contingencies and resource dependence   the sources of one department's power to control another, rooted in the powerful unit's control over processes or resources the latter depends on.

Additional Terms

Hierarchical authority
Resource control
Network centrality
Coercive, utilitarian, and normative powers
Reward, legitimate, referent, and expert
  powers
Dependence
Authority, ideology, expertise, and political
  systems
Dominance
Empowerment
Resistance
Delegation
Interdependence
Lobbying
Coalition building
Direct ownership, direct interlock ties, and
  indirect interlocks
Joint ventures

POWER SHIFT AT BANK OF AMERICA

Precipitated by rumors of impending failure, confronted with takeover bids, and facing continuing huge loan losses on foreign and farm loans, Bank of America was in dire straits. Under the circumstances, the resignation of President and Chief Executive Officer (CEO) Samuel Armacost in October of 1986 was predictable; however, the return of former President and CEO A. W. "Tom" Clausen was a surprise to many observers. Soon after Clausen's return was announced, he made moves to consolidate his power.

When Clausen was renamed as CEO, the board of directors made another move. Thomas Cooper, who had recently joined the bank, was moved into a position to share power with Clausen. But this two-party power arrangement developed by the board of directors was to be very short-lived. Approximately seven months after the board announced the resignation of Samuel Armacost, the rehiring of Tom Clausen, and the retention of Thomas Cooper, Clausen remained alone with the reins of power at Bank of America. Events preceding the rehiring of Tom Clausen and events leading to Cooper's resignation provide the background for this internal shift in power at America's fifth largest commercial bank.

During Tom Clausen's first (1970–1980) reign as Bank of America's president and CEO, the bank rose to become the world's largest commercial bank. Citicorp of New York had long held this number one ranking, and it was no secret that the Clausen-led Bank of America coveted this crown. The two giant banks raced to see who would be first to open offices in iron curtain countries, to be the syndicate loan leader on loans valued at hundreds of millions of dollars to Third World nations, and in sum, to be the biggest commercial bank in the world.

Clausen had worked at Bank of America for over 20 years when he first became CEO in 1970. Beginning as a vault clerk, he developed a reputation for being hard working, autocratic, even "dictatorial" during his career. As evidence of this style, he reportedly was responsible for driving out the bank's best managerial talent, including Joe Pinola, who later led First Interstate Bankcorp's merger bid for Bank of America in 1986. Clausen also reportedly focused more on short-term profits than on long-term strategy. Although this focus produced asset growth and record dividends during his 11 years as CEO, it may also have played a role in the bank's heavy loan losses during the tenure of the successor he appointed in 1980, Samuel Armacost.

Under Clausen, the bank vigorously pursued Third World loans, decentralized lending operations, and authorized overseas managers to make medium-sized loans. These Third World loans were strongly encouraged by the United States government, but billions of dollars in loans to Brazil and other nations became noninterest earning bad debts in the Armacost years as interest rates soared and payment of interest became impossible for these nations. Additionally, Clausen's growth strategy left Armacost with billions of dollars of fixed, low-rate agricultural loans, the result being an even greater interest-rate squeeze as the costs of deposits went up in the early 1980s. Before departing in 1980, Clausen also reportedly approved some creative accounting practices that converted a loss of $7 million into $7 million in earnings for 1980. One example was booking mortgage loans rather than amortizing them over a period of years, the more common bankers' practice. In sum, the bank suffered hundreds of millions in loan losses during the Armacost years, forcing it to report its largest ever single write-off of $1.1 billion in bad loans in the spring of 1987, just six months after Clausen's return.

Armacost was staunchly supported by the board for several years. He had won support by automating the bank's operations, bringing it into the 21st century and overcoming the neglect of the Clausen years, during which the bank lagged technologically behind most major commercial banks. That support continued even to 1985, when the bank posted $337 million in losses, began its first personnel layoffs, cut dividends for the first time in its history, and sold its world headquarters building for cash to reduce losses. However, this combination of events seriously weakened support for Armacost. Support was diminishing further in the fall of 1986 amidst rumors in the press and on Wall Street of the bank's impending failure. A persisting takeover/merger bid by First Interstate Bankcorp and the expectation that dividends would not be paid for the first time in bank history worsened the bank's problems.

Faced with these difficulties, the directors began searching for a replacement for Armacost. Eight of the ten outside members of the board (six members were from inside the bank) had actually been appointed during Clausen's first presidency, including the leader of the replacement search, John Beckett, the investment banker who had expanded Transamerica during the Clausen years with loan assistance from Bank of America. Beckett was reportedly aided by the former Bank of America president and honorary board director, Rudolph Peterson, who had chosen Clausen as his replacement in 1970. All eight of these members were also reportedly members of the Pacific-Union Club, an old-line, all-male network. It was reported that Beckett had even solicited Clausen's suggestion for a replacement for Armacost, further indicating a close relationship.

The board's decision to replace Armacost was not simply an issue of hiring one new leader; the bank also needed to restore customer, stockholder, and employee faith. Much had transpired at Bank of America during the six years since Clausen had left. Now he was faced not with the growth challenge of the 1970s but with the need to reduce expenses and find ways to curtail heavy loan losses. A two-man power structure was suggested by the board for the bank's immediate future. Clausen would be chairman and CEO and Thomas Cooper would be president and chief operating officer. Cooper had come to Bank of America from Mellon Bank if Pittsburgh in 1985 and as an executive vice president proceeded to eliminate jobs at a rate of 1,000 per month and targeted to reduce Bank of America's excessive costs by $180 million. Considered a hard-nosed manager and a tough cost cutter, Cooper was to complement Clausen, who was perceived as not being disposed to laying off large numbers of workers.

Indeed, Cooper found himself in the midst of a corporate culture that had a long tradition of never changing dramatically or of down-sizing. For example, the bank's history of zero layoffs during the Great Depression was often noted with pride during personnel socialization activities.

However, this dual power arrangement created in October 1986 was to be a short-lived one. In May of 1987, Cooper resigned. Preceding his resignation, Cooper had stepped up the pace of staff reductions, but Clausen was reportedly unhappy with the retail and corporate banking operations, which were directly under Cooper's control. Clausen named Richard Rosenburg vice chairman and chief of the California retail operations, thus making him report directly to Clausen, not to Cooper. Clausen also named Vice Chairman Robert Frick (Corporate Banking Chief) as a director, giving Frick an independent power base, further eroding Cooper's power. Although Cooper made no mention of a power struggle in his resignation, he did state that "the bank's needs . . . are changed from those that were present when I assumed the position of chief operating officer." Total control of Bank of America appeared once again to be in the hands of Tom Clausen.

Before announcing he was stepping down as CEO in late 1989, Clausen articulated five basic management steps that were taken during Bank of America's recovery:

> A management team of proven winners was built, and everyone understood that the company's survival depended on how well each job was done.

> The entire business was reassessed, and top management faced the reality that what was successful in the past no longer worked.

3. Top management focused on how to generate maximum value for the bank's shareholders.

4. Top management concentrated on actions with an immediate impact, but that would not curtail the future of the bank.

5. Top management communicated constantly, consistently, and credibly both inside and outside the bank.

Sources: Adapted from A. W. Clausen, "Strategic Issues in Managing Change: The Turnaround at Bank of America Corporation," *California Management Review* 32 (1990): 98–105. Copyright © 1990 by the Regents of the University of California. Reprinted by permission of the Regents. Also from G. Hector, *Breaking the Bank: The Decline of Bank America* (New York: Little, Brown, 1988).

Although power has existed in organizations from their very inception, organizational researchers were little interested in it until about 1975. "Few researchers were inclined to knock on the organization's door to announce: 'I'm here to find out who has the power in this place'" (Mintzberg, 1983, p. 3). There were several reasons for this reluctance. Possibly the most important was that it was somehow unseemly in a democratic society to be too worried about issues of dominance, dependence, and control. If students were schooled to view business organizations as groups of people obsessed with power, the businesses might have had serious recruitment problems. It was far more socially acceptable for the student to think of himself as developing skills to allocate resources efficiently rather than learning to engage with others in political struggles over values and preferences (Pfeffer, 1981). Even Thomas Cooper seemed to be reluctant to relate his departure from Bank of America to a power struggle with Tom Clausen. But power and influence in organizations are quite real, as the bank case clearly illustrates. Understanding them is critical to the success of every manager.

Until 1975, to the extent that organizational power was studied at all, it was studied by sociologists who took an external perspective, studying power at a distance. The Watergate affair, culminating in President Nixon's resignation in 1974, left managers and researchers alike extremely disturbed by the engagement of top-level U.S. government officials in activities designed purely and simply to increase power. With this impetus, the study of power in organizations became more intense, yet another example of how much of what organizational researchers study is in response to historical events.

In this chapter, we will draw upon this growing body of research to study power and politics. We will first study the bases of power within organizations. With that grounding, we will be able to explore how power is manifested among individuals and groups within the same organization and among different organizations. We will then look at the political tactics that members of organizations employ and consider the attitudes that managers take toward the politics of organizations.

What Are Power and Politics?

Most of the numerous definitions of power and politics have to do with dependence, control, authority, and influence. The definition we prefer is that "power is the capability of one social actor to overcome resistance in achieving a desired action or result" (Pfeffer, 1981, p. 2). **Power** is a relationship among people in which one person is able to get another to do something he would not otherwise do. **Politics**, on the other hand, is the study of who gets what, when, and how (Lasswell, 1936). "Organizational politics involves those activities taken by organizations to acquire, develop, and use power and other resources to obtain one's preferred outcomes in a situation in which there is uncertainty or dissent about choices" (Pfeffer, 1981, p. 71). **Authority** is differentiated from power; it is the right to command and decide.

We can see these three concepts at work in the Bank of America case. Tom Clausen was granted the authority to command by reason of his appointment as chairman and CEO by the bank's board of directors. Clausen's subsequent political moves—putting his appointees in key positions and thus causing the departure of CEO Cooper—were effective in increasing his power base into bank operation activities controlled by Cooper.

Most discussions of power view organizations as settings in which rational decision making is driven out by a political process in which decision making is based on relative power. One writer ascribes this to what he calls

> the Law of Political Entropy: given the opportunity, an organization will tend to seek and maintain a political character. The argument is that once politics is introduced into a situation, it is very difficult to restore rationality. Once consensus is lost, once disagreements about preferences, technology and management philosophy emerge, it is very hard to restore the kind of shared perspective and solidarity which is necessary to operate under the rational model. If rationality is indeed this fragile, and if the Law of Political Entropy is correct, then over time one would expect to see more and more organizations characterized by the political model. (Pfeffer, 1981, p. 32)

Looking more closely, however, one might use both rational and political models to explain what goes on in a particular organization at any given moment. Some activities are probably driven by rational behavior, whereas others are controlled through political processes. All in all, however, power is a subtle phenomenon, "its origin and impact . . . embedded in the symbols and systems that evolve out of contests and struggles among organizational actors" (Frost, 1987, p. 505).

The existence of politics in organizations should not be a surprise; politics, involved as it is with the distribution of resources and outputs, is inevitable in any entity that includes more than one individual or group. The distinction between rational and political processes for arranging that distribution is the differentiation between decisions made on the basis of reasoned analysis and those based on relative power (or the desire for such power). The commonly held view that the former method is honorable and the latter tainted may be nothing but prejudice. Political moves may, in fact, enhance one's ability to pursue rational objectives. Clausen may have eased Cooper out to establish total control for himself, thereby reducing the chance for disagreements of any kind from his top-level executives so he could implement his rebuilding plan for the bank.

One set of writers (Velasquez, Moberg, and Cavanagh, 1983) addressed this equation of political maneuvering with unsavory behavior. They distinguished between "dirty politics" and what they referred to as "organizational statesmanship," arguing that actions based on ethical considerations, even if clearly political, need not be undesirable. The authors presented three fundamental approaches to ethical behavior: the utilitarian approach, which views behavior in terms of the greater good for the greater number; the rights approach, which evaluates actions as ethical or not based on whether individual rights are protected; and the justice approach, which identifies as ethical that which fairly apportions the benefits of an action. These criteria can be used in consonance in many situations to determine how to proceed in an ethical manner while still practicing politics. The authors argued that these principles permit a reasonable and frank disagreement on goals or strategies, but that organizational diplomats can work fairly to settle those disagreements. They acknowledged, as well, that conflict between criteria or within criteria or the lack of power to apply the criteria can hamper the manager's capacity to apply them.

Sources of Power

In the Bank of America case we find a clear illustration of the realignment of interpersonal power based on hierarchy and the division of tasks. Clausen used structural power adjustments to consolidate operations under his own control. The case also demonstrates how individuals obtain power. In some cases it is formally conferred, as in Clausen's reappointment by the board. Such power corresponds to authority. Sometimes it is developed through relationships; Clausen's close ties with board members put him in a powerful position to regain control of the bank. The sources of power bear close scrutiny; we will first examine those that derive from structural arrangements and then investigate interpersonal bases of power.

Structural Aspects of Power

Most studies of power in organizations focus on hierarchical power, either the power of supervisors over subordinates (e.g., Kanter, 1977) or the power of lower- over higher-level participants (Mechanic, 1962; Porter, Allen, and Angle, 1981). Hierarchical power is important in understanding what goes on in organizations, but it is not the only dimension of power. (For a detailed description of hierarchy, see Chapter 2.) In complex organizations, tasks are divided among departments or subunits, and some are more powerful than others (Perrow, 1986). Structural power, then, is not only hierarchical but also created by the division of tasks.

Some writers focus solely on structural bases of power, believing they are far more important in complex organizations than interpersonal bases of power. Most of these two types of bases apply equally to individuals and to subunits in organizations. In the Bank of America case—and quite probably in many real-world situations—it is also difficult to distinguish between structural and interpersonal power bases.

Astley and Sachdeva (1984) discussed three structural sources of power. The first, not surprisingly, is **hierarchical authority**, or the position in the chain of command. **Resource control** is the second structural source of power. Those actors who obtain the resources that are both the most critical and the most difficult to secure have the most control. The third structural source of power is **network centrality**. To the extent that people are located at key connection points in networks, they gain power because others depend on them.

Related to the concept of centrality is the idea that organizational members accrue power by their ability to affect the decision process (Pfeffer, 1981). There are a number of ways to do this. A person might have control over the premises of organizational decision making. These "premises" revolve around the goals and objectives of the organization and around constraints on behavior. Goals, norms, and rules are all developed on these premises and influence decision processes. The person who establishes goals, controls constraints, and develops norms accrues power.

Another way to control decision processes is to control the alternatives considered. For example, a project team charged with making recommendations about the kind of computer system an organization should buy will probably present key decision makers with only a few of the large number of possible alternatives. This narrowing of choices is a kind of exercise of power. A final way to control decision processes is to control the information about alternatives. Workers who present or withhold facts about such factors as assembly processes or customer relations are exerting power over their supervisors, who are more or less in the know depending on how much they are told.

Kanter (1989) suggested that structural sources of power are changing as rapidly changing environments and increasing competitiveness break down organizational hierarchies and promote new bases of power based on "the number of networks in which [managers] are centrally involved." Kanter terms this environment "postentrepreneurial" because it requires "the application of entrepreneurial creativity and flexibility to existing businesses." In this new environment, negotiating ability becomes a key to managerial success and power. Managers must be open to many channels of communication. Further, they must abandon such tools of motivation as financial reward or promotion because the fluctuating environment does not permit them the certainty of granting such rewards. The new motivators become such factors as mission, professional growth, and pride in making a contribution. If Kanter is correct, the structural bases of power will soon give way to the interpersonal bases of power. In fact, a recent study of antecedents to power shows that past power is a better predictor of future power than are structural characteristics (Lachman, 1989).

Interpersonal Bases of Power

Power bases come from many different sources. One discussion (Etzioni, 1961) identified three types of power: **coercive power**, or forcing someone to comply with our wishes; **utilitarian power**, or power derived from control over performance-reward contingencies; and **normative power**, based on the belief of people in the right of others to control their behaviors. Etzioni argued that organizations can be classified on the basis of the prevalence of each of these types of power. Thus a prison is coercive, a business organization utilitarian, and a church normative. Clausen's actions at Bank of America were examples of utilitarian power so frequently seen in business. Although this classification is somewhat helpful, it cannot address certain aspects of power, such as the interpersonal power shifts seen at the bank.

To better understand how power comes to be held, power may be described in terms of how it is exerted. Taking this perspective, French and Raven (1959) identified five types of power. **Reward power** exists when one person controls the rewards of another. Supervisors are thought to control the primary direct rewards of their employees. However, if we look closely, major rewards in most organizations, such as pay and other benefits, are often under only partial supervisory control—the department head may be able to determine the amount of a raise, but not the amount of health insurance. If the organization has workers under union contract, a given manager may have very little reward power available.

Coercive power is based on fear. Also called punishment power, it is exercised through reliance on physical strength, verbal facility, or the ability to grant or withhold emotional support and rewards from others.

Legitimate power is based on the right or authority of one person to control another. It is derived from cultural norms, accepted social structure, or designated responsibility. The power parents have over children is endorsed by cultural norms; the power wealthy families have in many nations derives from social structure. Clausen, given command of Bank of America by the board of directors, had designated power.

Referent power emanates from the fact that someone is looked up to, perhaps because of her personal qualities, characteristics, or reputation. Referent power, often called charismatic power, is the kind of power possessed by some leaders (see Chapter 8).

Expert power derives from knowledge. Staff specialists such as lawyers and tax accountants are in those positions, and command attention, because of their specialized knowledge.

To these bases, Kotter (1977) added several other dimensions. He discussed how managers develop among their subordinates a sense of obligation to the manager, belief in managerial expertise, and identification with and perceived dependence on a manager. He also noted the formal authority derived from the management situation.

A model that synthesizes these differing views and provides an overview of intraorganizational power and politics appears in Figure 6.1. A manager's authority, or formal power, includes the attributive bases of power: legitimate, coercive, and reward powers. These powers are exerted to achieve organizational objectives. A manager's influence on subordinates is enhanced or reduced based on the informal bases of power, expert and referent powers. These are characteristics of the individual, not attributes conferred by the organization. Political actions involve influencing both the organization's objectives and subordinates' actions in achieving those objectives. The manager can use political approaches to enhance her influence; similarly, other managers—or even the subordinates being managed—can use their own political techniques to affect that manager's influence. Political pressures are exerted not only to enhance or undermine influence, however. Members in the organization also use political maneuvering to help define the objectives themselves.

FIGURE 6.1

An Influence-Based Model of Intraorganizational Power and Politics

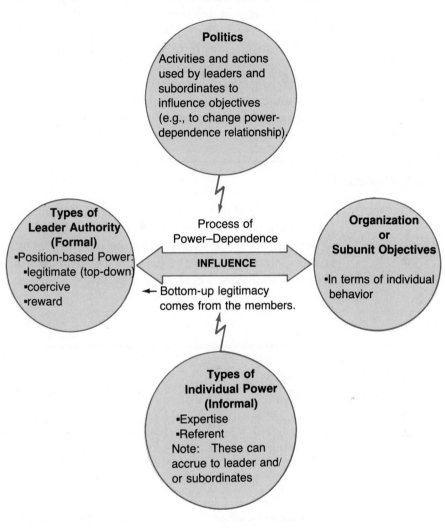

Politics

Activities and actions used by leaders and subordinates to influence objectives (e.g., to change power-dependence relationship)

Types of Leader Authority (Formal)
- Position-based Power:
  - legitimate (top-down)
  - coercive
  - reward

Process of Power–Dependence

INFLUENCE

← Bottom-up legitimacy comes from the members.

Organization or Subunit Objectives
- In terms of individual behavior

Types of Individual Power (Informal)
- Expertise
- Referent

Note: These can accrue to leader and/ or subordinates

The model in Figure 6.1 is somewhat oversimplified, of course. As we will see, the actions of one manager occur within the context of the entire organization, which means the involvement of other managers and their groups, the interaction between groups, and even contact with other organizations. In other words, power relationships take place in two contexts—within organizations and between organizations. Power within organizations includes situations in which one member controls resources that another wants, such as pay or benefits, or even his very job, as in Thomas

Cooper's case at Bank of America. Intraorganizational power also includes the relationships of different groups within the same organization. Cooper's control over the daily operations of the bank were diminished by Clausen's appointment of two executives to deal directly with operational activities without going through Cooper.

Interorganizational power exists when one organization controls whatever another organization needs. It is now time to study those power relationships in detail, beginning with intraorganizational power.

Intraorganizational Power

No discussion of intraorganizational power is complete without some mention of the players in the power game, and there is where we shall begin. Mintzberg (1983) identified ten groups of possible influences, five outside the organization, called the **external coalition**, and five inside, called the **internal coalition**. These groups are listed in Figure 6.2. Which of these

FIGURE 6.2
Cast of Players in the Organizational Power Game

External Coalition

Owners	Give birth to the organization and provide its capital.
Associates	Suppliers, clients, partners, or competitors.
Unions	Employee organizations (usually lower-level).
Professional associations	Employee organizations (usually higher-level).
Publics	A constituency that bears some special relationship to the organization.

Internal Coalition

Chief executive officer	The head of the organization. Control over him is diffuse.
Middle line managers	Managers below the chief executive officer. Control over them is concentrated.
Operators	Skilled and unskilled workers.
Analysts	Planners, operations researchers, budget analysts, and other specialists (staff or support).
Support staffs	People who provide a wide range of services (i.e., public relations, personnel).

Source: Adapted from H. Mintzberg, *Power in and Around Organizations* (New York: McGraw-Hill, 1983), pp. 27–28.

groups are involved in any given organization depends on the organization itself; the players will vary from one firm to another.

The External Coalition

Owners have legal title to the organization. They contribute to organizational viability in two ways: they often set up the organization, and they contribute capital. Owners, clearly, have the ultimate in legitimate power; depending on the role they play in the organization, they may have other bases of power as well. That role is measured on two dimensions—involvement and concentration. Involved owners are directly and intimately concerned with the organization's operations, whereas detached owners are totally removed from them, usually leaving operations to their elected representatives (e.g., the board of directors at Bank of America). Dispersion (as opposed to concentration) is the degree to which organizations are closely held (for example, hundreds of thousands of shareholders make Bank of America widely dispersed).

Mintzberg hypothesizes that the more involved the owners and the more concentrated their ownership, the greater their power. In an involved, concentrated ownership, the owners belong to both an external and an internal coalition. Such a situation can occur with organizations of various sizes, ranging from the mom-and-pop grocery store to CBS. William Paley and Lawrence Tisch are large shareholders as well as executives in CBS. This position and their high interest in the medium's news function in many ways colors the direction CBS takes as a company.

Associates are suppliers, clients, partners, or competitors who engage in purely economic relationships with an organization. In a pure market relationship, an associate buys or sells to an organization when the prices and products are right. Otherwise he goes elsewhere and makes no attempt to influence the policies of the organization.

Not all associates are disinterested. Three factors, which lead to dependency, govern the power relationships between an organization and its associates: necessity, substitutability, and concentration. That is, the more essential the resource to an organization, the more irreplaceable the supplier, and the more concentrated the suppliers, the greater their power. For example, because there are only a few suppliers of aircraft to the military, the military is dependent on them. The same, of course, is true of the organization in relation to its clients. The organization that is essential, irreplaceable, and concentrated is powerful in relation to its suppliers. The military, in turn, has significant power over defense contractors because it provides those contractors with one of their very few markets.

This kind of influence of one group over another reflects coercive power. When the relationship is based on one group's possessing a special expertise—as, for example, when a firm hires an outside consultant to structure a new benefits package—the consultant relies on expertise as his base of power. An organization may also model itself on another, successful firm, an example of referent power.

Sometimes employees go outside their organizations to exert influence. They do so through two kinds of associations: *unions*, which represent lower-level employees, and *professional associations*, which represent highly trained operators and staff personnel. As individuals these people may exercise power in internal coalitions, but their associations outside the organization allow them to act collectively to bring their combined power to bear on their organizations. It is often so difficult for employees to change jobs that they are better off trying to change the behavior of their organizations. In terms of employees, these outside associations possess referent power, rooted in the complex social and economic history of collective employee action. In regard to the organization itself, they may exert coercive power, depending on their strength relative to the organization; strikes and work slowdowns are two examples of potentially coercive collective action.

The various *publics* of an organization are technically most detached from it. A public is a constituency or group of people who bear some special relationship to the organization and whose actions or opinions are important to it (e.g., stockholders, suppliers, customers, regulators, legislators). These publics feel sufficiently affected by the organization's actions to try to influence it.

Publics come in a variety of forms. One category is comprised of the purveyors of public interest—newspapers, friends, spouses, and so on. The second category is government; the third, special interest groups. The power possessed by publics derives from different bases. A government agency with the regulatory authority over a business has coercive and legitimate power. An environmental group can have coercive or referent power, depending on its relationship to the organization and to the public at large.

Two general arguments justify the rights of external publics to try to exert control over organizations. One viewpoint says that organizations exist to fulfill a societal purpose and that society therefore has a right to worry about what organizations do. The other view dismisses legitimacy entirely and sees the issue as a power game; organizations should be controlled by whatever constituents can amass the forces to control them.

Two major factors give outsiders control over organizations. One is access, as when a board member, Beckett, called Clausen, then an outsider, for advice about a replacement for Armacost. The other is the ability to disrupt the organization's activities, as when rumors circulating in the news media and the pressure exerted by stockholders, clients, and Wall Street forced Bank of America's board of directors to fire Armacost.

The Internal Coalition

The *chief executive officer* (CEO) is usually the single most powerful individual in an organization. This does not mean that there are not other powerful people in organizations, but the CEO is in a unique position, one that affords maximal power, as Tom Clausen demonstrated. The CEO serves in a formal sense as the board of director's trustee to manage the organization, and in an informal sense as the reconciler of pressures placed on the organization by various external influences. In the Bank of America case, the fact that several board members owed their jobs to Clausen enhanced his power and influence. The CEO has the best access to external influences. In addition, he has a number of bases for internal power.

Without looking very far we can see that CEOs typically have four of French and Raven's five bases of power (coercive, reward, legitimate, and referent; some may also possess expert power). In addition to these bases of formal power, CEOs have substantial informal power. They typically have as their goals the survival and growth of their organizations (Chandler, 1977; Galbraith, 1967). As the most important people in the organization's power game, they can orient their organizations toward their goals.

Everything said about the CEO applies to *middle line managers*, but to a decreasing degree as one moves lower in the organizational hierarchy. Those executives nearest the top share the CEO's goals and power. If they do not, they may be removed. Those near the bottom share far less power. There is a fundamental difference between managers and the CEO, however. Control over managers is concentrated in someone else (their superior), whereas control over the CEO is diffused. Some is held by the external coalition, some by various members of the organization, for example, the board of directors.

Skilled and unskilled *operators* work in organizations. Since unskilled operators cannot call on expert power and since they lack power as individuals, their power is based on that of the group. Consequently, shared goals rather than individual goals are reflected in the demands of the group.

Professional operators, on the other hand, rely on their expertise as their basis of power. They can band together and impose standards on organizations; sometimes those standards can be determined from outside the organization when allegiance to a professional association is involved. Medical doctors are an example. Appropriate behaviors for doctors are typically spelled out in medical schools and by their professional associations.

Analysts are planners, operations researchers, budget analysts, and other specialists who usually do staff or support work in an organization. According to Mintzberg (1983), analysts have no formal authority, usually are professionals, are committed to organizational change yet are obsessed with stability, and require operational goals in order to apply their techniques. Because analysts are hired by organizations to use complex techniques they have learned outside those organizations, their power is derived from their expertise.

Support staffs provide a wide range of services, from running the plant cafeteria to providing its public relations. Organizations can either internalize these services or buy them from outside. Unskilled support staffs are not very critical to the organization and consequently have little power, although the extent to which they have many members and are organized can give them greater influence. Professional support staffs rely on their expertise for power. Whereas professional analysts deal with organizational change, professional support staffs deal with environmental change. Thus support staffs too are in the position of favoring change but working toward stability. In theory, once environmental change is dealt with successfully, stability occurs and there is no further need for the professional support staff. (Managing change will be examined in greater detail in Chapter 11.)

The organizational stage, then, is peopled with a large number of actors making different demands on the organization and entering the power game from different bases. Now let us examine how these various players attempt to influence each other within organizations.

Theories of Intraorganizational Power

In the last few years a number of theories of intraorganizational power have been advanced. Each offers managers a slightly different view of the development and acquisition of power. We will focus in detail on one of these theories—strategic dependencies—and then offer brief comments on others.

Strategic Contingencies and Resource Dependence   In 1971 a group of British researchers advanced a theory of organizational power that rested on the control of strategic contingencies (Hickson, Hinings, Lee, Schneck, and Pennings, 1971), rather than focusing selectively on individual exchange or on identifying organizational systems. These authors focused on organizational subunits that vie for scarce resources and that engage in often asymmetrical exchange relationships. At the heart of their thinking was the notion of **dependence**. A department is said to have control of a **strategic contingency** to the extent it can control activities of another department relevant to its strategic function and thereby creates in that other department dependence upon itself. Such is the case on a modern aircraft carrier, where squadrons are dependent for flight hours on the admiral's staff, which decides on the exercises to be conducted on any particular day, on deck personnel who keep the decks ready for aircraft catapults and recoveries, on the ship's maintenance units, and on a myriad of other departments.

A department has power to the extent that it can do three things:

1. Reduce unpredictability that results from a lack of information about future events—that is, cope well with uncertainty

2. Do work that is nonsubstitutable—that is, handle tasks that other departments in the organization cannot

3. Be at the center of the information flow among departments—that is, have high centrality

The strategic contingency theory was supported by empirical work done in five breweries (Hinings, Hickson, Pennings, and Schneck, 1974), although a replication of this study (Saunders and Scamell, 1982) found only partial support for the original theory. It has been found as well that people central to networks are perceived to be influential (Boje and Whetten, 1981; Brass, 1984). Saunders (1981) portrayed the strategic contingency theory graphically, as shown in Figure 6.3 (page 294). Note that, in this view, the critical nature of the department's tasks is also a factor.

Several authors (see Mechanic, 1962; Crozier, 1964) argue that the power of lower-level organizational participants derives from their control of scarce and important resources. For example, Crozier (1964) noted that maintenance workers in a French factory had more power than their positions would have suggested because they controlled the one remaining organizational uncertainty in the firm—the breakdown of the machinery.

Pfeffer (1981) supported many aspects of the theory of strategic contingencies. He noted that most treatments of the sources of power emphasize the critical role of **resource dependence**. From this perspective, power derives from having something that someone else wants or needs. Pfeffer and Salancik (1978) noted that those units that control scarce resources develop power.

Pfeffer (1981) added to this perspective several additional sources of power. He discussed power that comes about through providing resources, noting with regard to monetary resources that a new Golden Rule was becoming popular—"he who has the gold makes the rules" (p. 101). Another important resource, discussed earlier, is the ability to control decision premises—that is, influencing the goals or objectives served by the decision or the constraints under which the decision is made, controlling the alternatives

FIGURE 6.3

The Strategic Contingency Theory of Power

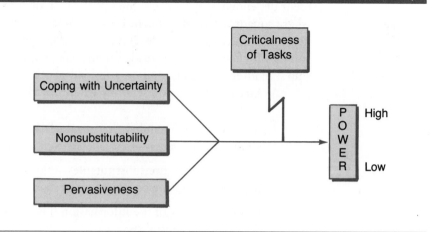

Source: C. S. Saunders, "Managerial Information Systems, Communications, and Departmental Power: An Integrative Model," *Academy of Management Review* 6 (1981): 439. Reprinted by permission.

considered, or controlling the information about alternatives that are considered.

The final source of power discussed by Pfeffer is the power of consensus, or power derived from developing norms of agreement within a group. This power of consensus is not equally descriptive of individuals and subgroups but applies to subgroups alone. Consensual work groups are often in a position to influence decisions. To the extent that their members share perspectives and values and are likely to act in concert in a consistent manner, they have power. For example, a subgroup in the organization may strongly favor one brand of computer equipment and be large enough to have a significant voice in the decision about which equipment to purchase.

Consensus contributes to power in several ways (Pfeffer, 1981). The ability to argue that results will be more certain and predictable in one subunit over another causes the allocation of resources to shift to that unit. Then, too, consensus facilitates cohesion, and cohesion in an otherwise uncertain world provides the subunit with additional power.

Other Theories of Intraorganizational Power   A network approach examines the recurrent aspects of power (Bacharach and Lawler, 1980; Lawler and Bacharach, 1983). Power is embedded in social relationships and is not an attribute of a single person, group, or organization. According to this view, power has three formal dimensions: its relational aspect, its dependence aspect, and its sanctioning aspect. All organizations are networks of interest groups composed of professional groups, work groups, divisions, and so on. Organizational politics involve the efforts of interest groups to influence decisions that affect their positions in the organization. Interest groups have to decide whether to go it alone in these attempts or to form coalitions with other groups in pursuit of common goals.

A third theory focuses on organizational systems rather than individuals or groups as repositories of power (Mintzberg, 1983). Four systems operate simultaneously, although very differently, within organizations. The **authority system** draws power into the middle line of the organization and from there to its apex. By contrast, the **ideology system** diffuses power widely to all who share its norms. The **expertise system** gets the work done but distributes power unevenly in the internal coalition, acting as a force of disintegration. Finally, the **political system** is both disintegrative and parochial.

Internal influence systems act in concert, at times to concentrate power in the internal coalition and at other times to diffuse power. The ideology system infuses life into the shell of the organization created by the authority and expertise systems and overcomes isolationist tendencies in other systems by inducing insiders to consider the needs of the whole organization. The political system is necessary to correct deficiencies and dysfunctions in the authority, ideology, and expertise systems and to provide for certain forms of flexibility that those other systems deny.

Hollander and Offermann (1990) view power in terms of what it is used for. They distinguish three types:

1. *Power over.* This is the familiar form of power, which could also be termed **dominance**—the power to make another act in a certain way.

2. *Power to.* This form of power provides others with the means to act more freely themselves; it is also called **empowerment**.

3. *Power from.* This form of power is **resistance**, the ability to protect oneself from the power of others.

Hollander and Offermann reviewed the mixed results of studies on the connection between participative decision making (see Chapter 7) and job satisfaction and concluded that another vehicle may be the most effective way to empower organizational members: **delegation**. They pointed to studies that indicated that delegation does promote better performance and suggested that the selectivity involved in delegation is a key to its success. Unlike participatory decision making, which indiscriminately provides groups with decision-making power, delegation selectively offers opportunities to individuals deemed ready. Some managers are particularly good at empowering subordinates.

Three obstacles may hinder the widespread use of delegation as a method of empowering workers. First is the erroneous notion that power is finite and to apportion it to others is to lose it oneself. Second is the tendency of some managers to see the use of the first form of power, dominance, as central to their jobs. Third is the contradiction between endorsing delegation while holding higher-level managers responsible for their subordinates' actions. Nevertheless, the capacity to distribute power remains a promising vehicle for managers. A number of books attempt to teach managers the benefits of delegation and how to do it (Nelson, 1988).

Interorganizational Power

No discussion of power in organizations would be complete without a discussion of interorganizational power and control, particularly because they are so pervasive in everyday life. Interorganizational power can be thought of in two ways: (1) attempts to control other organizations and what takes place within them and (2) attempts to control legislative processes that ultimately affect the organization. We will look at both approaches.

Organizational Attempts to Influence Other Organizations

The major theory of external control of organizations is closely akin to resource dependence theory. In fact, the major differences are solely due to the former's focus on external rather than internal control of organizations (Pfeffer and Salancik, 1978). That is, external control focuses on those aspects of control outside the organization's boundaries, on the assumption that organizations are interdependent. **Interdependence** arises when one organization does not entirely control all the conditions necessary for achieving its objectives. Interdependence is a function of the availability of resources relative to demand. When a large number of resources exist relative to demand, the organizations that require those resources are not very interdependent. As an example, when many businesses produce automobile mirrors, the automobile manufacturers requiring those mirrors can act relatively independently of one another and of the suppliers.

Interdependence is revealed through transactions between organizations, the nature of which causes uncertainty and unpredictability. Organizations faced with uncertainty therefore attempt to alter their exchange relationships by attempting to reduce their uncertainties—finding an additional or alternative supplier, say—but their actions increase uncertainties for other organizations in the same environment.

FIGURE 6.4
Conditions That Affect an Organization's Compliance with an Attempt to Control

An organization will comply to the extent that:
1. It is aware of the demands.
2. It obtains some resources from the person or unit making the demands.
3. The resources obtained are a critical or an important part of the organization's operation.
4. The person or unit controls the allocation, access, or use of the resource; that is, alternative sources for the resource are not available to the organization.
5. The organization doesn't control the allocation, access, or use of other resources critical to the person or unit's operation and survival.
6. The actions or outputs of the organization are visible and can be assessed by the person or unit to judge whether they comply with its demands.
7. The organization's satisfaction of the person or unit's requests is not in conflict with the satisfaction of demands from other components of the environment with which it is interdependent.
8. The organization does not control the determination, formulation, or expression of the person or unit's demands.
9. The organization can develop actions or outcomes that will satisfy the external demands.
10. The organization wants to survive.

Source: Figure adapted from *The External Control of Organizations* by Jeffrey Pfeffer and Gerald R. Salancik. Copyright © 1978 by Jeffrey Pfeffer and Gerald R. Salancik. Reprinted by permission of HarperCollins Publishers.

In general, organizations are influenced by those who control the resources they require. A number of conditions, though, affect the extent to which an organization complies with attempts to control it (see Figure 6.4). It is not necessary for all of these conditions to be present for control to take place.

It is clear that these conditions are at least partly consistent with models of intraorganizational power. For example, we saw that the strategic contingencies model states that power accrues to those within organizations who are able to reduce uncertainties, and the more central the uncertainties, and the more irreplaceable the associate, the more influential she will be. This notion matches Pfeffer and Salancik's theory of the external control of organizations. Research also shows that interpersonal power is magnified through interdependent relationships.

There are a number of conceptual and empirical studies of interorganizational power and influence. Some look at issues of interdependence (e.g., Koot, 1983), some examine organizational responses to outside political pressures (e.g., Fisher, 1983), and others analyze organizational strategies to change their environments (e.g., Aplin and Hegarty, 1980). One interesting study (Useem, 1982) showed that in both American and British businesses the highest echelons were tightly interconnected with government. A select group of business leaders, the dominant segment of the business elite, also helped run the affairs of the country. This practice is clearly a strategy to reduce uncertainty.

Controlling Legislative Processes

Although little research has been done on the best corporate strategies to influence legislative decisions, this is obviously an important issue. Laws are constantly made that influence what corporations can do. One need only think about the application of antitrust legislation in the middle of the 20th century and ongoing corporate responses to legislation of the 1960s to realize the far-reaching organizational implications of legislation.

One strategy to influence legislation was just alluded to: establishing links between the corporation and the government. This strategy can take two forms. The first is the practice previously mentioned, in which business elites also serve in government capacities. The other is the reverse: government workers are recruited by business. The revolving door between the armed forces and defense contractors in the United States is a clear example of this.

Two authors (Keim and Zeithaml, 1986) identified five corporate political strategies common among firms: constituency building, campaign contributions through political action committees (PACs), advocacy advertising, lobbying, and coalition building. The feature on Pacific Gas & Electric shows how one organization employed a number of these techniques.

FEATURE: *How One Organization Successfully Lobbied to Protect Its Interests*

The nation's electric utilities, led by Pacific Gas & Electric Co. of San Francisco, waged and won a major lobbying effort to protect their hydroelectric plants from takeover by municipal utilities. The battle, which took place between 1980 and 1986, had its origins in 1920 when Congress passed what is now called the Federal Power Act, creating the Federal Power Commission (FPC) and authorizing it to issue hydroelectric project licenses. The licenses typically run for an initial period of 50 years, before which the license holder is required to apply for relicensing.

Pacific Gas & Electric (PG&E) held 29 licenses from the FPC, now known as the Federal Energy Regulatory Commission (FERC). These licenses covered 64 operating plants, all of which had been built with conventional utility financing—an initial stockholder investment supported by customer rate payments after the plant became operational.

The Federal Power Act gave a "preference" for developing new hydroelectric sites to government-owned utilities if they were "equally well adapted" to fully utilizing and conserving the resource in the public interest. The preference applied to initial licensing before any significant investment was made. Upon relicensing, the preference would favor municipalities only against other newcomers trying to get the project and not against the project's original owner.

In 1980, however, the FERC announced that it would give municipally run systems a relicensing preference even against the project's owner, and a federal appeals court upheld the ruling. In 1983 the FERC reversed itself, but by this time several municipal utilities in California had geared up to contest four of PG&E's licenses for projects with a combined generating capacity of 588 megawatts. The municipalities and their national lobbying organization appealed the 1983 FERC ruling and prepared for hearings on the contested licenses, which would expire in the late 1980s.

Faced with the uncertainty over the municipalities' appeal and the prospect of hearings getting under way, PG&E launched a major effort to get federal legislation passed to do away with any notion of municipal relicensing preference and require just compensation for any takeover. The strategy adopted was to make the dispute a consumer issue and position PG&E and other investor-owned utilities on the side of the consumer. The heart of the argument went as follows: municipally run utilities serve fewer customers than investor-owned utilities and already enjoy access to federally subsidized power. Therefore, if they should take over licenses for existing hydro facilities, their already low rates would go lower. At the same time, with low-cost hydro power removed from their generating mix, investor-owned utilities would have to raise rates to their customers, who had already paid to build, develop, and improve the projects. Thus customers of investor-owned utilities—the majority of electric customers across the country—would lose not only an investment but a reliable, renewable, and inexpensive energy source. Thus, the investor-owned utilities maintained, taking these benefits away from the many to enrich the few would be poor public policy.

PG&E took the initiative and framed the issue for public debate along the lines of this argument, winning the first round by not letting the municipalities frame the issue as an "investor-owned versus public-owned" battle. But hydro relicensing was not a common breakfast table topic. Before grass-roots action would be possible, those involved had to understand and be able to discuss the issue. PG&E developed and widely distributed a comprehensive background paper detailing the history and current status of the hydro controversy, as well as shorter informational pamphlets and question-and-answer pieces.

The company's early efforts included securing letters and resolutions of support from the cities and counties where its customers lived. By 1986, 138 California cities and 38 counties were formally on record with the FERC in support of PG&E's retention of the projects. At the same time, a campaign to get news stories and editorial support was begun. Major in-depth features appeared in the California press and on television and radio. Once explained, PG&E's side of the issue received nearly unanimous editorial support from the print and electronic media. By 1986, 68 California newspapers as well as the *Wall Street Journal* and the *New York Times* had endorsed the position against municipal preference.

Educational material was also sent to employees, stockholders, and customers. Updates were sent when corrective legislation was being introduced in Congress and at crucial points during the legislative debate. Extensive records were kept so that supporters were continually updated, thanked, urged to new efforts, and kept on board for repeated support. Nontraditional alliances were sought and gained with such groups as senior citizen and ethnic organizations, agricultural groups, and other consumer organizations.

PG&E enlisted and received the support of other investor-owned utilities. Through the industry's national trade association, the Edison Electric Institute, a national grass-roots program was developed, including targeted efforts aimed at key congressional districts and a broadened campaign to win editorial support. By the time the bill eliminating preference reached the floor of Congress in 1986, some 9,000 Californians had written individual letters to their representatives supporting it. Nearly 5,000 utility stockholders wrote letters to Congress. A major appeal to customers through an insert in customer bills resulted in nearly 120,000 returns, which were computerized by congressional district and shared with the respective congressional office.

The result of this effort came in late 1986 with the passage of the Electric Consumers' Protection Act. The cost of winning the battle was evident in the final terms of the act. Overall environmental requirements were increased and the utilities had to pay some compensation to the municipal utilities for their expenses in mounting the cases to take over the licenses. But the preference issue on relicensing was unquestionably laid to rest.

Source: Pacific Gas & Electric Company, personal interviews and company literature, 1981–1987.

Constituency building consists of efforts to identify, educate, and motivate political action among those people who are likely to be affected by public policies that influence the organization. A corporation's natural constituencies are usually employees, shareholders, suppliers, dealers, and the communities in which the organization is important. An organization may use many methods (letters, phone calls, and so on) to inform its constituents and solicit their political participation on relevant issues.

Corporate PACs make contributions to candidates and support campaigns advocating specific issues. These PACs solicit money for these contributions from employees and sometimes from shareholders. PACs have one drawback: the combination of money and politics raises ethical questions that may reflect negatively not just on the officeholder but also on the business or industry supporting the PAC.

Often, corporations use advocacy advertising to reach a general audience with messages about public policy issues. Source credibility, accuracy, and a noncoercive approach are basic requirements for corporate advocacy advertising programs.

Corporations often engage in lobbying. **Lobbying** consists of efforts by political professionals or company executives to communicate with regulatory bodies, legislators, and their staffs. Lobbying conveys the sentiments of the company on major issues of concern, provides position papers on issues and the implications for corporations of legislation on these issues, monitors legislation, and attempts to influence decisions of legislators.

Coalition building consists of efforts made by corporations to find other groups of voters who share common political perspectives on specific issues. Like other kinds of coalition building, this strategy often temporarily unites groups with few common interests except for a particular issue. These alliances sometimes turn into formal associations such as the Business Roundtable.

The Use of Power: Power Tactics

As we learned at the beginning of the chapter, power is a potential state—a capacity to influence others. That capacity is activated when the holder of power wants to exert the influence to get something done. The purpose may be to redirect goals, accomplish a task, or begin a new venture.

To the inexperienced, such an aim may seem simple to achieve—one need merely state the goal and tell the other person or group to attain it. Such an approach may be appropriate in clear-cut situations, as when a manager instructs a subordinate to investigate alternatives for solving a problem and make a report. In complex situations, however, this approach is often self-defeating. It can alienate the subordinate person or group, sabotaging the accomplishment of the desired objective. In the case of attempts to use power to influence others higher up the hierarchy or in other organizations, such a heavy-handed approach is impossible. If Kanter (1989) is correct about the shape of things to come in organizations, the use of dictatorial behavior even with lower-level employees is bound to backfire. Whereas traditional managers "were trained to know their place, to follow orders, to let the company take care of their careers, to do things by the book," times have changed. "The book is gone. In the new corporation, managers . . . must learn to operate without the crutch of hierarchy" (Kanter, 1989, p. 88).

Aware of the need for more subtlety, managers choose from among a variety of tactics for exercising power. Most of these tactics are designed to be as unobtrusive as possible, because that is when the use of power is most effective.

A recent extensive analysis of political strategies and tactics in organizations (Pfeffer, 1981) concentrated on attempts to make the use of power less obtrusive, on the exercise of power in legitimizing and rationalizing decisions, and on the building of additional support and power behind a favored position. A number of tactics emerged from this analysis. Some of these tactics are applicable to interpersonal interactions, and some focus on interorganizational power. We discuss both kinds of tactics here.

Interpersonal Power Tactics

A simple and direct approach to identifying tactics people use in power relationships is to ask them, "How do you get your way?" One researcher (Falbo, 1977) asked psychology students to write paragraphs answering this question and then inductively arrived at 16 approaches to getting one's way. The mechanisms fell on two dimensions: the tactics were based more on reason (rational) than emotion (nonrational), and they were open and direct (direct) or subtle (indirect). This list of strategies, including as it does such behaviors as deceit, persuasion, persistence, and hinting, is probably most appropriate to thinking about interpersonal power and politics. Two other studies (Kipnis, Schmidt, and Wilkinson, 1980) studied the organizational scene and arrived at eight dimensions of influence: assertiveness, ingratiation, rationality, sanctions, exchange, upward appeals, blocking, and coalitions.

Porter, Allen, and Angle (1981) noted that much of what has been written about organizational politics addresses such microissues as the bargaining processes organizations use in formulating their goals. They believe that from the point of view of the individual, the microprocesses that have been addressed are attempts at downward influence covered by the management and leadership literatures (see Chapter 8) and lateral influence attempts discussed by writers exploring group dynamics (see Chapter 4) and socialization (see Chapter 3). Downward influence occurs when a supervisor uses motivational strategies to control subordinate behavior. Lateral influence is seen in a group's efforts to socialize its members to behave in ways acceptable to it.

Porter, Allen, and Angle contended, however, that most political behavior in organizations involves attempts at *upward influence*, as when subordinates try to influence their supervisor's behavior. This view is based on the assumption that the typical object of influence is someone with more formal, legitimate power than that of the person attempting to influence him. Although Porter and colleagues do not deny the importance of influence attempts by and aimed at groups, they feel the one-on-one political influence situation is particularly prevalent and little understood.

These authors presented an "episodic model of the upward political influence process" (1981, pp. 136–137), which is depicted in Figure 6.5 (page 304). The model has five major components, each either a thought process or a specific decision.

These steps take place in a context established by five broad collections of factors: situational factors (characteristics of the organization or of the issue at stake); agent characteristics (personal traits of the individual who may or may not attempt the influence); target characteristics (traits of the person to be influenced); agent–target relationship (the relationship between the two individuals); and agent belief system (the things the agent believes in). Particular considerations within each of these groups of factors can positively or negatively influence the agent at each of the five steps. The strengths of these influences are depicted in the figure by pluses and minuses.

In viewing this figure, it is important to keep in mind that the process is not inevitably followed from beginning to end. Each stage is a decision point at which the agent can choose *not* to proceed to the next step. When viewed in their entirety, the five steps of the process are:

1. Recognizing an opportunity to promote or protect self-interest. A person must believe that an opportunity exists to change things.

2. Deciding whether or not to make the attempt.

3. Deciding whom to influence. The prime consideration is the potential capacity of the target to accomplish the agent's objective.

4. Choosing a method for exerting influence. Positive or negative sanctions are unlikely methods, the first because of the limited range of rewards available and the second because of the target's potential for retaliation. Upward influence is pursued for the most part through informational means. Three ways to exert informa-

FIGURE 6.5
Episodic Upward Political Influence Model

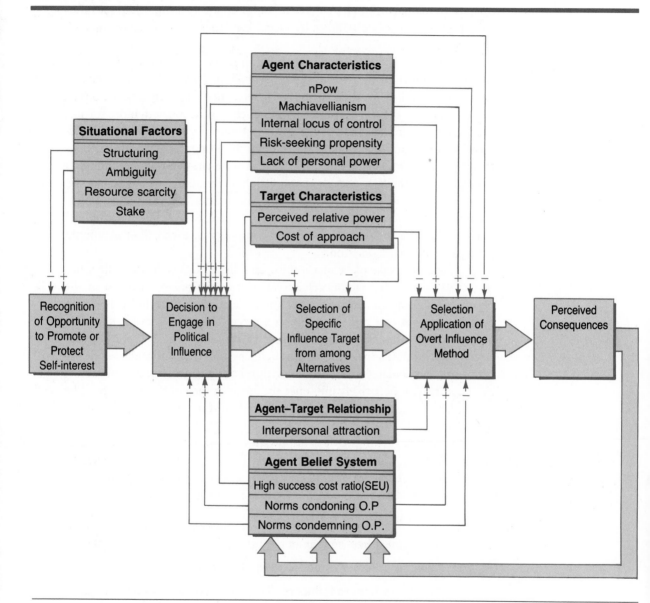

Source: L. W. Porter, R. W. Allen, and H. L. Angle, "The Politics of Upward Influence." In L. L. Cummings and B. M. Staw (eds.), *Research in Organizational Behavior*, vol. 3 (Greenwich, CT: JAI Press, 1981), p. 136. Copyright © 1981 by JAI Press. Reprinted by permission.

tional influence are persuasion, manipulative persuasion, and manipulation. The first two methods are overt, the third covert. Overt methods result in greater commitment than covert methods because they are more public and reveal the motives of the person trying to exert the influence.

5. Once the attempt has been made, the actor perceives the consequences of what he did. Knowledge of results modifies his beliefs about what leads to what. He may either raise expectations about certain actions leading to certain outcomes or he may lower them. In addition, he may learn something new about the norms that operate in the organization.

This model in Figure 6.5 depicts a normal sequence of events in an attempt to influence higher-level persons. Few of the model's linkages have been subjected to research, but the model itself suggests both a rich research agenda for any organizational scholar interested in micropolitical behavior and a set of potential linkages managers should think about when faced with an opportunity to enhance or protect self-interest.

Other power tactics can be employed in organizations as well; some of these have been touched on earlier. We have already mentioned the importance of controlling decision premises, or the goals, norms, and rules involved in a given decision. Another tactic related to decision making is to control access to the decision maker. The gatekeeper plays a significant role in many organizations by allowing or preventing individuals to reach a significant decision maker.

A similar approach to exercising power is controlling the agenda. The person who frames the debate on a given issue is in a powerful position to channel alternatives. As an example, simply by defining a company's problem as a need for growth into a certain market, rather than the need to increase existing market share, a sales manager is forcing decision makers to consider only a limited number of options and to ignore other possibilities.

The possession of information was mentioned earlier as a source of power; the manipulation of the availability of that information is a common power tactic. By presenting or withholding information, or by presenting it only in small stages, a worker constrains the behavior of a superior.

Each of these tactics may also be employed in the interactions of organizations as they engage in power struggles. It is to the tactics unique to the interorganizational playing field that we now turn.

Interorganizational Power Tactics

Individuals use power tactics within organizations to extend their control over the organization's objectives, resources, or processes. Organizations use power to attempt to control their environments; they try to reduce the uncertainty caused by interdependence on other organizations or influence by other external constraints. Many political tactics used by organizations have corollaries at the intraorganizational level. An example is the formation of coalitions. However, several do not, simply because organizations, whether attempting to limit controls placed on them by their environments or attempting to exert controls on their environments, face different problems than they do in dealing with internal constituencies. An example of a tactic unique to interorganizational power is the merger. Let us examine these various tactics in more detail.

Organizations form coalitions and more permanent mechanisms for cooperation and the enhancement of their power (Pfeffer and Salancik, 1978). Organizations get together through cooperation, trade associations, cartels, reciprocal trade agreements, coordinating councils, advisory boards, and linked boards of directors. These linkages provide four advantages to an organization attempting to manage environmental interdependence. First, linkages among organizations provide information about what each is doing. Second, they provide channels for communication. Third, in part from the exposure they provide, linkages are important first steps in obtaining commitments of support from important elements of the outside environment. Fourth, they legitimize focal organizations (for example, prestigious or legitimate persons on the board serve to tell the rest of the world about the value of the organization).

The practice of interlocking boards of directors provides the opportunity to evolve a stable collective structure of coordinated action through which interdependence is managed. By providing at least the appearance of participating in organizational decisions, co-optation increases support for the organization by those co-opted. Board members are expected to become committed to the organizations they serve; the development of such commitment is promoted by the fact that a board member is publicly identified with an organization and expected to be responsible for it. Such a situation promotes the development of conformity between the organizations thus linked.

Burt (1980, 1982) studied interlocking corporate boards of directors. He looked at three kinds of ties among organizations: **direct ownership**; **direct interlock ties**, such as when two establishments are owned by separate firms that share one or more directors; and **indirect interlocks**, such as when two establishments owned by separate firms are connected indirectly through a financial institution interlocked to them both. Burt found that all three types of ties among establishments have co-optive potential for creating preferred trade partners among establishments. "As conduits for information, advice, and influence, all three create nonmarket contexts in which essential buying and selling can be transacted between establishments in the absence of market constraints characterizing those same transactions when conducted in the open market" (Burt, 1982, p. 168). As Burt pointed out, a firm's co-optive network can be extended to include other kinds of potentially co-optive interorganizational relations such as mergers (Pfeffer, 1972), personnel flows (Baty, Evan, and Rothernel, 1971; Pfeffer and Leblebici, 1973), joint ventures (Pfeffer and Nowak, 1976), and information and support (Galaskiewicz and Marsden, 1978; Galaskiewicz, 1979).

Joint ventures are creations of new separate entities jointly owned and controlled by parent organizations. They permit a forum for information exchange among top executives. Pricing is done jointly, and production decisions are made jointly. All in all, things are set up in such a manner that the joint venture is unlikely to compete with the parent firms. Joint ventures are probably entered into to share risk (Pate, 1969), overcome resource limitations of a single organization (Aiken and Hage, 1968), and reduce uncertainty and promote environmental stability (Pfeffer and Salancik, 1978). All of these outcomes are designed to enhance the power of the participants. In other words, they are engaged in to maximize influence.

Mergers and growth are also strategies for managing interdependence and enhancing power by extending control over an organization's environment. Recall our discussion of organizational structure (Chapter 2), which addressed vertical and horizontal differentiation. There are also vertical and horizontal mergers. A vertical merger—such as the recent uniting of Time, with its cable TV movie services, and Warner Communications, possessed of a movie library—is a mechanism for extending control over resources vital to organizational survival. Horizontal expansion is a method for attaining dominance and reducing uncertainty caused by competition. Examples of this approach are the many recent acquisitions in the airlines industry, as detailed in the feature "Airlines Mergers: A Co-optive Shootout." Diversification reduces an organization's dependence on other dominant organizations. In this strategy, a business branches out into other industries to protect itself from overexposure to the uncertainties of one market. The recent moves of tobacco companies to acquire businesses in the food industry are examples of this kind of attempt to reduce risk. Thus one reason mergers are undertaken is to restructure an organization's interdependence and achieve stability in its environment.

FEATURE: *Airlines Mergers: A Co-optive Shootout*

The use of mergers to gain competitive advantage—and to discourage competing firms—was the dominant corporate strategy in the bruising shootout that followed airline deregulation in 1978. In less than a decade, most of the small airlines that sprang up immediately after deregulation had been absorbed, as had many established carriers.

The merger wave hits its peak in 1985 and 1986. People Express bought Frontier; United bought Pan Am's Pacific Division; corporate raider Carl Icahn took over TWA, then Ozark; Northwest and Republic merged; Texas Air bought Continental, then Frontier and People Express, and finally Eastern; American bought Air Cal; USAir bought Piedmont; and Delta and Western merged.

By 1987 the industry was dominated by just five companies: American, United, Delta, Texas Air, and Northwest. In the process, the industry was transformed from a gentleman's club to a fiercely competitive battleground where the objective was to outmaneuver your competitor, primarily with three weapons: fare wars, computer reservation systems, and control of hub airport terminals.

Deregulation eliminated controlled ticket prices, opening the way for carriers to stimulate demand and meet other market pressures by manipulating fares. Vast computerized reservation and ticketing systems quickly became a necessity for maximizing revenues. Because travel agents sell about 70% of airline tickets, the aggressive carriers rushed to install terminals for their systems in agents' offices. Once the system was installed, the airline could offer incentives to the travel agent to favor it when arranging travel plans for customers. The agent also pays the airline a rental fee for use of the terminal. And when the agent books a flight on the system through another airline, the second airline has to pay a service charge to the airline owning the system.

More important, these systems permit their owners to manipulate prices to fill their planes with passengers, with as many as possible paying full fare. Although discounted fares and bargain-basement prices are widely advertised, few of them are available on the most widely used flights. On a given day a single carrier may adjust as many as 100,000 fares across its system to meet and shape market demand. These adjustments are far from trivial. One airline chief executive said he could add between $40 million and $50 million in operating profits a year if he could raise average revenue per passenger mile by one-tenth of one cent.

Another cooptive strategy was control of key cities. Each of the surviving large carriers has a system of hub airports which have become the heart of airline operations. The spokes of the system are dozens of feeder flights into the hub airport coinciding with a carrier's fewer long-haul routes. When the system works properly, each feeder flight will add a few passengers and additional revenue to the more profitable long-distance flights. By dominating a market, a carrier can be more certain that flights take off with high load factors, that it can predict traffic with reasonable accuracy. This knowledge can enable the airline to use its other competitive weapons, the reservation system and ticket prices, with more confidence and effectiveness.

These examples of the use of various means to gain power were made possible by the removal of another kind of power—that of the government to regulate the industry. As the shakeout continued, yet one more kind of power began to emerge—the power of the customers. In their drive to lower costs and thereby gain competitive advantage, many carriers allowed significant erosion in the quality of their service. Growing numbers of complaints were prompting some in government and the media to call for reregulation. These calls were fueled by increasing concern over airline safety, which, it was feared, was being weakened by deferred maintenance to cut costs, increased traffic from airlines competing to get into the same terminals at the same time, and weary airline crews and attendants driven too hard by overly competitive management.

Source: From "Winners in the Air Wars" by Kenneth Labich. *FORTUNE* Magazine, May 11, 1987. © 1987 Time Inc. All rights reserved. Reprinted by permission.

Co-optations and mergers are ways organizations deal with uncertainty and external constraints through absorbing interdependence or negotiating arrangements that coordinate behavior. When interdependence cannot be managed in these ways, organizations try to use the greater power of the larger social system to meet their needs. Organizations may seek direct financial support from government, as was the case with Chrysler Corporation some years ago. They may seek market protection (as has recently happened with the auto and semiconductor industries), they may engage in litigation, or they may act to have the laws themselves changed (recall the Pacific Gas case presented earlier). Organizational attempts to alter and to adapt to the political environment are almost endless. "Organizations are constrained by the economic, social, political, and legal environments, [and] law, social norms, values, and political outcomes reflect, in part, actions taken by organizations in their interests of survival, growth, and enhancement" (Pfeffer and Salancik, 1978, p. 190). In Chapter 11 we discuss other ways to manage change and uncertainty.

The list of power tactics could go on and on. The choice of tactics is constrained by the power bases underlying the players, by their situations, and by the personal characteristics of the participants (Goodstadt and Kipnis, 1970). Decisions to use power are not simple. Few people are so powerful they can use power indiscriminately, and few are so powerless they cannot accomplish a substantial amount through judicious use of the power they have. Power is simply a tool; it is inherently neither good nor bad. The challenge for managers is to use power judiciously and to constructive ends while encouraging others to do likewise.

What Managers Think of Organizational Politics

Two investigations examined what managers think about organizational politics. In one study (Gandz and Murray, 1980), young managers were asked about the extent to which politics is discussed in organizations, the perceived politicalization of their organizations, where political behavior occurs in organizations, their attitudes and beliefs about workplace politics, and factors influencing perceptions of political behavior.

The managers responded that politics was the subject of much casual conversation at work. They indicated that promotions, transfers, demotions, and dismissals were the most politicized organizational processes. Stories about these processes focused on perceived inequities in superiors' decisions about their subordinates. A common theme was that employees were bypassed in favor of someone with "pull." Performance evaluations were another commonly mentioned theme; many stories dealt with avoiding blame for poor performance, fear of superiors, superiors judging performance on hidden or uncontrollable criteria, superiors who were nonsupportive, and superiors and colleagues who spent most of their time in building alibis or defenses in case of subsequent failures. Another process frequently mentioned was interunit competition for authority over functions and special projects.

In this study the climate was seen as more political at higher levels of this organization by the junior managers, but more senior managers viewed the climate as less political at all levels than did junior-level managers. These managers were ambivalent about organizational politics. Most agreed that workplace politics is common, that successful and powerful executives act politically, and that one must be a good politician to get ahead. They also said that weak people play politics. But they added that people would be happier in organizations free of politics, that politics is detrimental to organizations, and that top management should work to get rid of organizational politics.

A second study looked at the perceived incidence of organizational politics, organizational characteristics thought to be associated with increased political activity, and the positive and negative use organizational politics is thought to have for the attainment of individual and organizational goals (Madison, Allen, Porter, Renwick, and Mayes, 1980). Managers perceived politics as a common organizational activity occurring more frequently at middle and upper than at lower levels and more commonly in staff than line positions. The highest levels of political activity were perceived to take place among marketing staff, followed by the board of directors and sales personnel. Least political activity was perceived to take place in production. Overall, power was seen as strongly related to political activity.

Three underlying conditions were related to high levels of political activity: uncertainty, the importance of uncertainty to the organization, and the salience of the issue to the individual. Finally, organizational politics was seen to be useful in achieving both positive and negative outcomes for individuals and for the organization as a whole.

Together these studies illustrate that organizational politics is perceived as being pervasive and taking place more at higher than at lower organizational levels and more in certain functions than others. Managers see politics as useful in obtaining desired ends, but they do not like the political milieus of their organizations. The studies suggest that people usually perceive politics as detrimental to the organization, rather than embrace the view taken here: that politics is inevitable in organizations and can be used to enhance both organizational and individual desires.

SUMMARY

This chapter began by distinguishing between the notions of power and politics in organizations. We noted that organizational power and politics, while pervasive in practice, have not until recently been given much attention by academicians. Power is described as the capacity of one person to get another to do what he or she wants. Political approaches to organizations are said to focus on what goes on in them that departs from rationality. Power is seen as having structural bases in the hierarchy and in the division of tasks. The five bases of interpersonal power were identified as reward, coercive, legitimate, referent, and expert.

The cast of players in the organizational political game includes the external coalition—owners, associates (suppliers, clients, partners, or competitors), unions, professional associations, and the general public (purveyors of the public interest, governments, and special interest groups). The cast also includes the internal coalition (the CEO, middle line managers, operators, analysts, and support staff).

Theories of intraorganizational power were discussed. These theories are not integrated with one another, but they offer different perspectives from which managers can think about various aspects of power in their organizations. Dependence is a key to power. The degree to which a person or unit can reduce unpredictability, cannot be substituted for, and sits at the center of the organization's information flow is the degree to which that person or unit has power.

Other perspectives approach power differently. The systems approach elucidates four systems operating simultaneously in organizations; it focuses on how each contributes to the operation of organizational power. The network approach focuses on the emergent properties of groups and the importance of network centrality. Growing in prominence is the idea that power is not a finite resource that is subtracted from when given away, but that it is an expandable force that can be cultivated in workers. Delegation is presented as the technique most suited to foster worker growth.

Next we discussed three approaches to interorganizational power. The first theory focuses on the notion of interorganizational dependence and directs our attention once again to resource control. The research in this area examines interdependence and the responses organizations make to external political pressures. This perspective defines strategies for controlling legislative decision making and identifies situations in which various strategies might be best.

The chapter then considered a number of power tactics. Within organizations, some authors believe, the most frequent exercises of power are attempts at upward influence. A model of this behavior summarizes the situational factors as well as the personal characteristics (of both the potential exerciser of power and of the target) to come into play in the decision whether to attempt upward influence. Other tactics—including controlling decision premises, controlling access to the decision maker, controlling the agenda, and controlling information—are also common in organizational politics.

Some organizations use similar power tactics in attempting to influence other organizations, but there are clearly specific techniques that are unique to intraorganizational developments. Organizations often form alliances and linkages in order to manage their turbulent environments. Joint ventures, co-optations, and mergers among organizations are all tactics aimed primarily at reducing uncertainty.

Although politics is pervasive in organizations, many organizational participants deride it. It is not necessary to do so; the use of politics can be an effective way to pursue individual and organizational goals.

MANAGERIAL INSIGHT

To: *Student Managers*
From: *Veteran Manager*
Subject: *Power*

The chapter describes the legitimate power of managers as that which has been designated as theirs, a domain over which they have authority and responsibility. The implication is that they use this power (along with other types of power) to *get* others to do work. I like to think of managers using power in a different context—*letting* others do work.

The difference is between exercising power yourself or giving it to others. The currently popular term for giving power to your people is "empowering" them. There are several ways you can empower the people you manage.

According to Tom Peters, the most essential way you empower people is by delegating. In *Thriving on Chaos*, he energetically describes how important it is to let go entirely when delegating, not to "take back," to set high standards, and to develop a shared vision of the objective. Though I don't wish to take issue with his point, I can say that delegation isn't the only way to give power to your people—there are others that are both useful and effective.

1. *Give them what they need.* Make sure they have good tools with which to work. Good tools might include anything from the latest in office technology to a smoothly running organizational structure. Good tools certainly include good information about the organization, its strategy and direction, and how the manager's unit fits in and contributes to the total.

2. *Disencumber them.* "Get the organization off their backs," to adapt the phrase that former President Reagan used so effectively when he was campaigning for less government. Many times I've seen employees struggling not against competition or exceptionally complex problems, but against themselves or their organization. Bureaucracy, red tape, useless regulations and paperwork, required reports that contribute no value, following procedures for their own sake and not because they make sense, are all disempowering encumbrances. By removing or reducing them, you free up your people to make their best contribution.

3. *Run interference.* Use the weight of your position to win support of other departments or your boss for the project you've entrusted to your people. The physical analogy is that of bodyguards escorting a famous person through a crowd of well-wishers, or blockers "running interference" for a halfback running with a football. This is not the same thing as running with the ball yourself. It is giving somebody else the ball and taking a supporting role so they can succeed.

4. *Give your expertise to them.* If you have expert power, you can give it away by being a good coach and teacher. I've seen managers who were technically strong in their field but very reluctant to teach their subordinates to become experts, perhaps because they

were afraid of losing stature to the subordinate. In fact, I have never seen such a loss happen to a teaching manager. On the contrary, I have found that more interpersonal power actually accrues to the manager who gives it away by teaching and coaching. Such a manager doesn't actually *lose* any expertise but gains in reputation as a developer of others. Such a practice over time also generates another kind of power—the emergence of a network of loyal "students" who have benefited from your coaching and monitoring.

I have the real-world notion—not demonstrated by any certifiable research but sincerely believed—that there isn't a fixed amount of power that is somehow assigned to any manager's department. Authority and responsibility, yes; these are usually quite specifically limited. But whatever legitimate power the manager inherits can be expanded, by the counterintuitive process of giving it away.

It has always worked for me.

REVIEW QUESTIONS

1. Was Clausen practicing "dirty politics" or "organizational statesmanship"?

2. Identify three structural sources of power. Give reasons to support your answer, and explain which you think is the most important.

3. Which of Etzioni's three bases of power—coercive, utilitarian, and normative—are present in the armed forces?

4. Name French and Raven's five bases of power.

5. How does lack of support from higher in the organizational hierarchy undercut a manager? Explain in terms of each of French and Raven's five bases of power.

6. What groups are included in the external coalition?

7. What factor will influence how much power the owners of a corporation will have?

8. What individuals or groups are included in the internal coalition?

9. According to resource dependency theory, what three factors affect the power of an organizational unit?

10. What sources of power are identified by Pfeffer?

11. What factors may hinder the use of delegation as a vehicle for empowering subordinates?

12. What are six techniques organizations can use to influence governments?

13. Why do Porter, Allen, and Angle focus on the politics of upward influence?

14. What four power tactics can be used in attempts at interpersonal influence?

15. What four general power tactics can organizations use to reduce uncertainty in their environment?

REFERENCES

Aiken, M., and Hage, J. (1968). Organizational interdependence and intraorganizational structure. *American Sociological Review* 33:912–930.

Aplin, J. C., and Hegarty, W. H. (1980). Political influence: Strategies employed by organizations to impact legislation in business and economic matters. *Academy of Management Journal* 23:438–450.

Astley, W. G., and Sachdeva, P. S. (1984). Structural sources of intraorganizational power: A theoretical synthesis. *Academy of Management Review* 9:104–113.

Bacharach, S. B., and Lawler, E. J. (1980). *Power and Politics in Organizations*. San Francisco: Jossey-Bass, 1980.

Baty, G. B., Evan, W. M., and Rothernel, T. W. (1971). Personnel flows as interorganizational relations. *Administrative Science Quarterly* 16:430–443.

Boje, D. M., and Whetten, D. A. (1981). Effects of organizational strategies and constraints on centrality and attributions of influence in interorganizational networks. *Administrative Science Quarterly* 26:378–395.

Brass, D. J. (1984). Being in the right place: A structural analysis of individual influence in organization. *Administrative Science Quarterly* 29:518–539.

Burt, R. S. (1980). Cooptive corporate actor networks: A reconsideration of interlocking directorates involving American manufacturing. *Administrative Science Quarterly* 25:557–582.

Burt, R. S. (1982). *Toward a Structural Theory of Action*. New York: Academic Press.

Chandler, A. D. (1977). *The Visible Hand: The Managerial Revolution in American Business*. Cambridge, MA: Harvard University Press, 1977.

Cole, R. E. (1985). The macropolitics of organizational change: A comparative analysis of the spread of small group activities. *Administrative Science Quarterly* 30:560–585.

Crozier, M. (1964). *The Bureaucratic Phenomenon*. Chicago: University of Chicago Press.

Etzioni, A. (1961). *A Comparative Analysis of Complex Organizations*. New York: Free Press.

Falbo, T. (1977). Multidimensional scaling of power strategies. *Journal of Personality and Social Psychology* 35:537–547.

Fisher, D. W. (1983). Strategies toward political pressures: A typology of firm responses. *Academy of Management Review* 8:71–78.

French, J. R. P., and Raven, B. (1959). The abuses of social power. In D. Cartwright (ed.), *Studies in Social Power*. Ann Arbor: Institute for Social Research, University of Michigan.

Frost, P. J. (1987). Power, politics, and influence. In F. M. Jablin, L. L. Putnam, K. H. Roberts, and L. W. Porter (eds.), *Handbook of Organizational Communication*. Beverly Hills: Sage, pp. 503–548.

Galaskiewicz, J. (1979). *Exchange Networks and Community Politics*. Newbury Park, CA: Sage.

Galaskiewicz, J., and Marsden, P. V. (1978). Interorganizational resource networks: Formal patterns of overlap. *Social Science Research* 7:89–107.

Galbraith, J. K. (1967). *The New Industrial State*. Boston: Houghton Mifflin.

Gandz, J., and Murray, V. V. (1980). The experience of workplace politics. *Academy of Management Journal* 23:237–251.

Goodstadt, B. E., and Kipnis, D. (1970). Situational influence on the use of power. *Journal of Applied Psychology* 54:201–207.

Grimes, A. J. (1978). Authority, power, influence, and social control: A theoretical synthesis. *Academy of Management Review* 3:724–736.

Hickson, D. J., Hinings, C. R., Lee, C. A., Schneck, R. E., and Pennings, J. M. (1971). A strategic contingencies' theory of intraorganizational power. *Administrative Science Quarterly* 16:216–229.

Hinings, C. R., Hickson, D. J., Pennings, J. M., and Schneck, R. E. (1974). Structural conditions of intraorganizational power. *Administrative Science Quarterly* 19:22–44.

Hollander, E. P., and Offermann, L. R. (1990). Power and leadership in organizations. *American Psychologist* 45:179–189.

Kanter, R. M. (1977). *Men and Women in the Corporation*. New York: Basic Books.

Kanter, R. M. (1989). The new managerial work. *Harvard Business Review*, November–December, 85–92.

Keim, G. D., and Zeithaml, C. P. (1986). Corporate political strategy and legislative decision making: A review and contingency approach. *Academy of Management Review* 11:828–843.

Kipnis, D., Schmidt, S. M., and Wilkinson, I. (1980). Intraorganizational influence tactics: Explorations in getting one's way. *Journal of Applied Psychology* 65:440–452.

Koot, W. (1983). Organizational dependence: An exploration of external power relationships of companies. *Organizational Studies* 4:19–38.

Kotter, J. P. (1977). Power, dependence, and effective management. *Harvard Business Review*, July–August, 125–136.

Krackhardt, D. (1990). Assessing the political landscape: Structure, cognition, and power in organizations. *Administrative Science Quarterly* 35:342–369.

Lachman, R. (1989). Power from what? A reexamination of its relationships with structural conditions. *Administrative Science Quarterly* 34:231–251.

Lasswell, H. D. (1936). *Politics: Who Gets What, When, How.* New York: McGraw-Hill.

Lawler, E. J., and Bacharach, S. B. (1983). Political action and alignments in organizations. In S. B. Bacharach (ed.), *Research in the Sociology of Organizations.* Greenwich, CT: JAI Press, 83–108.

Madison, D. L., Allen, R. W., Porter, L. W., Renwick, P. A., and Mayes, B. T. (1980). Organizational politics: An exploration of managers' perceptions. *Human Relations* 33:79–100.

Mechanic, D. (1962). Sources of power of lower level participants in complex organizations. *Administrative Science Quarterly* 7:349–364.

Mintzberg, H. (1983). *Power in and Around Organizations.* Englewood Cliffs, NJ: Prentice-Hall.

Nelson, R. B. (1988). *Delegation: The Power of Letting Go.* Glenview, IL: Scott-Foresman.

Pate, J. L. (1969). Joint venture activity, 1960–1968. *Economic Review, Federal Reserve Bank of Cleveland,* 16–23.

Perrow, C. (1986). *Complex Organizations,* 3rd ed. New York: McGraw-Hill.

Pfeffer, J. (1972). Merger as a response to organizational interdependency. *Administrative Science Quarterly* 17:382–394.

Pfeffer, J. (1981). *Power in Organizations.* Boston: Pitman.

Pfeffer, J., and Leblebici, H. (1973). Executive recruitment and the development of inter-firm organization. *Administrative Science Quarterly* 18:449–461.

Pfeffer, J., and Nowak, P. (1976). Joint ventures and interorganizational interdependence. *Administrative Science Quarterly* 21:398–418.

Pfeffer, J., and Salancik, G. R. (1978). *The External Control of Organizations: A Resource Dependence Perspective.* New York: Harper & Row.

Porter, L. W., Allen, R. W., and Angle, H. L. (1981). The politics of upward influence in organizations. In L. L. Cummings and B. M. Staw (eds.), *Research in Organizational Behavior.* Greenwich, CT: JAI Press.

Saunders, C. S. (1981). Management information systems, communications, and departmental power: An integrative model. *Academy of Management Review* 6:431–442.

Saunders, C. S., and Scamell, R. (1982). Intraorganizational distributions of power: Replication research. *Academy of Management Journal* 25:192–200.

Useem, M. (1982). Classwide rationality in the politics of managers and directors of large corporations in the United States and Great Britain. *Administrative Science Quarterly* 27:199–226.

Velasquez, M., Moberg, D. J., and Cavanagh, G. F. (1983). Organizational statesmanship and dirty politics: Ethical guidelines for the organizational politician. *Organizational Dynamics,* Autumn, 65–84.

7

Decision Making in Organizations: How We Make Choices

CHAPTER OVERVIEW

In this chapter we discuss how decision making, the process of choosing between alternatives, is at the heart of organization management. Decisions are made by individuals, groups, and entire organizations. Each has open to it a variety of techniques for making the process easier. This chapter discusses the similarities and differences of decision making at each of these levels and presents some specific techniques that have been found successful in promoting effective decisions.

THEME CASE

"The Corvair Decision" relates how General Motors executives made the decision to produce the Corvair even though it was known to have design and safety problems.

CHAPTER OUTLINE

- What Is Decision Making?
- Individual Decision Making
- Group Decision Making
- Organizational Decision Making
- Aids to Decision Making
- Summary
- Managerial Insight

KEY DEFINITIONS

Decision making   choice behavior in the face of alternatives.

Rational model   assumes that the decision maker has perfect knowledge of values, alternatives, outcomes, and probabilities, and selects the alternative that maximizes the attainment of values.

Administrative model   recognizes the limitations of the rational model and introduces the concept of "satisficing," or searching for an outcome that is satisfactory but less than perfect.

Participative decision making   allows larger numbers of organization members to take part in a decision process.

Risky shift   the tendency shown by some groups to make decisions involving higher risks that individuals would not make if operating alone.

Groupthink   the sharing of illusions and related norms among members of small groups that interfere with critical thinking and reality testing.

Additional Terms

Bounded rationality
Satisficing
Standard operating procedures
Suboptimal behavior
Incrementalism
Transfer effects
Functional fixedness
Risk-taking propensity
Mixed scanning
Garbage can model
Organizing model
Brainstorming
Nominal group technique
Synectics
Input-output model
Decomposable matrices
Morphology
Delphi technique
Policy capturing

THE CORVAIR DECISION, OR HOW MORAL MEN MAKE IMMORAL DECISIONS

"We feel that 1972 can be one of Chevrolet's great years. . . . Most of the improvements this year are to engines and chassis components aimed at giving a customer a better car for the money. . . . I want to reiterate our pledge that the 1972 Chevrolets will be the best in Chevrolet history. . . . We recognize that providing good dealer service is the surest way to keep quality-built Chevrolets for 1972 in top quality condition. . . . This is the lineup of cars for every type of buyer that we offer for 1972. Cars that are the best built in Chevrolet history . . ."

The words seemed to fall out of my mouth like stones from an open hand. Effortlessly. Almost meaninglessly. It was August 31, 1971. I was powergliding through the National Press Preview of 1972 Chevrolet cars and trucks at the Raleigh House, a mock-Tudor restaurant-banquet hall complex in suburban Detroit. The audience was filled with reporters from all over the country. In their midst was a plentiful sprinkling of Chevrolet managers. The new product presentation and question-answer session went smoothly, and I was stepping down from the podium and receiving the usual handshakes and compliments from some of the sales guys and a few of the members of the press when a strange feeling hit me: "My God! I've been through all this before." . . .

Never once while I was in General Motors management did I hear substantial social concern raised about the impact of our business on America, its consumers or the economy. When we should have been planning switches to smaller, more fuel-efficient, lighter cars in the late 1960s in response to a growing demand in the marketplace, GM management refused because "we make more money on big cars." It mattered not that customers wanted the smaller cars or that a national balance-of-payments deficit was being built in large part because of the burgeoning sales of foreign cars in the American market.

Refusal to enter the small-car market when the profits were better on bigger cars, despite the needs of the public and the national economy, was not an isolated case of corporate insensitivity. It was typical. And what disturbed me is that it was indicative of fundamental problems with the system. . . .

The whole Corvair case is a first-class example of a basically irresponsible and immoral business decision which was made by men of generally high personal moral standards. When [Ralph] Nader's book [*Unsafe at Any Speed*] threatened the Corvair's sales and profits, he became the enemy of the system. Instead of trying to attack his credentials or the factual basis of his arguments, the company sought to attack him personally. This move failed, but, in the process, GM's blundering "made" Ralph Nader.

When the fact that GM hired detectives to follow and discredit Nader was exposed, the system was once again threatened. Top management, instead of questioning the system which would permit such a horrendous mistake as tailing Nader, simply sought to preserve the system by sacrificing the heads of several executives who were blamed for the incident. Were the atmosphere at GM not one emphasizing profits and preservation of the system above all else, I am sure the acts against Nader would never have been perpetuated.

Those who were fired no doubt thought they were loyal employees. And, ironically, had they succeeded in devastating the image of Ralph Nader, they would have been corporate heroes and rewarded substantially. I find it difficult to believe that knowledge of these activities did not reach into the upper reaches of GM's management. But, assuming that it didn't, top management should have been held responsible for permitting the conditions to exist which would spawn such actions. If top management takes credit for a company's successes, it must also bear the brunt of the responsibility for its failures.

Furthermore, the Corvair was unsafe as it was originally designed. It was conceived along the lines of the foreign-built Porsche. These cars were powered by engines placed in the rear and supported by an independent, swing-axle suspension system. In the Corvair's case, the engine was all-aluminum and air-cooled (compared to the standard water-cooled iron engines). This, plus the rear placement of the engine, made the car new and somewhat different to the American market.

However, there are several bad engineering characteristics inherent in rear-engine cars which use a swing-axle suspension. In turns at high speeds they tend to become directionally unstable and, therefore, difficult to control. The rear of the car lifts or "jacks" and the rear wheels tend to tuck under the car, which encourages the car to flip over. In the high-performance Corvair, the car conveyed a false sense of control to the driver, when in fact he may have been very close to losing control of the vehicle. The result of these characteristics can be fatal.

These problems with the Corvair were well documented inside GM's Engineering Staff long before the Corvair ever was offered for sale. Frank Winchell, now vice-president of Engineering, but then an engineer at

Chevy, flipped over one of the first prototypes on the GM test track in Milford, Michigan. Others followed.

The questionable safety of the car caused a massive internal fight among GM's engineers over whether the car should be built with another form of suspension. On one side of the argument was Chevrolet's then General Manager, Ed Cole, an engineer and product innovator. He and some of his engineering colleagues were enthralled with the idea of building the first modern, rear-engine, American car. And I am convinced they felt the safety risks of the swing-axle suspension were minimal. On the other side was a wide assortment of top-flight engineers, including Charles Chayne, then vice-president of Engineering; Von D. Polhemus, engineer in charge of Chassis Development on GM's Engineering Staff, and others.

These men collectively and individually made vigorous attempts inside GM to keep the Corvair, as designed, out of production or to change the suspension system to make the car safer. One top corporate engineer told me that he showed his test results to Cole but by then, he said, "Cole's mind was made up."

Albert Roller, who worked for me in Pontiac's Advanced Engineering section, tested the car and pleaded with me not to use it at Pontiac. Roller had been an engineer with Mercedes-Benz before joining GM, and he said that Mercedes had tested similarly designed rear-engine, swing-axle cars and had found them far too unsafe to build.

At the very least, then, within General Motors in the late 1950s, serious questions were raised about the Corvair's safety. At the very most, there was a mountain of documented evidence that the car should not be built as it was then designed.

However, Cole was a strong product voice and a top salesman in company affairs. In addition, the car, as he proposed it, would cost less to build than the same car with a conventional rear suspension. Management not only went along with Cole, it also told the dissenters in effect to "stop these objections. Get on the team, or you can find someplace else to work." The ill-fated Corvair was launched in the fall of 1959.

The results were disastrous. I don't think any one car before or since produced as gruesome a record on the highway as the Corvair. It was designed and promoted to appeal to the spirit and flair of young people. It was sold in part as a sports car. Young Corvair owners, therefore, were trying to bend their car around curves at high speeds and were killing themselves in alarming numbers.

It was only a couple of years or so before GM's legal department was inundated with lawsuits over the car. And the fatal swath that this car cut through the automobile industry touched the lives of many General

Motors executives, employees and dealers in an ironic and tragic twist
of fate.

The son of Cal Werner, general manager of the Cadillac Division,
was killed in a Corvair. Werner was absolutely convinced that the design
defect in the car was responsible. He said so many times. The son of Cy
Osborne, an executive vice-president in the 1960s, was critically injured in
a Corvair and suffered irreparable brain damage. Bunkie Knudsen's niece
was brutally injured in a Corvair. And the son of an Indianapolis Chevrolet
dealer also was killed in the car. Ernie Kovacs, my favorite comedian, was
killed in a Corvair.

While the car was being developed at Chevrolet, we at Pontiac were
spending $1.3 million on a project to adapt the Corvair to our division.
The corporation had given us the go-ahead to work with the car to give it
a Pontiac flavor. Our target for introduction was the fall of 1960, a year
after Chevy introduced the car.

As we worked on the project, I became absolutely convinced by
Chayne, Polhemus and Roller that the car was unsafe. So I conducted a
three-month campaign, with Knudsen's support, to keep the car out of the
Pontiac lineup. Fortunately, Buick and Oldsmobile at the time were tooling
up their own compact cars, the Special and F-85, respectively, which featured conventional front-engine designs.

We talked the corporation into letting Pontiac switch from a Corvair
derivation to a version of the Buick-Oldsmobile car. We called it the Tem-
pest and introduced it in the fall of 1960 with a four-cylinder engine as
standard equipment and a V-8 engine as an option.

When Knudsen took over the reins of Chevrolet in 1961, he insisted
that he be given corporate authorization to install a stabilizing bar in the
rear to counteract the natural tendencies of the Corvair to flip off the road.
The cost of the change would be about $15 a car. But his request was re-
fused by The Fourteenth Floor as "too expensive."

Bunkie was livid. As I understand it, he went to the Executive Committee and told the top officers of the corporation that, if they didn't re-
appraise his request and give him permission to make the Corvair safe,
he was going to resign from General Motors. This threat and the fear of
the bad publicity that surely would result from Knudsen's resignation forced
management's hand. They relented. Bunkie put a stabilizing bar on the
Corvair in the 1964 models. The next year a completely new and safer
independent suspension designed by Frank Winchell was put on the Corvair. And it became one of the safest cars on the road. But the damage
done to the car's reputation by then was irreparable. Corvair sales began to
decline precipitously after the waves of unfavorable publicity following

Nader's book and the many lawsuits being filed across the country. Production of the Corvair was halted in 1969, four years after it was made a safe and viable car.

To date, millions of dollars have been spent in legal expenses and out-of-court settlements in compensation for those killed or maimed in the Corvair. The corporation steadfastly defends the car's safety, despite the internal engineering records which indicated it was not safe, and the ghastly toll in deaths and injury it recorded.

There wasn't a man in top GM management who had anything to do with the Corvair who would purposely build a car that he knew would hurt or kill people. But, as part of a management team pushing for increased sales and profits, each gave his individual approval in a group to decisions which produced the car in the face of the serious doubts that were raised about its safety, and then later sought to squelch information which might prove the car's deficiencies.

The corporation became almost paranoid about the leaking of inside information we had on the car. In April of 1971, 19 boxes of microfilmed Corvair owner complaints, which had been ordered destroyed by upper management, turned up in the possession of two suburban Detroit junk dealers. When the Fourteenth Floor found this out, it went into panic and we at Chevrolet were ordered to buy the microfilm back and have it destroyed.

I refused, saying that a public company had no right to destroy documents of its business and the GM's furtive purchase would surely surface. Besides, the $20,000 asking price was outright blackmail.

When some consumer groups showed an interest in getting the films, the customer relations department was ordered to buy the film, which it did. To prevent similar slip-ups in the future, the corporation tightened its scrapping procedures.

Source: From J. P. Wright, *On a Clear Day You Can See General Motors: John DeLorean's Look Inside the Automotive Giant* (New York: Avon Books), 1979. Copyright © 1979 by J. Patrick Wright. Available in paperback from Avon Books.

What Is Decision Making?

At General Motors in the late 1950s and 1960s, executives were faced with a critical decision: whether or not to produce the Corvair, the first American rear-engine car, even though it was known to have design problems. The desire for short-term profits led them to go ahead with production; yet those profits were clearly diminished by accidental deaths and subsequent lawsuits caused by the car's poor design. But why and how was this unfortunate decision made? What got in the way of good critical thinking processes? One difficulty in answering this question is that we do not think very much about the processes we use to make decisions. How many of us have deliberated about what we are actually doing when choosing the flavor of ice cream we want or picking out lunch in a cafeteria line? Then, too, there is the possibility that even when making choices we do so in relatively unthinking ways. When pressed, however, we can no doubt think of reasons for any recent decision we made. Are these reasons factors that we used in making the decision or are they justifications developed after the fact?

Decision making is of more than passing interest to most of us, not only because we make decisions every day but also because large decisions are made that influence large numbers of people and situations. We are fascinated by what led General Motors executives to produce a potentially unsafe car or what lured John F. Kennedy into the Bay of Pigs and kept him away from disaster in the Cuban Missile Crisis (Allison, 1969). We are influenced by the Federal Reserve Board's decisions to raise and lower interest rates or by our firm's decisions to open and close plants. At every level of our lives we are influenced by our own and others' decisions.

In broad terms, we think of **decision making** as choice behavior in the face of alternatives. Yet we should differentiate between the information acquisition stage and information use stage, rather than focus entirely on the latter (O'Reilly, Chatman, and Anderson, 1987). Herbert Simon (1976) viewed the entire business of management as decision making. It probably is fair to say, however, that managers often feel that neither they nor anyone else makes decisions very often and that the decisions they do make are made in a hurried fashion. Over the years, in fact, a number of researchers have studied what managers really do (e.g., Mintzberg, 1973; Kurke and Aldrich, 1983; Kotter, 1982; McCall and Kaplan, 1985; Nutt, 1989). They find that managers operate in work settings characterized by fragmentation of activities, brief in-person interactions, and dependence on others for initiating contacts. These are hardly settings conducive to pondering and searching for information and alternatives, the basics of the classic decision-making model.

We will divide our discussion of decision making into three parts. Because decision making is a complex process, we will begin by examining how it is performed by only one person. By focusing first on the individual, we can thoroughly study the various models for decision-making behavior. From that starting point, we will examine group decision making, including the influence of groups, and then we will explore characteristics of organizational decision making.

Scholars who study decision making ask very different questions at the individual, group, and organizational levels of study. Research on individual decision making stresses its cognitive aspects. Research on group decision making focuses on personal interaction (avoiding altogether the process of decision making itself); these studies focus on the benefits of participative decision making. Research on organizational decision making focuses on the constraints placed on the process by formal structures and the resolution of conflicts of interest through political processes.

Our discussion of individual, group, and organizational decision making will be followed by a review of strategies for making decisions and for altering current decision approaches. Many such strategies have been developed over the years as practical aids and tools for improving performance.

Individual Decision Making

One approach to individual decision making centers on the use of reinforcements to get people to make choices. We cover the major features of reinforcement theories in our discussion of motivation (see Chapter 9). This approach takes an outside-in look, asking how managers can get employees to alter their behaviors. In the Corvair case, Knudsen's threat to resign served to alter the General Motors board members' decision to build a safer rear suspension system. For another example, management might get a pharmaceutical company's research and development people to examine more thoroughly the possibilities of risk in a new drug by changing the rewards and punishments for doing so. Thus these employees would expand their information search and alter their decision criteria before deciding the safety of a drug.

The vast majority of research about individual decision making, however, has dealt not so much with reinforcements and outsiders changing people's decision-making behavior as with two other issues: the construction of models to describe the process of decision making and psychological influences on decisions. These will be the focus of our discussion.

Models of Individual Decision Making

Decision-making researchers have approached behavior from a number of perspectives. One approach focuses on identifying the problem, searching for alternatives, and evaluating and selecting among those alternatives. The two models reflecting this perspective are the rational and the administrative models. A second approach concentrates not on search and acceptance, but on the issues raised by the exercise of judging alternatives; this is the judgment approach.

Rational Model A pervasive model of decision making is the **rational**, or economic, **model**. The basic tenets of this model are that decision makers define problems and then search for alternative solutions. Once the search is complete, they assess the probability that each alternative will result in some desired outcomes, assign values to the different outcomes, and select the alternative that produces the outcome with the highest value. This model is so pervasive that it has become the touchstone of the study of decision making; all other models either incorporate or react against the notions of value and outcomes.

The model assumes that the decision maker:

1. Knows his values precisely

2. Has all possible information about alternatives

3. Understands all possible outcomes of any alternative

4. Knows the probability of any alternative's leading to a desired outcome

5. Can judge how much each alternative is likely to contribute to overall values

6. Selects the alternative that maximizes value

This model is not a good representation of individual decision making, however, because these assumptions usually cannot be met. It is also a poor model because our emotions frequently become involved (Etzioni, 1989). Clearly, with regard to the Corvair, General Motors executives did not consider all alternatives and outcomes nor choose the decision that maximized both short-run profits and long-range consumer image.

Etzioni (1989) summarized the limitations of the rational model. First, three cognitive attributes of humans are inconsistent with the rational model: the human brain cannot process multitudes of facts, our ability to combine more than two probabilities is low, and we learn slowly, often repeating the same mistakes. This model's second group of limitations is based on actual behavior. Emotions cloud judgment. Also, decision makers' use of such patterns as delaying decisions, making decisions impulsively, or obsessively collecting information renders decisions less than rational. Political factors, too, are ignored by the rational model.

Administrative Model In response to the deficiencies of the rational model, researchers relaxed some assumptions and formulated the **adminis-**

trative model of decision making. This model introduces two important concepts (March and Simon, 1958; Simon, 1972). The first is the notion of **bounded rationality**, which recognizes that people cannot know everything; they are limited by such organizational constraints as time, information, resources, and the like, and by their own mental capacities. The second notion is that of **satisficing**, a hybrid word meaning to search for and accept something that is satisfactory rather than perfect. The "satisficer" does not try to find optimal solutions to problems but searches until she finds an acceptable or satisfactory solution and adopts it. Thus, for example, you do not wait around for the perfect husband or wife to come into your life. You have an idea of what an acceptable husband or wife would be like; when someone with those characteristics comes into your life, you ask that person to marry you. Acceptance of administrative model has become widespread.

This model assumes the following:

1. People are willing to settle for less than the best.

2. Only a limited set of alternatives are searched for and examined. Search continues until a good enough solution is reached.

3. Few if any possible consequences are considered.

4. Probability is either not considered or is only considered in a simple rather than rigorous way.

5. One major factor is likely to determine choice.

The administrative model recognizes that most decisions follow a particular course of action. For decisions that are similar time and time again, we try to develop **standard operating procedures** (SOPs), or rules that can simply be applied over and over as the problem is met repeatedly. SOPs may also be shortcut schemes that people use when faced with familiar problems; in a sense, habits are SOPs. Many organizational policies, from personnel to manufacturing to purchasing, have been reduced to standard operating procedures to ensure uniformity of implementation and predictability of outcome and to reduce the need to "reinvent the wheel" hundreds of times each day.

The administrative model offers a benefit over the rational model in that, by denying the perfect rationality of the actor, it admits that people's decision-making propensities will be guided by their own characteristics. Their beliefs, attitudes, and values will determine the kinds of issues about which they make decisions, how they will search for information, when a satisfactory solution will appear, what it will look like, and so on. This model thus accepts the reality that decision makers from different cultures bring to the decision process different beliefs, leading to distinct decision-making styles. Europeans, for instance, tend to base decisions on past experiences, whereas Americans are more future oriented (Ronen, 1986).

Evidence shows that one not only searches just until a satisfactory solution is found but that one also tends to use sources of information that are accessible whether or not they are of the highest quality (O'Reilly, 1982). The reason may be that organizational structure restricts the availability of information, that reward systems guide the type of information sought (Feldman and March, 1981), or that because information is vague and incomplete, trustworthy sources are sought. Whatever the cause, it is clear that individuals do not perform as perfectly as the rational model predicts.

Judgment Models Another approach to decision making focuses on how judgments are made and what influences a person's judgments. The springboard for these models is the gap between actual behavior and the predictions of probability theory. People do not behave according to probability theory—an example is the gambler who assures herself that because her last 20 bets were losers, the next will pay off. This practice of ignoring the probabilities is called **suboptimal behavior** (Einhorn and Hogarth, 1975).

Of great concern to researchers interested in how people make judgments is how they represent "problem space" (Newell and Simon, 1972). How one represents the problem space determines the probabilities associated with the various outcomes; that is, how one defines the problem shapes the possible outcomes and their likelihood. One thought is that when faced with a new problem, people make use of scripts or schemas of similar past events and integrate the new problem into those scripts. These scripts suggest appropriate choices. (We discuss scripts and schemas in more detail in Chapter 10.)

Judgment comes into play in the acquisition of information, whether people acquire information from their own memories or from the environment around them (see Chapter 10). Central to the acquisition of information is *selective attention:* we are most likely to attend to cues that are either similar to or different from what is in our experience, salient (or perceived to be relevant to what we are doing), and redundant (Einhorn and Hogarth, 1981). In the Corvair case top management seemed to select only information supporting their decision to proceed with the Corvair as it was originally designed. Often, decision makers attend to the wrong information (Connolly and Thorn, 1987). The sequence in which information is received affects salience by creating both shifts in our perceptions and different demands on attention and memory. (Recall the discussion of memory in Chapter 5.)

The development of judgment models is an important step in analyzing choice behavior. However, they are deficient in conceptualizing tastes and preferences (March, 1978). People are often unsure of their preferences, as we mentioned before, and uncertainties about future preferences complicate the modeling of choice even more.

Incrementalism

One kind of decision-making style can occur within any of the models noted previously. Called **incrementalism**, this approach, rather than the rational model, is probably used in most decision-making situations (Connolly, 1988). When faced with a problem like cutting a hedge, a homeowner does not acquire a fancy set of information, note salient information, engage in a cost/benefit analysis of the outcomes of clipping away at various branches, or attempt to reduce conflict through leaving the situation or compromising on which branches to cut. Instead he snips away a little here and a little there until the overall look seems acceptable. The incremental approach is discussed more fully when we take up organizational decision making, but a few points can be made here.

As Connolly noted, "It is not difficult to suggest classes of problems for which [this] approach will fail. Nuclear wars and child bearing decisions are poor settings for a strategy of 'try a little of one and see how it goes'" (1988, p. 45). Connolly's argument is not that the incremental strategy is always superior to rational strategies, but that there may be situations in which it is. These are situations characterized by conflict, turbulence, extremely difficult problems, poorly defined goals and alternatives, and ambiguity.

A set of interesting studies shows the fallibility of incrementalism. Staw and his colleagues (Staw, 1976; Staw and Fox, 1977; Staw and Ross, 1978) investigated how decision makers became committed to courses of action. In situations in which people experienced negative consequences, they tended to commit even more resources to the course of action that produced those consequences, possibly trying to turn the situation around. They were also likely to continue committing resources if they themselves were responsible for the decision. They tended to quit committing resources when the explanation for failure had something to do with problems internal to the program they were investing, but to continue to invest resources when the explanation was external to that program. Perhaps this helps explain why even after several lawsuits, General Motors executives continued to pursue the production of the Corvair; only when a significant internal threat—Knudsen's threat to resign—was present did they decide to improve the car's safety.

Staw (1981) created a model indicating that commitment to a given course of action is a function of four factors: the motivation to justify previous decisions, norms for consistency, the perceived probability of future outcomes, and the perceived value of those outcomes (see Figure 7.1). Given

FIGURE 7.1
A Model of the Commitment Process

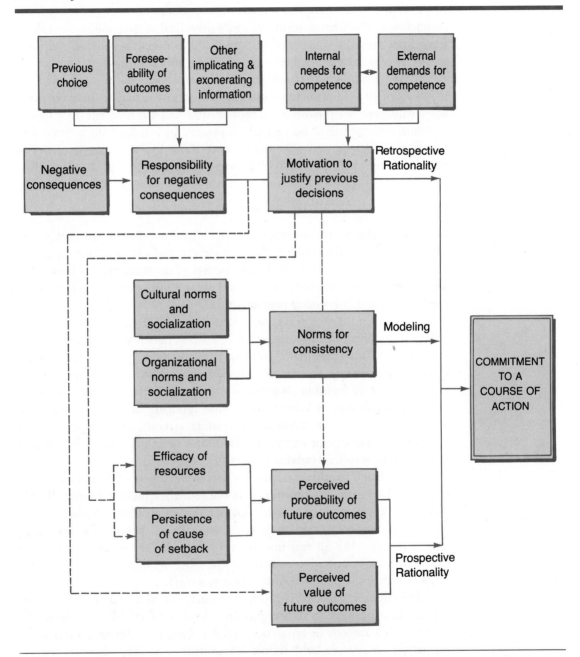

Source: From B. M. Staw, "The Escalation of Commitment to a Course of Action," *Academy of Management Review* 6 (1981): 582. Reprinted by permission.

the built-in bias to create the appearance of rationality in decision making, the motivation to justify decisions is a significant factor. This motivation is a function of responsibility for negative consequences as well as demands for competence. But what determines one's perceived responsibility for a decision? Staw sees the sources of responsibility in previous choices, the foreseeability of outcomes, and other implicating information.

Managers might be taught to ignore "sunk cost," but it is terribly hard to ignore prior commitments. One way is to expose managers to other managers who have not thrown good money after bad but have cut their losses. Another approach may be related to power. In a recent study Staw and Boettger (1990) showed that people were more likely to expose errors in past decisions when they were given some power.

Influences of Personality, Attitudes, and Values on Decision Making

It is obvious that what we bring to the decision situation influences whether we look at a particular problem, how we view it, and what decision strategies we are likely to invoke. At least four aspects of decision makers have been given considerable attention: perceptual ability, information capacity, aspiration level, and risk-taking propensity.

A decision maker's perceptions depend on his premises about a situation as well as his prior experience and resulting personality and values. It is often said, for instance, that a problem with the military is that they are always busy preparing to win the previous war. Thus armed forces faced World War II by focusing on ground-based steps to thwart tanks, the technological revolution of World War I, and ignoring defenses against what would become the main threat of that conflict, aircraft. The degree to which a decision maker's prior experience facilitates or inhibits the solution of a new problem is called **transfer effects** (Taylor, 1975).

Functional fixedness is another perceptual aspect of decision making, one that always inhibits transfer. It is the tendency to view as inapplicable a solution previously used to solve another kind of problem (Dunker, 1944–1945). This tendency occurs only in the transfer of a familiar solution to an unfamiliar one. We all run into it every day. We are so used to putting papers into the "out box" on our desks that when we need to carry coffee we often overlook the potential of that box as a tray.

Information capacity is crucial to much decision making. A decision maker's susceptibility to information overload is affected by the degree to which he is a *concrete* or an *abstract thinker*. Concrete thinkers use few information dimensions and simple integrating schemes, whereas abstract thinkers tend to process many dimensions of information and use complex integrative schemes. Abstract thinkers are more information oriented and use more information to reach decisions than concrete thinkers do (Schroeder, Driver, and Streufert, 1965).

Dogmatism also influences information capacity. Dogmatic individuals make rapid or "snap" decisions based on little information and adhere to these decisions confidently and inflexibly (Block and Peterson, 1955).

A decision maker's level of aspiration strongly influences her effectiveness in applying different decision strategies, including identifying problems, evaluating alternative courses of action, and setting up negotiations (MacCrimmon and Taylor, 1976). One's level of aspiration, for example, will detemine the kinds of negotiations she is willing to accept.

Risk-taking propensity, too, influences the adoption of various decision-making strategies (Kogan and Wallach, 1967). A high-risk taker will consider more options than one who avoids risk, because he will include as possible alternatives many risky courses the conservative person would ignore. The high-risk taker thus may be able consistently to produce more creative ideas—but the low-risk taker is more predictable. And conservative superiors, peers, and subordinates desire predictability in a manager. It might be useful for managers to measure their risk-taking propensities and those of their fellow workers to get information about the kinds of decisions work groups are likely to make. We will return to the issue of risk in our discussion of group decision making.

One study (Trevino, 1986) suggested that another personality characteristic is involved in making decisions that involve ethical questions. Trevino proposed that the manager will perceive the problem based on his stage of moral development. (Trevino uses a well-known theory of moral development that comprises six stages.) The actual decision taken, influenced in part by this perception, is also shaped by three "individual moderators" and by three "situational moderators." The individual factors are the manager's ego strength, degree of field dependence, and external or internal locus of control. The situational factors are the immediate context of the job, the organizational culture, and the characteristics of the work.

Group Decision Making

Two issues have been at the forefront of research on group decision making. The first is whether groups are better than individuals at making decisions. Clearly, John DeLorean, the GM executive from whose perspective the Corvair story was told, was in conflict with General Motors' other top management, but the case provides little evidence that his decisions would have been superior to those of top management as a group. The second is how groups facilitate or constrain decision making. At General Motors, executives together exhibited a level of immorality they clearly did not have individually. We will discuss these two issues.

Group Versus Individual Decision Making

Many organizational decisions are made by groups simply because the information, authority, and other resources required to make decisions in complex settings are not available to any single individual. Managers, who repeatedly face the choice of assigning problems either to individuals or to groups for resolution, would be helped if there were clear-cut evidence as to which process is better. Unfortunately, research into individual versus group performance has a long history fraught with inconsistencies. Several studies suggested that individual efforts are superior to group efforts, but several others concluded the opposite (see, for example, Taylor, Berry, and Block, 1958; Laughlin and Barth, 1981). A frequent finding of these studies is that group performance is superior to the performance of the average individual in the group but inferior to the performance of the best individual in the group.

What factors make group decisions less than perfect? Differences between potential and actual group performance can be explained by social loafing, inappropriate resource utilization, and the adoption of satisficing rather than maximizing strategies, among other factors. Some factors, too, make group decision making superior to individual decision making. The two most important are the capacity of an individual to learn in a group and opportunity provided by many contributors to stimulate thinking (Latane, Williams, and Harkins, 1979; Steiner, 1972; Maier, 1967; Hill, 1982).

Participation

Participative decision making, in which large numbers of organization members share in decision making, has received a good deal of attention. Because we live in a democratic society, we probably feel that participation will result in a number of good outcomes. For managers, the issue is one of engaging in cost-effective behavior. Participation is advocated as having three advantages: it improves the quality of decisions, it improves the resulting commitment to decisions, and it increases employee satisfaction. Results do not always bear out these claims, however. A recent review of 43 studies showed no relationship between participation and satisfaction in 40 percent of the studies (Locke and Schweiger, 1979; Locke, Schweiger, and Latham, 1986).

There is considerable discussion about the relationship of participation and the effective completion of tasks. Some research showed a positive relationship (e.g., Miller and Monje, 1986) and some showed participation had little impact on effective task completion (Wagner and Gooding, 1987). A recent investigation showed that assigned goals were as effective as participatively set goals in obtaining high performance (Latham, Erez, and Locke, 1988).

Participation can take a number of forms. For example, it can be forced or voluntary. Union contracts often build in participation on some issues; with political decisions about broad social issues, the participation of certain groups is required by virtue of their relative power, if not by law. Participation varies in degree and scope and can be direct or indirect, as was apparent at General Motors regarding the Corvair decision. One thing is certain: participation in organizations cannot work unless management is clearly behind it (Krishna, 1974).

Baloff and Doherty (1989) focused on an interesting aspect of the negative side of participative decision-making programs: negative effects on employees. They pointed out that employees who join a participative decision-making program may be subjected to pressure from other workers who label their participation as collaboration with management. The result is not only stress for the employee, but a crippling of the participative program. A second threat to participators is coercion from or punishment by managers. A third problem associated with participation is the adjustment that participants must undergo after the program has ended. Baloff and Doherty suggested that programs established by those unattuned to the subtleties of participative decision making are likely to suffer these negative outcomes.

Vroom and Yetton (1973), updated by Vroom and Jago (1987), offered an articulate prescription for the appropriate use of participation. They began by identifying five degrees of possible participation, each labeled as A (autocratic), C (consultative), or G (group):

- *The manager makes the decision alone based on information she possesses (method AI).*

- *The manager makes the decision alone based on information supplied—at the manager's request—by subordinates (method AII).*

- *The manager makes the decision alone but first consults with relevant subordinates individually; the decision may or may not reflect their counsel (method CI).*

- *The manager makes the decision alone but first holds a group meeting at which alternatives are discussed; the decision may or may not reflect the subordinates' views (method CII).*

- *The group analyzes the problem, identifies alternatives, evaluates the alternatives, and makes a decision. The manager acts as a co-*

ordinator of the discussion but does not influence the outcome (method GII).

Vroom and Jago said the appropriate degree of participation is determined by the nature of the decision itself. They presented 12 diagnostic questions managers should ask before selecting a degree of participation (the original Vroom and Yetton model had 7 such questions), as shown in Figure 7.2. In other words, there are times when participation is useful and times when it is not. The Vroom and Jago model is meant to help identify each of these times. If subordinates have useful information, their commitment to the decision is essential, they share the organization's goals, timeliness is not crucial, and conflict is unlikely, then participation is useful.

A decision tree is used to follow each of the factors through to the appropriate level of decision making. For the sake of simplicity, the decision tree treats each question as having only two answers, yes and no or high and low. The model tree also assumes that the two motivational factors are weighted a certain way (other weights produce alternative decision trees) and that the time necessity and geographic dispersion are held constant. The resultant tree is shown in Figure 7.3; each outcome identifies by code which of the five decision-making styles previously outlined is appropriate.

FIGURE 7.2
Vroom and Jago's Diagnostic Questions for Participative Decision Making

- *Quality requirement.* Does a quality requirement make one solution more rational than another?
- *Commitment requirement.* Is a high level of commitment required from subordinates?
- *Leader information.* Does the manager have enough information to make a high-quality decision?
- *Problem structure.* Is the problem well structured, such that the manager knows what information is required and where it is?
- *Commitment probability.* If the manager were to make the decision, would subordinates likely be committed to it?
- *Goal congruence.* Do subordinates share the goals to be attained by solving the problem?

- *Subordinate conflict.* Are subordinates likely to show conflict over possible solutions?
- *Subordinate information.* Do the subordinates have enough information to make a high-quality decision?
- *Time constraints.* Does a time constraint limit the manager's ability to involve subordinates?
- *Geographical dispersion.* If subordinates are geographically dispersed, do the benefits of involving them in the decision outweigh the costs of bringing them to the same place?
- *Motivation—time.* How much importance does the manager place on saving time?
- *Motivation—development.* How much importance does the manager place on developing the abilities of subordinates?

Source: Based on V. H. Vroom and A. G. Jago, *The New Leadership: Managing Participation in Organizations* (Englewood Cliffs, NJ: Prentice-Hall, 1987).

FIGURE 7.3
The Vroom and Jago Decision Tree

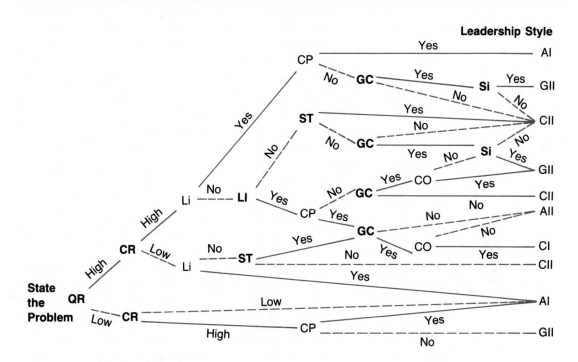

Problem Attributes

QR	Quality requirement:	How important is the technical quality of this decision?
CR	Commitment requirement:	How important is subordinate commitment to the decision?
LI	Leader's information	Do you have sufficient information to make a high-quality decision?
ST	Problem structure:	Is the problem well structured?
CP	Commitment probability:	If you were to make the decision by yourself, is it reasonably certain that your subordinate(s) would be committed to the decision?
GC	Goal congruence:	Do subordinates share the organizational goals to be attained in solving this problem?
CO	Subordinate conflict:	Is conflict among subordinates over preferred solutions likely?
SI	Subordinate information:	Do subordinates have sufficient information to make a high-quality decision?

One aspect of participation in decision making that merits consideration is the degree to which it improves "buy in" and minimizes later resistance to change. If a corporation is considering a reorganization that significantly reduces the authority of corporate staff and increases the authority of line managers, allowing members of both groups to participate in the design of the reorganization (a form of participating in the "decision") may be critical to later acceptance. As the change progresses from initial recommendation to detailed design, pilot testing, and full implementation, successively larger numbers of individuals can be brought into the process. Participation can give a sense of ownership in the decision, reduce the "unknown" factor, heighten understanding in the decision, and ease the way for smooth implementation. The decision thus reached may appear to be "better" than one made without participation when, in fact, it is the same decision. The difference in outcomes colors the evaluation of the decision itself.

The downside of participation is that it may induce stagnation if participants are unable to agree on a course of action. Allowing participation means allowing others the opportunity to block a desired outcome. Participative decision making usually takes longer and is more costly in terms of individuals' time and, to a lesser extent, other expenses, such as travel. (Recall that the importance of timeliness was one of Vroom and Jago's factors in evaluating the appropriateness of participative decision making.)

Some research supports the assumption that more participation takes place at high levels of the hierarchy than at low levels (Blankenship and Miles, 1968; Heller and Yukl, 1969). The research suggests that in situations demanding high-quality solutions, the appropriateness of participation is perceived as no different at high and low levels (Jago, 1981). Some evidence suggests that participation is problem dependent (Koopman, Drenth, Bus, Kruyswijk, and Wierdsma, 1981). Participation is called for when tasks are difficult to analyze and quite different from one another, where environments are changing rapidly, and where there is considerable interdependence among employees (Nutt, 1976; Roberts and Gargano, 1989; Sashkin, 1976).

This approach to decision making may be more widely used outside the United States. When participation is institutionalized nationally, it goes by a variety of names and includes a variety of schemes, some of which are shown in Figure 7.4. These schemes all emphasize participation in the overall governance of the firm and participation at lower levels. Divergence between what is legally sanctioned and what occurs is often wide; informal arrangements may have as much impact on what goes on as do legal prescriptions. Participation has been more successful in Japan, the Scandinavian countries, and West Germany than in the United States, Great Britain, and

FIGURE 7.4
*National Schemes
of Industrial
Democracy*

Country	Political Context	In-Company Arrangement
United Kingdom	Law on board level representation being discussed, but now vociferous employer opposition and unions only moderately interested. Traditionally, law keeps out of industrial relations. Collective bargaining is not legally enforceable.	No statutory works councils, but shop stewards committees are prevalent. Growth in decentralized power (de facto) in recent years.
Belgium	Multiparty system not yet federalized. Communitarian problems and multiunionism according to political, religious, and linguistic divisions. Bargaining on centralized and decentralized basis. High unionization with Christian, socialist, and liberal confederations.	No worker representatives on supervisory boards. Works councils, safety and health committees, and union delegations. Former two have consultative role; last bargains. Christian and socialist unions disagree on forms of worker representation at company level.
Yugoslavia	Socialist country organized on decentralized community-based self-government. Capital communally owned.	Plant run by elected committee (workers council). Each unit (basic association of organized labor) has its own representative committees.
Sweden	Strong union movement negotiating centrally with a likewise centralized employers' federation. Up to 1976 very little state interference in industrial relations.	Union "clubs" that bargain with management mainly over wages. Safety committee with union majority. Works council for information and consultation. Two workers directors on the (only) board.
Holland	Parliamentary democracy with multiparty system. Moderate level of unionization organized according to political/religious lines. Bargaining takes place at central level in which government participates also, and at branch level worker participation regulated mainly through national laws.	No representation of workers on supervisory board. Most important representative organ is works council. It has mainly advisory and consultative character. Recent development toward more authority for the works council. Some activities of union representatives on the shop floor. Some developments toward institutionalization of consultation supervisor—work groups on day-to-day activities.

(continued)

FIGURE   7.4
(*Continued*)

Country	Political Context	In-Company Arrangement
Germany (West)	Long-standing tradition of introducing worker participation at company/plant level by way of statutory regulations (national laws). Collective bargaining (wages/working conditions) mainly above company level between well-organized, industry-based unions and employers associations.	Works council is central body for employee representation at plant/company level with information, consultation, or codetermination rights depending on issues. Generally, large companies have 1/3 (500 employees) or 1/2 (2,000 employees) of seats on supervisory boards for employee representatives. Two-tier company structure.
France	Politicized arena of collective bargaining. Numerically weak union movement, divided by confederal allegiances, resists reformist solutions.	Works council (*Conseil d'enterprise*) has consultative role. Few workers on board.
Finland	Centralized bargaining and high level of unionization. Degree of statutory participation behind pace of other Nordic countries.	Productivity committee for plants over 60 people, but are of low importance. Shop stewards and work protection delegates important.
Israel	Strong labor movement has institutionalized worker participation in its federation's own enterprises and public sector.	Works committees in company and plant. Joint productivity councils in industrial plants and joint management in some Histadrut industrial plants only.
Italy	Politicized union movement, moderately well organized in manufacturing, but little state/legal interference vis-à-vis participation.	Factory councils, but not prescribed by legislation, depend on union strength.
Denmark	Strong labor movement cooperating with Labor Party and worker minority representatives on boards. High degree of unionization and centralized collective bargaining.	Cooperative committees in which workers shop stewards take part (joint consultation) affect day-to-day situations. Shop stewards important.

FIGURE 7.4
(*Continued*)

Country	Political Context	In-Company Arrangement
Norway	Mixed economy. Strongly centralized and united labor movement with national unions bargaining 2-year collective agreements with equally centralized employers confederation. Close cooperation between trade unions and dominant social-democratic labor party. High degree of unionization. Increasing state participation in national collective bargaining.	Local union representatives bargain with management with basis in collective agreement. Shop stewards take part in joint consultation/information bodies and safety committees. One-third of board of directors and supervisory board members are elected by and among employees, after nomination by local unions.

Source: International Research Group, *Industrial Democracy in Europe* (Oxford: Oxford University Press, 1981), pp. 13–14. Copyright © 1981 by the International Research Group. Reprinted by permission of the Oxford University Press.

France (Strauss, 1982). Recently, Lincoln (1989) reported that in Japan decision making is both participatory and centralized and that participation operates differently at higher and lower organizational levels. Some decentralization apparently has also occurred in China.

It is difficult to provide simple rules about the appropriateness of participation because it is connected to so many other things. The issue is clearly related to managerial style (e.g., forcing a manager to use an uncomfortable style may impede decision making). Also, organizations develop norms that become a part of their cultures, which are understood by employees—who may have even selected the employer in part because of such intangibles. Forcing compliance to a particular form of decision making may be dysfunctional if some other comfortable style has developed over the years. On the other hand, if an organization has limped along under a management style that impedes flexibility and creativity, it may be time for an entire overhaul. Perhaps John DeLorean was suggesting this when he criticized General Motors for not being creative, stating in reference to the cosmetic changes made for 1977's new line of cars that "we were kidding ourselves that these slight alternatives were innovative."

Risk and Groupthink

In Chapter 4, when discussing group processes in some depth, we noted that a number of problems occur in groups. They are brought about by the fact that some people talk more than others, high-status people have more impact on decisions than low-status people, groups often have to spend a good deal of time dealing with interpersonal interactions, groups lose sight of their goals and get off on tangents, and groups exert extreme pressure to conform. The Corvair decision illustrates many of these issues. Here we will extend our discussions of polarization and conformity (see Chapter 4) because these processes can be absolutely deadly to decision making.

An important body of research asks what groups do in decision situations involving risk. Common sense leads us to think that individuals will make riskier decisions than groups because groups have to adopt more conservative, middle-of-the-road positions to accommodate the varied perspectives of their members. It turns out, however, that groups often make riskier decisions than individuals do alone. This phenomenon is called the **risky shift** (Stoner, 1961).

The shift toward risk, however, does not always occur. Some studies have shown groups to make more conservative decisions than individuals, but these decisions seem to revolve around culturally accepted standards. For example, individuals made riskier decisions than groups when asked to make a recommendation about marriage for two people who had recently been having problems and when given a situation involving the protection of the endangered life of an expectant mother (Stoner, 1968).

There are three possible explanations of shifts toward risk or conservatism. The first is a social comparison explanation: people shift after discussion because they want to appear to have better views than other group members. A second explanation, related to information acquisition, holds that people change their minds once they are exposed to arguments they had not thought about before. The third explanation is the tendency for group members to polarize or shift their views to extremes in the same direction as their previous views. Coca-Cola's decision in 1985 to abandon its classic formula is an interesting example of various forces that influenced a risky decision.

FEATURE: *How Coca-Cola Executives Made the New Coke–Old Coke Decisions*

The Decision to Change the Formula

1. *The Pepsi Challenge.*   In 1974, Coca-Cola's leading rival, Pepsi Cola, launched "The Pepsi Challenge," a taste-test campaign in which consumers were given a choice of two unmarked drinks and asked to say

which tasted better. The majority consistently chose Pepsi. Coca-Cola's reaction to the challenge was first haughty and disdainful, but it soon began to fight back directly. During the period of the challenge (1974–1979), Pepsi's market share increased modestly, primarily at the expense of other brands. Coke's share also showed fractional gains during the period. The key impact of the campaign was psychological. Coke's corporate pride was wounded, and in response the company became obsessed with the brand's image as number one. For the first time since the company's founding, Coca-Cola had to question its famous secret formula. In 1979 the company's market research department began testing the first of several new colas formulated by the technical division. . . .

2. *The Change of Corporate Culture.* In 1980 Roberto C. Goizueta, a Cuban who had fled to the U.S. after Castro took over, was named president of Coca-Cola and in 1981 succeeded to the chairman's position. At a meeting of top company executives in March 1981, he called for a radical change in the company's culture, citing among other reasons Pepsi's steady gains, the fact that Coke's sales were growing slower than the soft drink market and that shareholder return had been essentially flat for a number of years. In the windup of his speech he said, "Just to give you an example that there are no sacred cows . . . , let me assure you . . . that such things as the reformulation of any or all of our products will not stand in the way of giving any of our competitors a real or a perceived product advantage." . . .

3. *The Proliferation of Colas and the Success of Diet Coke.* By the early 1980s Coke's competitors had introduced a rash of new products—Diet Pepsi, Pepsi Light, Pepsi Free and Sugar-Free Pepsi Free from Pepsi Cola alone, as well as numerous others from Royal Crown, 7-Up and Dr. Pepper. Coca-Cola had two low-calorie entries, Tab and Fresca, but was stymied over introducing a diet drink with Coca-Cola in the name. It was doctrine in the company that a 1920 Supreme Court ruling over trademark disputes between Coke and competitors somehow prevented the company from marketing any other drink with Coke in the name. This tenet of corporate culture had been swept aside by Goizueta when he assumed power. Finally, in 1982, Coca-Cola introduced Diet Coke, and it became the most successful new product in the beverage industry. By the end of 1983 it was the best selling diet drink in the U.S. and by 1984 the number three soft drink overall.

4. *Pepsi's Relentless Growth and Coke's Loss of Market Share.* Coca-Cola's market share lead over Pepsi had fallen from 2-to-1 in the fifties to a mere 4.9 percentage points. In the grocery store market, Coke was trailing by 1.7 percentage points (in the soft drink market, 1 percentage point represents $250 million in sales). Yet Coca-Cola spent far more on advertising and was more widely distributed than Pepsi, so marketing technique was

not the problem. In the end company executives had no choice but to consider the product itself. . . . Coca-Cola USA President Byson and market research director Roy Stout put increasing pressure on top management to consider a change in formula. . . . In the fall of 1983 senior management gave the go-ahead to "explore the possibility of a reformulation."

5. *Decisive Research.*   Research into the *idea* of changing Coca-Cola showed that Pepsi drinkers, who were thought to be more loyal to their brand than Coke drinkers, would be interested in a new Coke. At the same time, it was learned that some Coke drinkers were strongly opposed to any tampering with Coke and did not think the drink could be improved. In September 1984 the technical division came up with a formulation that showed dramatically favorable results when tested against Pepsi. By late 1984, President Keough, who had initially had a negative instinctive reaction to changing the formula, gave in. During the holiday season at the end of 1984, senior management unanimously agreed to change the taste of Coke. The new Coke was announced with great fanfare on April 23, 1985.

The Decision to Bring Back "Old Coke"

1. *The Public Outcry.*   Consumer reaction to new Coke was swift and almost overwhelmingly negative. Between the day it was introduced and the announcement of old Coke's return on July 11, the Company received more than 40,000 letters, most of them protesting the decision. The company also received 557 petitions signed by 28,138 distraught consumers. . . . Up to 8,000 calls a day poured in on the company's 83 WATS lines. The issue became a cause célèbre in media throughout the nation, and numerous jokes and stunts poked fun at the new drink. . . .

2. *Disappointing Sales.*   Despite massive promotion, discounting, and giveaways, the new formula didn't ring up impressive sales. New Coke had completely replaced old Coke by Memorial Day, but in June the product was selling only at about the level the older product had attained a year earlier.

3. *Pressure from Bottlers.*   Regional bottlers, who exercise a great deal of influence in the Coca-Cola organization, were becoming increasingly unhappy over the new product and began to exert pressure on senior management to take corrective action. They didn't like the uproar because it undermined their pride in their own product. Rather than supporting the new Coke, they began to agree with critics that old Coke was better. Many began to demand that old Coke be brought back.

4. *Dyson's Acceptance of the Situation.*   New Coke was actually the responsibility of Coca-Cola USA, headed by Dyson. Goizueta and Keough, who outranked Dyson in the hierarchy, concluded they would have to bring back old Coke but held off making an executive decision, wanting

Dyson to come to the same conclusion first. On July 8, Dyson met with the board of governors of the Coca-Cola Bottlers Association. Although no formal vote was taken, Dyson understood the consensus of the bottlers: bring back old Coke. Late that afternoon he reported to Keough that he concurred with those who favored bringing back old Coke. On July 9, the decision was reached, and on July 11 the senior officials held a press conference to announce that old Coke, renamed "Coke Classic," would be brought back.

Source: From Thomas Oliver, *The Real Coke—The Real Story* (New York: Penguin Books, 1987), Chapter 10. Copyright © 1987 by Thomas Oliver. Reprinted by permission of Random House, Inc.

Irving Janis (1972) examined a number of group decision-making situations, including Admiral Kimmel's handling of the Pearl Harbor situation just prior to December 7, 1941 and John Kennedy's handling of the Bay of Pigs, and identified the development of a highly cohesive form of conformity that he called groupthink. **Groupthink** occurs when members of small groups develop shared illusions and related norms that interfere with critical thinking and reality testing.

Antecedents to groupthink are high cohesiveness and the insularity of the decision-making group, lack of methodological procedures for searching for and appraising information, directive leadership, and high stress combined with low hope for finding a better solution than the one favored by the leader or other influential people. Particularly when under stress, decision makers develop a number of cognitive defenses that result in a collective pattern of avoidance. These defenses include (1) misjudging relevant warnings, (2) inventing new arguments to support a chosen policy, (3) failing to explore ominous implications of ambiguous events, (4) forgetting information that would enable a challenging event to be interpreted correctly, and (5) misperceiving signs of the onset of actual danger.

Symptoms of groupthink are:

1. An illusion of invulnerability shared by most or all members, which creates excessive optimism and encourages taking extreme risks

2. Collective efforts to rationalize in order to discount warnings that might lead members to reconsider their assumptions before they recommit themselves to their past policy decisions

3. An unquestioned belief in the group's inherent morality, inclining the members to ignore the ethical or moral consequences of their decision

4. Stereotyped views of rivals and enemies as too evil to warrant genuine attempts to negotiate, or as too weak or stupid to counter whatever risky attempts are made to defeat their purposes

5. Direct pressure on any member who expresses strong arguments against any of the group's stereotypes, illusions, or commitments, making clear that such dissent is contrary to what is expected of all loyal members

6. Self-censorship of deviations from the apparent group consensus, reflecting each member's inclination to minimize to himself the importance of his doubts and counterarguments

7. A shared illusion of unanimity, partly resulting from this self-censorship and augmented by the false assumption that silence implies consent

8. The emergence of self-appointed "mindguards"—members who protect the group from adverse information that might shatter their shared complacency about the effectiveness and morality of their decisions

Executives at General Motors suffered from several of these symptoms of groupthink when making the decisions that led to the construction of the Corvair.

The major factor differentiating group and individual defective decision making, then, is that for each member of a relatively cohesive group one particular incentive looms large: the approval or disapproval of his fellow group members and their leader. A model of groupthink and how it relates group cohesion and performance is shown in Figure 7.5; notice the six defects in the decision making of groups affected by groupthink. This figure is probably an incomplete model of group decision making, if for no other reason than it fails to consider that decision makers in situations that have resulted in fiascos probably frame the problem facing them as having two or more negative and no positive outcomes (Whyte, 1989).

Groups can take a number of steps to reduce the probability of groupthink. They can develop strong norms of critical appraisal. Their leaders can abstain from pushing their own views and using their influence, and instead encourage genuine debate. Groups can attempt to avoid isolation by involving more than one group in the decision-making process. Finally, they can program conflict into the decision-making situation (Cosier and Schwenk, 1990; Janis, 1989).

FIGURE 7.5
*A Model of
Groupthink*

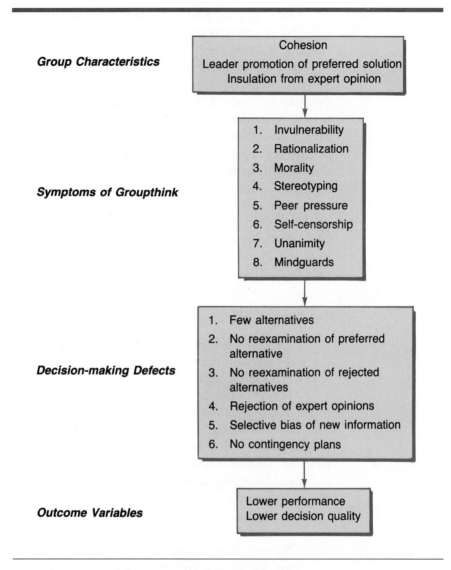

Group Characteristics

Cohesion
Leader promotion of preferred solution
Insulation from expert opinion

Symptoms of Groupthink

1. Invulnerability
2. Rationalization
3. Morality
4. Stereotyping
5. Peer pressure
6. Self-censorship
7. Unanimity
8. Mindguards

Decision-making Defects

1. Few alternatives
2. No reexamination of preferred alternative
3. No reexamination of rejected alternatives
4. Rejection of expert opinions
5. Selective bias of new information
6. No contingency plans

Outcome Variables

Lower performance
Lower decision quality

Source: Adapted from Gregory Moorhead, "Groupthink: Hypothesis in Need of Testing," *Group and Organization Studies*, December 1982, p. 434. Copyright © 1982 by Sage Publications, Inc. Reprinted by permission of Sage Publications, Inc.

Organizational Decision Making

Certain processes in organizations combine individual and group decisions to arrive at organizational decisions. In fact, much of the interesting work of organizations is in their decision making and implementation. Organizations learn about themselves through their decision-making activities. The countries of Eastern Europe began making decisions in 1989 and 1990 that, both through the processes used and the results obtained, will enhance their learning of themselves.

Researchers recognize that organizations are messy places and that organizational decision making is something other than the sum of individual or group decisions. The kinds of issues they talk about implicitly, if not explicitly, recognize that organizational decision makers frequently operate in ambiguity and uncertainty, which are generated from both inside and outside the organization. Coca-Cola had to face its internal questions as well as the changing competitive environment influenced by Pepsi.

Just as individual attitudes and values influence individual decision making and group attitudes and values influence group processes, the assumption that organizational values, norms, and ideologies color organizational decisions underlies two of the three major approaches we will study here. Initially, we will turn our attention to how this process occurs. We will then look at those three approaches to organizational decision making.

The Influence of Values, Norms, and Ideologies on Organizational Decision Making

Attitudes, values, and ideologies shape two steps early in the organizational decision-making process. These are defining the problem and determining who will make the decision.

"In traditional theory, a decision problem arises when a gap exists between a current state and some desired state, someone becomes aware of this gap, wants to reduce it, and has access to resources to eliminate the gap" (Beyer, 1981, p. 180). No doubt, how a problem is defined determines the kinds of solutions available to resolve it by focusing attention on certain issues and providing interpretations of those issues. The GM norm of team playing led management to define its problem not as engineering or design lapses in the Corvair but as the inability of dissident managers to support production of the new car. The solution, then, was not to revise the design but to threaten those managers into compliance.

However, little is known about problem finding (Connolly, 1977). Organizations rarely choose their problems. Sometimes problems are forced on them by the environments in which they exist—Coca-Cola would not have had a problem were it not for the aggressive marketing of Pepsi. Those environments may even constrain the kinds of problems that will occur. Another flaw in the traditional view is that problem definition is not always solely in response to gaps between the current situation and a desired situation. Sometimes potential solutions are used to help define problems (Cyert, Dill, and March, 1967). The rapid and widespread introduction of personal computers into organizations provides instances of a solution in search of problems. Often, someone buys a PC without a very good idea about how it will be used. He then tries it out for various kinds of projects until a valid function can be found.

A second limitation on problem finding is prior definitions. Organizations work to develop commitment to their goals, plans, programs, and activities, and once developed, they codify as much of this commitment as they can into SOPs. Managers want to weave the corporate objectives somehow into every employee's daily "to do" list. Commitment, the existence of SOPs, the stability of organizational structures, organizational culture, and inertia all work against redefinition of problems once they are defined.

The second early step in the decision-making process that is influenced by organizational values, norms, and ideologies is the selection of who will make the decision. Organizations vary in the degree to which they encourage wide participation. Those who participate actively often have vested interests in particular outcomes. One might argue that if diverse interests are represented in the decision-making process, at least someone's interests will be served by the decision (Lindblom, 1965). Organizations usually generate only a few alternative decision strategies, not only because of the cost of an information search but also because participants are more interested in controlling choices than in creating them. Indeed, participants in the decision process can wield a considerable amount of influence. We saw that Cole and Knudsen both influenced key decisions, to produce the Corvair in one instance and to make it safer in another.

As we already know, wide participation in decision making is prescribed by many writers in the interest of securing employee commitment and perhaps satisfaction. (Narrow, autocratic decision-making systems in Eastern Europe contributed to the democratic uprising in many countries.) Recall that participation can occur in a number of different forms. The feature on CEOs and decision making describes how different CEOs used participation to help get their management team committed to important and dramatic decisions.

FEATURE: *A Look at How Seven CEOs Made Critical Decisions*

Decision maker: William Ylvisaker, CEO of Gould, Inc.
Decision: To transform Gould from a car battery and electrical equipment manufacturer into a high-tech electronics business.
The process: Ylvisaker decided to sell off the low-tech three quarters of the $2.2 billion a year company and replace those parts with electronics firms.

Half the management committee left the company. Because investment bankers had been skeptical he could sell off the assets for reasonable value, he decided to do it without them. He enlisted the help of the heads of the units to be sold off by promising bonuses and equity participation. In deciding on acquisitions, he subjected them to full-scale debates on the deal's merits between a pro and a con team of Gould senior managers.

Decision maker: Allen Neuharth, CEO of Gannett Co.
Decision: To launch *USA Today*, a national newspaper.
The process: Extensive market research provided a "hazy" answer—there'd be a market for the right kind of product. Neuharth judged the research to provide a "go" decision and succeeded in convincing his directors to approve. Neuharth says the decision was not based on logic alone. "Quite a number of us in Gannett were still fairly young and aggressive and hungry. We wanted to expand an empire we had inherited, not just preserve it." . . .

Decision maker: Ward Hagan, former CEO of Warner Lambert.
Decision: Make health care the dominant part of the company instead of consumer products.
The process: Hagan didn't know how to make all the little decisions needed to make the big decision happen. He hired McKinsey and Co. to teach his people strategic planning. The effect was a mini-cultural revolution. "It opened doors," said Elizabeth Tallet, chief planner. "The company became more participative." Questioning and opposition began to replace the company's tradition of waiting for orders. Hagan sent his top 500 managers through a program to train them to be more critical and probing, and took care to show by promotions that he valued such behavior. As a result his troops were able to show him how to implement his strategy.

Decision maker: Kenneth Oshman, CEO of Rolm Corp.
Decision: To find a second business to supplement the military computer business, which he feared was going to top out soon. The product selected was computerized telephone systems.
The approach: Research produced a disappointing conclusion: to gain a worthwhile share of the market, you'd have to go in with full manufacturing, sales, and service capabilities, which Rolm didn't have. Oshman spent several months sounding out skeptical telephone experts, then hired a technical expert and a marketing veteran to make Rolm's top management feel more committed to the decision. Despite the inconclusive reseach and against the advice of experts in the field, Rolm jumped in anyway, and succeeded. The product worked, bringing Rolm nine years of growth at a 57% compounded rate and a merger with IBM.

Decision maker: Alfred Brittain III, CEO of Bankers Trust.

Decision: To sell off the bank's retail division and emphasize the wholesale (corporate) business.

The approach: First efforts to negotiate a sale to the Bank of Montreal failed. Hardest part of the decision was deciding to try to sell it again. Convinced his original decision was right, he went back into the ring and sold it off piecemeal over five years.

Decision maker: William Woodside, American Can CEO.

Decision: To make a major diversification move to energize a business that was sliding downhill.

The process: Woodside told subordinates that the company would have to decide to do something big. To develop options, he would "gradually start with the easy stuff and then work up to the things that are unthinkable. You sort of ratchet yourself along by having a picture of the future that gradually changes as you learn more facts and add more pieces to it." The paper division came up with a plan to sell one mill and enter a joint venture with another. But Woodside felt this would make no difference to the corporation. So he told the division to go back and consider every possible scenario, including selling the business. He established a "strategic work group" of half a dozen officers to help him study the alternatives, which the group discussed every week or two with everyone in top management. This process helped convince Woodside that only the sale of a big chunk of the company would do, that the can business wasn't easily salable, and that the paper unit, although the better business, was thus the only candidate. The process also served another purpose. "The process itself was part of the selling of the decision," said Robert Abramson, senior vice president for strategic planning. "You must allow senior managers to get a fair hearing, so you'll end up making a decision not that everyone will agree to, but all will carry out." . . .

Decision maker: Howard Lowe, CEO of National Intergroup (formerly National Steel)

Decision: Whether to continue to invest in the company's steel business in the face of declining market share.

The approach: The decision came to a head when it came time for the regular rebuilding of the burned-out coke ovens at the company's big Weirton, West Virginia, mill, a $100-million-plus capital expenditure. Lowe asked himself the unaskable question: Why do we need to make our own coke? That first taboo question led to another, and another. If we don't make our own coke, can our coal business stand on its own? And is our iron business competitive? "Once you start this peel-the-onion type of approach, you can find yourself with some pretty interesting questions," said Lowe. A study commissioned by the company predicted zero growth for the U.S. steel industry, not the 5% to 7% the company had been predicting. This led to the ultimate unaskable question: Why should National be in the steel business at all? Lowe answered this question by selling off the Weirton mill to company employees in 1983 and later sold a Japanese company 50% of the remaining steel operations, declaring that henceforth steel would be a stand-alone business, not *the* business of the company.

Low-level workers may participate as well, especially in decisions about changing SOPs. In fact, because they are the ones actually carrying out the SOPs, they can be a good source of information on how to improve them. Organizational suggestion systems, many of which have produced phenomenal savings and improvements through the ideas of lower-level employees, are based largely on this notion. So are quality circles. (For more on various techniques for redesigning organizations to promote participation, see Chapter 11.)

Three Approaches to Organizational Decision Making

The Incremental Approach   The incremental approach begins by saying that even if values, norms, and ideologies are at play in organizations, they are so amorphous that decision makers cannot easily use them to attach value to particular alternatives. Then, too, a value may be held with regard to one kind of decision that is different for another kind of decision. One often cannot rank values when they conflict with one another. The result is that decisions are made incrementally.

> In summary, two aspects of the process by which values are actually handled can be distinguished. The first is clear: evaluation and empirical analysis are intertwined; that is, one chooses among values and among policies at one and the same time. Put a little more elaborately, one simultaneously chooses a policy to attain certain objectives and chooses the objectives themselves. The second aspect is related but distinct: the administrator focuses his attention on marginal or incremental values. Whether he is aware of it or not, he does not find general formulations of objectives very helpful and in fact makes specific marginal or incremental comparisons. Two poli-

cies, X and Y, confront him. Both promise the same degree of attainment of objectives a, b, c, d, and e. But X promises him somewhat more of f than does Y, while Y promises him somewhat more of g than does X. In choosing between them, he is in fact offered the alternative of a marginal or incremental amount of f at the expense of a marginal or incremental amount of g. The only values that are relevant to his choice are these increments by which the two policies differ; and when he finally chooses between the two marginal values, he does so by making a choice between policies. (Lindblom, 1959, pp. 82–83)

Decision makers change policy only a little at a time. Perhaps this helps explain the slowness of GM executives to change their response to lawsuits and bad publicity surrounding the early models of the Corvair. We do not see massive changes in welfare policy; we see demonstration projects. We do not see large increments or decrements in budgets; we see small changes, as discussed in the feature "Budgeting as an Incremental Model."

FEATURE: *Budgeting as an Incremental Model*

Simplification

Participants in budgeting deal with their overwhelming burdens by adopting aids to calculation. They simplify in order to get by. They make small moves, let experience accumulate, and use the feedback from their decisions to gauge the consequences. They use actions on simpler matters they understand as indices to complex concerns. They attempt to judge the capacity of the men in charge of programs even if they cannot appraise the policies directly. They may institute across-the-board ("meat-axe") cuts to reduce expenditures, relying on outcries from affected agencies and interest groups to let them know if they have gone too far.

Incremental Method

By far the most important aid to calculation is the incremental method. Budgets are almost never actively reviewed as a whole in the sense of considering at once the value of all existing programs as compared with all possible alternatives. Instead, this year's budget is based on last year's budget, with special attention given to a narrow range of increases or decreases. The greatest part of any budget is a product of previous decisions. Long-range commitments have been made. There are mandatory programs whose expenses must be met. Powerful political support makes the inclusion of other activities inevitable. Consequently, officials concerned with budgeting restrict their attention to items and programs they can do something about—a few new programs and possibly some cuts in old ones.

Expectations of Participants

Incremental calculations proceed from an existing base. By "base" we refer to commonly held expectations among participants in budgeting that programs will be carried out at close to the going level of expenditures. The base of a budget, therefore, refers to accepted parts of programs that will not normally be subjected to intensive scrutiny. Since many organizational units compete for funds, there is a tendency for the central authority to include all of them in the benefits or deprivations to be distributed. Participants in budgeting often refer to expectations regarding their fair share of increases and decreases. The widespread sharing of deeply held expectations concerning the organization's base and its fair share of funds provides a powerful (though informal) means of coordination and stability in budgetary systems which appear to lack comprehensive calculations proceeding from a hierarchical center.

Source: M. Murray, *Decisions: A Comparative Analysis* (Marshfield, MA: Pitman, 1986).

Lindblom (1959; Lindblom and Cohen, 1979) argue for the value of successive limited changes and evaluations. He states that it is the system most administrators use (Allison, 1971) and contends that it is superior in many situations to any other decision-making method available for the solution of complex problems, especially superior to futile attempts at superhuman comprehensiveness required by the rational model.

Etzioni (1989) distinguishes between incrementalism, which he identifies as timid and conservative, and a strategy he called mixed scanning. Incrementalism is flawed because the small adjustments are not part of any larger direction, meaning that they cannot be properly evaluated. **Mixed scanning**, on the other hand, involves making broad choices about the organization's development and then identifying a number of particular partial steps that can be taken and evaluated. The method is superior to the rational model because it recognizes the necessity to make decisions before the accumulation of all information—the gathering of which is impossible and the waiting for which may fatally delay a decision. This technique, which Etzioni believes is the method practiced by most decision makers, is ideal for organizations in ambiguous, changing environments because it promotes adaptability.

One shortcoming of the incremental model is that, by observing what appear to be incremental choices, one cannot really infer that this model of decision making and change has been followed. Relative stability in patterns of allocation over time may be the result of the rational model instead of incremental decision making. If the allocation was correct in the first place, one would not expect more than minimal shifts over time. Rather than true incrementalism, it may be a process of fine-tuning. The competition for and exercise of power by various members of an organization may also dampen the magnitude of changes. This dampening or moderating effect contributes to stability and the misleading appearance that incrementalism has been used. Another shortcoming to the incremental model is that experience may be a poor teacher (Levitt and March, 1988).

The Garbage Can Model   Decision making attempts to order the confusions of life. This assumes events and activities can be ordered into chains of ends and means. It also assumes that organizations are hierarchies in which higher levels have control over lower levels. A more confusing picture results when one actually observes an organization, however. Actions in one part of the organization may be only loosely connected to those in another. Pontiac clearly took a different path than Chevrolet in choosing the F-85 rather than the Corvair. Solutions may seem only vaguely related to problems, policies may not be implemented, and decision makers may wander in and out. The decision-making process has been described as a funny soccer game:

> Consider a round, sloped, multi-goal soccer field on which individuals play soccer. Many different people (but not everyone) can join the game (or leave it) at different times. Some people can throw balls into the game or remove them. Individuals, while they are in the game, try to kick whatever ball comes near them in the direction of goals they like and away from goals they wish to avoid. (March and Romelaer, 1976, p. 276)

To explain what happens in such situations, which they call "organized anarchies," Cohen, March, and Olsen (1972) viewed organizations not as places where the identification of problems leads to the creation of solutions but as garbage cans into which are poured problems, solutions, participants, and choice opportunities (or the **garbage can model**). How decisions are made is influenced by these four streams entering the garbage can, the amount of energy supplied by participants, organizational structure, and external institutions (Levitt and Nass, 1989). Cohen and co-workers (1972) identify three ways that decisions are made: by a choice resolving the problem, by a choice being made irrespective of its applicability to a problem, or by a problem attaching to a new choice.

Working with a computer simulation that manipulated many of these variables, Cohen, March, and Olsen concluded that the first approach, choices resolving problems, is the least likely to occur (even though it is the model most often used in decision-making literature). The other two approaches are both used with greater frequency, even though they do not resolve problems. The authors reached other conclusions as well. The decision-making process is sensitive to the number of decisions in the garbage can (the more there are, the less resolution will occur) and the variables modeled are highly interactive, meaning that different combinations of variables produce different results. Perhaps the most interesting findings are that important problems are more likely to be solved than unimportant ones, but important choices are somewhat less likely to actually resolve problems than are unimportant choices.

The Organizing Model   The third approach to organizational decision making is also a response to the rational actor approach; **the organizing model** emphasizes ambiguity in organizations and focuses specifically on the interpretation of events.

Many writers assume that organizations work under conditions of uncertainty (Duncan, 1972; Downey and Slocum, 1975; Manning, 1977) and ambiguity (Lerner, 1976). Weick used this as a jumping-off point and focused on organizational inputs, which he considered equivocal because they have multiple potential meanings. An example of an input with multiple potential meanings is a pun. As Weick (1979) sees it, "Organizational puns are everywhere. Car buyers frequently run into pun-like information when automobile makers raise their prices and at the same time give large discounts" (p. 171). Organizations then select meanings for the inputs, which now make sense because of how they are transformed during meaning selection.

The process of selection is influenced by two factors: enactment and retention. Enactment, the process of interpreting experience, can take place either by acting or by defining limitations to one's actions. Weick used playing charades (in which the individual acting out a phrase uses reactions of the other players to understand what he is acting out) as a metaphor for enactment in organizations: "People in organizations need to act to find out what they have done" (p. 152). Enactments, these interpretive definitions of reality, shape the meanings that are selected for equivocal inputs. When existing enactments are used to interpret new situations, they do so through the vehicle of retention, which is simply the individual's set of beliefs, or retained enactments. The result of these processes is that mental constructs are used to reduce equivocality and give meaning to experience.

Weick introduces one other factor: retrospect. The selection process can be seen as writing a history to make sense of what has been perceived as having occurred. As a result, decisions are not made so much as they are interpreted. The implications are clear: decision making is conservative because "selection is abbreviated, reflection is rare, and habitual interpretations dominate. Managers don't have much time for retrospection or for deliberated selection" (p. 204).

Aids to Decision Making

Managers can choose from among a large number of decision aids designed to address two kinds of problems associated with decision making: the uncertainty and complexity of environments. We saw both of these conditions present at General Motors with regard to the Corvair decision. Another approach is to reduce conflict in the decision-making process; for a discussion of methods for reducing conflict, see Chapter 4. Recently, a number of computer programs have been developed to facilitate planning and decision making; these are discussed in the feature "Software Planning and Decision-Making Aids."

FEATURE: *Software Planning and Decision-Making Aids*

By becoming easier to use . . . , microcomputers are slowly winning over even the most reluctant senior executives. And the spread of computer databases gives executives more reason to become computer literate. Access to more data, especially when desktop computers are "networked" to other desktops and to the data contained in head-office mainframes, helps managers to make better-informed decisions.

Simply getting better numbers to executives more quickly is a huge aid to planning and decision-making. . . . But better numbers are only half the decision-making battle. The other part is getting a tighter grip on subjective factors, . . . [and] business-school researchers are trying. . . .

. . . Decision technology, with a lot of help from desktop computers, allows an executive—or, better still, a company's senior management team—to recreate their own business as an on-line case study. Instead of asking their strategic planners "what if?" or, "how should we react to?" and then waiting days for an answer, executives can now model their business on a microcomputer and get answers in minutes.

According to Mr. Derek Bunn, chairman of London Business School's Decision Sciences Unit, the answers churned out by the computers are almost a by-product. The big gains from modeling come from building the model. To do that, an executive must clarify how he thinks his company works—and see if that internal model really responds to change as he thinks it will. . . .

Three main tools are now used to help managers think more clearly about their businesses.

Cognitive mapping is intended to bring some order to chaotic thoughts, and is used when decision makers have little or no idea of what decisions are needed to solve a particular problem. Cognitive mapping simply seeks to "make a map of thinking," symbolically representing all the ideas that the managers believe may be relevant to their current problem—in essence, a brainstorming approach. By structuring these ideas, the cognitive map attempts to show how various factors in a decision are connected.

. . . The cleverest programs can transform a cognitive map into a decision map, which is the next stage of analyzing decisions.

Decision mapping may be used to distill a cognitive map into a hierarchical set of objectives and alternatives. But if the management team already has a good idea of the objectives and decisions it wants to consider, decision mapping may be the starting point. The technique encourages executives to think about their business in terms of a number of linked parameters and objectives; for example, will a bigger sales force necessarily increase market share?

Decision mapping aims to establish simple algebraic links (e.g., sales effort equals the size of sales force times the number of selling hours per month). These are then manipulated by the computer. What makes this useful is that the links and feedback loops between various elements of even simple models can bring unexpected results. . . .

Microworlds is a term coined by a mathematician, Mr. Seymour Papert of MIT, to describe the simulation of a company's activities by a computer. Having constructed a computerized model of their business, executives can then "play" with it in varying circumstances, or microworlds, fiddling with strategic assumptions and searching for winning strategies. . . .

How do top executives react to such wizardry? Most decision technologists say that they get a frosty reception at first. But they are making some progress. Big multinationals . . . believe it does give them a competitive edge by increasing their senior executives' knowledge of how the company will respond to changes in its operations and its environment.

Others are less convinced. Some business strategists argue that, once executives are familiar with their microworld, they play with it much as they would with a video game: too quickly and with little time for reflection or discussion. Other research suggests that a disappointingly small proportion of executives are capable of applying the lessons learnt in the simulation to the real world—and vice versa. On the other side of the screen, some executives worry that, by reducing decision making and planning to a computer-aided routine, their creative insights and business flair may be stifled.

Undaunted, decision technologists say that two new developments will make their systems even better proxies for real life—and better tutors for executives. The first is the increasing integration of decision-analysis software with the sort of spreadsheet package that many young executives now use. . . .

The second development, still in its infancy, is the idea of "decision conferencing" rooms . . . [in which] decision makers sit around a circular table surrounded by screens . . . [onto which] can be projected slides, diagrams, and graphics generated by a computer model of the company and its markets.

Source: Adapted from "Decisions, Decisions," *The Economist,* July 22, 1989, pp. 64–65. Copyright © 1989 by The Economist Newspaper Limited. Reprinted with permission.

Aids to Dealing with Uncertainty

Decision makers may be uncertain about the nature of the problems they face, about when or whether those problems should be resolved, about available alternative actions and the availability of resources to take those actions, and about external events that may influence the situation. Control over uncertainty is always obtained at a cost. In selecting decision aids, managers have to decide which costs they can bear. The new Coke marketing decision by Coca-Cola was made amidst uncertainty and with high risk. The outcry from original formula loyalists, however, bailed the company out of a costly loss of customers and reversed the situation.

Some strategies are aimed, consciously or unconsciously, at reducing the perception of uncertainty; these techniques are based on the perception that uncertainty causes anxiety, which is undesirable. One way to reduce that anxiety is to ignore the uncertainty. Another way is to change the uncertainty to certainty by pretending the events are more certain than they really are. Uncertainty may be absorbed by passing information about the decision to various decision units. During transmission the information loses some of its uncertainty; as the information is passed along, it gains the attribution of certainty.

More active ways to handle uncertainty may take one of three general approaches: (1) modeling the uncertain aspects of the environment, (2) more actively generating alternatives, or (3) acquiring new information. Clearly, these approaches were not followed at General Motors in the Corvair case.

In modeling uncertainty, decision makers try to identify patterns and to fit events into simple models. A problem with this approach is that people tend to assign patterns to events even when they know the patterns are random. Decision makers should be wary of this tendency. A variety of techniques are available for dealing with time series data and trying to obtain from them some pattern of events (Chambers, Mulick, and Smith, 1971; Vroom and MacCrimmon, 1968). These methods are generally good for short-term forecasting but poor for long-term predictions.

Other ways to model uncertainty involve efforts to quantify it. One approach is to attempt to compute the amount of uncertainty in a situation in order to determine how much additional information must be collected or what credence to attach to a predicted outcome. Another approach is to externalize vague beliefs about what will occur by assigning subjective probabilities to alternatives and outcomes. Managers should be cautious, however, of the biases likely to occur with this technique. Too often we are too confident in our own beliefs and consequently give more weight to them than we should, ignoring other possible alternatives. This may well have been the case with Cole in the Corvair decision.

Three popular decision aids—brainstorming, the nominal group technique, and synectics—focus on the generation and testing of alternatives. **Brainstorming** is designed to generate creative decision alternatives by separating decision making into two phases: the idea generation phase and the evaluation and selection phase. During the first phase, brainstorming groups work under three rules: (1) ideas are freely expressed without consideration of their quality, (2) group members are encouraged to modify and combine previously stated ideas, and (3) no ideas are evaluated until all are stated. By delaying the evaluation of ideas, this technique opens group participants to generating more creative solutions to a problem. The research suggests that in generating unique and high-quality ideas, the pooled efforts of individuals working in isolation are superior to the ideas of brainstorming groups (Taylor, Berry, and Block, 1958).

The **nominal group technique** (Delbecq, Van de Ven, and Gustafson, 1975) is a more frequently used version of brainstorming. This method follows the first phase of brainstorming and then reaches judgment in three steps. The first is a secret ballot, in which individuals rank the alternatives that have been identified. Next, members hold a brief discussion of the preliminary vote. The last step is a final voting by secret ballot.

Another strategy aimed at generating creative alternatives is **synectics** (Gordon, 1961). A carefully selected and trained group views the problem situation in various ways until its members discover an innovative solution. To generate creative alternatives, the procedure forces participants to use analogies that make the familiar strange. Participants may have to play the role of some part of the problem (for example, a broken machine), or make direct analogies between the problem and nature, or make fantasy analogies; the goal is to break up familiar ways of thinking. The requirement that the synectic group be specially selected and trained is a limitation to this technique.

Uncertainty can also be reduced by acquiring and processing more information. Sometimes decisions are postponed until more information can be gathered—the presidential "blue ribbon commission" is an example. Two dangers imperil decision makers using this approach. The first is the possibility that participants will lose sight of the real goal—making a decision—and transform the process of gathering information into the goal. The second danger is that the decision maker will forget that he cannot gather enough information to reduce uncertainty completely. At some point, a decision must be made, whether all uncertainties are resolved or not. Setting that point—identifying how much information is enough—is a key decision-making skill.

The final approach to reducing uncertainty is to attempt to change adverse consequences. These strategies operate through two mechanisms: (1) they diffuse responsibility for the risky decision by reducing the potential loss or gain resulting from the decision, or (2) they build up a capacity to respond to potentially adverse consequences. An example of the former approach is the Japanese *ringi* system, in which a lower-level manager drafts a petition (*ringisho*) that is passed up the hierarchy to acquire the approval (using a *chop*, which is akin to the rubber signature stamp) of relevant people (Lincoln and McBride, 1987). An example of the latter strategy is the development of a contingency plan.

Aids to Dealing with Complexity

Decision makers find complexity a major barrier to effective decision making. To reduce that complexity, they adopt all manner of simplifying strategies and devices that prepackage information. The reader can evaluate whether the following approaches would have helped GM regarding the Corvair.

One approach is to model complexity either through the development of input-output models or the use of decomposable matrices. **Input-output models** (Leontief, 1966) represent the relationships of inputs and outputs in a system. These models have been used primarily to analyze production and sales patterns, but they could be useful with other complex organizational processes such as information flow. **Decomposable matrices** (Simon, 1976) break up complex structures into semi-independent components corresponding to functional parts. The underlying rationale here is that systems are constructed as hierarchies of levels in which the operation of a system at any level can be described in terms of its components. An example is viewing an organization as a set of barely connected departments rather than taking on the complexity of the whole.

Strategies for reducing perceptions of complexity recognize the limitations of humans as information processors. Two kinds of strategies are common. One is to search for information locally, either in the neighborhood of the problem or in the neighborhood of the current alternative. Such a search may derive from an overly simplistic perception of the complex decision environment (Cyert and March, 1963), and its failure may result in widening the search. The other mechanism for changing the perception of complexity is to apply incrementalism, as described previously in this chapter. This strategy attempts to reduce the demand placed on the decision maker by reducing the number of decision alternatives and potential consequences.

Complexity is also reduced by formulating alternatives. A promising approach is to relate previously unrelated elements of the decision problem. **Morphology** (Wills, Wilson, Manning and Hildebrandt, 1972) provides a structured procedure for systematically relating combinations of factors to form new alternatives. This approach requires the decision maker to identify key elements needed in a solution. Values of these elements are then identified and considered in all possible combinations. Large numbers of alternative solutions are identified, most worthless but a few possibly novel and promising.

Highly complex environments tax decision makers in their attempts to diagnose problems. As we discussed earlier, the way a problem is defined influences the types of alternative solutions considered and resources used. Decision strategies designed to help in problem definition are (1) determining the problem's boundaries by focusing on what is not a part of the problem, (2) examining changes in the decision environment or decision makers that may have precipitated the problem, (3) factoring complex problems into subproblems, and (4) focusing on the controllable components of a decision situation.

Complex decision environments tend to place extreme demands on the information processing capacity of the decision maker, thereby constraining the ability to make a decision. Thus decision makers try to reduce complexity through aggregating information. These strategies include "chunking" information into categories and using an optimal level of aggregation for a problem at hand. For example, in some cases the information may be too detailed for the problem (for example, store-by-store sales), and in other cases it may be too aggregated (for example, national sales). The use of reliable information is another strategy to reduce this kind of complexity. Managers learn, often by trial and error, what sources to rely on for information about particular kinds of problems.

Setting up appropriate communication networks and allowing for participation are further strategies for handling the demands of information processing in complex decision situations. The most formally developed such strategy is the **Delphi technique** (Dalkey, 1969), which employs interaction among decision makers but attempts to prevent forceful group members from dominating discussion and stifling the contributions of others. This technique isolates participants in the decision-making process from one another and presents them with a series of questionnaires soliciting their opinions and the bases for those opinions. After each round of questionnaires is completed, information from participants is consolidated and circulated anonymously to each group member. This procedure is widely used in many contexts. Figure 7.6 summarizes the advantages and disadvantages of the Delphi technique.

There are strategies for reducing complexity through aggregating preferences (MacCrimmon, 1973). When decision makers make large numbers of similar decisions, it is possible to build a simple statistical model of their behavior. For example, personnel selection can use individual characteristics of job candidates (such as education and experience) as inputs and ratings as outcomes.

Linear equations can be developed to model the decision maker's behavior. As it turns out, on subsequent decision-making occasions the linear models often make better decisions than the decision makers. This approach is used in many situations (Slovic and Lichtenstein, 1971). A commonly used

FIGURE 7.6
Advantages and Disadvantages of the Delphi Technique

Advantages	Disadvantages
■ Allows group decision making over long distances.	■ A complex method requiring a trained coordinator.
■ Reduces social pressure and conflict, allowing decision making to proceed without undue influence from one or more members.	■ A slow method.
■ Makes for clear decisions.	■ Consensus is not always the best decision.
■ Promotes the generation of more possible solutions and sometimes better-quality solutions.	■ Costly to administer a series of questionnaires.
	■ Results are not known, which may lower commitment.
	■ No sense of teamwork.

version of the approach is called **policy capturing** because it captures whatever policy the decision maker adheres to. Approaches that model decision-maker behavior focus on what decision makers do. One could change the model slightly and ask decision makers their preferences, using these figures to derive statistical models of choice.

An interesting group of voting procedures designed to reduce complexity through aggregation of preferences is called SPAN (MacKinnon and MacKinnon, 1969). In SPAN, each member of a decision-making group is given a fixed number of votes that he may allocate directly to alternatives or to other voters. The rationale is that each member should allocate votes to other members when he has limited knowledge and can identify experts. The process is continued until all votes are allocated to alternatives.

Some organizational decisions are of the make-or-break variety, such as the development of new products or the Eastern Airlines negotiations with a striking labor force in 1989. These are "tough" decisions according to Paul C. Nutt (1989). When organizational decision makers are faced with these decisions, they may want to consider Nutt's guidelines as well as avoid the frequent traps associated with these critical decisions. Nutt suggested a process of decision making to uncover and overcome these pitfalls by exploring and assessing options, experimenting, and searching for missed opportunities. The feature "Tough Decisions" reproduces one of the five cases that Nutt used to illustrate tough decisions that have turned into debacles.

FEATURE: *Tough Decisions*

ITT's Paper Pulp Plant. In the late 1970s, International Telephone and Telegraph (ITT) built a plant in the Province of Quebec to produce high-grade paper pulp. The opportunity to acquire logging rights in Quebec for an area nearly the size of the state of Tennessee made the decision to build the plant seem low risk. Although revenue estimates were modest, the value of the timber rights seemed substantial. The Province of Quebec offered these rights at a large discount in the hope of increasing employment. The shrinking of harvestable timber stands implied a shrinkage of the supply of high-grade paper pulp to ITT decision makers. The continued growth and demand for this product seemed a reasonable assumption. Decisions to close high-grade paper pulp plants in Canada and Scandinavia were noted and used to justify the prospect of strong markets in both North America and Europe.

The chief executive officer (CEO) of ITT first became aware of plans for the pulp plant at the close of a board meeting. The size of the timber stand attracted his attention. Participants left the meeting thinking that the project had been approved. Studies and negotiations followed in which estimates of the plant's potential were made. Doubts about market and financing were uncovered by divisional executives but were not offered to the CEO, in the belief that he had approved the project and would not want to hear negative information at this point. In 1971 the decision was announced. The plant was to be one of three that ITT would build to process timber obtained from the logging rights negotiated with Quebec.

Problems plagued plant operation from the outset. The market was soft; long-term sales contracts were impossible because of a glut of high-grade pulp on the market. Firms that exited this market signaled a problem, not an opportunity. Labor difficulties arose. The plant was located in a foreign country with a history of militant unions and fierce nationalistic pride. ITT mismanaged Canadian workers by failing to understand these instincts. ITT's political acts in Chile during the period further riled the workers by giving the impression that management could not be trusted. The plant was completed six months late and $60 million over budget, in part because ITT had problems dealing with the complex pollution-control devices required by Canadian law. Because of the harsh climate and short growing season, the timber stands were made up of low-yield, slow-growing trees.

The operation costs for the plant were driven up by labor disputes made worse by language incompatibility between the French-speaking union members and English-speaking managers. Logging costs increased because of a shortage of loggers to meet production schedules. Logs had to be obtained from other areas, adding transportation expenditures to the mounting costs. Production problems stemmed from ice embedded in the bark of trees, which reduced the quality of the pulp. Because the plant was designed with a production-line approach, problems in one area (for example, ice removal) shut down large segments of the production process. Only 13 percent of the plant's capacity was achieved after the first year of operation. After five years, the plant managed to average just 75,000 tons of the projected annual volume of 375,000 tons, all of it low-grade pulp. Expensive advertising designed to dramatize the value of ITT's pulp for use in products such as rayon proved futile. The plant was closed in 1979 with a pretax loss of $200 million.

The hidden conflict that often occurs in firms emerges to a degree in the ITT paper plant decision. The CEO of ITT made an off-the-cuff remark at a board meeting that was interpreted as approval of the project. Subsequent doubts were not expressed. As the old story goes, the messenger bearing bad news is often executed. In such a situation, both supervisor and subordinate can come to view each other as incompetent, which also leads to conflict. Ambiguity in the decision was dismissed on the assumption that the timber could be processed to produce high-quality pulp and to fill a market void. When key line managers saw the folly of their earlier assumptions, they became anxious but saw no way to express their concerns. Uncertainty was dismissed on the assumption that a strong prospect for sales was signaled by the market exit of European firms when the reverse was true. No one attempted to explore the uncertainty in the paper pulp market or to make cost estimates with both favorable and unfavorable assumptions about factors that influence cost. Again, the key characteristics of a tough decision appear to have been ignored.

Source: Adapted from Paul C. Nutt, *Making Tough Decisions* (San Francisco: Jossey-Bass, 1989), pp. 23–25. Copyright © 1989 by Jossey-Bass, Inc. Reprinted by permission of Jossey-Bass, Inc.

SUMMARY

General Motors' decision to produce the Corvair illustrated many of the issues surrounding individual, group, and organizational decision making. The propensity of groups to make more risky decisions was clearly at issue in the Corvair case. And GM's executives appeared to be suffering from several symptoms of groupthink, which got in the way of their making effective decisions.

In a broad sense, decision making is choice behavior in the face of alternatives. Choices, however, may have to be made in situations in which people differ in their values and goals, situations characterized by conflict. In a very real sense, decision making is what managing is all about: making and implementing choices for ourselves and our employees.

There are a number of models of individual decision making. The rational view requires too perfect knowledge by the decision maker of the problem, the alternatives, and the probabilities of those alternatives to be an accurate portrayal of what goes on in decision making. The administrative model accepts the imperfections of decisions, introducing the notions of bounded rationality and satisficing, or settling for a less-than-perfect alternative. Judgment models focus on how people depart from probability theory in forming judgments at each stage in the decision process.

Decision making is influenced not only by the strategies adopted by decision makers but also by their personalities, attitudes, and values. The four characteristics of decision makers given the most attention are perceptual ability, information capacity, aspiration level, and risk-taking propensity. Prior experience affects how decision makers will meet new problems.

Group decision making focuses on the processes through which people work together to solve problems, rather than the models they may use to assess alternative choices. One important issue in group problem solving is the use of participation. Often, groups are no better problem solvers than their best members, but participation provides other benefits beside solving problems. It often helps participants to understand the problem better and commits them to solutions. The Vroom and Jago model of group decision making focuses on identifying when participation is appropriate and when it is not.

Two other aspects of group decision making have received a good deal of attention. Groups sometimes make riskier decisions than individuals. Several theories have been advanced to explain this shift toward risk, as well as the shift toward conservatism that has also been observed. A second frequently observed aspect of group decision making is groupthink, an extreme form of conformity that occurs when members of groups develop shared illusions and related norms that interfere with critical thinking and reality testing. Several strategies may be employed to reduce groupthink.

Organizational values, norms, and ideologies significantly influence problem finding and decision making, but little is known about how. There are three major approaches to organizational decision making. The first is the incremental approach: organizations change their past policies and activities only a little. The garbage can approach to decision making conceptualizes organizations as garbage cans into which are poured problems, solutions, participants, and choice opportunities. In this view, problems are rarely resolved and solutions often go in search of problems. The third approach to organizational decision making emphasizes the role of equivocality in organizations and focuses on how events are interpreted. The problem for the decision maker is to attach meaning to equivocal inputs; decision making becomes a matter of interpreting.

A large number of decision aids are used to enhance decision quality amidst uncertainty and complexity. Most popular among decision aids are techniques like brainstorming, the nominal group technique, and the Delphi method. Modeling is also popular.

MANAGERIAL INSIGHT

To: *Student Managers*
From: *Veteran Manager*
Subject: *Decision Making*

When you graduate from school and head for your first organizational job as a real manager, you will probably be rubbing your hands in anticipation over your role as decision maker. Think about how prepared you will be: you will have all the analytical tools that are worth having, a personal computer with enough power to move mountains, and a knowledge from this course of all the secrets of how organizations decide things. Even though you know you will not have perfect information, you will know how to assess risks under uncertainty and find the optimum course. You will definitely be ready to make Big Decisions.

If you get any. Chances are, you won't for a while.

What you will get, more likely, are opportunities to make very small incremental decisions and to help influence somewhat larger incremental decisions. The point is that most decisions in organizations are not the bet-your-company type, but are more mundane. The opportunities to set grand strategies do not come along every day. What do come along every day are decisions of lesser moment that go into the larger fabric of your organization.

I believe this is true even in smaller companies, though to a lesser degree than in larger ones.

The value of studying about how an organization makes its decisions lies in the clues it gives you for developing influence strategies. Most important, you want to study how your boss makes decisions, because she presumably has learned to fit her decision-making style into the company's culture and therefore is worth emulating to some degree.

Some bosses make decisions on numbers, some on persuasive arguments. Some like to have a staff member play devil's advocate and take a deliberately contrary point of view for the sake of teasing out the weaknesses of the opposing position. Others like to see the alternatives vetted and arrayed like soldiers standing for inspection. Some love to engage with staff in free-swinging dialogue that may resemble a parliamentary debate. Still others tend to rely more on hunches and intuition.

Learning the pattern your boss follows in a given type of situation— and most bosses will use more than one method of arriving at a decision— will enable you to be most effective at influencing the decision.

This skill, if learned well, should prepare you more thoroughly for the day when you may have the boss's responsibility and may be expected to make the decision she is making now.

REVIEW QUESTIONS

1. What does the Corvair case suggest about the potential contribution of socialization to groupthink?

2. What assumptions underlie the rational model of decision making? Are these assumptions reasonable in the real world?

3. What assumptions underlie the administrative model of decision making?

4. Can Etzioni's objections to the rational model of decision making be applied to the administrative model as well?

5. According to the work on selective attention, what is characteristic of the kinds of cues people pay attention to?

6. Under what circumstances, according to Connolly, is incrementalism an appropriate strategy?

7. What tendency undercuts the effectiveness of incrementalism? What can be done to overcome this tendency?

8. Habits can impair the individual's capacity to make good decisions, an example of functional fixedness. Why is that true? Is the same true of organizations?

9. Do groups make better decisions than individuals? If not, are there any advantages to group decision making?

10. What are the five decision-making styles in the Vroom and Yetton and Vroom and Jago models? Which method do these writers assert is superior?

11. Is groupthink more likely to occur in a weekly production meeting or in a crisis meeting? Why?

12. How do organizational values, norms, and ideologies influence problem definition and the determination of who makes the decision?

13. What disadvantage of incrementalism does Etzioni suggest that his decision-making method, called mixed scanning, replaces?

14. What two problem-solving outcomes do March et al. suggest are the most frequent events when they describe their garbage can model of decision making?

15. How, according to Weick, do individuals attempt to interpret the world around them?

16. Name three techniques for reducing uncertainty in making decisions.

REFERENCES

Allison, G. T. (1969). Conceptual models and the Cuban missile crises. *American Political Science Review* 63:689–718.

Allison, G. T. (1971). *Essence of Decision.* Boston: Little, Brown.

Anderson, P. A. (1983). Decision making by objection and the Cuban Missile Crisis. *Administrative Science Quarterly* 28:201–222.

Baloff, N., and Doherty, E. M. (1989). Potential pitfalls in employee participation. *Organizational Dynamics* 17:51–62.

Beyer, J. M. (1981). Ideologies, values, and decision making in organizations. In P. C. Nystrom and W. H. Starbuck (eds.), *Handbook of Organizational Design*, vol. 2. London: Oxford University Press, pp. 166–202.

Blankenship, L. V., and Miles, R. E. (1968). Organizational structure and managerial decision behavior. *Administrative Science Quarterly* 13:106–120.

Block, J., and Peterson, P. (1955). Some personality correlates of confidence, caution, and speed in decision situation. *Journal of Personality and Social Psychology* 51:34–41.

Bowen, M. G. (1987). The escalation phenomenon reconsidered: Decision dilemmas or decision errors. *Academy of Management Review* 12:52–66.

Chambers, J. C., Mulick, S. K., and Smith, D. D. (1971). How to choose the right forecasting technique. *Harvard Business Review* 49:45–74.

Cohen, M. D., March, J. G., and Olsen, J. P. (1972). Garbage can model of organizational choice. *Administrative Science Quarterly* 45–74:1–25.

Connolly, T. (1977). Information processing and decision making in organizations. In B. Staw and G. Salancik (ed.), *New Directions in Organizational Behavior*. Chicago: St. Clair, pp. 205–243.

Connolly, T. (1988). Hedge-clipping, tree-felling, and the management of ambiguity: The need for new images of decision making. In L. R. Pondy, R. J. Boland, Jr., and H. Thomas (eds.), *Managing Ambiguity and Change*. New York: Wiley, pp. 37–50.

Connolly, T., and Thorn, B. K. (1987). Predecisional information acquisition: Effects of task variables on suboptimal search strategies. *Organizational Behavior and Human Decision Processes* 39:397–416.

Cosier, R. A., and Schwenk, C. R. (1990). Agreement and thinking alike: Ingredients for poor decisions. *Academy of Management Executive* 4:69–74.

Cowan, David A. (1986). Developing a process model of problem recognition. *Academy of Management Review* 11:763–776.

Cyert, R. M., Dill, W. R., and March, J. G. (1967). The role of expectations in business decision making. In M. Alexis and C. Z. Wilson (eds.), *Organizational Decision Making*. Englewood Cliffs, NJ: Prentice-Hall, pp. 134–147.

Cyert, R., and March, J. G. (1963). *A Behavioral Theory of the Firm*. Englewood Cliffs, NJ: Prentice-Hall.

Dalkey, N. (1969). *The Delphi Method: An Experimental Study of Group Opinion*. Santa Monica, CA: RAND.

Delbecq, A., Van de Ven, A., and Gustafson, D. (1975). *Group Techniques for Program Planning*. Glenview, IL: Scott, Foresman.

Donaldson, G., and Lorsch, J. W. (1983). *Decision Making at the Top*. New York: Basic Books.

Downey, H. K., and Slocum, J. W. (1975). Uncertainty: Measures, research, and sources of variation. *Academy of Management Journal* 18:562–578.

Duncan, R. B. (1972). The characteristics of organizational environments and perceived environmental uncertainty. *Administrative Science Quarterly* 17:313–327.

Dunker, K. (1944–1945). On problem solving. *Psychological Monographs* 58:1–111.

Einhorn, H., and Hogarth, R. M. (1975). Unit weighing schemes for decision making. *OBHP*, pp. 171–192.

Einhorn, J. J., and Hogarth, R. M. (1981). Behavioral decision theory: Processes of judgment and choice. In L. W. Porter and M. Rosenzweig (eds.), *Annual Review of Psychology* 52:53–88.

Etzioni, A. (1989). Humble decision making. *Harvard Business Review*, pp. 122–126.

Frankenstein, J., and Chao, C. N. (1988). Decision-making in the Chinese foreign trade administration: A preliminary survey. *Columbia Journal of World Business* 23:35–40.

Feldman, M., and March, J. G. (1981). Organizational communication systems and the decision process. *Management Science* 17:1383–1396.

Gordon, W. J. J. (1961). *Synectics*. New York: Harper & Row.

Grandori, A. (1984). A prescriptive contingency view of organizational decision making. *Administrative Science Quarterly* 29:192–209.

Heller, F. A., and Yukl, G. (1969). Participation, managerial decision-making, and situational variables. *O.B.H.P.* 4:227–241.

Hill, W. (1982). Group versus individual performance: Are N+1 heads better than one. *Psychological Bulletin*, pp. 517–539.

Jago, A. (1981) An assessment of the deemed appropriateness of participative decision making for high and low hierarchical levels. *Human Relations* 34:379–396.

Janis, I. L. (1972). *Victims of Groupthink: A Psychological Study of Foreign-Policy Decisions and Fiascos*. Boston: Houghton Mifflin.

Janis, I. L. (1989). *Crucial Decisions: Leadership in Policy Making and Crisis Management*. New York: Free Press.

Kogan, N., and Wallach, M. A. (1967). Group risk taking as a function of members' anxiety and defensiveness. *Journal of Personality* 35:50–63.

Koopman, P. L., Drenth, P. J., Bus, F. B. M., Kruyswijk, A. J., and Wierdsma, H. M. (1981). Content process and the effects of participative decision making on the shop floor. *Human Relations* 34:657–676.

Kotter, J. (1982). *The General Managers*. New York: Free Press.

Krishna, R. (1974). Democratic participation in decision making by employees in an American corporation. *Academy of Management Journal* 17:339–347.

Kurke, L. B., and Aldrich, H. C. (1983). Mintzberg was right. A replication and extension of managerial work. *Management Science* 29:975–984.

Latane, B., Williams, K., and Harkins, S. (1979). Many hands make light the work: The causes and consequences of social loading. *Journal of Personality and Social Psychology* 37:822–832.

Latham, G. P., Erez, M., and Locke, E. A. (1988). Resolving scientific disputes by the joint design of crucial experiments by the antagonists: Application to the Erez-Latham dispute regarding participation in goal setting. *Journal of Applied Psychology* 73:753–772.

Laughlin, P. R., and Barth, J. M. (1981). Group-to-individual and individual-to-group problem-solving transfer. *Journal of Personality and Social Psychology* 41:1081–1093.

Leontief, W. (1966). *Input-Output Economics*. Oxford: Oxford University Press.

Lerner, A. W. (1976). On ambiguity and decision maker relations in organizations. Unpublished manuscript. Lehman College, City University of New York.

Levitt, B., and March, J. G. (1988). Organizational learning. In *Annual Review of Sociology*. Palo Alto, CA: Annual Reviews 14:319–340.

Levitt, B., and Nass, C. (1989). The lid on the garbage can: Institutional constraints on decision making in the technical core of college-text publishers. *Administrative Science Quarterly* 34:190–207.

Lincoln, J. R. (1989). Employee work attitudes and management practice in the U.S. and Japan. *California Monthly Review* 32:89–106.

Lincoln, J. R., and McBride, K. (1987). Japanese industrial organizations in comparative perspective. *Annual Review of Sociology* 13:289–334.

Lindblom, C. E. (1959). The science of "muddling through." *Public Administration Review* 19:79–88.

Lindblom, C. E. (1965). *The Intelligence of Democracy*. New York: Macmillan.

Lindblom, C. E., and Cohen, D. K. (1979). *Usable Knowledge: Social Science and Problem Solving*. New Haven: Yale University Press.

Locke, E. A., and Schweiger, D. M. (1979). Participation in decision making: One more look. In B. Staw (ed.), *Research in Organizational Behavior*, vol. 1. Greenwich, CT: JAI Press.

Locke, E. A., Schweiger, D. M., and Latham, G. P. (1986). Participation in decision making: When should it be used? *Organizational Dynamics* 14 (Winter): 65–79.

Lounaman, P. H., and March, J. G. (1987). Adaptive coordination of a learning team. *Management Science* 33:107–123.

McCall, M. W., Jr., and Kaplan, R. E. (1985). *Whatever It Takes: Decision Makers at Work*. Englewood Cliffs, NJ: Prentice-Hall.

MacCrimmon, M. K. (1973). An overview of multiple objective decision making. In J. L. Cochrane and M. Zeleny (eds.), *Multiple Criteria Decision Making*. Columbia, SC: University of South Carolina Press, pp. 18–44.

MacCrimmon, K., and Taylor, R. (1976). Decision making and problem solving. In M. D. Dunnettee (ed.), *Handbook of Industrial and Organizational Psychology*. Chicago: Rand McNally, pp. 1397–1453.

MacKinnon, W. J., and MacKinnon, M. J. (1969). Computers: The decisional design and cyclic computation of SPAN. *Behavioral Science* 14:244–277.

Maier, N. R. F. (1967). Assets and liabilities in group problem solving: The need for an integrative function. *Psychological Review* 74:239–249.

Manning, P. K. (1977). *Police Work: The Social Organization of Policing*. Cambridge, MA: MIT Press.

March, J. G. (1978). Bounded rationality, ambiguity, and the engineering of choice. *Bell Journal of Economics* Autumn: 587–608.

March, J. G., and Simon, H. A. (1958). *Organizations*. New York: Wiley.

March, J. G., and Romelaer, P. J. (1976). Position and presence in the drift of decisions. In V. G. March and J. P. Olsen (eds)., *Ambiguity and Choice in Organizations.* Bergen: Universitetsforlagel.

Miller, K. I., and Monje, P. R. (1986). Participation, satisfaction, and productivity: A meta analytic review. *Academy of Management Journal* 29:727–753.

Mintzberg, H. (1973). *The Nature of Managerial Work.* New York: Harper & Row.

Newell, A., and Simon, H. A. (1972). *Human Problem Solving.* Englewood Cliffs, NJ: Prentice-Hall.

North, D. M. (1987). Military accident rates parallel 1986's low levels. *Aviation Week and Space Technology,* June 8, pp. 66–70.

Nutt, P. C. (1976). Models for decision making in organizations and some contextual variables which stipulate optimal use. *Academy of Management Review* 1:94–98.

Nutt, P. C. (1989). Types of organizational decision processes. *Administrative Science Quarterly* 29:414–450.

O'Reilly, C. A. (1982). Variations in decision makers' use of information sources. The impact of quality and accessibility of information. *Academy of Management Journal* 25: 756–771.

O'Reilly, C. A., Chatman, J. A., and Anderson, J. C. (1987). Message flow and decision making. In F. M. Jablin, L. L. Putnam, K. H. Roberts, and L. W. Porter (eds.), *Handbook of Organizational Communication.* Beverly Hills, CA: Sage, pp. 600–623.

Pinfield, L. T. (1986) A field evaluation of perspective on organizational decision making. *Administrative Science Quarterly* 31:365–388.

Roberts, K. H., and Gargano, G. (1989). Managing a high reliability organization: A case for interdependence. In M. A. Von Glinow and S. Mohrman (eds.), *Managing Complexity in High Technology Organizations: Systems and People.* New York: Oxford University Press.

Rohrbaugh, J. (1981). Improving the quality of group judgment: Social judgment analysis and the nominal group technique. *Organizational Behavior and Human Performance* 28:272–288.

Ronen, S. (1986). *Comparative and Multinational Management.* New York: Wiley.

Sashkin, M. (1976). Changing towards participative management approaches: A model and methods. *Academy of Management Review* 1:75–86.

Schroeder, H. M., Driver, M. H., and Streufert, S. (1965). *Information Processing Systems in Individuals and Groups.* New York: Holt, Rinehart and Winston.

Shrivastava, P. (1987). *Bhopal: Anatomy of a Crisis.* Cambridge, MA: Ballinger.

Simon, H. A. (1972). Themes of bounded rationality. In C. B. McGuire and R. Radner (eds.), *Decision and Organization.* Amsterdam: Elsevier North-Holland.

Simon, H. A. (1976). *Administrative Behavior: A Study of Decision Making Processes in Administrative Organizations,* 3rd ed. New York: Free Press.

Slovic, P., and Lichtenstein, S. (1971). Comparison of Bayesian and regression approaches to the study of information processing in judgment. *Organizational Behavior and Human Performance* 6:649–749.

Staw, B. M. (1976). Knee-deep in the Big Muddy: A study of escalating commitment to a chosen course of action. *Organizational Behavior and Human Performance* 16:27–45.

Staw, B. M. (1981). The escalation of commitment to a course of action. *American Management Review* 6:577–587.

Staw, B. M., and Boettger, R. (1990). Task revision as a form of work performance. *Academy of Management Journal* 33:534–559.

Staw, B. M., and Fox, F. V. (1977). Escalation: The determinants of commitment to a chosen course of action. *Human Relations* 30:431–450.

Staw, B. M., and Ross, J. (1978). Commitment to a policy decision: A multitheoretical perspective. *Administrative Science Quarterly* 20:546–558.

Steiner, I. D. (1972). *Group Process and Productivity*. New York: Academic Press.

Stoner, J. A. F. (1961). A comparison of individual and group decisions involving risk. Unpublished master's thesis. School of Industrial Management, MIT.

Stoner, J. A. (1968). Risky and cautious shifts in group decisions: The influence of widely held beliefs. *Journal of Experimental Social Psychology* 4:422–459.

Strauss, G. (1982). Workers' participation in management: An international perspective. In B. M. Staw and L. L. Cummings (eds.), *Research in Organizational Behavior*. Greenwich, CT: JAI Press, pp. 173–265.

Taylor, R. N. (1975). Perception of problem constraints. *Management Science* 22:22–29.

Taylor, D. W., Berry, P. C., and Block, C. H. (1958). Does group participation when using brainstorming facilitate or inhibit creative thinking? *Administrative Science Quarterly* 3:23–47.

Thompson, J. D. (1967). *Organizations in Action*. New York: McGraw-Hill.

Trevino, K. E. (1986). Ethical decision-making in organizations: A person-situation interactionist model. *Academy of Management Review* 11:601–617.

Ungson, G. R., Braunstein, D. N., and Hall, P. D. (1981). Managerial information processing: A research review. *Administrative Science Quarterly* 26:116–134.

Vroom, V. H., and Jago, A. G. (1987). *The New Leadership: Managing Participation in Organizations*. Englewood Cliffs, NJ: Prentice-Hall.

Vroom, V. H., and MacCrimmon, K. (1968). Toward a stochastic model of managerial careers. *Administrative Science Quarterly* 13:26–46.

Vroom, V. H., and Yetton, P. W. (1973). *Leadership and Decision Making*. Pittsburgh: University of Pittsburgh Press.

Wagner, J. A., and Gooding, R. Z. (1987). Shared influence and organizational behavior: A moderator meta-analysis of situational variables expected to moderate participation-outcome relationships. *Academy of Management Journal* 30:524–541.

Weick, K. E. (1979). *The Social Psychology of Organizations*. Reading, MA: Addison-Wesley.

White, S. E., Dittrich, J. E., and Lang, J. R. (1980). The effects of group decision making process and problem-situation complexity on implementation attempts. *Administrative Science Quarterly* 25:428–440.

Whyte, G. (1989). Groupthink reconsidered. *Academy of Management Review* 14:40–56.

How We Work Through Others

Leadership: Showing the Way to Others

CHAPTER OVERVIEW

This chapter defines leadership, viewing it as a special aspect of management, addresses the question of whether leadership matters, examines several theoretical approaches to leadership from those focusing on personality to those focusing on situations, and discusses various leadership training programs.

THEME CASE

"Government Leadership: An Assistant Secretary of Commerce" relates Elsa Porter's stance against the traditional autocratic style of leadership often associated with government settings, and her style of encouraging employee participation, building trust, and satisfying individual needs. In short, her style of leadership focuses on getting things done through people.

CHAPTER OUTLINE

- Why Study Leadership?
- What Is Leadership?
- The Study of Leadership
- Theoretical Approaches to Leadership
- Environmental and Organizational Influences on Leadership
- Leadership Training
- Summary
- Managerial Insight

KEY DEFINITIONS

Leadership   interaction amongst members of a group in which the leader acts as an agent of change.

Headship   the nominal or hierarchical top position in a group.

Charisma   that quality possessed by leaders who, by the force of their personal abilities, have extraordinary influences on their followers.

Additional Terms

Manager roles: figurehead, leader, liaison, monitor, disseminator, spokesperson, entrepreneur, disturbance handler, resource allocator, negotiator
Demands, constraints, choices

Instrumental, or task, leader
Socioemotional leader
Idiosyncrasy credits
Gamesman
Hawthorne effect
Consideration
Initiating structure
Contingency theories
Situational variables
Path-goal theory
Locus of control
Subordinate maturity
Cognitive theories
Managerial grid
Leader match
Telos
Center for Creative Leadership

GOVERNMENT LEADERSHIP:
AN ASSISTANT SECRETARY OF COMMERCE

Most of the federal executives who are jungle fighters and gamesmen are political appointees; a few are successful civil servants. The jungle fighters conquer turf and build baronies with their henchmen. Rivals are cut up and out by office intrigue and well-placed leaks. The gamesmen play for the limelight and headlines. They find young, ambitious comers to join an entrepreneurial team, in search of issues that can be leveraged into power. The majority of federal executives who are institutional loyalists and craftsmen have moved up the ranks of the civil service. At best, they administer the rules fairly and craft the often ambiguous policy directives from Congress so they are workable. They make the system function, but surrounded by the jungle fighters and gamesmen, they avoid unnecessary risks.

. . . Elsa Porter is an institutional loyalist with dominating tendencies kept under control. Her achievement has been to demonstrate how to bring out the best in the civil service. As the first woman to become an assistant secretary for administration during the Carter presidency, she struggled at the Commerce Department against the irrationality of regulations, the hopelessness of career civil servants, and the power games of those at the top. . . .

. . . Since a new administration generally arrives fresh from a campaign against the bureaucracy, with promises to cut costs and red tape, political appointees of all ideological persuasions take pride in cracking the whip. The assumption is that the civil service is a recalcitrant mule that must be bribed and beaten with carrots and sticks. . . .

Elsa Porter maintains that management will bring out the best in civil servants only by respecting their best motives and developing trust by satisfying their needs for security, equity, participation, and individual development. Beneath the disillusionment, most of the civil servants we have interviewed are motivated by a combination of careerism and craftsmanship, with the desire to serve the public. Porter points out that the system now brings out the worst in both managers and employees, fear and obstinacy. Mechanistic management-control systems and rigid hierarchies combine to cause insecurity, inequity, and human stagnation. She believes that the macho power drives of managers are reinforced by rewards and hierarchy whereas employees on a lower level, in uniform, routinized jobs do not even know how their small piece of fragmented work furthers the public good. She argues that the modern federal employee, concerned with career and increasingly with the new goals of "self-development," resents dead-end jobs, disrespectful management, and intellectually barren tasks. . . .

As employees defend themselves against their bosses and the personnel system, it becomes increasingly difficult to manage them and attempts to tighten up intensify resistance. Even the best-intentioned employees will do little or nothing to put pressure on their most unproductive colleagues, because no one wants to make enemies, and the rewards for cooperation are meager.

A hierarchical controlling structure of work may be efficient provided there is a clearly measurable product, a stable market, submissive employees, and assembly-line technology. But this is a poor organization for most government work, which requires high levels of flexibility and interdependency with highly educated employees capable of constructive criticism. Since the output of work is so often service, where payment is not negotiated with a customer, its value cannot be measured quantitatively but requires qualitative analysis. . . . In many areas, especially administration, which includes such functions as personnel policy, budgeting, financial auditing, and accounting for the whole department, Porter found that employees tended to define service in terms of policing only, rather than also helping. Although it is easier and safer to measure performance as a policeman than as a helper, advances in "productivity" may also end up undermining policy.

For example, the Carter administration was committed to helping minority business, partly through granting government contracts. Commerce Department auditors found that many of the black or Hispanic business people, inexperienced about government contracts, made mistakes in their financial systems. The auditors could either help them to avoid problems or wait to point an accusing finger. Helping was risky; the auditor lost independence and might be blamed for errors. Also, how do you measure a "help" that avoids a problem? Infractions are "cleaner," easier to count, and the more you find, the higher the "policeman's" productivity (output per manhour) as is measured by economists.

Elsa Porter decided this made no sense. She saw the same problem of policing vs. service at the root of problems between government and business. If government auditors and regulators were to work cooperatively with other sectors, they needed the confidence that they would be supported in their own organization. At age fifty, after twenty years in the federal bureaucracy, struggling against irrationality and male chauvinism, she had not lost a sense of indignation and mission. She was determined to push the limits of the system to create a true civil service.

Her predecessors had the reputation of [being] intimidating managers who used their power over the budget, space, and resources to dominate the department. Porter inherited ten senior civil servants, tough and skeptical men who ran the offices in her domain, and who were used to being dominated rather than led.

One described his first meeting with Porter: "This little blond blue-eyed person introduced herself and I felt like running to defend her. I felt like saying, 'Listen you guys, leave her alone.' But she didn't need it." Her subordinates learned that while she did not like to push people around, she had her own agenda.

In attempting to transform her organization of more than 600 employees, to develop trust and greater participation in management, Porter was moving against the tide of the Carter administration, presenting a model of leadership in contrast to most of her superiors. For the first two years, Under Secretary Sidney Harman was an ally, but he was becoming angry and frustrated by the job. The Secretary was Juanita Kreps, a brilliant and charming economist, formerly dean at Duke University's School of Business and a member of corporate boards on which she represented women and stood for social responsibility. Regal, insecure as a manager, she was made nervous by the missionary zeal of Harman and Porter and leaned on aides who flattered her and appeared more protective.

When Porter's attempts to improve management began to bear fruit, she and I reported to Kreps who listened graciously and said, "This seems to me very precious, and I mean that in both senses of the word." That was the end of her response. Porter was disappointed, but continued with her program; however, it was only after Kreps had left the department that she again publicly reported on the results.

Porter had begun her campaign to change management style by inviting me to lead a monthly seminar on human development with the office directors subordinate to her. We explored theories and new models of management. . . . Porter took her team on trips to see new technology at IBM and to open themselves to new ideas.

Impatient to change the cautious, anxious bureaucrats, she fed them "third-wave" books and articles. Porter's early speeches were saved from being purely sermons only by her insistence on paying attention to the technical aspects of personnel and financial management, to analyze how control systems determine human relationships.

I worried that she was out of touch with civil servants when she told a crowd of personnel specialists that while they were going through a period of change in how they evaluated people and work, "evolutionary changes were taking place in the human species." She said, "I really think you need to see how big the issues are, how crucial they are to human survival and how important the role you play is to the survival of the species. We are moving to the dream of human maturity and human potential. We are, in this country, and in some of the other industrial countries, I believe, moving into the S-curve of change, the possibility of realizing that potential. We are moving to the end of a millennium. We are approaching the dawn of a new age and we have within ourselves an enormous power either to cross that threshold into the new age or go close the doors of history upon people, upon civilization as we know it. Just think of the power we have to destroy ourselves or to remake ourselves and to rekindle the life that sustains the human species."

Afterward, one of the office directors said, "No one knew what she was talking about. It was all sailing through the blue sky. We took ratings on all the speeches from the audience and she got one of the lowest." . . .

One of Porter's strengths is her ability to listen to criticisms and learn from her mistakes. In a spirit of good-humored determination, she took the protest and invited other speakers and consultants to meet with her subordinates. As a result of our seminar on work and human development, two office directors, Dave Farber of the Publications Office and Joe Sickon, who ran the Office of Audits, volunteered to lead work improvement programs, provided a majority of employees in their offices approved. . . .

The project in Audits involved 170 professionals and office workers. A committee of fifteen people was chosen, representing different regions of the country and types of work. After meeting for two days, the committee approved the idea of a program "to: (1) improve the quality of work, (2) improve the quality of work environment, and (3) develop, establish, and clarify Office policies. Our goal is to carry out this purpose through the spirit of participation in the decision-making process by all levels of the Office. The Committee's work will also be guided by the desire to create an atmosphere of mutual trust and to foster individual employee fulfillment."

An Office of Audits Council was established and soon after, Margaret Duckles began to work with the group and with its subcommittees, dealing with issues that had been raised, including travel policy for auditors, flexitime, and training.

Duckles also organized a research committee to study differences in the approach of auditors in relation to the policy goals of the office. She found that some auditors felt comfortable only as monitors, noting the facts from a neutral point of view. Others were motivated to be policemen, detectives, and, in some cases, crusaders, uncovering fraud and abuse of public funds. A few were most satisfied when their work allowed them to be helpful as teachers or management consultants. Taking note of these differences, the auditors recognized that improving the effectiveness of their service required clarification of auditing policy, fitting auditors to the type of work they did best, and supporting that approach. An auditor with a policing approach would be most effective where there was a suspicion of fraud, but in the case of those minority businesses lacking experience, a helping auditor would best serve the policy goals of the department. However, the helping auditor would need to talk over his or her observations with other auditors, to secure support and protection for moving into an area of judgment not defined by rigid rules.

The project in audits began with a goal of "participation," but it soon became necessary to define this concept more carefully. As Michel Crozier points out, bureaucrats are ambivalent about participation in making decisions that will affect them. On the one hand, they are attracted by the promise of gaining control over their environment. For example, auditors were able to determine their own job assignments in a way that was more satisfying than if the decision had been made by the office director. On the other hand, they have reason to fear that if they participate in making decisions that affect them, they may lose their autonomy and their right to protest.

Management may talk about sharing power, but the responsibilities of civil servants and political appointees are determined by law. The president and his appointees are accountable to Congress, and invitations to participate can be withdrawn unilaterally and indeed may have to be on occasion, if legality is to be preserved.

It became necessary in the Office of Audits and with the directors under Porter to clarify the difference between *participative* and *consultative* management. Employees could participate in studying work and in analyzing problems, but decision making remained essentially consultative. This was, to be sure, an advance over autocratic management. Employees were motivated to cooperate once they trusted that managers like Porter, Farber, and Sickon cared and believed in principles that expressed shared values of craftsmanship and individual development at work. Above all, they had to trust the leader would not punish them for telling unpleasant truths, nor abandon them in principled battles with other parts of the bureaucracy. Within this context, areas of consultation and participation were established through trial and error. However, cooperation lasted only as long as there was trust in the leader. When Sickon left the Office of Audits, the program ended.

Elsa Porter also learned that she was unwilling to allow those who did not share her values to prevail in disagreements about policy. The jungle fighters would use her principles against her, organizing others through intimidation, unless she was prepared to use her power in defense of principle. . . .

Porter was learning that resistance to participation was not just because her people were used to authoritarianism. . . . Civil servants had legitimate reason to fear terms like "participation" or "humanistic . . ." which might end up undermining their rights and sense of autonomy. Porter's education was in first understanding rather than attacking resistances with either force or inspirational appeals. Once she and her subordinates understood resistance better, they were able to cooperate in proposing ways to improve both service and the quality of life at work. . . .

[After reviewing Porter's life and early career in government, Maccoby summarizes.] . . . as Porter reviewed her failures in trying to improve the civil service, she concluded that she had been groping around for magical techniques, organizational nostrums. She decided that government cannot be changed merely by legislating new pay and job classification systems. Techniques are useless without leadership that clarifies goals and defends the best values of the civil service.

From the successful experiments in the Department of Commerce she says that she has learned "the importance of defining a work group's mission and values as a first step in the learning process. One needs bedrock to stand on—so the first step is to describe what should *not* change. . . . People will experiment if they are assured their basic values are protected."

In the process of experimentation, Porter has herself developed from a critic, an angry outsider, to a leader now respected throughout government (although not by everyone at Commerce) as a pioneer in the improvement of government work. . . .

There were two views of Porter among the employees of the Commerce Department. One was that she had no power, was a fuzzy-minded romantic who did not lead. According to this view, she got pushed around by other assistant secretaries and did not fight with the weapons at hand. One of her deputies, when asked to draw a picture of administration symbolized by some form of transportation, drew a ship in shark-infested waters, trying to avoid torpedoes while Porter steered the ship toward the land of angels. Another who supports Porter's view of leadership noted that, "we are *programmed* to expect a 'kick ass' leadership role from our 'bosses.' Any deviation is construed as a weak or incompetent management resulting in chaos and ultimate destruction of an organization. Many managers seem to prefer tough bosses as they feel somewhat tougher and more secure themselves through the transferred power."

The second view was that Porter had gotten office directors to work more cooperatively and administration had been of greater service to the department than ever before. Information was shared and priorities determined cooperatively. It happened gradually and was not noticed by many people, least of all those who were involved. . . .

I have met a number of women in government and business who are successful gamesmen, able to operate more easily than does Porter at high levels. They are more oriented to personal glory and less questioning of the rules of the game. But none has created a new model of management, none has demonstrated a new direction to improve public service.

In Elsa Porter's position, her jungle fighting predecessors have used the power of administration, control of resources, and the budget process, to dominate the department, present themselves as indispensable to the secretary, and gain a major say in policy. A gamesman would have focused first on gaining a winning reputation by improving whatever could be measured. One approach would be to place hotshot managers into key positions. Porter recognized that it is difficult to replace people in government and hard to find good federal managers. By supporting those she had and emphasizing both professional and personal development, she gained high performance without decimating the organization. Everyone benefited.

In her personality Elsa Porter integrates positive aspects of the traditional character types: the jungle fighter's protectiveness and bravery, the company man's caring and loyalty, with flexibility and openness to self-criticism. One reason the participative-consultative approach works for her is that she gains strength and improves herself by inviting others to criticize her and join her.

Why Study Leadership?

In addition to planning, meeting, making decisions, talking, analyzing, and paying attention to their bosses, managers know they must ultimately get things done through other people. In this interaction, they must provide leadership. Thus we need to know something about leadership if we are to fully understand our own and others' roles in organizations. Different organizational cultures and climates foster different kinds of leadership. We need to think about these differences when choosing the kinds of organizations to join. We also need to know what kinds of leadership styles we can engage in, what we can bring to the workplace. Elsa Porter clearly felt that she could bring out the best in civil servants only by respecting their best motives and developing trust by satisfying their needs. By studying what happened to her, we can see how some organizational cultures raise obstacles to that leadership style.

We will study leadership by first defining it and distinguishing it from mere authority; this differentiation will include addressing the question of how leadership emerges within a group. With this basic understanding of what leadership is, we will begin to explore the study of leadership—including the relatively new notion that leadership is not a worthwhile area of study. From this base, we will examine the leadership research in greater depth, exploring the various approaches to this aspect of management. Although this chapter generally follows an historical flow from trait approaches to attribution theory, the theories presented should not be seen as competing views. As we will see at the end of the chapter, they each contribute something valuable to a complete view of the complex concept of leadership.

What Is Leadership?

There are as many definitions of leadership as there are people to do the defining, but they have enough in common that we can fashion from them one definition as representative of all. Over the years the trend in defining leadership has moved toward a focus on the importance of group properties. (As we will see, however, studies of leadership are not as quick to catch up in their attention to group processes.) A leader is the person whose behavior has a determining effect on the behavior of other group members. Keep in mind that groups include vocal people who affect them but do not have a following—they are not leaders. This consideration leads to a refinement of the definition: a leader is someone who can help the group maintain its motivation. Even more inclusively, **leadership** is the interaction among members of a group in which leaders are agents of change. A leader is the person whose acts, more than anyone else's, affect the motivation and competencies of the group.

Here we differentiate leadership from **headship,** which is the nominal or hierarchical "top" position in a group. Headship is maintained through the system and not through the relationships that leaders establish with their followers. With headship there is not necessarily a sense of shared feeling or joint action, and the authority of the head is derived from some power external to the group that he exercises over group members. Both leadership and headship derive from the bases of power discussed in Chapter 6. The head possesses legitimate power, the authority conferred by the hierarchy. The leader has referent power, the capacity to exert influence on others. Both headship and leadership may occur in the same individual—Elsa Porter was not only the titular head of the administrative group, she was also, quite clearly, the leader, someone with the vision to take that group to a new way of acting.

Are Managers Leaders?

For a long time managers and organizational scholars relied on the notion that the primary functions of management should be planning, organizing, staffing, directing, coordinating, reporting, and budgeting. Managers were given one of their first acronyms, POSTCORB, from these seven functions (Gulick and Urwick, 1937). No doubt these tasks are performed, but viewing management in terms of such general functions inhibited a more searching inquiry.

In the 1950s interest developed in looking at how managers actually spend their time. Many studies (see, for example, Stogdill and Shartle, 1955; Prien, 1963; and Tornow and Pinto, 1976) examined what kind of tasks were handled by managers at different levels. They concluded that first-line managers spent most of their time interacting with superiors and peers and focused on task-related issues such as organizing, planning, and supervising work. Upper-level managers spent more time interacting with subordinates (including lower-level managers) and focused on strategic and organizational tasks, including planning for the future, coordination of units, and internal business control.

A number of other studies examined in more detail how managers work (Mintzberg, 1973; Lombardo and McCall, 1981; Carlson, 1951; Kurke and Aldrich, 1983; Guest, 1956). Studies in the United States, Canada, Sweden, and Great Britain observed all kinds of managers, from foremen to staff managers, from company presidents to street gang leaders. The results of these studies should put to rest four major myths about the average manager (Mintzberg, 1975):

1. *"The manager is a reflective, systematic planner."*   The evidence on this issue is overwhelmingly to the contrary. Managers work at an unrelenting pace, and their activities are characterized by brevity, variety, and discontinuity. They are strongly oriented to action and dislike reflection.

2. *"The effective manager has no regular duties to perform."*   In addition to handling everything that goes wrong, managers perform a number of regular duties, including ritual and ceremony, negotiations, and information processing that links organizations to their environments.

3. *"Senior managers need the kind of aggregated information that a formal management information system best provides."*   Evidence shows that formal MIS systems don't work and that managers don't use them. Managers actually process information that reaches them through documents, phone calls, scheduled and unscheduled meetings, and

observational tours. They strongly prefer the verbal media, phone calls, and meetings.

4. *"Management is quickly becoming a science and profession."* Brief observation of any manager will lay to rest the notion that she practices science. Science involves the application of systematic, analytically determined procedures. We don't even know what procedures managers use; how can we prescribe them by scientific analysis? Management is hardly a profession if we can't specify what managers should learn.

The Roles of Managers

Another way of approaching managers' work is to consider what roles they play as they go about their day. The most discussed investigation of this sort was done by Mintzberg (1973). Based on a variety of intensive observational techniques, managerial activities were divided into three roles: interpersonal, informational, and decisional.

The interpersonal category contains three types of roles: (1) in the **figurehead** role, managers perform symbolic duties of a legal or social nature because of their obligations as head of the organization or subunits; (2) in the **leader** role, managers establish the work atmosphere and motivate people; (3) in the **liaison** role, managers develop and maintain webs of contact outside their organizations or units to obtain information or favors.

The informational category also includes three roles: (1) in the **monitor** role, managers collect information relevant to the organization; (2) in the **disseminator** role, managers transmit information from outside to members of the organization; (3) in the **spokesperson** role, managers transmit information from inside the organization to outsiders.

There are four decisional roles: (1) managers adopt the role of **entrepreneur** when they initiate controlled change in their organization to adapt to changing environmental conditions; (2) they are **disturbance handlers** when forced to deal with unexpected changes; (3) they become **resource allocators** when they make decisions concerning the use of organizational resources; and (4) they act as **negotiators** when they handle major negotiations with other organizations or individuals.

Other researchers asked about the universality of these roles for all managers. One study found that the roles held up fully a decade after the initial research (Kurke and Aldrich, 1983). Another (Pavett and Lau, 1983) found that some roles (the disseminator, figurehead, negotiator, liaison, and spokesperson) were more important for high-level than low-level management. They also concluded that functional area influenced the perceived importance of various roles. General managers rate human skills as more important than do research and development managers.

Other authors attempted to reduce the number of roles. One study reduced the ten roles to two facets: roles dealing with the generation and processing of information and roles that involve decisions (Shapira and Dunbar, 1980).

Stewart (1982) developed a model in contrast to Mintzberg's, noting particular flaws in his approach. Stewart's model, shown in Figure 8.1,

---

FIGURE 8.1
Demands, Constraints, and Choices Affecting Managerial Action

Demands

Overall, meeting minimum criteria of performance. Doing certain kinds of work. Such work is determined by:
- The extent to which personal involvement is required in the unit's work
- Who must be contacted and the difficulty of the work relationship
- Contacts' power to enforce their expectations
- Bureaucratic procedures that cannot be ignored or delegated
- Meetings that must be attended

Constraints

Resource limitations
Legal and trades union constraints
Technological limitations
Physical limitations
Organizational constraints, especially extent to which the work of manager's unit is defined.
Attitudes of other people to:
- Changes in systems, procedures, organization, pay, and conditions
- Changes in the goods or services produced
- Work outside the unit

Choices

In *how* work is done
In *what* work is done:
  Choices within a defined area:
  - To emphasize certain aspects of the job
  - To select some tasks and to ignore or delegate others
  Choices in boundary management
  Choices to change the area of work:
  - To change the unit's domain
  - To develop a personal domain
  - To become an expert
  - To share work, especially with colleagues
  - To take part in organizational and public activities

Source: R. Stewart, "A Model for Understanding Managerial Jobs and Behavior," *Academy of Management Review* 7 (1982): 7–13. Reprinted by permission.

focuses on three kinds of managerial activity: demands, constraints, and choices. **Demands** are what anyone in the job has to do. **Constraints** are factors that limit what the jobholder can do; they can be internal or external. **Choices** are the activities a manager can do but does not have to do. The model can be viewed as consisting of an inner core of demands, an outer boundary of constraints, and an in-between area of choices. These three kinds of activity are dynamic, changing over time due to situational changes.

The Mintzberg model of managerial activity stresses fragmentation and the necessity of concentrating on a variety of roles. The Stewart model stresses opportunities for managers to do what they want and asserts the existence of considerable flexibility in managerial jobs. Stewart's approach also alerts us to specific constraints that will influence what can be done.

Yet we are left with the question posed earlier in the chapter—are managers leaders? In the view of these researchers, leadership is one aspect of management, one role that managers may play. Other researchers take a different approach, best summarized recently by Zaleznik (1989, 1990), who defined managers and leaders as two distinct species (though a leader may certainly have a managerial position). In Zaleznik's view, managers deal with style and process—how things are done. Leaders, he believes, focus on substance—whether the right thing is being done. Leaders are not afraid to take risks, be aggressive, or use their imaginations to identify opportunities and convince others to follow. Another popular writer (Bennis, 1989a, b) approaches leadership in a similar way: leaders use instinct, are aggressive and open to trying anything, and willing to take risks.

This perspective brings us back to our original definition of leadership: it is the capacity to act as an agent of change. A leader is someone who can take the organization in a new direction. Such a leader is undoubtedly a manager—or will rise to become one. But all managers are not leaders.

The Emergence of Leadership

The distinction between leadership and management raises the question of how leadership emerges. A manager has status conferred from a higher power; the leader must somehow claim the prize of leadership through her own effort. Since the 1950s a considerable amount of attention has been given to how leadership emerges in groups. The first explanation offered was reinforcement. In this view, the process begins when a group member makes statements he feels will contribute to the group's task. If he is encouraged to continue (his conduct is reinforced), the group may see him as helpful and therefore provide him with status. The group expects more and is given more, raising the status of the speaker further. Ultimately, the group accepts that person as the leader (Bales, 1953).

Two kinds of leadership can emerge. The group member perceived as having the best ideas emerges as the **instrumental,** or **task, leader;** the member who can reduce tension, reassure members, express solidarity, and so on emerges as the **socioemotional leader.** These two kinds of leadership can emerge in the same person or in different people. The notion of task versus interpersonal leadership is carried out through much of the research on leadership, as we shall see.

The Phases of Leadership Emergence   Leadership emerges in three phases. First, those who are unsuitable are eliminated. Then one potential leader is selected. Finally, there is a probationary period during which the leader must continue to demonstrate her skills (Bormann, 1969).

Some researchers (Stein, Hoffman, Cooley, and Pearse, 1979) view the emergence of leadership as a solution to two problems that groups experience: (1) what functions have to be performed by the group to accomplish the task, and (2) what member of the group is best able to perform these functions and guide the group in performing them. According to this view, differences in member status are the basis for attributing leadership potential in the early stages of group interaction. During this phase, group members perform a variety of task-related functions, including defining the task, suggesting solutions, and recommending procedures to follow. By virtue of how they participate in this process, various members announce their candidacy for leader (this need not be explicit). The acts themselves help define the nature of leadership for this particular group.

If one member consistently initiates and guides group activity and controls the behaviors of others, that candidate will pass the "candidacy threshold" into the second stage of leadership emergence. In some groups, one member takes charge early and continues over the long haul to suggest procedures, define problems, or just control. In other cases, two people may pass the candidacy threshold about the same time, thus creating conflict. One of the two candidates may exert herself more, recruit followers, or have a particularly attractive way of accomplishing the task, thus surpassing the other and emerging as leader. Or the two candidates may be neck and neck, causing a search for a third candidate acceptable to each of the other two and to the membership at large.

The third stage begins after one member has passed the candidacy threshold. At that point the group has adopted someone who continues to earn points as a leader and to consolidate her leadership position. The turmoil in Eastern Europe that began in 1989 resulted in a pluralism of ideas and a leadership vacuum in many countries. The processes through which leaders will emerge there will probably resemble the leadership emergence process.

Lord and his colleagues (Cronshaw and Lord, 1987; Lord, 1985; Lord and Alliger, 1985; Lord, Foti, and DeVader, 1984) extensively studied the role of attributions in the emergence of leaders. In their view, group members possess images of what a leader is; these images influence who in the group is perceived as a leader. Essentially, groups look for members who match their preconceived notions.

Banking Idiosyncrasy Credits   Hollander (1958, 1964) offered an interesting notion about how status accrues: the idea of idiosyncrasy credits. **Idiosyncrasy credits** are gained and lost based on how a person conforms to a group's expectations and contributes to its tasks. Deviance and poor performance are like taking money out of a bank account: they reduce built-up credits.

Initially people accrue credits based on their personal characteristics, which shape first impressions (see Chapter 5). Factors leading to low status and elimination as a candidate for leadership include inappropriate leadership style, gender (women were eliminated in the past), irritating personality, inflexibility, and undue emphasis on either maintenance or task activities (Stein et al., 1979). More recent evidence shows that women are not necessarily prevented from emerging as leaders (Schneier and Bartol, 1980) or, once in managerial positions, seen as having less power than men (Ragins, 1989). These are hopeful findings, indeed.

At some point the person may accrue sufficient credits to attain the role of leader. The role is a set of expectations about the person; he continues to accrue credits to the extent that he meets those expectations. The expectations include providing structure and setting goals, maintaining flexibility in handling new and different situations, and establishing good social relationships. Only after accruing a large number of idiosyncrasy credits is deviance acceptable. Elsa Porter's role as a deviant in the civil service system would likely have failed had she not first created sufficient idiosyncrasy credits.

Managers seem to be intuitively aware of these issues of leadership emergence. Typically, managers new to a group do not take action about much of anything during their initial time in the group. Perhaps they are building idiosyncrasy credits, perhaps attempting to engage in behaviors to prove their worth to the group.

The Study of Leadership

Leadership and a related concept, motivation, have received far more attention from management scholars than any other topics in this book. From the

1950s to the present, literally hundreds of studies of both have appeared in scholarly journals (Life, 1986), and the issues raised are often the same. Despite the abundance of research, there are gaps. First, the research rarely examines the broad notions of leadership symbolized by the persuasive power of a Churchill, Gandhi, or Hitler to sway groups for good or ill. Rather, the focus has much more often been on narrow studies of leadership as a matter of style. A second limitation to leadership research is the failure to explore leadership in all its complexity.

One scholar (Dubin, 1979) formulated a set of metaphors for leadership, each expressing one of many common attitudes toward leaders and how they lead. These metaphors offer compelling insights into the phenomenon (see the feature "Metaphors and Leadership"), but as yet no research has addressed them. Indeed, Dubin's list leads to far more complex issues of organizational leadership than we generally see discussed in the management literature.

FEATURE: *Metaphors of Leadership*

1. *"The buck stops here" metaphor.*   According to this metaphor, at the top of the organization a final decision is made—in the words of virtually every politician campaigning for an executive office, the leader "makes the tough choices." Many organizations attempt to make the stopping place a committee rather than one person. Yet the buck often stops not at the top of an organization but with middle- or lower-level managers, who actually make the decisions.

2. *The "batting a thousand" metaphor.*   This metaphor suggests that leaders make good decisions every time. Acceptance of this myth can harm the leader, who may despair when failure occurs, or undermine organizational effectiveness if subordinates work to cover for the boss's mistakes.

3. *The "wisdom versus expertise" metaphor.*   This metaphor concerns the values placed on judgment and technical knowledge. Both qualities are important. But while lip service is paid to wisdom (probably the more important trait for leaders), promotions usually reward expertise.

4. *The "n of one" metaphor.*   This metaphor states that leaders are perceived—by themselves and by others—as occupying a class whose membership is one. There are ill effects of such a view: for

leaders, it produces arrogance and authoritarianism; for subordinates, deference and subservience.

5. *The "lone ranger" metaphor.* This metaphor exalts the loneliness of the top position. A leader who believes in this metaphor increases the burden of responsibility for decisions that do get made. Subordinates who accept it may not give the leader the support he needs.

6. *The "confidant" metaphor.* This metaphor addresses the role of the confidant to the leader. Crucial to the leader is independence of mind in advisers. Renaissance writers aptly called flattery and unquestioning support from aides the "malady of princes."

The "chosen one" metaphor. According to this metaphor, some groups make their own leader. Although such a leader may represent the group, her leadership may be constrained by the group's attitudes. The group that perceives itself as kingmaker, however, often believes that it has the power to unmake that king whenever it desires.

8. *The "charismatic leader" metaphor.* This metaphor asserts that the leader is leader because of something distinctive about him. We will have more to say about charisma, literally "the gift of grace," later in the chapter.

9. *The "office makes the man" metaphor.* This metaphor assumes that someone thrust into a high position can become a leader. Harry Truman, a little-known politician who became a president admired for his decisiveness and frankness even by many who criticized his policies, is pointed to as an example. But if the office does make the man, the man must be changing, which is highly improbable. It is, perhaps, more accurate that the office allows new scope to the man.

10. *The "zone of indifference" metaphor.* This metaphor addresses followers, not the leader. The vast majority of a leader's decisions affect only a small portion of her followers. This probably combines with the legitimacy of the leadership role to lead to compliance based on a "zone of indifference." Of course, leaders must recognize the borders of that zone and know when they are entering areas where issues are salient to followers, who may not as readily comply.

11. *The "power corrupts" metaphor.* This metaphor recognizes Lord Acton's statement that power corrupts and absolute power corrupts absolutely. Leaders may abuse their position for personal

gain. While there are both corrupt and non-corrupt or incorruptible leaders, no one has provided any way of predicting how or why corruption develops in some but not in others.

Source: Adapted from R. Dubin, "Metaphors of Leadership: An Overview," in J. G. Hunt and L. L. Larson (eds.), *Crosscurrents in Leadership* (Carbondale: Southern Illinois University Press, 1979), pp. 225–238.

Leadership Does Not Matter

One prominent management theorist presented the notion that leadership does not really matter (Pfeffer, 1977). A number of reasons are given to support this notion (Meindl and Ehrlich, 1987):

1. There is nothing unique in the concept of leadership that cannot be explained under more general theories of social interaction.

2. The breadth of behavior in which leaders engage is very small. Obtaining a leadership position requires selection, and perhaps only certain limited behavior styles are chosen. Once a person is in a leadership position, discretion and behavior are constrained.

3. Leaders typically influence only a few of the variables important in organizational performance.

4. Leaders serve as symbols, and whether or not a leader's behavior actually influences performance is important only because people believe it does.

An example of leaders serving as symbols is provided in professional sports (Gamson and Scotch, 1964) when the manager or coach is fired because the team is losing. The owner cannot fire the whole team for poor performance, but he must do something to demonstrate to the players that they must improve their record and to reassure the ticket-buying fans that losing is not tolerated.

Yet the notion that leadership does not matter seems of limited usefulness. A leader is indeed constrained in his actions—by the amount of power granted from above and by the willingness of those below to follow where he leads—and it is also true that some individuals have taken their organizations to higher levels of performance because they were effective leaders. In some instances they are individuals who rescued the organization in a crisis—Lee Iacocca is one such example. Other times, they are people who are able to point their companies in a new direction or meet a new challenge (see the theme case of Chapter 11 about Roger Milliken).

All organizations need leaders because leaders help them surmount challenges, keep an established business growing, or prevent decline. Organizations have universal problems that must be met by their leadership. Leaders have to evaluate continually the coordination and integration of company operations. They have to recognize conditions that require new adaptations and get their company adapting in the appropriate way. They must resolve functional conflicts so that poor performers do not feel permanently defeated and can find ways to modify their performance. The importance of attending to these functions is clearly demonstrated in the feature on the leadership of Coca-Cola, which allowed the distraction of legal problems to pull it away from its main tasks, resulting in the loss of market share. Lee Iacocca, in his popular autobiography published in the mid-1980s and as excerpted in the next feature, offered his own thoughts on the importance of leadership.

FEATURE: *Leadership Missing in Action: Coca-Cola's Management in the 1970s*

To the world that watched upbeat Coke ads, packed Coke for every picnic, and stocked Coke for every party, the Coca-Cola Company appeared huge and healthy throughout the seventies. But behind the scenes, executives were ensnared in a very different drama, bickering among themselves, distracted by tangential issues, and losing sight of the heart of the matter—Coke itself. The top executives of the Coca-Cola Company of the late seventies actually paid less and less attention to the marketing and sale of their central product, so caught up were they in dodging government allegations, fighting with bottlers over the price of syrup, and squabbling over whether or not to control who owned the company franchises. Gone were the days of the inspired entrepreneur and the spritely intellect, gone the days of unswerving leadership.

The FTC opened fire on Coca-Cola in 1971, charging that the bottlers' contracts guaranteeing territorial exclusivity restricted competition. The prospect of a "walls down" world was unacceptably distasteful to almost everyone in the Coca-Cola family. Robert Woodruff, the 82-year-old patriarch who still controlled the company from his specially created position of chairman of the finance committee, was so anxious over the impending change that he told Coca-Cola's president, Lucian Smith, he would preserve the status quo even if he had to commit the huge Woodruff personal fortune to the cause. The obsessiveness of Woodruff fairly hypnotized the company.

"Our system was immobilized," said Donald R. Keough, who, as president of the company's domestic soft-drink unit, Coca-Cola USA, found himself in the thick of it. It is astounding to imagine it now, but the first *fifty* meetings he attended after assuming office in 1974 were legal briefings on the FTC battle. And, said one senior executive, "After hearing discussion after discussion of the 'walls down' possibility, you felt too despondent to get on with business." Keough confessed that long-range planning was thwarted, too. "We always had to confront the reality that the system as we knew it might not exist, and we were painting the worst-case scenario." So obsessed was everyone with the FTC that they forgot the essence of what they were fighting for—the right to sell Coke, with the emphasis on "sell." The battle was to last a decade, ten years in which officials amidst the company took its eye off the ball while its rival, Pepsi, kept its own cola sharply in focus. With its image rejuvenated by the "Pepsi Generation" campaign and the product itself more generally available, Pepsi-Cola in 1975 pulled ahead of Coca-Cola in supermarket sales.

Source: From Thomas Oliver, *The Real Coke—The Real Story* (New York: Penguin Books, 1987). Copyright © 1987 by Thomas Oliver. Reprinted by permission of Random House, Inc.

FEATURE: *Lee Iacocca on Leadership*

If I had to sum up in one word the qualities that make a good manager, I'd say that it all comes down to decisiveness. You can use the fanciest computers in the world and you can gather all the charts and numbers, but in the end you have to bring all your information together, set up a timetable, and *act.*

And I don't mean act rashly. In the press, I'm sometimes described as a flamboyant leader and a hip-shooter, a kind of fly-by-the-seat-of-the-pants operator. I may occasionally give that impression, but if that image were really true, I could never have been successful in business.

Actually, my management style has always been pretty conservative. Whenever I've taken risks, it's been after satisfying myself that the research and the market studies supported my instincts. I may act on my intuition—but only if my hunches are supported by the facts.

Too many managers let themselves get weighed down in their decision-making, especially those with too much education. I once said to Philip Caldwell, who became the top man at Ford after I left, "The trouble with you, Phil, is that you went to Harvard, where they taught you not to take any action until you've got *all* the facts. You've got ninety-five percent of them, but it's going to take you another six months to get that last five percent. And by the time you do, your facts will be out of date because the market has moved on you. That's what life is about—timing."

A good business leader can't operate that way. It's perfectly natural to want all the facts and to hold out for the research that guarantees a particular program will work. After all, if you're about to spend $300 million on a new product, you want to be absolutely sure you're on the right track.

That's fine in theory, but real life just doesn't work that way. Obviously, you're responsible for gathering as many relevant facts and projections as you possibly can. But at some point you've got to take that leap of faith. First, because even the right decision is wrong if it's made too late. Second, because in most cases there's no such thing as certainty. There are times when even the best manager is like the little boy with the big dog waiting to see where the dog wants to go so he can take him there.

. . . In addition to being decision makers, managers also have to be motivators. . . . The only way you can motivate people is to communicate with them. . . . A good manager needs to listen as much as he needs to talk. Too many people fail to realize that real communication goes in both directions.

In corporate life you have to encourage all your people to make a contribution to the common good and to come up with better ways of doing things. You don't have to accept every single suggestion, but if you don't get back to the guy and say, "Hey, that idea was terrific," and pat him on the back, he'll never give you another one. That kind of communication lets people know they really count.

You have to be able to listen well if you're going to motivate the people who work for you. Right there, that's the difference between a mediocre company and a great company. The most fulfilling thing for me as a manager is to watch someone the system has labeled as just average or mediocre really come into his own, all because someone has listened to his problems and helped solve them.

. . . It's important to talk to people in their own language. If you do it well, they'll say, "God, he said exactly what I was thinking." And when they begin to respect you, they'll follow you to the death. The *reason* they're following you is not because you're providing some mysterious leadership. It's because you're following them.

Source: Excerpts from *Iacocca: An Autobiography* by Lee Iacocca with William Novak, copyright © 1984 by Lee Iacocca. Used by permission of Bantam Books, a division of Bantam, Doubleday, Dell Publishing Group, Inc.

Substitutes for Leadership

A related notion is that organizations possess *substitutes for leadership.* These are subordinate characteristics, task or group factors, or organizational factors that reduce the necessity of manager leadership (Kerr and Jermier, 1978). These authors studied the effect of these factors on both task leadership and socioemotional leadership.

Three characteristics of subordinates are relevant to this view. First, a worker with a large amount of experience or special expertise or training might be less susceptible to his leader's suggestions on how to work. Second, workers with professional training may follow the principles set by professional standards rather than the leader's prescriptions. Finally, employees high in self-confidence may need less socioemotional leadership.

Task and group factors may decrease the need for leadership as well. Satisfying tasks require little motivating effort from the leader; routine tasks require less task-oriented leadership, as do tasks in which supervisor feedback is less important or that are governed by established group norms. Work done by highly cohesive groups requires neither task nor socioemotional leadership.

Formal rules and policies in the organization and an extensive support staff also reduce the need for task leadership. When a leader has little reward power or coercive power, the need for both kinds of leadership lessens. The same is true if distance separates leader and subordinate (Kerr and Jermier, 1978).

The point of these findings is not that leadership is unnecessary, but as a reminder that members of organizations do not simply follow the leader. Other individuals and the context within which they work shape their behavior as well.

The Significance of Followers

Kerr and Jermier's work does not dismiss the importance of leaders, but it shifts the focus of study somewhat from leader to subordinate. Hollander and Offermann (1990) take this emphasis further, pointing out that "leadership clearly depends on responsive followers" and arguing that,

> because the leader cannot do everything, [leadership] functions need to be dispersed and involve sharing power and engaging others' talents through empowerment. . . . Both leadership and followership can be active roles, given the reality that hierarchical organizations require both at every level. The traditional view of the follower role as mainly passive is misconstrued. Although leaders command greater attention and influence, there is more awareness now of follower influence on leaders. (p. 179)

Some of the work cited in the discussion of the emergence of leaders reflects the increased awareness of followers. Lord's work with attribution theory identifies followers' expectations as significant factors in the emergence of leaders. Similarly, the idea of idiosyncrasy credits emphasizes the role of subordinates in the emergence of leaders. Hollander and Offermann pointed to the growth of participative decision making (see Chapter 7) and new work group arrangements (see Chapter 11) as evidence of the growing acceptance of the importance of followers in the actual practice of organizations.

Theoretical Approaches to Leadership

Four different approaches have been taken to the study of leadership: those that look for characteristics that might make people good leaders, those that examine leadership behaviors, those that look at situational constraints on leader behavior, and those that focus on the importance of leader and follower cognitive processes. The first two approaches were more popular areas of study in the past, although some interest in the trait approach to leadership still remains. Largely, though, current research into leadership focuses on the latter two lines of inquiry.

Trait Approaches

The earliest attempts to understand what constitutes good leadership looked for traits that differentiated leaders from followers. All in all, this approach was disappointing because very few traits were decidedly associated with leadership. When traits were found that seemed to be related to leadership, it was virtually impossible to decide what combination would yield most effective leadership. For instance, if leaders are vigorous and intelligent, need they be very vigorous or only a little vigorous? In either case, need they be quite intelligent or only moderately intelligent?

A recent review (Bass, 1985) summarized the findings of the trait approach:

> The leader is characterized by a strong drive for responsibility and
> task completion, vigor and persistence in the pursuit of goals, ven-
> turesomeness and originality in problem solving, drive to exercise
> initiative in social situations, self-confidence and sense of personal
> identity, willingness to accept consequences of decision and action,
> readiness to absorb interpersonal stress, willingness to tolerate frus-
> tration and delay, ability to influence other persons' behavior, and
> a capacity to structure social interaction systems to the purpose at

hand. . . . The characteristics generate personality dynamics advantageous to the person seeking the responsibilities of leadership. (p. 81)

That trait approaches are not completely dead is evidenced by studies of the influence of such characteristics as Machiavellianism on leadership behavior (Drory and Gluskinos, 1980) and of leadership differences between men and women. Early studies of sex differences found women to be unsuccessful leaders or not to assert leadership roles at all. More recent studies, however, indicate that few differences in leadership are attributable to sex (Rice, Instone, and Adams, 1984; Brenner, 1982; Jago and Vroom, 1982; Stevens and DeNisi, 1980; Petty and Bruning, 1980).

Gamesmanship   An interesting set of traits is at the heart of Michael Maccoby's (1976) provocative insights about leadership, already introduced in the Elsa Porter case. Maccoby (1979) asserted that over the last 200 years there have been three different types of ideal social character in America. These ideal types are associated with the dominant modes of production at different periods of our history. By modeling these traits, leaders have performed the changing functions of leadership and projected an image that others in their era can copy. The three ideal types are the independent craftsman (from the late 18th century to the Civil War); the paternalistic empire builder (from after the Civil War to the 1950s); and the gamesman (from 1960 to the present).

Benjamin Franklin described the virtues of the ideal craftsman: moderation, silence, orderliness, resoluteness, thriftiness, industry, sincerity, justice, temperance, cleanliness, imperturbability, chastity, and humility. These traits served a businesslike, male-dominated society of independent craftsmen. George Washington was probably as close as anyone could come to representing this ideal type. As organizations grew more powerful, self-employment declined and the new leader had to have entrepreneurial skills and toughness to build industries, manage a flood of new immigrants, and survive the competition. Andrew Carnegie most closely personified this model, the paternalistic empire builder.

As social character became more self-affirmative and the national spirit more meritocratic, a new image of leadership appealed to Americans: the gamesman, adventurous and ambitious, but fair and flexible. The arrival of the gamesman coincided with the election of John F. Kennedy to the presidency. Unlike the paternal leader, who demanded deference, the gamesman enjoys challenge. The **gamesman** has a boyish, informal style, and controls subordinates through persuasion, enthusiasm, and seduction, rather than through heavy and humiliating commands. He is fair but detached and welcomes the era of equal opportunity as a fair way to get to the top.

The problem with the gamesman is that he cannot provide appropriate leadership in an era of shrinking resources. The gamesman has no vision of development beyond winning, and though he may move up the organizational pyramid, he fails to change it. Leaders typically do not exemplify one of these types but are a combination of all of them, as in the case of Elsa Porter.

Charisma A trait that has received renewed research interest is **charisma,** used to describe leaders who, by the force of their personal abilities, have extraordinary influence on their followers. One recent study found that people working under charismatic leaders performed better and adjusted to the group better than other workers (Howell & Frost, 1989). For many years people have spoken of charismatic leaders and pointed out leaders who seem to embody this trait, but no one has described the trait itself very well. Charisma is probably a complex interaction of personal characteristics, leader behaviors, characteristics of followers, and situational factors. A charismatic leader models a value system for followers, engages in behavior that exudes competence and success, articulates a transcendent goal that is ideological rather than pragmatic, exhibits high expectations, shows confidence in his followers, and arouses some motivation in them. From the next feature, we can see that Steve Jobs, one of the founders of Apple Computer, was a charismatic leader even if we cannot pinpoint exactly why. House (1977) attempted to describe charisma and to predict some of its potential effects on followers:

> [Charismatic leadership] is born out of stressful situations. It is argued that such leaders express sentiments deeply held by followers. These sentiments are different from the established order and thus their expression is likely to be hazardous to the leader (Friedland, 1964). Since their expression is hazardous, the leader is perceived as courageous. Because of other "gifts" attributed to the leader, such as extraordinary competence, the followers believe that the leader will bring about social change and thus will deliver them from their plight. (pp. 203–204)

FEATURE: *Steve Jobs at Apple Computer*

Steve was their inspirational leader, and they idolized him. . . . That was Steve's power—to make people believe in him.

. . . Steve made every decision [about the Macintosh], from whether the computer should have a fan in it (he opposed them because they were too noisy) to what final shape it should take. . . . He didn't create anything, really, but he created everything. And when his decisions didn't make sense, members of the team would make others behind his back. "The Macintosh," Steve would say, "is inside of me, and I've got to get it out and turn it into a product."

. . . Steve provided phenomenal inspiration and demanding standards to get his team to do such things. He pushed them to their limits, until even they were amazed at how much they were able to accomplish. He possessed an innate sense of knowing exactly how to extract the best from people. He cajoled them by admitting his own vulnerabilities; he rebuked them until they, too, shared his uncompromising ethic; he stroked them with pride and praise, like an approving father.

. . . In his quest for perfection, Steve put many people on the defensive. He'd fix his intense, dark eyes on you in an intimidating stare, focusing his eyes in and out. It was a stare that bore down on you, froze you like a 100-ampere headlight, a what-makes-you-think-you're-so-smart look. He could tell you things that only you really knew yourself. At one moment, he could drain all your self-esteem. At the very next, he could praise you, offering just a few complimentary crumbs that somehow made all the angst worthwhile.

. . . He instinctively knew how to reach people. One time, his fourth-grade teacher, Teddy Hill, came to visit Steve at Apple. She brought with her a photograph of the class on Hawaiian day. Steve apparently showed up without his Hawaiian T-shirt, yet there he was in the middle of the picture proudly dressed in one. Teddy lovingly recalled that he had conned the shirt off the back of one of the other children. It was typical of Steve.

Source: Excerpt from John Sculley with John A. Byrne, *Odyssey: Pepsi to Apple . . . A Journey of Adventure, Ideas and the Future.* (New York: Harper & Row, 1987). Copyright © 1987 by John Sculley. Reprinted by permission of HarperCollins Publishers.

Most writers agree that the effects of charismatic leadership are more emotional than calculative (Conger, 1989). Conger and Kanungo outline possible differentiating behaviors of charismatic and noncharismatic leaders, as summarized in Figure 8.2. They later expanded on this outline (Conger and Kanungo, 1988).

Though charismatic leadership is probably not seen frequently in work organizations, it is an extreme anchor on the continuum of personal characteristics. A recent review (Nadler and Tushman, 1990) suggests that char-

FIGURE 8.2

Behavioral Components of Charismatic and Noncharismatic Leadership

	Noncharismatic Leader	Charismatic Leader
Relation to status quo	Essentially agrees with status quo and strives to maintain it	Essentially opposed to status quo and strives to change it
Future goal	Goal not too discrepant from status quo	Idealized vision which is highly discrepant from status quo
Likableness	Shared perspective makes him or her likable	Shared perspective and idealized vision makes him or her a likable and honorable hero worthy of identification and imitation
Trustworthiness	Disinterested advocacy in persuasion attempts	Disinterested advocacy by incurring great personal risk and cost
Expertise	Expert in using available means to achieve goals within the framework of the existing order	Expert in using unconventional means to transcend the existing order
Behavior	Conventional, conforming to existing norms	Unconventional or counter-normative
Environmental sensitivity	Low need for environmental sensitivity to maintain status quo	High need for environmental sensitivity for changing the status quo
Articulation	Weak articulation of goals and motivation to lead	Strong articulation of future vision and motivation to lead
Power base	Position power and personal power (based on reward, expertise, and liking for a friend who is a similar other)	Person power (based on expertise, respect, and admiration for a unique hero)
Leader-follower relationship	Egalitarian, consensus seeking, or directive	Elitist, entrepreneurial, and exemplary
	Nudges or orders people to share his or her views	Transforms people to share the radical changes advocated; possibility of uncovering specific personal attributes that make for good leadership in various situations.

Source: Adapted from J. A. Conger and R. N. Kanungo, "Toward a Behavioral Theory of Charismatic Leadership," *Academy of Management Review* 12 (1985): 637–647. Reprinted by permission.

ismatic leadership is ever more important in turbulent environments, but that such leadership must also be supported by "institutional leadership"— sound management practices—to ensure organizational health.

To date researchers have not uncovered identifiable leadership traits. Perhaps now, however, with more emphasis on the interaction of manager and followers and the situations in which they find themselves, the possibility of identifying such traits is greater.

Behavioral Approaches to Leadership

The majority of research attention on leadership asks what the leader's behavior is and how it influences followers. Modern behavioral research on leadership probably has its origins in a study by Kurt Lewin and his colleagues Lippitt and White (1939) and in research conducted in the Hawthorne Works of Western Electric Company. Leadership research seems particularly embedded in current social values. As shown in the next feature, the questions asked and the outcomes of the research of Lewin et al. were consistent with the values of a nation entering war with Nazi Germany, in which the virtues of democracy over tyranny were on many people's minds.

FEATURE: *A Classic Leadership Study*

Lewin, Lippitt, and White (1939) formed clubs in which 11-year-olds made masks and did other things boys' club members did in the 1930s. They assigned to these clubs authoritarian, democratic, and laissez faire adult leaders. Authoritarian leaders gave orders, democratic leaders developed goals and the means for attaining them with the boys, and laissez faire leaders gave out information only on request and did not enter into the spirit of the task. Production was highest in the authoritarian groups, but fell off when the leaders departed. It was sustained in the democratic groups when their leaders left. Production was low in the laissez faire groups. Satisfaction was high in the democratic groups and low in the other two groups. These kinds of results continue to be fairly typical for groups in which authoritarian and democratic leadership styles are compared; their influence on production is not as clear-cut as it is on satisfaction.

Interestingly, numerous studies of some sort of democratic versus some sort of authoritarian leadership done over the years have turned up fairly similar results, suggesting that these results can be generalized to other situations. We found it to be true in the Elsa Porter case; her participative style was contrasted with the traditional autocratic style of civil service leaders. Some evidence (Hofstede, 1980), however, suggests that the participative strategies touted in the United States are not appropriate in other cultures.

Also noteworthy is that management texts have reported the Lewin, Lippitt, and White study (1939) as an example of how adult leaders should behave in adult work groups despite the fact that the study used boys' clubs. One should question whether boys' clubs are prototypes of adult work groups. This concern alerts managers to question the extent to which their own situations correspond to any other situations they are examining as models of what to do.

The Hawthorne Studies   Between 1927 and 1932 a series of studies were done at the Hawthorne Works of the Western Electric Plant (Roethlisberger and Dickson, 1939). In one of these studies a group of women workers assembling relay switches for telephones was moved to a special room, a number of innovations were introduced, and the impact of these changes on productivity was studied. When lighting was dimmed in the room, production increased. When coffee breaks were introduced, production increased. When the workday was shortened, production increased. When the workday was lengthened, production increased. In short, every change increased production. Researchers concluded that change itself—whatever its nature—led employees to conclude that management cared about them and so responded by working more productively. This was the first demonstration of the impact of leadership on the fabric of the group. The **Hawthorne effect** is the label for this phenomenon of working harder because of feelings of participation in something special.

The Ohio State and University of Michigan Studies   Two major leadership research programs begun in the late 1940s produced similar results. These Ohio State University and University of Michigan studies attempted to identify dimensions that characterize differences in leaders. At Ohio State two dimensions of leadership were identified: consideration and initiating structure. **Consideration** is supervisory behavior that is "indicative of friendship, mutual trust, respect, and warmth"; **initiating structure** is behavior whereby "the supervisor organizes and defines group activities and his relation to the group" (Halpin and Weiner, 1957).

At Michigan, two distinct leadership styles were also observed: the "person-centered" style and the "job-centered" style. Job-centered leaders practice close supervision, and subordinates perform their work using specified procedures. Employee-centered leaders delegate decision making and help followers satisfy their needs by creating a supportive work environment (Katz, Maccoby, and Morse, 1950; Katz, Maccoby, Gurin, and Floor, 1951).

When either of these two pairs of dimensions are related to such important organizational outcomes as performance and satisfaction, the results are not unlike those from the original Lewin, Lippitt, and White (1939) study. High consideration or employee-centered leaders tend to have more satisfied subordinates than do high-initiating structure or job-centered leaders. The relationship of these dimensions to performance is not as clear. Both negative and positive effects on performance have been reported for all four styles (Vroom, 1976; Bass, 1985).

Recently, these dimensions have also been related to organizational communication. Supervisors thought to be high on consideration are suggested to be more responsive and to communicate more task- and career-related messages than other supervisors. High-initiating structure supervisors were seen as clarifying policy and letting employees know what needed to be done (Penley and Hawkins, 1985). Similar leadership dimensions have been studied in a systematic way since 1949 in Japan (Misumi, 1985).

These concepts are rather broad, however, and offer managers no prescriptions about specific behaviors to use. Yet these concepts may be true and nevertheless accepted by managers with drastically different leadership styles. To say that a manager should be concerned about both production and her employees is not saying much about what she should do in particular situations.

Theories of Participation   When boiled down, investigations of authoritarian versus democratic groups, initiating structure versus consideration, and people orientation versus job orientation are studies of the degree to which subordinates participate in controlling their own work activities. The Vroom and Jago (1988) model discussed in Chapter 7 is yet another observation of conditions under which participation can be a useful strategy. With its creation of a decision tree to determine the appropriate style for a given situation, it may be more helpful to managers as well.

Participation is frequently considered in discussions of leadership, as well as in decision making. The Vroom and Jago model considers subordinate and organizational factors as well as simple interactions between superiors and subordinates. It is realistic in that it points out real constraints on what one can do as a manager. Evidence supports the original (Vroom and Yetton, 1973) version of this model (Field, 1982) and suggests that the leadership behavior of women may agree more with its prescriptions than that of men (Jago and Vroom, 1982).

To be more complete, prescriptions about leadership should specifically address the nature of the relationship between superiors and subordinates. One perspective on leadership (Graen, 1976; Graen and Cashman, 1975) focuses on the role-making process and sees the leader and subordinate agreeing over time as to the general and specific nature of their interaction. Agreement is reached by using reciprocal rewards and punishments. Thus leadership is a dyadic exchange in which leaders behave differently with different subordinates rather than act relatively similarly across the board.

Here leadership is a developmental process in which change is inherent through learning and socialization. Recent work that focuses on this developmental process of exchange is illustrated in Figure 8.3. In this view, both initial interactions and the complex interactions of the subordinate's behavior and attributes, the leader's attributions, and the leader's responses affect the nature of the exchange between the leader and the subordinate. In addi-

FIGURE 8.3
The Leader-Member-Exchange Developmental Process

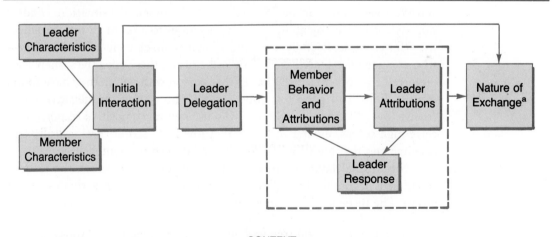

-CONTEXT-

[a] After the nature of the exchange has been determined it is assumed that the reciprocal process between leader and member will continue.

Source: From R. M. Dienesch and R. C. Liden, "Leader-Member Exchange Model of Leadership: A Critique and Further Development," *Academy of Management Review* 11 (1986): 627. Reprinted by permission.

tion, subordinates in high-quality dyadic relationships had more positive perceptions of and higher consensus about their organizational climate (Kozlowski and Doherty, 1989). In a 13-year study of Japanese managers, Wakabayashi and Graen (1989) found that the quality of a manager's vertical exchange with his superior contributed uniquely to the development of the subordinate's career.

Much research has focused on the use of reinforcements by leaders (Mitchell, 1979; Scott, 1977; Ashour and Johns, 1983). Since the notions discussed are complementary to how rewards and punishments are used for motivating employees, we reserve the topic for Chapter 9.

Contingency Approaches to Leadership

Contingency theories of leadership take a wider and more complex view than the models previously discussed by identifying individual personal characteristics and situational constraints that should be thought about simultaneously. Few leadership contingency models are available. The two most prominent kinds focus on the characteristics of either the situation or the subordinates.

Situational Variables   According to Fiedler (1967, 1978), leadership style and effectiveness are contingent on the favorableness of the situation. Leadership style is gauged by an individual's responses to a set of 18 bipolar adjectives (for example, friendly/unfriendly, inefficient/efficient). Respondents— who are managers—are asked to describe, using these adjectives, their least preferred co-worker (LPC), that is, that person with whom they have found it most difficult to get a job done. Those who respond in negative terms receive low LPC scores, and those who use neutral or positive responses receive high scores. Fiedler proposes that low LPC scorers are basically task oriented and that high LPC scorers are relationship oriented.

Situational favorableness refers to the degree to which the leader's situation is favorable for influencing and controlling the activities of the group. The three major components of situational favorableness follow:

1. Support by followers and endorsement of the leader's position: the more support and the higher the degree of endorsement, the more favorable the situation.

2. Structure of the group's task: the more highly structured, the more favorable the situation.

3. Formal power of the leader's position in the group: the more power, the more favorable the situation.

FIGURE 8.4
Fiedler's Contingency Model

	CELL	1	2	3	4	5	6	7	8
Situational Factors	Leader/Member Relations	Good	Good	Good	Good	Poor	Poor	Poor	Poor
	Task Structure	Structured	Structured	Unstruc-tured	Unstruc-tured	Structured	Structured	Unstruc-tured	Unstruc-tured
	Leader Position Power	Strong	Weak	Strong	Weak	Strong	Weak	Strong	Weak
Situational Favorableness		Favorable			Moderately favorable			Unfavorable	
Situational Certainty		Very certain situation			Moderately certain situation			Very uncertain situation	
Recommended Leadership Style		Task	Task	Task	Employee	Employee	Employee	Task	Task

Source: From Fred E. Fiedler, *A Theory of Leadership Effectiveness* (New York: McGraw-Hill, 1967), p. 176. Copyright © 1977 by Fred E. Fiedler. Reprinted by permission of the author.

The model proposes that task-oriented (low LPC) leaders are more effective than relationship-oriented (high LPC) leaders in situations that are either very favorable or very unfavorable. In situations that are intermediately favorable, relationship-oriented leaders are more effective. The model is diagrammed in Figure 8.4.

The utility of this model has been hotly debated. Research by Fiedler and his group generally supports the model (for example, Fiedler, 1970, 1978), but other research fails to do so (for example, Graen, Alvares, Orris, Martella, 1970; Schriesheim and Kerr, 1977). Despite these disparate findings, this approach does offer insight into situational characteristics that may determine the appropriateness of different leadership styles.

In another view, more structured, directive leadership is more effective for groups working on unstructured tasks. When the task is more structured, more supportive leadership seems best. As an example, if you are called on to fix a car but you do not know the first thing about mechanical objects, you would probably appreciate specific structure and guidance. But if you are an expert mechanic, you want general support, not someone looking over your shoulder. A number of studies support this model (Fulk-Schriesheim, 1980; Fulk and Wendler, 1982).

Subordinate Variables Another kind of approach to contingency models focuses not on the situations, but on the subordinates. One such view, called the **path-goal theory** of leadership (House, 1971; House and Dessler, 1974; House and Mitchell, 1974), presents a somewhat more complex classification of both leader and situational variables than those developed by Fiedler and his co-workers. The major concern is how a leader's behavior is motivating or satisfying to a follower because of its impact on her perceptions of her goals and the paths to those goals. The model is diagrammed in Figure 8.5.

Four leadership styles are introduced: directive, supportive, participative, and achievement oriented. Two types of situational variables are important to the leader: (1) subordinate ability and personality characteristics such as authoritarianism and internal versus external locus of control and (2) environmental factors such as the task and the structure, power, and interpersonal relations in the work group. (**Locus of control** refers to an individual's consistent view that things happen either because of what she does to make them happen—an internal locus of control—or because of external factors over which she has no control—an external locus of control.

By taking into account leadership style and contingency factors, one can predict who among a pool of potential leaders will perform best. For example, research has shown that employees with an internal locus of control are more satisfied with participative leadership than employees with an external locus of control (Mitchell, Smyser, and Weed, 1975). Similarly, in situations requiring clarity in job expectations, directive supervision is as-

FIGURE 8.5
House's Path-Goal Theory of Leadership

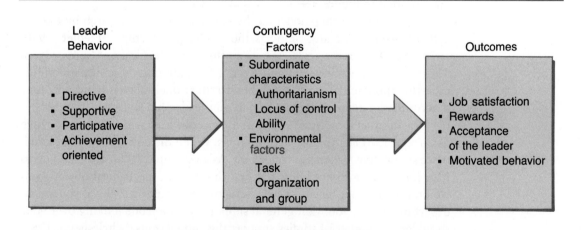

Source: From R. J. House and T. R. Mitchell, "Path-Goal Theory of Leadership," *Journal of Contemporary Business* 3 (1974): 81–97. Reprinted by permission.

sociated with high job satisfaction (Keller, 1989). It makes intuitive sense that more independent internal people prefer more autonomy and that the more dependent externals prefer leadership that structures the environment for them.

Another contingency theory of leadership that focuses on subordinates was introduced by Hersey and Blanchard (1982). According to this view, the primary situational determinant of whether a leader should exhibit initiating structure or consideration behavior is **subordinate maturity.** Maturity, which reflects how much responsibility the individual takes for his own work, results from experience and training. Hersey and Blanchard identified two kinds of maturity: job maturity, the ability to take responsibility, and psychological maturity, the willingness to take responsibility.

Within the two dimensions of task and relationship behaviors, Hersey and Blanchard identified four leadership styles that are appropriate given various levels of subordinate maturity:

1. *Telling* is a high task-oriented, low relationship-oriented style in which the leader directs subordinates. This style is appropriate for subordinates who are low in willingness and low in ability.

2. *Selling* is a high task-oriented, high relationship-oriented style in which the leader provides directive and supportive behavior. This style is useful if workers are willing to do tasks but not yet fully able.

3. *Participating* is a low task-oriented, high relationship-oriented style in which the leader emphasizes support and communication. The leader uses this style for subordinates who are able but unwilling to do what the leader wants.

4. *Delegating* is a low task-oriented, low relationship-oriented style, in which the leader allows subordinates wide latitude for action. The leader uses this style for subordinates who are both willing and able.

It is probably a good idea for managers to think about their subordinates' levels of job maturity in deciding what leadership styles are appropriate to their situations. However, since the formal properties of this situational leadership model have not yet been well developed, we cannot offer prescriptions about leadership behavior based on it (Graeff, 1983; Vechio, 1987).

The contingency approaches to leadership offer considerable sophistication when compared to what was previously known. They provide a set of individual and environmental variables managers can think about when leading employees. For example, Elsa Porter clearly was aware of the need for employee trust and good leader–member relations in order to effect change. These approaches, like the model of manager roles discussed early in the chapter, assume that leaders can change their behaviors to meet various situations.

In the future, such a capacity for behavior change may be significant for organizational survival. Particularly because of the potential for new market development in diverse locations unavailable to Western business interests before the 1990s, managers and researchers alike need to think about increasing their understanding of the greater range of situational variables rooted in international diversity.

A Cognitive Approach to Leadership

A new perspective on leadership is beginning to emerge. Here the emphasis is not on leader behavior per se, but on **cognitive theories,** on what is perceived to cause leader behavior. Proponents of this perspective, called the attribution theory of leadership, state that leaders have their own theories about what they and their subordinates do, and that understanding leadership requires getting into the heads of leaders and their subordinates to comprehend those expectations. We discussed attribution theory in Chapter 5 (on communication) and will see it again in Chapter 9 (when we discuss motivation). Needless to say, leaders are subject to all the biases in information processing discussed in Chapter 5.

The first stage in making an attribution is observation of some behavior and the effects of that behavior, which is followed by making a cause-effect judgment. This process can be seen at work in a number of different attributions about leadership. For example, much research shows that people who talk frequently are perceived as leaders (Bavelas, Hastorf, Gross, and Kite, 1965; Zdeo and Oakes, 1967). Because talking is associated with directing and with expertise, two traits associated with leadership, those who are voluble are perceived as leaders.

Recall also from our discussion of interpersonal communication that observers are more likely to attribute the actions of actors to internal characteristics, whereas actors are more likely to attribute them to external factors. Thus subordinates see leaders as possessing leadership characteristics, but the leaders themselves probably think much of what they do has external causes. Thus, when a leader behaves in supportive ways toward his subordinates, those subordinates perceive the behavior as due to personality traits of the leader and the leader views it as necessary because of the particular leadership situation: being supportive is what a leader is supposed to do.

The characteristics attributed to anyone are not constant; perceptions can change. Any behavior or effect of behavior that is sufficiently extreme can override previously made attributions. This phenomenon is called "engulfing the field" (Heider, 1958). The rumor that a given leader once punched out a subordinate is sufficiently extreme to override a generally favorable previous impression of that leader (Calder, 1977).

Leaders and subordinates also make attributions about the causes of subordinate behavior (Mitchell, Green, and Wood, 1981; Martinko and Gardner, 1987). The perceived causes of a subordinate's performance have clear implications for how a leader responds to that performance. For example, if high performance is perceived as a result of effort, it is rewarded. If poor performance is perceived as due to lack of effort, it is punished, but if it is ascribed to bad luck, the leader provides sympathy, encouragement, and support.

A number of factors influence the attribution process. Key among these are the self-serving biases of the leader (Miller and Ross, 1975; Bradley, 1978). People regularly take responsibility for positive outcomes of their behaviors and deny responsibility for negative ones. As we will see in Chapter 9, one popular theory of motivation is based on this notion.

What can managers do to reduce the influence of the attribution process? Two major conditions seem to limit or alter attribution effects. First is restrictions on leader behaviors. Examples are social norms, pressure from others, union contracts, governmental regulations, or other constraints that prevent the leader from taking actions based on negative attribution. The second restraint is developing organizational personnel policies that provide alternative explanations for behavior other than attributions. Examples are personnel policies that trigger responses in increasing severity as infractions continue; by codifying the behavior and response, the judgment calls required by attribution are removed. In thinking about cross-national interaction, one might add to this list the training of managers in the meanings attached to behaviors in other cultures.

The attribution researchers themselves say they do not believe attributions account for a large part of leadership. They feel that an attribution view is consistent with the "interactionist" views of leadership that have popped up in recent years. The shift from total emphasis on the consequences of leadership behavior to some thinking about causes and interactions is probably healthy. We will study this approach to leadership next.

Environmental and Organizational Influences on Leadership

Like so many other areas, leadership has not been tied into the main body of macro-organizational research (that research dealing with larger organizational issues such as structure or environment). Yet, it is obvious that leadership is constrained or enhanced by environmental and organizational characteristics (Behling and Rauch, 1985). Yet very little is known about such influences (Melcher, 1977). When writers try to relate macro-environmental characteristics to leader-subordinate interaction, they do not focus on the same kinds of issues as the leadership researchers.

For example, an open systems view (Buckley, 1968) suggests that what takes place outside organizations will influence what goes on inside. Considerable work has been done on the influence of such environmental characteristics as stability and turbulence on the structure of organizations. In stable organizations all departments can be similarly structured, but turbulent organizations require diversified organizational structures to be successful (Lawrence and Lorsch, 1969).

Some evidence indicates that the most effective groups are characterized by a leader style that matches environmental variety. That is, workers in low-variety environments with low-variety leaders are high performers, as are workers in high-variety environments with high-variety leaders (Osborn, Hunt, and Busson, 1977).

Studies of political, social, and legal influences on leadership are also not helpful to managers trying to decide what to do about the leadership in their unit or work group. Some evidence suggests that managers who see economic influences as important are more directive than those who do not (Bass, Valenzi, and Farrow, 1977; Farrow, Valenzi, and Bass, 1980). Macro-environmental events are probably sufficiently removed from leadership behavior on a day-to-day basis that they really do not influence it, except through influence on organizational characteristics such as structure or culture. Research has not yet identified these environmental-organizational-behavioral linkages.

It is clear, however, that the emphasis on global competition is changing the way organizations must think about developing their leadership. "When managers move into this high level arena, they must become holistic thinkers. They must dig below surface explanations and take advantage of all factors, even those which are beyond the obvious . . ." (Marsick and Cederholm, 1988, p. 5). Tichy provides an interesting example of how General Electric attempted to do this at its Crotonville Management Development Institute (Tichy, 1989).

Relationships between superiors and their subordinates are, of course, strongly influenced by the policies and culture of the larger organization. For example, restrictive structures are associated with directive, constraining leadership. In more open structures, where jobs are clearly spelled out, less directive leadership is found (Bass, 1985). Sometimes managerial policy increases worker authority and autonomy. Such policies are possibly best carried out by decentralized organizations.

Managers should sensitize themselves to the characteristics of their or-

FIGURE 8.6
*A Conceptual
Framework of
Leadership*

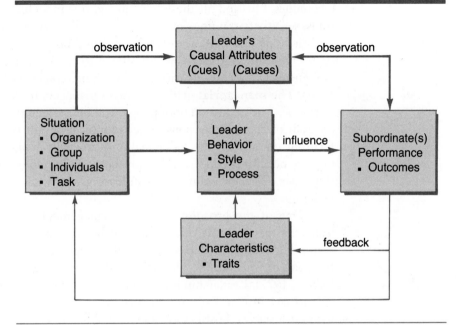

ganizations and cultures that are likely to influence superior–subordinate interaction (Bennis, 1989). They might think about leadership styles that are most comfortable for them and then consider how these styles might be related to other organizational characteristics. Perhaps they can change organizational characteristics that are inconsistent with their preferred leader styles or change their styles to be harmonious with unchangeable organizational characteristics. It may be that organizations changed so dramatically in the 1970s and 1980s that whole new styles are called for (Byrd, 1987).

From these various approaches to leadership, we can construct a conceptual framework to identify the contribution each perspective can make to understanding the phenomenon as a whole; such a framework is shown in Figure 8.6. Figure 8.6 shows how such leader factors as characteristics and attributes (the latter affected by subordinates' perceptions), as well as the organizational context and the specific situation, help shape leader behavior. This behavior influences subordinate performance, the outcomes of which will feed back into the situation and to the leader.

Leadership Training

There are probably more programs to train various kinds of leaders than any other kind of training program. There are, as well, a number of training techniques. On- and off-the-job lecturing, role modeling, computer simulations, sensitivity training, and behavior modeling are frequently used. Here we briefly describe just a few of the training programs currently available.

One training package was designed to teach leaders that they can simultaneously use consideration and initiating structure (Blake and Mouton, 1964). The **managerial grid** encourages managers to develop a 9,9 leadership style, 1 being low on both people and task orientation and 9 being high on each of these dimensions. The training program consists of six steps, focusing initially on the individual and gradually building up to addressing organizational concerns, that promote the development of a 9,9 leadership style. The program uses seminars, group work, and self-evaluation techniques.

One of the broadest forms of management training encompassing leadership principles is that conducted by American Telephone and Telegraph. For years AT&T has supported the operation of assessment centers, the goals of which are to identify and develop leadership skills (Moses and Byham, 1977). Leadership is defined as the extent to which an individual in face-to-face interaction can influence others to resolve problems effectively without arousing hostility (Moses and Byham, 1977). A variety of techniques are used, including unstructured, highly competitive leaderless group exercises and highly structured, cooperative business games. Exercises are designed to reflect organizational problems and goals.

Fiedler developed a leadership training program based on his contingency theory. **Leader match** (Fiedler and Chemers, 1984) is a workbook with self-paced programs of study. Since contingency theory sees the LPC (least preferred co-worker) score as a relatively unchangeable personality trait, the focus of this training program is on changing the situation to make it more favorable to the leader. Leader match teaches leaders how to (1) assess their own leadership style based on their LPC scores, (2) assess the amount of situational favorability, and (3) change the situation so it matches their style. The program has come under some criticism.

The **Telos** program is a two- to two-and-a-half day program based on the Vroom and Yetton model. Named from a Greek word meaning goal-directed or purposeful, the aims of the program are to (1) determine when and how to involve people in resolving specific situations, (2) establish differences between manager's intuitive approaches and the Vroom-Yetton model, (3) help managers to formulate a personally effective leadership choice model, and (4) work out individual developmental plans and build desired changes into the manager's work plans.

The seven-day leadership development program at the **Center for Creative Leadership** (Campbell, 1979) is an ambitious leadership training program using elements of many theoretical approaches. Emphasis is on expanding self-knowledge through assessment, exercises, didactic presentations, feedback, and future planning. The seven days involve (1) assessment center exercises, (2) an inventory, peer feedback, and exercises in decision making based on the Vroom-Yetton model, (3) work with the Blake-Mouton and Fiedler models, (4) discussion and skill building involving creativity, (5) giving and receiving feedback, (6) goal setting and individual career analysis, and (7) actualizing goal setting.

Hersey and Blanchard developed a training program called LEAD that is based on their model. The program uses a questionnaire with 12 situations reflecting different levels of subordinate maturity. For each situation, the respondent is to pick one of four responses, each representing one of the four leadership styles. The questionnaire is then scored by the respondent and the choices analyzed.

SUMMARY

The Elsa Porter case serves to illustrate the role of participation in leadership. Central to Porter's leadership style are her efforts to implement participative management in the midst of a traditionally autocratic civil service bureaucracy. Her efforts are both innovative and insightful when taken in light of the following remarks on the study of leadership.

Leadership is different from mere headship, or the authority conveyed by upper echelons; leadership involves the ability to motivate subordinates and affect change. Managers engage in a variety of functions, not all of them leadership roles. Researchers have also shown that those functions vary according to the managerial level. The study of managers has also exploded four myths of management, revealing that management is an action-oriented, regularized, interpersonal, and unscientific activity. Management is also varied: managers can perform a wide variety of roles, one of which is leadership.

To understand the difference between management and leadership, we must understand how leadership emerges. The leadership process takes place through three steps involving the contributions that individuals make to groups. Group members' preconceptions of what leaders are possibly contribute to who is selected as leader. In one view, leaders may obtain "idiosyncrasy credits," increasing their own status as they build rather than use these credits. Once a sufficient store of credits has been banked, the leader can exhibit deviant behavior and, drawing on those credits, retain support.

To further understand the concept of leadership, we presented a set of myths about leadership that seem to capture the truth and yet are unsupported by research. Two perspectives suggest that leadership may not matter. In one view, the constraints on leader behavior are so great, and the latitude for leader action so narrow, that it is misguided to focus much attention on this aspect of organizational life. In the other view, subordinate or organizational characteristics can provide substitutes for leadership that render it unnecessary. Although these views are a useful caution, the real need for direction and motivation in organizations argues that leadership is a valuable phenomenon.

We studied four approaches of research into leadership: trait, behavioral, contingency, and attribution. Trait approaches to leadership have not gotten us very far; only a few traits of successful leaders have been identified. Recently, the trait theory has reappeared in a slightly different form, with emphasis on charismatic leadership, or the ability of the leader to move followers.

Two early behavioral studies of leadership stand out. One was a study of boys' clubs that concluded that democratic leadership is superior to authoritarian or laissez-faire leadership in terms of subordinate satisfaction and performance. The other study, at the Hawthorne Works of the Western Electric Company, uncovered the fact that people will perform better merely when they feel they are given attention. These studies were supplemented by work at the University of Michigan and Ohio State, where studies of leadership identified two dimensions of leadership, one focusing on the task and the other on the people performing the task. Consideration and people orientation have been found to be consistently related to subordinate satisfaction, but not as consistently related to performance.

Participation (discussed in more detail in Chapter 7) relates to the question of leadership. Vroom and Jago's decision-making theory proposes that different degrees of participation are appropriate in different circumstances. Role-making theory sees the leader and subordinate negotiating the leader's role over time. This model suggests as well that leaders may employ different arrangements with different subordinates.

Contingency theories identify characteristics of subordinates or of situations that call for different leadership styles. Fiedler's work, which received much attention in the last 25 years, assumes that people have relatively unchanging personalities giving rise to relatively unchanging leadership styles. Appropriate leadership style depends on the favorableness of the situation. Because personality is relatively unchanging, leaders must change situational favorableness to fit their personality styles.

House's path-goal theory considers the situation and the leader-subordinate relationship simultaneously. The job of the leader is to clarify goals and objectives for subordinates that are consistent with subordinate expectations and to clarify paths to those goals. House, unlike Fiedler, sees the leader as able to adopt different leadership styles depending on appropriateness. A similar view, from Hersey and Blanchard, identifies as a key variable the subordinate's maturity, expressed as ability and willingness to go where the leader wants to lead.

Recent approaches to leadership have focused on perceptions by leaders and subordinates of each other's behavior. To understand leader and subordinate behavior, one must observe the attributions each makes about the situation. Subordinates interpret leader behavior based on their attributions to the leader and the situation; leaders behave toward subordinates based on their attributions. These attributions are often flawed by biases.

Environmental factors affect leadership as well, although largely by shaping the organizational structure and culture. Environmental turbulence is best met with differentiated organizations, whereas in stable environments organization units might not need to be as flexible to be responsive to environmental demands. This suggests there will be more variability in leadership in organizations facing turbulence than in stable environments.

Many organizations use leadership training programs to develop desirable leadership styles in their managers. Those selected for mention here cover many of the approaches to leadership described in the chapter.

MANAGERIAL INSIGHT

To: *Student Managers*
From: *Veteran Manager*
Subject: *Leadership*

Most of the examples of leadership discussed in this chapter—and indeed, in most books on the subject—are about people at the top of their organizations. CEOs, generals, and presidents are our most visible and hence most studied leaders.

Unless you are starting your own business, however, you probably won't go straight from business school to the top of an organization. You'll probably find yourself somewhere in the middle. How do you lead from the middle? Here are some thoughts on how to carry out this role:

1. In the middle, you have to lead and follow at the same time. This can be tricky, but it is the only way you will succeed at this level. As a leader, you have to be the one to size up the situation, decisively select a course from all that are available, and get others to willingly go along with you. As a follower, you have to make sure your choice of direction is in synchronization with where your boss wants to go.

2. Getting a clear fix on your boss's vision for the organization is absolutely crucial to your success in leading from the middle. Your ability to lead will hinge on your ability to translate the larger vision into relevant work for those who report to you. In effect, you are an interpreter, translating the language of your boss into the language of your employees. If you can't make this link, your employees will probably not want to follow you.

3. Once you've grasped and become a believer in this idea, your task becomes to create followers. People respond differently to different leadership styles. This means you may have to be an authoritarian leader with some and a coaching leader with others. It is at this point that your study of leadership becomes highly relevant.

Leadership styles are like a kit of tools to help you get things done through other people. If you can become adept at several, and learn when to select the right one for the conditions, you will be well along the road toward becoming a truly successful leader.

Learning to lead from the middle is essential in another regard. Your future in any organization (assuming you don't own it) is shaped in large part by those above you. If you understand their vision and direction, and lead your unit in the direction they are trying to take the whole organization, you will be perceived from above as a leader. Leaders get promoted and get larger groups to lead. So if you see your ultimate place being the head of the parade, learn to march smartly in the middle.

REVIEW QUESTIONS

1. Do you think that Elsa Porter's reforms outlived her tenure at the Department of Commerce? Why or why not?

2. Contrast leadership and headship.

3. What four myths about managers have been put to rest by various studies of how managers spend their time?

4. What roles does Mintzberg say that managers play? Is any role more important than the others?

5. What are the benefits of Stewart's model, with its identification of demands, constraints, and choices?

6. How has the study of attributions helped in our understanding of the emergence of leadership?

7. Do you agree with the view that leadership does not matter? Give examples, and explain why or why not?

8. Assume that organizations in the future will be characterized by cohesive groups of highly trained workers with task expertise. According to Kerr and Jermier, would leadership in such organizations be more or less necessary? What if the organizations' environment was characterized by frequent and radical change—would that alter the need for leadership?

9. What problem limits the effectiveness of identifying traits of leadership, including charisma?

10. What are the two types of leadership styles identified in the Ohio State and University of Michigan studies? Which is preferable for job satisfaction? Which is preferable for task performance?

11. How does Fiedler's model work?

12. What is the focus of House's path-goal model? What leadership styles does it address?

13. What variable do Hersey and Blanchard see as the key to identifying an appropriate leadership style? What two dimensions must be considered?

14. What paradox is presented by the differing attributions of leaders and followers?

15. Contrast the goals of such training programs as the managerial grid and the AT&T program with those of the Fiedler leader match program.

REFERENCES

Ashour, A. S., and Johns, G. (1983). Leader influence through operant principles: A theoretical and methodological framework. *Human Relations* 36:603–636.

Bales, R. F. (1953). The equilibrium problem in small groups. In T. Parsons, R. F. Bales, and E. A. Shils (eds.), *Working Papers on the Theory of Action*. Glencoe, IL: Free Press.

Bass, B. M. (1981). *Stogdill's Handbook of Leadership*. New York: Free Press.

Bass, B. M. (1985). *Leadership and Performance Beyond Expectations*. New York: Free Press.

Bass, B. M., Valenzi, E. R., and Farrow, D. L. (1977). External environment related to managerial style. Rochester: University of Rochester, U.S. Army Research Institute for the Behavioral and Social Sciences, Technical Report 7702. Also (March 1–4, 1977) in the *Proceedings of the International Conference on Social Change and Organizational Development*, Dubrovnik, Yugoslavia.

Bavelas, A., Hastorf, A. H., Gross, A. E., and Kite, W. R. (1965). Experiments on the alternation of group structure. *Journal of Experimental Social Psychology* 1: 55–70.

Behling, O., and Rauch, C. F. (1985). A functional perspective on improving leadership. *Organizational Dynamics* 13 (4): 51–61.

Bennis, W. (1989a). *On Becoming a Leader*. Reading, MA: Addison-Wesley.

Bennis, W. (1989b). *Why Leaders Can't Lead*. San Francisco: Jossey-Bass.

Blake, R. R., and Mouton, J. S. (1964). *The Managerial Grid*. Houston: Gulf.

Bormann, E. G. (1969). *Discussion and Group Methods: Theory and Practice*. New York: Harper & Row.

Bradley, G. W. (1978). Self-serving biases in the attribution process: A re-examination of the fact or fiction question. *Journal of Personality and Social Psychology* 36: 56–71.

Brenner, O. C. (1982). Relationship of education to sex, managerial status, and the managerial stereotype. *Journal of Applied Psychology* 67: 380–383.

Buckley, W. (ed.). (1968). *Modern Systems Research for the Behavioral Scientists*. Chicago: Aldine.

Byrd, R. E. (1987). Corporate leadership skills: A new synthesis. *Organizational Dynamics* 16 (1): 34–43.

Calder, B. J. (1977). An attribution theory of leadership. In B. M. Staw and G. R. Salancik (eds.), *New Directions in Organizational Behavior*. Chicago: St. Calir Press, pp. 179–204.

Campbell (1979). In B. M. Bass (ed.), *Stogdill's Handbook of Leadership*. New York: Free Press.

Carlson, S. (1951). *Executive Behavior: A Study of the Work Load and the Working Methods of Managing Directors*. Stromberg, Stockholm.

Conger, J. A. (1989). *The Charismatic Leader*. San Francisco: Jossey-Bass.

Conger, J. A., and Kanungo, R. N. (1985). Toward a behavioral theory of charismatic leadership in organizational settings. *Academy of Management Review* 12: 637–647.

Conger, J. A., and Kanungo, R. N., and associates (1988). *Charismatic Leadership: The Elusive Factor in Organizational Effectiveness*. San Francisco: Jossey-Bass.

Cronshaw, J. F., and Lord, R. G. (1987). Effects of categorization, attribution, and encoding processes on leadership perceptions. *Journal of Applied Psychology* 72:97–106.

Dienesch, R. M., and Liden, R. C. (1986). Leader-member exchange model of leadership: A critique and further development. *Academy of Management Review* 11: 618–634.

Drory, A., and Gluskinos, U. M. (1980). Machiavellianism and leadership. *Journal of Applied Psychology* 65: 81–86.

Dubin, R. (1979). Metaphors of leadership: An overview. In J. G. Hunt and L. L. Larson (eds.), *Crosscurrents in Leadership*. Carbondale: Southern Illinois University Press, pp. 225–238.

Farrow, D. L., Valenzi, E. R., and Bass, B. M. (1980). A comparison of leadership and situational characteristics within profit and non-profit organizations. *Proceedings of the Academy of Management*.

Fiedler, F. E. (1967). *A Theory of Leadership Effectiveness*. New York: McGraw-Hill.

Fiedler, F. E. (1970). A contingency model of leadership effectiveness. In L. Berkowitz (ed.), *Advances in Experimental Social Psychology*. New York: Academic Press, pp. 149–190.

Fiedler, F. E. (1978). The contingency model and the dynamics of the leadership process. In L. Berkowitz (ed.), *Advances in Experimental Social Psychology* 11: 60–112.

Fiedler, F. E., and Chemers, M. M. (1984). *Improving Leadership Effectiveness: The LEADER MATCH CONCEPT* (2nd ed.). New York: Wiley.

Field, R. H. G. (1982). A test of the Vroom-Yetton model of leadership. *Journal of Applied Psychology* 7: 523–532.

Friedland, W. H. (1964). For a sociological concept of charisma. *Social Forces* 43: 18–26.

Fulk, J., and Wendler, E. R. (1982). Dimensionality of leader-subordinate interactions: A path-goal investigation. *Organizational Behavior and Human Performance* 30: 241–264.

Fulk-Schriesheim, J. (1980). The social context of leader-subordinate relations: An investigation of the effects of group cohesiveness. *Journal of Applied Psychology* 65: 183–294.

Gamson, W. A., and Scotch, N. A. (1964). A scapegoat in baseball. *American Journal of Sociology* 70: 69–72.

Graeff, C. I. (1983). The situational leadership theory: A critical view. *Academy of Management Review* 8: 285–291.

Graen, G. (1976). Role making processes within complex organizations. In M. D. Dunnette (ed.), *Handbook of Industrial and Organizational Psychology*. Chicago: Rand-McNally, pp. 1201–1246.

Graen, G., Alvares, K., Orris, J. B., and Martella, J. A. (1970). Contingency model of leadership effectiveness: Antecedent and evidential results. *Psychological Bulletin* 74: 285–296.

Graen, G., and Cashman, J. F. (1975). A role making model of leadership in formal organizations: A developmental approach. In J. G. Hunt and L. L. Larson (eds.), *Leadership Frontiers*. Carbondale: Southern Illinois University Press.

Guest, R. H., (1956). Of time and the foreman. *Personnel* 32: 478–486.

Gulick, L. H. and Urwick, L. F. (eds.). (1937). *Papers on the Science of Administration*. New York: Columbia University Press.

Halpin, A. S., and Weiner, B. J. (1957). A factorial study of the leader behavior descriptions. In R. M. Stogdill and A. E. Coons (eds.), *Leadership Behavior: Its Description and Measurement*. Columbus: Ohio State University, Bureau of Business Research.

Heider, F. (1958). *The Psychology of Interpersonal Relations*. New York: Wiley.

Heller, F. A., and Clark, A. W. (1976). Personnel and human resources development. In M. R. Rosenzweig and L. W. Porter (eds.), *Annual Review of Psychology* (vol. 27). Palo Alto, CA: Annual Review, pp. 405–436.

Hersey, P., and Blanchard, K. H. (1982). *Management of Organization Behavior: Utilizing Human Resources* (4th ed.). Englewood Cliffs, NJ: Prentice-Hall.

Hofstede, G. (1980). *Culture's Consequences: International Differences in Work-related Values*. Beverly Hills, CA: Sage Publications.

Hollander, E. O. (1958). Conformity, status, and idiosyncrasy credit. *Psychological Review* 65: 117–127.

Hollander, E. P. (1964). *Leaders, Groups, and Influence.* New York: Oxford University Press.

Hollander, E. P., and Offermann, L. R. (1990). Leadership in organizations: Relationships in transition. *American Psychologist* 45:179–189.

Hornstein, H. A., Heilman, M. E., Mone, E., and Tartell, R. (1987). Responding to contingent leadership behavior. *Organizational Dynamics* 15 (4): 56–65.

House, R. J. (1971). A path goal theory of leadership effectiveness. *Administrative Science Quarterly* 16:321–338.

House, R. J. (1977). A 1976 theory of charismatic leadership. In J. G. Hunt and L. L. Larson (eds.), *Leadership: The Cutting Edge.* Carbondale: Southern Illinois University Press, pp. 189–207.

House, R. J., and Dessler, G. (1974). The path goal theory of leadership. Some post hoc and a priori tests. In J. G. Hunt and L. L. Larson (eds.), *Contingency Approaches to Leadership.* Carbondale: Southern Illinois University Press, pp. 29–55.

House, R. J., and Mitchell, T. R. (1974). Path-goal theory of leadership. *Journal of Contemporary Business* 3:81–97.

Howell, J. M., and Frost, P. J. (1989). A laboratory study of charismatic leadership. *Organizational Behavior and Human Decision Processes* 43:243–269.

Jago, A. G., and Vroom, V. H. (1982). Sex differences in the incidence and evaluation of participative leader behavior. *Journal of Applied Psychology* 67:776–783.

Katz, D., Maccoby, N., Gurin, G., and Floor, L. (1951). *Productivity, Supervision, and Morale Among Railroad Workers.* Ann Arbor: University of Michigan, Institute for Social Research.

Katz, D., Maccoby, N., and Morse, N. C. (1950). *Productivity, Supervision, and Morale in an Office Situation.* Ann Arbor: University of Michigan, Institute for Social Research.

Keller, R. T. (1989). A test of the path-goal theory of leadership with need for clarity as a moderator in research and development organizations. *Journal of Applied Psychology* 74:208–212.

Kerr, S., and Jermier, J. (1978). Substitutes for leadership: Their meaning and measurement. *Organizational Behavior and Human Performance* 22:375–403.

Kotter, J. (1982). *The General Managers.* Cambridge, MA: Harvard University Press.

Kozlowski, S. W. J., and Doherty, M. L. (1989). Integration of climate and leadership: Examination of a neglected issue. *Journal of Applied Psychology* 74:546–553.

Kurke, L. B., and Aldrich, H. E. (1983). Mintzberg was right! A replication and extension of the nature of managerial work. *Management Science* 29:975–984.

Lawrence, P. R., and Lorsch, J. W. (1969). *Organization and Environment: Managing Differentiation and Integration.* Homewood, IL: Irwin.

Lewin, K., Lippitt, R., and White, R. K. (1939). Patterns of aggressive behavior in experimentally created social climates. *Journal of Social Psychology* 10:271–301.

Life, H. (1986). Strategy: Corporate leadership. *Journal of General Management* 12:72–91.

Lombardo, M. M., and McCall, M. M. (1981). Looking glass inc: An organizational simulation. In J. G. Hunt, M. Sekaran, and C. A. Schriesheim (eds.), *Leadership: Beyond Establishment Views*. Carbondale: Southern Illinois University Press.

Lord, R. G. (1985). An information processing approach to social perceptions, leadership and behavioral measurement in organizations. *Research in Organizational Behavior* 7:87–128.

Lord, R. G., and Alliger, G. M. (1985). A comparison of four information processing models of leadership and social perceptions. *Human Relations* 38:47–65.

Lord, R. G., Foti, R. J., and DeVader, C. L. (1984). A test of leadership categorization theory: Internal structure, information processing, and leadership perceptions. *Organizational Behavior and Human Performance* 34:343–378.

Maccoby, M. (1976). *The Gamesman*. New York: Simon & Schuster.

Maccoby, M. (1979). Leadership needs of the 1980s. *Current Issues in Higher Education, 1979*. Washington, D.C.: American Association of Higher Education, pp. 17–34.

Marsick, V. J., and Cederholm, L. (1988). Developing leadership in international managers—An urgent challenge. *Columbia Journal of World Business* 23:3–11.

Martinko, M. J., and Gardner, W. L. (1987). The leader/member attribution process. *Academy of Management Review* 12:235–249.

Meindl, J. R., and Ehrlich, S. B. (1987). The romance of leadership and the evaluation of organizational performance. *Academy of Management Journal* 30:91–109.

Melcher, A. J. (1977). Leadership models and research approaches. In J. G. Hunt and L. L. Larson (eds.), *Leadership: The Cutting Edge*. Carbondale: Southern Illinois University Press, pp. 94–108.

Miller, D., and Ross, M. (1975). Self serving biases in the attribution of causality: Fact or fiction? *Psychological Bulletin* 82:213–225.

Mintzberg, H. (1973). *The Nature of Managerial Work*. New York: Harper & Row.

Mintzberg, H. (1975). The manager's job: Folklore and fact. *Harvard Business Review*, July–August.

Misumi, S. (1985). *The Behavioral Science of Leadership: An Inter-disciplinary Japanese Research Program*. Ann Arbor: University of Michigan Press.

Mitchell, T. R. (1979). Organizational behavior. In M. R. Rosenzweig and L. W. Porter (eds.), *Annual Review of Psychology* (vol. 30). Palo Alto, CA: Annual Reviews, pp. 243–281.

Mitchell, T. R., Green, S. G., and Wood, R. (1981). An attributional model of leadership and the poor performing subordinate. In L. L. Cummings and B. M. Staw (eds.), *Research in Organizational Behavior* (vol. 3). Greenwich, CT: JAI Press, pp. 197–234.

Mitchell, T. R., Smyser, C. M., and Weed, S. E. (1975). Locus of control: Supervision and work satisfaction. *Academy of Management Journal* 18:623–630.

Moses, J. L., and Byham, W. C. (1977). *Applying the Assessment Center Method*. New York: Pergamon Press.

Nadler, D. A., and Tushman, M. L. (1990). Beyond the charismatic leader: Leadership and organizational change. *California Management Review* 32:77–97.

Osborn, R. N., Hunt, J. G., and Busson, R. S. (1977). On getting your own way in organizational design: An empirical illustration of requisite variety. *Organizational Administrative Science* 8:295–310.

Pavett, C. M., and Lau, A. W. (1983). Managerial work: The influence of hierarchical level and functional specialty. *Academy of Management Journal* 26:170–177.

Penley, L. E., and Hawkins, B. (1985). Studying interpersonal communication in organizations: A leadership application. *Academy of Management Journal* 28:309–326.

Petty, M. M., and Bruning, N. S. (1980). A comparison of the relationships between subordinates' perceptions of supervisory behavior and measures of subordinates' job satisfaction for male and female leaders. *Academy of Management Journal* 32:717–725.

Pfeffer, J. (1977). The ambiguity of leadership. *Academy of Management Review* 2.

Prien, E. P. (1963). Development of a supervisor position description questionnaire. *Journal of Applied Psychology* 47:10–14.

Ragins, B. R. (1989). Power and gender congruency effects in evaluations of male and female managers. *Journal of Management* 15:65–76.

Rice, R. W., Instone, D., and Adams, J. (1984). Leader sex, leader success, and leadership process: Two field studies. *Journal of Applied Psychology* 69:3–11.

Roethlisberger, F. J., and Dickson, W. J. (1939). *Management and the Worker*. Cambridge, MA: Harvard University Press.

Schneier, C. E., and Bartol, K. M. (1980). Sex effects in emergent leadership. *Journal of Applied Psychology* 65:341–345.

Schriesheim, C. A., and Kerr, S. (1977). Theories and measures of leadership: A critical appraisal of present and future directions. In J. G. Hunt and L. L. Larson (eds.), *Leadership: The Cutting Edge*. Carbondale: Southern Illinois University Press, pp. 9–44.

Scott, W. E. (1977). Leadership: A functional analysis. In J. G. Hunt and L. L. Larson (eds.), *Leadership: The Cutting Edge*. Carbondale: Southern Illinois University Press, pp. 84–93.

Shapira, Z., and Dunbar, R. (1980). Testing Mintzberg's managerial roles classification using an in-basket simulation. *Journal of Applied Psychology* 65:87–95.

Stein, R. T., Hoffman, L. R., Cooley, S. J., and Pearse, R. W. (1979). Leadership valence: Modeling and measuring the process of emergent leadership. In J. G. Hunt and L. L. Larson (eds.), *Crosscurrents in Leadership*. Carbondale: Southern Illinois University Press, pp. 126–247.

Stevens, G. E., and DeNisi, A. (1980). Women as managers: Attitudes and attributions for the performance of women. *Academy of Management Journal* 23:355–361.

Stewart, R. (1982). A model for understanding managerial jobs and behavior. *Academy of Management Review* 7:7–13.

Stogdill, R. M., and Shartle, C. L. (1955). *Methods in the Study of Administrative Leadership*. Columbus: Ohio State University Press, Bureau of Business Research.

Tichy, N. M. (1989). GE's Crotonville: A staging ground for corporate revolution. *Academy of Management Executive* 3:99–106.

Tornow, W., and Pinto, R. R. (1976). The development of a managerial job taxonomy: A system for describing, classifying, and evaluating executive positions. *Journal of Applied Psychology* 61:410–418.

Vecchio, R. P. (1987). Situational leadership theory: An examination of a prescriptive theory. *Journal of Applied Psychology* 72:444–451.

Vroom, V. (1976). Leadership. In M. D. Dunnette (ed.), *Handbook of Industrial and Organizational Psychology*. Chicago: Rand-McNally, pp. 1527–1552.

Vroom, V. H., and Jago, A. G. (1988). *The New Leadership: Managing Participation in Organizations*. Englewood Cliffs, NJ: Prentice-Hall.

Vroom, V. H., and Yetton, P. (1973). *Leadership and Decision Making*. Pittsburgh: University of Pittsburgh Press.

Wakabayashi, M., and Graen, G. (1989). Human resource development of Japanese managers: Leadership and career investment. In A. Nead (ed.), *Research in Personnel and Human Resources Management*. Greenwich, CT: JAI Press, pp. 235–256.

Zaleznik, A. (1989). *The Managerial Mystique: Restoring Leadership in Business*. New York: Harper & Row.

Zaleznik, A. (1990). The leadership gap. *The Executive* 4:7–22.

Zdeo, S. M., and Oakes, W. F. (1976). Reinforcement of leadership behavior in group discussion. *Journal of Experimental Social Psychology* 3:31–320.

CHAPTER 9

Motivation:
Convincing Others to Follow

CHAPTER OVERVIEW

This chapter examines the various theories of motivation that have been used to help explain behavior in organizations. Within each of two broad categories of theory the principal researchers and their ideas are explained. After reviewing the main theoretical bases for studying motivation, various programs for applying these theories are discussed.

THEME CASE

The Abraham Rosner Case describes a man who got laid off by an insurance company, worked for about 10 years with various brokerage firms, then lost his job again. He discusses what motivated him to work and how his motivation changed under the pressure of joblessness.

CHAPTER OUTLINE

- What Is Motivation?
- Early Theories of Motivation
- Content Theories
- Process Theories
- Stir Gently and Apply
- Summary
- Managerial Insight

KEY DEFINITIONS

Motivation   psychological processes that cause the arousal, direction, and persistence of behavior; these processes are voluntary although they may be influenced.

Content theories   explanations of motivation that are psychological in nature and focus on individuals' needs.

Process theories   explanations of motivation that focus on factors that determine the kind of choices individuals make.

Additional Terms

Hedonistic
Rationality
Scientific management
Human relations movement
System 4
Instinct
Manifest needs
Competence
Hierarchy of needs
Self-actualization
ERG theory
Motivation-hygiene theory

Dissatisfiers (hygiene factors)
Satisfiers (motivating factors)
Achievement
Affiliation
Power
Operant conditioning
Reinforcement
Rewards
Omission
Punishment
Reinforcement schedule
Expectancy theory
Expectancy
Valence
Effort-performance expectancies
Performance-outcome expectancies
Self-efficacy
Goal setting
Outcome feedback
Process feedback
Equity theory
Political theory
Management by objectives (MBO)
Behavior modification

THE ABRAHAM ROSNER CASE

In 1964 I got laid off from an insurance company. Well, I had been interested in the stock market for some time. I'd been doing some dabbling and had some investments. One day I was talking to my broker, who had become assistant manager of his office. I was unemployed, and I was sort of jokingly saying that I'd make a million dollars if I had his job. I said, "You've got the greatest job in the world." He said, "Why don't you come in and apply?" Then I got a call from him two days later that somebody had just left and there was an opening. He said, "Just come around and throw your hat in the ring." I did, and I got the job.

At that time I was already pretty knowledgeable about stocks. In fact, when I got in I soon discovered that I knew more than most of the people in the place. And I had had one big winner, which makes a difference. In other words, I knew it could be done. I had had a stock that went up twenty times beyond what I paid for it. Which has an effect on people's lives. . . . But that's a subject for another story. Anyway, it so happened that a new manager came there a couple of months after me who wanted his own trainees. So I wound up out. Eventually I got another job with another brokerage firm. I stayed there four years. Then I went with somebody else for a year, and they merged, and I wound up out of there. Probably there were other reasons, too. I might have offended some people. I guess I was doing pretty well, and I didn't care. After that I worked for another insurance firm for a while. I wasn't very successful at that. Then I managed to get into another stock brokerage firm. But I had a hard time and they got a little impatient. They wanted more business. I wound up out of there, and I've been mostly unemployed since 1974.

I'm not sure just what went wrong at the last firm. Coming back there from insurance, I just didn't have many customers, and I wasn't the type who was going to go ringing doorbells or spinning the phone all the time. I don't know, I felt that it was rubbing me the wrong way. In the brokerage house they essentially wanted salesmen. The manager of one house told me, "I'd rather have a successful Fuller Brush man than a Harvard M.B.A. I need somebody who can sell. I don't need your knowledge. The brokerage house will give you all the ideas you want. All you do is convince people to buy and sell stocks. That's where we make our money." The ethics of the brokerage industry are far from what they try to make them out to be.

I don't know, I just can't get on a phone and do that kind of selling. I guess I've always looked down on people who did that. I built up the business before without doing that by having a very good batting average. I came up with a lot more winners than losers. I got a lot of business by word of mouth. But when I came back to the business again, one of two things had happened. There had been some bad years in between, and the customers had pretty much lost their money, whatever broker they were dealing with. And those who were fortunate enough to be dealing with a broker who didn't lose their money, they were inclined to be loyal to that broker. So it was a bad scene. And the manager finally said, "Look, you're simply not doing the business, and I don't know how you're gonna get business unless you want to spend a lot of time on the phone. You're not inclined to do that. So I would suggest you resign."

I was a little bit discouraged by it all. I decided I would never go back to a brokerage house because I just couldn't be a salesman like that. I also knew it was ridiculous even to try and get another brokerage job. After that failure, it just wouldn't work. Nobody was gonna buy me. . . .

I didn't take it as too much of a personal failure when I left the brokerage house because I'd been successful in my own speculation in stocks. I've made a lot more from buying and selling stocks than I ever made from salaries and commissions. Which has had its effect as far as my family is concerned. In other words, my son grows up and he sees that I didn't make my money from hard work or labor. I made it from shrewdness. What does that do to a young fellow who's growing up? He thinks that the way to make out is to be shrewd. Or maybe even just to be lucky, coming in and out of the stock market at the right time. It's like being a winner in a poker game. Is it because you're smart or you're lucky? I think a little of each. But recently I haven't been a big winner. There aren't too many people who know more about the game than I do, but for the past few years I haven't been that good at it. I'd say for the last five years I haven't done anything brilliant in the stock market. It's just more difficult for me, and I think it's my mental attitude. I think half the battle is being in the right frame of mind.

See, this unemployment is bad for people. I could adjust to it in some ways. But even though I'm sure I have more assets than most people, I feel insecure. I don't know how far inflation is gonna go. I might easily make the wrong moves in the stock market. Another tumble would really hurt me if I'm in it. I don't have any pension. There's a feeling of insecurity about the future. So let's say my broker suggests a course of action and gives me the reasons for taking it. If he catches me on a day when I'm in one frame of mind, I will act on it. And if he catches me on a day when maybe I'm in a negative frame of mind, I'll find reasons for not doing it. Even though I'm the same person. I don't think I have as balanced an outlook as I used to have when I was doing better. The insecurity preys on me. It affects my judgment. It affects my moods. So much of this is psychological.

There was a period of time when everything I did seemed to work out beautifully. . . . Every move turned out brilliant. I know I did better than the other brokers in the office because one of them told me. He said, "You've done far better than anybody else. If I'd just been doing the same as you were doing, instead of listening to the manager and the house, I would have been infinitely better off." And that was true. I had a feel for doing the right thing. It's an intangible. I remember reading a story of a gambler who was successful. He did pretty well. But he broke a promise to a friend, and psychologically that hurt him because until then his word had always been good. He was supposed to take a trip and he didn't make the trip, or something like that. He left his friend hanging. And he was a loser after that.

While things were going well, I really enjoyed it. Business was picking up. Everything was breaking right. I got much more satisfaction out of choosing a stock that did well than out of making a big sale, like some of the others did. They were excited if they sold, say $20,000 worth of mutual funds and got a $1,000 commission. I always came up with unique ideas, too, that other brokers would never think about. But on a couple of these deals I got in hassles with the house. On one unusual deal—most brokers have never even heard of it—the house made an error which cost them quite a few thousand bucks. They wanted it to come out of my account, and I had a big hassle that wound up with my leaving that house. Actually I got everything adjusted to my satisfaction, but in the meantime, I'd made all the arrangements to leave. Which turned out to be a poor move, because at the next place things didn't go right anymore.

I guess you could say I should have been more loyal to that house because they gave me a really good break when I came up there, and I did pretty well. They carried me when I was doing poorly. But it got to be an impossible argument, and I guess I was looking for greener pastures. I thought it'd be better somewhere else. That was a mistake, looking back on it. And I was hurt by the bear markets over the last few years. However, I could have sold short as easily as bought stocks if I'd been smart enough to do that. Maybe it's possible that I could've made myself a fortune and wound up with a lot of self-esteem that I was one of the few people who was smart enough to recognize what was happening and make the right moves.

These days I spend a lot more time studying than actively trading stocks. I do a reasonable amount of trading, and I devote a lot of time and attention to it. But I don't think I can beat the game from where I'm sitting this time. I don't think my chances of doing things right are much better than random. The commissions are higher, so it's harder to trade actively and be successful. And my sources of information are not as good as when I worked for that particular brokerage house. I try to check with other brokers, but I find there are few decent brokers around who can come up with good information. I would love to find a broker who is the same broker I was in my good days. But it isn't to be.

But I still work at it. I read the *Wall Street Journal* every day. I get it from a neighbor who finishes it before he runs to work. He leaves it in front of the door, and I pick it up, so it saves me the job of buying it. Otherwise, I'd probably go over to the library and read it there. My wife yells that I spend too much time reading it, which I probably do. But I'm not pressed for time. Generally I get out of the house in the afternoon and go to the library. I enjoy reading all kinds of magazines, mostly nonfiction. And it ties in with the stock market if I read something like *Business Week* or *Fortune*. Occasionally I might get some ideas that might help me.

I often think of a customer of mine who was the president of a small company. His father had also been in the stock market. He quit somewhere in the 1930s, and for the rest of his life he never went to work again. He'd go to the poolroom every afternoon. Or he'd bet on horses. That's the way he spent his time. And sometimes I wonder where the hell my time goes at the end of the day. What did I do? And I don't enjoy the leisure. If I'm at home too much I get into hassles with my wife. I'm not inclined to do anything. We cut down those branches yesterday and they're still lying around. The shower needs fixing. The house needs work. But you get lazy.

It also affects your ethical outlook. I used to have contempt for people who cheat on their income tax. Now I'm becoming aware of how unfair the tax laws are, and I realize that people just do whatever is to their advantage. I'm no longer eligible for unemployment compensation, but if I found some gimmick that made me eligible, I'd use it. And I don't look down on somebody who does some work and is getting unemployment. I might if he was working full time, but if someone makes $50 a week and doesn't tell them, I think that's fine. So your ethical outlook changes. You feel inflation is hurting you, and you figure that certain people have things stacked to their advantage. Like government employees, who automatically get increases. And people in powerful unions and in certain occupations like lawyers and doctors. Everything goes their way. They strike; they get increases; they raise their fees. Sometimes I wish I was in one of these powerful unions. Or working for the government. Though I'm sure some people would envy my position if they knew it. My capital situation is quite strong. I could go a number of years without working. But eventually I would run out. Well, it depends how smart I am with the stock market. Maybe I'll never run out. But you kind of run scared all the time. Which is not a good way to be. . . .

We haven't been hit too hard financially, though if I had a job and was making $1,000 a month or so, I'd be a lot more free with my spending than I am now. I'd be pretty well on top of things because I have a pretty good capital situation. I try to save where I can, but in many ways it gets a little hopeless. For example, let's say this was a down week in the stock market. My stocks may go down several thousand dollars. And that's a real loss, like it came out of your pocket. So I may save a couple of dollars eating at home, but I can lose a couple of thousand in a week. So what does it all mean in the end? From that perspective, all the saving doesn't mean that much.

I think a lot about what I should have done. I should have stayed with that one house where everything was breaking right. Maybe with the changing market I would have fallen into trouble anyhow, but I always managed to come up with unique deals there. Maybe I would have sold short and come up rich. I'm a little sorry I didn't get into real estate a little heavier. I almost got into it a couple of times, but the deals fell through both times. I suppose if I was more persistent, maybe I could've gotten into it. I kind of let things fall where they may. I have this feeling of insecurity. Fear, sometimes. There have been times, not too much recently, when I felt a little bit suicidal. I don't think I was ready to do it, but I was thinking, "What the hell." One of my friends asked, "What happens if your money runs out?" And I said, "How does the song go? 'Suicide is painless, it brings on. . . .'" Some song from TV. That shocked him [laughs].

It's the loss of self-esteem, I guess. I sort of gave up the fight after a while. I've been unemployed at various times before, and it was a bit of a struggle to get something; but I always had reasonable confidence I'd get it. This time, after a while I decided that nothing is going to happen. This is pretty hopeless. And even though you rationalize and say, "Well it's not my fault. It's the fault of the economy. It's beyond my control," you still feel it. If I had done something brilliant with the stock market or commodity market in the last few years, my self-esteem would be much higher. If I'd become a millionaire or successful, maybe I'd have said, "Gee, I'm really brilliant." Or, "I'm smart," or something. But I kind of feel like the years are wasting away and I'm not accomplishing a damn thing. I don't think my life has been a fruitful or a happy one.

What Is Motivation?

Motivation is a stimulant to action. If goals are destinations, motivation is the impetus to choose one destination over another and also the fuel that moves the car along the road. A more technical definition of **motivation** sees it as "the psychological processes that cause the arousal, direction, and persistence of behavior. . . . Many authors add a voluntary component or goal-directed emphasis to that definition" (Mitchell, 1982, p. 81). Typically, we speak of a "highly motivated employee" as one with a strong drive to do a job well or to succeed. Someone lacking motivation is at best a clock-watcher and at worst a loafer. In this expanded form, motivation is something every manager wants to encourage in employees. The underlying assumptions are that employees or their managers, or both, can create conditions that arouse employees to action, direct that action toward fulfilling the goals of the organization, and make that action persistent.

In this view of motivation, the issue of individual differences arises. The manager's job becomes one of identifying the right chords to play to influence each group member to achieve the group's goals. Some of those chords will be the same. One goal of socialization (see Chapter 3) is to mold a team spirit, a common identity, that creates not only shared goals but also shared motivations for achieving them. In the end, however, the study of motivation addresses the distinctiveness of each individual, for each individual has a number of different motivators at work. This idea finds common expression in the newspaper's sports pages, where virtually every manager of every professional team sums it up the same way: "With some players, you have to stroke them. With other players, you have to know when to kick them in the butt."

Even if influenced as by a kick in the butt, motivation is essentially voluntary rather than coerced. The prisoner who follows the prison routine is not motivated but obedient. The employee who studies on her own to learn advanced features of a new computer program is motivated to increase her skills, perhaps because of a desire for promotion. Abe Rosner was motivated at various times by different needs: first by the need for security during a time of inflation, then by the excitement over choosing a stock that did well during good times, and finally by trying to keep his self-esteem even in his latest prolonged period of unemployment.

Motivation is intangible and must be inferred. We cannot state unequivocally that Abe Rosner was lazy or belligerent or just unlucky. We assume a hard-working employee is motivated, and a slow-moving worker is unmotivated, but motivation and performance are not perfectly related. The slow-moving employee may be ill, not know how to do the job, not understand the manager's instructions, or—as with Rosner—be running too low on self-esteem to take up the gauntlet yet one more time. In some cases, speed is not an appropriate measure of work anyway. The "slow-moving" employee, after all, may be more careful than the faster, and seemingly more motivated, one. The perfectionist may be motivated by a sense of craft and pride in output that can be equally beneficial to the employer.

One study summed up five reasons for difficulty in inferring motives from observed behavior: "(1) any single act may express several motives; (2) motives may appear in disguised forms; (3) several motives may be expressed through similar or identical acts; (4) similar motives may be expressed in different behavior; and (5) cultural and personal variations may significantly moderate the modes of expression of certain motives" (as reported in Steers and Porter, 1983, p. 5).

Further complicating the situation is that motivation is not simple, but multifaceted. Each worker has a number of different motivators that impel him to commute to work and confront the day's tasks. The factor at work on any given day may differ from the impetus on another day. Some days a worker feels on top of the world and wants to surmount a challenge. On other days, tired and plagued by problems, he may go to work simply out of a sense of duty or to get out of the house.

Organizations devote valuable resources to selection, training, evaluation, and compensation programs. Underlying such programs is the assumption that if employees are selected correctly, know how to do their jobs, understand how they are doing, and are compensated properly, they will be motivated to engage in behavior directed to attaining both their own and their organizations' goals. Another aspect of motivation that managers should know about is the increasing need to use existing personnel better due to legal, environmental, and economic constraints on organizations. If managers can learn more about motivation, the thinking goes, they will be better able to make employees more productive.

Of all the topics studied by researchers interested in behavior in organizations, those that historically have received the most attention are motivation, leadership (see Chapter 8), and learning (see Chapter 10). All three are closely connected. Early learning studies in psychology could not avoid motivation and vice versa. Did a rat successfully clamber through a maze to some end-point for food because he wanted the food or because he had learned the route to it? When psychology moved out of the laboratory and into industry, managers' key questions concerned all three of these interrelated phenomena: finding effective ways of teaching employees how to do something, motivating them to do it, and providing overall leadership.

It has been popular to divide discussions of various approaches to, or theories about, motivation into two classes: content theories and process theories. This chapter will follow that approach after noting that several early theories of motivation effectively fall into both the content and process camps. **Content theories** typically discuss internal states that lead an individual to engage in various behaviors and ask questions about what starts, stops, and sustains behavior. They are psychological in nature and focus on individuals' needs. **Process theories** are concerned with how behavior is started, stopped, and sustained. These theories focus on factors that determine the kind of choices individuals make when they are satisfying their needs. In a sense, content theories focus on employee motivations (what makes each person tick?), whereas process theories emphasize what managers can do to channel motivation in desirable directions or engender it at desirable levels.

Two assumptions underlie most motivational theories. The first, dating as far back as Aristotle (384–322 B.C.), is the assumption that we are all **hedonistic;** that is, we will do whatever is necessary to avoid pain and seek pleasure. The other is the assumption of **rationality** coming from the Enlightenment ideas of French philosopher and mathematician René Descartes (1596–1650): humans are rational animals and make choices based on sound evaluation of available information. Current thinking (you will recall from Chapter 7) modifies this premise somewhat by introducing the idea of limited rationality to recognize the fact that complete information is frequently unavailable; thus individuals make choices using less than perfect information.

Although hedonism and rationality underlie all theories of motivation, both assumptions are often violated in real life. Abe Rosner's hindsight shows one example. In retrospect, he believes that he never should have left the brokerage job he describes as his most successful; in pursuing pleasure (greener pastures), he clearly did not act rationally.

As we discuss various approaches to motivation we shall forget, for the moment, that there are limits to what managers can do to alter performance (a supposed outcome of motivation). None of the theories address important factors that can affect the dynamic of any given situation, such as union agreements, which often control what can and cannot be done in the workplace; different managerial styles, which determine which issues will be prioritized; or intergroup relations, which constrain the development of programs and policies intended to enhance motivation. We can safely ignore these issues here to focus specifically on motivation, but in the real world managers need to keep their own situational constraints in mind when deciding which motivational strategies will work best for them.

Early Theories of Motivation

One set of early motivational theories falls into both the content and process camps. These are motivational approaches designed by management theorists as management in the first half of the 20th century. As industrialization progressed and the assembly line became a more widespread technique for production, it became necessary to redefine both what constitutes work and the nature of social relationships among people at various levels in the workplace. During this period, one philosophy of management that emerged held that the average worker was lazy and motivated almost entirely by money. According to this view, the way productivity was manipulated was to restructure it to be as simple as possible and then to offer employees piece rates consistent with the amount they produced.

Frederick Taylor, the father of **scientific management,** assumed that individuals were rational; if they were shown how better methods of work were more efficient and led to earning better rewards, they would adopt them. Representative of Taylor's approach is his analysis of the job of a pig-iron handler named Schmidt at Inland Steel Company. First, Taylor ascertained that Schmidt really did want money, and then through time-and-motion study he redesigned the way Schmidt did his job:

> Schmidt, are you a high-priced man? . . . . What I want to find out is whether you want to earn $1.85 a day or whether you are satisfied with $1.15. . . . If you are a high-priced man you will load that pig iron on that car tomorrow for $1.85. . . . That is what a high-priced man does, and you know it just as well as I do. (quoted in Braverman, 1974, pp. 104–105)

This approach represents both a content and process perspective. It assumes that Schmidt has some need or desire to earn money (the content) and designs a strategy by which he can do that (the process). It is both rational and hedonistic as well. Interestingly, in some important senses scientific management presages various elements of more recent approaches to work motivation, first by using incentive rather than the presence of an intimidating supervisor as a motivating force and second by creating a unified system of management rather than relying on hit-or-miss techniques (George, 1972).

From the 1930s through the 1960s management thinkers developed a quite different view that became known as the **human relations movement.** Management writers were increasingly aware of two realities: factors other than money motivated performance, and some workers were self-starters who did not need the close supervision prescribed by scientific management. In addition, there were many instances in which management instituted job simplification models without instituting commensurate pay, a strategy that annoyed workers and became an important issue between unions and management. Employee distrust was heightened.

In response to these factors, management adopted strategies to make employees feel more important. Morale surveys, departmental meetings, company newspapers, and a plethora of other devices were instituted to make employees feel wanted (and often to discourage union entry to plants). The human relations movement attempted to secure employees' compliance with company rules and policies by increasing their satisfaction. Operations research and human engineering methods came along to replace scientific management techniques.

These new approaches are applicable to tasks that the tools of scientific management cannot address. Scientific management is appropriate when tasks can be simplified, structured, and arranged and less effective with tasks that are messy, broad, or cannot be broken apart. As Leavitt (1965) noted, these two management approaches nevertheless had fundamental similarities. Both use technical methods to solve work problems, both separate the development of problem-solving strategies from the implementation of solutions, and both require a cadre of staff specialists to develop and implement the programs.

Ironically, as the workplace in the late 1960s and 1970s increasingly reflected tight technical control and the separation of planning from work, management-derived theories of motivation (and many other approaches to motivation) emphasized the importance of worker autonomy. These theories assumed that people wanted a variety of benefits from their work, ranging from remuneration to self-actualization, that different people wanted different things, and that employees wanted to contribute to the welfare of their organizations.

Illustrative of this broader approach is Likert's interaction-influence theory (1961). Likert envisioned organizations as capable of becoming overlapping groups in which every member would feel that the organization's values and goals reflected his, that every member would identify with the objectives of the organization and the goals of his work group, and that every member would be motivated "to behave in ways best calculated to help the organization accomplish its objectives" (Likert, 1961, p. 182).

Likert (1967) later extended his thinking, identifying several attributes characteristic of effective firms, including people orientation and the development of work teams that pursue high-performance goals. This is what he called the **system 4** design, the "participative group model." System 1 firms, characterized by "primitive authoritarianism" are classic bureaucracies. System 2 organizations employ "benevolent authoritarianism," and system 3 organizations are "consultative." Figure 9.1 (page 440) profiles the differences between the four approaches in terms of leadership, motivation, communication, decisions, goals, and control.

According to Likert, the system 4 design increases employee motivation by promoting fair and equitable treatment from managers and by encouraging managers to treat subordinates as human beings and not merely as inputs into a task process. Employees theoretically perceive this managerial attitude favorably and respond with higher motivation. The amount of

FIGURE 9.1
Likert's Profile of Organizational Characteristics

	Organizational variables	System 1	System 2	System 3	System 4
Leadership	1. How much confidence is shown in subordinates?	None	Condescending	Substantial	Complete
	2. How free do they feel to talk to superiors about job?	Not at all	Not very	Rather free	Fully free
	3. Are subordinates' ideas sought and used, if worthy?	Seldom	Sometimes	Usually	Always
Motivation	4. Is predominant use made of 1 fear, 2 threats, 3 punishment, 4 rewards, 5 involvement?	1, 2, 3 occasionally 4	4, some 3	4, some 3 and 5	5, 4 based on group
	5. Where is responsibility felt for achieving organization's goals?	Mostly at top	Top and middle	Fairly general	At all levels
	6. How much cooperative teamwork exists?	None	Little	Some	Great deal
Communication	7. What is the direction of information flow?	Downward	Mostly downward	Down and up	Down, up and sideways
	8. How is downward communication accepted?	With suspicion	Possibly with suspicion	With caution	With a receptive mind
	9. How accurate is upward communication?	Often wrong	Censored for the boss	Limited accuracy	Accurate
	10. How well do superiors know problems faced by subordinates?	Know little	Some knowledge	Quite well	Very well
Decisions	11. At what level are decisions made?	Mostly at top	Policy at top, some delegation	Broad policy at top, more delegation	Throughout but well integrated
	12. Are subordinates involved in decisions related to their work?	Not at all	Occasionally consulted	Generally consulted	Fully involved
	13. What does decision-making process contribute to motivation?	Nothing, often weakens it	Relatively little	Some contribution	Substantial contribution
Goals	14. How are organizational goals established?	Orders issued	Orders, some comments invited	After discussion, by orders	By group action (except in crisis)
	15. How much covert resistance to goals is present?	Strong resistance	Moderate resistance	Some resistance at times	Little or none
Control	16. How concentrated are review and control functions?	Highly at top	Relatively highly at top	Moderate delegation to lower levels	Quite widely shared
	17. Is there an informal organization resisting the formal one?	Yes	Usually	Sometimes	No—same goals as formal
	18. What are cost, productivity, and other control data used for?	Policing, punishment	Reward and punishment	Reward, some self-guidance	Self-guidance problem-solving

Source: R. Likert, *The Human Organization* (New York: McGraw-Hill, 1967), pp. 14–25, 120–121. Copyright © 1967 by McGraw-Hill. Reprinted by permission of McGraw-Hill, Inc.

employee involvement in decision making, the leadership style, and the reliance on self-guidance for control, rather than coercive control, also contribute to motivation.

Content Theories

As noted earlier, all content theories of motivation are psychological in nature. That is, they focus on people's internal characteristics as goads to their behavior. The basic process illustrated in Figure 9.2 underlies all content theories. The individual is spurred to action toward a goal by a feeling of discomfort or disequilibrium caused by a perceived need or lack; the achievement of that goal—or the failure to achieve it—feeds back to affect the inner state, possibly modifying it. The model is intuitively satisfying. You feel a hankering for something sweet, identify the best solution as an ice-cream cone, buy one, and, after eating it, feel satisfied. As this simple model shows, process theories are both rational (you choose how to satisfy your sweet tooth on the basis of rational considerations such as the availability of sweets or your cash on hand) and hedonistic (you are driven by the desire for pleasure).

Content theories are no longer widely accepted; essentially, they have crumbled under the pressure of excess. Various writers have listed such a

FIGURE 9.2
A Model of Basic Motivational Processes

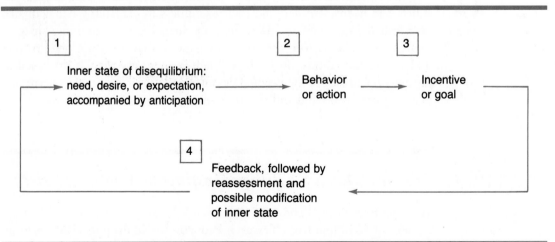

Source: From *Introduction to Organizational Behavior*, 3rd ed., by Richard M. Steers. Copyright © 1988, 1984 by Richard M. Steers. Reprinted by permission of HarperCollins Publishers.

variety of needs that it is difficult for managers to select which to emphasize in developing a personnel program. Also, most need theories were not developed specifically to deal with people at work, but rather to talk about people in general.

We study need theories despite these limitations for two reasons. First, because each theory is derived from a somewhat different perspective, each alerts managers to different approaches to motivating employee behavior. Second, together they offer a relatively large set of categories of internal human factors that probably do drive behavior. Managers can think about which categories are most appropriate to their situations. Need theories are both rational and hedonistic.

Instinct Theory

One of the earliest of the content approaches is instinct theory. An **instinct** is "an inherited or innate psychophysical disposition which determines its possessor to pay attention to objects of a certain class, to experience an emotional excitement of a particular quality upon perceiving such an object, and to act in regard to it in a particular manner, or at least, to experience an impulse to such an action" (McDougall, 1908, p. 39). To some writers, instincts are purposive and goal directed; to others they are blind and mechanical. Instincts include such basic drives as the impulses for self-protection, aggression, procreation, and nurturance. Instincts can, of course, be overcome; many drivers skidding on an icy road have triumphed over the instinct to step on the brakes and steered into the skid instead.

By the time the theory died of its own weight, many thousands of instincts had been identified and their usefulness in explaining behavior had been called into question. We mention them here to caution managers against overreliance on someone's statement that he "felt the instinct to. . . ." As the feature on J. Hugh Liedtke suggests, what is proposed as instinct may in fact be the rational pursuit of self-interest, perhaps occurring in a calculation so rapid and subconscious so as to be misidentified.

FEATURE: *Turning Down $2 Billion: Instinct or Cool Analysis?*

What motives drove Pennzoil's Chairman J. Hugh Liedtke to turn down an offer of $2 billion from Texcao if Pennzoil would drop its claims arising from Texaco's takeover of Getty Oil? Was he acting on instinct, or a more analytical, rational basis?

Many observers wondered that when Liedtke made his famous or infamous decision in the spring of 1987. *Fortune* magazine said, "the whole amazing story is beyond anyone's previous experience in business or law. Pennzoil's celebrated suit arose from Texaco's takeover of Getty Oil, which allegedly wrecked a planned Pennzoil-Getty deal. A Texas jury decided in November 1985 that Texaco owed Pennzoil $10.5 billion—the largest award in history. A higher court later reduced it to $8.5 billion, but by mid-April [of 1987] interest and penalties had brought it up to $11 billion. Texaco offered to pay Pennzoil around $2 billion if Pennzoil would drop its claims. . . . Liedtke—in what must be the biggest turn-down of cash ever—looked that ten-figure sum in the eye and said no. The next day Texaco filed for bankruptcy protection, the biggest company ever to do so."

Asked by *Fortune* whether he was the greediest man in the world or simply in need of psychiatric help, Liedtke chuckled and said, "Maybe both. I don't think 'greed' is fair, I really don't. . . . Pennzoil is unmoved by Texaco's dramatic gesture. Maybe now we should sit back awhile and see how they like bankruptcy—the euphoria should wear off in about a week. We will not take an unreasonably low settlement, whether it takes six months or four years."

Liedtke and his opposite number at Texaco, James W. Kinnear, refused at any point in the lengthy dispute to sit down and negotiate seriously. *Fortune*'s assessment was that the two genuinely did not understand or respect each other enough to communicate effectively. For 16 months, Texaco threatened to file for bankruptcy if Liedtke pushed too hard. He pushed anyway, and Texaco made good on its threat.

Asked why he continued to push, Liedtke offers this story: "When my daughter Kristie was a little girl, she'd threaten to hold her breath until she died if she couldn't have her way. She'd turn red and scare her mother and me to death. On our pediatrician's advice, one time we just let her hold her breath until she keeled over. She never did it again. She has a very sweet disposition now."

Liedtke was a gambler, "an entrepreneur and a rebel who named his first major company, Zapata Petroleum, after the famous Mexican revolutionary." Following his turn-down of the $2 billion offer, Liedtke told *Fortune*, he made a counteroffer of between $3 billion and $5 billion. He argued that having won $11 billion in a court decision, he had a fiduciary duty to Pennzoil's stockholders to collect as much of it as possible.

Related to instinct theory is unconscious motivation. Freud (1949) advocated the existence of such a phenomenon, the idea being that people are driven by unconscious forces. Modern psychiatry may also be driven by this notion, but it appears nowhere in theories of work motivation.

An underlying assumption of instinct theory is that if we look hard enough, we can find those factors that direct and mold behavior. This theoretical approach denies the assumption of rationality but accepts the assumption of hedonism. An instinct for pugnacity, for example, is not rational but may well provide pleasure for its quarrelsome owner.

Murray's Manifest Needs Theory

One of the most important need classification schemes was developed by Henry Murray (1938), who presented a list of more than 20 motives. The list never took hold among managers because, like lists of instincts, it is simply too long to deal with easily. The items from Murray's list, presented in Figure 9.3, are self-explanatory overall; infavoidance, the most unusual term, is the need to avoid humiliation or inaction due to fear of failure. The 20 main needs are accompanied by 3 factors (defined in the figure) that are related to other needs. In addition, Murray noted the existence of many more needs that can motivate behavior but which were not part of his study. Many of the needs he described, in both of these lists, appear in original or revised form in other need theories.

In Murray's view, these needs become manifest when triggered by environmental factors. The need to understand, for instance, would be activated by the challenge of new situations. If confronted only by the routine, that need would not direct behavior. Murray's work is called the theory of

FIGURE 9.3
Murray's List of Needs

Abasement	Dominance	Nurturance	Succourance
Achievement	Exhibition	Order	Superiority (a
Affiliation	Harmavoidance	Play	composite of
Aggression	Infavoidance	Rejection	achievement
Autonomy	Inviolacy (a composite	Seclusion (the opposite	and recognition)
Counteraction	of infavoidance,	of exhibition)	Understanding
Deference	dependence, and	Sentience	
Defendence	counteraction)	Sex	

Source: Adapted from H. A. Murray, *Explorations in Personality* (New York: Oxford University Press, 1938), pp. 144–145. Copyright © 1938 by Oxford University Press. Reprinted by permission of the Oxford University Press.

manifest needs because these drives are seen as significant only when they become activated or manifest.

Competence

Other needs classification theories did not come up with long lists. One of the most elegant small theories of needs, developed by Robert W. White (1959), was labeled "the concept of competence." After examining a variety of studies, White presented the notion that **competence** is an organism's capacity to interact with its environment, which is slowly attained by people through prolonged learning experiences. "The human learning that is needed to gain competence is characterized by high persistence and a strong goal orientation. Because of this dedication to learning, White argues that it is necessary to treat competence as having a motivational aspect that is separate from motivation derived from primary drives or instincts" (Lawler, 1973, p. 23).

White argued that the need to gain competence is aroused when people are faced with new situations and wanes when situations become familiar. There are a number of interesting examples of the concept of competence. Children learn to walk, though with frequent falls that learning must often be painful. High school graduates suddenly thrown onto large college campuses are at first taut and fearful but become more comfortable as they master the new situations. Managers suddenly introduced to new groups of employees to manage are frequently uncertain, but as familiarity grows so does their feeling of competence and control. In some sense this approach may not seem entirely rational. Why would children endure the pain required to learn to walk, given the costs? More students might simply leave large and unfriendly campuses, given their costs. But one cannot limit the definition of rationality to the consideration of short-term effects. In the theory of competence, one has to assume that larger, more long-term benefits prevail.

Competence theory has its benefits. Thinking about the effect of new and strange situations is helpful; individuals probably attempt to learn about those situations to make them less strange. It might also be helpful if training programs for new managers included the notion that it is perfectly normal to feel strange and ill prepared in new situations.

Hierarchical Needs

The **hierarchy of needs** posited by Maslow (1943), has been seminal for people interested in work motivation. A developmental theory, it was directed at understanding how motivation changes throughout the life of an individual. This is one reason that tests of this theory using samples of people at work can never prove or disprove it: those samples consist of adults, not people at all stages of growth and development.

Underlying Maslow's theory are two basic premises. The first follows the basic motivational model illustrated earlier. People are primarily "wanting" creatures, motivated by a desire to satisfy specific needs (clearly a hedonistic view). When these needs go largely unsatisfied, they create tensions, leading the individual to behave in ways aimed to reduce the needs and restore internal equilibrium. Once a need is satisfied, it loses its potency as a motivating force until reactivated.

The second basic tenet of the theory is that the needs people pursue are universal. That is, unlike Murray and some instinct theorists, Maslow identified few needs but said they were characteristic of all people. These needs are:

1. *Physiological.* The need for such things as water, food, and sex

2. *Safety.* The need to be in safe and secure physical and emotional environments

3. *Belongingness.* The need to develop friendships and to be accepted by one's peers

4. *Esteem.* The need to have a positive self-image and to receive recognition, attention, and appreciation from others

5. *Self-actualization.* The need to develop one's fullest potential and to become all that it is possible for one to become

According to Maslow, people are first concerned with their basic needs. As these needs are satisfied, people move on to concern for safety needs, then belongingness needs, and so on up the hierarchy. However, Maslow added that all people do not feel the push of the highest level of needs, **self-actualization.** And for those who do, satisfaction of these needs, far from reducing their potency, leads to further wanting. Research demonstrates similar but not identical rank ordering of needs across cultures. Such diverse cultures as those of Peru (Stephens, Kedia, and Ezell, 1979), India (Jaggi, 1979), the Middle East (Badawy, 1979), and Mexico (Reitz and Grof, 1973) have been involved in this research.

Some companies (e.g., Kuriloff and Hemphill, 1978) have used this set of categories to design personnel policies and management strategies. It does offer a relatively simple set of categories managers might think about in developing compensation and training programs. Thus managers could create work groups or at least promote group feeling to fulfill belongingness needs and establish clear rewards for performance to meet esteem needs. Salary, of course, is a straightforward way of meeting security needs.

Alderfer's ERG Theory

In response to criticism of Maslow's theory, Clayton Alderfer (1972) proposed a modified needs theory that essentially collapsed Maslow's five needs into three—existence needs, relatedness needs, and growth needs—which he called **ERG theory,** an acronym of those three needs. Existence needs are concerned with survival, relatedness needs with social interactions, and growth needs with self-esteem and self-actualization.

In general, Alderfer, too, said that people move up a hierarchy of needs, but he said that people will regress to lower categories if frustrated by an inability to satisfy higher categories. When Abe Rosner was both unemployed and afraid that inflation would erode his investments, he reverted to the need for security. In addition, Alderfer stated that more than one need category may be active simultaneously. These additions make his theory a little less rigid than Maslow's, though problems involved in testing still abound. Another difference from Maslow's work is that ERG theory was developed with people at work in mind.

Again, such categorical schemes are useful because they imply which internal individual facets managers should give attention. If an astute manager carried around in his head just the three concepts existence, relatedness, and growth, she might manage employees more sensitively than if she had no notion at all about what they need from their jobs.

Motivation-Hygiene Theory

Another need theory in wide use in business and government today is elegant in its simplicity. Called the two-factor, or **motivation-hygiene, theory** of motivation (Herzberg, Mausner, and Snyderman, 1959), it embraces both the rational and hedonistic explanations of behavior. The theory is unique in saying that satisfaction and dissatisfaction are not opposite ends of the same continuum but different constructs. It is possible for employees to be both satisfied and dissatisfied at the same time—a possibility that makes sense to most of us. It is not difficult to imagine a worker who is quite happy with his job but not with his paycheck. According to Herzberg, employee responses can run from dissatisfied to neutral and from some neutral zone to positive, thus breaking a continuum into two independent scales (see Figure 9.4, page 448).

The theory distinguishes **dissatisfiers,** or *hygiene factors*, from **satisfiers,** or *motivators*. Dissatisfiers are factors external to the employee and

FIGURE 9.4
Herzberg's Two-Factor Theory of Motivation

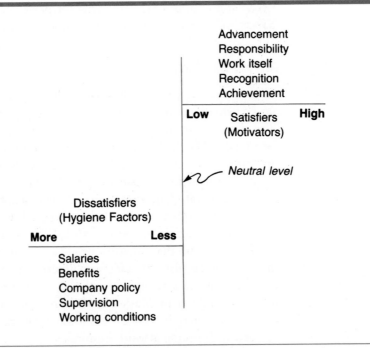

include salaries, benefits, company policy, supervision, and working conditions. Satisfiers are internal to the employee and include achievement, recognition, work itself, responsibility, and advancement. Herzberg said that one can manipulate external factors and improve working conditions to some neutral level by reducing dissatisfaction to a neutral level. Further manipulations of these external factors, however, will not change responses to work. For example, painting the walls, adding water coolers, and so on, will work to a point by reducing dissatisfaction, but after some point no further change in affect can be expected from these kinds of manipulations. Once managers reach this point of no further return on their investment, they are urged to begin working on internal motivational factors. According to Herzberg, manipulating these factors will improve employee motivation, and the sky's the limit in terms of expected positive outcomes.

During the 1960s this theory received an enormous amount of research attention, in some ways derailing work motivation research. All of Herzerg and his colleagues' research produced evidence supporting the theory; most studies by others, however, failed to produce supporting evidence.

Research done in other cultures often fails to support the theory as well (Crabbs, 1973; Hines, 1973b). In the end, Herzberg's theory has fallen into disrepute among researchers.

What, then, can this theory do for managers? It highlights a list of job factors that are probably important to many employees and that might well be changed in the interests of greater job satisfaction, and maybe even improved performance. In addition, it alerts managers to think about both intrinsic and extrinsic job factors.

Three Needs Emphasized

As a direct extension of the manifest needs theory of Murray, McClelland, Atkinson, and their colleagues (McClelland, Atkinson, Clark, and Lowell, 1953; McClelland, 1961, 1971, 1976) focused on three needs: achievement, power, and affiliation. Earliest attention was given to the need for **achievement** (called *nAch*), which is "a desire to do well; a desire to appear intelligent and demonstrate some leadership capacity" (McClelland, 1961, p. 40). In this theory, high need for achievement is characterized by four factors:

1. A strong desire to assume personal responsibility for finding solutions to problems

2. A tendency to set moderately difficult achievement goals and take calculated risks

3. A strong desire for concrete feedback on task performance

4. A single-minded preoccupation with task and task accomplishment

That many management positions require such a drive for success seems common sense, so it is logical that people with high achievement needs might tend to self-select into management jobs. It is important to keep in mind that for the achievement need to be activated, people must be placed in demanding positions. Routine, nonchallenging jobs do not activate achieving behaviors. For example, a high-achievement person would not respond with much enthusiasm to an assembly-line job, but would respond energetically to a problem-solving task such as how to schedule production. Comparative research on the need for achievement shows it to be relatively consistent across cultures (Hines, 1973a).

The second need given some attention by this group was the need for **affiliation** (nAff), or attraction to another person for purposes of obtaining reassurance and approval. Not a great deal of effort has been devoted to the implications of need for affiliation at work. People with high nAff probably work better in situations of cooperative work norms, where pressure to get things done is primarily exerted by friends (Atkinson, 1964, DeCharms, 1957).

The final need focused on by this group was the need for **power** (nPow), or an employee's need for control. Power comes in two forms, personal power and socialized power. People with high needs for personal power dominate for the sake of dominating. Those with high needs for socialized power, on the other hand, are more concerned with the problems of the organization and what they can do to help facilitate organizational goals (McClelland, 1976). Feeling personal responsibility for building organizations, such people seem willing to give up some of their own personal interests for the interests of the organization. They have a strong sense of justice or equity and maturity. A study of managers and their motives that reached the nonfiction bestseller list supports these notions about power (Maccoby, 1976).

But which of these needs is most important in determining managerial success? Managers with high needs for achievement focus their energies on personal accomplishments. This drive may be quite consistent with entrepreneurial success but leaves much to be desired in a large corporation. High needs for affiliation may get in the way of decisiveness and focus attention on the happiness of subordinates to the exclusion of their performance. High needs for personal power may, too, get in the way of obtaining good organizational performance (McClelland, 1976). McClelland found that managers with high needs for socialized power had high-performing and satisfied work groups. Whatever else organizations are, they are political structures that operate through the distribution of authority and resources. People with high needs for socialized power can help provide the structure, drive, and support necessary to facilitate an organization's reaching its goals. The combination of high achievement motivation and high socialized power motivation is associated with managerial success (McClelland, 1985). However, high need for power is also associated with health problems (House and Singh, 1987).

McClelland's theory provides a twist not seen in the other needs approaches. Training programs based on Maslow, Alderfer, or Herzberg focus on changing jobs to address the supposed needs of people in those jobs better. McClelland, on the other hand, did not focus on changing something to meet individual needs. He argued that achievement motivation can be taught, in the following four steps:

1. Teach participants how to think, talk, and act like a person with a high need for power or achievement (role playing).

2. Stimulate people to set carefully planned, realistic, and high work goals for themselves.

3. Give participants knowledge about themselves.

4. Create group cohesiveness by focusing on each other's hopes and fears, successes and failures, and by going through the emotional experience together.

Some evidence indicates that training programs designed along these lines are successful. However, one must keep in mind that although people exposed to the training move along in their organizations faster than others, they were possibly identified as movers in the first place.

Content Theories in Review

Though the various content theories are useful to managers, we should be aware of a number of problems with these approaches to motivation. These theories assume that people have stable needs and that jobs are stable. The most obvious prescription is to tinker with one or the other or both until an adequate fit between needs and jobs is reached. But what if people's needs change frequently or jobs are not as stable as we wish, as was the case over Abe Rosner's lifetime? Then all this tinkering may well go for naught.

A second assumption is that attitudes and behaviors are linked. We assume that if workers' needs are reduced, and they are fairly well satisfied, they will perform maximally on the job. Yet each of us can think of situations in which that assumption is called seriously into question. Consider Abe Rosner: while a broker, his need for money was essentially reduced, but his performance was not maximal. He quit. Perhaps his other work-related needs were not being met. In this view, he quit because he needed autonomy.

A third assumption of these theories is that job characteristics are realities, that we do not subjectively interpret or construe our jobs in our minds. Yet mental constructs of jobs clearly go on, and in some situations we define our jobs through the social norms of others in similar jobs (O'Reilly and Caldwell, 1979; White and Mitchell, 1979). We might find a butchering job in a meat packing plant very exciting, complex, and rewarding if all those around us feel similarly about that same job. Alternatively, the job of veterinarian can be seen as dirty, monotonous, and back breaking if that's the way the other veterinarians see it.

Thus, in deciding whether to tamper with jobs and needs along the lines suggested by the content models, we should first ask ourselves if we are dealing with conditions under which those models of human behavior are likely to apply. After all, to some degree need satisfaction is necessary for survival (Alderfer, 1977)—no one would deny the necessity of food and water. Recently, we have been witness to both scientifically based and popular press arguments about the relationship of loneliness (relatedness needs) to the onset of illness and death. Few would deny that meaningful work was a necessary prerequisite for Abe Rosner's assessment of his self-worth.

Why are needs satisfaction models popular? There are a number of reasons, beginning with the fact that they are simple descriptions of human behavior and its correlates. Needs models also attribute to people pleasing characteristics, such as rationality and freedom, that we like to think we demonstrate, when in actuality our behavior may be shaped by situational factors such as external constraints, norms, and so on. Recall the finding (Nisbett and Ross, 1980) that people like to attribute the behavior of others to internal states rather than to environmental or other conditions (see Chapters 5 and 8).

Process Theories

One writer has identified the major process theories as operant conditioning, expectancy theory, goal setting, and equity theory (Mitchell, 1982). We add to these two more: social information processing theories and political theories of choice. As indicated earlier, process theories focus on factors that determine the kinds of choices we make.

Operant Conditioning

Operant conditioning is an aspect of classic learning theory developed in psychology and offers us a powerful set of behavioral controls. In its modern form, operant conditioning was developed by B. F. Skinner (his book *Beyond Freedom and Dignity*, 1971, provides a complete review of his position).

The basic tenets of **operant conditioning** are that some stimulus leads an actor to exhibit some voluntary behavior, which in turn results in some consequences that may or may not lead to the behavior's repetition. The process can be managed or manipulated to influence the actor to learn desired behaviors. The theory is hedonistic; behavior is driven by the desire for pleasure.

Positive and Negative Reinforcement Behaviors can be responded to in different ways. A response that promotes repetition of the behavior is called a **reinforcement.** Some reinforcements are positive—they give the person exhibiting the behavior pleasure. These are called **rewards.** Some reinforcements are negative, in response to which the actor acts either to remove an unpleasant stimulus or to prevent an unpleasant stimulus from taking place. Two other responses to a behavior are possible. In **omission,** reinforcement is stopped, which eventually reduces the frequency of the behavior. This technique is used to eliminate behaviors that are undesirable; it requires that managers identify the factor that reinforces that undesirable behavior. The other possible response is **punishment,** or the provision of an unpleasant event in response to a behavior.

A central tenet of operant conditioning is that reinforcement is preferable to omission or punishment. First, punishment involves ethical issues; indeed, much of the criticism of operant conditioning focuses on the ethics of punishment. Beyond this concern, positive reinforcement is also more effective. Then, too, more information is provided through positive reinforcement. When rewarded for something, the employee knows what he did right, but when punished he only knows what not to do; he still does not have specific information on what to do. Managers must keep in mind the necessity to associate with punishment information about how to change behavior.

To use operant conditioning, managers have to find reinforcers that are truly important to employees. It does absolutely no good for a manager to decide she will reward an employee's overproduction of widgets with a two-week vacation for him and his family if the employee is trying to get away from his family in the first place. Rewards that matter have to be found.

The second thing managers have to do is to design situations in such a way that they can reliably induce desired responses. If the responses never occur, there is no opportunity to reward them. The feature on Lincoln Electric is a good example of a successful motivation program.

FEATURE: *Lincoln Electric:*
Successful Employee Motivation Program

A great variety of productivity incentive programs have been tried in various industries, ranging from industrial engineering-based incentive-pay programs of the 1920s to the more "humanistic" or "organization climate" programs of the 1960s and 1970s. Yet none of these programs has enjoyed a sufficiently long period of success to indicate that it might be the ultimate solution—or best solution—to the problem of employee motivation. The experience of Lincoln Electric stands out from the above experiences because of its continuous operation and success over the last 45 years. It is this long period of successful operations that indicates a study of the nature of the program; and its performance contains useful lessons for a manager. It also raises some interesting questions for the theorist because of the remarkably small amount of attention this program has received, despite its success. It is difficult to understand why no other firm has attempted to copy or otherwise employ a similar concept to the compensation, evaluation, and motivation of its employees. In this program Lincoln stands alone.

From an economic point of view the program is based on maximizing output, minimizing inputs, and increasing efficiency. The inputs, in men's [or women's] time, materials, and capital equipment, are watched closely to reduce waste and achieve maximum output. The savings so generated are passed on to the customer (in this case an industrial customer who is probably quite price-elastic), which permits economies of scale to further the use of electric welding. The additional earnings so generated are apportioned between the customer in terms of lower prices and the employee in terms of an annual bonus. Both the customer and the employee share in the gains from the increased efficiency. Thus, the partnership between the employees and the customers is emphasized. Both are essential for the success of the enterprise and both share the gains from increased productivity. . . .

In James Lincoln's philosophy: "The incentives that are most potent when properly offered and believed in by the worker" are the following: (1) money in proportion to production; (2) status as a reward for achievement; and (3) publicity of the worker's contribution and skill and imagination and the reward that is given for it. This results in added status.

From a behaviorist's point of view, this program appears to be based upon the assumption that economic motivation is the major factor. However, this is an oversimplification and ignores the third element in Mr. Lincoln's list of incentives. When a $7,000-a-year floor sweeper receives a $10,000 annual bonus at the end of the year and is then written up in an article in the *Cleveland Plain Dealer*, such recognition by his superiors and peers in so tangible a form has to be far more significant than the traditional paternalistic company gift of a turkey at Thanksgiving or Christmas.

Each employee is evaluated regularly by his immediate superior. In the case of the engineering department, the chief engineer showed this author the personnel records of his employees. He made annotation on their performance at least monthly and often more frequently when a particular event justified this. The importance of the evaluation of workers by their superiors, and direct connection between this evaluation and the dollar bonus paid at the end of the year, emphasizes the relationship between the employee, his superior, and the overall performance of the company. The better the performance of the company in economic terms, the larger dollar pool from which bonuses will be paid; and the higher the employee is rated by the supervisor, the greater his share of this pool will be. The combination of these two factors results in the annual bonus the employee receives. Thus the relationships among the employee, the supervisor, and the company as a whole are directly tied together; and this relationship is demonstrated in very tangible terms: a check at the end of the year. The recognition is further emphasized by in-house publications and also in newspaper and magazine articles released by the company's public relations department.

Another factor that behaviorists have failed to recognize is the scope of the program. All employees are included in this program: production employees, support employees (like floor sweepers), and management. The fact that the total group of employees are all included in the program and treated in a similar manner adds an element that is absent in most so-called incentive programs. It tends to emphasize the unity of purpose and the common objectives of all employees, regardless of status or function, as they work toward the success of the common enterprise.

The philosophy of James Lincoln is well expressed in the following statement:

> It is well to keep in mind in applying any incentive system, that money of itself is not as great an incentive to any of us as self-respect and status. We all will sacrifice money to keep our self-respect and to gain the respect and admiration of our contemporaries. This is shown by the enthusiasm of the amateur athlete in playing a game. The only reward he can have is self-respect and the respect of others whose good opinion he values. He will generally try harder than the professional who gets paid for his performance.

Source: D. Piehl, "Lincoln Electric: Successful Employee Motivation Program," in J. E. DiHrick and R. A. Zannicki (eds.), *People in Organizations,* 2nd ed. (Plano, Texas: Business Publications, 1985). Copyright © 1985 by Business Publications, Inc. Reprinted by permission of Richard D. Irwin, Inc.

Rate of Reinforcement   A second factor affecting the effectiveness of operant conditioning is the frequency with which reinforcement takes place. There are two general classes of **reinforcement schedules,** or the timing of reinforcement. The first class is continuous reinforcement, reinforcing a behavior every time it occurs. Continuous reinforcement is not as effective at producing repeat behavior as the second class of reinforcers, intermittent reinforcement. Continuous reinforcement increases behavior very rapidly, but when the reinforcement stops so does the behavior—quickly. It is also difficult to manage continuous reinforcement schedules.

Intermittent reinforcement comes in a variety of forms, some which are also difficult to manage. The most commonly implemented schedule is a fixed-ratio schedule, wherein reinforcers are delivered when a certain number of responses have occurred. This is at the base of piece-rate pay schedules, whereby employees are paid for producing a particular number of products. Probably the best reinforcement schedule around by which to design a pay scheme is a fixed interval schedule: assuming adequate performance, an employee is rewarded at some known interval—paid every two weeks, for instance.

Other reinforcement schedules contain a degree of randomness. Praise is most often given at random intervals, and the employee never knows when it will occur. For such things as praise, but not for such things as money, random reinforcement schedules produce the best behavior. Because the employee does not know when the reinforcement is coming, behavior is maintained at a high level. Random reinforcement schedules are probably the most common. To illustrate, you put together an excellent report about new product innovation and your boss means to praise you, but forgets. You do six other major things very well, and they all go unnoticed. Then, on a lark, you remember that it might be useful to include the company's public affairs people at your next meeting about company-sponsored child care. Your boss extols your virtues for the afternoon.

To be effective, a schedule must include information about the exact behavior that will produce reward. Most pay and performance appraisal schedules are not good at this. There are several rules of thumb on using operant conditioning (Hamner, 1974) that managers should keep them in mind, as listed in Figure 9.5.

FIGURE 9.5
Rules for Using Operant Conditioning

1. Don't reward all people the same way. Differentiate so employees can tell who's doing better.
2. If you find it too difficult to make differentiations, think about the consequences of your failure to do this on your employees. Both action and failure act to modify the behavior of employees.
3. Be sure to let employees know what they need to do to receive rewards. That is, make the contingencies of rewards so workers know what is expected of them.
4. Be sure to inform employees about what they are doing wrong and how to change their behavior. This introduces necessary information into the situation.
5. Don't punish in front of others. Punishment in front of others can obviously lead to loss of face and encourage retaliation.
6. Be fair. Make the consequences match the behavior. Neither rewards nor punishments should be disproportional to behavior.

Source: Adapted from H. L. Tosi and W. C. Hamner (eds.), *Organizational Behavior and Management: A Contingency Approach* (Chicago: St. Clair Press, 1974). Copyright © 1990 by PWS-KENT Publishing Company. Reprinted by permission.

Expectancy Theory

Expectancy theory and operant conditioning are based on very different philosophies. **Expectancy theory** focuses on what people expect from their jobs and what they value. It is a cognitive theory, both rational and hedonistic. An **expectancy** is a belief about the likelihood that a particular behavior will result in a particular outcome. For example, we all carry in our heads some expectancy about the outcomes of working hard at our jobs: some people think that if they work harder, their boss will notice them; others, that if they work harder, they will earn more money.

In this theory, outcomes have positive or negative values. The term **valence** refers to the value people attach to outcomes. Thus, if you like chocolate ice cream, chocolate ice cream is valued. If you do not like chocolate ice cream, that particular outcome has no value for you. The level of satisfaction you think you will receive from the outcome, not its actual value, determines valence. If you believe your efforts to receive this outcome will be successful, your expectancy is high. If you believe no effort you can make will result in attainment of this outcome, your expectancy is low. If, like Abe Rosner, I am already comfortable due to personal wealth, the valence of earning more money will not be high. But notice that Rosner valued other outcomes, such as the esteem of others and a feeling of self-worth.

The model, shown in Figure 9.6, details two kinds of expectancies. The first is **effort-performance expectancies,** or the belief that effort actually leads to performance. To be effective, such expectancies should be challenging but not impossible. Great as my efforts at brain surgery might be, I

FIGURE 9.6
A Model of Expectancy or Valence Theory of Motivation and Performance

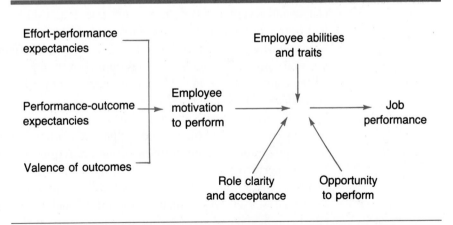

Source: Adapted from L. W. Porter and E. E. Lawler, *Managerial Attitudes and Performance* (Homewood, IL: Irwin, 1968), p. 17. Copyright © 1968 by Richard D. Irwin, Inc. Reprinted by permission.

have little faith that they will lead to adequate performance. Abe Rosner was discouraged from looking very hard for a bank job by a low expectancy that his effort would result in getting hired. Three factors influence these expectancies: level of self-esteem, past experience in similar situations, and perceptions of the actual situation (Lawler, 1973). Rosner's case showed all these elements. In addition, it was recently shown (Miller and Grush, 1988) that if people are sensitive only to their own expectations, they behave in a manner predicted by the model. If, however, they are sensitive to expectations of others or to norms of the situations, they may engage in behaviors that appear irrational based on this model.

The second kind of expectation, **performance-outcome expectancies,** is the belief that certain performances will, in fact, lead to certain outcomes. Abe Rosner had "one big winner," so he "knew it could be done." "If I work hard I will get more money" is such an expectancy. Performance-outcome expectancies are also influenced by past experiences and perceptions of the situation. Three other influences are present as well: the valences of various outcomes, the extent that the individual believes he can control the environment, and effort-performance expectancies.

Both kinds of expectancies combine with valences to determine effort or motivation to perform. The higher the two expectancies and the higher the value placed on the outcome, the higher the motivation. Motivation is a multiple of these three factors. For it to be high, therefore, all three must be high.

Three other factors influencing effort-performance-outcomes expectancies are shown in Figure 9.6. First, abilities and traits mediate whether effort will lead to performance (if I am not skilled at brain surgery, my efforts at that job cannot lead to adequate performance). The second is role clarity and acceptance (I do not accept myself as a skilled brain surgeon, so I had better not try to be one). This probably best describes Abe Rosner's situation when he was faced with a "salesman's" job he felt was unethical and not well suited to his skills. Third is opportunity to perform (I may have had all the training required for brain surgery but never had the opportunity to actually use those skills).

Closely allied with effort-performance expectancy is the notion of **self-efficacy** (Bandura, 1986), defined as "people's judgments of their capabilities to organize and execute courses of action required to obtain designated types of performances. It is concerned not with skills one has but with judgments of what one can do with whatever skills one possesses" (p. 391). Perceived self-efficacy enhances organizational performance through its effects on managers' goal setting and the quality of their analytic strategies (Wood and Bandura, 1989). This concept is broader in scope than effort-performance expectancy.

FIGURE 9.7
Managerial Implications of Expectancy Theory

1. *Clarify effort-performance expectancies.* Sometimes this can be done through training or other kinds of guidance. The result is that employees believe that they can achieve high-level performance.
2. *Clarify performance-outcome expectancies.* Design reward systems based on performance (as prescribed by operant conditioning). Let employees know what they can expect to get from high performance.
3. *Match rewards to what employees want.* Again, as prescribed by operant conditioning, find out what the really nitty gritty reinforcers are and provide them. Not all employees want the same things. Where feasible this argues for offering "cafeteria-type" benefit packages.
4. *Recognize conscious behavior.* Unlike operant conditioning, this approach says that people are rational and weigh choices. They reassess their situations. Managers should recognize this; one implication is the need for flexibility and change.
5. *Select people who can do the job.* The role of abilities, traits, and role acceptance should not be minimized. Training may be important here. Sometimes changing one's role concept is important. If women feel they cannot be good managers because these are jobs men do, they probably won't be very good managers.
6. *Clarify role expectations.* This is not independent of point 1. Let people know exactly what is expected of them.
7. *Provide opportunities to perform.* If you hire a freshly minted MBA and never provide her with opportunities to apply her skills, she probably won't be very motivated.

Source: Adapted from R. M. Steers, *Introduction to Organizational Behavior*, 3rd ed. (Glenview, IL: Scott, Foresman, 1988), p. 204.

Research support for expectancy theory is not strong, though there is some support for it cross-nationally (Matsui and Terrai, 1979). Like Herzberg's motivation-hygiene theory, it generated an enormous amount of research and maybe it, too, side-tracked motivation researchers a bit. For managers, expectancy theory offers a nice set of conceptual boxes for thinking about different strategies to motivate employees. Some of its managerial implications are indicated in Figure 9.7.

Goal Setting

Goal setting is related to expectancy theory, but focuses on a limited aspect of behavior and is therefore a simpler approach to motivation (Locke, 1968). The theory argues that behavior can be understood solely in terms of setting goals and that one does not need such concepts as the strength of the link between behavior and the likelihood of some outcome. This theory is a prime example of a rational approach to motivation.

Goal setting is elegant in its simplicity. It focuses on three issues: goal specificity, goal difficulty, and goal acceptance. The theory argues that people perform better if they are given very specific goals, as opposed to more general goals such as "do your best." Further, the more difficult the goal, the better the performance—up to some limit (Earley, Connolly, and Ekegren, 1989; Vance and Colella, 1990). Recall from expectancy theory that the effort-performance expectancies should be challenging but not impossible. (Need for achievement theory is consistent with goal theory.) The Pygmalion effect (see Chapter 10) establishes that external expectations set by others can provide the setting for attempting to select and achieve challenging goals (Eden, 1988). Finally, people need to be encouraged to accept goals. There is no assurance that goals set by managers will be embraced by employees (see Chapter 1), a fact that is too often forgotten. For example, Abe Rosner did not embrace the goals inherent in the brokerage house statement, "I need somebody who can sell. I don't need your knowledge."

Three other factors influence employee performance, according to goal theory. Competition is one. Competition increases quantity of output, although not quality, rendering it less desirable in situations where quality is important. For tasks requiring interdependence, competition may be a destructive strategy. In situations where only one winner is possible, competition may be useful, but if more than one winner is allowed, its utility decreases (Steers, 1988).

The second factor affecting performance is participation in setting goals. The virtues of employee participation in decision making have long been extolled (see Chapter 7). Unfortunately, little evidence suggests that participating in goal setting enhances job performance, though it may enhance satisfaction and attendance (see Latham, Mitchell, and Dossett, 1978; Latham and Yukl, 1975). An alternative view is sumarized by the statement, "It is not so important how a goal is set as that a goal has in fact been set" (Latham, Erez, and Locke, 1988, p. 758).

One study (Cotton, Vollrath, Froggatt, Lengnick-Hall, and Jennings, 1988) reviewed all studies on participation to summarize the findings. The authors reached the following conclusions about the main forms of participation:

1. Formal, long-term participative schemes in which workers help determine how tasks are handled increase productivity.

2. Formal, long-term consultation in decisions regarding job issues may or may not contribute to increased productivity; the results are inconclusive.

3. Formal, short-term participation programs produce few effects on productivity, and the results of such programs on satisfaction and motivation are mixed.

4. Informal participation (essentially due to the interrelationship of supervisors and workers) is related to productivity and satisfaction, but whether participation is cause or effect is unclear.

5. Employee ownership is positively related to profitability and employee satisfaction, involvement, commitment, and motivation.

6. Representative participation (in which workers are selected for management councils or the board of directors) has not been studied extensively, and the results concerning its impact on productivity, motivation, and related issues are inconclusive.

The third factor affecting performance is feedback. Most experiments on goal setting include feedback; one wonders whether any performance improvements observed are the result of the goal setting itself or the feedback. One would think that feedback enhances performance by acting as a directive and serving as an incentive. Unfortunately, there is no simple feedback-performance relationship. People use various kinds of feedback information differently (Vance and Colella, 1990), and some people need feedback and others do not (as suggested by McClelland's nAch). For example, you may be infuriated if a manager stands over you commenting on your performance in developing a spreadsheet, but someone else might appreciate those comments and improve his performance based on them.

One study (Earley, Northcraft, Lee, and Lituchy, 1990) distinguished between two types of feedback. **Outcome feedback** helps the individual determine the degree to which behavior contributes to achieving the desired goal. **Process feedback** is more specific information about the correct strategies to employ to improve the efficacy of behavior. Both process and outcome feedback improve task performance. The less well learned or structured the task, the greater the need for process feedback.

As managers we should be interested in how to obtain commitment to goals from our employees. We can obtain higher commitment if our employees participate in goal setting or if, in telling them the goals, we attempt to sell them on the goals rather than simply relating those goals to them (Latham, Erez, and Locke, 1988). Generally, the determinants of goals can be thought of as falling in three major categories (Locke, Latam, and Erez, 1988). First are factors external to employees: the legitimate authority of those assigning the goals, peer pressure, and the rewards for accepting goals. The second category addresses interactive factors and includes participation

FIGURE 9.8
*Principles for the
Design of an
Effective Goal-
Setting System*

1. Make goals measurable and related to organizational objectives.
2. Create an effective feedback system—one that focuses on smaller rather than larger groups, restricts itself to factors that employees can control, provides for regular feedback, and should be private if related to individual workers.
3. Determine whether the method employed will be targeted goal setting, focusing on specific aspects of work, or overall goal setting, relating to broader work questions.
4. Use a single performance measure. If multiple measures are used, set a goal for each important activity or devise a system of awarding points for given levels of performance.
5. Involve both supervisors and employees in setting goals.
6. Make goals difficult but attainable.
7. Make goals public to heighten employees' awareness of them and their motivational level. Make goals private to overcome the tendency of employees to set their own goals too low.
8. Create goals that can be measured within the logical completion cycle of the job; evaluate performance at the end of the cycle and act to improve performance if necessary.
9. Reevaluate goals at the end of each goal-setting period; allow changes to goals if necessary.
10. Train supervisors to create and implement a goal-setting system.

Source: R. D. Pritchard, P. L. Roth, S. D. Jones, P. J. Galfay, and M. D. Watson, "Designing a Goal-Setting System to Enhance Performance: A Practical Guide," *Organizational Dynamics* 17 (1988): 69–78.

in goal setting and the existence of competitiveness. The third set of factors is internal to the employee and includes her expectation of success and self-efficacy, as well as self-administered rewards such as saying, "I did well on this."

Goal theory has undergone extensive testing, probably because the activities it prescribes are relatively straightforward. Its clarity also makes the theory easy for managers to think about and use: help employees set specific and relatively difficult goals and make sure they accept the goals. The relationship of these issues to management by objectives is discussed later in this chapter. Figure 9.8 presents ten principles that can be followed in designing an effective goal-setting system.

Equity Theory

As tested in organizations to date, **equity theory** speaks to only a very small part of the employment relationship: the perceptions of equity in employee pay (Adams, 1965, 1976). Equity in this case means the employee's perception of the association between her effort or performance on the job and the pay she receives relative to the same association for others. The notion is that employees view their contributions and pay in light of the contributions and pay of others. No one is quite sure how others are selected for comparison, but such selection may be based on available information or on liking (Goodman, 1974). The result of this comparison is that one's pay is judged equitable or nonequitable. "Equity is said to exist whenever the ratio of a person's outcomes to inputs is equal to the ratio of others' outcomes and inputs" (Mowday, 1983, p. 93).

The theory makes a counterintuitive prediction. It argues that inequity will be perceived not just when people are underpaid but also when they are overpaid. Dissatisfaction may occur in either situation. Several authors question the extent to which overpayment may lead to perceived inequity (Locke, 1976; Campbell and Pritchard, 1976). They note that most of the evidence about this theory is from laboratory studies and that in real organizations employees are seldom told they are being overpaid, as they were in the experiments. It is further argued that even if employees know they are overpaid, they simply adjust their idea of equitable payment to justify their pay. Organizations, too, take action when they feel they are overpaying employees. They may, for example, demand continued education to raise the ostensibly overpaid individual's skills to meet the level of payment. In unusually inequitable situations, employees may actually be downgraded in pay level or "frozen" in a pay grade to allow for inflation or others' advancement to "catch up" with them, either of which will, in effect, lower their relative pay.

The motivational component of equity theory is derived from the consequences of perceived inequity. The theory postulates that perceived inequity creates tension proportionate to the perceived magnitude of the inequity. The presence of tension motivates the individual to reduce it; the strength of that motivation is proportionate to the amount of tension.

When faced with this tension, an individual may restore equity in any of six ways:

1. Altering inputs: work less hard (if underpaid) or harder (if overpaid).

2. Altering outputs: try to secure a more equitable pay.

3. Distorting inputs or outputs: begin to define either inputs or outputs differently to match the pay.

4. Leaving the field: transfer or quit.

5. Distorting the inputs or outcomes of the person with whom comparison occurs: begin to define the other person's level of effort or quality of work differently.

6. Changing the person with whom comparison occurs: find an object of comparison providing more equity.

The suggestion was recently made that all people are not equally sensitive to equity (Huseman, Hatfield, and Miles, 1987). These authors propose that individual reactions to inequity are a function of the individual's preferences for equity. Individuals called "benevolents" prefer that their outcome/input ratios be less than those of persons to whom they compare themselves. "Equity sensitives," on the other hand, desire ratios equal to those of their comparison others. "Entitleds" prefer ratios more favorable than those of the comparison others.

Unfortunately, organizational research has generally not studied notions of equity as they apply to factors other than pay. Many behaviors might be explained in terms of relative fairness. And many other factors interact with equity perceptions to determine performance. One study showed that perceived similarity of co-workers, in addition to pay equity, influenced performance (Griffin, Vecchio, and Logan, 1989). One problem that managers have thinking in these terms is that the trade-offs are often subtle, and teasing them out may be quite difficult.

A Social Information Processing Perspective

The social information processing perspective was developed as an antithesis to need theories (see Chapters 5, 8, and 11 for more on this theory). In this view, what helps us understand the behavior of people at work is their informational and social contexts and their past choices (Ilgen and Klein, 1989; Salancik and Pfeffer, 1977). The argument is that environments are not given, but that people create or enact their environments through their perceptions (Weick, 1979). Perception is a retrospective process that is derived from recall and reconstruction. We all know of examples in which people interpret situations differently from one another; it is these interpretations, derived from social information and past experience, that determine behavior. A person's own behaviors and cognitions help him construct this social reality (Thomas and Griffin, 1989).

Individuals rationalize behavior because they view it vis-à-vis aspects of the environment that justify it. As people attempt to make sense of their environments and their behaviors, their cognitive formulation of the environment becomes a function of their behaviors. This process takes place in social contexts in which norms and expectations operate to influence behaviors and rationalizations. The Jonestown episode, in which over 600 religious cult members committed suicide in Guyana, is an extreme example of a situation to which this kind of theorizing applies. People believed Jim Jones when he told them others would destroy them, and they interpreted various situational factors as consonant with this belief. Many were even willing to kill themselves because of their beliefs. (See *Black and White* by John Griffin for a detailed description of the Jonestown tragedy.) To a lesser degree, but perhaps in the same vein, daily life at Citibank, the University of North Carolina, Sears, Roebuck and Company, the U.S. Congress, and any military post offers examples of this.

Social information influences attitudes and behaviors in several ways. One influence is the direct effect of a worker's statements on a co-worker. Abe Rosner's self-esteem was enhanced by a fellow broker who said, "You've done far better than anybody else." If a worker remarks that the team seems to be performing better than usual, a co-worker may pay attention to this statement and actually improve his own output. Another way social influence operates is to structure and limit a person's attention, by making certain aspects of the environment more or less salient. For example, in organizations in which error can lead to serious consequences, such as nuclear power plants, employees are continually reminded about the possibility of committing errors and about safety measures that must be followed.

A third way social information affects people is through the interpretation of environmental cues. Meaning is given to behaviors through social information. For example, a manager might behave in an aloof, stern way toward subordinates, who might interpret this behavior as insensitive management or as preoccupation with getting out a good product for the benefit of the company. Which interpretation is chosen may well depend on norms operating in the firm, the manager's past behavior, expectations developed about behavior, and so on. Abe Rosner's reluctance to go to work for a firm that just wanted him to "convince people to buy and sell stocks" was influenced by his perception of questionable ethics in the brokerage industry.

It requires little imagination to think of situations that can be explained by social information processing. Only equity theory and social information processing theory, to this point in our discussion, recognize the possibility that our perceptions of other people in organizations help determine our behavior. Although the research jury is still out on the utility of this theoretical approach, we can be assured it is going to be around for quite some time as an explanation of motivated behavior.

In opposition to social information processing theories are notions that people really do not think much about why they do various things. In this view, behavior is guided more by scripts and schemas (see Chapter 5 for more on this perspective). If this is true, managers should try to figure out what scripts and schemas they and their employees carry around in their heads.

Political Theories

As discussed in Chapter 6, political theories are gaining prominence as descriptions of behavior. This view is quite different from the others we have discussed, first because it is less prescriptive and more descriptive than the others, and second because it considers groups as determining behavior. This view not only assumes that people's behaviors are based on their own self-interest, but it also acknowledges that aggregated behaviors of organizations are less than rational because they represent a blend of these individual self-interests.

Political theories view organizations as pluralistic entities composed of interests, subunits, and subcultures. The concept of power—where power rests, how much is available, how it is exercised, and so on—is fundamental. These "power factors" determine action. Abe Rosner's comments on powerful unions and governments clearly show that power was a factor in his understanding which occupations best survived inflationary times. Little can be said as yet about linkages between motivation and power, as little research has been done on this issue.

Process Theories in Review

As a group, the process theories are the major approaches to motivation dominating the field in the last two decades (Mitchell, 1979). Although some attempts have been made to integrate process theories (e.g., Fedor and Ferris, 1981), they have met with little success.

A recent attempt (Klein, 1989) builds on control theory, the central image of which is the feedback loop (see Figure 9.9). The model combines a number of theoretical perspectives to outline the basic motivating process. Goals determine behavior; feedback on performance is evaluated through a comparison. If the outcome matches the desired goal, the behavior may be repeated. If the outcome does not match the desired goal, the next step is to employ unconscious scripted responses or to find another solution. If the latter, the value of the goal (box 10) is evaluated; this evaluation is influenced by individual and situational factors. The result of this evaluation is change of either goals (box 12) or behavior (box 13).

An integrated approach is required because on their own each of the process theories is lacking. If one took a strict operant conditioning view of motivation, any reference to internally determined drives, which are at the

FIGURE 9.9
An Integrated Model of Motivation

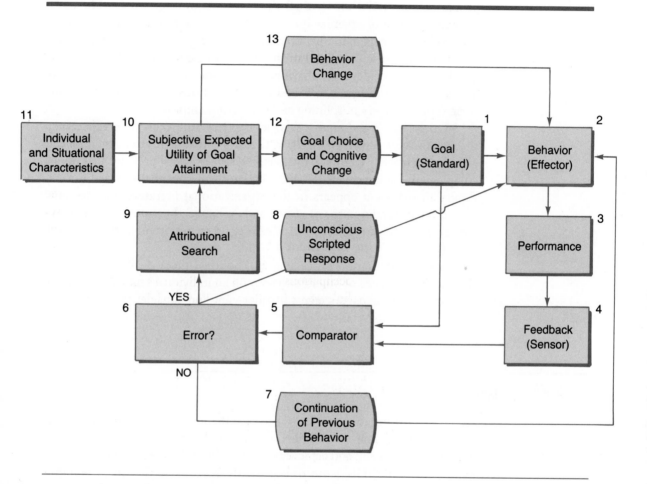

Source: From H. J. Klein, "An Integrated Control Theory Model of Work Motivation," *Academy of Management Review* 14 (1989): 153. Reprinted by permission.

heart of all other motivation theories, is irrelevant. In practice such a one-sided view is rarely taken, but it is one of the conceptual problems with the theory: we know that people's thoughts at least occasionally determine their behavior.

Expectancy theory also has its problems. It argues that "if people (a) knew all the alternatives, (b) knew all the outcomes, (c) knew all the action-outcome relationships, and (d) knew how they felt about these outcomes, they would use a rather complex formula to come up with an estimate of the best choice action" (Mitchell, 1979, p. 255). The problem, of course, is that people obviously do not have all that information, nor would they use a complex formula to organize it if they did. The theory is useful as a general approximation of people's behavior. Someone applying expectancy theory might use the basic principles of the theory to think about what causes or gets in the way of desired behavior. For example, effort-performance linkages are influenced by abilities and role perceptions, which should be considered by managers in training and socializing employees.

Goal-setting and equity theories are less ambitious than expectancy theory. A problem with goal-setting theories is that little attention has been given to such other factors as financial rewards or social pressure that might complement, enhance, or act independently of the goal-setting process. Equity theory, as it appears in the organizational literature, has not embraced the general notions of justice and exchange. The subtle forms of exchange in organizations are probably every bit as important as the exchange of work for pay.

Social information processing and political theories focus our attention on the influence of others' behavior on an individual's motivation. They both argue that managers take a broader view and consider the meaning of the situation in its totality.

Stir Gently and Apply

As the Abe Rosner case demonstrates, each theory of motivation explored in this chapter can help shed light on this complex area of human behavior. Security, self-esteem, and achievement needs all motivated Rosner at several points in his life. His sense of self-worth was clearly tied to meaningful work; it was also quite clearly tied to how he compared himself to others (equity theory). His effort-to-performance expectancies came into play in his last brokerage job, from which he was dismissed because, as he stated, "I just couldn't be a salesman like that." Reinforcement for Rosner should probably have been more in the form of recognition than commissions. Analysis based on the social information processing perspective helps us understand Rosner's actions as well; recall that he was reluctant to work for one firm because he perceived it as having questionable ethics. In sum, in terms of motivation theories, Abe Rosner's life can best be explained by an integrative approach to motivation, not by any one theory. If such is true of one individual, imagine the variety of techniques that must be employed in an organization of many employees.

A number of application strategies of various motivation models are available to managers. In fact, applications of motivational models to actual management situations are better developed than are applications of any other models of management behavior. These applications, however, may not be appropriate in countries other than the United States or Canada. One author (Kanungo, 1983) concluded that innovation strategies used in the West have limited applicability in those Third World countries that do not, like the West, value individualism.

A number of companies have developed management systems based on needs models. One can work such notions into training, benefits, and other aspects of personnel management. Explicit attention to such factors as job security and the implementation of social and job growth opportunities can be worked into personnel management programs. Managers might examine the situational relevance of maximizing such needs as achievement, institutional power, or affiliation, or of having people high on such needs manage in various environments.

Herzberg (1982) has his own training program that sharply divides motivators and hygienes and illustrates ways managers can work on both kinds of factors. McClelland (McClelland and Winter, 1969) also developed a training program designed to teach managers how to increase their performance and that of subordinates by increasing one or more of the three primary motivators he studied.

Management by objectives (MBO) is a simple program that, hand in hand with good everyday management, addresses various theoretical formulations about motivation but also draws primarily from goal-setting theory (see also Chapter 10). In companies with MBO programs, managers and their subordinates sit down uninterrupted at stated intervals and develop a set of goals to be reached in specified periods of time. During the interval, sessions might be scheduled to assess progress and refine goals, but during the primary goal-setting meetings dates are established for completing specific tasks. When those dates are reached, appraisal interviews are held. The discerning manager can see that MBO might meet some employee needs and certainly can be used to implement operant conditioning, expectancy, goal-setting, equity, and social influence notions. MBO procedures can be tailored to an organization's situation, culture, and leadership profiles (Muczyk and Reimann, 1989).

Another frequently used application is **behavior modification** (Luthans and Kreitner, 1975). This strategy manages reinforcement contingencies simply by setting up reinforcement schedules for completing certain jobs.

Because political approaches to motivation are relatively new in the management literature, no training programs to teach their application exist. About all we can recommend is that managers be sensitive to organizations as political milieus, pay attention to the development and location of power, and perhaps locate people with high needs for institutional power in units that can benefit from their attention to developing organizational resources.

Katzell and Thompson (1990) reviewed studies of the effects of a number of different variables on motivation, from personal characteristics of workers to work structure. They concluded that effective motivational programs rest on seven principles:

1. Ensure that workers' motives and values match their jobs.

2. Ensure that jobs match and appear attractive to workers' motives and values.

3. Create goals that are clear, challenging, attractive, and attainable.

4. Provide workers with resources they need to be effective.

5. Create a supportive environment.

6. Effectively reinforce desirable behavior.

7. Blend all the elements into an effective work system.

Clearly, such a program would provide workers with a congenial, challenging, and rewarding work environment.

SUMMARY

Three major approaches to motivation dominate the literature. The classical studies—embracing scientific management and the human resources movement—focused on issues that in effect combined the two main theoretical approaches, content theories and process theories. Scientific management defined the need for money as the worker's main motivator, then attempted to structure tasks in such a way as to feed that motivation. The human relations movement attempted to meet employees' need for satisfaction by manipulating elements of the organization's atmosphere. But the main research attention has been given to the two types of theories mentioned earlier, content theories and process theories.

Content theories are psychological in nature and focus on internal dispositions that purportedly influence behavior. These theories focus on needs; some focus on long lists of needs, others on shorter lists.

Murray's need classification scheme, which identified 20 needs, was among the first such theories developed; many of these needs have appeared in later needs theories. White emphasized the need for competence, which helps explain the motivation of individuals facing new situations. Maslow focused on a hierarchy of needs ranging from those that support basic survival up through the need to achieve a state of fulfillment of potential that he termed self-actualization. Alderfer tried to modify Maslow's five categories of needs into three: existence, relatedness, and growth.

Herzberg changed the debate on needs by differentiating two sets of job factors. External factors, called hygiene factors, can be manipulated only to eliminate dissatisfaction. To motivate employees, organizations need to address motivating factors. McClelland's studies focused on three particular needs, those for achievement, affiliation, and power.

Some need theories are of limited utility because they are virtually untestable. Nevertheless, need theories offer managers categories of factors to think about in designing training programs, evaluation schemes, pay and benefit packages, and so on. Underlying most need theories is the assumption that one would have to change the situation to meet existing needs. However, in the case of McClelland's need for achievement there is the assumption—and some evidence—that achievement motivation can be taught.

Process theories are a little broader in their coverage than content theories. Operant conditioning theory focuses exclusively on the role of reward and punishment in shaping behavior. Expectancy theory bases motivation on what employees expect from their jobs, what they predict their own performance to be, and how they value the factors identified in their expectations.

A related view, goal-setting theory, focuses on the specificity of goals, the difficulty of attaining them, and the degree to which the individual accepts the organization's goals as her own. Feedback is an important factor in this view. The question of employee participation in setting goals is also central to this theory.

Equity theory predicts that individuals will be motivated depending on how they perceive the fairness of their treatment compared to others. Social information processing theory is similarly based on perceptions. It suggests that a worker's behavior is determined not by objective realities but by how he perceives his situation and the actions of others. The political approach to motivation focuses on different issues than those having solely to do with individual differences. It turns our attention to the various ways groups and organizations push and pull their participants.

A number of these theoretical approaches have received practical application in training programs. The wise manager, however, is probably better off taking elements from the various theoretical approaches to motivation and building management systems suitable to her own situation.

MANAGERIAL INSIGHT

To: *Student Managers*
From: *Veteran Manager*
Subject: *Motivation*

For a manager, the good news about motivation theories is that they all work. The bad news is that they only work some of the time, with some of the people.

What most of the theories have in common is that motivation resides inside a person and must be released. Few researchers or practitioners believe motivation can be applied wholly from outside. What can be managed, though, are the outside factors that elicit the drive, or remove the barriers.

Viewed in this light, motivation takes on attributes of appetite and taste for food. Different foods appeal to different people. Some people like apricots, others don't. Some people like their food spicy, others prefer it bland. It is futile to try to get people voluntarily to eat food they don't like.

In your department Person A may be motivated by a desire to perform a task better than anyone else, Person B may respond more readily to praise, and Person C may be best persuaded by money. In other words, different strokes for different folks. Or more precisely, different strokes for different folks at different times in different jobs in different situations—because on a given day with a given task, competence won't be what pushes Person A; she wants more income, or more recognition, or more vacation time.

It's important to look at the entire environment of a person's job to assess the motivational climate. Compensation, job design, independence of action, power, perceptions of contribution to the unit and the larger organization, recognition, opportunity for advancement, physical surroundings, perceptions of equity, treatment as a person—all these and more can affect a person's motivation and therefore job performance.

Your job as a manager will be to get things done through other people. To use an elegant analogy, you will have a task akin to that of an orchestra conductor. You have to know when to call on which people and what kind of gesture will work to get the desired effect.

Where the analogy breaks down—and makes the manager's job more difficult than the conductor's—is that the manager doesn't have a musical score that specifies exactly who is supposed to be doing what at any given time. So don't worry if you are trying to manage without *having* a score. The time to worry is when you are trying to manage with *knowing* the score. Keep that in mind to keep yourself motivated.

REVIEW QUESTIONS

1. How does the Rosner case demonstrate the effect of situations on motivation?

2. Contrast the underlying assumptions of process and content theories of motivation.

3. What is the premise on which scientific management is based, and what conclusion is drawn from that premise?

4. Briefly characterize Likert's system 4 organization.

5. Describe the model that underlies all content theories of motivation.

6. According to Murray, what activates the motivators on his list of needs?

7. What are the five levels of needs identified by Maslow?

8. What is unique about Herzberg's theory of motivation? How are factors manipulated to achieve desirable results?

9. What attribute was found by McClelland and co-workers to be associated with successful work groups? Why is success more likely when managers possess this trait than others they studied?

10. According to operant conditioning theory, which is more effective, rewards or punishments?

11. Explain the three key variables in expectancy theory and how they interact to affect motivation.

12. What three factors related to goals are judged important to motivation in goal theory? Explain how each is seen as affecting motivation.

13. If poorly structured or learned tasks require process feedback, what qualities must be possessed by the manager giving that feedback?

14. If comparative wages are unknown, can the motivations proposed by equity theory be in effect? Why or why not?

15. What do equity theory and social formation processing theory have in common?

REFERENCES

Adams, J. S. (1965). Integrity in social exchange. In L. Berkowitz (ed.), *Advances in Experimental Social Psychology*. New York: Academic Press.

Adams, J. S. (1976). The structure and dynamics of behavior on organization boundary roles. In M. Dunnette (ed.), *The Handbook of Industrial and Organizational Psychology*. Chicago: Rand-McNally.

Alderfer, C. P. (1972). *Existence, Relatedness and Growth: Human Needs in Organizational Settings*. New York: Free Press.

Alderfer, C. (1977). A critique of Salancik and Pfeffer's examination of need satisfaction theories. *Administrative Science Quarterly* 22:658–669.

Atkinson, S. W. (1964). *An Introduction to Motivation*. Princeton: Van Nostrand.

Badawy, M. K. (1979). Managerial attitudes and need orientations of Mideastern executives: An empirical cross-cultural analysis. *Academy of Management Proceedings* 39: 293–297.

Bandura, A. (1986). *Social Foundations of Thought and Action: A Social Cognitive View*. Englewood Cliffs, NJ: Prentice-Hall.

Braverman, H. (1974). *Labor and Monopoly Capital: The Degradation of Work in the Twentieth Century*. New York: Monthly Review Press.

Campbell, J. P., and Pritchard, R. D. (1976). Motivation theory in industrial and organizational psychology. In M. D. Dunnette (ed.), *Handbook of Industrial and Organizational Psychology*. Chicago: Rand-McNally, pp. 63–130.

Cotton, J. L., Vollrath, D. A., Froggatt, K. L., Lengnick-Hall, M. L., and Jennings, K. R. (1988). Employee participation: Diverse forms and different outcomes. *Academy of Management Review* 13:8–22.

Crabbs, R. A. (1973). Work motivation in the culturally complex Panama Canal Company. *Academy of Management Proceedings*, pp. 119–126.

DeCharms, R. (1957). *Personal Causation: The Internal Affective Determinants of Behavior*. New York: Academic Press.

Earley, P. C., Connolly, T., and Ekegren, G. (1989). Goals, strategy development, and task performance: Some limits on the efficacy of goal setting. *Journal of Applied Psychology* 74:24–33.

Earley, P. C., Northcraft, G. B., Lee, C., and Lituchy, T. R. (1990). Impact of process and outcome feedback on the relation of goal setting to task performance. *Academy of Management Journal* 33:87–105.

Eden, D. (1988). Pygmalion, goal setting, and expectancy: Compatible ways to boost productivity. *Academy of Management Review* 13:639–652.

Fedor, D. B., and Ferris, G. R. (1981). Integrating OB mod with cognitive approaches to motivation. *Academy of Management Review* 6:115–125.

Freud, S. (1949). In *Collected Papers of Sigmund Freud* (vol. 4, original edition, 1915; Riviere, J., trans.). London: Hogarth Press.

George, C. (1972). *The History of Management Thought*. Englewood Cliffs, NJ: Prentice-Hall.

Goodman, P. S. (1974). An examination of referents used in the evaluation of pay. *Organizational Behavior and Human Performance* 12:170–195.

Griffin, J. H. (1977). *Black Like Me.* Boston: Houghton Mifflin.

Griffin, R. W., Vecchio, R. P., and Logan, J. W. (1989). Equity theory and interpersonal attraction. *Journal of Applied Psychology* 74:394–401.

Hamner, W. C. (1974). Reinforcement theory and contingency, management in organizational settings, in H. G. Tosi and C. W. Hammer, (eds.), *Organizational Behavior and Management: A Contingency Approach.* Chicago: St. Clair Press.

Herzberg, F. (1982). *The Managerial Choice: To Be Efficient and to Be Human.* Salt Lake City: Olympia Publishing.

Herzberg, F., Mausner, B., and Snyderman, B. (1959). *The Motivation to Work* (2nd ed.). New York: Wiley.

Hines, G. H. (1973a). Achievement motivation, occupations, and labor turnover in New Zealand. *Journal of Applied Psychology* 58:313–317.

Hines, G. H. (1973b). Cross-cultural differences in two-factor theory. *Journal of Applied Psychology* 58:375–377.

House, R. J., and Singh, J. V. (1987). Organizational behavior: Some new directions. *Annual Review of Psychology* 38:669–718.

Huseman, R. C., Hatfield, J. D., and Miles, E. W. (1987). A new perspective on equity theory: The equity sensitivity construct. *Academy of Management Review* 12:222–234.

Ilgen, D. R., and Klein, H. J. (1989). Organization behavior. In M. R. Rosenweig and L. W. Porter (eds.), *Annual Review of Psychology* (vol. 40). Palo Alto, CA: Annual Review, pp. 327–351.

Jaggi, B. (1979). Need importance of Indian managers. *Management International Review* 19:107–113.

Kanungo, R. N. (1983). Work alienation: A pancultural perspective. *International Studies of Management and Organization* 13:129–138.

Katz, F., and Kahn R. (1978). *The Social Psychology of Organizations.* New York: Wiley.

Katzell, R. A., and Thompson, D. E. (1990). Work motivation: Theory and practice. *American Psychologist* 74:144–153.

Klein, H. J. (1989). An integrated control theory of work motivation. *Academy of Management Review* 14:150–172.

Kuriloff, A., and Hemphill, J. M. (1978). *How to Start Your Own Business and Succeed.* New York: McGraw-Hill.

Latham, G. P., Erez, M., and Locke, E. A. (1988). Resolving scientific disputes by the joint design of crucial experiments by the antagonists: Application to the Erez-Latham dispute regarding participation in goal setting. *Journal of Applied Psychology* 73:753–772.

Latham, G. P., Mitchell, T. R., and Dossett, D. L. (1978). Importance of participative goal setting and anticipated rewards on goal difficulty and job performance. *Journal of Applied Psychology* 63:163–171.

Latham, G. P., and Yukl, G. A. (1975). A review of research on the application of goal setting in organizations. *Academy of Management Journal* 18:824–845.

Lawler, E. E. (1973). *Motivation in Work Organizations.* Monterey, CA: Brooks/Cole.

Leavitt, H. (1965). Applied organizational change in industry: Structural, technological, and humanistic approaches. In J. G. March (ed.), *Handbook of Organization.* Chicago: Rand-McNally, pp. 1144–1170.

Likert, R. (1961). *New Patterns of Management.* New York: McGraw-Hill.

Likert, R. (1967). *The Human Organization.* New York: McGraw-Hill.

Locke, E. A. (1968). Toward a theory of task motivation and incentives. *Organizational Behavior and Human Performance* 3:157–189.

Locke, E. A. (1976). The nature and causes of job satisfaction. In M. Dunnette (ed.), *Handbook of Industrial and Organizational Psychology.* Chicago: Rand-McNally, pp. 1297–1349.

Locke, E. (1982). The ideas of Frederick W. Taylor: An evaluation. *Academy of Management Review* 7:14–24.

Locke, E. A., Laham, G. P., and Erez, E. A. (1988). The determinants of goal commitment. *Academy of Management Review* 13:pp. 23–29.

Locke, E. A., Shaw, K. N., Saari, L. M., and Latham, G. P. (1981). Goal setting and task performance: 1969–1980. *Psychological Bulletin* 90:125–152.

Luthans, F., and Kreitner, R. (1975). *Organizational Behavior Modification.* Glenview, IL: Scott, Foresman.

McClelland, D. C. (1961). *The Achieving Society.* Princeton, NJ: Van Nostrand Reinhold.

McClelland, D. C. (1971). *Assessing Human Motivation.* Morristown, NJ: General Learning Press.

McClelland, D. C. (1976). *Power: The Inner Experience.* New York: Irvington-Wiley.

McClelland, D. C. (1985). *Human Motivation.* Glenview, IL: Scott, Foresman.

McClelland, D. C., Atkinson, J. W., Clark, R. A., and Lowell, E. L. (1953). *The Achievement Motive.* New York: Appleton-Century Crofts.

McClelland, D. C., and Winter, D. G. (1969). *Motivating Economic Achievement.* New York: Free Press.

McDougall, W. (1908). *An Introduction to Social Psychology.* London: Methuen.

McGregor, D. (1960). *The Human Side of Enterprise.* New York: McGraw-Hill.

Maccoby, M. (1976). *The Gamesman, the New Corporate Leader.* New York: Simon & Schuster.

Maslow, A. H. (1943). A theory of human motivation. *Psychological Review* 50:370–396.

Matsui, T., and Terrai, I. (1979). A cross-cultural study of the validity of the expectancy theory of work motivation. *Journal of Applied Psychology* 60:263–265.

Miller, L. E., and Grush, J. E. (1988). Improving predictions in expectancy theory research: Effects of personality, expectancies, and norms. *Academy of Management Journal* 31:107–122.

Mitchell, T. E. (1982). Motivation: New directions for theory, research, and practice. *Academy of Management Review* 7:80–88.

Mitchell, T. R. (1979). Organizational behavior. In M. R. Rosenzweig and L. W. Porter (eds.), *Annual Review of Psychology* (vol. 30). Palo Alto, CA: Annual Reviews, pp. 243–282.

Mowday, R. (1983). Equity theory predictions of behavior in organizations. In R. M. Steers and L. W. Porter (eds.), *Motivation and Work Behavior*. New York: McGraw-Hill.

Muczyk, J. P., and Reimann, B. C. (1989). MBO as a complement to effective leadership. *Academy of Management Executive* 3:131–140.

Murray, H. A. (1938). *Explorations in Personality*. New York: Oxford University Press.

Nisbett, R. E., and Ross, L. (1980). *Human Inference: Strategies and Shortcomings of Social Judgment*. Englewood Cliffs, NJ: Prentice-Hall.

O'Reilly, C. A., and Caldwell, D. (1979). Informational influence as a determinant of perceived task characteristics and job satisfaction. *Journal of Applied Psychology* 64:157–165.

Porter, L. W., and Lawler, E. E. (1968). *Managerial Attitudes and Performance*. Homewood, IL: Irwin-Dorsey.

Pritchard, R. D., Roth, P. L., Jones, S. D., Galfay, P. J., and Watson, M. D. (1988). Designing a goal-setting system to enhance performance: A practical guide. *Organizational Dynamics* 17:63–74.

Reitz, J., and Grof, G. (1973). *Similarities and Differences Among Mexican Workers and Attitudes to Worker Motivation*. Bloomington: Indiana University Press.

Salancik, G. R., and Pfeffer, J. (1977). An examination of need satisfaction models of job attitudes. *Administrative Science Quarterly* 23:224–253.

Skinner, B. F. (1953). *Science and Human Behavior*. New York: Macmillan.

Skinner, B. F. (1971). *Beyond Freedom and Dignity*. New York: Knopf.

Steers, R., and Porter, L. W. (1983). *Motivational and Work Behavior*, 3rd ed. New York: McGraw-Hill.

Steers, R. (1988). *Introduction to Organizational Behavior* (3rd ed.). New York: Wiley.

Stephens, D., Kedia, B., and Ezell, D. (1979). Managerial need structures in U.S. and Peruvian industries. *Management International Review* 19:27–29.

Taylor, F. W. (1903). *Shop Management*. New York: Harper.

Taylor, F. W. (1967, originally published 1911). *The Principles of Scientific Management*. New York: Harper.

Taylor, S. E., and Fiske, S. T. (1978). Salience, attention, and attribution: Top of the head phenomena. In E. Berkowitz (ed.), *Advances in Experimental Social Psychology* (vol. 15), pp. 249–288.

Thomas, J. G., and Griffin, R. W. (1989). Work motivation: Theory and practice. *American Psychologist* 74:144–153.

Vance, R. J., and Colella, A. (1990). Effects of two types of feedback on goal acceptance and personal goals. *Journal of Applied Psychology* 75:68–76.

Weick, K. (1979). *The Social Psychology of Organizing*. Reading, MA: Addison-Wesley.

White, R. W. (1959). Motivation reconsidered: The concept of competence. *Psychological Review* 66:297–333.

White, S. E., and Mitchell, T. R. (1979). Job enrichment versus social cues: A comparison and competitive test. *Journal of Applied Psychology* 64:1–9.

Wood, R., and Bandura, A. (1989). Social cognitive theory of organizational management. *Academy of Management Review* 14:361–384.

Individual Differences: Learning About Others

CHAPTER OVERVIEW

This chapter examines several individual differences that people bring to their jobs in organizations and reviews the training, reward, and punishment strategies that organizations use to enhance or modify those individual characteristics.

THEME CASE

"Ellen Randall: The Ceiling and the Wall" illustrates the impact of individual differences (e.g., gender, social perceptions and attributions, values and attitudes) on the training, evaluation, and promotion of a woman near the ceiling or top job in her organization.

CHAPTER OUTLINE

- Why Study Personality?
- Personality
- Social Perception
- Values and Attitudes
- Training
- Performance Evaluation
- Rewards, Discipline, and Responses to Discipline
- Summary
- Managerial Insight

KEY DEFINITIONS

Personality traits   hypothetical entities that account for the tendency for an individual to behave similarly in diverse situations.

Attribution theory   the theoretical perspective that addresses how our own perceptions color the characteristics of what we perceive.

Social perception   the study of how we try to understand the behavior of others based on the situation rather than on dispositional factors.

Values   normative beliefs about desirable goals and modes of conduct.

Attitudes   mental constructs comprised of affective, cognitive, and behavioral components.

Needs assessment   component of training system in which the nature and amount of training is determined by using organizational analysis, task analysis, and person analysis.

Transfer of training   the degree to which what is learned is actually used in work.

Additional Terms

Personality
Intelligence
Achievement
Uniqueness
Masculinity, femininity, androgyny
Authoritarianism
Machiavellianism
Schemas
Prototypes
Scripts
Dynamic self-concept
Reliability
Validity
Consistency, distinctiveness, and
    consensus information
Programmed instruction (PI)
Computer-assisted instruction (CAI)
Teletraining
Simulations
Case studies
Role playing
Relapse
Behavioral rating scales
Management by objectives (MBO)
Simple ranking
Paired comparison

479

Forced distribution
Unclear performance standards
Halo effect
Central tendency

Leniency or strictness error
Bias
Progressive discipline
Discipline without punishment

ELLEN RANDALL: THE CEILING AND THE WALL

The interviewer was embarrassingly late for the 9:00 A.M. appointment. She had come in the wrong entrance area, and someone had to be summoned by the receptionist to escort her through the huge building. The walk seemed at least two miles long, although the secretary who accompanied her was hospitable and talkative. Finally, the secretary showed her into a modest office, all glass on the inside wall, and introduced her to the head of the corporation's largest division, Ellen Randall (not her real name).

Ellen Randall was a distinguished-looking woman. Her hair had turned from brown to mostly gray and the interviewer was surprised to learn later that she was forty—she could have been older. She didn't appear bothered by the delay. Instead, she smiled warmly, got the interviewer seated comfortably at the round table at the other end of her office from the desk, arranged for coffee to be brought, and began commenting on the study. She obviously had read the background information and the interview questions sent a couple of weeks earlier. The interview was in full swing within a few minutes.

The first story she told was about an experience that had led to a lasting change in her approach to management. She was about twenty-eight years old when opportunity knocked at her door:

> My job change came about when I got a phone call from personnel. They said my name had come out of a computer [as a candidate for a job opening], but no one knew who I was. They were all curious.

Ann Morrison, R. P. White, Ellen Van Velsor, and the Center for Creative Leadership, *Breaking the Glass Ceiling: Can Women Reach the Top of America's Largest Corporations* (Reading, MA: Addison-Wesley, 1987), pp. 1–5. Copyright © 1987, Addison-Wesley Publishing Co., Inc. Reprinted by permission.

This was the first time I realized that to get ahead, you have to let people know who you are. I had thought hard work was enough. I started the interview process, but I wasn't sure I wanted it. My supervisor, a woman, took me aside after I'd been offered the job. Her boss had asked me to stay because they needed me in the department; she said, "I'd take the risk and leave. Don't end up like me, after twenty years." She pushed me out of the nest. I learned that you have to take care of yourself. Management won't always help you. You have to take a risk.

My first quantum leap was the move into personnel. Before this, I'd managed ten professionals; now I was managing one hundred clericals. My budget responsibilities jumped from $350,000 to $4.5 million. With professionals, you can give some direction and back off. With a large clerical staff, the issues are different: lots of rumors; a nonsmoker seated next to a smoker becomes a crisis; getting out early around holidays is an issue. There was more pressure from customers, too. They are all around you, and they think they can do your job better than you.

I learned that you have to roll up your sleeves and get interested in your people. I knew everyone's name and something personal about each; you've got to manage by walking around. My predecessor didn't do this. You've also got to dig in and learn the business; you can't leave it all to your direct subordinates—otherwise you can't help them solve problems. If your subordinates see you as there for two years to pick up a management stripe, they'll resent you.

While I had responsibility for the training department, I interviewed a man that I knew was the wrong person. But the job had been open so long, and I had other irons in the fire. It was over six months before I admitted it wasn't good. After nearly a year, I told my boss's boss I had made a hiring mistake. He said, "We had to give you time to see that and correct it." I learned to never discount your intuition. A bad decision isn't the end of the world, and relief comes when you correct a bad fit. It won't go away and problems add up. Additional pressure comes from the fact that we had an unhappy staff, and he had a heart attack in the middle of all this. I felt guilty that I gave him the heart attack. I don't want to feel that way ever again. He looked outside the company and got a great job.

She had been in staff jobs with the company for six years, and then she moved into her first line position—another significant event for her:

I didn't know the business. I had to prove my credibility by learning the business. One man there thought he had been the best choice and should have been promoted. I let that go longer than I should have. It was terribly disruptive to everyone in the department by the end. They were just waiting to see what would happen. Having to prove myself to everyone [with that on top of it] was very tough. We finally sat down to talk. We're good friends now. I learned to get things out on the table early. Now that's easier for me to do.

During this period, I went to a convention for the first time. I went with my direct reports, all men. I overpacked. No one had told me about business versus social, and no one offered to help me with my bags. They also did not bother to introduce me to people. The second convention was very different, four or five months later; I'd cleared up things with the male subordinates by then. They introduced me as their boss.

[During a merger and after moving into a line management position] a year ago, I picked up more people and responsibilities. My boss was dishonest and artificial, and gave little direction. There was no cohesiveness among the five people directly under him, except that none of us liked him. The business was being deemphasized and down-scaled. I began to wonder, Do I really need this? Is it worth it all? I know this attitude started to show through. I decided to do something about it. I compared my business to another and realized the other one was entrepreneurial. I put those things into my job objectives and found new niches, new opportunities, new products, and new clients. The job started to have momentum on its own.

I received feedback from two subordinates here. One man said, "You tend not to use your womanhood. You try to neutralize it. For example, you wear a suit instead of a dress." I said I did not want people to use it as a barrier. He felt it could be a tool used in a positive way. Another man asked me, "Why do you sometimes soften things afterward?" I responded that I did not want to be seen as an aggressive female. Maybe I work too hard to neutralize. Now, I sometimes wear a dress, and I don't apologize as much for giving orders.

Her family life wasn't always a picnic, either:

There has been a real strain on our marriage which comes and goes. In a previous job, my salary jumped much higher than my husband's. Then he caught up. When I took my present job, the salary and bonuses put me way above him again. He changed jobs in January after four months of interviewing. He did this without telling me a thing. My husband said one reason was that I did not think enough of the people he had been associating with. I think the real reason is he could become a partner one day and reach parity with me.

Ellen Randall is an impressive figure. She has worked her way up the ranks to become president of a business unit with full bottom-line responsibility, taken over in tough situations and worked things out, and added executive's stripes to her sleeve. She is obviously the one in charge, but she is also warm and open. She makes you think that she's going places, that you'll be reading about her future promotions in the *Wall Street Journal*. She's going to the top, you think.

But Ellen's future doesn't look so bright to her. When she looks ahead, she sees no realistic possibility for further advancement in her corporation. Instead, she senses a wall, a barrier between her—a woman—and a top job in her corporation:

> People tell me that I've moved quickly in fifteen years, but I think I would have been in the executive group earlier [if I were a man]. Men with less experience were promoted sooner. After eighteen months in a job, I was told I had to stay longer. They need to test women more. If the boss who hired me for this job had not been there and asked for me, I would have had a lateral transfer once, maybe twice more, before I got to this level.

Why Study Personality?

As the Ellen Randall case demonstrates, the characteristics that one person brings to an organization make a difference to that organization. Randall is an impressive person, indeed, the head of the corporation's largest division at the young age of 40, a woman poised near the top. She is a highly capable manager who has been able to take on and master a number of different assignments, both line and staff, of increasing responsibility. Her abilities have clearly stood out in her firm and enabled her to get ahead. Yet the Randall case also demonstrates that individual characteristics make a difference to the organization in another, more negative, way. For example, she mentions that her first break taught her that one needs to stand out to get ahead; hard work is not enough. Also, and more significantly, the highest reward available within the company may be denied her because she is a woman.

People bring with them various personality characteristics when they come through an organization's doors. These characteristics determine or are at least related to people's social perceptions, which are influenced by, and in turn influence, values and attitudes. Recall the reaction of Randall's subordinate when she first took over a staff management post. He thought he was better prepared for the job. How much of that perception was influenced by Randall's being a woman?

Since organizations cannot survive with members who possess such wide differences in personality traits, social perceptions, attitudes, and values that the people cannot work together, organizations take certain steps to reduce those differences and mold a work force that can proceed along the road to common goals. We have already studied one aspect of those steps in examining socialization (see Chapter 3). Other steps include training employees to engage in goal-directed behaviors, evaluating performance to ensure that the training results in the desired behaviors, and using reward and punishment systems to reinforce the desired behaviors.

We will examine three sets of issues in this chapter. First we will study the characteristics that individuals bring to the organization—personality, social perceptions, and values and attitudes. Then we will examine the training techniques that organizations use to modify or enhance those characteristics. These attributes and processes come together and find expression in the worker's behavior, or job performance. Our third subject will be how organizations evaluate that performance and apply rewards or punishments to try to remove undesirable behavior and reinforce desirable actions. These responses provide feedback to the individual, which will (or will not) result in modified behavior. The process also provides feedback to the organization. The overall process, modeled in Figure 10.1, provides a blueprint for the chapter.

We will talk about each of these issues in turn since they are not well integrated in the psychological literature. That is, those researchers who study evaluation or rewards are not likely to simultaneously think about the individual differences people bring to organizations. But managers have to. One has to think about how to tailor reward systems both to what employees bring with them in the first place and how they change once inside the organization. Some employees respond better to monetary rewards alone; others need praise and recognition. Some workers want to take on greater challenges—Ellen Randall is certainly an example. Others may be happiest and most productive when performing at peak ability in the same position.

Personality

People differ in an infinite variety of ways. Not only do they possess physical differences—size, gender, race, among others—but each person has a unique combination of characteristics that encompass such dimensions as demeanor and behavior. These differences are recognized in conversation. One person is called "cheerful" and another "aggressive." The sum of these various characteristics, unique to each individual, is that person's **person-**

FIGURE 10.1
A Model of the Interaction of the Individual and the Organization

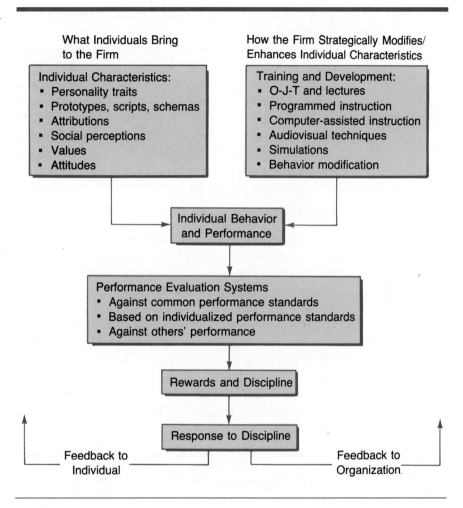

What Individuals Bring to the Firm

Individual Characteristics:
- Personality traits
- Prototypes, scripts, schemas
- Attributions
- Social perceptions
- Values
- Attitudes

How the Firm Strategically Modifies/Enhances Individual Characteristics

Training and Development:
- O-J-T and lectures
- Programmed instruction
- Computer-assisted instruction
- Audiovisual techniques
- Simulations
- Behavior modification

Individual Behavior and Performance

Performance Evaluation Systems
- Against common performance standards
- Based on individualized performance standards
- Against others' performance

Rewards and Discipline

Response to Discipline

Feedback to Individual

Feedback to Organization

ality. Personality psychologists have studied these differences and their significance to understanding people's lives. Yet studying personality differences is extremely hard to do, made harder, perhaps, by the fact that our language contains as many as 30,000 words to describe individuals (Allport and Odbert, 1936).

Generally, psychologists have moved from discussing large clusters of words that seem to describe the individual's enduring dispositions toward defining what they call **personality traits.** These are hypothetical entities that account for the tendency of an individual to behave similarly in diverse situations (Brody, 1988). Someone who is introverted, for example, will be more oriented to abstract ideas and feelings. An extraverted person will respond more to objects; such an individual may have less sensitivity to the feelings of others.

The study of personality has focused on two different approaches. For years, the emphasis was on the investigation of individual traits. There was much controversy as to whether these traits are determined genetically or acquired by simple stimulus response learning, but regardless of the putative source, the focus of study was on characteristics. Another, more recent view sees traits as a function of the interaction of environment and person. These researchers discuss the importance of scripts and schemas that govern people's social interactions. We will take each of these two perspectives in turn.

Personality Traits

Researchers have identified a large number of personality traits. Due to limitations of space, we cannot explore each of these in depth. As a result, we will focus on a few to which managers might be sensitive because of their influence on organizational life. Some characteristics people bring with them to the workplace provide greater challenges for management than others, as we will see. We begin our discussion with four traits that might be of general concern to managers—intelligence, achievement, uniqueness, and masculinity/femininity—and follow that with a discussion of two traits often linked to power—Machiavellianism and authoritarianism. Some additional traits that have received research attention are listed in Figure 10.2.

In studying these traits, it is important to think of each individual as

FIGURE 10.2
Additional Personality Traits

Trait	Explanation
Dogmatism	The degree to which an individual's beliefs are held firmly
Introversion/Extraversion	The individual's tendency to be directed inward (introversion) or outward (extraversion)
Locus of control	The extent to which the individual believes that he or she is in control of events (internal locus of control) or that control lies outside (external locus of control) (see Chapter 6)
Risk propensity	The degree to which an individual is willing to take risks (see Chapter 7)
Self-esteem	The way an individual evaluates his or her abilities and worth

being somewhere on a continuum from high to low rather than in binary states of either yes or no. Achievement motivation, for instance, is possessed by all individuals to some degree of being achievement oriented or not. The manager needs to see staffers, then, not as being on or off in terms of achievement motivation, but as being located somewhere on an achievement motivation scale.

Intelligence   Intelligence has long been of interest to psychologists—and is controversial as well. **Intelligence** is the individual's mental ability, which is measured through the administration of tests. The use of such tests is hotly debated, but research shows that achievement and success are related to higher scores on intelligence tests.

An explicit rationale for defining intelligence was presented in 1904 (Spearman, 1904). In Spearman's theory intelligence has two components: general intelligence (G) and special intelligence (S). Spearman proposed that if you give an individual a number of intelligence tests, what they all measure in common is G, but what each specific test measures is S. Spearman's major critics (Guilford, 1956) postulated the existence of more than 100 independent intelligence factors. Yet the body of data they collected provides one of the most comprehensive sources of support for Spearman.

How one scores on an intelligence test often results in the kinds of social situations (for example, school levels) he will be exposed to. So although we may think of intelligence as a relatively enduring trait, it is probably influenced by social setting and in turn influences that setting. As the feature on the Pygmalion effect reveals, a form of research bias or self-fulfilling prophecy can affect the perception of intelligence. Eden and his colleagues (Eden and Shani, 1982; Eden and Ravid, 1982) studied the military to show that the Pygmalion effect can improve performance in organizational settings as well. A more recent study, in this instance of retail workers (Sutton and Woodman, 1989), indicated that the effect may not operate in all situations.

FEATURE: *The Pygmalion Effect*

Pygmalion is a character in Greek mythology, a sculptor from Cyprus who carved and then fell in love with the statue of a beautiful woman. His devotion to Aphrodite, the goddess of love, was such that she rewarded him by turning the statue into a living human being.

In the original experiment demonstrating the Pygmalion effect (Rosenthal and Jacobson, 1968), the results were created by the inadvertent conveyance of researchers' expectations to subjects, and not by independent variables. Teachers in the study were told that several students were intelligent, regardless of those students' actual performance on intelligence tests. The teachers subsequently perceived those students to have higher intelligence and performance and, accordingly, treated those students differently. As a result of this differential treatment, these students actually increased their intelligence, as measured by test scores, whereas students who had not received such treatment improved less or not at all.

Intelligence is a factor that managers must confront in workers. One might be able to create situations in which employees can exercise their intellectual capacities to the maximum. Alternatively, all of us have been exposed to jobs that are below, or beyond, our intellectual capabilities. People become frustrated by being required to reach too high as well as by being underutilized (see the discussion in Chapter 1 on setting goals).

Achievement   The motive to achieve success has been examined as a personality trait for over 30 years. Because we more fully discuss this motive in Chapter 11, we will only summarize here. The motive for **achievement,** which includes meeting standards of excellence, seems deeply rooted in our society, but researchers have also found substantial evidence of its manifestation in other societies (Heckhausen, 1967; McClelland, Atkinson, Clark, and Lowell, 1953). However, the 1980s saw few cross-national studies of achievement motivation because the construct seems to have different cultural connotations (Maher, 1980).

At the opposite end of the continuum from achievement motivation is the motive to avoid failure. People with high achievement motivation enjoy activities that require skill because they enjoy the challenge of doing well. In contrast, people with a high need to avoid failure are threatened by failure and avoid activities in which their performance will be measured against that of others. As we indicate in Chapter 11, knowing an employee's degree of achievement motivation helps predict whether that employee will respond favorably to challenging tasks. Perhaps we can train people who fear failure to develop achievement skills.

Uniqueness   All individuals, of course, are unique; no two are the same. Nevertheless, we all have certain drives to be like others around us, to conform, which often stems from the desire to be accepted. Some individuals emphasize their differences, however; these people are considered high in a personality trait that has received research attention recently, **uniqueness.** A variety of studies show its importance in explaining some human differences (e.g., Snyder and Fromkin, 1980; Brandt, 1976). People high in uniqueness apparently enjoy being deviant and are drawn to rarities. Thus we would expect products that are advertised as rare to appeal to them. Such individuals may also be useful in helping to avoid groupthink (see Chapter 7).

Not much is known about how uniqueness develops, but one study suggests the importance of characteristics that originate early in life. It showed that people with unusual first names were more likely to rate high on uniqueness than people with more common first names (Snyder and Fromkin, 1980). Managers might want to think about how to channel the activities of employees high in uniqueness so that those activities serve the goals of the organization, particularly since deviance can be counterproductive.

Masculinity/Femininity   Psychologists perceive that using gender alone to distinguish personality is inappropriate. Accordingly, they have sought a personality measure of **masculinity** and **femininity** that could be used with individuals of either gender. Such a measures assumes that some men and women may be psychologically more similar to one another than they are different. Most recently, psychologists have argued that masculinity and femininity are separate sets of characteristics, with both men and women possessing varying degrees of each set. Examples of masculine characteristics are independence, competitiveness, and self-confidence. Feminine characteristics include kindness, gentleness, and warmth. A person can score high on both scales, low on both scales, or high on one scale and low on another. The term developed to refer to people high on both the masculine and feminine scale is **androgyny.**

Although most psychologists agree about the existence of androgyny, there is considerable disagreement about its implications. Bem (1974), the original researcher in the area, said that the androgynous person is the ideal we should strive for. In Bem's view such a person can function effectively in a wide variety of situations that call for either masculine or feminine behavior. She believes that gender-typed people are more limited because they can function effectively in some situations but not in others. Critics of this position are numerous. Some researchers argue that androgyny is a phenomenon peculiar to the United States, where individuality is valued and interdependence scorned (Sampson, 1977). Traditional sex roles and characteristics may be functional in most societies at most times.

Many leadership prescriptions (see Chapter 8) appear to support the notion of androgyny, advocating behaviors that are at once people oriented and supportive as well as task oriented and competitive. Ellen Randall implicitly acknowledged this dual approach when she discussed her tendency to "soften things" after giving an order. On the other hand, Randall also identified a gender barrier between herself and the top job, indicating that leadership may be androgynous but not gender blind.

Authoritarianism   The construct of authoritarianism was initially viewed as composed of anti-Semitism, ethnocentrism, and political and economic conservatism. Central to the construct was the study of prejudice, a prominent object of research for many social and personality psychologists. Following many years of research, the construct has been broadened to include nine elements, as shown in Figure 10.3.

The general label **authoritarianism** was given to the construct, but since the earliest studies prejudice has been repeatedly shown to be related to authoritarianism. This is true whether the focus is white prejudice against blacks (Martin and Westie, 1959), Arab prejudice against Jews (Epstein, 1966), or Israeli prejudice against Arabs (Siegman, 1961).

FIGURE 10.3
Elements of Authoritarianism

1. *Conventionalism.*   *Rigid* adherence to and *over*emphasis on middle-class values, and overresponsiveness to contemporary *external* social pressure.
2. *Authoritarian submission.*   An exaggerated, emotional need to submit to others; an uncritical acceptance of a strong leader who will make decisions.
3. *Authoritarian aggression.*   Favoring condemnation, total rejection, stern discipline, or severe punishment as ways of dealing with people and forms of behavior that deviate from conventional values.
4. *Anti-intraception.*   Disapproval of a free emotional life, of the intellectual or theoretical, and of the impractical.
5. *Superstition and stereotypy.*   Superstition implies a tendency to shift responsibility from within the individual to outside forces beyond one's control. Stereotypy is the tendency to think in rigid, oversimplified categories.
6. *Power and toughness.*   The aligning of oneself with power figures, thus gratifying both one's need to have power and the need to submit to power.
7. *Destructiveness and cynicism.*   Rationalized aggression; for example, cynicism permits the authoritarian person to be aggressive because "everybody is doing it."
8. *Projectivity.*   This disposition to believe that wild and dangerous things go on in the world.
9. *Sex.*   Exaggerated concern with sexual goings-on, and punitiveness toward violators of sex norms.

Source: From *Social Psychology*, 5th ed., by Kay Deaux and L. S. Wrightsman. Copyright © 1972, 1977, 1981, 1984, 1988 by Wadsworth, Inc. Used with permission of Brooks/Cole Publishing Company, Pacific Grove, CA 93950. (Based on Cherry and Byrne, 1977.)

Prejudice is, of course, morally reprehensible. An encouraging sign of the past few decades is that people are gradually realizing that all individuals are worthy and that prejudice harms the bigot as well as the object of prejudice. Were the immorality of prejudice not enough of a dissuasion, external factors exist that should help convince people to set aside their prejudices. The blocking of a skilled worker's career out of unthinking, unwarranted prejudice is inefficient; it costs the organization valuable skills. Further, the law punishes those who put their prejudices into action. Astute managers should be able to identify people with prejudiced attitudes and either arrange reward systems to prevent their implementation of these attitudes or engage in training programs directed to changing them.

Machiavellianism   How some people are able to manipulate others has been a topic of fascination for centuries. In the early 1500s Niccolo Machiavelli wrote a collection of essays called *The Prince* and a history called *The Discourses* that presented both a philosophy and a practical guide to manipulation. These essays were used by Christie and Geis (1970) to launch a series of studies of a trait they called **Machiavellianism.** High-Machiavellian people have a greater capacity for interpersonal manipulation and exploitation and are less susceptible to social pressure and influence than people low on Machiavellianism. They also seem to be more adept than others at imposing their own definition and structure on interpersonal activities. "In summary, if the high-Mach individual is the prototypic con man, the low-Mach individual appears to be the prototypic mark" (Snyder and Ickes, 1985, p. 891).

Christie and Geis speculate that people in the United States are becoming increasingly Machiavellian over time. The implications of this view for managing are unclear, though if true, the speculation suggests that influencing others may become increasingly difficult. One might speculate that the numerous mergers, acquisitions, and leveraged buyouts of the 1980s may reflect this growing Machivellianism.

An Information Processing View of Personality

As we discussed earlier, another perspective views personality as the product of the interaction of the individual and his environment. With this approach to personality, it makes sense to think of people as using scripts to organize past experience and to direct current and future understanding and behavior.

Scripts, Schemas, and Prototypes   During the 1970s personality and social psychologists attempted to distinguish among various kinds of cognitive structures. It was thought that information could be processed only if the perceiver had some sort of internal perceptual or cognitive structure to receive and organize it. One of the first labels for these internal organizers was schemas (Neisser, 1976). **Schemas** are like the knowledge structures discussed in Chapter 5, that is, frameworks for organizing and interpreting the social environment.

A **prototype** is a little different. It is an "abstract set of features commonly associated with members of a category, with each feature assigned a weight according to the degree of association with the category" (Cantor, 1981, p. 27). Thus the prototype of a fighter pilot contains a large and varied set of features built from our experiences either with fighter pilots or at the movies and focusing on athletic, masculine attributes. This prototype distinguishes them from other categories of people such as accountants and bank managers.

Scripts are different yet. They contain our expectations or theories about events in the social world (Schank and Abelson, 1977). A **script** is a conceptual structure of the roles, objects, conditions, and results of a stereotyped sequence of events, such as going grocery shopping, preparing for an exam, or taking someone out to dinner. Scripts differ from schemas and prototypes in that they are concerned with action and the temporal sequence of events.

Powerful, emotion-laden scripts originating in childhood have been shown to increase in strength throughout adult life (Tomkins, 1980). Emotionally charged memories and events are linked together and form dominant themes that guide cognitive processing and social behavior through life (Carlson and Carlson, 1984). We can all think of events in our early lives that continually seem to influence how we interpret and respond to new information. Managers must keep in mind that employees will experience such influence throughout their working lives.

A fascinating study (Helson, Mitchell, and Moane, 1984) examined a particular script: the "social clock" of a number of women. The significance of the work is summarized by other writers (Singer and Kolligan, 1987, p. 560):

> The term social clock suggests both a social group's agreement about when certain events ought to occur in life (e.g., marriage before age 30) and one's own personal set of goals or personal script for achieving such states as intimacy, childbearing, or financial security. In the study's twenty-year follow-up of female college graduates, Helson et al. (1984) were able to identify those women adhering to the traditional feminine social clock, those willing to postpone but not give up on such expectations of marriage and childbearing, and those women who eschewed such a script early in life or who, by age 28, had chosen career lines that conformed in the 1960s to the masculine social clock. In sum, this study provided preliminary evidence for the existence of "life-span schemas" that

are consistent across individuals and time. (Frieze, Bailey, Mamula, and Moss, 1985)

The question of social scripts for women received much attention recently when Schwartz unleashed a storm of controversy with an article in the *Harvard Business Review* about the different paths chosen by women who wish to pursue a conventional career and those who wish to combine career and family (see the feature on management women).

FEATURE: *Management Women*

. . . Let me focus on . . . what I call the career-primary woman and the career-and-family woman.

   Like many men, some women put their careers first. They are ready to make the same trade-offs traditionally made by the men who seek leadership positions. . . . The secret to dealing with such women is to recognize them early, accept them, and clear artificial barriers from their path to the top. . . .

   . . . The majority of women, however, are what I call career-and-family women, women who want to pursue serious careers while participating actively in the rearing of children. These women are a precious resource that has yet to be mined. Many of them are talented and creative. Most of them are willing to trade some career growth and compensation for freedom from the constant pressure to work long hours and weekends. . . .

   . . .The price you must pay to retain these women is threefold: You must plan for and arrange maternity, you must provide the flexibility that will allow them to be maximally productive, and you must take an active role in helping to make family supports and high-quality, affordable child care available to all women.

   . . . For all the women who want to combine career and family—the women who want to participate actively in the rearing of their children and who also want to pursue their careers seriously—the key to retention is to provide the flexibility and family supports they need in order to function effectively. . . . In its simplest form, flexibility is the freedom to take time off—a couple of hours, a day, a week—or to do some work at home and some at the office, an arrangement that communication technology makes increasingly feasible. At the complex end of the spectrum are alternative work schedules that permit the woman to work less than full-time and her employer to reap the benefits of her experience and, with careful planning, the top level of her abilities.

. . . On balance, employing women is more costly than employing men. Women can acknowledge this fact today because they know that their value to employers exceeds the additional cost and because they know that changing attitudes can reduce the additional cost dramatically. Women in management are no longer an idiosyncrasy of the arts and education. They have always matched men in natural ability. Within a very few years, they will equal men in numbers as well in every area of economic activity.

The demographic motivation to recruit and develop women is compelling. But an older question remains: Is society better for the change? Women's exit from the home and entry into the work force has certainly created problems—an urgent need for good, affordable child care; troubling questions about the kind of parenting children need; the costs and difficulties of diversity in the workplace; the stress and fatigue of combining work and family responsibilities. Wouldn't we all be happier if we could turn back the clock to an age when men were in the workplace and women in the home, when male and female roles were clearly differentiated and complementary?

Nostalgia, anxiety, and discouragement will urge many to say yes, but my answer is emphatically no. Two fundamental benefits that were unattainable in the past are now within reach. For the individual, freedom of choice—in this case the freedom to choose career, family, or a combination of the two. For the corporation, access to the most gifted individuals in the country. These benefits are neither self-indulgent nor insubstantial. Freedom of choice and self-realization are too deeply American to be cast aside for some wistful vision of the past. And access to our most talented human resources is not a luxury in this age of explosive international competition but rather the barest minimum that prudence and national self-preservation require.

Source: F. Schwartz, "Management Women and the New Facts," *Harvard Business Review,* January–February 1989, pp. 65–76. Copyright © 1989 by the President and Fellows of Harvard College; all rights reserved. Reprinted by permission of *Harvard Business Review.*

It was realized at the end of the 1970s that scripts, schemas, and prototypes are more similar than they are different. Thus the term *schema* seems to be settling in as the accepted label for all such cognitive structures. Taylor and Crocker (1981) identified three general classes of schemas:

1. Person schemas, or schemas of one's self or other people

2. Role schemas, or schemas for occupations, social roles, or social groups

3. Event schemas, or practical behavioral scripts

Perceptions of the Self   Personality research probably deals more with the development and functioning of person schemas than with the other two kinds. In fact, much research focuses on self-image. Markus and Wurf (1987) identified the idea of the **dynamic self-concept,** emphasizing that self-image is not a constant but can change (see Figure 10.4). From the individual's self-concept is drawn what Markus and Wurf call the working self-concept, which is simply those features of the self-concept that regulate the individual's actions in a given situation. This working self-concept can vary from situation to situation or time to time as one attribute or another is selected.

FIGURE   10.4
Formation of the Dynamic Self-Concept

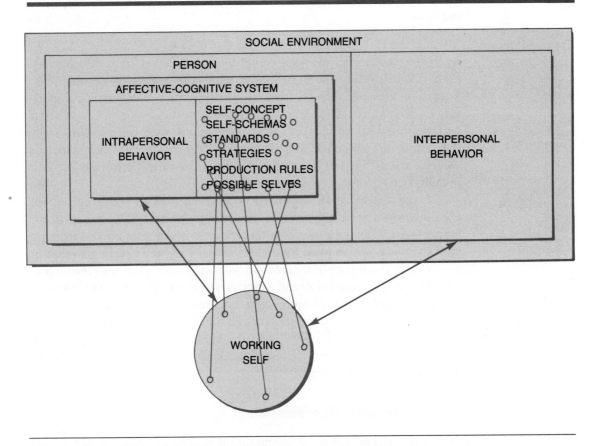

Source: H. Markus and E. Wurf, "The Dynamic Self-Concept: A Social Psychological Perspective," in M. Rosenzweig and L. W. Porter (eds.), *Annual Review of Psychology* 38 (1987):315. Reproduced, with permission, from the *Annual Review of Psychology,* © 1987 by Annual Reviews Inc.

FIGURE 10.5
Information Processing Consequences of Self-Structuring

1. People have heightened sensitivities to self-relevant stimuli. People respond to information relevant to their self-concepts and ignore that which is not.
2. Information congruent with what one believes about oneself is efficiently processed. People high on Machiavellianism, for example, read more stories about Machiavellianism than those who are low on that trait.
3. Information about one's own behavior is recognized and recalled faster than information relevant to someone else's behavior.
4. People make confident predictions about self-relevant behavior, attributions, and inferences.
5. People are resistant to information that is incongruent with how they see themselves. They often reject accounts of their behavior that differ from their own accounts.

Source: Adapted from H. Markus and E. Wurf, "The Dynamic Self-Concept: A Social Psychological Perspective," in M. Rosenzweig and L. W. Porter (eds.), *Annual Review of Psychology* 38 (1987):315. Reproduced, with permission, from the *Annual Review of Psychology,* © 1987 by Annual Review Inc.

The working self-concept comes into play in two kinds of behaviors. First, it affects intrapersonal processes, which include the processing of information relevant to the self-concept, the regulation of feelings, and motivation. Second, it influences interpersonal processes, which include social perception, social comparison, and interactions with others. One study (Greenhaus, Parasuraman, and Wormley, 1990) shows that black managers perceive themselves less positively and were treated less positively by their organizations than their white counterparts.

A self-schema is an organized body of knowledge and beliefs about one's intentions and capacities that is stored in long-term memory. Its major function is anticipatory in that it incorporates hypotheses about incoming information, as well as plans for gathering and interpreting schema-relevant information about the self (Singer and Salovey, 1985). Thus the schema is at once a definer of personality and a motivator (see our discussion of information processing models of motivation in Chapter 9). The research on self-structuring shows significant implications for information processing, which may be seen as somewhat similar to the biases discussed in Chapter 5 on communication. The main consequences identified by the research are listed in Figure 10.5.

Personality Assessment in Organizations: Testing

Personality assessment plays an important part in personnel selection and placement, whether it is done in an informal or formal way. Professional interviewers and performance appraisers describe people with phrases like "she seems friendly and would be a good bank teller" or "he seems gruff enough to be a good bouncer." However, managers are often inaccurate in their definitions of these constructs. In fact, most assessors cannot even define various personality traits consistently, let alone measure them accurately. Bass and Barrett (1981) asked 50 executives to define the word "dependability" and came up with 47 different definitions. Bernardin and Bownas (1985) pointed out that most organizational users of personality tests—vehicles often used to measure personality traits—do not know how to interpret research evidence about the usefulness of tests:

> The typical adoption scenario is for the practitioner first to be influenced by a slick brochure from a publisher of "Snake Oil Extraordinaire (SOE)." The brochure probably has guarded and ambiguous statements of support for the use of SOE. . . . The probability that the practitioner will purchase the test may be more a function of the slickness of the brochure and the fast-talking sales representative than of the actual validity of the instrument being peddled. . . . At one recent presentation for the American Society of Personnel Administrators, one of the authors found that 98 percent of practitioners thought personality/motivational constructs should be measured in selection/placement systems and 75 percent were doing it in one form or another. (p. vi)

Two aspects of any kind of paper-and-pencil test are important. The first is **reliability,** or whether the test measures consistently whatever it measures. The second is **validity,** or whether the test measures what it is purported to measure. Measurement is made more difficult because, as the evidence shows, personality traits are not fixed and unchanging. Test users must verify not only the qualifications of test developers and their products but their own sophistication. Both the American Psychological Association testing *Standards* and the *Principles* prepared by its Division of Industrial-Organizational Psychology (1980) emphasize that test users must have professional expertise and judgment to use tests properly. In terms of test reliability and validity, personality assessment is improving over time (Schmitt and Robertson, 1990).

Attribution Theory and the Assessment of Personality

Crucial to a discussion of personality is an understanding of how we, as individuals, interpret personality. This brings us to the realm of **attribution theory,** which essentially addresses how our own perceptions color the characteristics of what we perceive (Ilgen and Klein, 1989). In judging another's personality, we are not so much identifying key components of that individual's psyche as we are attributing characteristics, the assignment of which has much to do with our own personality and perceptions and which can change from one occasion to another. An example of various attributions of the same behavior is given in the feature "A Bad Day at the Office."

FEATURE: *A Bad Day at the Office*

Imagine that things haven't been going well at work recently. You haven't managed to get things done on time, and what you have managed to scrape through hasn't been up to standard. Things are coming to a head. A colleague stops you in the corridor and asks you whether you're feeling quite yourself. You overhear two others mention your name and one of them remarks to the other that you might not be up to the job any more. This morning in your mail is a memo from the boss saying she wants to see you. At your interview with her she opens the conversation by frankly saying that she's seen your work suffer, and that she suspects the explanation may be something to do with things at home.

By now you may well be wondering yourself quite what is up. People are attributing your current difficulties at work to ill-health, incapacity and family stress. But, you might say to yourself, all that's happening is that your work is going through the usual chaos that this time of the year brings. Or that it may look bad, but it's no worse than anyone else's work. Or that you're giving up cigarettes, this time for good, and it's bound to cause some temporary disruption. Or you might agree with the worst things that people are saying—that you can't cope any more, you're over the hill, and you might as well move over and let a younger person through.

I hope that story has been entirely imaginary—but I think that it should illustrate what could happen if things in one's life began to move out of their usual and comfortable orbit. In a case like this one, the importance of people's explanations of what's happening to them and around them . . . is, I hope, fairly clear; you, your colleagues and your employer will all be searching for an explanation of your behavior, and all of you will guide your actions by the explanations you finally arrive at. If your colleagues thought that the reasons for the poor work was that you were going downhill, the careerists would shun you (though, hopefully, the caring ones would befriend you); if they saw that it was the temporary effect of cigarette starvation they might tut-tut, but do nothing more than begrudge any extra work it meant for themselves; if they were told quietly that the reason was that your spouse had just left you, they might rally round and offer whatever help they could. If you yourself thought it was a temporary reaction to something in the office that would soon go away, you might carry on, entirely undisturbed. But if you thought that it was a signal of your declining abilities, on the other hand, you would be risking some degree of distress which, whatever the real cause of the problem at work, might only make things worse. The explanations one has of such things in one's everyday life have powerful effects on one's feelings, plans, hopes and well-being.

How do people decide why others behave as they do? What information do they work on and how do they put the information together? Do they use the same processes in interpreting their own actions? These are the questions of attribution theory. We already discussed attribution theories of leadership (Chapter 8) and motivation (Chapter 9), but we have not gone into much detail about the components of attribution theories in general.

Over the years there have been three major steps in the development of attribution theory. The first began in the 1950s when psychologists became interested in asking questions about how people attribute causes to action. This interest emanated from Fritz Heider's (1958) proposition that a major job of the perceiver in understanding the world is to find underlying causes of things he sees happening. Heider identified two broad classes of causes: personal and environmental. In other words, we attribute actions to dispositions or to situational factors. Extending on Heider's original proposition, Jones and Davis (1965) proposed the second major aspect of attribution theory, that the task of the explainer is to discount the operation of situational or external constraints on the person's behavior.

Together Jones and Davis (1965) and Kelley (1967) developed the third key notion, that the perceiver collects three kinds of information: how often another person took a similar action in a similar circumstance in the past (**consistency information**), how often that other person performed the same action in different circumstances (**distinctiveness information**), and how many other people did that sort of thing in similar circumstances (**consensus information**). If you find that a person has a long history of a particular kind of action in other places, that the circumstances now at work always provoke this action, and that no one else behaves this way, you attribute the action to the person and downplay the effect of surroundings.

Errors in Attributions   Unfortunately, the process of attribution introduces the possibility of numerous errors. Perhaps the most interesting work on attribution concerns identifying the kinds of biases that systematically influence our judgment. The research has uncovered four major biases: overestimating personal factors in relation to others, overestimating situational factors in relation to ourselves, underusing consensus information, and overattributing when affected by the other person.

People overemphasize the other person as the cause of events (Ross, 1977). Imagine you are watching one of your friends take an oral examination. The questioner, drawing on his own unique experiences, develops a set of questions that are difficult for your friend, who is only moderately successful at answering. Asked which person is more intelligent, you choose the questioner. In this judgment you neglect important situational factors: the amount of control and choice the questioner has (Ross, Amibale, and Steinmutz, 1977). This error can be pervasive in our estimates of the capabilities of those in power. We should be careful to avoid thinking of the CEO as all-knowing.

The general tendency to overestimate dispositional factors often stops short of our own behavior, which we perceive as situationally determined. Thus the hypothetical character in the feature presented earlier sees his current poor performance as due to the time of year or the fact that he is giving up cigarettes.

Attribution models assume that we explain the behaviors of some individuals by using information about what still other individuals do in similar situations. Research shows that such is not the case; in fact, people underutilize consensus information in forming attributions (Major, 1978; Nisbett and Borgida, 1975). We focus instead on salient information about the individual. Thus, for example, even though we have been refused a dozen times by colleagues who we have asked to volunteer for a particularly onerous assignment, we assume that Sam will distinguish himself from the other colleagues volunteering because he is a team player.

We also err when judging people who have some relationship with us. Two kinds of attribution errors are in this class. *Hedonic relevance* refers to the extent to which a person's actions are rewarding or costly to you. If someone else's actions affect you, you perceive that behavior to result from disposition rather than the situation. The second such error, called *personalism*, is closely related. If you believe that someone intended to affect you by his behavior, your attributions about him will be made more strongly (Jones and Davis, 1965).

Consequences of Attribution   The process of making attributions affects our behavior in many ways. If we think George's hesitance to speak reflects a lack of social skills rather than discomfort caused by the pressure of an interview, we are unlikely to hire him to be a salesperson. If we see Helen's quick responses to interview questions as indicative of a decisive personality, we will probably recommend hiring her and mark her for the fast track to management training. Careers can be made or broken, promotions won or lost, on the basis of a person's perception of another (Rodgers and Levey, 1987).

Heilman and Guzzo (1978) vividly demonstrated some consequences of attribution. They simulated an organization and asked business students to assume the role of employers and make pay raise and promotion decisions for a set of hypothetical employees. The subjects were provided with one of four types of information about employee job performance: high ability, considerable effort, an easy assignment, or pure chance. Supervisors recommended raises only for employees whose performance was explained by either ability or hard work. Promotion was given only to those who were said to be of high ability. Rewards, then, were reserved for those employees whose behavior was explained by internal rather than external causes.

Downey and Brief (1986) identified another set of organizational consequences of attributions. These are five important roles in organizational functioning for implicit organization theories that include attributions. These roles are (1) guiding organizational elites in designing organizations, (2) helping organizational members respond to the organization's structure, (3) contributing to the ability of the organization to satisfy members even though they possess different goals, (4) eliciting changes in organizational structure, and (5) bonding organizational members to each other and to the organization.

Social Perception

Social perception is an extension of attribution theory in that it takes as its main interest how people make sense of social situations. Traditionally, in psychology, perception has been concerned with how we attach meaning to physical stimuli. This view was found to be limiting, however, which led to the development of another perspective:

> Social perception was founded on the idea that internal factors such as values, needs, and expectancies influence the outcome of perception, so that [perception] could not be accounted for entirely in terms of stimulus qualities (e.g., Postman, Bruner, and McGinnies, 1948). And social cognition presented evidence that people typically did not reason about social information by weighing and combining available evidence in a rational and judicious manner (e.g., Heider, 1958; Mischel, 1968; Kahneman and Tversky, 1973).

Accordingly, social perception and cognition researchers have tended to take as their domain of inquiry the study of ways in which people go *beyond* the information given. (Higgins and Bargh, 1987, pp. 370–371)

Social perception, then, is the study of how we try to understand the behavior of others based on the situation rather than on dispositional factors. The study of social perception involves two factors: how we process information and how we interpret it to construct schemas of how the world works.

Information Processing

Making sense of our own behavior and that of others around us requires us to process information. Lord (1985) described a series of five steps in information processing, three input steps and two output steps. These steps represent the major points at which information is filtered or changed by social information processing:

Information input involves a *selective attention/comprehension* step in which relevant information is selected from a complex social environment, in part through the process by which it is comprehended or recognized; a step in which noticed information is *encoded and simplified* in a form more easily stored in long-term memory; and a *storage and retention* step during which information is frequently altered through integration with subsequent information concerning the stimulus person. Information output involves two conceptually distinct but highly related steps, the *retrieval* of relevant information and the translation of information into required *judgments* such as causal attributions or the selection of the appropriate response for each item on a questionnaire. (Lord, 1985, p. 89)

Lord argues that the net effect of these input and output steps is the distortion of social information, which can occur at any of the five steps. A diagram of this model is presented in Figure 10.6.

Think for a moment about the search processes we must go through in organizations. Information about other organizational members is generally available, but in complex and noisy environments (Feldman, 1981). We try to make sense of things while we are exposed to other people's behaviors, complex task or environmental information, and our own thoughts and memories. From these multiple sources we select relevant information and organize it into comprehensible patterns. Since people have limited attention capacities (Posner, 1982), this task is highly challenging. The net result is that much information to which we are exposed is filtered out before we become aware of it; it is not processed further. For example, American tele-

FIGURE 10.6
A Model of Information Processing

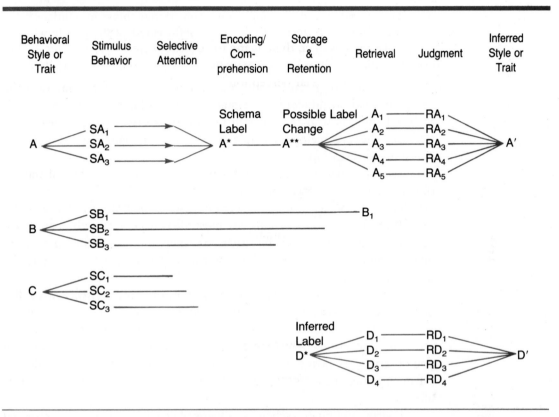

Source: R. G. Lord, "An Information Processing Approach to Social Perception Leadership, and Behavioral Measurement in Organizations," in L. L. Cummings and B. M. Staw (eds.), *Research in Organizational Behavior* (Greenwich, CT: JAI Press, 1985), p. 90. Copyright © 1985 by JAI Press. Reprinted by permission.

vision viewers could process only parts of the voluminous information presented to them about the upheavals in Eastern Europe in 1989 and 1990. Such filtering is shown in Figure 10.6 by the treatment of behavior C; selective attention filters it out and the behavior never reaches the encoding stage.

Information and Schemas

Once we obtain information we integrate it with existing schemas. Our schemas influence how we will process information in the future in at least four ways (Markus and Zajonc, 1985). First, they influence what information receives our attention and how it is encoded and organized. One experiment

(Bransford and Johnson, 1973) offers a nice example of how this is done. Subjects were exposed to the following nonsensical paragraph:

> The procedure is quite simple. First you arrange things into different groups. Of course, one pile may be sufficient, depending on how much there is to do. If you have to go somewhere else due to lack of facilities, that is the next step; otherwise you are pretty well set.

Subjects who were given the idea of washing clothes before they read the paragraph had no difficulty understanding it and later recalled more of it than did subjects who read it with no aid to its organization. Clearly the schema—the organizing principle provided beforehand—aided comprehension and retention.

Second, schemas influence information retention and retrieval and the organization of memory. A number of studies show that schemas have a variety of effects on retention and retrieval (Isenberg, 1986; Markus and Zajonc, 1985; Tesser, 1978). People are most likely to remember best and most confidently people, events, or situations when they are required to form general impressions. Most of the time that is probably what we try to do, just form general impressions.

Third, schemas act as interpretive frameworks and consequently influence our evaluations, judgments, predictions, and inferences. For example, you expect your boss to act responsibly—to come to work on time, to pay attention during meetings, and to approach serious problems seriously. If you observe your boss acting differently—arriving late every day or dozing off during meetings—your evaluation of your boss's performance will be affected.

Fourth, and finally, schemas influence behavior. Schemas are assumed to include plans of actions; insofar as they are tied to particular goals, they trigger these plans. For example, a goal like having fun in the snow is readily tied to the behavior associated with that goal. That behavior might be getting out of the house to enjoy the snow in the front yard or it might be getting into the car to drive someplace to ski.

Values and Attitudes

Two additional characteristics of the individual are important considerations in forming a full view of the person: values and attitudes. Difficult concepts to summarize, they are powerful determinants of personality and behavior. It is at the level of values and attitudes that organizations aim the kind of socialization techniques discussed in Chapter 3.

Values

Values are our normative beliefs about desirable goals and modes of conduct (Rokeach, 1979). Values do not have a specific object; rather, they are broad belief systems employed in making judgments and decisions. Largely ignored by researchers in the 1970s and 1980s, values are now receiving more attention. The notion of "symbolic attitudes" was recently introduced and refers to the strong feelings tied to important moral concerns or core values (Herek, 1986). The most frequently researched symbolic attitude—symbolic racism—provides an example. This complex of values is "a blend of anti-black affect and the kind of traditional American moral values embodied in the Protestant Ethic. Symbolic racism appears to partially underlie whites' opposition to welfare, 'reverse discrimination,' 'forced' busing, and other government programs that violate individualism" (Kinder and Sears, 1985, p. 416).

Employee values are significant variables in any organization, of course, but even more so in multinational organizations, where differing cultural values are likely to result in a work force with differing core values. One cross-national study (Hofstede, 1980) showed differences in values in the units of a multinational organization between both developed and less developed countries. A major finding of this study is that individualism is not as highly valued in less developed nations as in developed nations. Because of the diversity among Arab states, much attention has been given to similarities and differences in their values. Research shows that whether Arab states are modern or traditional, their values are remarkably similar (Muna, 1980). Although organizational structures are becoming more similar crossnationally (see Chapter 2), values are maintaining their cultural distinctiveness (Meindl, Hunt, and Lee, 1989).

In the early 1980s a great deal of attention was given to Japanese management practices. One study (Putti and Yoshikawa 1984) showed that these practices do not easily transfer to Singapore, where 76 percent of the population is Chinese. Japanese attention to "groupness" does not fit well with the Singapore manager's individualism. Another study looked at human resource management practices in Hong Kong and Singapore (Latham and Napier, 1987). In both countries, education and training are revered and people like working for North American rather than Chinese or Japanese companies.

Attitudes

Researchers divide the mental construct called **attitudes** into three components: cognitive, affective, and behavioral (Katz and Stotland, 1959; Zajonc and Markus, 1982). Another view of attitudes sees them as affective constructs only (Fishbein and Ajzen, 1975); that is, my attitudes reflect how good or bad I feel about something. But even with this approach, the cognitive and behavioral aspects of behavior are studied as well. More recently, this tripartite distinction has been relaxed, but the research still generally follows this kind of categorization (Tesser and Shaffer, 1990). Thus we will focus on the three components of attitudes.

The cognitive aspects of attitudes are the properties attributed to the object; a job could be viewed as challenging or boring, full of pressure or worry-free. Affect, the most heavily studied component of attitudes, is how much an individual likes the object—how does the employee feel about his job? The behavioral component, the person's behavior toward the object, is usually measured by what a person says she intends to do—"I intend to quit my job." Judging behavior from intention is valid because the relationship between behavioral intention and actual behavior is fairly high (Ajzen and Fishbein, 1980).

In organizational research the most frequently studied attitudes are those toward work. Job satisfaction studies have been done since the very beginning of research in organizations. One aim of all management and motivation theories is to have a satisfied work force, although an impediment to this research is disagreement about what constitutes satisfaction (Schneider, 1985). Despite this disagreement, satisfaction is significant for a number of reasons. First, it is an important human outcome in organizational life. In addition, it may be a predictor of other important behaviors like absenteeism and turnover, though the literature on this is not clear (Clegg, 1983). (See also the discussion of turnover in Chapter 3.) A longitudinal study (Staw, Bell, and Clausen, 1986) indicates that prior experience significantly affects job attitudes; this study showed a positive relationship between positive attitudes early in life, identified by these authors as "positive affect," and later job satisfaction. Individual positive and negative affect combine to determine positive or negative group affect, and affect is related to helping behavior in groups (George, 1990).

Attitudes and Behavior   Two models relate attitudes to behavior. The first says that behavior can be predicted if we know, first, a person's attitude toward that behavior and, second, the social norms that influence the likelihood of his performing that behavior. The problem is that we can never measure extraneous social norms or other external conditions perfectly. Thus, the failure of research to support this view unequivocally may be due to problems of measurement rather than to problems with the theory itself. The second approach questions how the activation of an attitude affects behavior. However, the notion that there is a clear causal link between attitudes and behaviors is not entirely supported by research (Chaiken and Stangord, 1987). The first study to show an imperfect relationship between attitudes and behavior is summarized in the feature on the LaPiere study (1934). Since the time of that study this relationship has fascinated researchers.

FEATURE: *The LaPiere Study*

All measurement of attitudes by the questionnaire technique proceeds on the assumption that there is a mechanical relationship between symbolic and nonsymbolic behavior. It is simple enough to prove that there is no *necessary* correlation between speech and action, between response to words and to the realities they symbolize. . . . There need be no relationship between what the hotel proprietor says he will do and what he actually does when confronted with a colored patron. Yet there may be. . . .

Beginning in 1930 and continuing for two years thereafter, I had the good fortune to travel with a young Chinese student and his wife. . . . Knowing the general "attitude" of Americans towards the Chinese as indicated by the "social distance" studies which have been made it was with considerable trepidation that I first approached a hotel clerk in their company. Perhaps that clerk's eyebrows lifted slightly, but he accommodated us without a show of hesitation. And this in the "best" hotel in a small town noted for its narrow and bigoted "attitude" towards Orientals. Two months later I passed that way again, phoned the hotel and asked if they would "accommodate an important Chinese gentleman." The reply was an unequivocal "No." That aroused my curiosity and led to this study.

In something like ten thousand miles of motor travel, twice across the United States, up and down the Pacific Coast, we met definite rejection from those asked to serve us just once. We were received at 66 hotels, auto camps, and "Tourist Homes," refused at one. We were served in 184 restaurants and cafes scattered throughout the country and treated with what I judged to be more than ordinary consideration in 72 of them. . . .

. . . Whenever possible I let my Chinese friends negotiate for accommodations (while I concerned myself with the car or luggage) or sent them into a restaurant ahead of me. In this way I attempted to "factor" myself out. . . .

In the end I was forced to conclude that those factors which most influenced the behavior of others towards the Chinese had nothing at all to do with race. Quality and condition of clothing, appearance of baggage (by which, it seems, hotel clerks are prone to base their quick evaluations), cleanliness and neatness were far more significant for person to person re-action in the situations I was studying than skin pigmentation, straight black hair, slanting eyes, and flat noses.

Source: R. T. LaPiere, "Attitudes vs. Actions," *Social Forces* 13 (1934):230–237. Reprinted by permission.

One interesting aspect of attitude research was the finding that "brain-washing" during the Korean War induced over 90 percent behavioral col-laboration by prisoners of war. The studies also showed that this was only overt compliance—unrelated to changes in belief (Schein, 1957). This suggests that there is not a perfect causal linkage between attitudes and behavior and suggests the need to distinguish between overt behavioral compliance and attitudinal conversion (Nail, 1986). However, a number of real-life incidents suggest that strong relationships between attitude and be-havior do occur. There are, for example, people who have been induced to join cults and who then behave consistently with the values of those cults. Japanese management techniques offer another example; they rely on group-oriented approaches designed to obtain homogeneity in attitude and behavior. In the Ellen Randall case, we saw such a connection as well. Ran-dall noted how an attitudinal turnaround improved performance: "The business was being de-emphasized and down-scaled. I began to wonder. Do I really need this? . . . I know this attitude started to show through. I de-cided to do something about it. . . . I put [an entrepreneurial approach] into my job objectives and found new niches, new opportunities, new products, and new clients."

Origins of Attitudes   Researchers postulate at least four major causes of attitudes. One is genetic. It may be that general liking of other people is a genetic characteristic (Lumsden and Wilson, 1981). Another cause is transi-tory physiological factors. Some attitudes may be associated with aging, as when men go through serious mid-life crises at about age 40, often changing their attitudes and values about key things in their lives (Levinson, 1978). A third cause of attitude is direct experience with the object of the attitude. Falling in love is certainly an example of this.

The fourth cause of attitudes is socialization. The institutions we are exposed to have both an intended and unintended impact on attitudes by determining what a person will be exposed to, what responses are available or appropriate, and what will be rewarded and punished (and when). Parents are important conveyors of attitudes and values. In fact, studies show that children usually share their parents' political values (e.g., Berger, 1980). At some point other vehicles of socialization take precedence; peer groups and the mass media become significant, for instance, diminishing parental impact on their children's attitude development. Schools and teachers surely influence attitude development and change. Institutions use rites and rituals to influence attitudes. Finally, "total institutions" such as prisons or military camps exert a great influence over attitudes (Goffman, 1959). The socialization techniques discussed in Chapter 3 represent the organization's attempts to shape attitudes.

Training

Some organizations focus heavily on selecting only those people with the skills desired in the organization. Others (for example, the military) are not as concerned with the selection of appropriate people; these organizations spend enormous resources on training. Most organizations fall somewhere in between these two extremes, and human resource managers often spend a good deal of time trying to identify training needs in their organizations.

Too often employees do not know why they should do something, how to do it, or what to do. They may think their way is better, your way will not work, or something else is more important. They may believe that there may be no positive consequences for doing what their managers want done, they may be rewarded for not doing it, or they may be punished for doing what they are supposed to do (Fournies, 1989).

Organizations can set up "instructional systems" (Goldstein, 1986) to help them in the ongoing process of defining training needs, actually performing the training, and then assessing the degree to which the training met organizational objectives. A model for an instructional system appears in Figure 10.7 (page 510). Its key features are the **needs assessment,** in which the nature and amount of training is determined; training and development, in which the program is designed and implemented; evaluation, in which the measure of effectiveness is devised and applied to the trainees; and the training goal, which is the aim of the training. Of course, it is crucial that the training system itself be evaluated to ensure that it works as planned.

In some countries industrial training has become a matter of government interest. Singapore levies a payroll tax on companies to support training. The Swedish government argues for supporting training, as does the West German government. The growth of multinationals will necessitate that organizations consider training and other human resource management issues as aspects of their overall strategy. Dowling (1988) cited a survey of

FIGURE   10.7
Model for an Instructional System

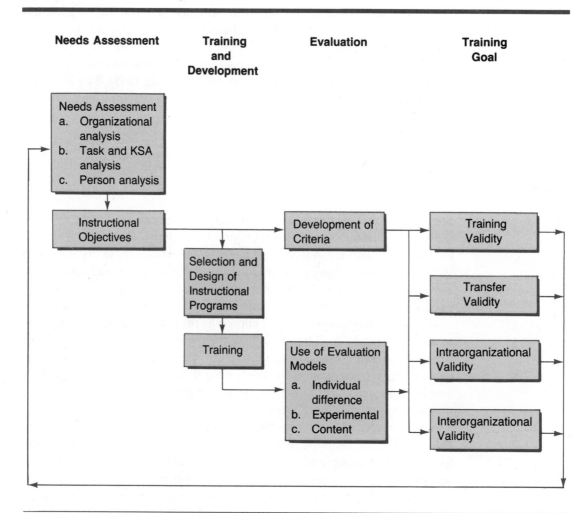

Source: From *Training in Organizations: Needs Assessment Development, and Evaluation,* 2nd ed., by I. L. Goldstein. Copyright © 1986, 1974 by Wadsworth, Inc. Reprinted by permission of Brooks/Cole Publishing Company, Pacific Grove, CA 93950.

human resources managers that indicated a particular training need for multinationals: the "development of managers into international managers; [and] the need to increase cross-training exposure of U.S. management to foreign operations and culture, while similarly exposing foreign management staff to U.S. operations and culture" (pp. 1-249–1-250). Recently, a special section of the *Wall Street Journal,* directed to college students, cautioned those entering the job market to look for employers committed to extensive training programs (Benjamin and Manter, 1990).

Needs Assessment

As we see from Figure 10.8, a needs assessment has three aspects. The first is an organizational analysis, an examination of the system-wide aspects of the organization that might influence training. Training needs must be linked to corporate strategy. In light of this, a recent report (Hussey, 1985) argued that training objectives, especially for managers, should be reviewed by top management whenever a major switch in strategy is planned. Hussey's study in the United Kingdom showed that most managers, however, felt that training should be tailored to individuals rather than to corporate needs.

A corporate analysis would include examination of the organization's goals, resources, climate for training, and internal and external constraints. The actual components of an organizational analysis depend on the characteristics of the organization, what it hopes to promote, and the kind of training program being instituted. Very early training research showed that

FIGURE 10.8
Three Aspects of
a Needs
Assessment

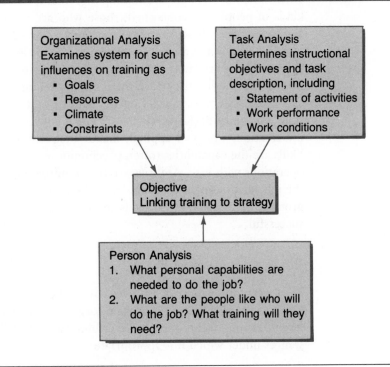

problems arise when the working environment and the training environment promote different values (Fleishman, Harris, and Burtt, 1955). In this study foremen were trained to be more considerate leaders. The training was successful, but the behavior was not maintained on the job because the day-to-day social climate was not conducive to consideration. The training could not transfer to the job, an issue we discuss later.

A task analysis determines the instructional objectives related to the performance of particular activities or job operations. This analysis results in a statement of the work to be performed and the conditions under which the job is done. It should cover all the essential job activities and include the worker's actions; the machines, tools and other work aids used; the materials, products, subject matter, or services involved; and the requirements of the worker (U.S. Department of Labor, 1972).

A study of British industry (Downs, 1985) showed that the tasks required of jobs in the future will be considerably different from those required of today's jobs. As a result, the kind of task analysis required may be shifting from an analysis of what is needed for jobs now to what will be required to do an effective job in the future. This approach would prevent skills obsolescence (Latham, 1988).

The organizational and task analyses provide a picture of the task and environmental setting. The missing ingredient, however, is the person. Two kinds of people are concerned: those who are already performing the job and those who will be trained to do the job. The key question here is, What personal capabilities are necessary to perform the job effectively? When these characteristics are known, the people who will do the job can be assessed to determine whether they have them now or require training to get them.

One system for specifying human capabilities emphasizes knowledge, skills, and abilities (KSAs) (Prien, 1977). Knowledge is an organized body of information, which, if applied, makes adequate job performance possible. Skills are the capabilities (often psychomotor) necessary to perform the job operations with ease. Abilities are the cognitive capabilities necessary to do the job. Instructional programs must be based on the characteristics of the group to be trained. Their needs and values are important if training is to be successful.

Training and Development

Before training will work, trainees have to be motivated to learn from it (see Chapter 9). Given that motivation, organizations employ a number of different training techniques. In describing each, we will consider the circumstances under which it is appropriate.

On-the-job Training and Lectures The two most frequently used kinds of training are on-the-job training and lectures, although little research exists as to the effectiveness of either. It is usually impossible to teach someone everything she needs to know at a location away from the workplace. Thus on-the-job training often supplements other kinds of training, e.g., classroom or off-site training; but on-the-job training is frequently the only form of training. It is usually informal, which means, unfortunately, that the trainer does not concentrate on the training as much as she should, and the trainer may not have a well-articulated picture of what the novice needs to learn. On-the-job training is not successful when used to avoid developing a training program, though it can be an effective part of a well-coordinated training program. Ellen Randall's training was mostly on the job. A disadvantage of this type of training, when it takes place in an unsupervised way, is that it permits the commission of mistakes, which can be costly to the organization and frustrating to the individual.

Lectures are used because of their low cost and their capacity to reach many people. Lectures, which use one-way communication as opposed to interactive learning techniques, are much criticized as a training device.

Programmed Instruction (PI) A number of **programmed instruction (PI)** devices exist. These devices systematically present information to the learner and elicit a response; they use reinforcement principles to promote appropriate responses. When PI was originally developed in the 1950s, it was thought to be useful only for basic subjects. Today the method is used for skills as diverse as air traffic control, blueprint reading, and the analysis of tax returns (Goldstein, 1986).

Computer-Assisted Instruction (CAI) With the computer revolution came an outbreak of various forms of **computer-assisted instruction,** or **CAI.** With CAI, students can learn at their own pace, as with PI. Because the student interacts with the computer, it is believed by many to be a more dynamic learning device. Educational alternatives can be quickly selected to suit the student's capabilities, and performance can be monitored continuously. As instruction proceeds, data are gathered for monitoring and improving performance (Odiorne and Rumler, 1988).

Audiovisual Techniques Both television and film extend the range of skills that can be taught and the way information may be presented. Many systems have electronic blackboards and slide projection equipment. The use of techniques that combine audiovisual systems such as closed circuit television and telephones has spawned a new term for this type of training, **tele-**

training. The feature on "Sesame Street" illustrates the design and evaluation of one of television's favorite children's program as a training device.

FEATURE: *"Sesame Street" as a Training Tool*

One of my favorite examples of [the audiovisual] technique comes from the television program "Sesame Street." . . . The reason I enjoy this example is that many readers of this book learned basic concepts from "Sesame Street," and very few people realize that this entertainment show was really a carefully designed training program. Basically, research on this program showed that (1) the children who watched the program learned more than those who didn't; (2) those skills that were emphasized on the program were learned best; and (3) disadvantaged children as compared with middle-class children began the program with lower achievement scores on the topics being emphasized, but their performance surpassed middle-class children who watched the program infrequently. Viewers who were not part of the experimental design often did not realize that this creative and entertaining program was an experiment designed to achieve specific behavioral objectives. These objectives were carefully determined in a series of workshops attended by representatives of all the pertinent fields, including psychologists, sociologists, teachers, filmmakers, writers, advertising personnel, and evaluators. They established objectives related to symbolic representation, cognitive processes, and physical and social environments. For example, behavioral objectives for symbolic representation might include: "Given a set of symbols, either all letters or all numbers, the child knows whether those symbols are used in reading or counting," or "Given a series of words presented orally, all beginning with the same letter, the child can make up another word or pick another word starting with the same letter." . . .

The evaluation design and criteria for "Sesame Street" were developed as part of the entire instructional program. The measures included outcome criteria, such as degree of learning, as well as process measures, which assessed what occurred during instruction. The process measures included the number of hours that the child viewed the program and the child's reactions while viewing. These measures also permitted the investigator to relate the number of hours of viewing to other criteria like learning. The pretests indicated that older children performed better than younger children. However, after viewing the program, the younger children who watched regularly often scored higher than older children who were infrequent viewers. This program is a fine example of the information that can be gained by the utilization of a variety of criteria developed from carefully defined goals and objectives.

Simulations   Training **simulations** replicate the essential characteristics of the real world that are necessary to produce both learning and the transfer of new knowledge and skills to application settings. Both machine and other forms of simulators exist. Machine simulators often have substantial degrees of physical fidelity; that is, they represent the real world's operational equipment. The main purpose of simulation, however, is to produce psychological fidelity, that is, to reproduce in the training those processes that will be required on the job. We simulate for a number of reasons, including to control the training environment, for safety, to introduce feedback and other learning principles, and to reduce cost. It is considerably safer and less costly, for instance, to have aviators practice aircraft carrier landings at the Navy's F-14 Tomcat fighter plane or E-2C Hawkeye simulator in San Diego than to have an aviator hit the stern of a carrier in order to learn how not to do that. Simulation is done to increase training transfer of training.

Business games are also simulations. They are the direct progeny of war games that have been used to train officers in combat techniques for hundreds of years. Almost all early business games were designed to teach basic business skills, but more recent games also include interpersonal skills. Monopoly might be considered the quintessential business game for young capitalists. It is probably the first place youngsters learned the words *mortgage, taxes,* and *go to jail.*

Case studies simulate an organization's conditions via a written report. The trainee analyzes the problems of the organization and offers solutions based on consideration of the people, the environment, and so on. In **role playing,** a slightly different simulation technique, trainees act out various roles. This method is used primarily in the analysis of interpersonal problems and the development of human relations skills (Bass and Vaughan, 1966).

The type of simulation that generated the most interest in the 1980s is behavioral role modeling. This approach is based on social learning theory (Bandura, 1977), which stresses the use of observation, modeling, and reinforcement as steps in changing behavior. This technique provides trainees with many vivid displays and considerable guidance of how they should act. As is true of many other training techniques, this technique is used a good deal, but there is a scarcity of research assessing its value (as an exception, see Latham and Saari, 1979).

Behavior Modification   Behavior modification (see Chapter 9) is a direct application of the principles of reinforcement developed by B. F. Skinner. Here an assessment is performed to specify the exact problems and determine the specific behaviors that require elimination or change. Reinforcers appropriate to the situation and to the individual are selected. Desired responses are immediately and continuously reinforced until the behavior is well established, when intermittent reinforcers are used.

Transfer of Training

Although the effectiveness of training is significant, an equally important aspect is **transfer of training**—the degree to which what is learned is actually used in work. Organizations do not want to spend money on training that is forgotten. There are two theories about transfer. One is that the elements common to the learning and work situation transfer (Thorndike and Woodward, 1901). A less restrictive assumption is that principles transfer. If we accept this assumption, we need not be terribly concerned that the learning and using situations are identical, as long as the underlying principles are clear to the learner. From an organization's standpoint the important issue is that the climate of the organization encourages transfer. At minimum this requires that top management support the training effort.

Figure 10.9 shows a model that deals with the opposite of transfer, **relapse.** It outlines the importance of having coping responses to prevent relapses of learned behavior. People have to be aware of relapse problems and learn to diagnose situations that are likely to sabotage the maintenance of learned behavior. These coping responses should lead to increased self-efficiency and decreased probability of relapse.

Performance Evaluation

Once employees are trained, managers need to evaluate their performance. Evaluations are used, in general, to control employee behavior and manage human resources. For this reason, the performance evaluation system should be tied to the organization's strategic and operational plans (Latham, 1984).

FIGURE 10.9
A Model of the Relapse Process

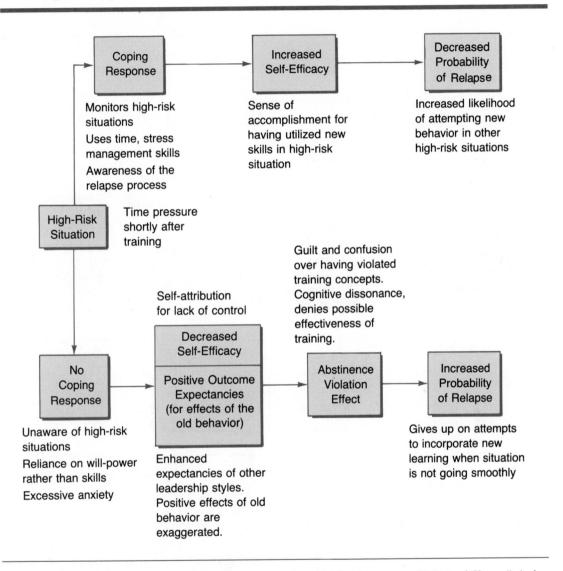

Source: R. D. Marx, "Relapse Prevention for Managerial Training: A Model for Maintenance of Behavioral Change," *Academy of Management Review* 7 (1982):434. Reprinted by permission.

FIGURE 10.10
Model of a Performance Evaluation System

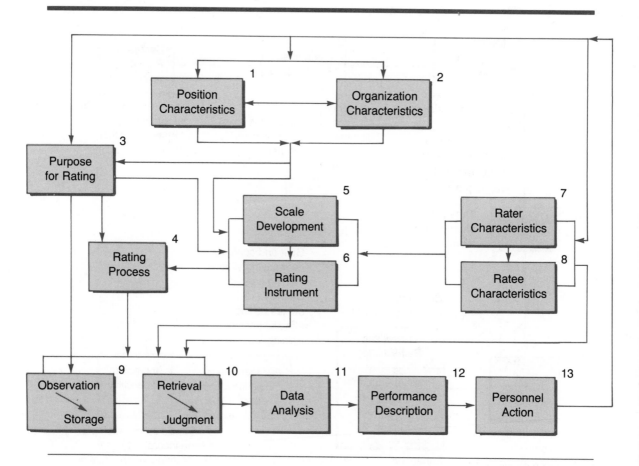

Source: F. J. Landy and J. L. Farr, "Performance Rating," *Psychological Bulletin* 87 (1980):72–107. Copyright © 1980 by the American Psychological Association. Reprinted by permission.

Just as an organization should have an instructional system, it should also have a performance evaluation system. A model for such a system is provided in Figure 10.10. Note that organizational and task analyses are as essential to the evaluation process as they are to the training process, because what employers evaluate must reflect what is required on the job (we discuss this further later). Note, too, that the personal characteristics of both the employee and the assessor will affect the outcome of the evaluation.

Performance evaluations are done for a number of reasons. They provide mechanisms for communicating with employees, documenting satisfactory and unsatisfactory performance, developing plans to improve or maintain performance, and ensuring fair treatment of all employees. They include assessment of traits, behaviors, and output.

Appraisal Methods

According to Scarpello and Ledvinka* (1988) there are three approaches to performance evaluation. The first evaluates employees against preestablished criteria. The employer might have developed a production standard in terms of the number of items to be produced per hour or day and quality standards for those items. For example, you might own a chain of hamburger stands and stipulate that at peak business hours each hamburger maker must produce at least 50 burgers, each with one-quarter pound of meat, one slice of tomato, one slice of onion, one piece of lettuce, and two tablespoons of your special dressing, all assembled in a particular manner.

The second evaluation approach is based on individual performance standards. Each employee may have individualized performance standards, which are meshed with the needs of the unit as a whole. An example is the manager of any store in the hamburger chain who establishes her performance goals for the month with her supervisor, depending on market conditions in the area, hours the store can remain open, staffing, and so on.

The third approach to evaluation ranks one employee's performance against that of other employees. We often rank order employees when deciding which ones to promote. As an example, the managers of the stores in the hamburger chain could be ranked by top management to decide who should be an area supervisor.

Evaluation Against Common Performance Standards   Rating scales are used to judge employee performance against common standards. Many different types of rating scales exist, the graphic rating scale being the oldest (Landy and Farr, 1983). Most graphic rating scales rate personality traits, although research shows such scales to be flawed (Bernardin and Beatty, 1984).

Such scales can be adapted to tasks, however. Such a scale asks the evaluator to rate the subject on a given dimension of behavior. In our hamburger restaurant example, the manager could rate each worker on the number of burgers made in a given time, the order of materials in each burger, the amount of materials used, and the neatness of the workstation. Each dimension could be evaluated using scales with intervals marked by numbers or phrases (for instance, very neat, somewhat neat, not very neat, messy).

---

*This section owes much to their discussion

The graphic rating scale has some popular variants. The mixed standards scale provides a description of the traits, behaviors, or job outcomes followed by a place for a rating. A description might be "averages 50 hamburgers per hour." The rater then marks the subject with a "+" if performance exceeds the description, "0" if it matches the description, and "−" if it falls short of the level set by the description. Checklists are similar to graphic rating scales. They typically use behavior derived from job analyses as item descriptors.

Behavioral rating scales, called *behaviorally anchored rating scales* (BARS), *behavioral expectation scales* (BES), or *behavior observation scales* (BOS), are also similar to graphic rating scales. Unlike graphic rating scales (particularly those assessing traits), they are based on thorough job analyses. Scale items are developed by gathering critical incidents associated with the job. In BARS and BES all items begin with the phrase "Could be expected to" to allow the evaluator to generalize from what he has observed the employee doing to what the employee might do.

Because BARS and BES are rather cumbersome to use (Cascio and Bernardin, 1981), BOS was developed. BOS group under a general performance category all behaviors that measure similar concepts. Each behavior is scaled from 1 to 5, and observers note how frequently they have seen the behavior. An example of BOS is shown in Figure 10.11.

Evaluation Against Individualized Performance Standards   The second type of evaluation system is called goal-oriented, results-oriented, or output-oriented performance evaluation. In these systems, the organization sets goals for specific departments, which in turn formulate their own objectives and distribute them among employees. Each employee's goals and expected outcomes are specified for some period of time, usually six months or a year.

Management by objectives (MBO) is the most commonly discussed technique of this type. The MBO process is based on three principles: (1) performance goals are set for a specified period, (2) the supervisor and subordinate both participate in goal setting, and (3) the supervisor provides the subordinate with performance feedback. Supervisor and subordinate always assess the subordinate's success in achieving past goals before setting new ones. This feedback is an important aspect of the MBO process; it influences performance when it is specific, timely, relevant, and accepted by the employee.

Evaluation Against Others   Managers do not always need to rank order employees. For example, in a shop of 15 welders, the foreman rarely needs to know who is number 1 and who is number 15. But on occasion ranking

FIGURE 10.11
Examples from a BOS Scale

1. Sees an employee packing poor-quality products for sale and opens the packaging to show the employee why the product is bad.

| Almost never | 1 | 2 | 3 | 4 | Almost always |

2. When calling an employee for overtime, asks about the employee's personal commitments and shows sensitivity and appreciation for those commitments by saying, "I know I'm asking a lot, but I need you to come in."

| Almost never | 1 | 2 | 3 | 4 | Almost always |

3. Suggests ways to make wearing safety equipment more comfortable and how to grip and carry products without getting hurt.

| Almost never | 1 | 2 | 3 | 4 | Almost always |

4. Gives the mechanic a clear description of the machine problem.

| Almost never | 1 | 2 | 3 | 4 | Almost always |

Source: V. G. Scarpello and J. Ledvinka, *Personnel: Human Resource Management* (Boston: PWS-KENT, 1988), p. 60. Copyright © 1988 by PWS-KENT Publishing Company. Reprinted by permission.

must be known, particularly when considering promotions. Three methods for ranking employees are common: simple ranking, paired comparison, and forced distribution. **Simple ranking** involves placing a group of individuals in order along some criterion (Landy and Farr, 1983).

Paired comparison is more complex; supervisors achieve an overall ranking of all employees by comparing every possible pair of individuals on overall performance or against specific performance categories (Guion, 1965). One way to do this is to write the name of each person to be ranked on a card and then compare any two people, putting one card in the winner pile and the other in the loser pile. The winner is then compared with a new person. The process is then repeated for second position, third position, and so on. By the time the task is complete, every person is essentially compared with every other person.

Forced distribution requires the ranker to distribute employees into specific performance categories, typically one of five ranging from very poor to outstanding. The number of people placed in each category is determined beforehand and usually represents a normal distribution curve. Thus only a few people are very poor or very good performers, many more are only a little above or below the middle, and the majority fall in the middle.

The Appraiser's Role

Appraisers are subject to a number of errors, five of major significance:

1. **Unclear performance standards** are one problem. Graphic rating scales are particularly prone to this. How much neatness is required on our hamburger maker's job?

2. The **halo effect** means that ratings given subordinates on one trait will influence how they are rated on another. An unfriendly employee is often rated low on other traits that he may or may not be low on.

3. The **central tendency** problem means that raters use the middle of scales, never the ends. That is, on a 5-point scale, 1 and 5 are avoided. This restriction can distort evaluation; a forced distribution scale helps prevent this problem.

4. The **leniency or strictness error** means that certain supervisors may tend to rate all their employees either very high or very low.

5. **Bias** is the tendency to allow individual differences, such as age, race, and sex, to affect employee appraisal.

A recent study (Schoorman, 1988) indicated another influence: a supervisor's approval or disapproval of the initial hiring decision influenced performance ratings upward or downward. The case of Ellen Randall's subordinate who thought he should have been given her job demonstrates that Schoorman's observation can manifest itself upward as well as downward, with morale and performance consequences.

Countering these errors requires training the evaluator; indeed, Cardy, Bernardin, Abbott, Senderak, and Taylor (1987) showed that experience in conducting appraisals increased evaluators' accuracy. Other studies (Athey and McIntyre, 1987; Hedge and Kavanagh, 1988) found training to be effective in increasing appraiser accuracy. Appraisers should be taught the importance of providing feedback on a regular basis and about common performance errors. They should also be trained to conduct the performance appraisal interview. There are four things to keep in mind:

1. Set the tone at the start of the interview.

2. Be as positive as possible in assessing strong and weak points.

3. Summarize your own and your subordinate's views.

4. Develop an action plan.

FIGURE 10.12
How to Encourage Your Subordinate to Talk in the Interview

Do

1. Try silence. When your subordinate says something, don't rush in with a comment; silence (plus an occasional nod or huh-huh) will often be enough to get the person to elaborate on what he or she means.
2. Use open-ended questions, such as, "What do you think we could do to improve sales in your region?"
3. State questions in terms of a problem, such as, "Suppose you were production manager and you thought there was too much waste?"
4. Use a command, such as "go on," "tell me more," and "keep talking."
5. Use choice questions, such as, "What are some things you don't like about working for the company?"
6. Restate the person's last point as a question. For instance, if he says, "I just don't think I can get the job done," try to draw him out by restating his point as a question, "You don't think you can get the job done?"
7. Try to get at the feelings underlying what the person is saying. Is the person frustrated by a lack of promotion possibilities? Does he or she think the treatment is unfair?

Don't

1. Do all the talking.
2. Use restrictive questions (like "would you" or "did you") that can be answered in one or two words.
3. Be judgmental by saying things like "you shouldn't have."
4. Give free advice, such as, "If I were you . . ."
5. Get involved with name calling (such as "Boy, that was stupid!").
6. Ridicule (for instance, by saying, "How did you manage that?").
7. Digress (for instance, by saying, "That reminds me of a funny story . . .").
8. Use sarcasm (for instance, by saying, "I'd hoped for more but I should have known better knowing you").

Source: G. Dessler, *Personnel Management*, 4th ed. (Englewood Cliffs, NJ: Prentice-Hall, 1988), p. 515. Reprinted by permission of Prentice-Hall, Inc.

The appraiser should encourage and help the employee to talk in the interview. Figure 10.12 suggests some do's and don'ts in this area.

Performance Evaluation and the Law

Because performance evaluation systems are used to make decisions about employees, they are subject to the law. The law's concern is not about whether a performance evaluation should be conducted but about the fairness of its conduct. Evaluations are subject to the Equal Employment Opportunities Commission's *Uniform Guidelines on Employee Selection Procedures.*

Based on court decisions, Bernardin and Beatty (1984) provided prescriptions for designing performance evaluation systems. They stated that standards for performance evaluation should be based on job analyses and communicated to employees. Employees should be evaluated on specific categories of job performance, and those categories should be defined in behavioral terms and supported by objective, observable evidence. Individual raters should be assessed for the validity of their ratings, or the degree to which they rate what they intend to rate. When possible, more than one rater should be used. Documentation of extreme ratings is required, and companies must provide a formal appeal process. Page and van de Voort (1989) presented a model job analysis for guidance in complying with the legal requirements.

Rewards, Discipline, and Responses to Discipline

Performance evaluations have a number of uses, including training needs determination. They are also frequently used as a basis for decisions about pay raises and promotions or disciplinary actions. That assumptions about rewards are not the same in different cultures was illustrated nicely by Von Glinow and Chung (1989). In Korea, as in the United States, financial compensation is the predominant reward, but human relationships with upper- and lower-level workers runs a close second as an important reward. Japan's system of rewards is based more on hierarchy than are the systems in other nations, and in China equality has been a predominant policy, which is only recently giving way to "more work, more pay." In another study (Kim, Park, and Suzuki, 1990), students from the United States and Japan exhibited a stronger preference for equitable rewards than did students from South Korea. In this section we talk generally about rewards and punishments and then discuss the basic elements of a discipline system.

Rewards and Punishments

Previously we mentioned operant conditioning as a strategy for delivering rewards and punishment (see earlier in this chapter and Chapter 9). The organizational research on reinforcement is mixed, with most demonstrating that operant conditioning techniques are useful controls for behavior (Pfeffer, 1985). The most frequently cited illustration of the use of operant conditioning in a company is the case of Emery Air Freight. Emery is a shipping business that in 1973 was worried about its container utilization rates. The firm measured container utilization and then designed a program for increasing the amount of freight packed into each container. Supervisors were trained in techniques of verbal reinforcement to improve container use. The results were instantaneous, and the program saved Emery millions of dollars. A number of other successful operant conditioning programs have been discussed (Hamner and Hamner, 1976).

The question of operant conditioning aside, organizations have used rewards for years, perhaps out of an intuitive understanding of their efficacy. That intuition has been borne out by years of research, which has shown that devising and using rewards effectively can have a positive effect on a wide range of attitudes and behaviors. Scant attention has been paid to negative outcomes and aversive control systems during this same time, perhaps because management views punishment as a last resort. Perhaps it is because organizational psychologists have generally not favored punishment out of a belief that punishment has undesirable side effects and produces unwanted employee reactions like aggression and hostility toward management.

Discipline should not be completely avoided. Discipline does serve a number of functions in organizations:

1. It can be used to control behavior directly. Employees learn from their own experiences that certain behaviors lead to aversive consequences.

2. It provides indirect signals to other employees about what constitutes acceptable behavior. They might learn by watching another employee's behavior and punishment.

3. It helps establish and maintain the "organizational boundary system." These are the formal and informal norms and rules employees are expected to follow.

4. It is used to maintain in-group and out-group relations with supervisors. Supervisors can use informal and formal disciplines to preserve the role and distance they want with employees.

5. It may be used harshly, inconsistently, and inappropriately to create an illusion of strict behavior control.

Basic Elements in a Discipline System

The most common approach to discipline is called **progressive discipline** (Zack and Block, 1979). In such a system, punishment increases in severity as the number of violations increases. The process is usually ordered as follows: informal talk, formal oral warning, formal written warning, suspension without pay, and discharge. For minor infractions, discipline starts with

FIGURE 10.13
Principles of a Progressive Discipline System

- *Specific rules,* which leave no doubt about when they have been violated
- *Job-related rules,* which are reasonably related to the employee's work or to some other legitimate organizational objective
- *Clearly stated punishments,* which leave no doubt about the consequences of violating those rules
- *Punishments that fit the crime,* which means that the infraction should be severe enough to warrant the disciplinary action taken
- *Careful investigation,* which ensures that the rules really were violated
- *Prompt* enforcement of rules
- *Consistent* enforcement of rules
- *Documentation* of all observed rule violations and disciplinary actions taken
- *Specific statement of the offense* in communicating with the employee at the oral and written warning steps
- *Confinement of discussion to the problem at hand;* does not question employee's overall worth
- *Effective communication* of the rules and punishments
- *Advance warning* of any change in the rules
- An *appeals process*

Source: V. G. Scarpello and J. Ledvinka, *Personnel: Human Resource Management* (Boston: PWS-KENT, 1988), p. 687. Copyright © 1988 by PWS-KENT Publishing Company. Reprinted by permission.

an informal talk, but for more severe infractions it might start with something more severe, and for the most serious infractions discipline may begin with discharge.

Figure 10.13 lists the principles required in a good progressive discipline program. The assumptions underlying this list are that the exercise of power should be based on a set of objective rules rather than on the personal preferences of those in power and that the rules respect the rights of the person against whom power is exercised.

Even when they include rewards and positive feedback, progressive discipline programs still focus on progressively negative steps. Such systems are also often quite rigid and overly legalistic. A newer approach, called **discipline without punishment** (Campbell, Fleming, and Grote, 1985), aims to avoid this negative approach to discipline. The process uses four steps: oral reminder, written reminder, decision-making leave with pay, and discharge.

In the first step, managers meet with employees to clarify procedure and standards of performance. No threats are made. The supervisor points out to the employee that it is her responsibility to abide by the rules of the organization. Following this conversation, the supervisor writes a memo reviewing the conversation and the employee's commitment.

If the problem behavior continues, the supervisor sends a second reminder. Consistent with the first, it emphasizes that the employee failed to live up to the agreed-on commitment. This step is designed to put the onus of responsibility on the employee. It does not focus on what management will do next but on what the employee will do, a much more positive way to handle the situation than provided under the traditional stepped plan.

The decision-making leave step shows the employee that the employer wants her to remain in the company. The assumption is positive—the employee is being given time off to reflect on how she will change. On returning to the job, the employee meets with the manager and indicates whether she plans to change her behavior and stay or leave the organization. If the decision is to stay, the employee and her supervisor develop specific goals and a plan to reach them. The supervisor points out that failure to live up to the agreement will result in dismissal. In addition to placing responsibility on the employee, this system eliminates the negativeness that might result in employee sabotage or grievance.

SUMMARY

Barriers to future promotions may exist for Ellen Randall because she is a woman, but it is also clear that she has been a competent—indeed, an impressive—manager for her corporation. Trained largely by on-the-job techniques and aided by advisers, she now feels that she has achieved the top level for a woman, though not the top job in her corporation. This barrier to the top job is what Morrison et al. (1987) call the "glass ceiling" that many women as well as members of ethnic minorities are believed to face. Ellen Randall has thus been denied the ultimate reward in her company— promotion to the top job. Will she take her talents elsewhere or persist and break through the glass ceiling? Only time will tell.

The study of individual differences opened with a discussion of the personality characteristics that people bring to organizations. Among all the available personality traits, we focused on six: intelligence, achievement motivation, uniqueness, masculinity/femininity, authoritarianism, and Machiavellianism. Attribution theory is significant to an understanding of personality as well; it helps account for which behaviors others perceive to be core to the individual's personality and which derive from the situation. An alternative view of personality focuses on schemas, prototypes, and scripts— the mental constructs we develop and against which actual behavior is assessed.

Social perception shows how people make sense of social situations. People form schemas, which have four influences on perception: they influence what information receives attention, what is retained and retrieved, how information is interpreted, and how people act.

Along with their personalities, people also bring their values and attitudes to their organizations. Cross-national studies show considerable differences in the values people hold. Attitudes are most usefully seen as having three main components: cognitive, affective, and behavioral. The most frequently studied attitudes in organizations are those toward work. In spite of the fact that we see examples every day of what we suppose to be connections between attitude and behavior, the research evidence about such connections is weak.

Training is one aspect of human resource management that should figure largely in organization strategy and planning. A needs assessment focusing on three areas—organizational needs, task needs, and person needs—is used to identify training needs. The major forms of training include on-the-job training and lectures, programmed instruction, computer-assisted instruction, audiovisual techniques, simulations, and behavior modification. Organizations need to ensure that their training transfers to the actual work setting, if not in detail at least in principle.

Performance evaluation, another important concept of human resource management, should figure prominently in strategic planning as well. One of the many purposes of performance evaluation is as a control mechanism. The three main approaches are evaluating employees against pre-established criteria, developing individual performance standards, and ranking employees against one another. Whatever the technique used, it must meet the requirements established by fair labor practices.

Performance evaluations are often used as bases for rewards and disciplinary procedures. Rewards are more useful than punishments in organizations. The basic elements of a progressive discipline system are to gradually increase the severity of the sanctions; a newer approach, called discipline without punishment, attempts to gain more favorable results by taking a more positive approach.

MANAGERIAL INSIGHT

To: *Student Managers*
From: *Veteran Manager*
Subject: *Tolerating Dissent*

The key to success as a manager is handling one of the results of individual differences: dissent. Managing dissent is one of the most difficult and challenging tasks you will have as a manager.

Just thinking about the subject is problematical. My dictionary defines *dissent* as "to think or feel differently; disagree; differ." Most modern managers operating in democratic societies would say such qualities are acceptable, perhaps even desirable, in a strong and dynamic organization. But when the verb becomes a noun, *dissension*, look at the negative meaning that appears: "a difference of opinion, especially one that leads to contention or strife." Few managers—or employees, for that matter—want contention or strife.

The ability to get the positive contribution of dissent without the negative consequences of dissension is, I believe, within the power of the manager. The key lies in the climate you establish by what you say and do, and what you permit and encourage in your employees.

Consider which of the following two managers you would prefer to work for: *Manager A* recognizes that her employees are adults and have experiences, attitudes, opinions, and views of their own. She encourages her employees to speak up, even when they disagree with her, and she honestly listens to and considers every point of view. Sometimes she changes her mind based on her employees' arguments. She makes it clear, however, that there is a time for dissent and a time when dissent is destructive, and she expects employees to support her decisions once they are made.

Manager B considers the expression of opposing views to be disloyal and subversive. She considers disagreement with her point of view as threatening and personal. She exhibits a low tolerance for disagreement and rarely changes her position on a subject as the result of an argument by an employee. She rewards those who always agree with her and punishes, either actively or passively, those who disagree.

I'd rather work for Manager A, and I bet you would, too. The difference sounds easy, doesn't it? It's not. As a manager seeking to tolerate dissent, you will find yourself dealing with at least three distinct kinds, each requiring a different set of tools to manage:

1. *Dissent from company policy.*   This kind of dissent might find expression on any topic from overall strategy to the policy on smoking in the workplace. Most organizational policies are based on sound principles that aren't always clear to the individual employee who thinks they should be different. What you as a manager have to do is to understand not only the policy but the reasons for it and be able to explain it, even when you may also personally disagree with it. You also have to be able to explain why it is best for the whole organization even though it may appear to be unfair or discriminatory to the dissenting employee.

2. *Dissent from what other employees do or say or are perceived to be able to "get away with."*   This kind of dissent will test your ability to administer your own and company policies and assignments with an

even hand. Managing this kind of dissent will require you, at various times, to draw on all the management techniques in this textbook. No one prescription will cover all cases.

3. *Dissent from your own views.*   This is the toughest kind of dissent you will have to deal with. You will need the self-confidence to listen to opposing views without feeling threatened and without becoming defensive. The knowledge, skills, and abilities you bring to the job, and the track record you make in the job, will build this self-confidence. You have to be able to acknowledge that you may not always have the right answer. Bradford and Cohen's book (1984) *Managing for Excellence* has some excellent suggestions on how to do this. If you let it be known, early in your assignment as manager of a particular group, just what the ground rules for dissent are going to be, you can establish reasonable and manageable expectations.

In my view, your ability to cope with this kind of dissent will be a direct measure of your ability to trust your employees. If you truly consider them as individuals, with minds of their own and valuable contributions to make, you can create a climate where dissent is not only welcomed, it is invariably expressed constructively.

It will not be enough to say you welcome opposing views and open discussion in your unit. You must demonstrate your tolerance by your actions. If you say it and then do the opposite, you can count on creating more dissent—about your ability to tolerate dissent!

As a practicing manager, there is little doubt that you will experience dissent. Start off your career by seeing it as a way of making your organization stronger. By doing so, you will harness the positive power of dissent and avoid the destructive power of dissension. It can be done!

REVIEW QUESTIONS

1. Explain what is meant in the theme case by the concept of "the ceiling." What significance does the concept have to the chapter?

2. Does an individual always follow the behavior described by a personality trait? Explain.

3. What does the Pygmalion effect suggest about attributions of intelligence? How might managers use the effect to get top performance?

4. How might a worker high in uniqueness present a manager with difficulties?

5. Since organizations—and managers—desire that workers yield to authority, is it desirable to have employees who are high in authoritarianism?

6. Distinguish between prototypes and schemas.

7. Identify each of the three types of schemas named by Taylor and Crocker.

8. Explain what is meant by each of the two significant measures of a personality test.

9. Describe the three types of information used in attribution theory and explain how each is used to identify causes that are attributable to personality rather than to situational factors.

10. What are the four main errors in attributions?

11. What are the five steps Lord identified in social information processing? Explain how any one of those steps can cause distortion.

12. Distinguish between values and attitudes.

13. Do attitudes influence behavior? If not, why study them?

14. What are the three components of a needs assessment?

15. What are four reasons that simulations are used in training programs? How do simulations affect transfer of training?

16. Discuss the advantages and disadvantages of each of the three approaches to performance evaluation.

17. What five sources of error may cloud the evaluations of a supervisor?

18. Does discipline have a useful function?

REFERENCES

Ajzen, I., and Fishbein, M. (1980). *Understanding Attitudes and Predicting Social Behavior.* Englewood Cliffs, NJ: Prentice-Hall.

Allport, G. W., and Odbert, H. S. (1936). Trait names: A psycholexical study. *Psychological Monographs* 47:171.

American Psychological Association, Division of Industrial-Organizational Psychology. (1980). *Principles for the Validation and Use of Personnel Selection Procedures* (2nd ed.). Berkeley, CA: *The Industrial-Organizational Psychologist.*

Athey, T. R., and McIntyre, R. M. (1987). Effect of rater training on rater accuracy: Levels-of-processing theory and social facilitation theory perspectives. *Journal of Applied Psychology* 72:567–572.

Bandura, A. (1977). *Social Learning Theory.* Englewood Cliffs, NJ: Prentice-Hall.

Bass, B. M., and Barrett, G. V. (1981). *People, Work, and Organizations.* Boston: Allyn & Bacon.

Bass, B. M., and Vaughan, J. A. (1966). *Training in Industry: The Management of Learning.* Belmont, CA: Wadsworth.

Bem, S. L. (1974). The measurement of psychological androgyny. *Journal of Consulting and Clinical Psychology* 42:155–162.

Benjamin, J. Y., and Manter, M. A. (1990). Excuse me, but where's my mentor? *Wall Street Journal* (College Edition, National Business Employment Weekly) (Spring: 16–17).

Berger, C. (1980). Power and the family. In M. E. Roloff and G. E. Miller (eds.), *Persuasion: New Directions in Theory and Research.* Beverly Hills, CA: Sage, pp. 197–224.

Bernardin, H. J., and Beatty, R. W. (1984). *Performance Appraisal: Assessing Human Behavior at Work.* Boston: PWS-KENT.

Bernardin, H. J., and Bownas, D. A. (eds.). (1985). *Personality Assessment in Organizations.* New York: Praeger.

Bradford, D. L., and Cohen, A. R. (1984). *Managing for Excellence.* New York: Wiley.

Brandt, J. M. (1976). Behavioral validation of a scale measuring need for uniqueness. Unpublished doctoral dissertation, Purdue University.

Bransford, J. D., and Johnson, M. K. (1973). Considerations of some problems of comprehension in W. G. Chase (ed.), *Visual Information Processing.* New York: Academic Press.

Brody, N. (1988). *Personality in Search of Individuality.* New York: Academic Press, p. 8.

Campbell, D. N., Fleming, R. L., and Grote, R. C. (1985). Discipline without punishment—at last. *Harvard Business Review* (July–August): 162–178.

Cantor, N. (1981). A cognitive-social approach to personality. In N. Cantor and J. F. Kihlstrom (eds.), *Personality, Cognition, and Social Interaction.* Hillsdale, NJ: Erlbaum.

Cardy, R. L., Bernardin, H. J., Abbott, J. E., Senderak, M. P., and Taylor, K. (1987). The effects of individual performance schemata and dimension familiarization on rating accuracy. *Personnel Psychology* 41:25–42.

Carlson, L., and Carlson, R. (1984). Affect and psychological magnification: Derivations from Tomkins script theory. *Journal of Personality* 52:36–45.

Cascio, W. F., and Bernardin, H. J. (1981). Implications of performance appraisal litigation for personnel decisions. *Personnel Psychology* 34:211–226.

Chaiken, S., and Stangord, C. (1987). Attitudes and attitude change. In M. Rosenzweig and L. W. Porter (eds.), *Annual Review of Psychology* 38:575–630.

Christie, R., and Geis, F. L. (1970). *Studies in Machiavellianism.* New York: Academic Press.

Clegg, C. W. (1983). Psychology of employee lateness, absence, and turnover: A methodological critique and empirical study. *Journal of Applied Psychology* 68:88–101.

Dessler, G. (1988). *Personnel Management* (4th ed.). Englewood Cliffs, NJ: Prentice-Hall.

Dowling, P. J. (1988). International HRM. In R. Dyer (ed.), *Human Resource Management: Evolving Rules and Responsibilities.* Washington, D.C.: Bureau of National Affairs, pp. 1-228–1-257.

Downey, H. K., and Brief, A. P. (1986). How cognitive structures affect organizational design: Implicit theories of organizing. In H. P. Sims and D. A. Gioia (eds.), *The Thinking Organization*. San Francisco: Jossey-Bass, pp. 165–190.

Downs, S. (1985). Retraining for new skills. *Ergonomics* 28:1205–1211.

Eden, D., and Ravid, G. (1982). Pygmalion vs. Self-expectancy: Effects of instruction and self-expectation on trainee performance. *Organizational Behavior and Human Performance* 30:351–364.

Eden, D., and Shani, A. B. (1982). Pygmalion goes to boot camp: Expectancy, leadership, and training performance. *Journal of Applied Psychology* 67:194–199.

Epstein, R. (1966). Aggression toward outgroups as a function of authoritarianism and imitation of aggressive models. *Journal of Personality and Social Psychology* 3:574–579.

Feldman, J. (1981). Beyond attribution theory: Cognitive processes in performance appraisal. *Journal of Applied Psychology* 66:127–148.

Fishbein, M., and Ajzen, I. (1975). *Belief, Attitude, Intention, and Behavior: An Introduction to Theory and Research*. Reading, MA: Addison-Wesley.

Fleishman, E. A., Harris, E. F., and Burtt, H. E. (1955). Leadership and supervision in industry. *Bureau of Educational Research, Report No. 33*, The Ohio State University.

Fournies, F. F. (1989). *Why Employees Don't Do What They're Supposed To Do*. Blue Ridge Summit, PA: Liberty House.

Frieze, I. H., Bailey, S., Mamula, P., and Moss, M. (1985). Life scripts and life planning: The role of career scripts in college women's career choices. *Imagination, Cognition, and Personality* 5:59–72.

George, J. M. (1990). Personality, affect, and behavior in groups. *Journal of Applied Psychology* 75:107–116.

Goffman, I. (1959). *The Presentation of Self in Everyday Life*. Garden City, NY: Doubleday.

Goldstein, I. L. (1986). *Training in Organizations: Needs Assessment, Development, and Evaluation*. Monterey, CA: Brooks Cole.

Greenhaus, J. H., Parasuraman, S., and Wormley, W. M. (1990). Effects of race on organizational experiences, job performance evaluations, and career outcomes. *Academy of Management Journal* 33:64–86.

Guilford, J. P. (1956). The structure of intellect. *Psychological Bulletin* 53:267–293.

Guion, R. M. (1965). *Personnel Testing*. New York: McGraw-Hill.

Hahn, D.C., and Dipboye, R. L. (1988). Effects of training and information on the accuracy and reliability of job evaluations. *Journal of Applied Psychology* 73:146–153.

Hamner, W. C., and Hamner, E. P. (1976). Behavior modification on the bottom line. *Organizational Dynamics* 4:3–21.

Heckhausen, H. (1967). *The Anatomy of Achievement Motivation*. New York: Academic Press.

Hedge, J. W., and Kavanagh, M. J. (1988). Improving the accuracy of performance evaluations: Comparison of three methods of performance appraiser training. *Journal of Applied Psychology* 73:68–73.

Heider, F. (1958). *The Psychology of Interpersonal Relations*. New York: Wiley.

Heilman, M. E., and Guzzo, R. A. (1978). The perceived cause of work success as a mediator of sex discrimination in organizations. *Organizational Behavior and Human Performance* 21:346–357.

Helson, R., Mitchell, V., Moane, G. (1984). Personality and patterns of adherence and nonadherence to the social clock. *Journal of Personality and Social Psychology* 46:1079–1096.

Herek, G. M. (1986). The instrumentality of ideologies: Toward a neofunctional theory of attitudes and behavior. *Journal of Social Issues* 42:99–114.

Higgins, E. T., and Bargh, J. A. (1987). Social cognition and social perception. In M. Rosenzweig and L. W. Porter (eds.), *Annual Review of Psychology*. Palo Alto: CA: Annual Reviews Inc., pp. 369–425.

Hofstede, G. (1980). *Culture's Consequences: International Differences in Work-related Values*. Beverly Hills, CA: Sage.

Hussey, D. E. (1985). Implementing corporate strategy: Using management education and training. *Long Range Planning* 18:28–37.

Ilgen, D. R., and Klein, H. J. (1989). Organization behavior. In M. R. Rosenzweig and L. W. Porter (eds.), *Annual Review of Psychology* 40:327–351.

Isenberg, D. J. (1986). The structure and process of understanding: Implications for managerial action. In H. P. Sims and D. A. Gioia (eds.), *The Thinking Organization*. San Francisco: Jossey-Bass, pp. 238–262.

Jones, E. E., and Davis, K. (1965). From acts to dispositions. In L. Berkowitz (ed.), *Advances in Experimental Social Psychology* (vol. 2). New York: Academic Press.

Kahneman, D., and Tversky, A. (1973). On the psychology of prediction. *Psychological Review* 80:237–251.

Katz, D., and Stotland, E. (1959). A preliminary statement to the theory of attitude structure and change. In S. Koch (ed.), *Psychology: A Study of Science*. New York: McGraw-Hill.

Kelley, H. H. (1967). Attribution theory in social psychology. In D. Levine (ed.), *Nebraska Symposium on Motivation*. Lincoln: University of Nebraska Press.

Kim, K. I., Park, H., and Suzuki, N. (1990). Reward allocations in the United States, Japan, and Korea: A comparison of individualistic and collectivistic cultures. *Academy of Management Journal* 33:188–198.

Kinder, D. R., and Sears, D. O. (1985). Public opinion and political action. In G. Lindzey and E. Aronson (eds.), *Handbook of Social Psychology* (3rd ed.). New York: Random House.

Landy, F. J., and Farr, J. L. (1980). Performance rating. *Psychological Bulletin* 87:72–107.

Landy, F. J., and Farr, J. L. (1983). *The Measurement of Work Performance Behavior, Methods, Theory, and Applications* (revised). New York: Academic Press.

LaPiere, R. T. (1934). Attitudes versus action. *Social Forces* 13:230–237.

Latham, G. P. (1984). The appraisal system as a strategic control. In C. J. Fombrun, N. M. Tichy, and M. A. Devanna (eds.), *Strategic Human Resource Management*. New York: Wiley, pp. 87–100.

Latham, G. P. (1988). Human resource training and development. In M. R. Rosenzweig and L. W. Porter (eds.), *Annual Review of Psychology* (vol. 39). Palo Alto, CA: Annual Reviews, Inc., pp. 545–582.

Latham, G. P., and Napier, N. (1987). Chinese human resource management practices in Hong Kong and Singapore. International Personnel and Human Resource Management Conference, Singapore, December.

Latham, G.P., and Saari, L. M. (1979). The application of social learning theory to training supervisors through behavior modeling. *Journal of Applied Psychology* 64:550–555.

Levinson, D. J. (1978). *The Seasons of a Man's Life*. New York: Knopf.

Lord, R. G. (1985). An information processing approach to social perception. In L. L. Cummings and B. M. Staw (eds.), *Research in Organizational Behavior* (vol. 7). Greenwich, CN: JAI Press, pp. 87–128.

Lumsden, C. J., and Wilson, E. O. (1981). *Genes, Mind, and Culture: The Coevolutionary Process*. Cambridge: Harvard University Press.

McClelland, D. C., Atkinson, J. W., Clark, R. A., and Lowell, E. L. (1953). *The Achievement Motive*. New York: Appleton-Century-Crofts.

Maher, M. L. (1980). *Culture and Achievement Motivation: Beyond Weber and McClelland*. Paper presented at the Annual Meeting of the American Educational Research Association, Boston.

Major, B. N. (1978). *Information Acquisition and Attribution*. Unpublished doctoral dissertation, Purdue University.

Markus, H., and Wurf, E. (1987). The dynamic self concept: A social psychological perspective. In M. Rosenzweig and L. W. Porter (eds.), *Annual Review of Psychology* 38: 299–338.

Markus, H., and Zajonc, R. B. (1985). The cognitive perspective in social psychology. In G. Lindzey and E. Aronson (eds.), *Handbook of Social Psychology* (vol. 1). Hillsdale, NJ: Erlbaum, pp. 137–230.

Martin, J., and Westie, F. (1959). The tolerant personality. *American Sociological Review* 24:521–528.

Meindl, J. R., Hunt, R. G., and Lee, W. (1989). Individualism-collectivism and work values: Data from the United States, China, Taiwan, Korea, and Hong Kong. In A. Nedd (ed.), *Research in Personnel and Human Resource Management*. Greenwich, CN: JAI Press, pp. 59–79.

Mischel W. (1968). *Personality and Assessment*. New York: Wiley.

Morrison, A., White, R. P., Van Velsor, E., and the Center for Creative Leadership. (1987). *Breaking the Glass Ceiling: Can Women Reach the Top of America's Largest Corporations*. Reading, MA: Addison-Wesley.

Muna, F. A. (1980). *The Arab Executive*. New York: Macmillan.

Nail, P. R. (1986). Toward an integration of some models and theories of social response. *Psychological Bulletin* 100:190–206.

Neisser, U. (1976). *Cognition and Reality*. San Francisco: Freeman.

Nisbett, R. E., and Borgida, E. (1975). Attribution and the psychology of prediction. *Journal of Personality and Social Psychology* 32:932–943.

Odiorne, G. S., and Rumler, G. A. (1988). *Training and Development: A Guide for Professionals*. Chicago: Commerce Clearinghouse.

Page, R. C., and Van de Voort, D. M. (1989). Job analysis and human resource planning.

In W. Cascio (ed.), *Human Resource Planning, Employment, and Placement.* Washington, D.C.: Bureau of National Affairs, pp. 2-34–2-72.

Pfeffer, J. (1985). Organizations and organization theory. In G. Lindzey and E. Aronson (eds.), *Handbook of Social Psychology* (3rd ed., vol. 1). New York: Random House, pp. 379–440.

Posner, M. I. (1982). Cumulative development of attention theory. *American Psychologist* 37:168–179.

Postman, L., Bruner, J. S., and McGinnies, E. (1948). Personal values as selective factors in perception. *Journal of Abnormal and Social Psychology* 43:142–154.

Prien, E. P. (1977). The function of job analysis in content validation. *Personnel Psychology* 30:167–174.

Putti, L., and Yoshikawa, A. (1984). Transferability—Japanese training and development practices. *Proceedings of the Academy of International Business, International Meetings, Singapore* 8:11–19.

Rodgers, B., with Levey, I. (1987). *Getting the Best out of Yourself and Others.* New York: Harper.

Rokeach, M. (ed.). (1979). *Understanding Human Values: Individual and Societal.* New York: Free Press.

Rosenthal, R., and Jacobson, L. (1968). *Pygmalion in the Classroom.* New York: Holt, Rinehart and Winston.

Ross, L. (1977). The intuitive psychologist and his shortcomings: Distortions in the attribution process. In L. Berkowitz (ed.), *Advances in Experimental Social Psychology* (vol. 10). New York: Academic Press, pp. 173–220.

Ross, L., Amabile, T. M., and Steinmutz, J. L. (1977). Social roles, social control, and biases in social perception. *Journal of Personality and Social Psychology* 35:485–494.

Sampson, E. E. (1977). Psychology and the American ideal. *Journal of Personality and Social Psychology* 35:767–782.

Scarpello, V. G., and Ledvinka, J. (1988). *Personnel: Human Resource Management.* Boston: PWS-KENT.

Schank, R. C., and Abelson, R. P. (1977). *Scripts, Plans, Goals, and Understanding: An Inquiry into Human Knowledge Structures.* Hillsdale, NJ: Erlbaum.

Schein, E. (1957). Reaction patterns to severe chronic stress in American army prisoners of war of the Chinese. *Journal of Social Issues* 13:21–30.

Schmitt, N., and Robertson, I. (1990). Personnel selection. In M. R. Rosenzweig and L. W. Porter (eds.), *Annual Review of Psychology* 41:289–319.

Schneider B. (1985). Organizational behavior. In L. W. Porter & M. R. Rosenzweig (eds.), *Annual Review of Psychology.* Palo Alto, CA: Annual Reviews Inc., 573–611.

Schoorman, F. D. (1988). Escalation bias in performance appraisals: An unintended consequence of supervisor participation in hiring decisions. *Journal of Applied Psychology* 73:58–62.

Schwartz, F. (1989). Management women and the new facts. *Harvard Business Review* (January-February):65–76.

Siegman, A. W. (1961). A cross cultural investigation of the relationship between ethnic prejudice, authoritarianism, ideology, and personality. *Journal of Abnormal and Social Psychology* 63:654–655.

Singer, J. L., and Kolligan, J. (1987). Personality: Developments in the study of private experience. In M. Rosenzweig and L. W. Porter (eds.), *Annual Review of Psychology* 38: 533–574.

Singer, J. L., and Salovey, P. (1985). Organized knowledge structures in personality: Schemas, self-schemas, prototypes, and scripts. A review and research agenda. Unpublished.

Snyder, C. R., and Fromkin, H. L. (1980). *Uniqueness: The Human Pursuit of Difference.* New York: Plenum Press.

Snyder, M., and Ickes, W. (1985). Personality and social behavior. In G. Lindzey and E. Aronson (eds.), *Handbook of Social Psychology* (3rd ed.). New York: Random House, pp. 883–948.

Spearman, C. (1904). General intelligence, objectively determined and measured. *American Journal of Psychology* 15:201–293.

Staw, B. M., Bell, N., and Clausen, J. A. (1986). The dispositional approach to job attitudes: A lifetime longitudinal test. *Administrative Science Quarterly* 31:56–77.

Sutton, C. D., and Woodman, R. W. (1989). Pygmalion goes to work: The effects of supervisor expectations in a retail setting. *Journal of Applied Psychology* 74:943–950.

Taylor, S. E., and Crocker, J. (1981). Schematic bases of social information processing. In E. T. Higgins, C. P. Herman, and M. P. Zanna (eds.), *Social Cognition: The Ontario Symposium on Personality and Social Psychology.* Hillsdale, N.J.: Erlbaum.

Tesser, A. (1978). Self generated attitude change. In L. Berkowitz (ed.), *Advances in Experimental Social Psychology* (vol. 11). New York: Academic Press.

Tesser, A., and Shaffer, D. R. (1990). Attitudes and attitude changes. In M. R. Rosenzweig and L. W. Porter (eds.), *Annual Review of Psychology* 41:479–523.

Thorndike, E. L., and Woodward, R. S. (1901). (I) The influence of improvement in one mental function upon the efficiency of other functions. (II) The estimation of magnitudes. (III) Functions involving attention, observation, and discrimination. *Psychological Review* 8:247–261, 384–395, 553–564.

Tomkins, S. S. (1980). Affect as amplification: Some modifications in theory. In R. Plutchik and H. Kellerman (eds.), *Emotion: Theory, Research and Experience: Theories of Emotion.* New York: Academic Press, pp. 141–164.

Triandis, H. C. (1960). Cognitive similarity and communication in dyad. *Human Relations* 13:175–183.

U.S. Department of Labor. (1972). *Handbook for Analyzing Jobs.* Washington, D.C.: U.S. Government Printing Office.

Von Glinow, M. A., and Chung, B. J. (1989). Comparative human resource management practices in the United States, Korea, and the People's Republic of China. In A. Nedd (ed.), *Research in Personnel and Human Resource Management.* Greenwich, CN: JAI Press, pp. 153–172.

Zack, A., and Block, R. (1979). *The Arbitration of Discipline Cases: Concepts and Questions.* New York: American Arbitration Association.

Zajonc, R. B., and Markus, H. (1982). Affective and cognitive factors in preferences. *Journal of Consumer Research* 9:123–131.

Managing Change: Organizational Success in the 1990s

CHAPTER OVERVIEW

This chapter has three basic objectives: to define and describe the process of change; to discuss a variety of techniques used to effect changes in job design and organizational culture; and to attempt an overview of the kinds of changes that can be expected in the next decade.

THEME CASE

"Milliken & Co.: Thriving on Chaos" tells of Roger Milliken's strategy of reevaluating his organization's competitive position and changing practices when necessary to maintain his company's edge; it is a paradigm for organizational survival in the 1990s.

CHAPTER OUTLINE

- Why Undertake Change?
- A Model of the Process of Managing Change
- Changes to the Structure of Work
- Changes in Organizational Culture
- The Shape of Things to Come: Environmental Impacts on the Organization in the 1990s
- Summary
- Managerial Insight

KEY DEFINITIONS

Change the process by which organizations adapt to new technologies and cultural or political pressures from both the external environment and the stakeholders they serve.

Change agent someone who facilitates effective change in an organization or in the behavior of its members.

Sociotechnical systems an approach to job design historically rooted in studies of the British coal mining industry. A balance of social and technical systems is sought by changing a number of specific organizational features and creating work groups.

Job characteristics an approach to task design derived as an alternative to the sociotechnical approach. This approach examines relationships among objective job attributes and employees' reactions to work.

Additional Terms

Evolutionary change
Strategic change
Force field analysis
Stream analysis
Needs analysis
Organizational development
Organizational transformation
Job rotation
Job enlargement
Job enrichment
Group working
Survey feedback
Team building
Quality circles (QCs)
Adviser-supportive techniques

MILLIKEN & CO.: THRIVING ON CHAOS

[In his book *Thriving on Chaos* Tom Peters starts out]

this book is dedicated to Roger Milliken of Milliken & Co. His genius in 1980 was to see that the answer to competition in the "mature" textile market was unparalleled quality attained largely through people. He revolutionized the company then. But he's almost unique because he saw in 1984 that the first revolution was wholly inadequate to meet the worldwide competitive challenge. So he made another revolution, reordering every relationship in the firm in pursuit of unparalleled customer responsiveness. Two revolutions in six years.

It is Roger Milliken's brand of urgency—and taste for radical reform—that must become the norm. For Milliken's two revolutions (and the firm was a star to begin with) are still only barely meeting the competitive challenge.

Milliken Mounts Another Revolution

It is becoming the norm at textile manufacturer Milliken. "It's a 'bet the company' move," an executive explains. That's a startling statement. The firm has long been its industry's leader in R&D and manufacturing technology. Finding that its traditional strengths were not adequate to meet the stepped-up challenges it faced from overseas, in 1981 Milliken mounted [an] all-out successful quality improvement program. . . .

Even so, the foreign onslaught continued unabated with most of the industry reeling from it. So Milliken mounted yet another revolution in 1985. Executives are now demanding, across the entire estimated $2.25 billion firm, nothing less than cuts of 90 percent in the time it takes to develop products and deliver them.

The first phase of Milliken's total customer responsiveness program consisted of mounting over 1,000 Customer Action Teams (CATs). Each was a self-contained effort to unearth new market opportunities in partnership with an existing customer. To launch a team, the customer had to agree to supply team members and join with Milliken representatives from manufacturing, sales, finance, and marketing in seeking creative solutions to better serving current markets or creating new ones. Each year hundreds of such projects are completed and hundreds of new ones are launched.

The details of a typical project make clear the sweeping nature of the firm's program. A two-year Partners for Profit program with apparel maker Levi Strauss has revolutionized the way the two firms do business together. First, Milliken capitalized on its unparalleled quality program. Given its belt, Milliken was even able to grasp some Limited Stores business that had long been filled by that firm's affiliated offshore plants.

The Milliken program is just gearing up, but cycle-shortening results are already astonishing. In a major carpet business, a six-week sample and product delivery cycle previously thought irreducible was cut to just five days. Another business's historic eighty-day cycle was reduced to three days—and twenty-four-hour response 100 percent of the time is now seen as an achievable goal.

Several elements, working in tandem, marked this latest Milliken revolution:

1. First, reminiscent of the quality revolution, was *top management commitment*. TCR was Revolution II. Letters from Roger Milliken never cease referring to the sense of urgency associated with this new operation.

2. Second, *the unparalleled success of the earlier quality program was the necessary foundation:* Without it, various partners such as Levi would have had no sound basis to move forward.

3. Third, the CATs and the projects with suppliers in the quality program paved the way for *a wholesale shift from adversarial to partnership relations* within and outside the firm. In 1980 Milliken epitomized the hierarchical, authoritarian, highly functionalized corporate organization. The CATs pulled sales, marketing, and the two strongest baronies, accounting and manufacturing, together, and this made possible the cooperation and the lowest-level, no-delay decision making that, much more than technology (as so many are finding out to their dismay), are the keys to TCR.

4. The fourth step was another breakthrough—*a complete shake-up, accomplished in 90 days across sixty plants, of the manufacturing organization structure*. In one move in 1985, the span of control in the plants went from one supervisor for every six nonsupervisors to a ratio of one to thirty-six. The freed-up supervisors, mostly called process engineers, are now first-class expediters. They ensure that new product samples are shepherded through the highly programmed system with alacrity and that phone calls from the various functions (customers, suppliers, etc.) are returned fast, with action taken. The increased number of in-plant process engineers is consistent with Japanese factory organization: in fact, Milliken

president Tom Malone launched the reorganization after carefully collecting data on Japanese factory organization in the course of over a dozen visits to that country.

Previously undreamed-of feats of multi-plant, multi-functional cooperation are now the daily norm with no letup in quality standards, which are constantly being tightened. This last point is vital. Since they were to be required to be so much more flexible, the company's plant managers at first pleaded for relief from quality standards. And indeed, the achievement of better quality and more flexibility simultaneously is a tall order. Perfection in production would seem to be at odds with satisfying small orders on a moment's notice. But once again, Milliken took chapters from Japan's book. Robert Hall, of Indiana University, elaborates in *Attaining Manufacturing Excellence:* "All Japanese motorcycle companies introduce several new models per month into plants already producing a large mix. Each day, after production is complete, some of the time remaining is used for trying the new tooling and arrangements for upcoming models. When it appears that production can go without a hitch, the new model is inserted into the production lineup for the succeeding schedule month. Any necessary finishing changes are incorporated at the end of the first or second month of production." This requisite increase in flexibility is possible only because of much tighter linkages among design, engineering, and manufacturing in Japan than in the United States. (This trait [was] also taught to the Japanese by American W. Edward Deming.) . . .

The Listeners

There's a certain image of Roger Milliken that I keep in my mind's eye. It's from his firm's annual strategy meeting at Calloway Gardens, Georgia, in 1986. Four grueling, down-to-the-wee-hours-of-the-morning sessions, no recreation—this is a survival exercise, as Roger sees it. He's just come out of a meeting with his company presidents and a few handpicked outsiders, in this case from Dana, IBM, and DuPont (and me). At the meeting, he probably asked sixty questions an hour. Each principal question was followed by five or ten more to get at the details, always the details—the real implementation story, not the gloss. In two-and-a-half hours he probably filled a quarter of a yellow legal pad with notes. (The next morning he'll turn the copious notes from this and other such sessions into his traditional meeting's-end speech—at which time he will announce a score of specific programs that will set the tone for the next twelve months.)

The participants of the meeting are exhausted from the intensity of this tireless 70-year-old, who's held the chief executive's job for over forty tumultuous years. We race back to our rooms for a fifteen-minute breather before the next grueling session commences—twenty-five action-packed small-group reports in ninety minutes. I happen to look up. There is Roger, pacing the corridor in front of his room, dictating at a staccato pace—yet more notes.

Listen. I don't know when it first occurred to me that I was observing a pattern. At our first Skunk Camp I watched Frank Perdue, the chicken king, and grocer sans pareil Stew Leonard engage in an Olympian struggle: Who would take the most notes?

Leonard won hands down, but even runner-up Perdue topped the rest of us put together, I'd bet. Both have been at their jobs, engaged, for decades. What was the subject? Milliken's president, Tom Malone, was describing the firm's quality program. Perdue, Mr. Quality to me already, rudely interrupted him dozens of times. He wanted clarification. Malone, a scientist, is as clear a speaker as I've heard, but he wasn't concrete enough for Frank. The reason became quickly clear. The next morning Perdue was up at 3 A.M. discussing with his people on the East Coast the implementation of the stuff he'd heard the day before. A major new executive compensation plan focused on quality and a landmark corporate training center were among the big ideas Perdue took from the seminar—and implemented in short order.

Stew Leonard didn't wait until 3 A.M. He was on the phone at lunch break. "Are you sure you know what this means?" I asked. "It makes sense, doesn't it?" was Stew's reply. Well, yes, I agreed. "So why wait?" Leonard snapped back. I had no rebuttal to that one.

Why Undertake Change?

When a business has invested billions of dollars in hiring and training its personnel, organizing their jobs into a coherent structure, developing plans for efficient communication, socializing those employees to adopt and pursue the organization's goals, and taking all the other myriad steps required to be successful, why would the organization's management want to change? The Milliken case suggests a major reason, growing competition. Other reasons can be imagined as well. Technological change can force, or provide the opportunity for, changes in processes. New environmental conditions— either opportunities such as the opening of new markets or constraints such as new regulations—can demand a response to maintain effectiveness. The list can go on, but the point is the same. As long as organizations exist in a world of environmental changes and competition, they will need to change. The need may not arise this year or even next, but it will come eventually, and the challenge must be met if the company is to succeed. The alternative is to perish.

It is not merely large organizations with long histories, like Milliken, that need to change. Any successful new venture is constantly facing the need to change, to adapt, to alter its products, procedures, or personnel policies as it grows and meets new challenges. Indeed, one of the major hurdles that a successful new business must cross is the transition from an energetic, entrepreneurial company capable of explosive growth to a larger, efficient, continuously responsive enterprise built for long-term profits and for maintaining a strong but less explosive rate of growth.

Given the need to change, organizational leaders have two choices. They can watch it happen, taking the role of observer. This approach to change is similar to the behavior described in the adage about the weather—everybody complains, but nobody does anything about it. The alternative course is to manage change.

Managing change is not an easy task. Organizations are complex entities composed of thousands of individuals and hundreds of groups. Structural and behavioral adjustments interact with one another as well as with technology and external forces (Leavitt, 1965; Friedlander and Brown, 1975; Peters and Waterman, 1982). Leavitt provides a model (see Figure 11.1) that recognizes that changes to structure, tasks, people, or technology cannot be made in an isolated manner. In essence, changing any one of these factors requires adjustment in the other three elements, as all are part of an interactive system.

Managing change may not be simple, but it is nevertheless the wiser of the two courses. Merely letting change wash over the organization allows

FIGURE 11.1
Factors That Interact in Organizational Change

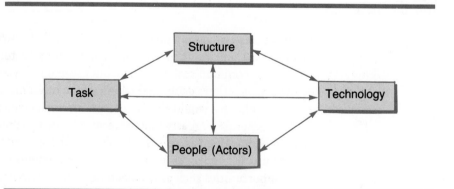

Source: H. J. Leavitt, "Applied Organizational Change in Industry: Structural, Technological, and Humanistic Approaches," in J. G. March (ed.), *Handbook of Organizations* (Chicago: Rand-McNally, 1965), p. 1145. Copyright © 1965 by Rand-McNally. Reprinted by permission.

the business to be swept this way and that by external or internal forces. Only by identifying the challenges that face the organization and choosing both direction and specific responses can the organization hope to ride the currents to a successful destination.

We will begin our exploration of managing change by first defining it and presenting a model for the process of managing it. We will then study how change is achieved by examining various techniques used to structure work tasks and detailing some principles of cultural change. We will close the chapter with a look ahead to the environmental conditions that managers may face in the 1990s.

Throughout this discussion, five issues will be apparent:

1. The degree of subordinates' participation in change

2. The selection and role of a change agent

3. The transferability of learned skills from the training room to the organization

4. The degree of top level support

5. The problem of resistance to change

The feature on the MSWD illustrates these five issues.

FEATURE: *The Case of the MSWD*

Changing the culture of an organization is a difficult, time-consuming, often gut-wrenching process. This is as true in public corporations as it is in the private domain. In fact, effecting such change in a public institution is, if anything, more difficult because of the number of legitimate constituencies—the public, legislators, unions, employees, special-interest groups—that can raise barriers to change. But change can be accomplished if a sufficient level of commitment is applied to the process for a long enough time. One example will reveal all the expenditures—of time, money, and morale—that are involved.

Metropolitan Sewer & Water District (MSWD—a major public wholesaler of these essential services to a large American city) is a public-sector corporation. It employs 2,500 people, has an annual budget of $75 million and spends $200 million a year on capital improvements. MSWD is one of the oldest public agencies of its kind in the country. . . .

[One of three problems] MSWD faced was rampant bureaucracy. . . . The state secretary on the environment was determined to "bring the MSWD into the twentieth century." . . . He knew, however, that revitalizing this moribund culture would be difficult and would have to be accomplished without major infusions of new management talent. Nevertheless, he and his new general manager, Ken Dillon (not his real name), were determined to take on the challenge.

Ken Dillon was a key figure in changing MSWD. Dillon was in his mid-fifties, semi-retired, and a successful entrepreneur when he took over the reins at MSWD. He was used to getting things done and making things happen. When he brought this attitude to the career-oriented bureaucratic environment of MSWD, it was like a breath of fresh air.

During the first several months in revitalizing MSWD, Dillon familiarized himself with the organization. . . . After six months of study, Dillon decided the time had come to act. To reshape the culture, he began by taking two major steps: he engaged consultants to supplement his staff in an aggressive change process, and he announced in a memo to MSWD's permanent complement of 2,500 employees that there would be no firings or layoffs as a result of the process he was launching. His objective, he said, was to work with the talented people of MSWD to improve its effectiveness. This second step turned out to be very significant later in the process since it helped buy time for some basic changes to take hold.

The team of four consultants spent its first six weeks learning about MSWD. In a meeting at the end of this period, the first gesture in the change process was decided on—to set up three major task forces of MSWD employees to work with the consultants on three commonly agreed-upon problem areas. The three areas selected were:

- Contracting . . .
- Operations and Maintenance (O & M) . . .
- Personnel . . .

. . . Meanwhile, Dillon initiated a weekly series of staff meetings with the chief operating officer, functional officer, functional managers, and their assistants. . . .

During their first week of work, the task forces accomplished little. Members were not used to working in this fashion; many of them felt uncomfortable in this new role. By the second week the members began to open up in their meetings. For example, engineers on the contracting task force admitted disappointment when projects they had worked on were not received warmly by operations personnel. They were astonished to learn that the operations people were often distressed when the engineers did not consult them about projects they were working on and when they delivered equipment that was hard to operate and maintain. Both sides agreed that better communication on projects between the two sides was definitely called for. In the other task forces, similar revelations occurred—to everyone's amazement.

By the third week, all three task forces were hard at work trying to formulate recommendations to deal with the problems they had identified. Their recommendations—delivered during the seventh week—were reviewed by Dillon, senior management, and the advisory committee.

Awaiting management's response, the task forces had gone back to work on their recommendations. . . . Everyone seemed more and more committed to the change process as time went on. . . .

Six months later, no one could doubt that the MSWD was significantly different. There was still too much paper and too much conformance to the book, but there was also a clear set of agreed-upon priorities, a sense of real urgency in pursuing these priorities, and the beginnings of a "we can make it happen" mentality.

Source: T. E. Deal and A. A. Kennedy, *Corporate Cultures: The Rites and Rituals of Corporate Life* (Reading, MA: Addison-Wesley, 1982), pp. 169–174. Copyright © 1982 by Addison-Wesley Publishing Company. Reprinted by permission of Addison-Wesley Publishing Company, Inc., Reading, MA.

A Model of the Process of Managing Change

Change is the process by which organizations adapt to new technologies and cultural or political pressures coming from the external environment or from any stakeholders, or constituents, whom they serve. Another definition of change (Schein, 1987) is the "induction of new patterns of action, beliefs, and attitudes among substantial segments of a population." As Tichy (1983) pointed out, this definition is somewhat ambiguous, sounding more like a definition of sociopolitical and economic trends than of something manageable. Yet if we accept that this induction can occur deliberately—can be impelled from within the organization—this definition adds a useful element to our understanding of change.

A more specific definition distinguishes two basic kinds of organizational change. **Evolutionary change** is brought on by external pressures, which are largely out of the realm of management control. Examples would be the dramatic changes in Eastern Europe in 1989 and 1990. **Strategic change** refers to non-routine pressures that cause organizational adjustments in structure, roles, and goals (Tichy, 1983). Though it is important to make this distinction, it is worth remembering that both types of change must be of concern to organizations that aim to grow and survive.

Bear in mind, as well, that whether the impetus for change is internal or external, the rate of change can vary from rapid to slow and the degree to which change can be anticipated can vary as well. The environmental changes associated with the establishment of one Western European market in 1992 have been building for years; many rules, regulations, and procedures were created in advance of 1992, giving organizations advance notice of how to behave. The changes wrought in Eastern Europe at the beginning of the 1990s, on the other hand, were dramatic, rapid, and unpredictable and will have unpredictable effects on planned change in Western Europe.

Lewin (1951) studied change using **force field analysis** to determine the factors that promote and impede change. His model proposes that planned change encompasses three phases:

1. *Unfreezing:* Preparing for change, creating a felt need for change, and coping with resistance to it

2. *Moving:* Implementing the change by modifying behavior, tasks, technology, or structure

3. *Refreezing:* Evaluating the change and reinforcing or modifying it

We expand on Lewin's basic model to establish the integrated framework of change shown in Figure 11.2. Like other models of change, this framework assumes a planned, problem-oriented, systematic, and system-wide approach to managing change. The major elements in this framework are problem awareness and diagnosis, selection and implementation of solutions, and assessment and evaluation of results of the attempted solution. We will examine each of these elements in detail.

Problem Awareness and Diagnosis

Becoming aware of problems and carefully delineating them represent the first step in nearly every model of the process of managing change. A common obstacle to change is the mistake of omission (Hartley, 1986), or being unaware of the need to change and therefore settling for the status quo. This was not the case at Milliken, where management clearly perceived the need to alter practices to remain competitive. Perceptual biases that all people share (see Chapter 5), however, may prevent managers in other organizations from correctly identifying the need for change.

Once the firm is aware of a need for change, diagnosis begins. A systematic diagnosis of an organization, its personnel, and their work provides

FIGURE   11.2
An Integrated Framework for Managing Change

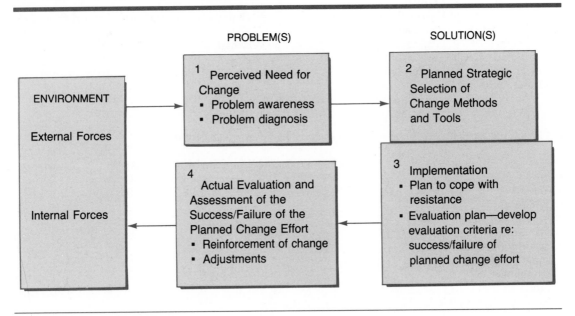

the basis for strategic actions that follow. It can be difficult, however, to diagnose and clearly define problems in a constantly changing environment.
Weisbord (1987) cautions that, with rapidly advancing technologies, rising
competition, and shifting worker needs, "nothing holds still long enough to
be diagnosed and changed anyway" (p. 13). Milliken is a good example. The
company was in the midst of one revolution when its chief decided that yet
other changes were needed. Yet the Milliken example also shows that problem diagnosis can occur even in the midst of a changing environment.

We offer one final note on diagnosis. To reduce resistance and help
prepare them for change, organizational members who will be affected by
the change should be involved in diagnostic efforts (see Chapters 4, 8, and 9
for discussions of participation). Knowing an organization needs to change
and getting it to change are two very different things. Employee involvement is a key to implementing change.

For the problem to be diagnosed correctly, information is needed.
There are a number of ways to gather such data.

Interviews and Questionnaires   Interviews offer a good deal of flexibility
to probe and seek out rich responses to questions. Questionnaires are usually more focused and are standardized to facilitate analysis. A sample page

FIGURE 11.3 *Sample Diagnostic Questionnaire*

SEX
○ Female
○ Male

SERVICE
○ Less than 1 year
○ 1–5 years
○ 6–10 years
○ 11–15 years
○ Over 15 years

RACE OR ETHNIC GROUP
○ White
○ Black
○ Hispanic
○ Asian/Pacific Islander
○ American Indian or Alaskan native
○ Other
○ I would prefer not to answer this question

2. What is your estimate of morale among people in this location?

	Exempt	Nonexempt
a. Very high	①	②
b. High	①	②
c. Neither high nor low	①	②
d. Low	①	②
e. Very low	①	②
f. Don't know	①	②

1. In terms of your present facilities (office, work area, etc.) how satisfied are you with the following?

	Very Satisfied	Satisfied	Neither	Dissatisfied	Very Dissatisfied
a. Space	①	②	③	④	⑤
b. Privacy	①	②	③	④	⑤
c. Equipment	①	②	③	④	⑤
d. Appearance and furnishings	①	②	③	④	⑤
e. Security (belongings, confidential material, etc.)	①	②	③	④	⑤
f. Cleanliness	①	②	③	④	⑤
g. Noise level	①	②	③	④	⑤
h. Function (how well it works)	①	②	③	④	⑤
i. Status (reflects your position to public and/or employees)	①	②	③	④	⑤

17. This firm clearly has a goal to be the "best" at what it does.　① ② ③ ④ ⑤ ⑥ ⑦ ⑨　Being the "best" is an idea that is rarely even mentioned.

26. In this firm, people are encouraged and given enough rein to be creative.　① ② ③ ④ ⑤ ⑥ ⑦ ⑨　Organizational procedures and rules actually discourage creativity.

54. How do you feel about the leadership and direction you receive? I am:
○ Very satisfied
○ Well satisfied
○ Only moderately satisfied
○ Somewhat dissatisfied
○ Very dissatisfied

75. For the job I do, I feel the amount of money I make is:
○ Very good
○ Good
○ Neither good nor poor
○ Poor
○ Very poor

89. The compensation system provides a real incentive for high performance.
○ Definitely yes
○ Yes
○ No

109. How do you generally feel about the peer group with whom you work?
○ They are the best group I could ask for
○ I work well with them
○ I have no feeling one way or the other
○ They are sometimes hard to work with
○ They are often very hard to work with

119. Belonging to this Organization automatically brings respect from other business or professional people.
○ Definitely yes
○ Yes
○ No
○ Definitely no
○ Don't know

Source: F. Smith and Organizational Studies, Inc., personal communication, (1986). Reprinted by permission.

from an employee survey questionnaire designed to examine workplace conditions is reproduced in part in Figure 11.3. Demographic questions (about the employee's gender, years of service, and race) should be included in such a survey instrument, as well as specific questions about satisfaction with work, pay and benefits, and other key components of the organization. Income and position are important demographic questions to ask as well.

Observation   Another common method of gathering data is observation, in which consultants observe the daily behaviors and work performance of individual managers and workers in the plant or office. This technique calls for highly skilled observers. Clearly, distortions may cloud results if the observer does not focus on behavior that is in fact typical of the observed person. Further distortion may occur if the observation is made at a time or a place that is out of the ordinary. The presence of an observer may in itself distort findings, as workers and managers alike try to please an expert, hide problems, or manipulate perceptions, rather than act normally.

Historical Records   Historical records, or secondary sources, can be used to provide a check or cross validation on perceptual findings. If the different methods garner similar results, validity is clearly more likely. If results are not the same, further analysis is needed to understand the differences that are found. Either way, the findings are enriched, and the results can be examined with more care. Examples of secondary data sources are records indicating past company performance; absenteeism, tardiness, and turnover rates; and quality and productivity information.

A note of caution: secondary data were most often gathered for purposes other than to diagnose the issue presently under study. As a consequence the data may not directly address the issues being investigated. Also, these data were gathered by persons other than the present researchers and therefore may contain unknown biases and inconsistencies.

Stream Analysis   The technique called **stream analysis** begins by identifying which organizational dimensions will be affected if change is to occur. Changes are seen as a stream or sequence of actions occurring over a period of time; the actions and their impact are constantly reevaluated and the course of action modified if necessary.

Members of the organization provide information on their perceptions of the problems and the strengths and weaknesses of the organization. However, identifying categories of information from streams goes beyond totaling members' beliefs about the nature of their problems. Graphic tools are used to depict these streams, and charts are created that lay out the change interventions to be made over time. The charts thus create a timetable and also show key linkages both between components of a stream and between different streams.

Needs Analysis   A less comprehensive approach to problem diagnosis, a **needs analysis** could be performed to gather data about a specific issue— say, personnel training needs within a firm. For example, a representative sample of a firm's work force might be interviewed or questioned about problems in their departments. Subsequently, leadership styles or motivational problems may be analyzed and uncovered as areas in need of improvement or change that can be affected by training. Performance evaluation data (see Chapter 10) can also be useful to identify career development needs for which an employee can get training and counseling.

Political Diagnosis   Researchers have only recently begun to study systematically the role of politics in organizational efforts to change. A political diagnosis attempts to identify the powerful players in an organization and their domains, examine the components of their power bases, and determine how and toward what ends a player uses her skills and power. Cobb (1986) suggests making this diagnosis at various levels: individual, group, coalitions, and within a network. He examines power in terms of resource allocation among players, their interests and characteristics, and the situational context within which they operate.

Cobb (1986) suggests three methods for use in a political diagnosis:

1. *Position analysis* identifies those with legitimate power and the issues they focus on. Formal organizational charts, the primary tool in this analysis, are extended to include positions not often found on the charts, such as legal counsel.

2. *Reputational analysis* identifies those with referent power. Because this analysis is based on information that organizational members supply, it extends political diagnosis to include informal elements.

3. *Decision analysis* seeks out those who have, in the past, influenced directly and indirectly decision making, including decision networks that cluster around key issues.

Selecting and Implementing Change Solutions

Once the problem is clarified and diagnosed, the next step is to select and implement a solution. Even though the step may be stated simply, it is, of course, quite complex. A key feature of choosing a course is using the diagnosis; the point of analyzing the problem is to provide answers to the question, "What's wrong?" If those answers are ignored, that first step was a worthless exercise. Unfortunately, biases and preconceptions and fears can lead managers to ignore or misinterpret the data provided.

Whatever solution is chosen must be sure to address the problem. If the problem is poor organizational performance due to low worker output, the change must address the cause of that low output. If outdated technology is the cause, the solution may be investment in new equipment. If low motivation leads to low output, a people-oriented solution is required.

Greiner (1967) suggested three approaches that managers can follow for selecting a solution: management can (1) share the decision about how to resolve the problem, (2) autocratically decide on a solution, or (3) delegate the responsibility for finding a solution. As we have discussed elsewhere on the question of participation (see Chapters 4, 7, and 9), opinion on which approach is best varies, but as the next feature indicates, participation may be an effective tool for reducing resistance.

FEATURE: *Overcoming Resistance to Change*

In the mid-1940s, Lester Coch and John French noticed that factory workers were resistant to changes in products and production methods. They asked two questions: why do people resist change? and what can be done to overcome that resistance?

They went to Harwood Manufacturing and examined the afterchange learning curves of several hundred workers rated as standard or better prior to job changes. They found that 38 percent of those workers achieved that standard of production shortly after change was introduced, but that "62 percent either became chronically substandard operators or quit" (Coch and French, 1948, p. 514).

Finding that relearning was often slower than initially learning the job, these authors designed two experiments to illustrate the forces creating resistance and to illustrate mechanisms for overcoming them. First they employed two variations of democratic procedures in handling groups to be transferred. In one group they used representatives of the workers in designing job changes. In two other groups they instituted total participation in designing job changes. A fourth group, with no participation at all, served as the control group.

After job changes were complete, the control group did not improve. Frustration was high, some aggression was seen, and 17 percent of the group quit. The group with representation improved markedly after the job changes, but the two groups with complete participation improved even more.

About three months after the initial experiment, what was left of the control group (13 workers) was brought together in a job change that involved total participation. With this approach, their performance improved rapidly—up to the level of the other groups.

Coch and French's study was repeated at a Norwegian shoe factory (French, Israel, and As, 1960), but without producing the same results. Whether cultural differences are contributing factors to these different results is not clear.

The planned change must consider ways of reducing resistance because resistance will inevitably occur. Some managers and workers, used to current policies, strategies, and structure, might actively suppress information that might bring about change. They might prefer the greater predictability of the status quo or wish to maintain a position of power that they fear would be jeopardized by change. As Fitzgerald (1988) points out, cultural change might also attack the workers' underlying values, which will surely beget resistance. Neumann (1989) believes that resistance has largely been ascribed to personality factors but evidence for this is lacking. She argued that structural, relational, and societal factors can promote resistance as well.

Implementing change includes determining when, where, and to what degree actions are to be taken. When and where to implement change are decisions influenced by external forces, as the Milliken example showed. The need to respond to the environment often compels change.

The issue of degree of change depends on how specific and focused change techniques will be—whether on certain jobs or individuals, on a key department, or on the total organization. Many organizations now pilot test new programs in one production unit. The future, however, calls for a system-wide cultural revolution of the type undertaken by MSWD and Milliken.

Whatever the approach, certain behavioral variables must be addressed if change is to succeed. Porras and Hoffer (1986) interviewed 42 leading theorists and practitioners of **organizational development,** the field concerned with devising structures to accommodate both organizational needs for effectiveness and individual needs for growth and satisfaction. These leaders described a set of behavioral variables fundamental to all successful efforts at organizational change, as summarized in Figure 11.4.

FIGURE 11.4
Behavioral Variables Required for Successful Organizational Change

At All Organizational Levels
Communicating openly
Collaborating
Taking responsibility
Maintaining a shared vision
Solving problems effectively
Respecting/supporting
Processing/facilitating interactions
Inquiring
Experimenting

At the Managerial Level
Generating participation
Leading by vision
Functioning strategically
Promoting information flow
Developing others

Source: Adapted with permission from NTL Institute, "Common Behavior Changes in Successful Organization Development Efforts," by Jerry I. Porras and Susan J. Hoffer, Table 3, p. 485, *Journal of Applied Behavioral Science*, Vol. 22, No. 4, copyright © 1986.

Monitoring and Evaluating Change

Many early models of the change process neglected the final stages of monitoring and evaluation, steps crucial to successful change. Seashore, Lawler, Mirvis, and Cammaunn (1983) presented a series of readings that offered a comprehensive look at the importance of accurately assessing the progress and impact of a planned change effort. Early cases of assessment were often limited to "testimonials" and lacked a scientific approach. Seashore pointed out that many problems with assessment were associated with poorly evaluated but popular change techniques, including the fact that time acts to contaminate findings. Longitudinal studies—of two, five, or ten years—are often called for by researchers but neglected by the consultants and change agents who implement the changes and then depart for other assignments.

Tichy (1983) points out that we must develop criteria for evaluating change during the planning phase of that particular change, before implementation begins. These criteria essentially consist of the desired goals of the change effort itself. In Chapter 1 we discussed the importance of setting clear and feasible operational goals. The same guidelines apply here, with the added proviso that the goals be measurable in some way so that they can indeed be evaluated.

Beer (1987) reminds us of another problem associated with assessing the progress of "soft" cultural change in organizations. Soft cultural change is directed more to issues like attitudes than to, for example, structural change. If attitudes are not measured to determine whether there is progress, organizational members will likely revert to "harder" pressures in response to change attempts.

The key to effective assessment is definition of clear objectives, but, as change progresses, progress toward these objectives should be monitored and desired behavior or other changes reinforced. Thus individuals are provided with critical feedback and reinforcement as the change takes place, thus improving the "refreezing" process.

If we view refreezing as a process, we may better avoid one clear danger of refreezing—implementation of an inflexible system that cannot adapt to future changes. The notion of a mid-point assessment allows the organization to fine-tune various elements of its change effort before unwanted refreezing occurs. In sum, assessment should be ongoing, and any new modes of behavior created by a change effort must be subject to future change if the need arises.

Hampden-Turner (1990) presents the necessity of constant reevaluation in his metaphor of the leader as helmsman. The helmsman sets a course and moves the wheel. The wind and current make the ship respond differently than intended, requiring the helmsman to set a new course, at which the cycle repeats itself. This useful metaphor is lacking in one respect: organizational leaders also must be attuned to the possibility that mere corrections in course are not the only possible responses to the environment. It may be necessary to redefine the destination, to remove the affects of wind and current by somehow changing the environment, or to overcome constant environmental constraints by changing technology—converting the ship into a plane, as it were.

The Role of the Change Agent

In the two sets of changes studied, Milliken and MSWD, we saw the importance of an individual committed to the idea of change overseeing the change process. This individual is a **change agent,** someone who facilitates effective change in an organization or the behavior of its members. Such an instigator may be a consultant, an outsider hired to take control (as Dillon was brought to MSWD), or an insider (Milliken).

If the change agent is an outsider, top management must provide her with strong support lest insiders resist her efforts. Since trust in the change agent is an essential part of effective change, top management must take steps to engender that trust. Obvious support such as an introductory letter or meeting, in which management presents the change agent and establishes the importance of her task, is useful. Employee participation in the selection of the change agent may be helpful in establishing trust. The external change agent must remember that she may be viewed suspiciously. The agent who is isolated, self-centered, or emotional may create problems for herself.

Weisbord (1973) notes the importance of a clear contract between the organization and the external change agent. The contract should spell out how the consultant will proceed from beginning to end. Weisbord distinguishes contracts involving the relationship of client to consultant from contracts involving the change agent role. In expert contracts, the consultant is hired to analyze and solve a problem using his expertise. Situations involving change agents are more collaborative, and the consultant's recommendations or actions must address the organization's expectations and wishes. In the end the effective change agent must mesh his role with the power systems and the business processes operating in the organization (Beer and Walton, 1990).

Internal change agents face different problems. Possessing a past history, as they do, they may be associated with one clique or another; thus power configurations or network interrelationships may affect how easily they are accepted. Yet familiarity with the organization may help in managing the change process, but actions might be perceived as favoritism. Kaplan, Drath, and Kofodimos (1987) suggest an important consideration for internal change agents: that psychological preparedness for change is a crucial characteristic of executives. They propose a method called "biographical action research" to study executives' character and to identify ways that such preparedness may be developed.

Shepard (1975) offers change agents a list of eight rules of thumb:

1. *Stay alive.* Do not self-sacrifice unnecessarily.

2. *Start where the system is.* Begin by diagnosing the current situation, even if diagnosis is resisted.

3. *Never work uphill.* Use a collaborative approach.

4. *Innovation requires a good idea, initiative, and a few friends.* Get allies to help contend with the myriad forces involved.

5. *Load experiments for success.* Make efforts to ensure that steps to be taken will work.

6. *Light many fires.* Because organizations involve many subsystems, actions must address more than one.

7. *Keep an optimistic bias.* Be alert to constructive forces as well as destructive ones.

8. *Capture the moment.* Have as many alternatives as possible.

The successful change agent recognizes that the answer is not always to overcome resistance to change (Harrison, 1970). Indeed, resistance to change may be valuable feedback that a good change agent may use to identify what some members of the organization feel is important. Change agents can use various techniques to work with resisters, including education, communication, participation, negotiation, and facilitation. Indeed, employee response to change, both the unplanned, environmental and planned, directed sorts, is coming under increasing scrutiny. *The American Psychologist* recently (February 1990) devoted an entire issue to this topic.

Fitzgerald (1988) offers some cautions to the would-be change agent—and to the organization that wants to change its culture. Reminding us that ethnologists now question the biases hidden in their studies of other cultures, he wonders if change agents are not guilty of a certain arrogance. "If I view as essentially insulting an uninvited attempt to make me over into someone else's vision of a better human being, should it be any less offensive to the hired hands?" (p. 13). He goes on to argue that resistance to change should not be viewed as the expression of a "frozen" attitude, which implies that the person holding the attitude is somehow wrong. Rather, change agents need to consider the question of the workers' right to maintain their long-held values.

This is essentially an argument of ethics. White and Wooten (1983) also pursued this issue by identifying five areas in which ethical dilemmas for change agents may arise: misrepresentation or collusion, misuse of data, manipulation and coercion, value and goal conflict, and technical ineptness. The authors point out that the great variety of change agents' backgrounds makes establishing common ethical standards and policing behavior problematical.

Changes to the Structure of Work

Change can affect the way work is performed, or it can be aimed at the organizational culture. Research into the restructuring of work, which has gone on for years, is the field known as *organizational development*. The study of company-wide reorientation may be called **organizational transformation**. As Bartunek and Louis (1988) point out, researchers in these two fields engage in somewhat similar work:

> Both groups are concerned about the culture of an organization, its shared meanings, beliefs, and values. Both groups have a special interest in how culture may change. Moreover, OD interventions sometimes require organizational transformation to be successful. . . . However, . . . they frequently address different questions regarding change. The primary focus of OD is on processes

through which to facilitate (often) pre-specified changes. . . . In contrast, the primary focus of organizational transformation is on a mapping of patterns of change in organizational form (such as, for example, changes in the organization's mission, values, and structure). (p. 99)

We will study the former type of change, organizational development, first. Numerous typologies of change techniques exist. We follow Friedlander and Brown's (1975) categorization of these techniques as technostructural, or system-wide, strategies and human-process, or behaviorally based, strategies. The former strategies are aimed at entire organizations or systems, though they focus on the structure of tasks. The latter attempt to resolve problems with or improve individual performance. The techniques within each of these two broad categories, which will be discussed in the following pages, are the following:

1. *Technostructural strategies:*   sociotechnical systems approach; job characteristics approach

2. *Human-process strategies:*   survey feedback, team building, quality circles, adviser-supportive techniques

Before examining these two sets of strategies, let us consider the more basic question: should jobs be restructured?

Job Restructuring

Deciding to Restructure   Campion and Thayer (1985) suggest that managers need to analyze job design efforts from more than one perspective. They differentiate among four different approaches to job design—the motivational, mechanistic, biological, and perceptual-motor approaches—and assigned different positive and negative outcomes to each approach (see Figure 11.5, page 560). They point out that too often jobs are developed in a haphazard manner without sufficient consideration of the needs of workers and their skills and limitations. Or, if consideration is given to workers, it is often based on only one of the four approaches and thus can have unintended consequences.

When contemplating job redesign, the first step is to determine whether the job is a good candidate for change. It is if the following characteristics exist (Aldag and Brief, 1979):

1. Workers perceive the job as monotonous and simple.

2. Rewards such as wages are sufficiently high that they are not perceived as problems.

FIGURE 11.5
Positive and Negative Relationships of Four Approaches to Job Design

Job Design Approach	Outcome
Motivational	+ Satisfaction − Efficiency
Mechanistic	+ Efficiency + Reliability − Satisfaction − Comfort
Biological	+ Comfort + Satisfaction + Efficiency + Reliability
Perceptual/Motor	+ Reliability + Comfort + Satisfaction + Efficiency

Source: M. A. Campion and P. W. Thayer, "Development and Field Evaluation of an Inter-disciplinary Measure of Job Design," *Journal of Applied Psychology* 70 (1985):29–43. Copyright © 1985 by the American Psychological Association. Reprinted by permission of the American Psychological Association and the authors.

3. It is possible to change production methods given the constraints of the existing facilities and technology or it is economically feasible to replace current technology.

4. Present and future workers are ready for job redesign.

How to Redesign a Job   If these criteria are met, job redesign efforts may lead to improved satisfaction and performance. The first step is to designate a task force to perform some type of job analysis. After examining the nature of the target job, the task force should examine how that job is linked to other jobs and how changes in it may influence them. Discussions should be held with job incumbents to supplement the other information collected. Then task force members should discuss their own thoughts about the value of changing the job; if they still feel that the job should be redesigned, they should then begin designing specific job changes.

Once mechanisms for change are decided, the task force should select a set of people to try out the redesign and then it should evaluate its impact on them. Change often brings about a number of unintended consequences; this process is a way to identify them. If the change works, steps can be taken to implement it elsewhere in the organization (Aldag and Brief, 1979).

Technostructural Techniques for Managing Change

Many strategies for changing organizations have been posited to deal with the total system, including Likert's systems 4 model, management by objectives, the managerial grid, and several others. These models attack problems by changing the structure, design, technology and tasks, leadership, and decision-making processes of an organization—in essence, its very fabric. We will now briefly describe two of these organization-wide change approaches and then explore some specific techniques for job restructuring.

The two system-wide approaches we will consider are the sociotechnical systems and the job characteristics approaches. The sociotechnical systems approach was developed at the Tavistock Institute in Great Britain and applied in a number of European countries. It traces its inception to the late 1940s. The job characteristics approach to change was developed in the United States beginning in the early 1960s (Turner and Lawrence, 1965). Task design studies derived from the job characteristics approach dominated the organizational literature in the 1970s and probably distracted many researchers from more fruitful pursuits (Roberts and Glick, 1981).

The Sociotechnical Systems Approach to Task Design   The basic tenets of the **sociotechnical systems** approach to job design can be traced back to work in the British coal industry in the late 1940s (Trist and Bamforth, 1951). In the coal mine studied, the cycle of getting coal involved three operations: preparation, concerned with making coal more accessible and workable; getting, in which the coal was loaded and transported away from the face; and advancing, in which roof supports, gateway haulage roads, and conveyor equipment were built. These jobs were done by independent, small teams, each working the whole cycle.

Mechanization and specialization were introduced with the expectation of achieving higher productivity. The organization now required different teams to work independently in shifts, but the nature of their tasks made them interdependent. Unfortunately, each team optimized each job for itself, but, in doing so, created safety problems for the next team. Instead of enabling the workers to cooperate, the new system created intergroup conflict, which resulted in backbiting, individualism, and high absenteeism, all contributing to low productivity.

The researchers realized that if one optimizes the technical system at the expense of the social system, the results will be less than optimal. Yet this happens in many organizations—such as rigorously routinized organizations like nuclear power plants or air traffic control systems.

From the coal mining experiments and a set of experiments on work restructuring at the Calico Mills in Ahmedabad, India (Rice, 1958), a set of general criteria were formulated pertaining to job content, design, and

FIGURE 11.6

*Changes
Suggested by the
Sociotechnical
Approach*

At the Individual Level
1. Optimum variety of tasks
2. A meaningful pattern of tasks that gives each job a semblance of an overall task
3. Optimum length for the work cycle
4. Some scope for setting standards of quality and quantity of production and suitable feedback on the results
5. Inclusion in the job of some auxiliary and preparatory (boundary) tasks
6. Inclusion in tasks of some degree of care, skill, knowledge, or effort worthy of respect in the community
7. Contributing in some way to the utility of the product for the customer

At the Group Level
1. Providing interlocked tasks, job rotation, or physical proximity where there is job interdependence
2. Providing interlocked tasks, job rotation, or physical proximity where individual jobs entail relatively high degrees of stress
3. Providing interlocked tasks, job rotation, or physical proximity where individual jobs don't make an obvious perceivable contribution to the utility of the end product
4. Where a number of jobs are linked by interlocking tasks or job relation, they should:
   a. Have some semblance of an overall task that contributes to the utility of the product
   b. Have some scope for setting standards and receiving knowledge of results
   c. Have some control over boundary tasks (tasks that are of a service or voluntary character)

Source: L. Klein (1976). *New Forms of Work Organization.* London: Cambridge University Press. Reprinted by permission.

meaning in the larger setting. These criteria were meant not only to supply technical efficiency but to meet the social needs of the workers. These general criteria were developed into a more specific set of objective criteria applicable to industrial jobs at both the individual and group level, as shown in Figure 11.6.

Most sociotechnical change projects involve two major facets: the adjustment of a number of specific organizational features and the creation of work groups. The features targeted may include jobs, rewards, physical equipment, spatial arrangements, work schedules, and so on. None of these is perceived as a primary focus of activity; rather, all aspects of organizational operations that might affect either how well work is done or the quality of member relations are examined. This is one reason such experiments are difficult to evaluate—it can never be known which change made a specific difference.

A major contribution of the sociotechnical systems approach to the theory and practice of work design is the *autonomous work group* (Cummings, 1978). Such groups are usually relatively small, and members share among themselves much of the decision making about how work should be done. These groups are related in some ways to quality circles, team building, and other group approaches to work restructuring.

Autonomous work groups are an increasingly popular innovation in and of themselves and are often seen in change projects that are not guided explicitly by a sociotechnical approach. One such example is the well-known case of the General Foods pet-food plant in Topeka, Kansas (Walton, 1972). The Topeka plant, completed in 1971, is a model of innovation in work organization and in the high degree of responsibility and freedom given its workers. The plant was developed to overcome absenteeism problems experienced elsewhere in the company, problems associated with poor motivation, high waste, costly recycling, and so on. The program was successful, but because employees in the plant were specially selected, the effort was criticized as nonrepresentative. The company later tried a similar effort in a new confectionery factory in Reims, France, with similarly good results (Bailey, 1983).

The generalizability of the sociotechnical systems approach to white-collar environments has been examined. Pava (1983) illustrated a case of sociotechnical change applied with success to such work. Barko and Pasmore (1986) and Cummings (1986) suggest that although concepts and research have primarily focused on blue-collar work environments, ample evidence suggests that sociotechnical change can be adapted to today's service organizations.

They also recognized that this approach to planned change is based on beliefs in workplace democracy and the importance of organizational choice, whose roots are more European than American. Perhaps modification of sociotechnical systems strategies are needed if its notions are to be more widely adapted around the world, where beliefs and values do not support these assumptions as consistently. These differing beliefs also serve to explain why the job characteristics approach to task design emerged in the United States as an alternative to the sociotechnical model.

The Job Characteristics Approach to Task Design   The **job characteristics** approach was introduced in the United States in the early 1970s (Hackman and Lawler, 1971). Its roots are in a study (Turner and Lawrence, 1965) that examined relationships among objective attributes of jobs and employees' reactions to their work. Job satisfaction was found to be higher when jobs where characterized by variety of work, employee autonomy in performing work, high degrees of interaction to carry out the task, a high number of opportunities for interaction, a high level of knowledge required to do the job, and a high degree of responsibility entrusted to the job holder.

Using the Turner and Lawrence work as a springboard, Hackman and his co-workers (e.g., Hackman and Lawler, 1971; Hackman and Oldham, 1975, 1980) initially focused on four job characteristics: variety, task identity (doing a whole piece of work), autonomy, and job-based feedback. They predicted that when these characteristics are present in a job, the jobholder feels more satisfaction. Later they added a fifth job characteristic: task significance.

These core characteristics promote job satisfaction and high-quality work if the worker measures high levels on three "critical psychological states": the employee has knowledge of the results of her work, she experiences responsibility for the work, and she experiences the work as meaningful. Because these are internal states, they are not manipulable. What can be manipulated are objective properties of the job that can influence these states—the core characteristics. The employee's reaction to the configuration of the core characteristics is influenced by three other factors. She must have the knowledge and skill to do the job, have a high level of growth-need strength (similar to Maslow's growth needs), and be satisfied with the overall organizational context (see Figure 11.7).

A number of criticisms have been leveled at the job characteristics approach (e.g., Roberts and Glick, 1981), chief among them being the question of whether employees respond to objective characteristics of jobs or redefine their situations, as suggested by social information processing theory (for example, Blau and Katerberg, 1982). Another concern is that the variations caused by individual differences may make the model too unwieldy—due both to the amount of individual variety and the changing nature of personal characteristics.

Various Forms of Work Change   It might be useful to think about work restructuring as occurring on either a horizontal or a vertical plane. Horizontal restructuring is concerned with the specialization of tasks at the same level, and vertical restructuring with specialization of functions and divisions at different organizational levels. Work restructuring can take a number of forms, the most popular being job rotation, job enlargement, job enrichment, and group working.

Job rotation involves rotating people among jobs at the same level. It can increase job variety and promote the use of different skills and the opportunity to learn. It can also give the manager increased staff flexibility. Workers view job rotation both positively and negatively because, although it may increase productivity, in some cases it simply represents more work for an employee.

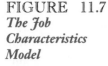

FIGURE 11.7
The Job Characteristics Model

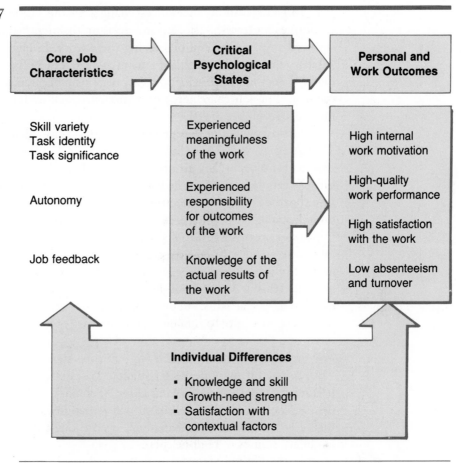

Source: H. R. Hackman and G. R. Oldham, *Work Redesign* (Reading, MA: Addison-Wesley, 1980), p. 90. Copyright © 1980 by Addison-Wesley Publishing Company. Reprinted by permission of Addison-Wesley Publishing Company, Reading, MA.

Job enlargement combines the number of tasks on a horizontal plane to create more complete and more meaningful jobs. It reduces specialization and the control of working pace established by an assembly line. If implemented poorly, the technique groups unrelated tasks, which minimizes its positive aspects. The value of job enlargement depends on the current skills and attitudes of employees; workers who cannot handle increased tasks or who perceive the change as a management attempt to exploit them will not benefit from this technique. Neither job enlargement nor job rotation are good techniques for increasing autonomy or decision making.

Job enrichment introduces changes in the vertical plane by giving employees more responsibility and decision making. People might be more involved in planning and organizing their work, in quality control, and in auxiliary tasks such as supply or maintenance. The aim of this strategy is to increase decision making, autonomy, responsibility, recognition, and development. The job characteristics approach is one example of a job enrichment program.

Group working recognizes the significance of interacting at work. This strategy is inherent in the sociotechnical systems approach to task design. Employers can group in any number of ways (Burbridge, 1976). Groups can be formed on the basis of common assembly work (e.g., the putting together of a car or electronic component). They can be formed based on a particular technology, as when machines are grouped for purposes of improving processing. Groups can be formed to join together operators who take responsibility for the output of a particular line, or they can be formed around office and service operations. Advantages of group structuring include increasing worker confidence through recognition of important skills; developing social skills, support, security, and encouragement; and providing the opportunity to influence and exercise leadership (Bailey, 1983).

Experience in Work Restructuring   Europe stands out in experience with work restructuring. One writer (Bailey, 1983) cites 1,000 restructuring experiments underway in Sweden alone. Denmark and Norway follow Sweden. Holland, France, and Italy provide some few examples. Work restructuring lags in the United Kingdom, even though the Tavistock Institute's landmark studies were done there.

In the United States work restructuring efforts have been limited primarily to departments or to small organizations. Here such efforts are often devoid of theory, though many are based on Herzberg's notions of motivation (see Chapter 9), which are not entirely inconsistent with the job characteristics approach. In the Far East there are few efforts at restructuring. One might categorize the Japanese use of quality circles as consistent with various aspects of the sociotechnical systems and job characteristics approaches. However, quality circles are derived from a different set of principles. Thus, they will be examined in the next section, which focuses on behavioral techniques for managing change.

Human-Process Techniques for Managing Change

The general emphasis of the second class of change strategies is a people orientation. Survey feedback, team-building, quality circles, and adviser-supportive techniques focus on departments, teamwork, and group performance.

Survey Feedback Questionnaires to examine employee attitudes about their work environment are the basis of **survey feedback.** Questions are asked about such factors as supervision, friendships at work, the degree of conflict within groups, values, degree of participation, and opportunities for innovation. The work group is subsequently provided with feedback on its attitudes and those of the organization as a whole.

A change agent then discusses these results with each group, perhaps comparing the results of different work groups and helping a particular group define problems and missed opportunities. Subsequently, the change agent can develop training programs to help resolve whatever problems are spotted and discussed. One department may actually receive training that is entirely different from what another department receives. The change agent both diagnoses these differing needs and selects and implements appropriate strategies for specific work groups.

Team Building A technique for both temporary task forces and permanent work groups, **team building** also focuses on aiding workers to learn to work together. The change agent is a facilitator who assists the group by improving its communications and its ability to deal with conflict. The bottom line is to build a cohesive work team. Problems associated with blocking the group from acting as a team are identified with the help of the change agent and then solutions are sought.

Early on in this technique a diagnostic meeting is held to examine group performance and problems that block effective performance. By sharing information, thoughts, and ideas about these problems, individual group members start to develop an understanding of the symptoms associated with those problems and an awareness of present organizational evaluation systems, goals, and rewards.

Next, a session is held where the focus turns to planning solutions for the identified problems. Again, as in other techniques, the change agent gathers questionnaire data, interviews some or all group members, and observes them to develop a database for discussions and analyses that follow. The data are subdivided into key categories for discussion, but it is up to the group to use the data, with some facilitation by the change agent. Quality circles, currently a popular technique for employee involvement, are essentially based on these team building notions.

Quality Circles Although introduced to America in the 1950s by William Deming, **quality circles (QCs)**—or, to be more accurate, quality control circles—received their popularity as a reimport from Japan, where they have made a wider impact on some industries from the 1960s to the present. The core concept of the quality circle is a simple one: labor and management representatives jointly identify areas or departments in an organization that might benefit from group discussion, analysis, and diagnoses of problems and opportunities. Circles, usually limited in size to 10 or fewer people, are formed within these areas or departments. These circles meet on a weekly basis to find solutions to problems involving productivity, quality, and individual performance.

Trained facilitators act as circle leaders and help by teaching the group how to use key statistical techniques for gathering and analyzing data. These statistical tools focus on waste reduction and the continual improvement of quality in all phases of procurement, production, sales, accounting, and customer service (Deming, 1982). Many organizations neglect teaching these critical statistical tools when implementing QC programs. Perhaps by neglecting this critical component, these abbreviated versions of QCs are merely reacting to a fad and not providing themselves with the real benefits associated with the complete implementation of QC. Indeed, Ferris and Wagner (1985) cautioned that many U.S. organizations adopt QCs on the basis of emotional appeals rather than sound advice and careful evaluation of their underlying assumptions.

Lawler and Mohrman (1987) pointed out other issues confronting firms that are considering the implementation of QCs. They suggest that the sequencing of change interventions is an important factor to consider when trying to develop a more participative management approach in an organization. Further, they recommend that QCs are not necessarily the best place to start such system-wide change efforts and point to the many cases where QCs had successful honeymoon periods but could not sustain enthusiasm over the long run. It is up to the members of the circle to take on the problems they identify and later present their suggested solutions to management. Thus, if QC sessions cease to uncover meaningful problems and instead turn to trivial gripes, they are likely to be counterproductive in the long run.

Adviser-Supportive Techniques

Advisor-supportive techniques are aimed at providing workers with support and advice on their jobs and careers. Performance evaluation and rewards systems, as well as the human resource management functions of selection, placement, training, and development, all provide the main support system for employee advancement and development. However, often the process of individual development needs the personal touch. This is especially true when members of an organization are confronted with changes. People may need advice and counseling on how to cope, or they may need to become aware that a problem even exists.

One way of providing that support is through the mentor relationship, which is traditionally an informal process whereby senior and junior artists, scholars, executives, and others discover one another and gradually develop a mutually beneficial relationship (Hunt, 1986). That such relationships traditionally have evolved may indicate that when we formalize the mentor relationship we change its very essence. However, this does not mean that we cannot develop formal or planned versions of adviser-supportive practices that take advantage of the benefits while avoiding the pitfalls of these essentially informal activities.

One view of the mentor relationship is to treat it as a process, thereby instilling a philosophy throughout an organization that senior personnel and executives will be evaluated and rewarded for their efforts to advise and support junior members of the firm. A second view of this phenomenon—coaching or counseling—treats these techniques as ways managers can provide employees with opportunities to develop.

Whatever support devices an organization or manager chooses to use, they must be a part of an organization-wide system of offerings. For example, career and job development counseling will be perceived as favoritism if not available to all personnel. Given this caveat, it is apparent that mentors or coaches can help junior members by providing political insights into the firm, by counseling them on advancement and career paths, and by supporting them when difficult decisions and actions of a controversial nature threaten their careers.

All is not a bed of roses for mentors and their protégés. If the mentor falls out of favor with top management, will the protege also sink? And what about company grapevines? Clearly, rumors of sexual relationships between a mentor and protege of different sexes can devastate careers, as in the over-reported case of Agee and Cunningham at the Bendix Corporation (Cunningham, 1984). Yet the danger of misinterpretation is ever present; Crary (1987) reminds us that attraction to a work colleague of the opposite sex is a common experience when men and women work together. Constructive organizational standards about male-female relationships must be developed to deal with this issue.

Changes in Organizational Culture

We have been focusing on the organization's decision to restructure tasks. As the feature on Bell shows, other kinds of organizational change, affecting the values and attitudes or organizational members, occur as well. In some cases, organizational transformation—a more radical overhaul of the entire organizational culture—is required. Torbert (1989) termed these changes "second-order, transformational changes" and contrasted them to first-order changes, which are merely aimed at improving effectiveness or efficiency. Wilkins (1989) suggested that companies with strong cultures can manage change most effectively.

FEATURE: *The Breakup of the Bell System:*
The Biggest Organizational Change

No organizational change of the magnitude of the breakup of the Bell System is likely to occur again any time soon. It is a rich source from which to learn. "Not surprisingly," wrote W. Brooke Tunstall, who was AT&T's corporate vice president for organizational and management systems at the time, "observers from academe, business, and the media [cited] AT&T as a living business case study—a virtual observatory of cultural change in 'real time'—not only because of the challenge to AT&T's management in adjusting a clear-cut, well-established cultural heritage to an entirely new business environment, but also because of the compressed time frame in which change had to occur."

The scope of the changes that management thought necessary were outlined in a speech by AT&T Chairman Charles L. Brown to his senior managers:

> Just as we have to sharpen our marketing focus, just as we have to shorten the journey of our goods from the laboratory to the marketplace, just as we have to produce goods and services more cost effectively, we also have to quicken our pace and sharpen our day-to-day management. We have to come to decisions faster. We have to lean more towards action than study. We have to learn to take more risks, and where we fail, to cut our losses. We have to open the channels of communication, so that ideas for improvement, cost savings, new opportunities, come to the fore in timely fashion and don't die on the organizational ladder. A more swift, more responsive, more accountable style of management will be required.
>
> In short, we need to establish and maintain an internal environment that commands excellence, that encourages a spirit of entrepreneurship and that rewards individual accomplishment.

To manage the massive cultural change that was necessary, AT&T determined that it would carry out a three-step process:

1. Determine the elements of the company's existing culture.

2. Decide which elements needed to be kept and which changed.

3. Take appropriate actions to effect the required changes while leaving the desirable elements unaffected.

AT&T's historic culture was easy to articulate: one superordinate goal—universal telephone service—supported by dedication to customer service, lifetime careers, up-from-the-ranks management succession, operational skills, consensus management, salary level consciousness, and a strong focus on regulatory matters.

As the company was broken up, management had to demonstrate consistently that it still cared about each employee as an individual and, at the same time, continue to foster the service doctrine as a strong corporate value. This historic vision of fairness and of service, the reinforcing sense of loyalty and unity and the valuing of operational and technical skills and safety standards were among the most prominent aspects of the culture that management wanted to protect.

What had to be changed was the mind-set of the company's managers: away from a regulatory environment and toward a market orientation. AT&T needed a new framework for its organization—in its simplest form, a drastic decentralization and downsizing of the corporate staff and the formation of two large sectors: one to conduct the regulated part of the business and the other the unregulated part. The corporate value system would have to recognize and reward a more entrepreneurial type of manager. The routes to managerial authority—for so long concentrated in line telephone operating jobs—would have to be broadened to include more characteristic routes upward, to include marketing and sales, finance, and production and engineering.

AT&T's senior management placed the management of change high on their agendas and took many actions to make it happen successfully.

Both words and deeds were important. Chairman Brown's speeches became closely watched sources of direction. He used them as occasions to establish a new mission for the business, articulate a new bias toward action, and announce an entirely new system of corporate positions and expectations.

Corporate actions were many and covered a broad front. They included:

- Changes in management processes (budgeting, decision making, delegation of authority, reporting, and so on)

- Changes in organizational structure

- Changes in management style

- New recruiting goals

- New kinds of management training (to teach managers to anticipate and respond to strategic issues in a rapidly changing business environment)

- New competitive steps

- A new corporate identity, mission, and organizational structure

- Early retirement packages to streamline the work force

- Profit-center management groups along market and product lines

- Numerous unprecedented joint ventures with other firms

- Numerous product and service innovations

These actions, probably more than anything management could have said or written, helped bring about the needed change by creating a "competitive frame of mind" in the company where no competition had previously existed.

Upon examination, in fact, it is clear that AT&T set about to make deliberate and drastic changes in most aspects of the entire organizational behavior spectrum. The reason it did so was that the changes forced upon it by environmental pressures were so great that only a virtually complete transformation in the organization would enable it to compete successfully in the new world.

Source: "The Breakup of the Bell System: A Case Study in Cultural Transformation," W. Brooke Tunstall, *California Management Review* 27, No. 2 (Winter 1986): 423. Copyright © 1986 by The Regents of the University of California. Reprinted by permission.

Managing Cultural Change

Organizational cultures usually change rather slowly except during times of major transitional events, in response to new market characteristics, when adding or changing product lines, when merging, and so on. Accounts have been written of the tensions created when two organizations with opposite cultures are merged (e.g., Sales and Mirvis, 1984). The type of merger influences the acculturation process. When the businesses are closely related, acquiring firms may exert considerable pressure on acquired units to adopt their cultures. The reason may be that the acquiring firm, not wishing to lose the market or production knowledge of the acquired firm, tries to bring the new staffers into the fold. When the two firms are in different businesses, the acquiring firm may be less willing to intervene, possibly because it does not have the knowledge required to operate the business (Shrivastava, 1986).

Another dynamic may be at work in a merger as well: the acquiring firm may pressure the acquired firm to adopt its culture because it perceives itself as having superior systems and values. By virtue of the fact that it did the acquiring, it views itself as the winner and wants the acquired firm (the loser) to adapt. Schein (1990) suggests that cultural clashes from mergers may be prevented if the acquiring firm assesses the culture of the firm to be acquired before the deal is completed.

Another major event that can trigger the need for a new culture is bankruptcy (Schein, 1990). Extreme measures may be required to rescue the firm. Often in such a case, experienced workers must be fired if they are unable to adapt to the new values that will be required. Borucki and Barnett (1990), in describing the restructuring of International Harvester into Navistar, described how the new company took steps to help those workers with separation packages and outplacement (finding new jobs) counseling.

Of course, organizations prefer to effect change before such drastic steps are required. But even if the change is not an attempt to bring the firm back from the brink of failure, the examples of Milliken, MSWD, and Bell show that cultural transformations can be profound. Large-scale change such as that called for in a change of organizational culture is difficult to deal with. During major transitions organizations tend to pay attention to technological change, letting the behavioral side evolve by default rather than by design (Kimberly and Quinn, 1984). The management of transition is largely the management of paradox, however, whereby transitions are not neatly compartmentalized and cannot be neatly managed according to the logic of technology.

Kilman and colleagues have identified four phases of cultural change: analysis of the current culture, presentation of new goals, modification of existing culture, and evaluation of results (Kilman, Saxton, and Serpa, 1985). Some common pitfalls to change (Davis, 1984) are:

1. Announcing a change with fanfare and then doing nothing

2. Paying lip service to something (in which actions do not follow the words)

3. Moving only to please the boss

4. The cynicism that occurs when management cannot stand behind what it says

5. The tail wagging the dog, or the daily beliefs rather than the guiding beliefs driving strategy and action

One prescription for managing cultural change focuses on honoring the organization's past (Wilkins and Bristow, 1987)—that is, reassuring those devoted to organizational traditions while energizing those hoping for change, without destroying a sense of pride and appreciation for what has been accomplished. Various strategies for honoring the past are presented in the next feature. This strategy gives workers a sense of stability and security in the midst of change and can therefore facilitate acceptance of that change.

FEATURE: *Honoring the Past*

Change that repudiates the cultural roots of the organization often leaves people without a usable past and may therefore seriously diminish their sense of competence and their faith in the organization's ability to change effectively. Here is a list of various ways organizations have managed to honor their past. . . .

1. *Return to the past for inspiration and instruction.* Simplot, a major producer of French fries for McDonald's, helped employees through a period of leveling off after rapid growth by reminding them of the entrepreneurial spirit of the company's founder, Jack Simplot.

2. *Back to basics.* A new division manager at GE changed the passive culture in his division by instituting budgeting and reporting practices that were common to the rest of the company. Because these changes were made to an existing culture and were already being widely used in the rest of the company, the manager was able to effect desired cultural change in a short period of time.

3. *Identify principles that will remain constant.* Hewlett-Packard helped manage a shift in its marketing orientation by emphasizing that the company would still be run "the HP way." This involved sticking with the principles of decentralized operations and autonomous division management even though the times called for increased coordination among divisions.

4. *Find examples of success within the current culture.* One company, seeking to overcome negative employee attitudes about a perceived management philosophy of "productivity through pressure," made examples of managers who were achieving high productivity with much higher motivation and morale by involving employees in goal attainment.

5. *Promote hybridization.* GE finds and promotes such exemplary managers—those who understand the old culture but can also serve as examples of the new. CEO Jack Welch himself was apparently picked because he not only fit at GE and understood the culture, but because he was also somewhat different.

6. *Label eras.* When a change is necessary in an organization, the management group and others may seek to understand and name a past era, and then label the upcoming era, to give employees a sense of continuity.

7. *Mourn the loss of a cherished past.* Until employees are able to mourn for and "bury" the past, the past seems to linger to haunt them. Without such acknowledgment, many people continue to live in the past, reminiscing through stories about "the good old days."

Source: A. L. Wilkins and N. J. Bristow, "For Successful Organization Culture, Honor Your Past," *Academy of Management Executive* 1 (1987): 221–229. Reprinted by permission.

Popular Books on Managing Change

Another view of change is provided by some popular books on change. Deal and Kennedy (1982) state that the business of change is cultural transformation. The question is how to do it in the most effective way possible. Deal and Kennedy (1982, pp. 164–166) offer five tips for the manager who takes on the challenge:

1. Recognize that peer group consensus is the major influence on acceptance or willingness to change.

2. Convey and emphasize two-way trust in all matters (and especially communications) related to change.

3. Think of change as skill building and concentrate on training as part of the change process.

4. Allow enough time for the change to take hold.

5. Encourage people to adapt the basic idea for the change to fit the real world around them.

Peters and Austin (1985) suggest "managing by wandering around" as a way for managers to take the pulse of the organization. Thus they can keep informed about gradual internal changes. This technique also helps managers spot lurking problems that require planned change to solve. To create and sustain superior performance, they offered these suggestions:

1. Take care of customers by supplying superior service and quality.

2. Motivate employees at all times.

3. Listen to employees and give them respect.

4. Lead by showing you are obsessed with key values.

5. Stay in touch with all variables so that you are ready to adapt.

Innovation is a major theme in these books. It is "the generation, acceptance, and implementation of new ideas, processes, products, or services" (Kanter, 1983, p. 20). Today's managers often face ambiguous or new problems that thwart their attempts to use familiar methods of attack; they must learn to manage the process of coping with poorly defined administrative situations (McCaskey, 1982). Change involves the identification, formation, and clarification of new possibilities, policies, behaviors, patterns, methodologies, products, or market ideas based on reconceptualized patterns in the organization (Kanter, 1983). Kanter speaks of "changemasters," or organizational leaders who build an internal culture that encourages innovation at all levels of a company.

All four books agree that the environment is turbulent. Political, technological, and cultural forces constantly change both inside and outside our organizations, placing a variety of complex and changing demands on organizations and managers. The external pressures that arise are often in the form of ambiguous problems for which no clear solutions are known. As McCaskey (1982) suggests, information may be incomplete, include errors, and present confusing issues; time may be short, creating a stressful crisis environment; employees may resist the solutions that are devised; or the problem itself may be poorly defined.

Pascale (1990) began by identifying four factors that can be managed to promote change: fit, or the organization's internal consistency; split, or techniques used to promote autonomy and diversity; contend, which introduces the value of constructive conflict; and transcend. This last is the management ability to handle the complexity caused by the other three factors. As a model of the ideal way to manage these factors, Pascale points to Honda.

Finally, all these books recognize that managing change is an ongoing process. Peters and Austin call for paying careful attention to detail in preparation and organizational planning. Deal and Kennedy focus on the identification of corporate cultures and awareness and diagnosis of a firm's present state as clearly important before proceeding to make adjustments in response to change. McCaskey deals with methods and strategies for coping with stress, ways to be creative, and ways to clear up ambiguity. Kanter encourages innovation and offers methods for enhancing one's power and influence. Pascale states that the new mindset required is a matter of maintaining vitality and flexibility.

The Shape of Things to Come:
Environmental Impacts on the Organization in the 1990s

Whenever a new decade begins we are inundated with predictions about coming events. Often these glimpses into the future are little more than extrapolations of the past (Coppo, 1990). Some of the major events that so dramatically altered the 1980s, however, will unquestionably reverberate into the 1990s.

Organizations in the United States are confronting some profound changes in the labor force. Demographics establish that fewer young workers will be entering the labor force in the next decade. Indeed, 80 percent of the growth in the labor supply will be from women, minorities, and immigrants. The average age of the labor force is increasing, which may have implications for mobility, ability to change, and the cost of labor. By 1995, as much as 90 percent of all new jobs in the United States are expected to come from the service sector of the economy, as manufacturing continues to decline in importance.

That service sector will be fueled by the continuing technological revolution. The growth in rapid means of communication, the spread of computers, the trend away from heavy manufacturing will all continue. Though we are no closer than before to the paperless office and electronic commuting is still a rarity, it is nevertheless clear that technological change is spawning profound changes in organizations and will continue to do so. Naisbitt and Aburdene (1990) offered an upbeat, if somewhat questionable view of the future. They say the U.S. budget deficit is declining, the trade deficit may not really exist, Japanese investment in the United States is good, and blacks are doing better than ever. They also note that there is a conflict between global business and local culture. As multinationals like Sony and Coca-Cola create a world culture, nations react by turning to local values. Much of that technological change centers on the new importance of information. As Drucker (1989) put it, knowledge is the new capital. The knowledgeable worker has power that provides greater influence within the organization and, at the same time, greater independence from it.

Perhaps the most significant recent trend, which will surely continue, is the growing internationalism of business. It is to this phenomenon and its implications that we turn our attention now.

Changes in the International Environment

Without question, the world is becoming one market. Currency exchange rates affect prosperity and growth, dislocations in stock and commodity markets in one country worry investors in another, businesses acquire new firms or build new plants in other countries to establish a market toehold. The new *transnational economy,* as termed by Peter Drucker (1989), does more than create new competitive challenges; in Drucker's view, it compels businesses to redefine their goals as market maximization, not profit.

In the midst of this evolution, major changes in Europe and Asia created a turbulent and very uncertain environment. "Europe 1992" was the cry of business leaders and pundits alike, as all looked ahead to the new European order based on a single market in Western Europe. This development was a major undertaking, but it pales in comparison to the revolution in Eastern Europe, where country after country has abandoned the inefficiencies of central planning and launched on a perilous voyage to a market economy. New markets, new labor forces, new uncertainties abound.

The uncertainties are greater nowhere than in the Soviet Union itself, where ethnic nationalism, pent-up frustration over material discomfort, and the existence of new opportunities of public expression combine with military cutbacks and a faltering economy. The outcome of these tensions is impossible to predict. Will Gorbachev manage this change and achieve growing prosperity, engender a level of democracy both satisfactory to the people and safe for the regime, and maintain the cohesion of Soviet territory? Or will all these forces plunge this huge and powerful nation into civil conflict? If so, will the result be a splintering of the country or a harsh counterreaction and return to the strict control of the past?

China seems to have chosen the latter course, at least for now. In doing so, it may have cast a shadow over another predictable transition—Hong Kong '97, when this island of capitalism becomes part of the communist state once again. Even with a smooth transition, the reverberations of this new status will be profound. But with the growing flight of money and people from Hong Kong to Canada, England, and the United States, it is clear that business will not be as usual in Southeast Asia.

Africa, too, is likely to see major changes in the new decade. In 1990 the government of South Africa seemed to be making advances toward a negotiated ending to apartheid, the policy that oppressed its black majority population and prompted international opposition harmful to its economy.

Should some settlement foster an end to that opposition, the country may take a new role as an economic force in the world.

The Western hemisphere is the scene of many questions as well. Hyperinflation in Brazil and Argentina is being confronted with draconian measures; drug lords who wield the economic power of whole nations threaten stability in the Andes region; and the continuing conflict between haves and have-nots threatens fragile democracies in Central America. Canada and the United States, by signing the Free-Trade Agreement of 1988, entered on a new economic policy, the consequences of which were frequently debated. The possibility of a similar agreement with Mexico creates the prospect of a single open North American market that may compete more effectively with Europe '92.

Implications for Business

The articles compiled and edited by Rosow (1989) identify seven steps that businesses must take for success in the 1990s: *globalization*

1. Use decentralized management, delegating responsibility and authority to overseas units.

2. Form transnational partnerships or joint ventures with overseas firms.

3. Establish trust, involvement, security, and motivation to encourage employee commitment to quality.

4. Have the capacity to move capital rapidly from one country to another when necessary.

5. Develop a sense of corporate citizenship to survive amid restrictive policies in some countries.

6. Create a high-quality universal product that can nevertheless appeal to local tastes.

7. Invest in research and development because product obsolescence now averages four to five years rather than ten to fifteen.

Bartlett and Ghoshal (1987) surveyed a number of successful transnational firms and found structural characteristics that contribute to success. The key is the capability to be multidimensional, with effective geographic, business, and functional management. The techniques are structural differentiation (establishing different organizational models in different locations), interdependence (built on good communication), and cooption (the communication of and identification with core values). These authors suggest that the solution is more than structural; organizations must develop a "managerial mindset that understands the need for multiple strategic capabilities, that is able to view problems from both local and global perspectives, and that accepts the importance of a flexible approach" (p. 52).

Ohmae (1989) also stresses one of these points—the need for "genuine equidistance of perspective." He points to Honda and Cascio as models of corporations that think globally; neither divides domestic from international operations but views all operations as important to the company. Another danger, in addition to compartmentalized thinking, is impatience. "Persistence and perseverance," Ohmae warns, are the secrets of international success. The problem of impatience is not merely attitudinal but may be institutionalized. Profit goals established in the home country for the home market may be inappropriate for a foreign market. One other implication of the growing internationalization of business is clear: managers, to be effective, will require global experience (see the feature).

FEATURE: *Going Global: The Chief Executives in Year 2000 Will Be Experienced Abroad*

Since World War II, the typical corporate chief executive officer has looked something like this:

He started out as a finance man with an undergraduate degree in accounting. He methodically worked his way up through the company from the controller's office in a division, to running that division, to the top job. His military background shows: He is used to giving orders—and to having them obeyed. As the head of the United Way drive, he is a big man in his community. However, the first time he traveled overseas on business was as chief executive. Computers make him nervous.

But peer into the executive suite of the year 2000 and see a completely different person.

His undergraduate degree is in French literature, but he also has a joint M.B.A./engineering degree. He started in research and was quickly picked out as a potential CEO. He zigzagged from research to marketing to finance. He proved himself in Brazil by turning around a failing joint venture. He speaks Portuguese and French and is on a first-name basis with commerce ministers in half a dozen countries. Unlike his predecessor's predecessor, he isn't a drill sergeant. He is first among equals in a five-person Office of the Chief Executive.

As the 40-year postwar epoch of growing markets and domestic-only competition fades, so too is vanishing the narrow one-company, one-industry chief executive. By the turn of the century, academicians, consultants and executives themselves predict, companies' choices of leaders will be governed by increasing international competition, the globalization of companies, the spread of technology, demographic shifts, and the speed of overall change. . . .

Until recently, the road to the top in a big corporation has been fairly well marked. General Motors Corp., for example, has been run by a finance man for 28 of the past 32 years. More than three-quarters of the chief executives surveyed in 1987 by the search firm Heidrick & Struggles had finance, manufacturing or marketing backgrounds. . . .

[In the future, however,] "it will be very difficult for a single-discipline individual to reach the top," predicts Douglas Danforth, former chairman of Westinghouse Electric Co. . . .

Intensifying international competition will make the home-grown chief executive obsolete. "Global, global, global," is how Noel Tichy, a professor at University of Michigan's Graduate School of Business, describes the wider-ranging chief executive of the future. "Travel overseas," Mr. Danforth of Westinghouse advises future chief executives. "Meet with the prime minister, the ministers of trade and commerce. Meet with the king of Spain and the chancellor of West Germany. Get yourself known." . . .

Others predict that by the next century, overseas executives will be equal contenders in the race for the top. This year, for the first time, Merck & Co. won't segregate its senior-executive training programs by country. "We have internationalized our training," says Art Strohmer, Merck's executive director of human resources. "We have high-level employees from Europe, Latin America, the U.S. and the rest of the world rubbing shoulders with each other." The model many cite for future chief executives is Coca-Cola Co.'s chairman, Roberto Goizueta, who started out with the company in Havana, Cuba, in 1954.

Computer-shy executives probably won't make it to the top of the company of 2000. Not that computer wizards or techies will be taking over—far from it. "The computer in the basement is a utility, not a source of competitive advantage," says Gerald R. Faulhaber, an associate professor at Wharton. Rather, chief executives will have to be comfortable exchanging information electronically and dealing with and ensuring organizational changes. . . .

In fact, some say that, with the increasing complexity and speed of decision making, the lone chief executive will be gone. Richard Vancil, a professor at Harvard Business School, notes the increasing popularity of the "office of the chief executive officer." By 1984, he found, 25% of American companies used this arrangement, which melds three to six top officers into a team led by the chairman; that's up from only 8% in the 1960s. . . .

"The undergraduate ought to concentrate on the humanities and social sciences," says Jack Sparks, retired chairman of Whirlpool. The future chief executive "can't have had his head buried in his briefcase, his test tube, or his computer." Graduate schools are struggling to figure out what they should teach.

But many say the disciplines that will be required of future corporate chiefs are too nebulous to be taught easily. Students often find courses in organizational behavior, for example, too "touchy-feely," says Donald Jacobs, the dean of Northwestern University's Kellogg graduate school of management. He says he understands that: "I'm an old finance professor. I have a model, and the model gives me a solution. That's easy. The problem is, that's not the way the world works."

Source: Amanda Bennett, "Going Global: The Chief Executives in the Year 2000 Will Be Experienced Abroad." *Wall Street Journal,* February 27, 1989, pp. A1, A4. Copyright © 1989 by Dow Jones & Company, Inc. All Rights Reserved Worldwide.

SUMMARY

The chapter opened with the example of Roger Milliken, who initiated two major company transformations within a decade. According to Peters, Milliken's dedication to success prompts an openness to change regardless of how thorough or profound it must be. This orientation seems to be the best adaptation to the turbulence that organizations will encounter in the coming years.

With this background understanding of one change in progress, we began to examine the many issues related to change. Change is what happens in the organization's environment when laws, the availability of resources, technology, or the competition is altered. But far more important to managers are their purposeful attempts to initiate change in their organizations, generally to respond to challenges.

To provide a way of grasping change, we developed a model of the process of managing change. The model had three main steps: problem awareness and diagnosis; selecting and implementing a solution; and monitoring and evaluating the change. A fully developed program of problem awareness requires the gathering of information, which can take the form of interviews or questionnaires, observation, analysis of the historical record, a stream analysis, a needs analysis, or a political diagnosis. Implementing change addresses the issues of deciding when, where, and to what degree the changes will take place. It must take into account ways to overcome employees' resistance to change.

Whatever solution is chosen, and however it is implemented, managers must clearly establish criteria for evaluating it in process. Only by monitoring the effects of the change can organizations ensure that the change will succeed—and prevent any unforeseen and undesirable consequences. Equally important is maintaining an openness to further change.

Some organizational changes are accomplished by relying on change agents, who are either outside consultants or leaders within the organization. Change agents are most effective when they have the trust of members of the organization.

We studied change by first distinguishing between two types. Some organizational changes, part of the field called organizational development, focus on the way jobs are structured. Other, more radical changes, may be called organizational transformation.

We explored in depth the process of redesigning jobs, pointing out that the process begins with the need to identify essential characteristics to determine whether a job is ripe for redesign. Once that determination is made, managers can choose a variety of tools to affect job redesign. These include job rotation, job enlargement, job enrichment, and group working.

Researchers have presented a number of models for job restructuring, which can loosely be gathered into two camps: those focusing on system-wide change and those focusing on individual or small group change. The former type is the sociotechnical approach. Born and flourishing in Europe, it tries to balance improvements in the technical aspects of work with the need to satisfy workers' social needs. Another type of system-wide change, the job characteristics approach, manipulates key traits of jobs to engender optimal worker motivation. Those traits are variety, task identity, autonomy, and job-based feedback.

The human, or behavior-based, techniques for managing change include survey feedback, team building, quality circles, and adviser-supportive techniques. The first technique is a way of using employee responses to questions to identify areas needing change; the second aims at improving the cohesiveness of the group. Quality circles have become fashionable recently, but it is important to recall that a major feature of this approach is the teaching of techniques of statistical analysis, thus arming circle members with necessary tools to make effective decisions. Adviser-supportive techniques confront a paradox: they require the formal implementation of the benefits of support generated in the past by naturally occurring informal relationships. Yet this paradox can be overcome if management creates a climate that fosters the support and advice that senior members can offer juniors.

The many techniques developed by research have achieved parallel expression in the observation of organizations in the real world, as evidenced by five popular books. The authors of these books, using actual businesses as case studies, emphasize some important points about change: system-wide change means cultural transformation; it is essential to develop techniques for overcoming resistance to change; change is a process. These books underscore the salience of change to the organization by analyzing the turbulence and ambiguity of the environment and the need for organizations to stay ready to adapt. Finally, they all stress a key characteristic that will be needed by all successful organizations in the future: the ability to innovate.

We concluded the chapter with an overview of the issues that will confront organizations in the 1990s. Though changing demographics and technology are profound environmental changes, the most significant change of all is undoubtedly the rise of the transcendence of nationalism as the milieu of business. The growth of regional economic agreements, the rising competition and, at the same time, interdependence of nations, and the turbulence within countries require organizations to infuse a new perspective into their activities. They can no longer focus on narrow, local concerns, but must develop ways of competing effectively on the international scene.

MANAGERIAL INSIGHT

To: *Student Managers*
From: *Veteran Manager*
Subject: *Change*

As a manager, you will be called on at times to manage stability and at other times to manage change. Neither is a snap, but in my experience, the latter is more demanding. What makes managing change tougher is that people have so many ways of resisting it.

If Newton had been a 20th-century management consultant, I believe he would have postulated a law that people at work tend to keep doing whatever it is that they are doing. Indeed, a fairly significant amount of managerial time is spent eliminating variety and standardizing every possible aspect of work. Without some degree of standardization, there would be only chaos in the office or the factory.

But the people I've worked with—an unscientific but probably reasonably representative sample of the population as a whole—have devised more ways to resist change than to resist stability. In lay terms, here are some forms I've seen this resistance take:

1. *Denying the need to change.* People send up all kinds of reasoned arguments that what exists is all right, that there is no need to "abandon what has made us successful to date."

2. *Denying the existence of a changed environment.* They look at changing conditions and swear that nothing has changed.

3. *Disagreeing on the proposed change.* They accept that change is necessary but have other ideas on what to do.

4. *Accepting the change on the surface but not internalizing it.* They give the outward appearance of having "bought in" but inwardly resist and perhaps even sabotage the planned change.

5. *Fearing the change and hiding from it.* They behave erratically and counterproductively in the face of change, beyond the natural anxiety that accompanies almost any change.

This short list doesn't exhaust the many forms of resistance you might encounter, but it is enough to make the point that you will need a great deal of patience and perseverance to accomplish organizational change of any magnitude. All the change management techniques discussed in this chapter will work in one situation or another. None work in all situations. It's important therefore never to assume that your first try will succeed, or that using just one technique will be enough to accomplish your ends.

Amazingly, some managers—even a few who have been around quite a while—think that the mere announcement of a change will cause it to happen. Anyone who has tried to change a personal habit (dieting, quitting smoking, starting an exercise program) merely by announcing his or her intentions to family or friends knows that this isn't true, but myths die hard, especially in organizational settings.

When you are faced with the need to manage some important change and the first two or three techniques you use don't overcome resistance, this doesn't mean that they should be discredited. They will work in another situation on another day. You may simply need to put them aside for the time being and try other approaches before finding the correct one for the present situation. Just as any great performer in sports or the arts or politics has a great repertoire of skills, so you as a manager can have a rich stockpile of tools and techniques for causing change to happen in the way you want it to.

Study the techniques discussed here. Observe them being used by leaders in every organization, from clubs to corporations to nations. Practice them. These are the tools of your trade. Knowing how to use them will not guarantee you success, but not knowing it will make your success very difficult.

REVIEW QUESTIONS

1. What is the key to Milliken's success in its major organizational changes?

2. According to Leavitt, what organizational factors can be manipulated in change situations, and what relationship of those factors, one to another, must be kept in mind?

3. Name the various methods of gathering information as part of problem diagnosis.

4. How might a political diagnosis be helpful in reducing resistance to change?

5. At what stage of developing a change strategy are the standards for evaluation created?

6. Is it preferable to have an inside or an outside change agent?

7. What characteristics must be present for a job to be a good candidate for restructuring?

8. What is the major goal of sociotechnical systems approaches to change?

9. Identify the three critical psychological states in job characteristics theory and contrast their treatment with that of the core job characteristics.

10. Contrast job rotation and job enlargement with job enrichment.

11. Contrast team building and quality circles with adviser-supportive techniques.

12. What is the benefit of honoring the past when managing a major organizational transformation?

13. What suggestion about change do Deal and Kennedy and Peters and Austin share?

14. Of the environmental changes described in the text—changes in the labor force, technological changes, and the growing internationalism of business—which do you think is the most important? Explain.

REFERENCES

Adler, N. (1991). *International Dimensions of Organizational Behavior*, 2nd ed. Boston: PWS-KENT Publishing Company.

Aldag, J. A., and Brief, A. P. (1979). *Task Design and Employee Motivation*. Glenview, IL: Scott, Foresman.

The American Psychologist. February 1990. Entire issue.

Bailey, J. (1983). *Job Design and Work Organization*. Englewood Cliffs, NJ: Prentice-Hall.

Barko, W., and Pasmore, W. (1986). Introductory statement to the special issue: Innovations in designing high-performance systems. JABS 22 (3):195–200.

Bartlett, C. A., and Ghoshal, S. (1987). Managing across borders: New organizational responses. *Sloan Management Review* 29:43–53.

Bartunek, J. M., and Louis, M. R. (1988). The interplay of organization development and organizational transformation. In W. A. Pasmore and R. W. Woodman (eds.), *Research in Organizational Change and Development* (vol. 2). Greenwich, CT: JAI Press, pp. 97–134.

Beer, M. (1987). Revitalizing organizations: Change process and emergent model. *Academy of Management Executive* February: 51–55.

Beer, M. and Walton, E. (1990). Developing the Competitive Organization: Interventions and Strategies. *American Psychologist* vol. 45 (2):154–161.

Bennett, A. (1989). Going global. *Wall Street Journal*, February 27, 1989, pp. A1, A4.

Blau, G. J., and Katerberg, R. (1982). Toward enhancing research with the social information processing approach to job design. *AMR* 7 (4):543–550.

Borucki, C., and Barnett, C. K. (1990). Restructuring for self-renewal: Navistar International Corporation. *Academy of Management Executive* 4:36–49.

Burbridge, J. L. (1976). *Group Productive Methods and the Humanization of Work*. Washington, D.C.: International Labor Office.

Campion, M. A., and Thayer, P. W. (1985). Development and field evaluation of an interdisciplinary measure of job design. *Journal of Applied Psychology* 70:29–43.

Cobb, A. T. (1986). Political diagnosis: Application in organization development. *AMR* 11 (3):482–496.

Coch, L., and French, J. R. P. (1948). Overcoming resistance to change. *Human Relations* 1:512–553.

Coppo, J. (1990). *Futurescape: Success Strategy for the 1990's and Beyond*. Chicago: Longman.

Crary, M. (1987). Managing attraction and intimacy at work. *Organizational Dynamics* 15:26–41.

Cummings, T. G. (1978). Self-regulating work groups: A sociotechnical synthesis. *Academy of Management Review* 3:625–634.

Cummings, T. G. (1986). A concluding note: Future directions of sociotechnical theory and research. *Journal of Applied Behavioral Science* 22:355–360.

Cunningham, M. (1984). *Powerplay: What Really Happened at Bendix*. New York: Random House.

Davis, S. (1984). *Managing Corporate Culture*. Cambridge, MA: Ballinger.

Deal, T. E., and Kennedy, A. A. (1982). *Corporate Cultures: The Rites and Rituals of Corporate Life*. Reading, MA: Addison-Wesley.

Deming, W. E. (1982). *Quality, Productivity, and Competitive Position*. Cambridge, MA: MIT Center for Advanced Engineering Study.

Drucker, P. F. (1989). *The New Realities*. New York: Harper & Row.

Ferris, G. R., and Wagner, F. A. III (1985). Quality circles in the U.S.: A conceptual reevaluation. *Journal of Applied Behavioral Sciences* 21:155–167.

Fitzgerald, T. H. (1988). Can change in organizational culture really be managed? *Organizational Dynamics* 17:5–15.

Friedlander, F., and Brown, L. D. (1975). Organization development. *Annual Review of Psychology* 25:313–341.

French, J. R. P., Israel, J., and As, D. (1960). An experiment on participation in a Norwegian factory. *Human Relations* 13:3–19.

Greiner, L. E. (1967). Patterns of organizational change. *Harvard Business Review* (May–June):119–130.

Hackman, J. R., and Lawler, E. E. (1971). Employee reactions to job characteristics. *Journal of Applied Psychology* 55:259–286.

Hackman, H. R., and Oldham, G. R. (1975). Development of the job diagnostic survey. *Journal of Applied Psychology* 60:159–170.

Hackman, H. R., and Oldham, G. R. (1980). *Work Redesign*. Reading, MA: Addison-Wesley.

Hampden-Turner, C. (1990). *Charting the Corporate Mind*. New York: Free Press.

Harrison, R. (1970). Choosing the depth of intervention. *Journal of Applied Behavioral Science* 6:181–202.

Hartley, R. F. (1986). *Management Mistakes*, Second ed. New York: John Wiley & Sons.

Hunt, D. M. (1986). Formal vs. informal mentoring: Towards a framework. *Mentoring: Aid to Excellence, Vol. II*. Proceedings of the First International Conference on Mentoring, pp. 8–14.

Kanter, R. M. (1983). *The Changemasters*. New York: Simon & Schuster.

Kaplan, R., Drath, W., and Kofodimos, J. (1987). High hurdles: The challenge of executive self-development. *The Academy of Management Executive* 1 (3):195–206.

Kilman, R. H., Saxton, M. J., and Serpa, R. (1985). *Gaining Control of the Corporate Culture*. San Francisco: Jossey-Bass.

Kimberly, J. R., and Quinn, R. E. (1984). *Managing Organizational Transitions*. Homewood, IL: Irwin.

Klein, L. (1976). *New Forms of Work Organization*. London: Cambridge University Press.

Lawler, E. E., and Mohrman, S. A. (1987). Quality circles: After the honeymoon. *Organizational Dynamics* 15:42–54.

Leavitt, H. J. (1965). Applied organizational change in industry: Structural, technological, and humanistic approaches. In J. G. March (ed.), *Handbook of Organizations.* Chicago: Rand McNally, p. 1145.

Lewin, K. (1951). *Field Theory in Social Science.* New York: Harper & Row.

McCaskey, M. B. (1982). *The Executive Challenge: Managing Change and Ambiguity.* Boston: Pitman.

Naisbitt, J., and Aburdene, P. (1990). *Megatrends 2000.* New York: William Morrow.

Neumann, J. E. (1989). Why people don't participate in organizational change. In W. W. Woodman and W. A. Pasmore (eds.), *Research in Organizational Change and Development* (vol. 3). Greenwich, CT: JAI Press, pp. 181–212.

Ohmae, K. (1989). Managing in a borderless world. *Harvard Business Review*, July–August, pp. 152–161.

Pascale, R. T. (1990). *Managing on the Edge.* New York: Simon & Schuster.

Pava, H. P. (1983). Designing managerial and professional work for high performance: A sociotechnical approach. *National Productivity Review.*

Peters, T. J., and Austin, N. K. (1985). *A Passion for Excellence.* New York: Random House.

Peters, T. J., and Waterman, R. H., Jr. (1982). *In Search of Excellence: Lessons from America's Best-Run Companies.* New York: Harper & Row.

Porras, J., and Hoffer, C. (1986). Common behavioral changes in successful OD efforts. *Journal of Applied Behavioral Science* 22:485.

Rice, A. K. (1958). *Productivity and Social Organization: The Ahmedabad Experiment.* London: Tavistock Publishers Ltd.

Roberts, K. H., and Glick, W. (1981). The job characteristics approach to job design: A critical review. *Journal of Applied Psychology* April: 193–217.

Rosow, J. M. (Ed.) (1989). *The Global Marketplace.* New York: Facts on File.

Sales, A. L., and Mirvis, P. H. (1984). When cultures collide: Issues in acquisition. In J. R. Kimberly and R. E. Quinn, *Managing Organizational Transitions.* Homewood, IL: Irwin, pp. 107–133.

Schein, E. H. (1987 revised). *Organizational Psychology*, 2nd ed. Englewood Cliffs, NJ: Prentice-Hall.

Schein, E. H. (1990). Organizational culture. *American Psychologist* 45:109–119.

Seashore, S. E., Lawler, E. E., Mirvis, P. H., and Cammaunn, C. (eds.). (1983). *Assessing Organizational Change.* New York: J. Wiley & Sons.

Shepard, H. A. (1975). Rules of thumb for change agents. *Organization Development Practitioner.* November: 1–5.

Shrivastava, P. (1986). Postmerger integration. *Journal of Business Strategy* 7:65–76.

Tichy, N. M. (1983). *Managing Strategic Change: Technical, Political and Cultural Dynamics.* New York: J. Wiley & Sons.

Torbert, W. R. (1989). Leading organizational transformation. In W. W. Woodman and W. A. Pasmore (eds.), *Research in Organizational Change and Development* (vol. 3). Greenwich, CT: JAI Press, pp. 83–116.

Trist, E., and Bamforth, K. (1951). Some social and psychological consequences of the longwall method of goal-getting. *Human Relations* 4:1–38.

Tunstall, W. B. (1986). The breakup of the Bell System: A case study in cultural transformation. *California Management Review* 27:110–124.

Turner, A. N., and Lawrence, P. R. (1965). *Industrial Jobs and the Worker.* Cambridge, MA: Harvard University Press.

Walton, R. E. (1972). How to counter alienation in the plant. *Harvard Business Review* Nov.–Dec.: 70–81.

Weisbord, M. R. (1973). The organization development contract. *Organization Development Practitioner* 5 (2):1–4.

Weisbord, M. R. (1987). Toward third wave managing and consulting. *Organizational Dynamics* Winter: 4–25.

White, L. P., and Wooten, K. C. (1983). Ethical dilemmas in various stages of organizational development. *Academy of Management Review* 8:690–697.

Wilkins, A. L. (1989). *Developing Corporate Character.* San Francisco: Jossey-Bass.

Wilkins, A. L., and Bristow, N. J. (1987). For successful organization culture, honor your past. *Academy of Management Executive* 1:221–229.

Name Index

Abbott, J.E., 522, *532*
Abelson, R.P., 492, *536*
Aburdene, P., 577, *589*
Adams, J.S., 400, *426*, 463, *474*
Adams, W., 33
Adeo, S.M., *427*
Adler, M.J., 265, *270*
Adler, N., 117, *158*, 186, *214*, *587*
Aiken, M., 66, 70, *105*, 307, *315*
Aikens, F., 245, *270*
Ajzen, I., 506, *531*, *533*
Albanese, R., 186, *214*
Aldag, J.A., 559–60, *587*
Alderfer, C.P., 447, 451, *474*
Aldrich, H.C., 325, *371*
Aldrich, H.E., 98, *104*, 386, 387, 389, *424*
Allaire, Y., 120, *158*
Allen, B.P., 259, *272*
Allen, R.W., 284, 302–5, 310–11, *317*
Alliger, G.M., 391, *425*
Allison, G.T., 325, 354, *369*
Allport, F.H., 188, *214*
Allport, G.W., 251, *271*, 485, *531*
al-Meer, A.R.A., 147, *159*
Alsing, C., 166, 167–72
Alvares, K., 409, *423*
Amabile, T.M., 500, *536*

Anderson, J.C., 325, *373*
Anderson, P.A., *370*
Anderson, T.R., 69, *104*
Angle, H.L., 36, *48*, 284, 302–5, *317*
Antaki, C., 499
Antal, A.B., 39, *48*
Aplin, J.C., 297, *315*
Arendt, C., 58, 59
Argote, L., 197, *215*
Argyle, M., 245, *270*
Aristotle, 437
Armacost, 290, 291
As, D., 554, *588*
Asch, S.E., 183, *214*
Ashour, A.S., 408, *421*
Astley, W.G., 284, *315*
Athey, T.R., 522, *531*
Athos, A.G., 12, 115, 143, *160*
Atkinson, J.W., 476, 488, *535*
Atkinson, S.W., 450, *474*
Aupperle, K.E., 32, *48*
Austin, N.K., 181, 575–76, *589*
Axtell, R., 242, *270*
Azma, M., 44, *48*

Bacharach, S. B., 294, *315*, 317
Badawy, M.K., 446, *474*
Bailey, J., 563, 566, *587*
Bailey, S., 493, *533*

Bales, R.F., 389, *421*
Baloff, N., 335, *370*
Bamford, J., *104*
Bamforth, K., 561, *590*
Bandura, A., 458, *474*, 477, 515–16, *531*
Banks, H., 92
Bannister, B.D., 261, *270*
Bargh, J.A., 236, *272*, 502, *534*
Barker, R.G., 230, *274*
Barko, W., 563, *587*
Barley, S.R., 95, 98, *104*, 123, *158*, 161
Barnett, C.K., 88, *105*, 573, *587*
Barnett, W.P., 185, *216*
Barrett, G.V., 497, *532*
Barth, J.M., 334, *372*
Bartlett, C.A., 579–80, *587*
Bartol, K.M., 391, *426*
Bartunek, J.M., 558, *587*
Bass, B.M., 399, 406, 414, *421*, *422*, 497, 515, *532*
Bates, P., 115, *158*
Baty, G.B., 307, *315*
Bavelas, A., 412, *422*
Beatty, R.W., 519, 524, *532*
Beckett, J., 279, 290
Beer, M., 555–56, 557, *587*
Behling, O., 414, *422*
Bell, M.A., 178, *214*
Bell, N., 506, *537*

591

Cosier, R.A., 346, *370*
Cotton, J.L., 460, *474*
Courtright, J.A., 89, *105*
Covault, C., 72
Cowan, D.A., *370*
Crabbs, R.A., 449, *474*
Crary, M., 569, *587*
Crocker, J., 494, *537*
Cronshaw, J.F., 391, *422*
Crozier, M., 71, *105*, 293, *315*, 382
Culnan, M.J., 251, *271*
Cummings, L.L., 304, 503
Cummings, T.G., 88, *106*, 563, *587*, *588*
Cunningham, M., 569, *588*
Curry, J.P., 148, *158*
Cusella, L.P., 259, 260, *271*
Cyert, R.M., 17–18, *48*, 348, 362, *370*

Daft, R.L., 74, *105*, 251, 253, 273
Dalkey, N., 363, *370*
Danforth, D.D., 55, 581
Darwin, C., 244, *271*·
Davenport, T., 59
David, F.R., 12, 95, *105*
Davis, K., 81, *105*, 499, 500, *534*
Davis, S., 573, *588*
Davis, S.M., 76, *105*
Davis, T.R.V., 173, *215*
Deal, T.E., 121, 122–23, *158*, 547, 575, 576–77, *588*
Dean, R.A., 260, *271*
Deaux, K., 188, *215*, 240, *271*, 490
de Castro, E., 168
DeCharms, R., 450, *474*
Delbecq, A., 360, *370*
DeLorean, J., 136–37, 333, 341
Dembroski, T.M., 259, *272*
De Meuse, K.P., 192, *217*
Deming, W.E., 542, 567, 568, *588*
Denis, H., 98, *106*
DeNisi, A., 400, *426*

De Paulo, B.M., 247, *275*
Descartes, R., 437
Dessler, G., 410, *424*, 523, *532*
Deutsch, S.J., 23, *48*
DeVader, C.L., 391, *425*
Dickson, W.J., 405, *426*
Dienesch, R.M., 407, *422*
Dierkes, M., 39, *48*
DiGaetani, J.L., 265, *271*
DiHrick, J.E., 455
Dill, W.R., 348, *370*
Dipboye, R.L., *533*
Dittrich, J.E., *374*
Dodd, N.C., 148, *159*
Doherty, E.M., 335, *370*
Doherty, M.L., 407–8, *424*
Donahue, P., 111
Donaldson, G., *370*
Dornbush, S.M., 73, *105*, 230, 274
Dorrycott, J., 57
Dossett, D.L., 460, *475*
Dowling, P.J., 509, *532*
Downey, H.K., 356, *370*, 501, *533*
Downs, S., 512, *533*
Drath, W., 557, *588*
Drenth, P.J., 338, *371*
Driver, M.H., 333, *373*
Drory, A., 400, *422*
Drucker, P.F., 31, *48*, 577, 578, *588*
Dubin, R., 392–94, *422*
Duckles, M., 381
Dunbar, R., 388, *426*
Duncan, D., 241, *271*
Duncan, R.B., 356, *371*
Duncan, W.J., 134, *158*
Dunker, K., 332, *371*
Dyer, W.G., *215*
Dyson, 344–45

Eagly, A.H., 201, 202, *215*
Earley, P.C., 261, *271*, 460, 461, *474*
Early, C., 187, *215*
Eddy, W.B., 177, 180, 193

Eden, D., 192, *215*, 460, *474*, 487, *533*
Efran, J., 246, *271*
Ehrlich, S.B., 394, *425*
Einhorn, J.J., 329, *371*
Eisenberg, E.M., 264, *271*
Ekegren, G., 460, *474*
Ekman, P., 242, 244, 245, 247, *271*
Ellsworth, P., 242, 244, 245, 246, 247, 256, *271*, *275*
Enz, C.A., 118, 119, *158*
Epstein, R., 490, *533*
Erez, E.A., 461–62, *476*
Erez, M., 259, *272*, 335, *371*, 460, 461, *475*
Etzioni, A., 16, *48*, 144, *158*, 285, *315*, 327, 354, *371*
Evan, W.M., 307, *315*
Evans, R.I., 259, *272*
Everett, J.E., 230, *272*
Exline, R.V., 246, *272*
Ezell, D., 446, *477*

Fairhurst, G.T., 89, *105*
Falbo, T., 302, *316*
Falvey, J., 253–54, 255
Farber, D., 381
Farr, J.L., 518, 519, 521, *534*
Farrell, D., 151, *158*
Farrow, D.L., 414, *421*, *422*
Faulhaber, G.R., 581
Faust, W.L., 191, *217*
Fedor, D.B., 466, *474*
Feldman, D.C., 140, 141, *158*
Feldman, J., 182, *215*, 502, *533*
Feldman, M., 124–25, *159*, 329, *371*
Ferris, G.R., 466, *474*, 568, *588*
Festinger, L., 184–85, *215*
Fiedler, F.E., 408–9, 416, *422*, *423*
Field, R.H.G., 406, *423*
Filley, A.C., 209, 210, *215*
Finholt, T., 173, *215*, 251, *272*
Firsirotu, M.E., 120, *158*
Fishbein, M., 506, *531*, *533*
Fisher, D.W., 297, *316*

Subject Index